The Beatles Diary
Volume 1: The Beatles Years

The Beatles Diary
Volume 1: The Beatles Years

Barry Miles

OMNIBUS PRESS
LONDON · NEW YORK · SYDNEY

Edited by Chris Charlesworth
Cover designed by Chloë Alexander
Picture research by Nikki Lloyd

ISBN: 0.7119.8308.9
Order No: OP48188

Exclusive Distributors
Book Sales Limited
8/9 Frith Street
London W1V 5TZ, UK

Music Sales Corporation
257 Park Avenue South
New York NY 10010, USA

Music Sales Pty Limited,
120 Rothschild Avenue, Rosebery
NSW 2018 Australia

To the Music Trade only:
Music Sales Limited
8/9 Frith Street
London W1D 3JB UK

Every effort has been made to trace the copyright
holders of the photographs in this book but one or two
were unreachable. We would be grateful if the
photographers concerned would contact us.

Printed by
MPG Books (Hartnolls) Bodmin
Typeset by
Galleon Typesetting Ipswich

A catalogue record for this book is
available from the British Library

www.omnibuspress.com

Contents

Introduction vii

Acknowledgements xi

Pre-1960 3

1960 17

1961 31

1962 53

1963 79

1964 123

1965 185

1966 223

1967 251

1968 289

1969 325

1970 365

Aftermath 379

Introduction

The Beatles were a Sixties band, the only band to encompass the entire decade, literally beginning in 1960, when they went to Hamburg, and ending in 1970, when Paul sued to end their partnership. Other bands, like The Shadows, lived through it, but they were a Fifties group who managed to hang on indefinitely. The Beatles both reflected the enormous changes in society through the decade and were themselves catalysts for that change. They came together during the era of 'How Much Is That Doggie In The Window?' and 'The Deadwood Stage', and went professional at the time of The Avons' 'Three Little Girls Sitting In The Back Seat' and Ricky Valence's 'Tell Laura I Love Her'. By the time they broke up, Jimi Hendrix, Brian Jones's Rolling Stones and Syd Barrett's Pink Floyd had been and gone. The Beatles were both precursors and survivors.

They started it all, entering the music business when the BBC had a monopoly on radio, and the industry giants EMI and Decca dominated the record charts. Before The Beatles, an American would have been hard pressed to name one British singer or group; after The Beatles, British acts occupied a large percentage of the American charts. They paved the way for The Rolling Stones, The Who, The Kinks, The Yardbirds, The Animals, Herman & The Hermits and scores of other bands that constituted "The British Invasion".

Pop music, as it was known in the days before "rock", was seen as part of show business: to their bosses at EMI, there was little difference between The Beatles and Alma Cogan. They were on the cusp between music hall and MTV, playing variety shows along with hoofers, jugglers and comedians, though there is no recorded instance of them following a performing dog act. It is unlikely that Oasis would consider sharing top billing on a TV show with a glove puppet, but The Beatles did. Pop groups were regarded as variety acts, and in these pages The Beatles can be seen playing *Saturday Night At The London Palladium*, and *Mike and Bernie Winters' Big Night Out*, along with Arthur Askey, Bruce Forsyth, Morecambe and Wise and the like, where they were expected to take part in skits as well as play their latest single. (In fact, as pop music has become more of a packaged commodity, new bands did much the same thing in the Nineties, but in the heady days of "rock" it was a point of principle for Led Zeppelin *never* to appear on television, regardless of the show.)

Live performance was more important to The Beatles than to many present day acts because that was how they made their money, at least in the early years. Their royalties from EMI were so derisory that the greatest benefit of having a record in the charts came from the ability to charge more for live performances. No-one expected to make serious money from record sales, but with records in the charts you could play a lucrative summer season in a seaside resort and a sold-out Christmas panto. The Beatles did all of this after their initial success. Of course, all that would change. Indeed, they sold so many records that even on a farthing per record each they were able to get rich, and when it came time to renew their contract with EMI they got their own back by driving an incredibly hard bargain.

Their work-load was astonishing: more than 800 hours on stage in Hamburg, 275 performances at The Cavern alone. On top of that, Brian Epstein experimented with bookings, trying out new markets, booking them into a public school here, a débutante dance there, three weeks at The Paris Olympia, Carnegie Hall. Brian was determined to present them as a class act. Looking through the chronology it is fascinating to see who else was on the bill, particularly in the early days. At The Cavern, with its origins as a jazz club, they were often as not sharing the bill with one or two traditional jazz bands. Trad jazz enjoyed a period of popularity just as The Beatles were getting going. It was a peculiar business, bearing little relationship to its supposed origins in Twenties' New Orleans. All its original practitioners were either dead or in their seventies and eighties. Acker Bilk headlined in bowler hat and striped waistcoat and The Temperance Seven were cool and languid in a smooth flapper style that owed little to a New Orleans street band. This was what The Beatles were up against. Not great competition admittedly, but their energy and belief in themselves and their music saw them through, blowing their rivals off the stage one by one, first in Hamburg, then Liverpool, London and then the world.

Why The Beatles and not, say, Rory Storm and The Hurricanes who already featured Ringo Starr? The answer lies in their extraordinary ability as composers. It was fortuitous that Lennon and McCartney should meet because not only were they rock'n'roll fanatics, but they were also both already writing songs. The chemistry between them worked perfectly and together they composed an extraordinary body of work. The Beatles recorded 184 original songs (some of which were by George) without which they would almost certainly not have enjoyed such worldwide success. It was remarkable that they wrote songs at all, coming from their background, but what made The Beatles unstoppable was the momentum they created in their work, striving to make each album and single different, relying not on a tried and tested blues format or a series of traditional pop hooks, but experimenting with harmonies and rhythms, changing tempos and even tagging on whole new melodies. Songs poured out of them, so many that they didn't need to use singles on albums to fill the space. In the modern era, up to three years or more often elapse between album releases by top recording acts, but The Beatles – *the* top act in the world – managed to release 12 original albums, including one double, in the eight years between 1963 and 1970, not to mention around 30 non-album tracks, including many of their biggest and best loved hit singles. Astonishingly, the third member of the group, George Harrison, also flowered as a songwriter. To his chagrin, Frank Sinatra always introduced 'Something' as "a Lennon and McCartney composition" and George didn't get his full due until after the band split up. Even Ringo wrote the odd song, such as 'Octopus's Garden', but his best songs came later: 'It Don't Come Easy', 'Back Off Boogaloo'.

They heralded the singer-songwriter, hastening the collapse of the Brill Building and its commercial song writing teams. Before The Beatles it was rare to sing your own material: Elvis never wrote a song. After The Beatles it was seen as a sign of weakness if you didn't sing your own stuff. As old time rocker Jerry Lee Lewis said, referring to the demise of Bobby Vee, Bobby Darin, Bobbie Vinton and all the other Bobbies as The Beatles wiped the board clean: "Thank God for The Beatles, they cut 'em down like wheat before the sickle."

They turned touring upside down too. Before The Beatles there were no stadium concerts: after they filled Shea Stadium to its 55,000 capacity – the biggest rock'n'roll audience ever assembled at that time – the American stadium tour became the norm for a world-class act. The Beatles toured America with two roadies and a driver, playing hockey arenas and baseball stadiums, using whatever existing PA there was and with no foldback speakers on stage. Modern groups tour with an entourage of 150 crew and have more volume in their stage monitors than The Beatles had for a whole stadium, but once again it was The Beatles that led the way.

As if all this wasn't enough, during the Beatlemania years of non-stop touring and recording they also somehow found the time to make two full-length feature films, scores of live radio and TV appearances and give more media interviews in a day than today's superstars are inclined to give in a year. Somehow, amidst all this, they also coped with being the most famous and sought after people on the planet. In some cities, notably in Australia, half the population would turn out to welcome them, crowding into the streets, waiting for them to make personal appearances on balconies just like the Royal Family.

No other group developed so much. It would have been easy to retire, or at least settle back into comfortable celebrity after Beatlemania, but instead the Four Moptops transformed themselves into the Princes of Psychedelia and began a whole new life and a whole new series of experiments, dragging pop music forever out of Denmark Street and Tin Pan Alley and into the realm of art. *Revolver* had been a landmark album, filled with beautifully crafted songs and yet using experimental studio techniques that had other groups consulting with their studio managers. It was hard to see how they could better it. Everyone was waiting to see what The Beatles did next.

Sgt. Pepper was the world's first "concept" album, the first to print the lyrics on the sleeve (another blow to Denmark Street), and musically, it blew everyone's minds. It had the huge iconic chord on 'A Day In The Life' and it even had an iconic sleeve that was much parodied and copied over the years. It was their "masterpiece" in the traditional Renaissance sense of a piece of work to prove you knew your craft.

Drugs certainly helped this transformation and, because LSD and marijuana were illegal, The Beatles found themselves assigned yet another pioneering role as spokesmen for the newly emerging drug culture: they signed (and paid for) the "pot ad" in *The Times*, they recorded psychedelic music that was banned by the BBC and were interviewed about LSD by serious newspapers. Naturally they were also busted. Having abandoned their identity as the Fab Four, the nation's favourite boys, they were fair game for the drugs squad, though it now seems likely that in the case of both John and George the drugs were planted in their homes by the police themselves.

The strain of it all took its toll. They were tired to their bones, stressed and taking too many drugs. John, perhaps, felt it most keenly. Once again they both mirrored and led the direction of Sixties' popular culture when they became involved in meditation and the Maharishi Mahesh Yogi. The Maharishi might have been a passing interest had Brian Epstein not died when The Beatles were on one of his meditation courses. His words helped them deal with their grief and the next year they set off to India, in John and George's case with no clear idea of when, if ever, they might come back.

In the event, they did not become yogis, but their period of enforced sobriety allowed scores of songs to come flowing from them, many of which appeared on the double white album and *Abbey Road*. Ultimately it all came to an end: first George, then Ringo left the group and both returned. Then John left and they told no-one. When Paul got fed up with waiting around instead of getting on with a solo career, he revealed that The Beatles were no more in a press release that accompanied his first solo album. The press misunderstood the story and thought that he was the one who had left. They soon found out the truth, and in looking for someone to blame, picked on Yoko Ono. Yoko certainly played a role in the break-up by sticking close to John in the studio, inhibiting the close-knit working relationship they had previously enjoyed, something that the other Beatles' wives and girlfriends did not do – and something that John would have objected to strenuously if anyone else had done it. But the band had run its course. They had grown apart. It was a marriage approaching divorce, and, as with many divorces, it was acrimonious, doubly so because it attracted the media spotlight. With so much money at stake there were powerful conflicting forces at work, one of which was their last "manager" Allen Klein, who later went to jail for financial skulduggery.

The Beatles have become icons: just as the Eiffel Tower is for Paris, Big Ben for London, The Empire State Building for New York, a clip of Hitler ranting locates us at the beginning of World War II. For the Sixties we have Harold Wilson puffing his pipe, Christine Keeler sitting astride her famous chair, and there, jigging their guitars on some forgotten stage, their fringes covering their foreheads, screaming girls drowning out their words: The Beatles – the last great band in black and white.

Miles

Acknowledgements

I first met The Beatles in 1965: George and John at Allen Ginsberg's 39th birthday party in London, Paul at Peter Asher's house and Ringo at a recording session at Abbey Road. Together with John Dunbar and Peter Asher, I founded a company called Miles Asher and Dunbar Limited (M.A.D. Ltd) and opened Indica Books and Gallery. Paul McCartney was then living in the Asher household and quickly became involved in the project: putting up shelves, plastering holes in walls and designing and printing the wrapping paper. In 1966 it was at Indica that John met Yoko Ono when we gave her her first European show.

That same year I co-founded *International Times* (IT) and once again Paul was the first Beatle to get involved. He suggested I interview him, and that on the strength of that we would be able to get record company advertising. I did, and he was right. It was my first interview. I followed it up with one with George, then Mick Jagger and many years of rock journalism followed. Paul and John came to Indica quite regularly, and I often hung out at their recording sessions, particularly when they were making *Sgt. Pepper*. When Apple was started, Paul made me the label manager for Zapple, the spoken word and experimental label. John and Yoko were very involved with Zapple and it was in 1969 that I did a two-day interview with them – once again for the underground press – this time for *Oz*.

Throughout the period I kept journal notes, as well as bulging clipping files and these have been the basis of much of this book. As the years went by, I also accumulated an enormous library of Beatles books and related trivia, always assuming they would come in useful one day. Well, that day finally came. As we were putting this book together new books on The Beatles were appearing at the rate of one or two a month, literally one every three weeks. I have details of more than 350, though many of these are little more than picture books, and I cannot claim to have referred to more than 150 of them. In the end there were a dozen or so essential source books that I found myself pulling from the shelf time and time again, the primary one of which was of course Mark Lewisohn's *The Complete Beatles Chronicle* (London, Pyramid, 1992). Anyone wishing to know the full details of every Beatles recording session will find Mark's book indispensable. Another key book was Kevin Howlett's *The Beatles At The BEEB, The Story of Their Radio Career* (London, BBC, 1982).

For early dates and addresses of homes and schools I used Hunter Davies' authorised *The Beatles* (London, Heinemann, 1968, revised and updated several times since then), and of course, another indispensable source of information was *The Beatles Book Monthly* 1–77 (August 1963–December 1969).

For John, by far the best for facts was Albert Goldman's *The Lives of John Lennon*, which added new information to the story (the name and dates of John's first school, for instance) even though the book is ungenerous in spirit. John's murder provoked about 100 "tribute" books of one sort or another, which I'll not list here. The following books proved useful in assembling this chronology: Baird, Julia, with Giuliano, Geoffrey: *John Lennon, My Brother* (London, Grafton, 1988); The editors of *Rolling Stone*: *The Ballad of John and*

Yoko (London, Michael Joseph, 1982); Fawcett, Anthony: *John Lennon, One Day At A Time* (New York, Grove, 1976); Harry, Bill: *The Book of Lennon* (London, Aurum, 1984); [eds] Herzogenrath, Wulf and Hansen, Dorothee: *John Lennon: Drawings Performances Films* (Stuttgart, Cantz Verlag, 1995); Lennon, Cynthia: *A Twist Of Lennon* (London, Star, 1978) [also updated and rewritten in *Hello!* magazine]; Lennon, Pauline: *Daddy Come Home* (London, Harper Collins, 1990); Miles, [Barry], ed: *John Lennon In His Own Words* (London, Omnibus Press, 1980); Peebles, Andy: *The Lennon Tapes* (London, BBC, 1981); Sheff, David: *The Playboy Interviews with John Lennon* (London, NEL, 1982); Shotton, Pete and Schaffner, Nicholas: *John Lennon In My Life* (London, Coronet, 1983); Wenner, Jan, ed: *Lennon Remembers* (Harmondsworth, Penguin, 1973).

For Paul I used his brother's three books: McCartney, Michael: *Mike Mac's White and Blacks* (London, Aurum, 1986); *Remember, The Recollections and Photographs of Michael McCartney* (London, Merehurst, 1992) and *Thank U Very Much, Mike McCartney's Family Album* (London, Arthur Barker, 1981). I also looked at the following and found the odd date or two among them: Benson, Ross: *Paul McCartney, Behind The Myth* (London, Victor Gollancz, 1992); Coleman, Ray: *McCartney, Yesterday and Today* (London, Boxtree, 1995); [duNoyer, Paul][ed]: *The Paul McCartney World Tour* (London, MPL/EMAP, 1989); Elson, Howard: *McCartney, Songwriter* (London, W.H. Allen, 1986); Flippo, Chet: *McCartney, The Biography* (London, Sidgwick & Jackson, 1988); Gambaccini, Paul: *Paul McCartney In His Own Words* (London, Omnibus Press, 1976); Giuliano, Geoffrey: *Blackbird, the Life and Times of Paul McCartney* (New York, Dutton, 1991.); Harry, Bill: *The McCartney File* (London, Virgin, 1986); Salewicz, Chris: *McCartney: The Biography* (London, Macdonald, 1986); Schwartz, Francie: *Body Count* (San Francisco, Straight Arrow, 1972); Welch, Chris: *Paul McCartney, the Definitive Biography* (London, Proteus, 1984) and Paul's fan club magazine: *Club Sandwich*.

For George I used his autobiography: *I Me Mine* (New York, Simon & Schuster, 1980); Giuliano, Geoffrey: *Dark Horse* (London, Bloomsbury, 1989), and Taylor, Derek: *As Time Goes By, Living In The Sixties* (San Francisco, Straight Arrow, 1973).

For Ringo I checked my dates and addresses against Clayson, Alan: *Ringo Starr, Straight Man or Joker?* (London, Sidgwick & Jackson, 1991).

As far as record releases went, I found Harry Castleman and Walter Podrazik's 1976 discography *All Together Now* to be the most accurate and complete of the dozens of Beatles discographies I have seen, though I also consulted Campbell, Colin and Murphy, Allan: *Things We Said Today,* (songs concordance) (Ann Arbor, Michigan, Pierian Press, 1980); Carr, Roy and Tyler, Tony: *The Beatles: An Illustrated Record* (London, Triune, 1978); Dowlding, William: *Beatlesongs* (New York, Simon & Schuster, 1989); Guzek, Arno: *Beatles Discography* (Hvidovre, Denmark, 1976); McGeary, Mitchell: *The Beatles Discography* (Olympia, Washington, Ticket To Ride, 1975); Reinhart, Charles: *You Can't Do That! Beatles Bootlegs & Novelty Records* (Ann Arbor, Michigan, Pierian Press, 1981); Russell, Jeff: *The Beatles: Album File and Complete Discography* (Poole, Dorset, Blandford, 1982); Stannard, Neville: *The Long And Winding Road, A History of The Beatles On Record* (London, Virgin, 1982); Turner, Steve: *A Hard Day's Write, the Stories Behind Every Beatles Song*

(London, Carlton, 1994); Wallgren, Mark: *The Beatles On Record* (New York, Simon & Schuster, 1982); Wiener, Allen: *The Beatles: The Ultimate Recording Guide* (London, Aurum, 1993) and *The Beatles For The Record* (Knutsford, Cheshire, 1981).

I think Tom Schultheiss's *A Day In The Life: The Beatles Day-By-Day, 1960–1970* (Ann Arbor, Michigan, Pierian Press, 1980) was the first day-by-day chronology though there have been many since and I have taken dates from all of them, in particular: *Beatles Diary for 1965* (Glasgow, Beat Publications, 1964); *Beatles Press Book* (London, Apple Records, 1969); Benson, Harry: *The Beatles In The Beginning* (Edinburgh, Mainstream, 1993); Bunt, Jan Van De: *The Beatles Concert-ed Efforts* (The Netherlands, 1979); Fulpen, H.V.: *The Beatles, An Illustrated Diary* (London, Plexus, 1982); Lewisohn, Mark: *The Beatles Live!* (London, Pavilion, 1986) and Pawlowski, Gareth: *How They Became The Beatles* (London, Macdonald, 1990). The source of many of the above books has been the (virtually identical) chronologies given in George Tremlett's two individual Beatle biographies: *The John Lennon Story* (London, Futura, 1976) and *The Paul McCartney Story* (London, Futura, 1975), an idea picked up by Ray Coleman in his useful *John Lennon* (London, Futura, 1985).

There have been books about most of The Beatles' tours and sometimes about individual concerts, and I have used them all. For their days in Hamburg, the following were useful: Williams, Allan: *The Man Who Gave The Beatles Away* (London, Coronet, 1976); Jürgs, Michael, Ziemann, Hans Heinrich and Meyer, Dietmar: *Das Album Der Beatles* (Hamburg, Stern, 1981); Rehwagen, Thomas and Schmidt, Thorsten: *Mach Schau! Die Beatles In Hamburg* (Braunschweig, EinfallReich, 1992); Zint, Günter: *Große Freiheit 39* (Munich, Wilhelm Heyne Verlag) and Vollmer, Jürgen: *Rock 'n' Roll Times* (New York, Google Plex, 1981).

There are two essential books about Liverpool: Thompson, Phil: *The Best of Cellars, the Story of the World Famous Cavern Club* (Liverpool, Bluecoat, 1994) and Harry, Bill, ed: *Mersey Beat, The Beginnings of The Beatles* (London, Omnibus Press, 1977) [facsimiles from *Mersey Beat* magazine]. Evans, Mike and Jones, Ron: *In The Footsteps of The Beatles* (Liverpool, Merseyside Council guidebook, 1981) was also valuable.

The Beatles In Sweden (London, City Magazines, 1963) was about just that and Glenn Baker's *The Beatles Down Under, the 1964 Australia and New Zealand Tour* (Glebe, Wild and Woolley, 1982) is the standard work on The Beatles in Australia, with so many facts and anecdotes your head spins. The Beatles in the USA were, naturally, very well covered. I made particular use of *26 Days That Rocked The World* (Los Angeles, O'Brien, 1978) which consisted entirely of facsimile newspaper clips of The Beatles' first US tour, and also found data in Leach, Sam: *The Beatles On Broadway* (Manchester, World Distributors, 1964), a souvenir of The Beatles' first visit to the USA; Cosham, Ralph: *The Beatles At Carnegie Hall* (London, Panther Pictorial, 1964); Freeman, Robert: *The Beatles In America* (London, Daily Mirror Publications, 1964); Freeman, Robert: *Yesterday, Photographs of The Beatles* (London, Weidenfeld & Nicolson, 1983); Rayl, A.J.S.: *Beatles '64. A Hard Day's Night In America* (London, Sidgwick & Jackson, 1989); Harrison, George [of the *Liverpool Echo*]: *Around The World With The Beatles* (Liverpool, Liverpool Echo, 1964). Alf Bicknell with

Gary Marsh:"*Baby You Can Drive My Car*" [np] (Number 9 Books, 1989) provided a few hotel names.

There are only a few books about Apple. The most useful were: DiLello, Richard: *The Longest Cocktail Party* (London, Charisma, 1972); Martin, George: *Summer of Love, The Making of Sgt. Pepper* (London, Macmillan, 1994); McCabe, Peter and Schonfeld, Robert: *Apple To The Core, the Unmaking of The Beatles* (London, Martin Brian & O'Keeffe, 1972) and Taylor, Alistair: *Yesterday, The Beatles Remembered* (London, Sidgwick & Jackson, 1988).

For the three films I consulted: Dellar, Fred: *NME Guide to Rock Cinema* (London, Hamlyn, 1981); Yule, Andrew: *The Man Who "Framed" The Beatles, A Biography of Richard Lester* (New York, Donald Fine, 1994); Matahira, Toru: *Beatles Movie Catalog* (Japan, 1979) and Cott, Jonathan and Dalton, David: *The Beatles Get Back* (London, Apple, 1969).

I should also mention: Black, Johnny: *The Beatles Complete* (London, HMV, 1988); Blake, John: *All You Needed Was Love* (London, Hamlyn, 1981); Braun, Michael: *Love Me Do! The Beatles Progress* (Harmondsworth, Penguin, 1964); Brown, Peter and Gaines, Steven: *The Love You Make* (London, Macmillan, 1983); Castleman, Harry & Podrazik, Walter: *The Beatles Again?* (Ann Arbor, Michigan Pierian Press, 1977); Castleman, Harry & Podrazik, Walter: *The End Of The Beatles?* (Ann Arbor, Michigan Pierian Press, 1985); Friede, Goldie, Titone, Robin and Weiner, Sue: *The Beatles A To Z* (New York, Methuen,1980); Harry, Bill: *The Ultimate Beatles Encyclopedia* (London, Virgin, 1992); Hoffmann, Dezo: *With The Beatles* (London, Omnibus Press, 1982); Schreuders, Piet and Smith, Adam: *The Beatles London*, (London, Hamlyn, 1994); Miles [Barry], ed: *Beatles In Their Own Words* (London, W.H. Allen, 1978); Schaffner, Nicholas: *The British Invasion* (New York, McGraw-Hill, 1982); Schaffner, Nicholas: *The Beatles Forever* (New York, McGraw-Hill, 1977); Southall, Brian: *Abbey Road, The Story of the World's Most Famous Recording Studios* (Cambridge, Stevens, 1982); Taylor, Derek: *It Was Twenty Years Ago Today* (London, Bantam, 1987).

Finally, I used the following Beatles internet sites, some of which will probably not still be up, but any search engine will take you to a site with links:

Dave Haber's Beatles page:
 http://www.primenet.com/~dhaber/beatles.html
The Official rec.music.beatles Home Page:
 http://kiwi.imgen.bcm.tmc.edu:8088/public/rmb.html
Troni's Beatles Page:
 http://nobile.wirtschaft.tuilmenau.de/~weigmann/beatles.html
Alan Braverman's Beatles Page:
 http://turtle.ncsa.uiuc.edu/alan/beatles.html
Mike Markowski's Beatles Page:
 http://www.eecis.udel.edu/~markowsk/beatles/
Aaron Gill's Paul McCartney page:
 http://www.halcyon.com/marieg/paul.html
Harald Gernhardt's Paul McCartney Home Page:
 http://131.188.139.62:8080/hyplan/gernhard/macca.html
and on usenet:
 rec.music.beatles

As this is the acknowledgements page, it is the correct place to thank my assistant Polly Timberlake for working so long and hard on this book as well and to give a nod to Chris Charlesworth and Bob Wise for commissioning it in the first place.

[Editor's note: The text in this edition of Barry Miles' *Beatles Diary* is substantially enlarged from the original illustrated 1998 edition. It benefits from incorporating much of the text from *The Complete Guide To The Music Of The Beatles* by John Robertson, and the inclusion of substantial additional material contributed by Peter Doggett. Reference sources for this included *Many Years From Now* by Barry Miles, *Fifty Years Adrift* by Derek Taylor, *The Beatles: Abbey Road & Let It Be* by Peter Doggett, *Lennon* by John Robertson and *The Beatles: From Cavern To Star Club* by Hans Olof Gottfridsson. Thanks also to Keith Badman for his suggestions.]

The Beatles Diary
Volume 1: The Beatles Years

Pre-1960

1933

February 18
Yoko Ono was born in Tokyo, Japan.

1934

September 19
Brian Epstein was born in Liverpool.

1938

December 3
Julia Stanley married Alfred Lennon at the Liverpool Register Office.

1939

September 10
Cynthia Powell was born in Blackpool, Lancashire.

September 15
John's Aunt Mimi married George Smith.

1940

June 23
Stuart Sutcliffe was born in Edinburgh, Scotland.

July 7
Richard Starkey was born at 9 Madryn Street, Liverpool 8, in the Dingle.

October 9
John Winston Lennon was born at Oxford Street Maternity Hospital, Liverpool, to Alfred Lennon and Julia Lennon, née Stanley. Contrary to other reports, there was no *Luftwaffe* raid that night. The previous raid had been on the night of September 21–22, and the next was on October 16, when the Walton and Everton districts were hit, causing 30 casualties. John lived at 9 Newcastle Road, Liverpool 15, with his mother, his Aunt Mimi and his grandparents. His father was away at sea, as he had been for most of his marriage to date.

1941

April 15
James McCartney married Mary Mohin in Liverpool and they went to live in furnished rooms in Sunbury Road, Anfield.

November 24
Randolph Peter Best was born in Madras, India.

1942

June 18
James Paul McCartney was born at Walton Hospital, Liverpool, to James McCartney, cotton salesman, and Mary Patricia McCartney, née Mohin, midwife. Because Mary had previously been a matron at the hospital she was entitled to a bed in a private ward. Jim's

job at Napiers aircraft factory was classifed as war work, so they were able to get a small house in Wallasey, at 92 Broadway, across the Mersey.

September 24
Linda Louise Eastman was born in Scarsdale, New York.

1943

February

FREDDIE LENNON
Freddie Lennon was a ship's steward on the liners, and had been in New York when the war broke out. He was transferred to a Liberty Boat, but demoted from head waiter to assistant steward. He purposely missed the boat and wound up spending three months in jail. His cheques to Julia stopped, and his marriage more or less ended because of it.

Aunt Mimi moved into "Mendips" when her husband, George, returned home from the war. She suggested that Julia and baby John move into a cottage owned by her husband at 120A Allerton Road, Woolton, which Julia did. She thought that her husband Freddie had deserted both her and the Navy. Free from the watchful eyes of her parents, she went out on the town, frequently leaving baby John alone in the cottage.

February 24 (not the 25th, as George himself believed for many years)
George Harrison was born at 11.42pm to Louise Harrison, née French, a Liverpool shopgirl, and Harold Hargreaves Harrison, a bus conductor since 1937 and for ten years before that a ship's steward on the Liverpool White Star Line. George was their fourth and last child, and grew up in a little two-up-two-down redbrick terraced house at 12 Arnold Grove, Wavertree, Liverpool 15.

1944

Julia Lennon became involved with another man in Liverpool, barman John Dykins.

January
The McCartney family moved to a bungalow in Roach Avenue, Knowsley Estate, Liverpool.

January 7
Paul's brother Michael McCartney was born in Liverpool.

1945

March 17
Patricia Boyd was born.

June 19
John's mother, Julia Lennon, gave birth to a daughter, Victoria, who was subsequently put up for adoption, and was raised in Norway.

November 12
John went to his first school: Mosspits County Primary School on Mosspits Lane.

1946

March
Freddie Lennon and John Dykins came to blows when Julia announced that she was going to live with Dykins. She moved in with him at 1 Blomfield Road, Liverpool 18. John was sent to live with Julia's sister Mimi and her husband George at "Mendips", 251

Menlove Avenue, Liverpool 25, because Dykins didn't want to bring up another man's son.

April 5
Jane Asher was born in London.

John was expelled from Mosspits County Primary School for misbehaviour. He was five and a half. John was enrolled in Dovedale Road Primary School.

JOHN'S UPBRINGING
Freddie Lennon returned to Liverpool in summer 1946 and took his five-year-old son to Blackpool for a holiday. Freddie was planning to emigrate to New Zealand, along with the man he was staying with in Blackpool, and intended to take John with him. After several weeks, Julia arrived at the door, wanting John back. Freddie invited her to come with them, but she declined. She just wanted John. Five-year-old John had to decide which parent he wanted, and inevitably chose his mother. But Julia did not intend to bring him up. He was delivered back to Aunt Mimi and Uncle George, this time for good.

August 4
Maureen Cox was born in Liverpool.

Aided by the money that Mary McCartney was now earning as a midwife, the McCartney family moved to a ground-floor flat in Sir Thomas White Gardens, Liverpool city centre, and not long afterwards to a new council house at 72 Western Avenue, Speke.

1947

March 5
Julia Lennon gave birth to another daughter, also named Julia; this time she and her partner, John Dykins, resolved to raise the child themselves.

September
Paul started at Stockton Wood Road Primary School, Speke. Within a year, he transferred to the Joseph Williams Primary School in Belle Vale, a bus ride away from his home.

1948

September
George went to Dovedale Road Primary School. John Lennon was still there but two years ahead, so they never met.

1949

George's family moved to a new two-up-two-down council house at 25 Upton Green, Speke. They had been on the council housing list for 18 years, ever since George's eldest sister, Louise, was born.

October 26
John's third half-sister, Jacqui, was born to Julia Lennon in Liverpool.

1952

Paul's family moved to 12 Ardwick Road, Speke.

September
John started at Quarry Bank High School, having left Dovedale Primary School in July. Within a few weeks, he had attracted a reputation as a troublemaker, having been discovered in possession of an obscene drawing.

QUARRY BANK

Quarry Bank was boys only, a grammar school with a high academic record and several cabinet ministers to its name. The masters wore black gowns and the school believed in discipline. To John the school was a challenge. He remembered his first day: "I looked at all the hundreds of new kids and thought, Christ, I'll have to fight my way through all this lot, having just made it at Dovedale." John's marks got steadily worse and his third-year report read: "Hopeless. Rather a clown in class. A shocking report. He is wasting other pupils' time." He often found himself up before the headmaster for six of the best.

1953

Spring
In his final months at Joseph Williams Primary School, Paul was awarded a prize at a ceremony in Picton Hall, Liverpool, for an essay he had written about the Queen's coronation.

September
Paul entered the Liverpool Institute school.

LIVERPOOL INSTITUTE

The Institute was the best known of Liverpool's grammar schools and had an impressive list of old boys, including High Court judges, politicians, even a Nobel Prizewinner. Exceptional 11 Plus results enabled the brightest children in Liverpool to be sent to the Institute. Paul was offered a place and took it up, even though it was a long bus ride from Speke.

1954

September
George started at the Liverpool Institute. Paul was already there, in the year above. George: "It took from four o'clock to five to get home in the evening to the outskirts of the Speke estate and it was on that bus journey that I met Paul McCartney, because he, being at the same school, had the same uniform and was going the same way as I was. So I started hanging out with him. His mother was a midwife and he had a trumpet."

1955

Paul's family moved to 20 Forthlin Road, Allerton, Liverpool 18. The property has since been bought by the National Trust, who have opened it to the public. It has been restored to the way it looked in 1955 in memory of its famous former inhabitant.

June 5
John's Uncle George, Aunt Mimi's husband, suffered a haemorrhage caused by an undiagnosed liver complaint, and died suddenly. John had been very close to him and was deeply shocked, though he found it difficult to express his emotions outwardly.

John Lennon: "I didn't know how to be sad publicly, so I went upstairs. Then my cousin arrived and she came upstairs as well. We both had hysterics. We just laughed and laughed. I felt very guilty afterwards."

September
John was now in the C stream at school because his marks were so poor. By the final term, he was 20th in the class: the bottom of the bottom class.

1956

April

John Lennon bought his first 78rpm single, Lonnie Donegan's skiffle hit, 'Rock Island Line'. He sold it the following year to a fellow member of The Quarry Men, Rod Davis.

June 18

For his 14th birthday, Paul's father bought him a trumpet. After taking a few lessons on the instrument, Paul swapped it at Rushworth & Drapers store in Liverpool for a Zenith acoustic guitar, priced £15.

September

A new headmaster Mr. Pobjoy, took over Quarry Bank High School. He recognised that John's poor marks were due to personal problems and that John was capable of much better work.

October 9

John spent some of the money he'd been given for his 16th birthday on two new 78rpm singles, Elvis Presley's 'Hound Dog'/'Don't Be Cruel' and the Goons' 'The Ying-Tong Song'.

October 31

Mary Patricia McCartney died of breast cancer, aged 47. For a few days after the tragedy, Paul and his brother Michael stayed with their Uncle Joe and Auntie Joan. From then on, Jim McCartney brought up Paul and Michael single-handedly, as well as holding down a full-time job.

Paul: "We didn't really know what was happening. We were shielded from it all by our aunties and our dad."

Within a few weeks of his mother's death, Paul had written his first song, 'I Lost My Little Girl'.

1957

George's mother bought him a guitar from a boy at school who was selling it for £3. It soon became obvious that he needed something better and his mother saved up her housekeeping money until she could buy him a £30 model with a cut-away neck.

John's Aunt Mimi lent him the money to buy a £17 Gallotone Champion guitar, complete with a sticker promising that the instrument was "Guaranteed not to split". Included in the deal was a book, *Play The Guitar*.

March

Inspired by Lonnie Donegan and fired up by Elvis Presley's 'Heartbreak Hotel', John and his school friend Pete Shotton started a skiffle group which they called The Blackjacks. John played guitar, bought for him for £17 from Hessy's Music Shop on Stanley Street and "guaranteed not to split". He played it with only four strings and used banjo chords taught to him by his mother as he worked out how to play songs from the repertoire of his idols, like Lonnie Donegan and Elvis Presley. Pete played washboard. The traditional skiffle-group line-up was completed shortly afterwards by the addition of Bill Smith on tea-chest bass. John handled almost all of the lead vocals, with the other members adding back-up support during the choruses.

Featured in the group's repertoire at this point were skiffle standards like 'Rock Island Line', 'Maggie Mae', 'Freight Train' and 'Don't You Rock Me Daddy-O', which were being performed by hundreds of teenage skiffle groups across the UK.

May

John was a difficult and argumentative band leader and the line-up changed rapidly. Since they were all from Quarry Bank High School, The Blackjacks changed their name to The Quarry Men, whose initial line-up was John on vocals and guitar; Eric Griffiths on guitar; Colin Hanton on drums; Len Garry, who quickly replaced Bill Smith on tea-chest bass; Pete Shotton on washboard; and Rod Davis on banjo.

May 24

The Quarry Men played their first gig: John: "Our first appearance was in Rose Street, it was their Empire Day celebrations. They all had this party out in the street. We played from the back of a lorry. We didn't get paid or anything."

June 9

The Quarry Men entered the ABC TV *TV Star Search* talent contest organised by "Mr Star Maker" Carroll Levis, held at the Empire Theatre, Liverpool. The contest was performed before a live audience and the winners of the audition went on to appear on television. It was a cheap way of producing a variety show, but sadly, The Quarry Men didn't pass the audition and the winners were The Sunnyside Skiffle from Speke fronted by a midget, Nicky Cuff, on vocals and tea-chest bass (he literally played it standing on top).

Among the songs performed by The Quarry Men during the contest was 'Worried Man Blues', recently popularised by skiffle king Lonnie Donegan.

June 22

The Quarry Men played at an outdoor street party at Roseberry Street, Liverpool, to celebrate the 750th anniversary of King John granting a charter to Liverpool making it a free borough. They played their sets from the back of a coal lorry, with the power leads running through the front window of number 76.

Summer

George and his brother Pete, together with Pete's school friend Arthur Kelly and Alan Williams (not to be confused with the future manager of The Beatles), played a gig at the British Legion Club in Speke calling themselves The Rebels. Since no other band scheduled to play had turned up, they were forced to play all through the evening.

George: "I remember The Rebels had a tea chest with a lot of gnomes around it. One of my brothers had a five shilling guitar which had the back off it. Apart from that it was all fine. Just my brother, some mates and me. I tried to lay down the law a bit, but they weren't having any of that. We thought we made a pretty good sound but so did about four million other groups."

The next morning on the bus to school, George told Paul about the gig. After that, Paul began to join George in the Harrisons' front room, where they played their way through his chord books.

George: "Paul was very good with the harder chords, I must admit. After a time though, we actually began playing real songs together, like 'Don't You Rock Me Daddy-O' and 'Besame Mucho'. Paul knocked me out with his singing especially, although I remember him being a little embarrassed to really sing out, seeing as we were stuck right in the middle of my parents' place with the whole family walking about. He said he felt funny singing about love and such around my dad. We must have both been really a sight. I bet the others were just about pissing themselves trying not to laugh."

Paul: "I knew George long before John and any of the others. They were all from Woolton, the posh district, and we hailed from the Allerton set which was more working class. George and I had got together to learn the guitar and we were chums, despite his tender years as it seemed to me then. In fact George was only nine months younger than I was but to me George was always my little mate. But he could really play the guitar, particularly a piece called 'Raunchy' which we all loved. If anyone could do something as good as that, it was generally good enough to get them in the group."

July 2

John and his friend Nigel Whalley signed on the seamen's unemployment register at the Merchant Navy Establishment at the Pier Head. They telephoned Mimi who was horrified at the idea that John might follow in his father's footsteps, and ordered him home at once.

July 6

John and Paul met for the first time, at the Woolton Parish Church Garden Fete, held at St. Peter's Church. The Quarry Men Skiffle Group were invited to perform three times that day, twice during the afternoon festivities in the Lower Church field at 4.15pm and 5.45pm, and again twice that evening (at 8.45pm and 10.00pm) at the church hall, where John's group were supporting The George Edwards Band. Between the two afternoon sets, the City Of Liverpool Police Dogs staged a display. The first evening set at the church hall was marked by a severe thunderstorm, which forced the group to stop performing for a few minutes.

After their 5.45 performance, McCartney was introduced to Lennon by their mutual friend, Ivan Vaughan.

Paul: "At Woolton village fête I met him. I was a fat schoolboy and, as he leaned an arm on my shoulder, I realised that he was drunk. We were 12 then, but, in spite of his sideboards, we went on to become teenage pals."

John: "The day I met Paul I was singing 'Be-Bop-A-Lula' for the first time on stage. There's a picture of me with a checked shirt on, holding a little acoustic guitar – and I am singing 'Be-Bop-A-Lula'."

Paul: "A mate of mine at school, Ivy Vaughan, had said, 'Come along and see this group, they're great.' We used to go to the fair together with these great jackets with flaps here, light blue with flecks in them . . . Sharp! . . . I went to see the group and loved it – it was a young group, instead of dance music. John was obviously leading this thing – he had an acoustic guitar, brown wood with a hole, and a bit of a crew cut, with a little quiff. He didn't know the words for anything, he'd obviously only heard the records and not bought them, but I was pretty impressed. I met up with John backstage in this little church hall, and just picked up his guitar (which I had to play upside down, because I'm left handed), and played 'Twenty Flight Rock'. They were all impressed 'cos I knew all the words, then somebody played the piano, somebody sang 'Long Tall Sally', and later they asked me to join."

John: "Shortly after that we started to do big beat numbers like 'Twenty Flight Rock' – funny really because we were meant to be a skiffle group. 'Let's Have A Party' used to be my big number."

Aunt Mimi: "When Paul first came to Mendips he had a buckle on his shoe. John had never seen anything like it."

Two songs from The Quarry Men's evening performance, which was reported and photographed by the local paper, survived on a reel-to-reel tape, which was made without the group's knowledge by 16-year-old Bob Molyneaux. This tape of 'Puttin' On The Style' and 'Baby Let's Play House' was sold at auction in London during 1994, and purchased by EMI Records for £78,500. Only 30 seconds of 'Puttin' On The Style' has ever been aired in public. Other songs The Quarry Men are known to have performed that day include 'Worried Man Blues', 'Come Go With Me', 'Railroad Bill', 'Maggie Mae' and 'Cumberland Gap'.

July 29

Paul and his brother Michael went to Scout camp at Hathersage in Derbyshire. A few days earlier, John's friend Pete Shotton had passed on the invitation for Paul to join The Quarry Men – an offer that he eagerly accepted.

August 7

The Cavern, with Ron McKay's Skiffle Group, Dark Town Skiffle Group and The Deltones Skiffle Group.

The Cavern in those days was a jazz club but skiffle was then seen as an offshoot of jazz and so was acceptable, and the evening was billed as a "Skiffle Session". John's group had gained the booking, their most prestigious to date, after the Cavern Club owner Alan Sytner heard them perform at Childwall Golf Club.

The Quarry Men Skiffle Group began with 'Come Go With Me' which was okay, but John blasted straight into 'Hound Dog' followed by 'Blue Suede Shoes', prompting club owner Alan Sytner to send a note on-stage reading "Cut out the bloody rock!"

Though Paul had been invited to join the group he was away at Scout camp with his brother Michael and did not play this gig, which marked John Lennon's début at The Cavern.

Summer
Paul and George took their guitars and hitchhiked to the south coast. George: "When I was 14 Paul and I went to Paignton in Devon on a hitchhiking holiday. It was a bit of a laugh, too, because we ran out of money and had nowhere to sleep. So Paul suggested we sleep on the beach. Sand, however, is as hard as concrete when you lie on it all night."

September
The McCartney family went to the Butlin's Holiday Camp at Filey in Yorkshire, where Paul and Michael entered *The People* National Talent Contest and, appearing as The McCartney Brothers, did a rendition of the Everly Brothers' 'Bye Bye Love' and Little Richard's 'Long Tall Sally'. As they were both under 16 they didn't qualify. It was Paul's first appearance on stage.

October
John began attending Liverpool Art School, where he was accepted into the 'Lettering' class.

October 18
Conservative Club, New Clubmoor Hall, Liverpool. Paul's first gig with The Quarry Men.
Paul: "That night was a disaster because I got sticky fingers and blew the solo in 'Guitar Boogie Shuffle', which is one of the easiest things in the world to play. That alone made me resolve never to become a lead guitarist."

Autumn
Paul and John began to practise their guitars together. Paul: "We never played our guitars indoors at Mimi's house. If we didn't go round to Julia's and we stayed there, then we practised outside the front door in the glass porch. John told me Mimi banished him out there from the first day he brought home his guitar on account of all the noise. He didn't mind, though. He liked it out on the porch as the echo of the guitars bounced nicely off the glass and the tiles."

By the end of the year they had begun to write songs together, after Paul revealed to John that he had composed a tune called 'I Lost My Little Girl'. John: "When Paul and I started writing stuff, we did it in the key of A because we thought that was the key Buddy Holly did all his songs in. Holly was a big thing then, an inspiration, sort of. Anyway, later on I found out he played in C and other keys but it was too late and it didn't worry us anyway. It all sounded okay in A so that's the way we played our stuff. Oh yeah, we keep up with all the keys – C, D, G, F but we keep out of B flat and that. It doesn't give you an artistic sound."

November 7
Wilson Hall, Garston.
A notorious teddy boy hangout. The Quarry Men played there four times on Charlie Mac's Thursday "Rhythm Nights".

November 16
Stanley Abattoir Social Club, Liverpool.
Good acoustics.

November 23
New Clubmoor Hall, Conservative Club, Liverpool.
The line-up of The Quarry Men at this point consisted of John, guitar and vocals; Paul, guitar and vocals; Eric Griffiths, guitar; Colin Hanton, drums; Len Garry, tea-chest bass.

Late in the year
Nigel Whalley resigned as the group's manager because he developed tuberculosis. Rod Davis also drifted out of the group, without ever resigning or being sacked.

December 7
Wilson Hall, Garston, Liverpool.
   A Saturday night hop.

Around this time George saw The Quarry Men play for the first time. George: "I'd been invited to see them play several times by Paul but for some reason never got round to it before. I remember being very impressed with John's big thick sideboards and trendy teddy boy clothes. He was a terribly sarcastic bugger right from day one, but I never dared back down from him. In a way, all that emotional rough stuff was simply a way for him to help separate the men from the boys, I think. I was never intimidated by him. Whenever he had a go at me I just gave him a little bit of his own right back."

1958

January 10
New Clubmoor Hall, Garston, Liverpool.

January 24
The Cavern (evening), with the Merseysippi Jazz Band.
   They were billed as "The Quarry Men Skiffle Group". This was Paul's Cavern début.

February 6
Wilson Hall, Garston, Liverpool.
   After the gig (or, according to some sources, the gig at the Morgue in March), John accompanied Paul and George part of the way home.
   Paul: "George slipped quietly into one of the seats on this almost empty bus we were on, took out his guitar and went right into 'Raunchy'. Some days later I asked John, 'Well, what do you think about George?' He gave it a second or two and then he replied, 'Yeah, man, he'd be great.' And that was that. George was in and we were on our way."
   The Quarry Men line-up now consisted of: John, Paul, George, Len Garry, Eric Griffiths and sometimes John "Duff" Lowe on piano.
   Paul: "We had a bloke called Duff as pianist for some time, but his dad wouldn't let him stay out late. He'd be playing away one minute, and the next he would have disappeared, gone home in the middle of a number."
   Griffiths left The Quarry Men soon after George was recruited.
   Despite joining The Quarry Men, George also continued to perform occasionally with his own band, The Rebels, and also guested with local groups like Rory Storm & The Hurricanes.

March 13
The Morgue Skiffle Cellar, Broadgreen, Liverpool.
   The first of several appearances at this illegal club held in the cellar of a Victorian mansion. The police closed it down a month later.

March 20
John and other members of The Quarry Men attended Buddy Holly & The Crickets' concert at the Liverpool Empire theatre.

Summer
Paul and George made another hitchhiking trip, this time to Wales.
   George: "We ran out of cash again, and Paul had the idea that we could sleep at the police station in one of the cells. Unfortunately the police refused but did suggest we could kip in the grandstand of the local football club. With great difficulty we climbed the wall surrounding the football ground, and with even greater difficulty got to sleep on the concrete steps of the grandstand. Just as day was breaking, I woke to see the caretaker standing over us.
   " 'What are you doing in my grandstand?' he demanded.
   " 'S-sleeping,' Paul croaked.
   " 'Well, you're not anymore!'
   "We didn't need telling twice."

July 15
John's mother, Julia, was killed in a road accident as she left her sister Mimi's house. She was run down by a policeman who was driving illegally alone on "L"-plates, speeding because he was late for work.

Paul: "When I look back on Julia's death, all I can see is the word TRAGEDY written in big black letters. The only way I could help John was to empathise, as I'd had the same thing happen to me. There wasn't anything I could say that would magically patch him up. That kind of hurt goes far too deep for words."

Julia's death affected John very deeply. His work at art college – poor at the best of times – suffered badly and he virtually lost interest in the group. The Quarry Men played very few gigs during 1958.

July 19
John's mother Julia was buried after a funeral service at Allerton Cemetery, Liverpool.

That year (in either late spring or early autumn; none of the participants can clearly remember the date) John Lennon arranged for a recording of The Quarry Men to be made at a small studio in the back room of a house at 38 Kensington, Liverpool 7, where Percy Phillips would record two sides of music for 17 shillings and sixpence. Phillips advertised himself as a "Professional Tape & Disc Recording Service", and continued to operate from the same address until the late 1960s.

Only one copy of the single was cut and the tape itself was destroyed 24 hours later, once the record had been paid for. The A-side featured John singing Buddy Holly's 'That'll Be The Day', while on the B-side was a love song credited to Paul and George (the only known example of them writing as a team) entitled 'In Spite Of All The Danger', loosely built around the tune of Elvis Presley's 'Trying To Get To You'. The line-up on the recording was John, Paul, George, Colin Hanton and John "Duff" Lowe.

On the day of the session, The Quarry Men could only muster fifteen shillings between them, so Phillips held on to the disc until one of the group returned the next day with the correct money.

John "Duff" Lowe: "It was just a shellac demo disc. The more you played it, the worse the quality became. It was just done for a giggle. It was passed around. Anyone who had a friend could borrow it for a couple of days. No one ever asked me to lend it, so it must have come to me after everyone else had had a go. People forgot about it, and it was at the bottom of a linen drawer in my house."

Paul bought the disc from John Lowe in 1981 for an unspecified sum in excess of £5,000. During the 1980s he pressed up a limited quantity of reproductions of the single, which he gave to friends. Edited versions of both songs eventually appeared on *Beatles Anthology 1*.

Autumn
John and fellow Liverpool Art College student Cynthia Powell began a relationship, after dancing together at a lunchtime party. Cynthia declined John's initial request for a date, but the couple still spent that night together at his Gambier Terrace flat.

December 20
The group played at the wedding reception of George's brother Harry to Irene McCann, in Speke.

Late in the year
The Quarry Men failed an audition for ABC Television in Manchester.

Drummer Colin Hanton left the group after an argument with Paul following a gig at Finch Lane Bus Depot. The lack of a regular drummer severely hampered The Quarry Men's progress over the next year.

1959

January 1
Wilson Hall, Garston, Liverpool. Speke Bus Depot Social Club.

George's father was chairman of the club so naturally The Quarry Men got the gig.

January 24
Woolton Village Club, Woolton, Liverpool.

February 4
The members of The Quarry Men were stunned to hear of the death the previous day of one of their rock'n'roll idols, Buddy Holly – a major influence both as a singer and a songwriter.

Summer
Because The Quarry Men were doing very little in the way of gigs, George began playing with other groups, particularly The Les Stewart Quartet.

July 20
John began a summer vacation job as a labourer at Barton's, an industrial firm based at the Scarisbrook Water Works near Ormskirk. He was booked to work there for two months, but was dismissed on 28th August – described on his official work-card as "unsuitable".

August 29
Casbah Coffee Club, West Derby, Liverpool.
   The Les Stewart Quartet (featuring George on guitar) was booked for the opening night of Mona Best's new club, held in the basement of her house, but that afternoon Les Stewart had a terrific row with his bass player, Ken Brown, resigned from the group and stalked off. Ken Brown asked George if he knew anyone who could help out and John and Paul were called in. The Quarry Men played the gig and every Saturday night for the next seven weeks. The Quarry Men line-up for these gigs had been reduced to John, Paul, George and Ken Brown. No drummer, but as they always told promoters, "The rhythm's in the guitars".

September 5
Casbah Coffee Club, West Derby, Liverpool.

September 12
Casbah Coffee Club, West Derby, Liverpool.

September 19
Casbah Coffee Club, West Derby, Liverpool.

September 26
Casbah Coffee Club, West Derby, Liverpool.

October 3
Casbah Coffee Club, West Derby, Liverpool.

October 10
Casbah Coffee Club, West Derby, Liverpool. Ken Brown left the group and the group left the Casbah over an argument about wages. Paul objected when Mona Best paid Brown his 15 shillings even though he had not played that evening because of a heavy cold. The future Beatles closed ranks and walked away.

Mid-October
The group changed their name to Johnny & The Moondogs for another audition for Carroll Levis' *TV Star Search* at the Empire Theatre (held on the 11th, 18th and 25th, though they appeared on only one of these dates). This time The Moondogs qualified for the final round which was held at the Empire Theatre between the 26th and 31st. They appeared twice during the week and qualified for the next round.

November 15
Hippodrome Theatre, Ardwick, Manchester. This was the final round of *TV Star Search*. If they qualified here they would have made it on to the TV show itself. Unfortunately they had nowhere in Manchester to stay, and as the voting was based on a "clapometer"

which measured the volume of the audience applause when the group made a brief reappearance, The Moondogs lost out because they had already caught the last train back to Liverpool, and weren't there to be clapped.

November 17

The Second Biennial John Moores Exhibition was held in Liverpool at the Walker Gallery. John's friend from art school, Stuart Sutcliffe, submitted the remains of a large canvas entitled "Summer Painting". It had begun life as a large abstract expressionist painting on two six-feet-by-four-feet panels, with a highly textured surface made from sand and wax. One panel had gone missing when Stuart was evicted from his flat in Percy Street, but his friend Rod Murray helped him to carry the other half to the gallery to submit it for the show. Not only was the painting accepted for the show (Stuart's work showed the influence of Peter Lanyon, the British abstract expressionist who happened to be on the selection panel), but John Moores himself bought it for £65 when the show ended in January.

ROYSTON ELLIS

The London "Beat" poet, 19-year-old Royston Ellis, author of *Jiving To Gyp: A Sequence of Poems* (Scorpion Press, London, 1959), was booked to read his poems at the University of Liverpool. He met The Beatles and convinced them to back him for a reading at the Jacaranda. At this time reading poetry to a jazz backing had been popularised in the US by Jack Kerouac, Kenneth Patchen and Lawrence Ferlinghetti, and in Britain by Christopher Logue. After the reading Ellis visited Gambier Terrace, where John and Stuart were then living, and showed them how to unscrew a Vick's inhaler to get the Benzedrine out. Years later it was Ellis who inspired John by introducing him to Polythene Pam.

January 17

The John Moores Exhibition ended and Stuart received £65 for his entry. John persuaded his friend that what he really wanted to do with this large sum of money was buy a bass guitar and join Johnny & The Moondogs. He bought a Hofner President, more for its looks than for its sound, since he was unable to play it.

March/April

Several hours of Quarry Men rehearsals, most likely recorded at the McCartney's home in Forthlin Road, and possibly also at the home of another member of the group, were preserved for posterity on reel-to-reel tape. The shambolic performances included the skeletons of several future Beatles tunes, including 'The One After 909', 'When I'm 64' and 'I'll Follow The Sun', covers of American standards, and numerous instrumental improvisations.

Among the other songs known to have been recorded were 'Hallelujah I Love Her So', 'Movin'n'Groovin', 'Matchbox', 'I Will Always Be In Love With You', 'The World Is Waiting For The Sunrise', 'That's When Your Heartaches Begin', 'Wildcat' and many Lennon & McCartney originals, among them 'Cayenne' and 'You'll Be Mine', which were released for the first time on *Beatles Anthology 1* (as was 'Hallelujah I Love Her So').

The Beatles took copies of these tapes to Hamburg with them later in the year, and gave them away freely to friends. Researchers have highlighted the existence of three different source tapes for these recordings – one of them owned by Astrid Kirchherr, Hamburg girlfriend of Stuart Sutcliffe. Another was given by Paul to his Liverpool friend, Charles Hodgson, who had loaned them the Grundig recorder on which these tapes were made.

The Quarry Men line-up heard on these tapes was John, Paul, George and Stuart; at this point, the group still did not have a permanent drummer. They are believed to be the only surviving recordings which feature Stuart Sutcliffe's very rudimentary bass guitar playing.

April 23

John and Paul hitchhiked down to Caversham in Berkshire, to stay with Paul's older cousin, Bett Robbins, who, together with her husband Mike, ran a pub called The Fox and Hounds. Prior to this they had been redcoats at Butlin's, and Mike had a small amount of showbusiness experience – appearing on the radio and being interviewed by local newspapers – which their visitors were delighted to hear about. John and Paul worked behind the bar and on Saturday night performed in the tap room as The Nerk Twins (they were advertised on the door of the saloon bar as such). They sat on high barstools with their acoustic guitars and opened with an old Butlin's favourite, 'The World Is Waiting For The Sunrise', before moving on to their usual repertoire.

April 24

The Fox and Hounds, Caversham.

The Nerk Twins performed in the tap room again this lunchtime before hitchhiking back to Liverpool.

May

Allan Williams was asked by John to be the band's manager. Williams owned the Jacaranda Coffee Bar on Slater Street, a regular meeting place for Liverpool groups such as Rory Storm & The Hurricanes and Derry Wilkie & The Seniors. The Jac featured live shows in the tiny basement which Williams had converted in to a tiny dance floor. His friends, The Royal Caribbean Steel Band, were the residents. Williams was not too impressed by The Moondogs but agreed to manage them.

Allan Williams: "I thought The Beatles were a right load of layabouts. It was true that they were different: they had strong personalities, somehow compelling, and they were oddly impressive in a way hard to define. There seems to be something about my personality that attracts the losers and fringe people of the world, and The Beatles just seemed to be part of the crowd."

The Moondogs were unhappy with their name. One night at Stuart's Gambier Street flat, John and Stuart came up with a new name for the group, taken from Marlon Brando's film *The Wild One*:

"Lee Marvin to Marlon Brando: 'You know I've missed you. Ever since the club split up I've missed you. Did you miss him?'

Motorcycle gang: 'Yeah.'

Lee Marvin: 'We all missed you,' points to the girls in the gang. 'The beetles missed yuh, *all* the beetles missed yuh. C'mon Johnny, let's you and I . . .'"

Stuart suggested The Beetles because it was like Buddy Holly's Crickets. John then modified the name by changing an "e" to an "a" to make a pun on beat. Allan Williams didn't like it and suggested Long John and The Silver Beatles. Other names considered at that time were The Silver Beats, Silver Beetles and Beatals.

May 5
Through Cass of Cass & The Cassanovas, Allan Williams found the group a drummer called Tommy Moore and allowed them to practise at the Jacaranda in return for doing odd jobs. Sometimes they filled in on The Royal Caribbean Steel Band's day off.

May 10
Wyvern Social Club.

Looking for musicians who would play for low wages, London promoter Larry Parnes came to Liverpool to audition groups to back Billy Fury (who was himself from Liverpool) on a tour of northern England and Scotland. Fury himself attended the auditions, as did every hopeful group in Liverpool. John dropped the "Long John" and they attended Parnes' audition as The Silver Beatles. Drummer Johnny "Hutch" Hutchinson of Cass & The Cassanovas stood in at the audition as Tommy Moore arrived late. Larry Parnes considered that the group, except for Tommy, had some potential – despite Stuart Sutcliffe's blatant deficiencies as a bassist – and a few days later he contacted Williams with a job offer.

May 14
Lathom Hall, Liverpool, as The Silver Beats, promoted by Brian Kelly ("Beekay").

Also on the bill were Cliff Roberts & The Rockers, The Deltones and King Size Taylor & The Dominoes. The Silver Beats had not been advertised to play but they were allowed to do a few numbers in the interval while Brian Kelly sized them up. He booked them for the following Saturday.

May 18
The group were offered a job by Larry Parnes as backing group for the little-known Liverpool pop singer Johnny Gentle on a nine-day tour of Scotland. They decided to adopt pseudonyms for the occasion; Paul changed his to Paul Ramon, George became Carl Harrison (after Carl Perkins) and Stu changed Sutcliffe to deStael (after the then-fashionable painter). They chose as their name The Silver Beetles. Tommy and George arranged time off work, John and Stuart skipped college and Paul somehow managed to persuade his father that the trip would enable him to study for his A-levels.

May 20
Town Hall, Alloa, Clackmannanshire (Johnny Gentle tour).

May 21
Northern Meeting Ballroom, Inverness (Johnny Gentle tour).

"The Beat Ballad Show" with Ronnie Watt and The Chekkers Rock Dance Band.

While they rocked upstairs Lindsay Ross and his Famous Broadcasting Band led the old-tyme dancing downstairs. In Liverpool Brian Kelly had advertised The Beatles as headliners at the Lathom Hall but they neglected to inform him that they were out of town.

May 23

Dalrymple Hall, Aberdeen (Johnny Gentle tour).

On the way to the venue, Johnny Gentle crashed the car. Tommy Moore was concussed and lost several teeth. He was taken to hospital but the manager of Dalrymple Hall was outraged that the group had no drummer and stormed into the hospital and dragged Tommy from his bed to take his place on stage.

May 25

St Thomas' Hall, Deith, Banffshire (Johnny Gentle tour).

May 26

Town Hall, Forres, Morayshire (Johnny Gentle tour).

The tour was not going well and The Silver Beetles did a runner from their hotel, The Royal Station, without paying the bill.

May 27

Regal Ballroom, Nairne, Nairnshire (Johnny Gentle tour).

May 28

Rescue Hall, Peterhead, Aberdeenshire (final concert of the Johnny Gentle tour).

May 29

The Silver Beetles arrived back in Liverpool, tired, exhausted and just as poor as the day they left but having clocked up their first road experience as a rock'n'roll band.

May 30

Jacaranda Coffee Bar, Liverpool.

Allan Williams engaged The Silver Beetles to play Monday night "fill-in" performances (when not otherwise engaged) on the evenings that the house band, The Royal Caribbean Steel Band, took the night off. Their fee was Coca-Cola and beans on toast.

At some stage over the next month, Allan Williams tape-recorded several of the groups whom he'd booked to play at the Jacaranda, including The Beatles, but none of these recordings is believed to have survived.

June 2

The Institute, Neston, Wirral.

An event promoted by Les Dodd's Paramount Enterprises arranged by Williams while the group had been away in Scotland. This was the first of their Thursday night sessions at this notoriously rough venue. During one Silver Beetles set at The Institute, a 16-year-old boy was nearly kicked to death.

The *Heswall And Neston News And Advertiser* documented the group's appearance: "A Liverpool rhythm group, The Beatles, made their début at Neston Institute on Thursday night". There was no mention of 'Silver Beatles' in this account, suggesting that the group were operating under both names at this time.

June 4

Grosvenor Ballroom, Liscard.

Les Dodd's other, even rougher, venue where he promoted his Saturday "Big Beat" nights.

June 6

Grosvenor Ballroom, Liscard, a special Whitsun bank holiday Jive and Rock session.

The Silver Beetles shared a bill with Gerry & The Pacemakers for the first time.

June 9

The Institute, Neston, Wirral.

June 11
The Grosvenor Ballroom, Liscard.

Another rowdy Saturday night. The group had no drummer since Tommy Moore had resigned, having had enough of John's malicious wit, and of the pressure from his girlfriend to "get a proper job". John asked if anyone in the audience could play drums and "Ronnie", the drunk, grinning leader of a local gang of teddy boys, settled himself behind Moore's kit (still on hire-purchase). Though Ronnie had obviously never played drums before, no one dared take them off him. In the interval John managed to phone Allan Williams who drove over to the Grosvenor and saved them.

June 13
The Jacaranda as The Silver Beetles.

This was Tommy Moore's last gig with the group before he went back to being a fork-lift truck-driver at the Garston bottle works. They were now a beat group without a drummer. As they used to try to convince local promoters, "the rhythm's in the guitars!"

June 16
The Institute, Neston, Wirral.

June 18
Grosvenor Ballroom, Liscard.

June 23
The Institute, Neston, Wirral.

June 25
Grosvenor Ballroom, Liscard.

June 30
The Institute, Neston, Wirral.

July
With no drummer The Silver Beatles (as they were now called) were reduced to playing at Williams' strip club. In early July Allan Williams and his friend "Lord Woodbine" opened an illegal strip club in Upper Parliament Street called the "New Cabaret Artists Club". He offered the group 10 shillings (50p) each every night to provide the music for a stripper called Janice.

Paul: "John, George and Stu and I used to play at a strip club in Upper Parliament Street, backing Janice the Stripper. At the time we wore little lilac jackets . . . or purple jackets or something. Well, we played behind Janice and naturally we looked at her . . . the audience looked at her, everybody looked at her, just sort of normal. At the end of the act she would turn round and . . . well, we were all young lads, we'd never seen anything like it before, and all blushed . . . four blushing, red faced lads.

"Janice brought sheets of music for us to play all her arrangements. She gave us a bit of Beethoven and the Spanish Fire Dance. So in the end we said, 'We can't read music, sorry, we can play the Harry Lime Cha-Cha which we've arranged ourselves, and instead of Beethoven you can have 'Moonglow' or 'September Song' – take your pick . . . and instead of the 'Sabre Dance' we'll give you 'Ramrod'. So that's what she got. She seemed quite satisfied, anyway. The strip club wasn't an important chapter in our lives, but it was an interesting one."

According to Williams they played two sets each night for a week, with Paul on drums.

The *Sunday People* newspaper featured photographs of John and Stuart Sutcliffe's flat in an exposé entitled "The Beatnik Horror, for though they don't know it they are on the road to hell". This dubious 'publicity', John's first appearance in the national press, was arranged by Allan Williams.

July 2
The Grosvenor Ballroom, Liscard.

Johnny Gentle, visiting his home in Liverpool on a weekend off, stopped by the

Jacaranda to look up his old backing group. Williams told him where The Silver Beatles were playing and Gentle and his father went over to the Grosvenor, where Gentle leaped up and joined the group on stage for a few numbers.

July 7
The Institute, Wirral.

July 9
Grosvenor Ballroom, Liscard.

July 16
Grosvenor Ballroom, Liscard.

July 23
Grosvenor Ballroom, Liscard.

July 30
Grosvenor Ballroom, Liscard.

Drummer Norman Chapman worked across the street from the Jacaranda as a picture framer, and would practise in his office after everyone had gone home. One night Allan Williams followed the sound and persuaded him to play with The Silver Beatles. After playing three gigs with them at The Grosvenor he was conscripted for his two years' National Service.

By the end of July the violence at The Grosvenor had become so bad that the local residents complained to Wallasey Council who owned it. They cancelled the rest of the season and reintroduced the Ballroom's "strict tempo" dances.

It was probably at one of these Grosvenor Ballroom gigs that Stuart Sutcliffe was beaten unconscious by teddy boy thugs in a fight. His injuries caused the blood clot on his brain which eventually killed him. He was rescued from his attackers by Pete Best and John Lennon.

THE HAMBURG CONNECTION
Without bothering to inform Allan Williams, his resident group at the Jacaranda, The Royal Caribbean Steel Band, had accepted an engagement at a club in Hamburg in late June and simply failed to turn up one night. They happily wrote to Williams telling him there was a good market for British bands in Hamburg and urging him to visit. Williams, always looking for a new angle, visited the city with his friend Lord Woodbine and met Bruno Koschmider, owner of the Kaiserkeller. Since American rock'n'roll bands would have been too expensive to bring over, Koschmider was delighted to find that cheap rock groups were available in Britain, and at the end of July Williams sent one of his groups, Derry & The Seniors, to Hamburg to play at the Kaiserkeller.

August 2
Things were going so well for Bruno Koschmider at the Kaiserkeller in Hamburg that he decided to open another music venue in a nearby strip club he owned. He wrote to Allan Williams asking if he could supply another group, and Williams in turn offered the engagement to The Silver Beatles, provided they could find a drummer.

Around this time, Paul wrote to a friend that since Norman Chapman's departure from the group, he had been acting as their drummer. He also noted that The Beatles had been promised a second tour of Scotland as a reward for completing their first trip successfully.

August 6
With their usual Saturday night engagement at the Grosvenor cancelled, the group went over to Mona Best's Casbah Coffee Club where they found The Blackjacks performing, with Mona's son, Pete, playing a brand new drum kit. The Blackjacks were about to split up, so The Beatles shrewdly asked Pete if he wanted to come to Hamburg with them and arranged for Pete to audition for them the following Saturday.

August 12

Pete Best was auditioned by John, Paul and George to be their permanent drummer and go with them to Hamburg. Since he was their only hope of getting a drummer and therefore getting the gig, he passed the audition. It was just before the Hamburg tour that the group changed their name to The Beatles.

Pete Best: "A few years ago I used to sit in with various groups at The Casbah, Heyman's Green, and also had a trio called The Blackjacks. The Beatles used to play at the club and I got to know them there. They were auditioning for a drummer at the Wyvern Club, Seel Street (now the Blue Angel) and asked me to come along. They desperately needed a drummer at the time as they had to go to Germany within a few days' time. They asked me to join the group and two days later I was in Hamburg with them . . ."

August 16

The Beatles, accompanied by Allan Williams, his wife, her brother and Lord Woodbine, left Liverpool for Hamburg in Williams' old Austin van. They stopped off in London for a further passenger, Herr Steiner, an Austrian then working at the Heaven & Hell coffee bar on Old Compton Street, who was to act as Koschmider's interpreter. They took the ferry from Harwich to the Hook of Holland.

August 17

The Beatles and company arrived in Hamburg in the early evening. The contract signed between Allan Williams' Jacaranda Enterprises and Bruno Koschmider was to provide a five-piece band called The Beatles who were to be paid DM30 per day of work.

They began work right away at the Indra, at 58 Grosse Freiheit. They were to play seven days a week from 8 until 9; from 10 until 11; 11 until 12 and from 1 until 2. On Saturdays they began work at 7, playing until 8. Then from 9 until 10; 10 until 11; 12 until 1 and 1 until 3am. On Sundays they began even earlier: 5 until 6, 6.30 until 7.30, 8 until 9, 9.30 until 10.30, 11 until 12 and 12.30 until 1.30.

Paul: "You revved your engines up so much that when you let them go, you just coasted. Like at Hamburg we often played an eight-hour day! Playing like that, you get to have a lot of tunes, if nothing else. So what we used to do, even on our eight-hour stint, was to try not to repeat any numbers. That was our own little ambition to stop us going round the bend. That gave us millions of songs, though some we could only just get away with – 'Dum-da-dum-da-dum-da-dum!' for half-an-hour! We'd shout out a title the Germans wouldn't understand to keep ourselves amused, like 'Knickers', but eventually we built up quite a programme."

George: "When you think about it sensibly, our sound really stems from Germany. That's where we learned to work for hours and hours on end, and keep on working at full peak even though we reckoned our legs and arms were about ready to drop off.

"Sure we come from Liverpool. There are hundreds of groups there, many on an R&B kick. But you won't hear us shouting about a Liverpool Sound, or Merseybeat, simply because it's been dreamed up as an easy way to describe what's going on with our music. 'Hamburg Stamp and Yell' music might be more accurate. It was all that work on various club stages in Germany that built up our beat."

Only John and Paul did vocals before the first Hamburg trip, but the eight-hour sessions meant that George had to share the work, and by the time they returned to Liverpool they had three vocalists.

Paul: "Hamburg was a good exercise really in commercialism – a couple of students would stick their heads round the door, and we'd suddenly go into a piece of music that we thought might attract them. If we got people in, they might pay us better. That club was called the Indra – which is German for India. We were nicking left, right and centre off other bands there; we'd see something that we'd like, and after they left Hamburg, we'd put it in our set. Well you've got to, haven't you? We used to like going up and watching Tony Sheridan, 'cos he was a little bit of the generation above us; he used to play some blues, real moody stuff."

The Beatles got on well with Tony Sheridan and his group, The Jets. Paul and Iain Hines, the keyboard player with The Jets, used to double date two Hamburg barmaids: Paul's was called Liane. Iain: "Every evening, when we'd finished working, Liane used to pick us up in her tiny Volkswagon and take us to her flat for coffee and a record session.

Paul and I used to play Elvis and Everly records while Liane prepared a supper of Deutsch Beefsteak (hamburgers) and coffee." It was already 4am when she picked them up from the club.

When The Beatles arrived at the Indra they were completely broke. Rosa, the cleaning lady, gave them a few marks so they could go across the street to Harold's café for a meal of potato fritters, cornflakes and chicken soup. Rosa washed their shirts and socks, gave them chocolate bars and, for a time, Paul lived in her small bungalow down on the docks.

Rosa: "I remember when young Paul used to practise guitar on the roof of my little place. We used to get crowds of burly old Hamburg dockers hanging around, just listening. They shouted out things in German, but Paul didn't understand them. It's odd. They were a very hard audience who didn't really know what Paul was playing, but somehow they took to him."

The Beatles' accommodation was two shared rooms behind the screen of the Bambi-Filmkunsttheater where they had to use the cinema bathrooms to wash. There were no cooking facilities and the group used to frequent the British Sailors' Society, where the manager, Mr Hawk, would feed them cornflakes and pints of milk.

September 1–30
Indra Club, Grosse Freiheit, Hamburg.

Paul: "The first time we went to Hamburg we stayed four and a half months. It's a sort of blown up Blackpool, but with strip clubs instead of waxworks; thousands of strip clubs, bars and pick-up joints, not very picturesque. The first time it was pretty rough but we all had a gear time. The pay wasn't too fab, the digs weren't much good, and we had to play for quite a long time."

Liverpool musician Howie Casey: "At the beginning, they still played a lot of The Shadows' numbers, but gradually turned to R&B. When they came over, they had very, very pointed shoes in grey crocodile. They had mauve jackets, black shirts and pants, and also brown jackets with half-belting at the back. The length of their hair caused a great stir – it was thick at the back, almost coming over their collars."

During their time at the Indra, Stuart Sutcliffe briefly left The Beatles to play with Howie Casey's group, The Seniors. "The Beatles did their nuts because Stu was playing with us", Casey recalled.

October 1–3
Indra, Grosse Freiheit, Hamburg.

October 4
Police pressure caused by noise complaints – mostly from the old woman who lived above the club – caused Bruno Koschmider to stop using the Indra as a music club and bring back the strippers. So after 48 nights on stage, The Beatles moved to the much larger Kaiserkeller, at 36 Grosse Freiheit. Here they alternated with Rory Storm & The Hurricanes who had arrived in Hamburg three days before, after playing a summer season at Butlin's. The drummer with The Hurricanes was Ringo Starr.

October 10
Allan Williams returned to Hamburg on a visit. The Beatles had a problem with the stage at the Kaiserkeller, which was much larger than they were used to and made them appear like frozen waxworks. Koschmider complained to Williams who yelled, "Make a show, boys!" and encouraged them to move around. Koschmider, who spoke no English, took up the chant: "Mach schau!" In future, every time they slowed down or looked tired, Koschmider would exhort them to "Mach schau!"

Their act was transformed: first John and then the others began to throw microphones and instruments about the stage. They smoked, drank and sometimes even fought on stage. John once performed wearing only his underwear and a toilet seat around his neck. They painted swastikas on old Afrikka Corps caps, and goose-stepped around the stage giving illegal Seig Heil salutes and yelling at the audience, "Clap your hands, you fuckin' Nazis". The audience loved it. Insulting the customers not only went down well but also began to attract large crowds. Half the time the band were drunk or – with the exception of Pete – on Benzedrine; there was no other way they could get through the two final sets. The gangsters in the audience would send up crates of beer and hand them preludin; it was sensible not to refuse gifts from these people.

The Beatles and Rory Storm had a competition to see which group could demolish the club's unstable and potentially dangerous stage. Rory Storm won the bet during an enthusiastic version of 'Blue Suede Shoes'. The outraged Koschmider fined him DM65 to pay for the damage.

October 15

Walter Eymond, the singer and bass player with The Hurricanes, made an amateur recording of 'Summertime' at the small Akustik studio by the railway station, at Kirchenallee 57, Hamburg – a place where messages to family and friends could be recorded on 78rpm discs. Eymond's stage name was Lou Walters but everyone knew him as Wally. Backing him were Ringo, also in The Hurricanes, and John, Paul and George from The Beatles. Stuart was there as an observer as he couldn't play well enough for recording, so for the first time on record, John, Paul, George and Ringo played together. Wally and Ringo also made recordings of 'Fever' and 'September Song', possibly during the same session. Nine copies of the 'Summertime' 78 were cut, but only one copy has surfaced.

Also in attendance when this record was made were The Beatles' manager, Allan Williams, and Johnny Byrne, another member of The Hurricanes.

October 16

The Beatles' contract was extended until December 31. They were making good money for Koschmider.

The audience was composed mostly of gangsters, people in the sex industry, rockers and visiting sailors. Then one day, an art student happened by, attracted by the sound of Rory Storm & The Hurricanes. Klaus Voormann was an "exi" – an existentialist – the sworn enemies of the rockers, and felt a certain trepidation at venturing into their territory, but having seen The Beatles do their set he was so excited that he returned the next day, and the one after, this time bringing with him the girlfriend, the photographer Astrid Kirchherr. Astrid and Stuart Sutcliffe soon became a couple (their engagement was announced in November), encouraging Astrid to take some of the best-known photographs of the group from that time.

Though Stuart was regarded by many as the most attractive member of the group, he had still not learned how to play his bass guitar, preferring to pose with it and look moody. This caused a tremendous friction in the group with Paul complaining to John, and both John and Paul complaining to Stuart. John was torn between friendship and his desire for the group to make it. He knew that Paul was right and The Beatles could never be any good musically as long as Stuart remained in the group. But at the same time he loyally defended his friend to the hilt, threatening to leave himself if Stuart was forced out.

Paul: "The problem with Stu was that he couldn't play bass guitar. We had to turn him away in photographs because he'd be doing F-sharp and we'd be holding G. Stu and I had a fight once on stage in Hamburg but we were virtually holding each other up. We couldn't move, couldn't do it. The thing that concerned me was the music, and that we get on musically, and we didn't. Same with Pete Best."

October 30

The Beatles made a verbal agreement with Peter Eckhorn to play the Top Ten Club in April provided that he sort out their immigration problems. Besides their commitment to the Kaiserkeller until the end of the year, the group had also made provisional plans to work in Berlin early in 1961 – suggesting that they were not intending to return to Liverpool for many months.

Tony Sheridan and Iain Hines joined The Beatles on-stage at the Top Ten for a jam session which ended with a 70-minute version of 'What'd I Say'.

November 1–30

Kaiserkeller, Grosse Freiheit, Hamburg.

Paul: "One night we played at the Top Ten Club and all the customers from the Kaiserkeller came along. Since the Top Ten was a much better club, we decided to accept the manager's offer and play there. Naturally the manager of the Kaiserkeller didn't like it. One night prior to leaving his place, we accidentally singed a bit of cord on an old stone wall in the corridor and he had the police on us.

"'Leave please, thanks very much, but we don't want you to burn our German houses.' Funny really because we couldn't have burnt the place if we had gallons of petrol – it was made of stone.

"There was an article on the group in a German magazine. I didn't understand the article, but there was a large photograph of us in the middle page. In the same article there was a photograph of a South African negro pushing the jungle down. I still don't quite know what he has to do with us, but I suppose it has some significance."

November 1
Bruno Koschmider terminated The Beatles' contract. His notice to quit read: "I the undersigned hereby give notice to Mr. George Harrison and to Beatles' Band to leave on November 30th, 1960. The notice is given to the above by order of the Public Authorities who have discovered that Mr. George Harrison is only 17 (seventeen) years of age."

Besides discovering that George was under age, Koschmider was more likely moved to dismiss The Beatles because he had discovered that they were planning to transfer to the Top Ten Club, run by his rival, Peter Eckhorn.

November 21
George was deported from Germany for being too young to work in nightclubs.

November 22
Despite the loss of their lead guitarist The Beatles were expected to continue playing at the Kaiserkeller normally. The work sheet for this date gives the exact times they were expected on stage: 7.30pm until 9; 9.30 until 11; 11.30 until 1; 1.30 until 2.30am: five and a half hours of playing time, seven days a week.

November 27
Paul wrote home to a friend: "All sorts of things have been happening here, but they're too complicated and too many of them to mention. We'll probably be staying over here till after Christmas, and playing at Munich before we come home."

November 29
During a change of digs from the Bambi-Filmkunsttheater to quarters provided by Peter Eckhorn, Pete and Paul accidentally set their old room on fire: there was no light and so as they were packing, they set fire to a condom in order to see. Though no damage was done except for one singe mark on the wall, Koschmider had them arrested and deported for arson.

Peter Eckhorn: "They were working at the Kaiserkeller in Hamburg at the time, but they didn't like it there and so they came to see me and ask if there was any work to be had at the Top Ten. To show what they could do they played a couple of numbers for me. I liked them. I said OK, I'd give them a job. But before I could hire them, the owners of the Kaiserkeller made a complaint about the boys to the police, saying they'd tried to set fire to the club! It wasn't true, of course, but the complaint had the desired effect: The Beatles were deported. It took seven months to get them back again. They stayed three months and were very popular, not so much for their music (which wasn't so different from the other groups), but for their personalities. Nobody in particular shone out – they were all well liked."

December 1
Paul and Pete arrived back in England after being deported from Germany.

December 10
John, who had decided to stay on in Germany with Stuart rather than returning home with Paul and Pete, finally set off for England by train. Stuart stayed on in Hamburg with Astrid, conveniently solving the problem of how to remove him from the group.

December 15
John finally contacted Paul, George and Pete, having arrived home broke and depressed

four days earlier. This was his first contact with his bandmates since their deportation, leading them to fear that he was no longer interested in playing with The Beatles.

December 16
George wrote to Stuart Sutcliffe in Hamburg: "Come home sooner . . . It's no good with Paul playing bass, we've decided, that is if he had some kind of bass and amp to play on!"

December 17
Casbah Coffee Club, West Derby, Liverpool.
   With Stuart still in Hamburg, and John's enthusiasm for The Beatles now confirmed, Pete Best contacted Chas Newby, the former rhythm guitarist with his group The Blackjacks, to play bass.

December 24
Grosvenor Ballroom, Liscard, with Derry & The Seniors.
   Rock dances had been resumed under the supervision of Wallasey Corporation itself.

December 27
Litherland Town Hall, where they were advertised as "Direct from Hamburg".
   This "Welcome Home" engagement had been booked for them by Bob Wooler with Brian Kelly (who had evidently forgiven them for letting him down on the May 21 booking). For a fee of £6, The Beatles played their normal Hamburg set, which had an electrifying effect on the young audience. Immediately after the show Brian Kelly booked them for another 36 dances – at £6 to £8 a gig – before any other promoter could get to them.
   John: "We'd been playing round Liverpool for a bit without getting anywhere, trying to get work, and the other groups kept telling us, 'You'll do all right, you'll get work someday.' And off we went to Hamburg, and when we came back, suddenly we were a wow. Mind you, 70 per cent of the audience thought we were a German wow, but we didn't care about that . . . In Liverpool, people didn't even know we were from Liverpool. They thought we were from Hamburg. They said, 'Christ, they speak good English!' Which we did of course, being English. But that's when we first stood there being cheered for the first time."

December 31
Casbah Coffee Club, West Derby, Liverpool.
   Chas Newby's final engagement with the group before returning to college.

NEIL ASPINALL

When Brian Kelly booked them for 36 gigs over the next three months, The Beatles decided that they needed a full-time roadie. Neil Aspinall, who was studying to become a chartered accountant, lived in Pete Best's parents' house and helped to run the Casbah Club in the basement while Pete was in Hamburg. He had helped with the gear at the Litherland Town Hall and the Casbah to augment his fifty shilling a week salary. When they asked if he would work for them full time, Neil gave up his studies, bought an £80 Commer van and has been with them ever since.

Neil was born on October 13, 1941, in Prestatyn where his mother had been evacuated at the height of the blitz on Liverpool. His father was in the navy. In 1942, with the end of the bombing, the family returned to Liverpool. He passed his 11 Plus exam at West Derby School and went to the Liverpool Institute where he took art and English lessons alongside Paul. George was one year below them, but they soon met.

Neil: "My first encounter with George was behind the school's air-raid shelters. This great mass of shaggy hair loomed up and an out-of-breath voice requested a quick drag of my Woodbine. It was one of the first cigarettes either of us had smoked. We spluttered our way through it bravely but gleefully. After that the three of us did lots of ridiculous things together. By the time we were ready to take the GCE exams we'd added John Lennon to our 'Mad Lad' gang. He was doing his first term at Liverpool College of Art which overlooks the

Institute playground and we all got together in a students' coffee bar at lunchtime."

Neil took nine GCEs and passed them all except for French. He stayed on at the Institute until July 1959, when he joined a firm of chartered accountants. He started working for The Beatles in December 1960. After acting as their senior road manager throughout the touring years of the 1960s, he finally received a job worthy of his examination grades in 1968, when he was appointed the Managing Director of Apple – a post he has held ever since.

January

When Chas Newby returned to college the group were left without a bass player. John tried to get George to play bass but this met with a solid refusal and so Paul, who had been playing both rhythm guitar and piano, was deputed to take the job. He put together a bass out of a Solid 7 model and three piano strings. It was not very satisfactory, but it still sounded better than Stuart had done.

After the "Welcome Home" concert Bob Wooler began to promote the group regularly, and to encourage other promoters to book them. He was often the MC at their gigs, making the performance as dramatic as possible by playing the *William Tell* Overture for their entrance or getting them to start playing before the curtain went up. Girls would start screaming and rushing the stage, mostly for Pete Best who on one occasion was nearly pulled into the audience. Beatlemania was beginning.

January 5

Litherland Town Hall.

The first of the engagements booked by Brian Kelly (Beekay). Ringo Starr, who had just returned from a stint in Hamburg with Rory Storm & The Hurricanes, was in the audience.

January 6

St John's Hall, Bootle in Lancashire.

January 7

Aintree Institute, Liverpool and Lathom Hall, Seaforth, Liverpool (both events were Brian Kelly promotions).

January 13

Aintree Institute, Liverpool.

January 14

Aintree Institute, Liverpool.

January 15

Casbah Coffee Club, West Derby, Liverpool.

January 18

Aintree Institute, Liverpool.

January 19

Alexandra Hall, Crosby, Liverpool.

January 20

Lathom Hall, Seaforth.

January 21

Lathom Hall, Seaforth and Aintree Institute, Liverpool.

January 25

Hambleton Hall, Huyton, Liverpool, with Derry & The Seniors and Faron & The Tempest Tornadoes.

January 26

Litherland Town Hall.

January 27

Aintree Institute, Liverpool.

January 28

Lathom Hall, Seaforth and Aintree Institute, Liverpool.

January 29
Casbah Coffee Club, West Derby, Liverpool.

January 30
Lathom Hall, Seaforth.

February 1
Hambleton Hall, Huyton, Liverpool.

February 2
Litherland Town Hall.

February 3
St. John's Hall, Bootle in Lancashire.

February 4
Lathom Hall, Seaford.

February 5
Blair Hall, Walton, Liverpool.

February 6
Lathom Hall, Seaforth.

February 7
Merseyside Civil Services Club, Liverpool.

February 8
Aintree Institute, Liverpool and Hambleton Hall, Huyton, Liverpool.

February 9
The Cavern (lunchtime).

THE CAVERN
This was the first time the group played The Cavern under the name of The Beatles. The club would become forever associated with the group. This was a humble beginning to the saga – an unadvertised lunchtime session. George arrived in blue jeans, which were banned from the club, but fortunately he was able to convince the bouncer, Paddy Delaney, that he was part of the act. The club was small – each of the three vaulted arches was only five chairs wide – and airless, but it was free of violence despite the tightly packed audiences.

John had first played The Cavern in August 1957 when The Quarry Men were a skiffle band, and skiffle was seen as an adjunct of jazz, but under the new management of Ray McFall, the venue had now adopted a broader booking policy.

February 10
Aintree Institute, Liverpool and Lathom Hall, Seaforth.

February 11
Lathom Hall, Seaforth and Cassanova Club, Sampson & Barlow's New Ballroom, Liverpool, the first booking for the group from promoter Sam Leach.

February 12
Casbah Coffee Club, West Derby, Liverpool.

February 14
Cassanova Club, Sampson & Barlow's New Ballroom, Liverpool and Litherland Town Hall, with Ray & The Del Rena's with Joan.

The second booking of the night was a St Valentine's Day Special. Paul sang Elvis' 'Wooden Heart' wearing a red satin heart bearing the names of the group pinned to his jacket. The heart was raffled but when the winner climbed up on stage to receive her prize and a kiss from Paul, the stage was inundated with squealing girls and the group had to be rescued by bouncers.

February 15
Aintree Institute, Liverpool and Hambleton Hall, Huyton, Liverpool.

February 16
Cassanova Club, Sampson & Barlow's New Ballroom, Liverpool and Litherland Town Hall.

February 17
St John's Hall, Tuebrook, Liverpool.
   This gig was promoted by Pete Best's mother, Mona, who negotiated a number of The Beatles' bookings at this stage in their career. It was probable that she also had ideas of managing them. The group were billed as The Fabulous Beatles Rock Combo.

February 18
Aintree Institute, Liverpool.

February 19
Casbah Coffee Club, West Derby, Liverpool.

February 21
The Cavern (lunchtime), Cassanova Club, Sampson & Barlow's New Ballroom, Liverpool and Litherland Town Hall.
   Three bookings in one day was not uncommon for The Beatles during 1961.

February 22
Aintree Institute, Liverpool and Hambleton Hall, Huyton, Liverpool.

February 24
Grosvenor Ballroom, Liscard.

February 25
Aintree Institute, Liverpool and Latham Hall, Seaforth.

February 26
Casbah Coffee Club, West Derby, Liverpool.

February 28
The Cavern (lunchtime), Cassanova Club, Sampson & Barlow's New Ballroom, Liverpool and Litherland Town Hall.

In late February, Stuart Sutcliffe returned to Liverpool to see his parents but stayed only for a couple of weeks – though that proved long enough to cause dissension within the Beatles' ranks, when John insisted that despite his musical shortcomings, Stu should resume his former role as the group's bass player.

March 1
Aintree Institute, Liverpool.

March 2
Litherland Town Hall.
   This was the date of the contract signed between Allan Williams' Jacaranda Enterprises and Peter Eckhorn of the Top Ten Club, Hamburg. The Beatles were contracted to play seven nights a week at DM40 per person per night. Williams was to receive £10 a week that The Top Ten management was supposed to deduct from the band's wages and pay into Williams' account at the Commerz Bank in Hamburg. From Monday to Friday The Beatles were to play from 7pm until 2am, on Saturday they were

to play from 7pm until 3am and on Sunday from 6pm until 1am. "After each hour of playing, there shall be a break of not less than 15 minutes."

March 3
St John's Hall, Bootle in Lancashire.

March 4
Aintree Institute, Liverpool.

March 5
Casbah Coffee Club, West Derby, Liverpool.

March 6
The Cavern (lunchtime) and The Liverpool Jazz Society (the previously named and later to be renamed Old Iron Door Club), with Gerry & The Pacemakers, Rory Storm & The Hurricanes, The Big Three, Derry & The Seniors and Kingsize Taylor & The Dominoes.

March 7
Cassanova Club, Sampson & Barlow's New Ballroom, Liverpool, with Derry & The Seniors.

March 8
The Cavern (lunchtime), Aintree Institute, Liverpool and Hambleton Hall, Huyton, Liverpool, with Rory Storm & The Hurricanes and Derry & The Seniors.

March 10
The Cavern (lunchtime), Grosvenor Ballroom, Liscard and St. John's Hall, Tuebrook, Liverpool.

March 11
Aintree Institute, Liverpool and Liverpool Jazz Society (Old Iron Door Club).
The latter was a 12-hour concert billed by adventurous promoter Sam Leach as "An All Night Rock Ball". Also on the bill were Rory Storm & The Hurricanes, Gerry & The Pacemakers, The Remo Four, Kingsize Taylor & The Dominoes, The Big Three, Dale Roberts & The Jaywalkers, Derry & The Seniors, Ray & The Del Renas, The Pressmen, Johnny Rocco & The Jets and Faron & The Tempest Tornadoes.

March 12
Casbah Coffee Club, West Derby, Liverpool and Cassanova Club, Sampson & Barlow's New Ballroom, Liverpool, with Kingsize Taylor & The Dominoes.

March 13
The Cavern (lunchtime) and Liverpool Jazz Society (Old Iron Door Club), with Kingsize Taylor & The Dominoes.

March 14
The Cavern (lunchtime).

March 15
The Cavern (lunchtime), Liverpool Jazz Society (afternoon), with Gerry & The Pacemakers and Rory Storm & The Wild Ones. This was a "Swinging Lunchtime Rock Session" running from 12 midday until 5pm which they went to straight after their lunchtime date at the Cavern.
Stuart Sutcliffe returned to Hamburg to his girlfriend, Astrid Kirchherr, and the State College of Art where he was studying painting.

March 16
The Cavern (lunchtime).

March 17
Mossway Hall, Croxteth and Liverpool Jazz Society (Old Iron Door Club).

March 19
Casbah Coffee Club, West Derby, Liverpool.

March 20
The Cavern (lunchtime) and Hambleton Hall, Huyton, Liverpool, with The Rockin' Ravens.

March 21
The Cavern (evening) with The Remo Four, Dale Roberts & The Jaywalkers and The Swinging Blue Genes, on a Blue Genes guest night. This was The Beatles' first evening gig at the Cavern.

March 22
The Cavern (lunchtime).

March 24
The Cavern (lunchtime).

March 26
Casbah Coffee Club, West Derby, Liverpool.

March 27
The Beatles returned to Hamburg by train to play at the Top Ten. They received DM35 per man per day and accommodation: the fourth-floor attic above the club.

April 1–30
Top Ten Club, Reeperbahn, Hamburg.

April 1
The Beatles began a three-month, 13-week season at The Top Ten Club, at Reeperbahn 136; a venue of about the same size as the Kaiserkeller, with a couple of dozen small tables surrounding a square dance floor by the stage. Their residency at the Top Ten Club lasted from April 1 until July 1, playing seven-hour sessions on week nights and eight hours at weekends with a 15-minute break every hour. They alternated first with The Jaybirds and later with Rory Storm & The Hurricanes. Beatles historian Mark Lewisohn has calculated that they spent 503 hours on stage over 92 nights.

In Hamburg they were reunited with Stuart Sutcliffe, who had returned there two weeks before and sometimes sat in with them. Stuart's decision not to remain in the band was now final. It was during this Hamburg visit that Astrid dressed Stuart in black leather, an outfit which the rest of the group then had copied by a tailor on the Reeperbahn. She also brushed Stu's hair forward, to look like her "exi" friends. The other Beatles did not go for this – yet.

April 20
Allan Williams in Liverpool had discovered that The Beatles did not intend to pay him his managerial commission on their earnings at The Top Ten Club, and that they considered he was no longer their manager. He wrote them a stormy letter, accusing them of forgetting who had helped them in the past, and describing them as "swollen-headed".

Allan Williams: "I am very distressed to hear you are contemplating not paying my commission out of your pay, as we agreed in our contract for your engagement at the Top Ten Club.

"May I remind you, seeing you are all appearing to get more than a little swollen-headed, that you would not ever have smelled Hamburg if I had not made the contracts.

"So you see, lads, I'm very annoyed you should welsh out of your agreed contract. If you decide not to pay I promise that I shall have you out of Germany inside two weeks through several legal ways and don't you think I'm bluffing.

"I don't want to fall out with you but I can't abide anybody who does not honour their word or bond, and I could have sworn you were all decent lads, that is why I pushed you when nobody wanted to hear you."

Williams no longer acted as The Beatles' manager after this point, and was unsuccessful in pursuing his financial claim against the group.

PAUL'S VIOLIN BASS

Paul: "I'd gone out there with a red Rosetti Solid 7, which was a real crappy guitar, but looked quite good. Stuart Sutcliffe was leaving the band and he wanted to stay in Hamburg, so we had to have a bass player. So I got elected bass player, or lumbered as the case may be. Stuart lent me his bass, so I got off the piano then and came up on the front line again to play it, but I actually played it upside down. I kind of wangled my way round that.

"I got my Hofner violin bass at the Steinway shop in the town centre. I remember going along and there was this bass which was quite cheap, it cost the German mark equivalent of £30 or so – my dad had always hammered into us never to get into debt because we weren't that rich. John and George went easily into debt and got beautiful guitars: John got a Club 40 and George had a Futurama – which is like a Fender copy – and then later Gretches. Then John got Rickenbackers. They were prepared to use hire purchase credit, but it had been so battered into me I wouldn't risk it. So I bought a cheap guitar. And once I bought it I fell in love with it."

Late May/early June

Having watched the group perform at The Top Ten Club in early May, German orchestra leader, composer and record label executive Bert Kaempfert signed The Beatles (John, Paul, George and Pete) to a recording contract with his production company, Der Bert Kaempfert Produktion. The deal officially ran from July 1st 1961 to June 30th 1962. Kaempfert had been alerted to their potential by one of his artists, German rock'n'roll singer Tommy Kent. Although he agreed to let them tape some of their own material, his primary interest in The Beatles was as a backing group for the London rock'n'roll singer, Tony Sheridan, whom he had also recently signed.

June 1–30

Top Ten Club, Reeperbahn, Hamburg.

John's girlfriend, Cynthia Powell, and Paul's Liverpool girlfriend, Dot Rohne, came to Hamburg on a visit. John and Cynthia stayed with Astrid while Paul and Dot stayed with Rosa down in the docks. John and Paul bought them both black leather skirts to make them look like Brigitte Bardot.

CYNTHIA

John met Cynthia at Art College and they began going steady in 1958. Brought up on the relatively affluent Wirrall, Cynthia appeared rather strait-laced for the now openly rebellious Lennon but their relationship flourished and they married in the summer of 1962. By this time Cynthia was pregnant and Mimi, John's aunt, refused to attend the wedding, stating that they were far too young. The marriage was kept secret at the outset but by 1964 it was fairly common knowledge and initial fears that it would affect The Beatles' popularity proved to be unfounded.

June 22/23

Friedrich-Ebert-Halle, Hamburg-Harburg.

The Beatles, with Paul on bass and Stuart Sutcliffe watching but not playing, backed Tony Sheridan on a recording session for German producer and orchestra leader Bert Kaempfert. For some reason the sessions spread over three days. However, since the equipment consisted of nothing more than a portable tape recorder set up on the stage of an orchestral hall with the curtains drawn, it was not as expensive or time consuming as real studio time would have been.

At the orchestral hall, they recorded four tracks backing Sheridan: 'My Bonnie Lies Over The Ocean', 'When The Saints Go Marching In', 'Why (Can't You Love Me Again)' and 'Nobody's Child'. They also did one of their own, 'Cry For A Shadow', an instrumental credited to John Lennon and George Harrison.

Kaempfert had arranged to collect The Beatles for the session outside The Top Ten Club, but they were not waiting for him when he arrived, so he had to climb up to their lodgings and shake them awake.

The single 'My Bonnie'/'The Saints' was released in Germany as Polydor 24673 in October. The Beatles were renamed "The Beat Brothers" for this release because their name sounded too much like "Peedles", a German slang term for male genitalia.

George: "The record of 'My Bonnie' goes like this: when Tony sings, then it's me playing lead, but the break in the middle is Tony playing. The shouting in the background is Paul."

June 24

Studio Rahlstedt, Rahlau 128, Tonndorf, Hamburg.

A further track with Tony Sheridan was recorded: Jimmy Reed's '(If You Love Me Baby) Take Out Some Insurance On Me', plus the pre-war standard 'Ain't She Sweet', recorded by The Beatles without Sheridan and with John on lead vocal.

June 28

The publishing contract with Bert Kaempfert's company Tonika Verlag for 'Cry For A Shadow' was signed by John and George.

July 2

The Beatles set off for Liverpool from Hamburg.

Liverpool impresario Brian Kelly: "When they returned, they had lost Stuart, and seemed downhearted. They had temporarily lost their lustre."

July 3

The Beatles arrived back in Liverpool.

July 6

Bill Harry published the first issue of his fortnightly beat music paper *Mersey Beat* which included a humorous article entitled "Being a Short Diversion on the Dubious Origins of The Beatles translated from the John Lennon":

"Once upon a time there were three little boys called John, George and Paul, by name christened. They decided to get together because they were the getting together type. When they were together they wondered what for after all, what for? So all of a sudden they all grew guitars and formed a noise. Funnily enough, no one was interested, least of all the three little men. So-o-o-o on discovering a fourth little even littler man called Stuart Sutcliffe running about them they said, quote, 'Sonny get a bass guitar and you will be alright' and he did – but he wasn't alright because he couldn't play it. So they sat on him with comfort 'til he could play. Still there was no beat, and a kindly old aged man said, quote, 'Thou hast not drums!' We had no drums! they coffed. So a series of drums came and went and came.

"Suddenly, in Scotland, touring with Johnny Gentle, the group (called The Beatles called) discovered they had not a very nice sound – because they had no amplifiers. They got some. Many people ask what are Beatles? Why Beatles? Ugh, Beatles, how did the name arrive? So we will tell you. It came in a vision – a man appeared on a flaming pie and said unto them. 'From this day on you are Beatles with an A'. Thank you, Mister Man, they said, thanking him.

"And then a man with a beard cut off said – will you go to Germany (Hamburg) and play mighty rock for the peasants for money? And we said we would play mighty anything for money.

"But before we could go we had to grow a drummer, so we grew one in West Derby in a club called Some Casbah and his trouble was Pete Best. We called, 'Hello, Pete, come off to Germany!' 'Yes!' Zooooom. After a few months, Peter and Paul (who is called McArtrey, son of Jim McArtrey, his father) lit a Kino (cinema) and the German police said, 'Bad Beatles, you must go home and light your English cinemas'. Zooooom, half a group. But even before this, the Gestapo had taken my friend little George Harrison (of Speke) away because he was only twelve and too young to vote in Germany; but after two months in England he grew eighteen, and the Gestapoes said, 'you can come'. So suddenly all back in Liverpool Village were many groups playing in grey suits and Jim said 'Why have you no grey suits?' 'We don't like them, Jim' we said speaking to Jim.

After playing in the clubs a bit, everyone said 'Go to Germany!' So we are, Zooooom. Stuart gone. Zoom zoom John (of Woolton) George (of Speke) Peter and Paul zoom zoom. All of them gone.

Thank you club members, from John and George (what are friends)."

July 8
Richard Starkey celebrates his 21st birthday in Liverpool, returning for the day from his season at Butlin's holiday camp with Rory Storm & The Hurricanes.

July 13
St John's Hall, Tuebrook, Liverpool.

July 14
The Cavern (lunchtime and evening), the latter a "Welcome Home Night", with Ian & The Zodiacs and The White Eagles Jazz Band.

July 15
Holyoake Hall, Wavertree, Liverpool.

July 16
Blair Hall, Walton, Liverpool.

July 17
The Cavern (lunchtime) and Litherland Town Hall.

July 19
The Cavern (lunchtime and evening), the latter with The Remo Four and The Pressmen.

July 20
St John's Hall, Tuebrook.

The second issue of *Mersey Beat* featured a picture of The Beatles on the cover with a report on their recording session with Tony Sheridan, under the grammatically dubious heading: "Beatle's Sign Recording Contract!' The report added that the group had agreed to record four numbers per year in their own right for Polydor, but that they were dissatisfied with the two songs taped at their first session. "Thus, in fact, under the contract the Beatles still have four more records to make this year."

The first record release from The Beatles' German recording sessions, 'My Bonnie' (credited to Tony Sheridan & The Beat Brothers), attracted heavy sales in Hamburg, but failed to reach the German national charts.

Noting the immediate popularity of *Mersey Beat*'s first issue, Brian Epstein ordered 12 dozen copies of the new edition for his record shop, NEMS.

July 21
The Cavern (lunchtime) and Aintree Institute, Liverpool, with Cy & The Cimarrons.

July 22
Holyoake Hall, Wavertree, Liverpool.

July 23
Blair Hall, Walton, Liverpool.

July 24
Litherland Town Hall.

July 25
The Cavern (lunchtime and evening), the latter with the Remo Four and Gerry & The Pacemakers on the Blue Genes Guest Night.

July 26
The Cavern (evening), with Johnny Sandon & The Searchers and The Four Jays.

July 27
The Cavern (lunchtime) and St John's Hall, Tuebrook, with The Big Three, Cass & the Cassanovas and Cilla White, whom The Beatles backed.
Brian Epstein later changed her name to the funkier sounding Cilla Black.

July 28
Aintree Institute, Liverpool.

July 29
Blair Hall, Walton, Liverpool.

July 30
Blair Hall, Walton, Liverpool.

July 31
The Cavern (lunchtime) and Litherland Town Hall.

August 2
The Cavern (lunchtime and evening), the latter with Karl Kerry & The Cruisers and Dale Roberts & The Jaywalkers.

August 3
Brian Epstein began his record review column for *Mersey Beat* magazine called "Stop the World – And Listen to Everything In It" by "Brian Epstein Of NEMS". His column frequently appeared opposite news stories about the latest exploits of The Beatles.

August 4
The Cavern (lunchtime) and Aintree Institute, Liverpool.

August 5
The Cavern (evening).
An all-night session with The Cimmerons, The Panama Jazz Band, The Mike Cotten Jazz Band, The Kenny Ball Jazzmen and The Remo Four.

August 6
Casbah Coffee Club, West Derby, Liverpool.

August 7
Town Hall, Litherland.

August 8
The Cavern (lunchtime).

August 9
The Cavern (evening).

August 10
The Cavern (lunchtime) and St. John's Hall, Tuebrook, Liverpool.

August 11
The Cavern (evening) with Alan Elsdon's Jazz Band.

August 12
Aintree Institute, Liverpool.

August 13
Casbah Coffee Club, West Derby, Liverpool.

August 14
The Cavern (lunchtime).

August 16
The Cavern (evening) with The Pressmen.

August 17
St John's Hall, Tuebrook, Liverpool, with The Big Three. Johnny Gustafson, bassist from The Big Three, sat in with them that night.
A further example of Lennon wit in this issue was the publication of an unsigned nonsense poem entitled 'I Remember Arnold'.

The first Beatles fan letters were printed in *Mersey Beat*, which also introduced a "Classified Ads" section full of private jokes between John Lennon and his friends: "Whistling Jock Lennon wishes to contact HOT NOSE . . . HOT LIPS, missed you Friday, RED NOSE . . . RED SCUNTHORPE wishes to jock HOT ACCRINGTON."
A further example of Lennon wit in this issue was the publication of an unsigned nonsense poem entitled 'I Remember Arnold'.

August 18
The Cavern (lunchtime) and Aintree Institute, Liverpool.

August 19
Aintree Institute, Liverpool.

August 20
Hambleton Hall, Huyton, Liverpool.

August 21
The Cavern (lunchtime).

August 23
The Cavern (lunchtime and evening), the latter with The Rockin' Blackcats and Kingsize Taylor & The Dominoes.

August 24
St John's Hall, Tuebrook, Liverpool.

August 25
The Cavern (lunchtime) and M.V. *Royal Iris*, River Mersey, with Acker Bilk and His Paramount Jazz Band.
A "Riverboat Shuffle" promoted by Ray McFall, owner of The Cavern, who closed the club for the event. The *Royal Iris* was a Liverpool institution, known as the "Fish & Chip Boat", which hosted dances and cruises for 40 years, until she was mothballed in January 1991. The Beatles were to play on the boat a number of times.

August 26
Aintree Institute, Liverpool.

August 27
Casbah Coffee Club, West Derby, Liverpool.

August 28
The Cavern (lunchtime).

August 29
The Cavern (lunchtime).

August 30
The Cavern (evening) with The Strangers.

August 31
St John's Hall, Tuebrook, Liverpool.
Mersey Beat reported that a "Beatles" fan club had been started with Bernard Boyd as President, Jennifer Dawes the Treasurer and Maureen O'Shea the Secretary. "The club will open officially in September . . ."

In the same issue, Cavern Club compere Bob Wooler claimed that "The Beatles are the biggest thing to have hit the Liverpool rock'n'roll set-up in years. They were, and still are, the hottest local property any Rock promoter is likely to encounter." Significantly, in the light of later events, the only member of the group whom Wooler singled out for special attention was Pete Best, whom he memorably described as "a sort of teenage Jeff Chandler".

September 1
The Cavern (lunchtime) with Karl Terry & The Cruisers, and (evening) with Dizzy Burton's Jazz Band.

September 2
Aintree Institute, Liverpool.

September 3
Hambleton Hall, Huyton, Liverpool.

September 6
The Cavern (evening) with Johnny Sandon & The Searchers and Ian & The Zodiacs.

September 7
The Cavern (lunchtime).

September 8
St John's Hall, Tuebrook, Liverpool.

September 9
Aintree Institute, Liverpool.

September 10
Casbah Coffee Club, West Derby, Liverpool.

September 11
The Cavern (lunchtime).

September 13
The Cavern (lunchtime and evening), the latter with The Remo Four and The Pressmen.

September 14
Litherland Town Hall.
John's satirical column "Around and About", written under the pseudonym Beatcomber, first appeared in *Mersey Beat* magazine, alongside another selection of his fake classified ads.

September 15
The Cavern (lunchtime), Grosvenor Ballroom, Liscard and Village Hall, Knotty Ash.
This second gig of the evening was promoted by Pete Best's mother, Mona, who was still interested in managing the group.

September 16
Aintree Institute, Liverpool.

September 17
Hambleton Hall, Huyton, Liverpool.

September 19
The Cavern (afternoon).

September 20
The Cavern (evening) with Karl Terry & The Cruisers and Ian & The Zodiacs.

September 21
The Cavern (lunchtime) and Litherland Town Hall, with Gerry & The Pacemakers and Rory Storm & The Hurricanes.

September 22
Village Hall, Knotty Ash.

September 23
Aintree Institute, Liverpool.

September 24
Casbah Coffee Club, West Derby, Liverpool.

September 25
The Cavern (lunchtime).

September 27
The Cavern (lunchtime and evening), the latter with Gerry & The Pacemakers and Mark Peters & The Cyclones.

September 28
Litherland Town Hall.

September 29
The Cavern (lunchtime) and Village Hall, Knotty Ash.

September 30
Paul and John set off to hitchhike to Paris, financed by some cash which John had been given as an early 21st birthday present.

During their time in Paris, the two Beatles attended several rock'n'roll concerts, including 'The Johnny Hallyday Rock Show' at the Olympia, and 'Les Rock Festival' at a Montmartre club, with British rocker Vince Taylor topping the bill.

October
The single 'My Bonnie'/'The Saints' by Tony Sheridan & The Beat Brothers was released in Germany on Polydor NH 24673.

The EP *My Bonnie* by Tony Sheridan and The Beat Brothers was released in Germany on Polydor EPH 21485: Side A: 'My Bonnie', 'Why'; Side B: 'Cry For A Shadow', 'The Saints'.

October 5
The Beatles were named as Liverpool's top group in Bob Wooler's regular column in *Mersey Beat*. Gerry & The Pacemakers and Rory Storm & The Hurricanes were the most popular runners-up.

October 9
John spent his 21st birthday in Paris with Paul.

THE ORIGINS OF THE 'BEATLE CUT'

John: "Paris has always been the object of English romanticism, hasn't it? I fell for Paris first of all, even before Hamburg. I remember spending my 21st birthday there with Paul in 1961 . . ."

In Paris they visited Jürgen Vollmer, a friend from the Reeperbahn, who had moved there to study photography. He wore his hair brushed forward in a fashion which was popular among some French youths, and was a style he had been introduced to by Astrid Kirchherr, who cut Stuart Sutcliffe's hair that way when they were all in Hamburg. John and Paul decided they wanted their hair like Jürgen's and asked him to do it. Jürgen Vollmer: "I gave both of them their first Beatles haircut in my hotel room on the Left Bank."

Paul: "Jürgen was in Paris on that trip, and we said, 'Do us a favour, cut our hair like you've cut yours.' So he did it, and it turned out different, 'cos his wasn't exactly a Beatle cut, but ours fell into The Beatles thing. We didn't really start that. The impression that got over was that it was just us, that we'd started it all. We kept saying, 'But there's millions of people in art schools who look like this. We're just the spokesmen for it.'"

Astrid had initially copied the style from a Jean Cocteau movie. Cocteau's favourite actor, Jean Marais, wore his hair brushed forward to play Oedipus in Cocteau's 1959 *Le Testament d'Orphée* and so that is the ultimate origin of the famous Beatles haircut.

Aunt Mimi told the *Liverpool Echo* that she remembered the time that John slipped off to Paris to "sell his paintings" and that some unsuspecting Frenchman has a Lennon original on his wall.

October 15
Albany Cinema, Northway (lunchtime).

The Beatles' first show after John and Paul returned from Paris was this charity concert promoted by Jim Getty (who had sold John his first guitar) in aid of the local St John's Ambulance Brigade. There were 16 acts on a three-hour bill, headed by local comedian Ken Dodd and ending with a ten-minute Beatles set.

Hambleton Hall, Huyton.

October 16
The Cavern (lunchtime).

October 17
David Lewis Club, Liverpool. Promoted by The Beatles' newly formed fan club.

October 18
The Cavern (lunchtime and evening), the latter with Ian & The Zodiacs and The Four Jays.

October 19
Litherland Town Hall with Gerry & The Pacemakers and Karl Terry & The Cruisers.

Halfway through the evening, The Beatles and The Pacemakers combined to form a "supergroup", The Beatmakers, with a line-up featuring: George, lead guitar; Paul, rhythm guitar; John, piano; Pete Best and Freddy Marsden, drums; Les Maguire, saxophone; Les Chadwick, bass; Gerry Marsden, lead guitar and vocals; Karl Terry, vocals. Among the numbers they performed were 'Whole Lotta Shakin' Goin' On', 'What'd I Say?', 'Red Sails In The Sunset' and 'Hit The Road Jack'.

October 20
The Cavern (lunchtime) and Village Hall, Knotty Ash.

October 21
The Cavern (all night session) with The Panama Jazz Band, The Remo Four, Gerry & The Pacemakers, The Yorkshire Jazz Band and The Collegians Jazz Band.

October 22
Casbah Coffee Club, West Derby, Liverpool.

October 24
The Cavern (lunchtime).

October 25
The Cavern (evening) with Gerry & The Pacemakers and The Strangers.

October 26
The Cavern (lunchtime).

October 27
Village Hall, Knotty Ash.

October 28
Aintree Institute, Liverpool.
   This was the legendary day on which Raymond Jones asked Brian Epstein for a copy of 'My Bonnie' by The Beatles at NEMS record store. The record was released only in Germany at that time and was by Tony Sheridan and The Beat Brothers, not The Beatles, so it took Epstein a little while to track it down. The Beatles had been enthusiastically 'plugging' the record during their shows around Liverpool, despite the fact that it was not available anywhere in the UK.
   Epstein's assistant, Alistair Taylor, subsequently claimed that this legendary occurrence was actually a myth, and that there was no 'Raymond Jones'. Alistair Taylor: "The truth is that we were being asked for 'My Bonnie', but no one actually ordered it. Brian would order any record once we had a firm order for it. I thought that we were losing sales, and I wrote an order in the book under the name 'Raymond Jones', and from that moment the legend grew."

October 29
Hambleton Hall, Huyton, Liverpool.

October 30
The Cavern (lunchtime).
   Two girls asked for 'My Bonnie' at NEMS, causing Brian Epstein to search foreign record importers' lists for this elusive record. Since he had sold 12 dozen copies of *Mersey Beat* and even wrote a column for the paper, it is virtually impossible that he didn't know who The Beatles were.
   Whether or not these girls or the mysterious Raymond Jones were the first customers to actually order 'My Bonnie', the result was that Brian Epstein ordered several copies of the single, which quickly sold out after he advertised the fact it was in stock with a small notice in the NEMS window. This rapid response encouraged him to re-order many times over, each time in larger quantities.

October 31
Litherland Town Hall.

November 1
The Cavern (lunchtime and evening), the latter with The Strangers and Gerry & The Pacemakers.

November 3
The Cavern (lunchtime).

November 4
The Cavern (evening) with The Collegians Jazz Band.

November 6
The British arm of Polydor Records decided to follow their German counterpart by releasing 'My Bonnie' by Tony Sheridan & The Beatles in the New Year.

November 7
The Cavern (lunchtime), Merseyside Civil Service Club and The Cavern again (evening), with Gerry & The Pacemakers and The Strangers on a Blue Genes guest night.

November 8
The Cavern (evening) with The Remo Four and Ian & The Zodiacs.

November 9
The Cavern (lunchtime) and Litherland Town Hall.
   Brian Epstein, accompanied by his assistant, Alistair Taylor, and wearing a rather incongruous pinstriped suit, visited the Cavern for the first time. His presence was announced by DJ Bob Wooler over the PA: "We have someone rather famous in the

audience today." It is a measure of how small-town Liverpool was in 1961 that a record shop owner could be regarded as a famous celebrity.

Brian was intrigued by all the publicity attending The Beatles, particularly by the speedy sales of their 'My Bonnie' single and the coverage that the band had been receiving in *Mersey Beat*, and had come to see what the fuss was about. Despite feeling very out of place amongst the lunch-time 'cave-dwellers' in the primitive, sweaty atmosphere of the Cavern, he began to visit the club regularly to see The Beatles, always taking time to have a few words with them.

George: "He started talking to us about the record that had created the demand. We didn't know much about him but he seemed very interested in us and also a little bit baffled.

"He came back several times and talked to us. It seemed there was something he wanted to say, but he wouldn't come out with it. He just kind of watched us and studied what we were doing. One day he took us to the store and introduced us. We thought he looked rather red and embarrassed about it all."

The evening show at Litherland was the group's last appearance at this venue.

BRIAN EPSTEIN

The man who became the manager of The Beatles had led an unsettled life, attending eight different schools throughout the UK, considering careers in dress design and the theatre before at the age of 16 settling into work in the family furniture store in Walton Road, Liverpool, where he proved to be an excellent salesman. Obliged to do National Service in 1952, Brian was subsequently arrested for impersonating an officer – a genuine misunderstanding that resulted from his refined manner – and subsequently discharged on 'medical grounds'. After an unsuccessful stint training to become an actor at RADA in London, he returned to Liverpool and took over a new store that the Epstein family had founded in Hoylake on the Cheshire Wirral.

Brian Epstein was homosexual and lived a double life, by day managing the furniture shop, by night visiting those areas of Liverpool where gay men gathered. Homosexuality was illegal in Britain in the Fifties and Brian was in constant fear of being exposed or beaten up. On one occasion he was arrested for soliciting, an incident which led him to consider taking his own life.

In 1958 Brian became the manager of the record department in the Epsteins' new shop, North End Music Stores, in Liverpool's Great Charlotte Street. Imaginative and artistic in his ideas for presentation and publicity, he made it immensely successful and was soon able to advertise its wares as 'the Finest Record Selection in the North'.

November 10
Tower Ballroom, New Brighton, Wallasey, with Roy Storm & The Hurricanes, Gerry & The Pacemakers, The Remo Four, Kingsize Taylor & The Dominoes, Village Hall, Knotty Ash.

The first of promoter Sam Leach's "Operation Big Beat" concerts. The Beatles played two sets, the first at 8 and the second at 11.30. In between sets they drove to Knotty Ash where they played another gig.

November 11
Aintree Institute, Liverpool.

To celebrate the success of "Operation Big Beat" the previous night, Sam Leach gave a late-night party at the Liverpool Jazz Centre which The Beatles all attended.

November 12
Hambleton Hall, Huyton, Liverpool.

November 13
The Cavern (lunchtime).

November 14
Merseyside Civil Service Club.

The Cavern, with The Remo Four and Gerry & The Pacemakers on a Blue Genes guest night.

November 15
The Cavern (lunchtime and evening), the latter with The Four Jays and Johnny Sandon & The Searchers.

November 17
The Cavern (lunchtime) and Village Hall, Knotty Ash.

November 18
The Cavern (evening) with The White Eagles Jazz Band.

November 19
Casbah Coffee Club, West Derby, Liverpool.

November 21
The Cavern (lunchtime) and Merseyside Civil Service Club.

November 22
The Cavern (evening) with Gerry & The Pacemakers and Earl Preston & The TTs.

November 23
The Cavern (lunchtime).

November 24
Casbah Coffee Club, West Derby, Liverpool and Tower Ballroom, New Brighton, Wallasey with Rory Storm & The Hurricanes, Gerry & The Pacemakers, The Remo Four, Earl Preston & The Tempest Tornadoes and Faron Young & The Flamingos.

The evening was Sam Leach's "Operation Big Beat II". The Beatles arrived for an 11pm set, and there were surprise appearances by Emile Ford, who performed with Rory Storm & The Hurricanes, and American singer Davy Jones, who did two numbers backed by The Beatles.

November 26
Hambleton Hall, Huyton, Liverpool.

November 27
The Cavern (lunchtime).

November 28
Merseyside Civil Service Club.

November 29
The Cavern (lunchtime and evening shows), the latter with Ian & The Zodiacs and The Remo Four.

December 1
The Cavern (lunchtime) and Tower Ballroom, New Brighton, Wallasey. The latter was another of Sam Leach's "Operation Big Beat" sessions, with The Beatles heading the bill of six groups.

December 2
The Cavern (evening) with The Zenith Six Jazz Band.

December 3
Casbah Coffee Club, West Derby, Liverpool.

The first meeting between the group and Brian Epstein to discuss his becoming their manager was held at Epstein's office at NEMS. Paul was late because he was having a bath, but once the full complement had gathered they retired to a milk bar for Brian to put his proposals to them.

George: "Eventually he started talking about becoming our manager. Well, we hadn't really had anybody actually *volunteer* in that sense. At the same time, he was very honest about it, like saying he didn't really know anything about managing a group like us. He sort of hinted that he was keen if we'd go along with him . . ."

Brian: "There was something enormously attractive about them. I liked the way they worked and the obvious enthusiasm they put into their numbers . . . It was the boys themselves, though, who really swung it. Each had something which I could see would be highly commercial if only someone could push it to the top. They were *different* characters but they were so obviously part of the whole. Quite frankly, I was excited about their prospects, provided some things could be changed."

The Beatles were not sure and went away to think about it. Meanwhile, a second meeting was arranged.

It appears that even in advance of this first meeting, Brian Epstein had already written to R. White, the General Marketing Manager of EMI Records, recommending that they should sign the group. He may have hoped that by the time he met The Beatles, he would already be able to show them definite interest in their career from one of Britain's major record companies.

December 5
The Cavern (lunchtime).

December 6
The Cavern (evening) with The Remo Four and The Strangers.

The Beatles' second meeting with Brian Epstein. John, acting as the spokesman for the group, accepted Brian's proposal but no documents were drawn up.

December 8
The Cavern (lunchtime), also backing Davy Jones whom Ray McFall had booked for the lunchtime session as well; and Tower Ballroom, New Brighton, Wallasey, with Danny Williams and Davy Jones, who headed the bill and for whom The Beatles again provided backing.

Although he had not yet signed The Beatles to a management agreement, Brian Epstein wrote again in that capacity to EMI Records, telling them that their main rival, the Decca group of labels, was interested in recording the group, but offering them first refusal. He also claimed that the group had recently been visited by a representative from Deutsche Grammophon Records – an exaggeration, but not entirely untrue, as the Polydor label in Germany was a division of Deutsche Grammophon.

Epstein concluded: "These four boys, who are superb instrumentalists, also produce some exciting and pulsating vocals. They play mostly their own compositions and one of the boys has written a song which I really believe to be the hottest thing since 'Living Doll'. This is a group of exceptional talents and appealing personalities."

December 9
Palais Ballroom, Aldershot, with Ivor Jay & The Jaywalkers.

Sam Leach's first attempt at promoting a concert in southern England ended in disaster. As he was not known to them, the local newspaper refused to accept his cheque for an advertisement, and as he neglected to leave his telephone number with them, his ad was not run. The Beatles arrived at an empty hall; no one in Aldershot knew the "Battle of the Bands" was happening. A quick run round the local coffee bars asking people to come to a free dance resulted in an audience of 18 people.

The Beatles had nowhere to stay so they drove into London to visit the Blue Gardenia, a Soho drinking club run by their old friend Brian Cassar, formerly of Cass & The Cassanovas. They jammed on stage (minus George) to an even smaller audience than in Aldershot.

The near humiliation of this venture outside Merseyside reinforced the idea that The Beatles desperately needed a full-time manager to take care of all aspects of their bookings.

December 10
Hambleton Hall, Huyton, Liverpool.

BRIAN EPSTEIN BECOMES THE BEATLES' MANAGER

The group came to an informal agreement with Brian Epstein, making him their manager providing he could get them a recording contract. He also promised to release them from their contract with Bert Kaempfert in Hamburg. Brian had very specific ideas about stage presentation. There was to be no eating, drinking or fighting on stage, nor were they to shout at the audience. Brian wanted them to be punctual and to plan their set in advance. His biggest change was to take them out of their black leathers and put them all into neat suits. The group assumed that he knew what he was doing and went along with it.

John: "We were in a daydream 'till he came along. We'd no idea what we were doing. Seeing our marching orders on paper made it all official. Brian was trying to clean our image up. He said we'd never get past the door of a good place. He'd tell us that jeans were not particularly smart and could we possibly manage to wear proper trousers. But he didn't want us suddenly looking square. He let us have our own sense of individuality. We respected his views. We stopped chomping at cheese rolls and jam butties on stage. We paid a lot more attention to what we were doing. Did our best to be on time. And we smartened up, in the sense that we wore suits instead of any sloppy old clothes."

December 11

The Cavern (lunchtime).

December 13

The Cavern (lunchtime and evening), the latter with Gerry & The Pacemakers and The Four Jays.

Brian Epstein used his influence as a major record dealer to persuade the A&R Manager of Decca Records, Mike Smith, to visit Liverpool to see them play The Cavern. After watching them play he agreed to audition them in London.

December 15

The Cavern (lunchtime) and Tower Ballroom, New Brighton, Wallasey, with a reformed Cass & The Cassanovas and The Big Three.

December 16

The Cavern (evening) with The White Eagles Jazz band.

December 17

Casbah Coffee Club, West Derby.

December 18

The Cavern (lunchtime).

EMI Records wrote to Brian Epstein, declining his offer that they should sign The Beatles, but enclosing an English translation of their German recording contract with Bert Kaempfert, which he had given them to explain their current commitments.

December 19

The Cavern (lunchtime).

December 20

The Cavern (evening) with The Strangers and Mark Peters & The Cyclones.

December 21

The Cavern (lunchtime).

December 23

The Cavern, all-night session with The Micky Ashman Ragtime Jazz Band, The Remo Four, Gerry & The Pacemakers, The Saints Jazz Band and The Searchers.

December 26
Tower Ballroom, New Brighton, Wallasey. The concert was billed as featuring "The Beetles" with Rory Storm & The Hurricanes and Tony Osborne & His Band for a "Boxing Night Big Beat Ball".

December 27
The Cavern (evening) with Gerry & The Pacemakers and Kingsize Taylor & The Dominoes. Advertised as "The Beatles' Xmas Party".

December 29
The Cavern (evening) with the Yorkshire Jazz Band.

December 30
The Cavern (evening) with The White Eagles Jazz Band.

January 1

The Beatles auditioned for Mike Smith, an A&R manager at Decca Records, at Decca's studios in Broadhurst Gardens, West Hampstead, north London. They arrived in London after a ten-hour drive through stormy conditions on New Year's Eve with the group and roadie Aspinall squashed into a van with all their equipment. Tony Meehan, the former drummer for The Shadows, had joined Decca as a producer the year before and was present in the control room, and the group were impressed to meet him. The Beatles were nervous and Mike Smith was late after an all-night party. When Smith saw the state of their amps he insisted that they use the unfamiliar studio equipment.

The group recorded 15 songs chosen by Brian Epstein. They got started at 11am and finished about an hour later. They recorded a mixture of oldies, some of their own compositions and a selection of recent chart hits, intending to show all sides of their ability, from rock'n'roll to ballad standards: 'Like Dreamers Do' (Lennon/McCartney), 'Money (That's What I Want)', 'Till There Was You', 'The Sheik Of Araby', 'To Know Her Is To Love Her', 'Take Good Care Of My Baby', 'Memphis, Tennessee', 'Sure To Fall (In Love With You)', 'Hello Little Girl' (Lennon/McCartney), 'Three Cool Cats', 'Crying, Waiting, Hoping', 'Love Of The Loved' (Lennon/McCartney), 'September In The Rain', 'Besame Mucho' and 'Searchin'.

Smith said he would let Epstein know and hurried them out of the studio because he was running late and had another appointment to see Brian Poole & The Tremeloes. He had been enthusiastic about their performance, and the group left feeling optimistic. The Beatles and Brian Epstein stayed at the Royal Hotel (27 shillings a night plus breakfast) and celebrated with rum and scotch-and-cokes.

Mike Smith cut a number of acetates for his boss Dick Rowe, the head of "Pop" A&R at Decca, to hear when he returned from America. He singled out the Lennon & McCartney songs 'Hello Little Girl' and 'Like Dreamers Do' as the most interesting items on the tape. But Rowe turned the group down, famously telling Brian Epstein: "Groups of guitars are on the way out, Mr Epstein. You really should stick to selling records in Liverpool." Electric guitars, he told him, were now "old hat". He became known as "The man who turned down The Beatles" but quickly made up for it by signing The Rolling Stones to Decca – on George Harrison's advice.

January 3

The Cavern (lunchtime and evening), the latter with Johnny Sandon & The Searchers and Kingsize Taylor & The Dominoes.

January 4

A poll of 5,000 readers of *Mersey Beat* magazine to find Liverpool's most popular group showed The Beatles at number one with Gerry & The Pacemakers in second place. "Beatles Top Poll!" screamed the front cover headline, over a moody photograph of the four Beatles in their leather jackets.

Mersey Beat also included a belated report on their Paris trip, written by John and Paul.

January 5

The Cavern (lunchtime).

The single 'My Bonnie'/'The Saints' was released in the UK as Polydor NH 66833 by Tony Sheridan and The (now-correctly-named) Beatles: an Epstein promotional plan which meant that "Polydor Recording Artists" could now be added to posters and advertisements even though there was little chance of the record getting into the charts.

January 6

The Cavern (evening) with The Collegians Jazz Band.

January 7

Casbah Coffee Club, West Derby, Liverpool.

January 9

The Cavern (lunchtime).

January 10
The Cavern (evening) with Gerry & The Pacemakers.

January 11
The Cavern (lunchtime).

January 12
The Cavern (evening) with The Mike Cotten Jazzmen.
Tower Ballroom, New Brighton, Wallasey, with Mel (King of Twist) Turner & The Bandits, Rory Storm & The Hurricanes, The Strangers. When Screaming Lord Sutch & His Horde of Savages didn't arrive, The Beatles took over the 11.30 headline spot.

January 13
Hambleton Hall, Huyton.
This was their last performance at this venue.

January 14
Casbah Coffee Club, West Derby, Liverpool.

January 15
The Cavern (lunchtime).

January 17
The Cavern (lunchtime and evening), the latter with Ian & The Zodiacs and The Remo Four.

January 19
The Cavern (lunchtime) and Tower Ballroom, New Brighton, Wallasey.

January 20
The Cavern (evening) with The Yorkshire Jazz Band.

January 21
Casbah Coffee Club, West Derby, Liverpool.

January 22
The Cavern (lunchtime) and Kingsway Club, Southport.
This was the first of The Cavern's five experimental one-hour lunchtime sessions (instead of two hours). Admission was one shilling (five pence).
Brian Epstein signed a deal with Manfred Weissleder, the proprietor of the soon to be opened Star-Club in Hamburg, for The Beatles to help launch the venue. They were initially booked from April 13th to May 31st, at a fee of 500DM per musician per week.

January 24
The Cavern (lunchtime and evening), the latter with The Four Jays and Gerry & The Pacemakers.
That afternoon The Beatles finally signed a management contract with Brian Epstein, witnessed by his assistant Alistair Taylor, at Brian's NEMS office. He was to receive 25 per cent of their gross earnings. The four Beatles divided what was left after their expenses had been deducted. This meant that Brian always received more money than any individual Beatle and, when their expenses became enormous, he received considerably more. The normal management percentage in those days was ten per cent.
The four of them wrote their signatures over four of the five sixpenny stamps attached to the document as was required in those days to make it legally binding. Then Brian announced that he was not going to sign, saying that he did not want The Beatles to feel tied to him in any way. Alistair Taylor was asked to witness his non-signing. Since Brian's original agreement with the band was that he would get them a recording contract, which he had not yet done, his decision not to sign was not that surprising.

January 26
The Cavern (lunchtime and evening), the latter with The Yorkshire Jazz Band, and Tower Ballroom, New Brighton, Wallasey.

January 27
Aintree Institute, Liverpool.
    This was the last time that the group played for promoter Brian "Beekay" Kelly. Brian Epstein was insulted when Kelly paid the group their £15 fee in loose change and ensured they never worked for him again.
    The *Liverpool Echo* published an account of the group's audition with Decca written by Tony Barrow who was later to become their publicist.

January 28
Casbah Coffee Club, West Derby, Liverpool.

January 29
Kingsway Club, Southport.

January 30
The Cavern (lunchtime).

January 31
The Cavern (evening) with The Remo Four and Kingsize Taylor & The Dominoes.

February 1
The Cavern (lunchtime) and Thistle Café, West Kirby, with Steve Day & The Drifters.
    Billed as "The Grand Opening of The Beatle Club", this was the first booking where Brian Epstein took a commission. (The Beatles never played there again.)

February 2
Oasis Club, Manchester, with The Allan Dent Jazz Band and Tony Smith's Jazzmen.
    This was their first professionally organised gig outside Liverpool.

February 3
The Cavern (evening) with The Saints Jazz Band and Gerry & The Pacemakers.

February 4
Casbah Coffee Club, West Derby, Liverpool.

February 5
The Cavern (lunchtime) and The Kingsway Club, Southport, with The Quiet Ones.
    Pete Best was ill and couldn't make these two gigs. Since Rory Storm & The Hurricanes had no bookings this day, Ringo Starr stood in as The Beatles' drummer for both performances.

February 7
The Cavern (lunchtime and evening), the latter with Dale Roberts & The Jaywalkers and Gerry & The Pacemakers.

February 8
Brian Epstein had the Decca audition tape made into 78rpm acetates at EMI's His Master's Voice record shop at 363 Oxford Street, London, which was managed by a friend of his called Bob Boast. Jim Foy, the disc-cutter who worked on the first floor, over the shop, was impressed by their performance, and when Brian told him that John and Paul wrote some of their own material, he suggested that Brian should meet Sid Coleman, the head of EMI's record publishing company, Ardmore & Beechwood, whose offices were on the top floor. Coleman eventually published two of John and Paul's songs, 'Love Me Do' and 'P.S. I Love You', which are now owned by Paul McCartney, the only Beatles songs in the MPL (McCartney Productions Ltd) catalogue. It was Sid Coleman who sent Brian to see George Martin, head of A&R at another of EMI's companies, Parlophone Records.

February 9
The Cavern (lunchtime and evening), the latter with Gerry & The Pacemakers and The Collegians Jazz Band, and Technical College Hall, Birkenhead.
   This was the first of three consecutive Friday night sessions at the Tech.

February 10
Youth Club, St. Paul's Presbyterian Church Hall, Tranmere, Birkenhead.

February 11
Casbah Coffee Club, West Derby, Liverpool.

February 12
The Beatles were auditioned by Peter Pilbeam, who produced BBC Radio programmes for teenage audiences made in the north of England. The Beatles did two numbers with Paul on vocals: 'Like Dreamers Do', which was his own composition, and Peggy Lee's 'Till There Was You'; and two with John singing: his own 'Hello Little Girl' and Chuck Berry's 'Memphis, Tennessee'. Pilbeam's notes read "Yes" for John and "No" for Paul. He concluded: "An unusual group, not as rocky as most, more C&W with a tendency to play music." He booked them to record a session for *Teenagers' Turn* on March 7. It was their first radio broadcast.

February 13
The Cavern (lunchtime).

February 14
The Cavern (evening), with Johnny Sandon & The Searchers and The Strangers.

February 15
The Cavern (lunchtime) and Tower Ballroom, New Brighton, Wallasey, with Terry Lightfoot and his New Orleans Jazz Band. Billed as the "Pre-Panto Ball" as there was to be a "Panto Ball" at the Tower the next night. Between them they drew a large audience of 3,500 people.

February 16
Technical College, Birkenhead, and Tower Ballroom, New Brighton, Wallasey.

February 17
The Cavern (evening) with Cyril Preston's Excelsior Jazz Band and The Zenith Six Jazz Band.

February 18
Casbah Coffee Club, West Derby, Liverpool.

February 19
The Cavern (lunchtime).

February 20
Floral Hall, Southport, with Gerry & The Pacemakers, Rory Storm & The Hurricanes and The Chris Hamilton Jazzmen.
   "A Rock 'n' Trad Spectacular" and their biggest venue booked by Brian Epstein to date. A contract was sent by BBC Manchester for The Beatles to record the *Teenager's Turn* radio show on March 7.
   Brian Epstein wrote to Bert Kaempfert in Hamburg asking him to release The Beatles from their recording contract of May 1961.

February 21
The Cavern (lunchtime and evening), the latter with Ken Dallas & The Silhouettes and Steve Day & The Drifters.

February 23
The Cavern (lunchtime), Tower Ballroom, New Brighton, Wallasey (sets at 9 and 10.45pm) and Technical College, Birkenhead.
   The group just had time between sets at the Tower to squeeze in a half-hour appearance at Birkenhead.

February 24
YMCA Wirral and The Cavern.
   The YMCA audience were bored by the group's long introductions between songs and booed them off the stage.
   The Cavern show was an all-night session which also featured The Red River Jazzmen, Tony Smith's Jazz Band, Ken Sim's Jazz Band, Gerry & The Pacemakers and Ken Dallas & The Silhouettes.

February 26
Kingsway Club, Southport.

February 27
The Cavern (lunchtime).

February 28
The Cavern (evening) with Gerry & The Pacemakers and The Searchers.

March 1
The Cavern (lunchtime) and Storyville Jazz Club, Liverpool.

March 2
St John's Hall, Bootle and Tower Ballroom, New Brighton, Wallasey, with Johnny Sandon's Searchers and The Tenabeats. Billed as the "Mad March Rock Ball".

March 3
The Cavern (evening) with Jim McHarg's Storeyville Jazzmen.
   Replying to Brian Epstein's request, Bert Kaempfert agreed to release the group from their May 1961 recording contract but asked that they agree to record for Polydor during their spring engagement in Hamburg.

March 4
Casbah Coffee Club, West Derby, Liverpool.

March 5
The Cavern (lunchtime) and Kingsway Club, Southport.

March 6
The Cavern (evening) with Gerry & The Pacemakers on the Blue Genes Guest Night.

March 7
The group drove to the Playhouse Theatre in Manchester to record their set for the BBC Light Programme show *Teenagers' Turn – Here We Go*. They did three numbers, all covers of American hits, before a teenage audience: Roy Orbison's 'Dream Baby (How Long Must I Dream)', Chuck Berry's 'Memphis, Tennessee' and the Marvelettes' 'Please Mister Postman'.

March 8
Storyville Jazz Club.
   The BBC Light Programme broadcast The Beatles' appearance on *Teenagers' Turn – Here We Go*.

March 9
The Cavern (lunchtime and evening), the latter with The Saints Jazz Band.

March 10
St Paul's Presbyterian Church Youth Club, Church Hall, Tranmere, Birkenhead.
Also on the bill were The Country Four with Brian Newman.

March 11
Casbah Coffee Club, West Derby, Liverpool.

March 12
The Cavern (lunchtime).

March 13
The Cavern (lunchtime).

March 14
The Cavern (evening) with Gerry & The Pacemakers and Clay Ellis & The Raiders.

March 15
The Cavern (lunchtime) and Storyville Jazz Club, Liverpool.

March 16
The Cavern (evening) with The Collegians Jazz Band.

March 17
Village Hall, Knotty Ash.
A "St Patrick's Night Rock Gala" which also featured Rory Storm & The Hurricanes. Afterwards the promoter, Sam Leach, held a memorable party to celebrate his engagement to be married, which did not end until the following afternoon.

March 18
Casbah Coffee Club, West Derby, Liverpool.

March 19
Kingsway Club, Southport.

March 20
The Cavern (evening) with The Remo Four, The Zodiacs and Johnny Sandon on a Blue Genes Guest Night.

March 21
The Cavern (lunchtime).

March 22
The Cavern (evening) with Peppy & The New York Twisters.
Mersey Beat's gossip column, 'Mersey Roundabout', hinted that Ringo Starr might soon be leaving Rory Storm & The Hurricanes to join another Merseyside group, Derry & The Seniors. Also mentioned in the same column was the fact that John Lennon and Paul McCartney had now written more than 70 original songs.

March 23
The Cavern (lunchtime and evening), the latter with Pete Hartigan's Jazzmen and Gerry & The Pacemakers.

March 24
Heswall Jazz Club, Barnston Women's Institute, Heswall, Wirral, with The Pasadena Jazzmen.
For the first time, The Beatles wore suits as stage costumes for this prestigious event.

March 25
Casbah Coffee Club, West Derby, Liverpool.

March 26
The Cavern (lunchtime).

March 27
Brian Epstein officially informed Bert Kaempfert that he was giving notice of The Beatles' wish to withdraw from their contract with the German producer when it expired on June 30th.

March 28
The Cavern (lunchtime and evening), the latter with Gerry & The Pacemakers and The Remo Four with Johnny Sandon.

March 29
Odd Spot Club, Liverpool, with The Merseybeats.

March 30
The Cavern (lunchtime and evening), the latter with The Dallas Jazz Band.

March 31
Subscription Rooms, Stroud in Gloucestershire with The Rebel Rousers.
    Punters warned: "At the request of the Council – No Teddy Boys and Ladies please do not wear stiletto heels."

April
The Lennon & Harrison instrumental composition 'Cry For A Shadow' appeared on record for the first time anywhere in the world, as part of the *Mister-Twist* EP issued by Polydor in France (no. 21914). Ironically, the record credited Tony Sheridan as the artist, without any mention of The Beatles or, indeed, The Beat Brothers. It is unlikely that The Beatles were ever informed of this release.

April 1
Casbah Coffee Club, West Derby, Liverpool.

April 2
The Cavern (lunchtime) and Liverpool Pavilion with "Ireland's Pride", the Royal Show Band from Waterford. The Beatles were billed as "Merseyside's Joy".

April 4
The Cavern (lunchtime and evening), the latter with The Searchers and Earl Preston & The TTs.

April 5
The Cavern (evening).
    Presented by The Beatles' Fan Club, called "The Beatles for their Fans, or an Evening with John, Paul, George and Pete". The compere was Bob Wooler, and The Four Jays were also on the bill. Ticket holders received a free photograph of the group. The Beatles played the first half in their old Hamburg black leathers before changing into their new Epstein suits and ties for the second half.

April 6
The Cavern (lunchtime) and Tower Ballroom, New Brighton, Wallasey.
    The Beatles (spelled "Beetles" on the poster) played support to Emile Ford & The Checkmates. Also on the bill were Gerry & The Pacemakers, Howey Casey & The Seniors, Rory Storm & The Hurricanes, The Big Three and The Original King Twisters. All for six shillings.

April 7
The Cavern (evening) with The Saints Jazz Band and Casbah Coffee Club, West Derby, Liverpool.
    The Cavern show was advertised as "The Beatles Farewell Show" before they left for Hamburg. George was ill and couldn't play these two gigs.

April 10
Stuart Sutcliffe, who had remained in Hamburg, was rushed to hospital with a brain haemorrhage, but died in the ambulance. He was 22.

April 11
The Beatles, except George, flew to Hamburg from Ringway Airport, Manchester. They were greeted on arrival by Stuart Sutcliffe's distraught girlfriend, Astrid Kirchherr, who managed to stammer her tragic news. To her surprise, John exhibited no outward emotion at all – though she later credited John as having "saved" her from her grief, by insisting that she come out to see The Beatles perform every evening rather than maintaining a lonely vigil in her room.

April 13–30
Star-Club, Grosse-Freiheit, Hamburg.
   The Beatles played a seven-week season at the Star-Club ending on May 31, with only one day off: April 20, when the club closed for Good Friday. For the first two weeks they were on the same bill as Gene Vincent.
   Mersey Beat described the club: "There are two bars, a refreshment counter and a small 'twistin' base' situated in the balcony. Over the ground floor and beneath the balcony a suspended trellis ceiling has been slung from which hang attractive lanterns which give the club an exciting and intimate atmosphere."
   The same report hinted at potentially exciting developments in The Beatles' career: "In the first night audience was a television producer, who was most impressed with the boys, and arrangements are being made for them to appear on German television. Several members of the press were there, and it is understood that a photograph and report of The Beatles has been published in the leading German National Newspaper *Bilt*."

April 23
The single 'My Bonnie'/'The Saints' was released in the US as Decca 31382, by Tony Sheridan and The Beat Brothers. The release wasn't considered prestigious enough for The Beatles themselves to be informed.

May 1–31
Star-Club, Grosse Freiheit, Hamburg.

May 8
In London on one of his regular missions to secure The Beatles a recording deal, Brian Epstein used his status as manager of an important Liverpool music store to win a meeting with Sid Coleman, a director of EMI's music publishing division, Ardmore & Beechwood. He was impressed by the acetate of the group's Decca audition, and put them in touch with a friend at Parlophone Records.

May 9
George Martin met with Brian Epstein at Abbey Road at the suggestion of Sid Coleman. On the strength of the Decca audition tapes, Martin offered Brian a provisional recording contract before he had even seen the group play. The paperwork was processed and Brian's signature added. All that remained was for George to audition the group at Abbey Road, and if he liked them, EMI's official signature could be added and the contract would be legally binding. A date was set of June 6 for The Beatles to make their first visit to Abbey Road. Brian sent a telegram to The Beatles in Hamburg which read, "Congratulations boys. EMI request recording session. Please rehearse new material." A second telegram was addressed to *Mersey Beat* editor Bill Harry in Liverpool.

GEORGE MARTIN
Born in 1926, George Martin, who would become The Beatles' producer and a key factor in their success and musical development, had joined EMI in 1950 as assistant to Oscar Preuss, the head of A&R. A trained musician, he had attended the London Guildhall and was proficient on the piano and oboe.

In 1954 Martin became the head of A&R at Parlophone, EMI's downmarket label which released comic dialogue records and novelty items such as the 1962 hit 'Stop, You're Driving Me Crazy' by The Temperence Seven. Most pop hits, such as those by Cliff Richard and The Shadows, appeared on EMI's more upmarket Columbia label.

Fortunately for The Beatles, George Martin, although conservative by nature, had an open mind and was constantly on the lookout for something new and original. He was also a generous collaborator who over the coming years would give unselfishly and unstintingly of his time and talent towards polishing the music of The Beatles, whilst simultaneously refusing to either impose his ideas dictatorially or take undue credit for his work.

May 24

Almost a year after their last recording session in Hamburg, and only a few weeks before their contract with Bert Kaempfert expired, The Beatles once again acted as Tony Sheridan's backing band at the Studio Rahlstedt. They were joined for the session, which began at 6pm, by Roy Young (piano) and Ricki Barnes (saxophone). Two songs were recorded, 'Sweet Georgia Brown' and 'Swanee River'. Paul was credited in Polydor's paperwork as the arranger for 'Sweet Georgia Brown'.

May 25

With their obligations to Bert Kaempfert complete, Brian Epstein and Kaempfert signed an agreement cancelling The Beatles' German recording contract with immediate effect. This freed The Beatles to record for George Martin at Parlophone a few days later.

May 28

The Beatles opened what the Star-Club billed as their "Rockin'-Twist Festival 62 mit Gene Vincent, King of Rock '61 in USA, Davy Jones, Tony Sheridan, The Bachelors, Tanya Day, Roy Young, Tex Roberg und den Rock-und-Twist-Bands: The Beatles, The Graduates, Gerry & The Pacemakers, The Starliners, Roy & Tony's Star Inc." which ran from May 28 until June 11.

Brian Epstein had originally booked today and tomorrow to hold a private recording session for The Beatles at Studio Rahlstedt, with Bert Kaempfert hired as the producer, when they were scheduled to record 12 songs for a possible album. But he cancelled the booking when he heard that George Martin would be holding a session with the group the following week in London.

May 31

Already anticipating the result of the group's forthcoming audition, Brian Epstein told *Mersey Beat* that he had "secured a recording contract with the powerful EMI organisation for The Beatles to record for the Parlophone label".

June

The album *My Bonnie* by Tony Sheridan & The Beat Brothers was released in Germany on Polydor LPHM 46612 (mono) and SLPHM 237112 (stereo). The album, the first anywhere in the world to feature The Beatles' work, included 'My Bonnie' and 'The Saints', credited on the rear cover as "Accompanied by The Beatles".

June 6

Abbey Road. The Beatles recorded four numbers in studio three: 'Besame Mucho', 'Love Me Do', 'P.S. I Love You' and 'Ask Me Why'. The session was produced by Ron Richards. George Martin was not at the session from the beginning, and only showed up when the balance engineer, Norman Smith, liked their first Lennon and McCartney composition and sent the tape operator, Chris Neal, to fetch him. George Martin saw the potential in what he heard, but he did not like Pete Best's drumming and said they could use a session drummer for the recording sessions. With this potential stumbling block resolved, George Martin ordered the final signature to be placed on the contract. The Beatles were now EMI artists.

George Martin: "If there's anything you don't like, just tell me."

George Harrison: "Well, I don't like your tie, for a start!"

June 9

The Cavern (evening): "The Beatles' Welcome Home Show" also featuring The Red River Jazzmen, The Spidermen, The Four Jays and Ken Dallas & The Silhouettes.

Nine hundred fans managed to squeeze into the airless basement for this gig, breaking The Cavern's attendance record.

June 11

The group recorded another set for the BBC Light Programme's *Teenagers' Turn – Here We Go*, at the BBC's Playhouse Theatre, Manchester. They played 'Ask Me Why', 'Besame Mucho' and 'A Picture of You'.

The Beatles' Fan Club in Liverpool organised a special bus trip to this event, collecting members from outside Brian Epstein's NEMS shop at 6pm and promising to deliver them back after the recording at 10.30pm.

June 12

The Cavern (lunchtime and evening) with no support.

June 13

The Cavern (lunchtime and evening), the latter with The Dakotas and The Dennisons.

June 15

The Cavern (lunchtime and evening), the latter with Group One and The Spidermen.

The Beatles' appearance on *Teenagers' Turn – Here We Go* was broadcast by the BBC Light Programme.

June 16

The Cavern (evening) with Tony Smith's Jazzmen.

June 19

The Cavern (lunchtime and evening), the latter with The Merseybeats and The Swinging Blue Genes.

June 20

The Cavern (lunchtime and evening), the latter with The Sorrals and Kingsize Taylor & The Dominoes.

June 21

Tower Ballroom, New Brighton, Wallasey.

Bruce Channel topped the bill with Delbert McClinton and The Barons as his backing group. Also on the bill were Howie Casey & The Seniors, The Big Three and The Four Jays.

McClinton played harmonica on Bruce Channel's smash hit, 'Hey Baby'. When he discovered that John also played the instrument, he gave the Beatles' leader several valuable hints on how to improve his technique. Thereafter John incorporated harmonica parts into most of the group's original compositions for the next two years.

June 22

The Cavern (lunchtime and evening), the latter with Clay Ellis & The Raiders and The Olympics.

June 23

The Victory Memorial Hall, Northwich in Cheshire.

Brian Epstein formed NEMS Enterprises Limited to deal with Beatles affairs.

June 24

Casbah Club, West Derby, Liverpool. The Beatles' final appearance at Mona Best's club.

June 25

The Cavern (lunchtime) and Plaza Ballroom, St Helens in Lancashire, with The Big Three "Big Beat Bargain Night".

June 26
EMI's General Marketing Manager R. White wrote to Brian Epstein, expressing his embarrassment that he had previously told The Beatles' manager that the company were not interested in the group. He ended his letter: "I know you will appreciate that even Artistes Managers are human and can change their minds!"

June 27
The Cavern (lunchtime and evening), the latter with The Swinging Blue Genes.

June 28
Majestic Ballroom, Birkenhead, "Merseyside's luxury ballroom".
   The Beatles' first booking with the Top Rank Organisation.

June 29
The Cavern (lunchtime).
   Tower Ballroom, New Brighton, Wallasey. "Operation Big Beat III", a five-and-a-half hour "Cavalcade of Rock 'n' Twist".

June 30
Heswall Jazz Club at the Barnston Women's Institute in Heswall, with The Big Three.

July 1
The Cavern (evening) with Gene Vincent & Sounds Incorporated.
   A bootlegged recording of Gene Vincent playing 'What'd I Say' is said to feature The Beatles sitting in with Sounds Incorporated at this gig.

July 2
Plaza Ballroom, St Helens in Lancashire.

July 3
The Cavern (lunchtime).

July 4
The Cavern (evening) with Group One and The Spidermen.

July 5
Majestic Ballroom, Birkenhead.

July 6
Riverboat Shuffle on board the M.V. *Royal Iris*, organised by The Cavern.
   Also on the bill were Acker Bilk's Paramount Jazz Band.

July 7
Golf Club Dance, Hulme Hall, Port Sunlight, Birkenhead.

July 8
The Cavern (evening) with The Swinging Blue Genes and Tony Smith's Jazzmen.

July 9
Plaza Ballroom, St Helens.

July 10
The Cavern (lunchtime).

July 11
The Cavern (evening) with The Statesmen and The Morockans.

July 12
The Cavern (lunchtime).
   Majestic Ballroom, Birkenhead.

July 13
Tower Ballroom, New Brighton, Wallasey.

July 14
Regent Dansett, Rhyl, Wales, with The Strangers.

July 15
The Cavern (evening) with The Saints Jazz Band, The Swinging Blue Genes and The Four Jays.

July 16
The Cavern (lunchtime) and Plaza Ballroom, St Helens in Lancashire.

July 17
McIlroy's Ballroom, Swindon.

July 18
The Cavern (lunchtime and evening), the latter with Ken Dallas & The Silhouettes and The Spidermen.

July 19
Majestic Ballroom, Birkenhead.

July 20
The Cavern (lunchtime) and The Bell Hall, Warrington.

July 21
Tower Ballroom, New Brighton, Wallasey.

July 22
The Cavern (evening) with The Swinging Blue Genes, The Red River Jazzmen and Ken Dallas & The Silhouettes.

July 23
Kingsway Club, Southport.

July 24
The Cavern (lunchtime).

July 25
The Cavern (lunchtime) with Gerry & The Pacemakers and (evening) with The Dakotas, Ian & The Zodiacs and The Dennisons; and Cabaret Club, Liverpool.
    The Cabaret Club show was a failed attempt by Brian Epstein to get The Beatles into the lounge band circuit. The audience hated The Beatles. The Beatles hated the audience.

July 26
Cambridge Hall, Southport, supporting Joe Brown & The Bruvvers.
    A NEMS Enterprises promotion.

July 27
Tower Ballroom, New Brighton, Wallasey, supporting Joe Brown & The Bruvvers. Also on the bill were The Statesmen, The Big Three, The Four Jays and Steve Day & The Drifters.
    A NEMS Enterprises promotion.

July 28
The Cavern (evening), with The Red River Jazzmen and Dee Fenton & The Silhouettes, and Majestic Ballroom, Birkenhead, Cheshire, with The Swinging Blue Genes and Billy Kramer & The Coasters.

July 30
The Cavern (lunchtime) and Blue Penguin Club, St John's Hall, Bootle in Lancashire, with The Merseybeats and The Sensational Sinners.

August 1
The Cavern (lunchtime and evening), the latter with Gerry & The Pacemakers and The Merseybeats.

August 3
Grafton Ballroom, Liverpool, with The Big Three and Gerry & the Pacemakers.
A "Holiday Spectacular!!"; the first time a rock concert was held here.

August 4
Victoria Hall, Higher Bebington in the Wirral.

August 5
The Cavern (evening) with The Saints Jazz Band and The Swinging Blue Genes.

August 7
The Cavern (lunchtime and evening), the latter with Wayne Stevens & The Vikings, Ken Dallas & The Silhouettes and The Swinging Blue Genes.

August 8
Co-op Ballroom, Doncaster.

August 9
The Cavern (lunchtime).

August 10
Riverboat Shuffle held on the M.V. *Royal Iris*, with Johnny Kidd & the Pirates and The Dakotas.

August 11
Odd Spot Club, Liverpool.
Around this date, John's girlfriend, Cynthia Powell, informed him that she was pregnant. John replied unenthusiastically that if that was the case, then the couple would have to get married.

August 12
The Cavern (evening) with The Swinging Blue Genes and The Red River Jazzmen.

August 13
The Cavern (lunchtime) and Majestic Ballroom, Crewe billed as "The Biggest Rock Since Blackpool Rock".

August 15
The Cavern (lunchtime and evening).
These were Pete Best's last performances with the group before he was unceremoniously fired.
John Lennon telephoned Ringo Starr in Skegness, where he was about to complete a summer season with Rory Storm & The Hurricanes at Butlin's Holiday Camp, and confirmed that he was to become The Beatles' new drummer. Ringo and The Beatles had already had several clandestine meetings about him replacing Pete Best.

August 16
Riverpark Ballroom, Chester.
In the morning, Brian Epstein told Pete he was no longer in The Beatles. Johnny "Hutch" Hutchinson, drummer with The Big Three, filled the empty drum stool at Chester.

THE SACKING OF PETE BEST

John, Paul and George couldn't face telling Pete that he was no longer in the group and asked Brian to do it on their behalf. The Beatles' roadie, Neil Aspinall, who lived in Pete's house and was a close friend of his, was going to quit in disgust but Pete insisted that he stay.

The Beatles' official comment was: "Pete left the group by mutual agreement. There were no arguments or difficulties, and this has been an entirely amicable decision." They had decided that he did not fit the image of the group they wanted: he was too moody, and would not wear his hair in the distinctive Beatle cut.

In 1963 Pete Best gave his version of what happened: "On our third trip to Hamburg we became the first group to play at a new venue, The Star-Club. Whilst over there we received a telegram saying we'd got a Parlophone contract. Just before the first release I was told that I would have to leave the group. The news came as a complete surprise to me as I had no hint that it would happen and didn't even have the opportunity of discussing it with the rest of the group."

August 17

Majestic Ballroom, Birkenhead, and Tower Ballroom, New Brighton, Wallasey.

Again "Hutch" Hutchinson played drums with The Beatles even though his own group had a date this night and had to find someone to replace him.

August 18

Horticulture Society Dance, Hulme Hall, Port Sunlight, Birkenhead, with The Four Jays.

This was Ringo's début as a Beatle. They managed a two-hour rehearsal together before the 10pm gig.

August 19

The Cavern (evening) with The Zenith Six Jazz Band, The Swinging Blue Genes and Peppy & The New York Twisters.

This was Ringo's Cavern début as a Beatle. Pete Best had many fans who were aggrieved at his dismissal, and the group were attacked as they entered the club. George got a black eye, the effects of which were still visible when the group had their first photographic session for EMI two weeks later.

August 20

Majestic Ballroom, Crewe.

August 22

The Cavern (lunchtime and evening), the latter with Gerry & The Pacemakers and Dee Fenton & The Silhouettes.

At lunchtime Granada Television filmed the group playing 'Some Other Guy' and 'Kansas City'/'Hey, Hey, Hey, Hey' for their *Know The North* programme. It was scheduled to be shown on November 7 but the film never actually went out. The film clips survived but the sound quality was found to be too poor for them to be used, so further sound-only recordings were made on September 5th.

August 23

Riverpark Ballroom, Chester.

Having come to an agreement that this was the only possible response to the news of Cynthia's pregnancy, John and Cynthia got married at the Mount Pleasant Register Office with Paul as best man. George, Brian Epstein, Cynthia's brother Tony and his wife Marjorie were the only guests. John's harridan Aunt Mimi boycotted the event. Most of the ceremony was drowned by the noise of a nearby pneumatic drill, making the party hysterical. Afterwards Brian Epstein took them all to Reece's café for a set lunch of roast chicken with all the trimmings followed by fruit salad. The café did not sell alcohol so they toasted each other with water. Brian allowed the couple to move into a small bachelor flat he maintained near the art college. John spent his wedding night on stage.

Mersey Beat announced the change in The Beatles' line-up, in a story which also revealed that the group would soon be travelling to London to make their first single for Parlophone: "They will be recording numbers that have been specially written for the group, which they have received from their recording manager, George Martin."

In the same issue of *Mersey Beat*, John Lennon published another of his occasional "Beatcomber" columns – a nonsense story entitled 'Small Sam'.

August 24
The Cavern (lunchtime) and Majestic Ballroom, Birkenhead, Wirral.

August 25
Marine Hall Ballroom, Fleetwood in Lancashire.

August 26
The Cavern (evening) with Mike Berry & The Phantoms, The Red River Jazzmen and The Swinging Blue Genes.

August 28
The Cavern (evening) with The Swinging Blue Genes and Gerry Levine & The Avengers.

August 29
Floral Hall Ballroom, Morecambe.

August 30
The Cavern (lunchtime) and Riverpark Ballroom, Chester, with Gerry & The Pacemakers, compered by Bob Wooler.

August 31
Town Hall, Lydney in Gloucestershire.

September 1
Subscription Rooms, Stroud in Gloucestershire.

September 2
The Cavern (evening) with Kingsize Taylor & The Dominoes and The Zenith Six Jazz Band.

September 3
The Cavern (lunchtime) and Queen's Hall, Widnes in Cheshire, with Billy Kramer & The Coasters, Rory Storm & The Hurricanes, Sonny Kaye & The Reds.

The first of three Monday evening gigs.

September 4
Abbey Road. The Beatles flew from Liverpool Airport to London, where they checked into a small hotel in Chelsea. Neil Aspinall had already driven their equipment down and was waiting with it at the studio. They rehearsed until 5pm, then George Martin took the group to his favourite Italian restaurant for dinner to get to know them a bit, entertaining them with reminiscences of his past work with comedians Peter Sellers and Spike Milligan.

They recorded a number of takes of 'Love Me Do' and, much against their wishes, 'How Do You Do It', a song written by professional pop composer Mitch Murray, which George Martin intended as their first A-side. The group's lack of enthusiasm was evident from the lacklustre performance captured on tape.

Photographer Dezo Hoffmann documented the session for posterity, and traces of the black eye that George received on August 19 can be seen in Dezo's photographs.

September 5
The Cavern (evening) with The Dennisons and Gus Travis & The Midnighters.

One hour of The Beatles' performance was professionally taped by a Granada TV engineer, with the intention of marrying up the tapes with the film shot at the same venue two weeks earlier. But the project was abandoned, and the tape was wiped. All that survived were two acetate recordings of 'Some Other Guy', one of which was matched with the existing film footage a year later, and one acetate of 'Kansas City'/'Hey, Hey, Hey, Hey'.

September 6
The Cavern (lunchtime) and Rialto Ballroom, Liverpool, with Rory Storm & The Hurricanes, The Big Three and The Merseybeats.
  Mersey Beat published 'A Little Bare', a brief account by Paul McCartney of the Beatles' early experiences backing a stripper at a Liverpool club. Also in this issue was another "Beatcomber" contribution from John Lennon, 'On Safairy With Whide Hunter'.

September 7
Newton Dancing School, Village Hall, Irby, Heswall in the Wirral.

September 8
YMCA Birkenhead, and Majestic Ballroom, Birkenhead.

September 9
The Cavern (evening) with Cyril Preston's Jazz Band with Clinton Ford and Billy Kramer & The Coasters.

September 10
The Cavern (lunchtime) and Queen's Hall, Widnes in Cheshire, the second of three Monday evening gigs supported by Geoff Stacey & The Wanderers and Rory Storm & The Hurricanes.

September 11
Abbey Road. The group recorded 'Love Me Do', 'P.S. I Love You' and 'Please Please Me' using session drummer Andy White. Ringo was relegated to tambourine and maracas, a demotion which led him to fear that he would soon be following Pete Best out of The Beatles. This was the recording of 'Love Me Do' which eventually appeared on most copies of their first single, plus their début LP, though the initial pressings of the single used the version with Ringo's drumming recorded on the 4th. The difference is minimal.

September 12
The Cavern (evening) with Freddie & The Dreamers, 16-year-old Simone Jackson (for whom The Beatles played backing), The Spidermen and Group One.

September 13
The Cavern (lunchtime) and Riverpark Ballroom, Chester.

September 14
Tower Ballroom, New Brighton, Wallasey.
  Sam Leach's "Operation Big Beat V" with Rory Storm & The Hurricanes, Gerry & The Pacemakers and Billy Kramer & The Coasters.

September 15
The Victory Memorial Hall, Northwich in Cheshire.

September 16
The Cavern (evening) with The Red River Jazzmen and Gerry & The Pacemakers.

September 17
The Cavern (lunchtime) and Queen's Hall, Widnes, the last of three Monday evening gigs supported by Billy Kramer & The Coasters and The Vikings.

September 19
The Cavern (evening) with The Dakotas and The Big Three.

September 20
The Cavern (lunchtime).
   Mersey Beat printed another of Paul McCartney's memoirs of the Beatles' career, this one simply entitled 'Hamburg'.

September 21
Tower Ballroom, New Brighton, Wallasey, with Rory Storm & The Hurricanes.

September 22
Majestic Ballroom, Birkenhead.

September 23
The Cavern (evening) with The Saints Jazz Band and Kingsize Taylor & The Dominoes.

September 25
Heswall Jazz Club, The Barnston Women's Institute, Heswall, with Gerry & The Pacemakers.

September 26
The Cavern (lunchtime and evening), the latter with The Spidermen and Kingsize Taylor & The Dominoes.

September 28
The Cavern (lunchtime) and "A Grand River Cruise" aboard the M.V. *Royal Iris*, with Lee Castle & The Barons and Freddy (The Teddy) Fowell.

September 29
Oasis Club, Manchester.

September 30
The Cavern (evening) with The Red River Jazzmen and Clay Ellis & The Raiders.

October
The EP *Ya Ya* by Tony Sheridan & The Beat Brothers was released in Germany on Polydor EPH 21485. The record included one song, 'Sweet Georgia Brown', on which Sheridan was backed by The Beatles.

October 1
The group signed a second management contract with Brian Epstein – which, unlike their deal in January 1962, the manager actually signed himself. It ran for five years and gave him 25 per cent of their gross earnings.

October 2
The Cavern (lunchtime).

October 3
The Cavern (evening) with The Echoes and Billy Kramer & The Dakotas.

October 4
The Cavern (lunchtime).

October 5
The single 'Love Me Do'/'P.S. I Love You' was released in the UK as Parlophone 45-R 4949. Brian Epstein is reputed to have bought 10,000 copies for his NEMS chain of record stores because he knew that was how many they would have to sell to make it into the Top 20. Whether or not this rumour is true, local sales across Liverpool were so heavy that the single immediately topped the 'official' Merseyside Top Twenty chart published in *Mersey Beat*.
   Radio Luxembourg played the record for the first time this evening, to the thrilled disbelief of The Beatles.

LOVE ME DO

"Our greatest philosophical song," Paul McCartney called it tongue-in-cheek. But it was, in this original version with Ringo Starr on drums, The Beatles' first single, later replaced on album and 45 by the version available on the 'Please Please Me' CD.

Despite the claim on the 'Please Please Me' album cover, the album track wasn't the one issued on the first Beatles single. It was the same song, true enough, but not the same recording. At the group's début session, on 4 September 1962, they had struggled through more than 15 takes of 'Love Me Do' before George Martin was remotely satisfied. A week later, they returned to London, to find session drummer Andy White ready to take Ringo Starr's place. Having only recently replaced Pete Best in the band, Ringo must have wondered whether his own days were numbered. White duly handled the sticks on a remake of the song, with Ringo dejectedly banging a tambourine on the sidelines.

For reasons that remain unclear, it was the initial version of 'Love Me Do' which appeared as the group's first 45. But when their album was assembled, George Martin elected to use the Andy White recording instead – presumably because the tape of the single had been sent overseas to an EMI subsidiary. Later in 1963, the decision was made to use the White take on all future pressings of the single, as well; and from then until 1982, Ringo's recording début with The Beatles remained officially unavailable.

The song itself was a genuine Lennon/McCartney collaboration, its plodding beat enlivened by Lennon's harmonica solo. That was a gimmick he picked up from Bruce Channel's spring 1962 hit, 'Hey Baby', and proceeded to use many times over the next two years. Without the gimmick, 'Love Me Do' hadn't previously been regarded as one of the highlights of the group's original repertoire.

P.S. I LOVE YOU

There's a clear division in The Beatles' early work between the songs they wrote before 'Please Please Me', and the ones that came immediately after. McCartney's 'P.S. I Love You' dated from the early months of 1962, and had the slightly forced feel of 'Love Me Do' and 'Ask Me Why' – with only Paul's swoop into the upper register for the last middle section to suggest that any great genius was on display.

October 6

Horticultural Society Dance, Hulme Hall, Port Sunlight, Birkenhead.

The Beatles arrived at Dawson's Music Shop, Widnes, at 4pm to autograph copies of 'Love Me Do'.

October 7

The Cavern (evening) with The Swinging Blue Genes, The Red River Jazzmen and Ian & The Zodiacs.

October 8

The Beatles recorded an interview session for EMI's *The Friday Spectacular* show on Radio Luxembourg. This consisted of new EMI releases played before a live audience of about 100 people at the company's London headquarters on Manchester Square. The audience danced and applauded the records and the artists were interviewed. Both sides of their new single were played.

October 9

The Beatles visited the offices of *Record Mirror* to try and drum up publicity for themselves.

They also visited Liverpool-born *New Musical Express* correspondent Alan Smith, who asked them what they thought of Londoners. "Not much," they told him. "If they know you come from the North, they don't want to know."

October 10

The Cavern (lunchtime and evening), with Ken Dallas & The Silhouettes and The Four Jays.

October 11

Rialto Ballroom, Liverpool.

October 12
The Cavern (lunchtime) and Tower Ballroom, New Brighton, Wallasey.

A five-and-a-half-hour NEMS presentation. Brian Epstein placed The Beatles second to Little Richard on a bill which also included The Big Three, Billy Kramer & The Coasters, Pete MacLaine & The Dakotas, The Four Jays, Lee Curtis & The All-Stars (with Pete Best on drums), The Merseybeats, Rory Storm & The Hurricanes, Guy Travis & The Midnighters and The Undertakers. The concert was a huge success.

Little Richard: "Man, those Beatles are fabulous. If I hadn't seen them I'd never have dreamed they were white. They have a real authentic negro sound."

The 'Love Me Do' single made its first appearance in a national sales chart, appearing at No. 49 in the listing published by the trade magazine *Record Retailer*.

EMI's *The Friday Spectacular* with The Beatles' record and interview was broadcast by Radio Luxembourg.

October 13
The Cavern (evening) with The Zenith Six Jazz Band, Group One and The Dennisons.

October 15
Majestic Ballroom, Birkenhead.

October 16
La Scala Ballroom, Runcorn in Cheshire, with The Chants.

October 17
The Cavern (lunchtime) with Johnny Sandon & The Remo Four and (evening) with Johnny Sandon & The Remo Four, Group One and The Swinging Blue Genes.

Between shows at the Cavern the group appeared on Granada Television's *People and Places* singing 'Some Other Guy' and 'Love Me Do', transmitted live from Manchester. This was their first television appearance to be broadcast, as their earlier Cavern performance was not screened at the time.

October 19
The Cavern (lunchtime).

October 20
Majestic Ballroom, Hull.

October 21
The Cavern (evening) with The Fourmost and The Red River Jazzmen.

October 22
Queen's Hall, Widnes, with Lee Curtis & The All-Stars, The Merseybeats and The Chants.

October 25
The group recorded 'Love Me Do', 'A Taste Of Honey' and 'P.S. I Love You' for the BBC Light Programme's *Here We Go* at the BBC studios in Manchester.

October 26
The Cavern (lunchtime) and Public Hall, Preston, with Mike Berry, The Outlaws and The Syd Munson Orchestra, presented by the Preston Grasshoppers Rugby Football Club.

The Beatles on *Here We Go* was broadcast by the BBC Light Programme.

'Love Me Do' entered the *New Musical Express* charts at number 49. Paul: "If you want to know when we knew we'd arrived, it was getting in the charts with 'Love Me Do'. That was the one – it gave us somewhere to go."

October 27
Hulme Hall, Port Sunlight, Birkenhead.

Before playing this gig the group recorded an interview with a boys' club to be broadcast to the patients of Cleaver and Clatterbridge Hospitals, Wirral, on the hospital radio show, *Sunday Spin*.

October 28
Liverpool Empire as support for Little Richard.
Also on this NEMS Enterprises *Pop Package Show* were Craig Douglas (backed by The Beatles), Jet Harris (formerly bassist with The Shadows) & The Jetblacks, Kenny Lynch, The Breakaways and Sounds Incorporated. Brian had tried to book Sam Cooke as a "surprise guest" but he was not available.
The Beatles' appearance on the hospital radio show, *Sunday Spin*, was transmitted.

October 29
The Beatles made a second visit to Granada Television's Manchester studios to record for *People and Places*. They performed 'Love Me Do' and 'A Taste Of Honey'.

October 30
The Beatles flew to Hamburg for 14 nights at the Star-Club sharing the bill with Little Richard. With her husband now likely to be absent for the rest of the year, Cynthia Lennon moved in with Aunt Mimi at Mendips, where she was quickly educated into the behaviour that her aunt-in-law expected from her.

November 1–14
Star-Club, Grosse Freiheit, Hamburg, with Little Richard.
The Beatles deeply resented having to fulfil this booking, at a time when it seemed as if their début single might be about to become a sizeable hit in the UK. A few days into their stay, Paul wrote home to a friend: "Nothing happened: a thoroughly uneventful week has passed . . . In fact Hamburg is dead as far as we're concerned."

November 2
The Beatles' second appearance on Granada Television's *People and Places* was aired.

November 15
The group flew to London from Hamburg.

November 16
The Beatles recorded a second appearance for EMI's *The Friday Spectacular* show on Radio Luxembourg, appearing on stage at EMI's headquarters for an interview between the playing of both sides of their record while the audience danced, applauded and even screamed.
The Beatles visited the Fleet Street offices of *Disc*, and garnered a few column inches in the next issue.

November 17
Matrix Hall, Coventry, with The Mark Allen Group and Lee Teri.
Regarded by the group as a disappointing performance.

November 18
The Cavern (evening) with The Merseybeats and The Pete Hartigan Jazz Band in a "Welcome Home" gig.

November 19
The Cavern (lunchtime), Smethwick Baths, Smethwick in Staffordshire and Adelphi Ballroom, West Bromwich.
Three gigs in one day.

November 20
Floral Hall, Southport. Two sets.

November 21
The Cavern (lunchtime and evening), the latter with Johnny Templar & The Hi Cats and Ian & The Zodiacs.

November 22
The Cavern (lunchtime) and Majestic Ballroom, Birkenhead.

November 23
St James' Church Hall, Gloucester Terrace, London, and Tower Ballroom, New Brighton, Wallasey.
In London The Beatles auditioned for Ronnie Lane, the Light Entertainment auditioner for BBC TV. They played a ten-minute set for him, and four days later Brian Epstein received a rejection letter.
The New Brighton show was the "12th Annual Lancashire and Cheshire Art's (sic) Ball", held in aid of a children's charity, with the Llew Hird Jazz Band, Billy Kramer & The Coasters and The Pipes and Drums of 1st Battalion Liverpool Scottish Regiment (Queen's Own Cameron Highlanders).
The Beatles' second appearance on Radio Luxembourg's *The Friday Spectacular* was aired.

November 24
Royal Lido Ballroom, Prestatyn, Wales.

November 25
The Cavern (evening) with The Zenith Six Jazz Band, The Fourmost and The Swinging Blue Genes.

November 26
Abbey Road. The group recorded 'Tip Of My Tongue', 'Ask Me Why' and 'Please Please Me'. George Martin was pleased with the results and told the group that 'Please Please Me' would be a number one hit. The 'Tip Of My Tongue' recording didn't survive, though George Martin commented: "It's a great number, but we'll have to spend a bit of time giving it a new arrangement. I'm not too happy with it as it is."
After the session, Martin told *NME* correspondent Alan Smith: "I'm thinking of recording their first LP at the Cavern. If we can't get the right sound, we might do the recording somewhere else in Liverpool, or bring an invited audience into the studio in London. The Beatles have told me they work better in front of an audience."

November 27
The group recorded 'Love Me Do', 'Twist And Shout' and 'P.S. I Love You' for the BBC Light Programme's *Talent Spot* at the BBC Paris Studio on Lower Regent Street.

November 28
The Cavern (evening) with Johnny Sandon & The Remo Four and Dee Young & The Pontiacs, and The 527 Club, top floor of Lewis' Department Store, Liverpool – "The Young Idea Dance" for the shop staff.

November 29
Majestic Ballroom, Birkenhead.

November 30
The Cavern (lunchtime) with The Dakotas and Town Hall, Earlstown, Newton-le-Willows in Lancashire – "The Big Beat Show".

December 1
The Victory Memorial Hall, Northwich in Cheshire, and Tower Ballroom, New Brighton, Wallasey.

December 2
Embassy Cinema, Peterborough.
The Beatles went down badly in both sets of this Frank Ifield concert. Also on the bill were Susan Cope, The Tommy Wallis & Beryl Xylophone Team, The Lana Sisters and The Tod Taylor Four.

December 3
The group appeared on *Discs-a-Go-Go*, live from Bristol's TWW (Television Wales and West) studio.

December 4
The Beatles sang 'Love Me Do', 'P.S. I Love You' and 'Twist And Shout' live on *Tuesday Rendezvous*, a children's show presented by Gary Marshall, transmitted live from Associated-Rediffusion's Kingsway Studio, London.
   The Beatles' appearance on *Talent Spot* was broadcast on the BBC Light Programme.

December 5
The Cavern (lunchtime and evening) with Gerry & The Pacemakers, Johnny Sandon & The Remo Four and The Statesmen.

December 6
Club Django, Queen's Hotel, Southport.

December 7
The Cavern (lunchtime) and Tower Ballroom, New Brighton, Wallasey.

December 8
Oasis Club, Manchester.

December 9
The Cavern (evening) with The Fourmost, The Swinging Blue Genes and The Zenith Six Jazz Band.
   George Martin attended this performance to see if a live album could be recorded at The Cavern.

December 10
The Cavern (lunchtime).

December 11
La Scala Ballroom, Runcorn in Cheshire, with Johnny Sandon & The Remo Four and The Merseybeats.

December 12
The Cavern (lunchtime and evening), the latter with The Fourmost, The Merseybeats, Robin Hall and Jimmy MacGregor.

December 13
Corn Exchange, Bedford, with Robin Hall and Jimmy MacGregor.

December 14
Music Hall, Shrewsbury.

December 15
Majestic Ballroom, Birkenhead.
   The regular evening show was followed at midnight by The *Mersey Beat* Poll Winners Award Show. The Beatles were voted most popular group for the second year running and closed the show at 4am.

December 16
The Cavern (evening), with The Fourmost, The Swinging Blue Genes, Gerry & The Pacemakers and The Red River Jazzmen.

December 17
The Beatles played live on Granada Television's *People And Places* show.

December 18–31
The Star-Club, Grosse Freiheit, Hamburg.

The Beatles' fifth and final residency in Germany, arranged before their chart success and growing concert revenues. As with the previous Hamburg booking they were reluctant to go, but had no option.

Despite their increasing fame at home, The Beatles were listed among the minor attractions in the Star-Club's advertising, alongside Carol Elvin, The Strangers, Kingsize Taylor and the inevitable Tony Sheridan & The Star Combo. Topping the bill above them all during December were visiting American rockers Johnny & The Hurricanes.

December 27
'Love Me Do' got to number 17 in the *Record Retailer*'s Top 50 charts, its highest position.

December 28
George wrote home to Liverpool: "I hope you had a good Christmas, or at least better than ours. We have only three more days to go, and then will be away from this place for good (I hope)."

December 28–31
Star-Club: On behalf of Ted 'Kingsize' Taylor, the leader of another Merseyside group, The Dominoes, Adrian Barber recorded several of The Beatles' performances, including their final night at the Star-Club, with a hand-held microphone and a 4-track Philips machine. In total, four separate sets were apparently recorded. 30 songs from these tapes were later released on a series of unauthorised albums – until Apple and The Beatles successfully mounted a legal challenge in 1998.

Barber's recordings revealed the natural spontaneity and chaotic wit of The Beatles' performances in the months before they became major national stars. But they also betrayed the frustration that the group felt at having to work out an ill-rewarded contract with a German club-owner, while their record was still on the hit parade at home. "Only The Beatles would be playing for you on New Year's Eve," Lennon quipped sarcastically during the show.

Two of the released songs on Barber's tapes, 'Hallelujah I Love Her So' and 'Be-Bop-A-Lula', featured the group supporting an unidentified singer, thought to be waiter Fred Fascher (brother of the Star-Club's manager, Horst Fascher).

One song from these Star-Club sessions, John performing 'Red Hot', remains officially unreleased, although it has surfaced on bootleg. Also unreleased to date are alternative versions of 'Ask Me Why', 'I Saw Her Standing There' (twice), 'A Taste Of Honey' (twice), 'To Know Her Is To Love Her', 'I'm Talkin' 'Bout You', 'Roll Over Beethoven' and 'Road Runner'. There is also a rendition of 'Money (That's What I Want)' on which The Beatles supported Tony Sheridan.

January 1
The Beatles' engagement at the Star-Club ended and they flew from Hamburg to London.

January 2
The group flew from London to Scotland but the plane, due to land in Edinburgh (where Neil Aspinall was waiting for them with the van), was diverted to Aberdeen. Their first night's booking at the Longmore Hall in Keith had to be cancelled because snowdrifts had blocked the roads and so, with nothing to do until the following evening, John flew back to Liverpool for a brief reunion with his wife (and aunt).

January 3
Two Red Shoes Ballroom, Elgin, Morayshire.
   John flew from Liverpool to Scotland, arriving barely in time for the show.

January 4
Town Hall, Dingwall, Ross and Cromarty.
   The Beatles' chart success with 'Love Me Do' won them 111th place in the annual survey of the previous year's most successful acts, published by the *New Musical Express*.

January 5
Museum Hall, Bridge of Allan, Stirlingshire. The group were billed for the night as "The Love Me Do Boys".

January 6
Beach Ballroom, Aberdeen.

January 8
The group appeared live on Scottish TV's *Round-Up*, transmitted locally from The Theatre Royal, Glasgow, and presented by Paul Young and Morag Hood. The band mimed 'Please Please Me'.

January 10
Grafton Rooms, Liverpool, where they headed a bill of five acts.

January 11
The Cavern (lunchtime) with Kingsize Taylor & The Dominoes, and Plaza Ballroom, Old Hill, Staffordshire.
   The single 'Please Please Me'/'Ask Me Why' was released in the UK as Parlophone 45-R 4983. It was given a favourable review in the country's leading pop paper, the *New Musical Express*, where DJ Keith Fordyce wrote: "I can't think of any other group currently recording in this style. I shan't be in the least surprised to see the charts invaded by Beatles."
   The Beatles appeared on ABC TV's *Thank Your Lucky Stars*, performing 'Please Please Me'.

PLEASE PLEASE ME
Though no evidence remains on tape, The Beatles' original arrangement of 'Please Please Me' was apparently closer to a Roy Orbison ballad than a beat group number. It was attempted during the group's second EMI session in September 1962, George Martin remembering it as "a very dreary song". He suggested that the group soup up the arrangement – something that was done to such effect that it became their first No. 1 at the end of February 1963.
   In up-tempo form, it became an overt sexual invitation on Lennon's part, and a clear sign that The Beatles were more than just another pop group. Their harmonies, the opening harmonica riff, and Ringo's accomplished drumming testified to a remarkable surge in confidence since their first EMI sessions.
   As with 'Love Me Do', there are two different versions of this song on EMI releases. The stereo mix, unavailable on CD, utilised an alternate take on which Lennon and McCartney

messed up their vocals. Quite how that blatant a mistake escaped the notice of George Martin remains to be answered.

ASK ME WHY

Unlike Paul McCartney, John Lennon took time to slide into the conventions of pop songwriting. 'Ask Me Why' illustrated what happened before he acquired the knack. From the difficult rhythm of the opening lines to the cut-and-paste structure of the middle section, it was a song that seemed to have been constructed painfully, bar-by-bar, rather than flowing naturally like McCartney's early efforts. Careful study of his role models, like Smokey Robinson and Arthur Alexander, soon rewarded Lennon with a keen grasp of the essentials of composing, though not in time to prevent this number being consigned to the flipside of 'Please Please Me'.

January 12

Invicta Ballroom, Chatham, Kent. This was their first South of England performance since signing their recording contract six months earlier.

January 13

Alpha TV Studios, Birmingham, where the group recorded an appearance on ABC TV's *Thank Your Lucky Stars.* They closed the first half of the show miming to 'Please Please Me'.

January 14

Wolverham Welfare Association Dance, Civic Hall, Wirral.

January 16

Granada TV Centre, Manchester. Rehearsal for a live appearance on the *People And Places* programme to be broadcast later in the day.

Playhouse Theatre, Manchester, to rehearse for a session on the BBC Radio programme *Here We Go*.

Granada TV Centre, for the *People And Places* transmission, for which they mimed to 'Please Please Me' and 'Ask Me Why'.

Playhouse Theatre, Manchester to record their spot on *Here We Go,* for which they sang 'Chains', 'Please Please Me', 'Three Cool Cats' and 'Ask Me Why'. 'Three Cool Cats' was edited out when the programme was broadcast .

January 17

The Cavern (lunchtime) and Majestic Ballroom, Birkenhead, where 500 disappointed fans had to be turned away.

'Please Please Me' entered the charts.

January 18

Floral Ballroom, Morecambe, Lancashire.

Roadie Neil Aspinall went down with flu so Les Hurst, Gerry & the Pacemakers' roadie, stood in for him.

January 19

Town Hall Ballroom, Whitchurch, Shropshire.

Once again, Les Hurst stood in for Neil Aspinall.

Thank Your Lucky Stars was broadcast.

January 20

The Cavern with Pete Hartigan's Jazzmen, The Dennisons, The Merseybeats and The Swinging Blue Genes.

Neil, sweating and feverish, hauled their gear. He explained to Brian Epstein that he just could not do the drive to London the next day. Fortunately, he bumped into Mal Evans on the stairs of the Cavern where he worked and asked, "Mal, can you run the boys to London and back for me?"

Mal, a GPO telephone engineer who had taken to dropping into The Cavern on his way back to the Post Office after lunch, agreed. After a while he extended his visits to include the evenings and got to know George Harrison. They left the club together one day and Mal invited him back to listen to some records. George suggested that Mal should work on the door of the Cavern; that way he would hear the music free and get paid in his spare time. Mal, an imposing 6 feet 2 inches, was gentle and polite, but had the outward appearance of a tough bouncer.

January 21
EMI House, London, to record EMI's plug show *Friday Spectacular* for Radio Luxembourg hosted by Shaw Taylor and Muriel Young with an audience of 100 teenagers. They were interviewed, and 'Please Please Me' and 'Ask Me Why' were played.

The Beatles were signed in the US by Vee Jay Records, who made immediate plans to release 'Please Please Me'.

January 22
BBC Paris Studio, London, where they were interviewed live on the radio programme *Pop Inn* to promote their new single 'Please Please Me'.

Playhouse Theatre, London, to rehearse and record their first appearance on the BBC pop radio programme *Saturday Club*, presented by Brian Matthew. They recorded 'Some Other Guy', 'Love Me Do', 'Please Please Me', 'Keep Your Hands Off My Baby' and 'Beautiful Dreamer'.

BBC Paris Studio, London, to record a BBC Light Programme show *The Talent Spot,* presented by Gary Marshall. They sang 'Please Please Me', 'Ask Me Why' and 'Some Other Guy' before a studio audience.

January 23
The Cavern (evening), with The Fourmost, Ken Dallas & The Silhouettes and Freddie Starr & The Midnighters.

MAL EVANS

The Beatles drove back to Liverpool from London for the gig in freezing temperatures. The windscreen of the van shattered and their stand-in roadie Mal Evans drove with no glass. The group were so cold they lay huddled on top of each other in the back.

John Lennon told Neil Aspinall what had happened: "You should have seen Mal. He had this paper bag over his head with just a big split in it for eyes. We were all in the back of the van doing the same thing. It was freezing. The windscreen shattered. Mal had to knock out the rest of the broken glass and just drive on. It was perishing. Mal looked like a bank robber."

The Beatles had a Cavern gig the next lunchtime and an out of town gig that evening. Mal showed up at Neil's with the van in perfect condition, windscreen replaced. Neil: "We never knew how he'd managed to get it fixed again so quickly and, even if we didn't say so, it was something we remembered. Ten out of ten to Mal for not just bringing back the van and leaving it for someone else to get a new windscreen put in." Mal's efficiency was to lead him to a career with The Beatles which lasted out the decade.

January 24
Assembly Hall, Mold, Wales.

Earlier, The Beatles signed copies of 'Please Please Me' at NEMS record shop in Liverpool and gave a short acoustic performance to the assembled fans.

January 25
Co-operative Hall, Darwen – a local Baptist Church youth club event billed as 'The Greatest Teenage Dance', with supporting acts The Electones, The Mike Taylor Combo and The Mustangs with Ricky Day.

The Beatles session on BBC Radio's *Here We Go* was broadcast, presented by Ray Peters.

Radio Luxembourg's *Friday Spectacular* broadcast.

January 26
El Rio Club, Macclesfield, Cheshire, with Wayne Fontana & The Jets, and King's Hall, Stoke-on-Trent in Staffordshire.

John and Paul began work on 'Misery', intended for Helen Shapiro, backstage at this gig. They completed the song en route to the following night's performance in Manchester.

The Beatles' first appearance on the BBC's *Saturday Club* was broadcast.

January 27
Three Coins Club, Manchester.

January 28
Majestic Ballroom, Newcastle upon Tyne.

January 29
BBC's *Talent Spot* broadcast.

January 30
The Cavern (evening) with Johnny Sandon & The Remo Four and The Dakotas.

January 31
The Cavern (lunchtime) and two shows (because of demand for tickets) at the Majestic Ballroom, Birkenhead.

February 1
Assembly Rooms, Tamworth, Staffordshire, and Maney Hall, Sutton Coldfield, Warwickshire.

New Musical Express printed the word "Beatles" on the cover for the first time, as reporter Alan Smith interviewed the group. He complimented them on their "clipped negro sound".

February 2
Gaumont Cinema, Bradford.

The first gig on their nationwide tour with Helen Shapiro, where they were effectively bottom of the bill. The programme opened with The Red Price Band, followed by The Honeys, compere Dave Allen, The Beatles, Dave Allen and Danny Williams who closed the first half. The Red Price Band again opened the second set, followed by The Kestrels and Kenny Lynch, and then David Allen introduced 16-year-old Helen Shapiro. The Beatles wore burgundy suits with velvet collars, designed by Paul, and their hair brushed forward "French style".

John: "We don't really bother about what we do on the stage. We practise what we call 'Grinning at nothings'. One-two-three, and we all grin at nothing! When we go out with Helen Shapiro I don't know how we'll manage. I thought I might lie on the floor like Al Jolson."

Their set was 'Chains', 'Keep Your Hands Off My Baby', 'A Taste Of Honey', and 'Please Please Me'.

John and Paul finished 'Misery' on the coach but Helen's management didn't even bother to show it to her. Kenny Lynch, however, was interested and has the distinction of being the first outsider to record a Lennon and McCartney song. It was also on the coach that John and Paul came up with the idea of running up to the microphone together and shaking their heads and singing, 'Whooooooo!', even though 'She Loves You' was not yet out.

'Please Please Me' entered the *Music Week* charts at number 16.

February 3
The Cavern (evening), an eight-hour "Blues Marathon" with The Fourmost, The Dominoes, The Hollies, Earl Preston & The TT's, The Merseybeats, The Swinging Blue Genes and The Roadrunners.

February 4
The Cavern (last lunchtime session).

February 5
Gaumont Cinema, Doncaster (Helen Shapiro tour).

February 6
Granada Cinema, Bedford (Helen Shapiro tour).

February 7
Regal Cinema, Wakefield (Helen Shapiro tour).

February 8
ABC Cinema, Carlisle (now in Cumbria) (Helen Shapiro tour).

The tour received national press publicity, when "a member of one of the supporting groups" (actually Ringo Starr, though neither he nor The Beatles were named in the press accounts) was banned from a dance after the show because he was wearing the uniform of the young tearaway, a leather jacket.

February 9
Empire Theatre, Sunderland (Helen Shapiro tour).

February 11
Abbey Road. All ten new tracks needed to make the *Please Please Me* album were recorded in one ten-hour session (the other four tracks were already out as sides A and B of their two singles). The tracks were chosen by George Martin from their Cavern set in an attempt to re-create the atmosphere of the group's live performance.

The marathon session was made all the more remarkable by the fact that John was suffering from a severe head-cold, and was in imminent danger of losing his voice – as a cursory listen to the rendition of 'Twist And Shout' that closed their début album will reveal.

Paul: "We'd been playing the songs for months and months and months before getting a record out. So we came into the studio at ten in the morning, started it, did one number, had a cup of tea, relaxed, did the next one, a couple of overdubs . . . we just worked through them, like the stage act. And by about ten o'clock that night, we'd done ten songs and we just reeled out of the studios, John clutching his throat tablets!"

John: "My voice wasn't the same for a long time after. Every time I swallowed, it was like sandpaper. We sang for 12 hours, almost non-stop. We had colds and we were concerned how it would affect the record. And by the end of the day, all we wanted to do was drink pints of milk."

February 12
Azena Ballroom, Sheffield, and Astoria Ballroom, Oldham.

February 13
Majestic Ballroom, Hull.

February 14
Locarno Ballroom, Liverpool – a St Valentine's Day dance.

February 15
Ritz Ballroom, King's Heath, Birmingham.

The Beatles racked up another showbiz milestone when *New Musical Express* subjected them to a 'Lifelines' questionaire, which revealed John and Paul's joint ambition to be "to write a musical".

February 16
Carfax Assembly Rooms, Oxford.

February 17
Teddington Studio Centre, Middlesex, to record an appearance on ABC TV's *Thank Your Lucky Stars* where they sang 'Please Please Me'.

February 18
Queen's Hall, Widnes – two sets, promoted by Brian Epstein.

February 19
Cavern Club (evening) with Lee Curtis & The All-Stars, The Pathfinders and Freddie Starr & The Midnighters.

The queue began to form two days before the doors opened. Bob Wooler announced from the stage that The Beatles' 'Please Please Me' now occupied the No. 1 position in the *NME* charts. It was also, apparently, the last time that any of The Beatles saw Pete Best, though they took great pains to ensure that their paths crossed at no time during the evening. Afterwards The Beatles drove through the night to London.

February 20
St James St Swimming Baths, Doncaster.

Earlier, the group appeared live on the BBC Light Programme's *Parade Of The Pops*, presented by Denny Piercy, singing 'Love Me Do' and 'Please Please Me'. This was their first live BBC transmission.

February 21
Majestic Ballroom, Birkenhead.

February 22
Oasis Club, Manchester.

The eagerly awaited publication of this week's *New Musical Express*, the first pop paper to reach the news-stands, confirmed that 'Please Please Me' had now reached the No. 1 position in the sales chart – albeit sharing that honour with Frank Ifield's 'The Wayward Wind'.

The music publishing company Northern Songs was set up by Dick James to control the rights to all compositions by John and Paul.

NORTHERN SONGS

Northern Songs Limited was set up to control John and Paul's songwriting copyrights. John and Paul naïvely thought that they would own 100 per cent of the company, but it turned out that Dick James and his accountant Charles Silver took 51 per cent, John and Paul had 20 per cent each and Brian Epstein owned 10 per cent. Dick James and Charles Silver always had the controlling vote. They both became multi-millionaires on the strength of a negligible investment.

Paul: "We just signed this thing, not really knowing what it was all about, that we were signing our rights away for our songs. That became the deal and that is virtually the contract that I'm still under. It's draconian!"

February 23
Granada Cinema, Mansfield in Nottinghamshire (Helen Shapiro tour).

'Please Please Me' reached No. 1 in its own right in the *Disc* singles charts. .

ABC Television transmitted The Beatles on *Thank Your Lucky Stars*.

February 24
Coventry Theatre, Coventry (Helen Shapiro tour).

February 25
Casino Ballroom, Leigh in Lancashire, for Brian Epstein's NEMS Enterprises "Showdance".

The single 'Please Please Me'/'Ask Me Why' was released in the US as Vee Jay VJ 498, The Beatles' first American record under their own name.

February 26
Gaumont Cinema, Taunton in Somerset, with Danny Williams heading the bill in place of Helen Shapiro who had a cold and Billie Davis standing in to complete the line-up (Helen Shapiro tour).

February 27
Rialto Theatre, York (Helen Shapiro tour, still without Helen Shapiro).

February 28
Granada Cinema, Shrewsbury (with Helen Shapiro back on stage).
   In the tour coach on the way to this gig, John and Paul wrote 'From Me To You', which later became their next single, in preference to the original choice of 'Thank You Girl'.

March 1
Odeon Cinema, Southport (Helen Shapiro tour).

March 2
City Hall, Sheffield (Helen Shapiro tour).
   Didsbury Studio Centre. After their second set, The Beatles drove to Manchester to be interviewed live with Brian Epstein by David Hamilton for ABC TV's evening talk show, *ABC At Large*. A short clip of them playing 'Please Please Me' was shown.

March 3
Gaumont Cinema, Hanley, Staffordshire.
   The last show on the Helen Shapiro tour. The Beatles now closed the first half of the show.

March 4
Plaza Ballroom, St Helens.

March 5
Abbey Road. The group recorded 'From Me To You', 'Thank You Girl' and one of the earliest Lennon/McCartney compositions, 'The One After 909'. They also took part in a photographic session at the EMI headquarters in Manchester Square, posing on a balcony in a shot that was subsequently used on the cover of their *Please Please Me* LP.

March 6
Playhouse Theatre, Manchester. The Beatles recorded another session for the BBC Light Programme's *Here We Go*, singing 'Misery', 'Do You Want To Know A Secret' and 'Please Please Me'.

March 7
Elizabethan Ballroom, Nottingham, with Gerry & The Pacemakers, The Big Three and Billy J. Kramer & The Dakotas.
   Everyone on the bill of this 'Big Beatle Show' was managed by Brian Epstein, who also promoted the event. This was the first of six "Mersey Beat Showcase" events promoted by NEMS, where the artists accompanied by 80 paying fans were taken by coach to venues across the country. Bob Wooler, DJ from The Cavern, was compere.

March 8
The Royal Hall, Harrogate.

March 9
Granada Cinema, East Ham, London.
   Their second package tour, this time supporting visiting American stars Tommy Roe and Chris Montez. The Beatles wiped the stage with them at the early show on this first night and took over top billing for the day's second performance. Their set for this tour was 'Love Me Do', 'Misery', 'A Taste Of Honey', 'Do You Want To Know A Secret', 'Please Please Me' and 'I Saw Her Standing There'.

March 10
Hippodrome Theatre, Birmingham (Roe/Montez tour).

March 11
This was the group's first day without a concert appearance in more than a month, but The Beatles still had career obligations, as they attended EMI House to record their last interview for *Friday Spectacular* to be broadcast on Radio Luxembourg.

March 12
Granada Cinema, Bedford (Roe/Montez tour).
   The strain of the group's relentless schedule took its toll, as John came down with a cold and was unable to play this concert. George and Paul took over all the singing for the night, fronting a three-man Beatles.
   The Beatles appeared on BBC Light Programme's *Here We Go*, presented by Ray Peters.

March 13
Abbey Road. John was considered well enough to take part in an over-dub session to put harmonica on to 'Thank You Girl', but not to sing, which meant he was unable to take part in the group's appearance that evening at the Rialto Theatre, York (Roe/Montez tour).

March 14
Gaumont Cinema, Wolverhampton (Roe/Montez tour, again without John).

March 15
Colston Hall, Bristol, with John back on stage to play both sets (Roe/Montez tour).

March 16
Broadcasting House, London. The Beatles performed live on the BBC Light Programme's *Saturday Club* presented by Brian Matthew. They sang; 'I Saw Her Standing There', 'Misery', 'Too Much Monkey Business', 'I'm Talking About You', 'Please Please Me' and 'The Hippy, Hippy Shake'.
   City Hall, Sheffield (Roe/Montez tour).

March 17
Embassy Cinema, Peterborough (Roe/Montez tour).

March 18
Regal Cinema, Gloucester (Roe/Montez tour).

March 19
Cambridge (Roe/Montez tour).

March 20
ABC Cinema, Romford (Roe/Montez tour).

March 21
BBC Piccadilly Studios, London, to record 'Misery', 'Do You Want To Know A Secret' and 'Please Please Me' for BBC Light Programme's *On The Scene*.
   ABC Cinema, West Croydon (Roe/Montez tour).

March 22
Gaumont Cinema, Doncaster (Roe/Montez tour).
   The album *Please Please Me* was released in the UK as Parlophone PMC 1202 (mono) and PCS 3042 (stereo). Side A: 'I Saw Her Standing There', 'Misery', 'Anna (Go To Him)', 'Chains', 'Boys', 'Ask Me Why', 'Please Please Me'; Side B: 'Love Me Do', 'P.S. I Love You', 'Baby It's You', 'Do You Want To Know A Secret', 'A Taste Of Honey', 'There's A Place', 'Twist And Shout'.

PLEASE PLEASE ME
It requires a leap of the imagination to return to the innocent days of 1963, when The Beatles recorded and released their first two long-playing albums. The common currency of teenage pop was the three-minute single, or at a stretch the two-for-the-price-of-two 45rpm extended player (EP). Albums, or LPs as they were universally known in the early Sixties, were regarded as being beyond the financial reach of most teenagers; and with the oldest of The Beatles themselves no more than 22 when their first album was recorded, the teen audience was definitely EMI's target.

Only adult performers like Frank Sinatra and Ella Fitzgerald were allowed to use the 30- or 40-minute expanse of the LP as a personal artistic statement. For the rest, the LP was unashamedly a cash-in – either for a film, or else for die-hard supporters entranced by a hit single or two. Hence the full title of The Beatles' début album, which defined its selling points precisely: Please Please Me, Love Me Do and 12 Other Songs.

Much has been made of the fact that 10 of the record's 14 tracks were recorded during one day; but that was the way the pop business operated in 1963. This haste was proof of The Beatles' junior status at EMI, and also of the company's desire to rush an LP onto the market before teenage Britain found a new set of heroes. Remember that the band had yet to score their first No. 1 when the album was recorded: the extended session represented a commendable act of faith on the behalf of producer George Martin.

Four of the album's titles were already in the can, via their first two singles, 'Love Me Do' and 'Please Please Me'. The rest – a mix of originals and covers – was a cross-section of their typical concert fare, with one exception: the group's penchant for covers of Chuck Berry and Little Richard rock'n'rollers was ignored, presumably because George Martin believed the era of rock'n'roll was past.

Recorded on two-track at Abbey Road, the album was mixed into mono and very rudimentary stereo – the latter format claiming only a tiny proportion of the market in 1963. Until 1968, The Beatles regarded the mono versions of their albums as the authentic representation of their work; and if they'd been asked, they would no doubt have agreed with George Martin's decision to prepare the CD mix of Please Please Me in mono. But stereo-philes, particularly in America, regarded this decision as barbarism in disguise, and continue to lobby for the release of the CD in stereo. Those tracks which didn't appear on singles are as follows:

I SAW HER STANDING THERE
With a simple count-in, Paul McCartney captured all The Beatles' youthful exuberance in the opening seconds of their début album. Lyrically naïve, melodically unpolished, 'I Saw Her Standing There' was still classic Beatles' rock'n'roll – Lennon and McCartney trading vocals as if they were chewing gum between syllables, the falsetto 'ooos' that soon became a Beatles trademark, the rising chords of the middle eight that promised some kind of sexual climax, and the tight-but-loose vigour of the playing. And the record ended with a triumphant clang of a guitar chord matched by a whoop from McCartney. No doubt about it, The Beatles had arrived.

MISERY
Right from the start of their recording career, The Beatles were encouraged by manager Brian Epstein to work as a songwriting factory, turning out hits to order for other artists. By February 1963, their reputation had yet to acquire its later power, and fellow performers more often than not turned them down. Helen Shapiro was offered this Lennon composition the week before The Beatles recorded it themselves, but her management declined. Unabashed, Lennon and McCartney romped through what was supposed to be a declaration of lovelorn anguish like two schoolboys on half-day holiday. Never has a song about misery sounded so damn cheerful.

Trivia note: the sheet music for this song, as copied by Kenny Lynch's early cover version, gives the first line as: "You've been treating me bad, misery." Lennon and McCartney sang something much more universal: "The world's been treating me bad".

ANNA (GO TO HIM)
If The Beatles had been allowed more than a day to make this album, they would no doubt have re-recorded the instrumental backing for this rather laboured cover of an Arthur Alexander R&B hit. But there was no faulting Lennon's vocal, which had already hit upon the mixture of romantic disillusionment and supreme self-interest that became his trademark when tackling a love song. It was almost sabotaged, though, by the pedestrian nature of McCartney and Harrison's backing vocals.

CHAINS
At The Beatles' Decca audition in January 1962, George Harrison threatened to surface as their prime lead vocalist. A year later, he'd already been relegated to cameo appearances, as on this charmingly cheerful cover of The Cookies' New York girl-group hit, which The Beatles had only recently added to their repertoire.

BOYS
If George was restricted to cameos, Ringo Starr's vocal contributions to The Beatles' recording career were purely tokens, to keep his fans from causing a fuss. He bawled his way through The Shirelles' 1960 US hit with enthusiasm if not subtlety, nailing the song in just one take. Presumably nobody in 1963 stopped to wonder why Ringo was singing a lyric that lauded the joys of boys, rather than the opposite sex. The song had been a Beatles standard for a couple of years, Ringo having inherited the number from former drummer Pete Best.

BABY IT'S YOU
Lennon may have sounded slightly ill-at-ease on his own songs, but with covers, he already had the confidence of a born interpreter. The group's boyish harmonies didn't distract him from giving another Shirelles hit a commanding vocal performance that marked him out as The Beatles' most distinctive voice.

DO YOU WANT TO KNOW A SECRET?
Given away simultaneously to fellow Brian Epstein protégé Billy J. Kramer (for a hit single), and to George Harrison (for this LP), 'Do You Want To Know A Secret?' was a Lennon composition — inspired by a line he remembered from a Disney song that his mother used to sing. "I thought it would be a good vehicle for George because it only had three notes and he wasn't the best singer in the world," Lennon explained charitably in later years.

A TASTE OF HONEY
In Hamburg and Liverpool, The Beatles were required to work up a sheaf of ballads and standards, which would melt the hearts of even the most anti-rock audience they would be forced to entertain. McCartney was the Beatle with the heritage in pre-Elvis pop, and it fell to him to perform the group's token demonstration of 'sophistication' – an American song recorded most notably by Lenny Welch, but fast becoming a favourite among sedate jazzmen and big bands around the world.

In retrospect, the inclusion of this song seems laughable – the Stones would never have made such a blatant cop-out – but in McCartney's capable hands, 'A Taste Of Honey' became another slice of Beatle music. The group didn't much care for the song, though: when they performed it live, Lennon invariably changed the chorus to 'A Waste Of Money'.

THERE'S A PLACE
Forget the theory that John Lennon only started singing about himself when he started taking drugs. Listen to the words of this cheery beat tune, and you'll find his first piece of self-analysis: "There's a place where I can go, when I feel low, when I feel blue. And it's my mind, and there's no time when I'm alone." No one – not even Bob Dylan – was writing songs like that in 1963. But nobody told John Lennon that. The result: the first self-conscious rock song, beating The Beach Boys' equally self-obsessed 'In My Room' by several months.

TWIST AND SHOUT
"I couldn't sing the damn thing, I was just screaming." So said John Lennon, about the first take of the final song recorded during The Beatles' marathon 11 February session. His voice shot by the rigours of the day's schedule, and unable to fall upon the twin crutches of pills and booze which had fuelled The Beatles on their night-long gigs in Hamburg, Lennon simply shredded his vocal cords in the interests of rock'n'roll.

Until McCartney matched it with 'Long Tall Sally' a year later, this was the supreme

Beatles rocker – a cover, ironically enough, of a tune that the Isley Brothers had rescued from an abysmal original recording by Phil Spector's charges, The Top Notes. In that one take, Lennon cut Britain's best rock'n'roll record to date, and the band kept pace with him, right down to Ringo's exultant flourish on the drums as The Beatles reached home.

March 23
City Hall, Newcastle upon Tyne (Roe/Montez tour).

March 24
Empire Theatre, Liverpool (Roe/Montez tour).

March 25
The Beatles spent the day being photographed and filmed by Dezo Hoffmann. Among the photos which resulted from this session were the famous 'bombsite' shot which was later used on the cover of the *Twist And Shout* EP.

March 26
Granada Cinema, Mansfield (Roe/Montez tour).

March 27
ABC Cinema, Northampton (Roe/Montez tour).

March 28
ABC Cinema, Exeter (Roe/Montez tour).
   The Beatles' recording for the BBC Light Programme's *On The Scene* was transmitted.

March 29
Odeon Cinema, Lewisham, London (Roe/Montez tour).

March 30
Guildhall, Portsmouth (Roe/Montez tour).

March 31
De Montfort Hall, Leicester.
   The last night of the Roe/Montez tour.

April 1
BBC Piccadilly Studios, London. The group recorded two shows for the BBC Light Programme's *Side By Side,* presented by John Dunn, in which the resident act, The Karl Denver Trio, invited a guest group each week. For the first show, The Beatles sang 'Side By Side' with The Karl Denver Trio, followed by 'I Saw Her Standing There', 'Do You Want To Know A Secret', 'Baby It's You', 'Please Please, Me', 'From Me To You' and 'Misery'. For the second show they once more sang 'Side By Side' with The Karl Denver Trio followed by 'From Me To You', 'Long Tall Sally', 'A Taste Of Honey', 'Chains', 'Thank You Girl' and 'Boys'.

April 3
Playhouse Theatre, London, to record a session for BBC Radio's *Easy Beat*, presented by Brian Matthew, before a teenage studio audience. The Beatles performed 'Please Please Me', 'Misery' and 'From Me To You'.

April 4
BBC Paris Studio, London, to record a third *Side By Side* broadcast. The Beatles performed 'Too Much Monkey Business', 'Love Me Do', 'Boys', 'I'll Be On My Way' and 'From Me To You'. The BBC already had two tapes of The Beatles playing the theme tune with The Karl Denver Trio.
   Roxburgh Hall, Stowe School, Bucks. After the recording session The Beatles went to play an afternoon session at the boys' public school in Stowe, where the all-male audience sat in neat rows and did not scream. The booking had been made by one of the

schoolboys, David Moores; Brian Epstein was so impressed by the professionalism of his approach that he agreed to this unusual request.

April 5
EMI House, London. During an award ceremony in which they were presented with their first silver disc for 250,000 sales of the single 'Please Please Me', the group gave a private performance for executives of EMI.

Swimming Baths, Leyton, London.

April 6
Pavilion Gardens Ballroom, Buxton, Derbyshire.

April 7
Savoy Ballroom, Portsmouth.

The Beatles' appearance on *Easy Beat* was aired by the BBC.

April 8
John and Cynthia's son, John Charles Julian Lennon, was born at 6am, at Sefton General Hospital, Liverpool.

JULIAN LENNON
It was three days before John went to visit Cynthia and his new son. Cynthia: "Years later, John said something in an interview which was to hurt me very much. He told *Playboy* magazine: 'Julian was born out of a bottle of whisky on a Saturday night.' John was with Yoko Ono then but I was still offended and so was Julian. It was so untrue. I could tell that John said it to impress the interviewer but it still hurt. For a start we didn't even drink whisky in those days, but the worst part was the implied denial of our love. We were very much in love and very happy – Julian truly was a love child."

Nevertheless, John was an absent father for much of Julian's childhood but behind the machismo that John displayed on the outside was a deep sense of regret that was only apparent when his second son, Sean, was born in 1975. For the first five years of Sean's life, John rarely left his side.

Julian's birth left Cynthia in the awkward position of having to look after a Beatle's son, while his father was out on the road, and she was living with John's Aunt Mimi. Worst of all, she was forced to conceal the birth from Beatles' fans, for fear that the knowledge that one of the group was married, and a father, might damage their collective popularity.

April 9
BBC Paris Studio, London, to do a live interview for the BBC Light Programme lunchtime show *Pop Inn,* during which their forthcoming single 'From Me To You' was played.

Associated-Rediffusion's Wembley Studios for a live appearance on the children's programme *Tuesday Rendezvous*. They mimed 'From Me To You' and 'Please Please Me'.

The Ballroom, Gaumont State Cinema, Kilburn, London.

April 10
Majestic Ballroom, Birkenhead.

John sneaked in to see Cynthia and Julian at Sefton General Hospital before the evening's show.

April 11
Co-operative Hall, Middleton in Lancashire.

The single 'From Me To You'/'Thank You Girl' was released in the UK as Parlophone R 5015.

FROM ME TO YOU
Like many of their early songs, The Beatles' third single was deliberately built around heavy use of personal pronouns – the idea being that their audience could easily identify with the 'me' and 'you' in the title.

The opening harmonica solo was George Martin's suggestion, and proved to be a major part of the record's appeal. Equally commercial was the simple melody line of the chorus, which leaves 'From Me To You' as one of the less durable Beatles 45s.

THANK YOU GIRL

Songwriting for The Beatles in 1963 was less about self-expression than it was about a constant search for hit records. John Lennon's 'Thank You Girl' was one of the attempts that didn't quite make it, despite all the usual ingredients – his harmonica showcase, an easy-on-the-ear melody and a vocal gimmick. This time simplicity was taken a step too far, and 'Thank You Girl' wouldn't have withstood the constant airplay that every Beatles single was treated to in the Sixties.

April 12

Cavern Club, for a Good Friday, eight-hour "R&B Marathon", with The Fourmost, The Dennisons, The Nomads, The Panthers, Faron's Flamingos, The Flintstones, The Roadrunners and Group One.

April 13

Studio E, Lime Grove Studios, London, for extensive rehearsals and the recording of an appearance on BBC Television's *The 625 Show*. They performed 'From Me To You', 'Thank You Girl' and were joined by the rest of the cast to close the show with 'Please Please Me'.

At a party held that evening by Shadows' guitarist Bruce Welch at his house in North Harrow, The Beatles met Cliff Richard for the first time. The meeting was regarded as a significant event by the British pop press, who saw the two acts as bitter rivals. In fact, despite some occasionally acerbic public comments in later years, The Beatles and Cliff Richard seem to have indulged in a mutual appreciation society in the initial years of the group's success.

April 14

ABC Television's Teddington Studio Centre, Teddington. The Beatles mimed to 'From Me To You' for an edition of *Thank Your Lucky Stars*.

That evening, The Beatles saw The Rolling Stones play at the Crawdaddy Club in the Station Hotel, Richmond. The Beatles appeared at the club identically dressed in long suede leather jackets with matching hats acquired in Hamburg. It was an intentionally intimidating image, later described by Jagger as a "four-headed monster".

April 15

Riverside Dancing Club, Bridge Hotel, Tenbury Wells in Worcestershire.

The Beatles' interview on *Friday Spectacular* was broadcast on Radio Luxembourg.

April 16

Granada TV Centre, Manchester. The Beatles mimed live to 'From Me To You' on *Scene At 6.30*.

BBC screened *The 625 Show* at the same time.

April 17

Majestic Ballroom, Luton.

April 18

Royal Albert Hall, London, with Del Shannon, The Springfields, Lance Percival, Rolf Harris, The Vernon Girls, Kenny Lynch, Shane Fenton & The Fentones and George Melly.

A two-part concert, the second half of which was broadcast live by BBC radio as *Swinging Sound '63*. In the first half The Beatles played 'Please Please Me' and 'Misery' and in the second 'Twist And Shout' and 'From Me To You'. The show closed with a fade-out from the entire cast performing Kurt Weill's 'Mack The Knife'.

After the concert, The Beatles taught American star Del Shannon the chords and lyrics to 'From Me To You', prompting him to record the song as a US single on his return. Shannon thereby became the first overseas act to cover a Lennon/McCartney composition.

JANE ASHER

During rehearsals The Beatles met 17-year-old Jane Asher in the Green Room. She was writing a celebrity piece about them for *Radio Times* magazine and was posed as a screaming fan by the BBC photographer. After the show, Jane returned with them to the Royal Court Hotel where they were staying and afterwards they all went to NME journalist Chris Hutchins' apartment on the King's Road. Jane and Paul started a relationship which would continue until 1968.

Paul: "We knew her as the rather attractive, nice, well-spoken chick that we'd seen that year on *Juke Box Jury*. We all thought she was blonde because we'd only ever seen her in black and white on television, and we went mad for blondes. Then she came backstage afterwards and so we all immediately tried to pull her. At the end of all that, I ended up with Jane. Maybe I'd made the strongest play, or maybe she fancied me, I don't know."

The Rolling Stones had received front-row tickets from The Beatles and back-stage passes. After the gig, Brian Jones and The Stones' then manager Giorgio Gomelsky helped Mal Evans and Neil Aspinall load the van with The Beatles' stage gear. Some fans mistook Brian for one of The Beatles and mobbed him for autographs. He was overwhelmed, and Gomelsky remembered Brian walking away afterwards in a daze, down the big steps at the rear of the building, saying: "That's what I want, Giorgio. *That's* what I want!"

Before the concert, Giorgio Gomelsky asked *Jazz News* reporter Peter Clayton to come and meet The Beatles at his Bayswater apartment in London, so they could discuss collaborating on a film project – which Gomelsky hoped to direct, with Clayton as screenwriter.

Peter Clayton: "I found The Beatles to be extremely intriguing people. I remember John picking quietly at a mandolin all the time we talked. It wasn't rudeness, but he accompanied his own conversation with these fragments of tunes. I found it impossible to know what to do with Paul McCartney at first, because until I knew him better he was a closed book."

April 19
King's Hall, Stoke-on-Trent. The second of Brian Epstein's "Mersey Beat Showcase" events.

April 20
Ballroom, Mersey View Pleasure Grounds, Frodsham, Cheshire.

April 21
Empire Pool, Wembley, for the *NME*'s '1962–63 Annual Poll-Winners' All Star Concert', starring Cliff Richard and The Shadows.

As the poll had been conducted in 1962, The Beatles hadn't actually won anything, but they were included because of their two recent number one singles. They played 'Please Please Me', 'From Me To You', 'Twist And Shout' and 'Long Tall Sally' to an audience of 10,000 people, and were regarded by media observers as having stolen the show from the headliners.

Pigalle Club, Piccadilly, London. The Beatles travelled into London's West End after their *NME* concert for a performance at this more select venue.

The BBC Light Programme broadcast the first of The Beatles' *Side By Side* programmes.

April 23
Floral Hall, Southport.

April 24
Majestic Ballroom, Finsbury Park, London.

Another of Brian Epstein's "Mersey Beat Showcase" promotions, with Gerry & The Pacemakers, Billy J. Kramer and The Big Three, to an audience of 2,000 people.

Writer Peter Clayton held another meeting with the group before the show, discussing further ideas for a possible feature film.

Peter Clayton: "The film never came to pass because of what happened when Giorgio Gomelsky and Brian Epstein got together. I remember seeing Brian backed against a brick wall in a rear passage. There was Giorgio with one hand firmly on the wall, as if to imprison Epstein, while the other hand gesticulated wildly like a lunatic. Clearly the man was telling Epstein what brilliant ideas the two of us had, and just as clearly Brian was terrified of, and utterly baffled by, the way Gomelsky was behaving. After I watched Gomelsky spluttering all over Epstein, I knew the two would never meet again."

April 25
Ballroom, Fairfield Hall, Croydon.
Another "Mersey Beat Showcase" evening, with Gerry & The Pacemakers, Billy J. Kramer and The Big Three.

April 26
Music Hall, Shrewsbury.

April 27
The Victory Memorial Hall, Northwich in Cheshire.

April 28
George, Paul and Ringo flew to Santa Cruz, Tenerife for a 12-day holiday.
At Brian's expense, John and Brian Epstein flew to Torremolinos, Spain, for a vacation together, leaving Cynthia and her new born baby in Liverpool. That decision alarms and hurts Cynthia, while the news that Lennon and his overtly gay manager had holidayed together prompted much amusement and gossip amongst the Merseybeat community.

JOHN'S HOLIDAY WITH BRIAN

John: "I was on holiday with Brian Epstein in Spain, where the rumours went around that he and I were having a love affair. Well, it was almost a love affair, but not quite. It was never consummated. But it was a pretty intense relationship. It was my first experience with a homosexual that I was conscious *was* homosexual . . . We used to sit in a café in Torremolinos looking at all the boys and I'd say, 'Do you like that one? Do you like this one?' I was rather enjoying the experience, thinking like a writer all the time: *I am experiencing this*." While John was there, he wrote 'Bad To Me' for Billy J. Kramer, one of Brian's artists.

May 9
The two parties of holidaying Beatles returned to Liverpool after their separate vacations.

May 11
Imperial Ballroom, Nelson. A record 2,000 attendance.

May 12
Alpha TV Studios, Birmingham, for another recorded *Thank Your Lucky Stars* appearance. They mimed 'From Me To You' and 'I Saw Her Standing There'.
The BBC Light Programme broadcast the second of The Beatles' *Side By Side* programmes.

May 14
Rink Ballroom, Sunderland.

May 15
Royal Theatre, Chester.

May 16
Television Theatre, London, for their second appearance on national BBC TV. They shared the bill with a glove puppet, Lenny the Lion, The Raindrops and Patsy Ann Noble on the children's programme *Pops And Lenny* which went out live before an invited audience. With the puppet, The Beatles performed 'From Me To You', a short version of

'Please Please Me' and then joined Lenny the Lion and the rest of the cast for a version of 'After You've Gone'.

May 17
Grosvenor Rooms, Norwich.

May 18
Adelphi Cinema, Slough, on tour with Gerry & The Pacemakers, Tony Marsh, Erkey Grant, Ian Crawford, The Terry Young Six, Daiv Macbeth, Louise Cordet and, initially heading the bill but rapidly demoted to second spot, Roy Orbison.

The Beatles' set for this tour was 'Some Other Guy', 'Do You Want To Know A Secret', 'Love Me Do', 'From Me To You', 'Please Please Me', 'I Saw Her Standing There' and 'Twist & Shout'.

Thank Your Lucky Stars was broadcast by ABC TV.

May 19
Gaumont Cinema, Hanley in Staffordshire (Roy Orbison tour).

May 20
Gaumont Cinema, Southampton (Roy Orbison tour).

May 21
Playhouse Theatre, London, to record the BBC Light Programme's *Saturday Club.* They were interviewed by presenter Brian Matthew and performed 'I Saw Her Standing There', 'Do You Want To Know A Secret', 'Boys', 'Long Tall Sally', 'From Me To You' and 'Money (That's What I Want)'.

They also recorded a session for a new radio programme *Steppin' Out,* for which they did 'Please Please Me', 'I Saw Her Standing There', 'Roll Over Beethoven', 'Thank You Girl' and 'From Me To You' before a live audience.

After the recordings were completed, writer Peter Clayton held his final discussion with The Beatles about a proposed film project, which was abandoned soon afterwards.

May 22
Gaumont Cinema, Ipswich (Roy Orbison tour).

May 23
Odeon Cinema, Nottingham (Roy Orbison tour).

May 24
Studio Two, Aeolian Hall, London, to record the first programme in their own BBC Light Programme series: *Pop Go The Beatles.* The programme began and closed with a rocked-up version of 'Pop Goes The Weasel' recorded by The Beatles with the aid of their guests for this programme, The Lorne Gibson Trio. The Beatles performed 'From Me To You', 'Everybody's Trying To Be My Baby', 'Do You Want To Know A Secret', 'You Really Got A Hold On Me', 'Misery' and 'The Hippy Hippy Shake' as well as bantering with presenter Lee Peters.

Granada Cinema, Walthamstow, London (Roy Orbison tour). The Beatles were now officially billed as the headliners for the tour, Roy Orbison having graciously bowed to public opinion.

May 25
City Hall, Sheffield (Roy Orbison tour).

The Beatles appear on the BBC Light Programme's *Saturday Club.*

May 26
Empire Theatre, Liverpool (Roy Orbison tour).

May 27
Capitol Cinema, Cardiff (Roy Orbison tour).

The single 'From Me To You'/'Thank You Girl' was released in the US as Vee Jay VJ 522, where it competed with Del Shannon's recently issued version of the song.

May 28
Gaumont Cinema, Worcester (Roy Orbison tour).

May 29
Rialto Theatre, York (Roy Orbison tour).

May 30
Odeon Cinema, Manchester (Roy Orbison tour).
   Future Beatles and Apple press officer Derek Taylor reviewed the show for the *Daily Express* newspaper: "I thought it was magnificent . . . Indecipherable, meaningless nonsense, of course, but as beneficial and invigorating as a week on a beach at the pierhead overlooking the Mersey . . . I suppose there is not – yet – a first-class musician among them . . . Their stage manner has little polish but limitless energy, and they have in abundance the fundamental rough good humour of their native city . . . Nobody could hear themselves trying to think. The act was largely drowned, but it didn't matter at all."

May 31
Odeon Cinema, Southend-on-Sea (Roy Orbison tour).

June 1
BBC Paris Studio, London. The Beatles recorded the second and third programmes in their *Pop Go The Beatles* series. On the second programme they sang 'Too Much Monkey Business', 'I Got To Find My Baby', 'Youngblood', 'Baby It's You', 'Till There Was You' and 'Love Me Do'. Their guests were The Countrymen. For the third programme they performed 'A Shot Of Rhythm And Blues', 'Memphis, Tennessee', 'A Taste Of Honey' and 'Sure To Fall (In Love With You)' with Carter-Lewis & The Southerners as their guests.
   Granada Cinema, Tooting, London (Roy Orbison tour).

June 2
Hippodrome Theatre, Brighton (Roy Orbison tour).

June 3
Granada Cinema, Woolwich, London (Roy Orbison tour).
   The Beatles on BBC Radio's *Steppin' Out* was broadcast.

June 4
Town Hall, Birmingham (Roy Orbison tour).
   The first of the *Pop Go The Beatles* programmes was broadcast by the BBC Light Programme.

June 5
Odeon Cinema, Leeds (Roy Orbison tour). Girls from local high schools were noticeably 'absent' during the few days preceding this event as they queued in shifts, day and night, in order to be sure of tickets.

June 7
Odeon Cinema, Glasgow (Roy Orbison tour).

June 8
City Hall, Newcastle upon Tyne (Roy Orbison tour).

June 9
King George's Hall, Blackburn.
   The last concert of the Roy Orbison tour.

June 10
The Pavilion, Bath, with The Colin Anthony Combo and Chet & The Triumphs.

June 11
The BBC Light Programme broadcast the second programme in the series *Pop Go The Beatles*.

June 12
Grafton Rooms, Liverpool.
   A charity event in aid of the NSPCC at which The Beatles played for free.

June 13
Palace Theatre Club, Stockport, and Southern Sporting Club, Manchester.

June 14
Tower Ballroom, Wallasey.
   Another of Brian Epstein's "Mersey Beat Showcase" promotions.

June 15
City Hall, Salisbury.

June 16
Odeon Cinema, Romford, with Billy J. Kramer & The Dakotas, The Vikings with Michael London, Gerry & The Pacemakers, and compere Vic Sutcliffe. The last of the "Mersey Beat Showcase" concerts.

June 17
BBC Maida Vale Studios, London, to record the fourth of the *Pop Go The Beatles* programmes, this time with The Bachelors as "guests". The Beatles recorded 'I Saw Her Standing There', 'Anna (Go To Him)', 'Boys', 'Chains', 'P.S. I Love You' and 'Twist And Shout'.
   Dezo Hoffmann photographed the session and did a separate photo session afterwards in Delaware Road.
   The group drove to Liverpool.

June 18
Paul's 21st birthday party was held in a marquee in the back garden of his Aunt Jin's house at 147 Dinas Lane, Huyton.

THE BOB WOOLER INCIDENT
The Beatles' old friend Bob Wooler teased John about his trip to Spain with Brian Epstein but John was drunk and in a belligerent mood. He leapt on Bob Wooler and beat him up. John said, "He called me a queer so I battered his bloody ribs in." Next John attacked a woman who was standing nearby. When Billy J. Kramer intervened, Lennon yelled, "You're nothing, Kramer, and we're the top." Brian Epstein drove Bob Wooler to the hospital to get his eye treated and to check for broken ribs.
   John: "The Beatles' first national coverage was me beating up Bob Wooler at Paul's 21st party because he intimated I was homosexual. I must have had a fear that maybe I was homosexual to attack him like that and it's very complicated reasoning. But I was very drunk and I hit him and I could have really killed somebody then. And that scared me . . . That was in the *Daily Mirror*, it was the back page . . ."

The BBC Light Programme broadcast the third edition of *Pop Go The Beatles*.

June 19
Playhouse Theatre, London, to record their second appearance on BBC Radio's *Easy Beat* before a live, screaming audience. They performed 'Some Other Guy', 'A Taste Of Honey', 'Thank You Girl' and 'From Me To You'.
   Derek Taylor of the *Daily Express* travelled to Liverpool to interview Brian Epstein.

June 20
Acting on orders from Brian Epstein, John sent Bob Wooler a telegram reading: "Really sorry Bob. Terribly worried to realise what I had done. What more can I say?"

The Beatles Limited was formed, as a corporate device to handle the group's legal and business affairs.

June 21
Odeon Cinema, Guildford.

News of John's assault on Bob Wooler belatedly reached the back cover of the *Daily Mirror* newspaper – the first negative press coverage the group ever received.

June 22
Television Theatre, London: John taped a BBC TV *Juke Box Jury*, hosted by David Jacobs, with fellow jurors Katie Boyle, Bruce Prochnik and Caroline Maudling. Unbowed by his villainous role in the previous day's press, John outspokenly voted every one of the records presented as a "miss".

Afterwards he was driven to the Battersea Heliport where he flew by specially chartered helicopter to join the others in Wales, landing at the Penypound Football Ground, in Abergavenny.

Ballroom, Town Hall, Abergavenny. A civic reception in which the group met the Mayor and Mayoress, Councillor and Mrs J.F. Thurston, was held when Paul, George and Ringo arrived in Abergavenny with Neil Aspinall in the group's van.

After the show, the group signed autographs at three pence each, proceeds going to the local committee of the Freedom From Hunger Campaign.

June 23
Alpha TV Studios, Birmingham, to tape a session for *Summer Spin* – the summer name for *Thank Your Lucky Stars*. The whole show was a celebration of the Mersey scene. The programme was presented by Pete Murray. The group mimed 'From Me To You' and 'I Saw Her Standing There'.

The Beatles' appearance on *Easy Beat* was transmitted.

June 24
Playhouse Theatre, London, for another recording session for BBC Radio's *Saturday Club* presented by Brian Matthew. The Beatles sang 'I Got To Find My Baby', 'Memphis, Tennessee', 'Money (That's What I Want)', 'Till There Was You', 'From Me To You' and 'Roll Over Beethoven'.

June 25
Astoria Ballroom, Middlesbrough.

The BBC Light Programme broadcast the fourth *Pop Go The Beatles* programme.

June 26
Majestic Ballroom, Newcastle-upon-Tyne.

Before this show Paul and John began to write their next single, 'She Loves You', in their room at Turk's Hotel.

June 27
Taking advantage of a rest day in The Beatles' schedule, Paul flew to London to attend Billy J. Kramer's recording session at Abbey Road, and to watch him cut John's 'Bad To Me' and 'I Call Your Name'.

June 28
Queen's Hall, Leeds, with Acker Bilk and his Paramount Jazz Band to an audience of 3,200.

June 29
The Beatles appeared on the BBC Light Programme's *Saturday Club*.

The Beatles' appearance on ABC TV's *Summer Spin* Mersey Beat special was aired. John's appearance on BBC TV's *Juke Box Jury* was broadcast, clashing with ABC TV's *Summer Spin*.

June 30
ABC Cinema, Great Yarmouth.
The first of a ten-week series of seaside concerts. They played 'Some Other Guy', 'Thank You Girl', 'Do You Want To Know A Secret', 'Misery', 'A Taste Of Honey', 'I Saw Her Standing There', 'Love Me Do', 'From Me To You', 'Baby It's You', 'Please Please Me' and 'Twist And Shout'.

July 1
Abbey Road. The Beatles recorded their next single, 'She Loves You'/'I'll Get You', and posed for another official EMI photographic session.

July 2
Maida Vale Studios, London, to record the first of 11 new *Pop Go The Beatles* programmes, this time presented by Rodney Burke. The Beatles performed 'That's All Right (Mama)', 'Carol', 'Soldier Of Love (Lay Down Your Arms)', 'Lend Me Your Comb', 'Clarabella' and 'There's A Place'. Their first guest act was Duffy Power with The Graham Bond Quartet.

July 3
Playhouse Theatre to rehearse and record a session for BBC Light Programme's *The Beat Show* with the NDO (Northern Dance Orchestra) and The Trad Lads. The show's host was Gay Byrne and The Beatles performed 'From Me To You', 'A Taste Of Honey' and 'Twist And Shout'.

July 4
The BBC Light Programme broadcast *The Beat Show*.
The Beatles, accompanied by Jane Asher's brother Peter, saw The Rolling Stones play the Scene Club, Soho.

July 5
Plaza Ballroom, Old Hill, Dudley, with Denny & The Diplomats.

July 6
Northwich Carnival, Verdin Park. That afternoon The Beatles attended the carnival and Paul crowned the Carnival Queen.
The Victory Memorial Hall, Northwich.

July 7
ABC Theatre, Blackpool.

July 8
Winter Gardens, Margate.
The Beatles' set: 'Roll Over Beethoven', 'Thank You Girl', 'Chains', 'Please Please Me', 'A Taste Of Honey', 'I Saw Her Standing There', 'Baby It's You', 'From Me To You' and 'Twist And Shout'.

July 9
Winter Gardens, Margate.

July 10
Aeolian Hall, London, to record two more *Pop Go The Beatles* shows. For the sixth programme they did 'Sweet Little Sixteen', 'A Taste Of Honey', 'Nothin' Shakin' (But The Leaves On The Trees)', 'Love Me Do', 'Lonesome Tears', 'In My Eyes' and 'So How Come (Nobody Loves Me)' and had Carter-Lewis & The Southerners as their guests.
For the seventh programme they recorded 'Memphis, Tennessee', 'Do You Want To Know A Secret', 'Till There Was You', 'Matchbox', 'Please Mister Postman' and 'The Hippy Hippy Shake' with The Searchers as their guests. After the recording session they drove back to Margate in time for the first house.
Winter Gardens, Margate.

July 11
Winter Gardens, Margate.

July 12
Winter Gardens, Margate.
    The EP *Twist And Shout* was released in the UK as Parlophone GEP 8882 (mono only): Side A: 'Twist And Shout', 'A Taste Of Honey'; Side B: 'Do You Want To Know A Secret', 'There's A Place'.
    As a spoiler for this release, Polydor chose the same day to issue *My Bonnie*, a four-track EP taken from The Beatles' Hamburg sessions with Tony Sheridan. The EP was released as Polydor H 21–610 (mono only): Side A: 'My Bonnie', 'Why'. Side B: 'Cry For A Shadow', 'The Saints'.
    John was forced to deny press rumours that he regarded Ringo Starr as "ugly". He also vowed that the rest of the group were not deliberately keeping the drummer in the background: "Ringo is still rather shy. But in six months, he will really be playing a major part in the act."

July 13
Winter Gardens, Margate.

July 14
ABC Theatre, Blackpool.

July 15
Paul was fined £17 at Birkenhead Magistrates Court for speeding. He did not attend.

July 16
BBC Paris Studio, London. Programmes eight, nine and ten of *Pop Go The Beatles* were recorded and stockpiled in one long session. For programme eight they recorded 'I'm Gonna Sit Right Down And Cry (Over You)', 'Crying, Waiting, Hoping', 'Kansas City'/'Hey, Hey, Hey, Hey', 'To Know Her Is To Love Her', 'The Honeymoon Song' and 'Twist And Shout'. They had as their guests The Swinging Blue Jeans.
    The ninth programme featured 'Long Tall Sally', 'Please Please Me', 'She Loves You', 'You Really Got A Hold On Me', 'I'll Get You' and 'I Got A Woman' and would have The Hollies as guests when it was broadcast.
    Programme ten featured 'She Loves You', 'Words Of Love', 'Glad All Over', 'I Just Don't Understand', '(There's A) Devil In Her Heart' and 'Slow Down', with guests Russ Sainty & The Nu-Notes.

July 17
Playhouse Theatre, London, to record a BBC Light Programme *Easy Beat*. They performed four numbers before the usual live teenage audience: 'I Saw Her Standing There', 'A Shot Of Rhythm And Blues', 'There's A Place' and 'Twist And Shout'.

July 18
Abbey Road. The Beatles worked on material for their second album: 'You Really Got A Hold On Me', 'Money (That's What I Want)', '(There's A) Devil In Her Heart' and 'Till There Was You'.

July 19
Ritz Ballroom, Rhyl.

July 20
Ritz Ballroom, Rhyl.
    Afterwards, The Beatles drove back to Liverpool.

July 21
Queen's Theatre, Blackpool.
    Four thousand fans blocked the streets of Blackpool before the concert, an early intimation of Beatlemania to come.
    The Beatles met with Don Haworth from BBC TV Manchester to discuss the

possibility of a serious half-hour documentary on The Beatles and the Mersey scene. They were interested and plans went ahead.

The recent *Easy Beat* recording was transmitted by the BBC Light programme.

July 22

Odeon Cinema, Weston-super-Mare. The opening of a six-night engagement.

Dezo Hoffmann spent the day with the group on the beach at Bream Down, where he got them to pose in Victorian swimming costumes, ride donkeys and also made an amateur film of them cavorting on the beach. Dezo Hoffmann: "I had the idea of hiring bathing huts, old-fashioned swimming costumes, etc. They loved dressing up in silly costumes. John kept his on back at the hotel long after the session was over." On the way back they stopped at a Go-Kart track.

July 23

Odeon Cinema, Weston-super-Mare.

Pop Go The Beatles was broadcast by the BBC Light Programme.

July 24

Odeon Cinema, Weston-super-Mare.

July 25

Odeon Cinema, Weston-super-Mare.

July 26

Odeon Cinema, Weston-super-Mare.

The album *Introducing The Beatles* was released in the US as Vee Jay VJLP 1062 (mono) and SR 1062 (stereo). Side A: 'I Saw Her Standing There', 'Misery', 'Anna (Go To Him)', 'Chains', 'Boys', 'Love Me Do'; Side B: 'P.S. I Love You', 'Baby It's You', 'Do You Want To Know A Secret', 'A Taste Of Honey', 'There's A Place', 'Twist And Shout'.

July 27

Odeon Cinema, Weston-super-Mare.

July 28

ABC Cinema, Great Yarmouth.

July 30

Abbey Road. The Beatles recorded 'Please Mister Postman' and 'It Won't Be Long' in a morning session.

Playhouse Theatre, London, for two BBC Light Programme recordings: an interview with Phil Tate for the "Pop Chat" spot on *Non Stop Pop*, and a session for *Saturday Club* where they played 'Long Tall Sally', 'She Loves You', 'Glad All Over', 'Twist And Shout', 'You Really Got A Hold On Me' and 'I'll Get You'.

Back at Abbey Road for an evening session, The Beatles worked on 'Till There Was You', 'Roll Over Beethoven', 'It Won't Be Long' and 'All My Loving'.

Pop Go The Beatles was broadcast by the BBC Light Programme.

July 31

Imperial Ballroom, Nelson.

August 1

Playhouse Theatre, Manchester, to record two more sessions for the BBC Light Programme's *Pop Go The Beatles*. For the 11th show in the series, they recorded 'Ooh! My Soul', 'Don't Ever Change', 'Twist And Shout', 'She Loves You', 'Anna (Go To Him)' and 'A Shot Of Rhythm & Blues' and their guests were Cyril Davies' Rhythm & Blues All-Stars with Long John Baldry. The 12th show featured Brian Poole & The Tremeloes as guests and The Beatles playing 'From Me To You', 'I'll Get You', 'Money (That's What I Want)', 'There's A Place', 'Honey Don't' and 'Roll Over Beethoven'.

The first issue of *The Beatles Book* was published by Beat Publications Ltd. publisher Sean O'Mahony, in collaboration with Brian Epstein. The A5 magazine continued to provide exclusive photographs of the group, plus detailed (and uncritical) news coverage of their activities, every month until the end of 1969.

August 2
Grafton Rooms, Liverpool.

August 3
Cavern Club.
   The Beatles' last performance at the club – officially documented by the Cavern management as their 292nd, although the complete accuracy of that figure has since been questioned. Tickets for the show understandably sold out within half an hour of going on sale.

August 4
Queen's Theatre, Blackpool.
   The Beatles had to enter the theatre through a trap door on the roof, reached through scaffolding in the next-door builder's yard, because the normal entrances were totally blocked by fans.

August 5
Urmston Show.
   An annual bank holiday show held in a giant marquee. The Beatles topped a four-act bill, which included Brian Poole & The Tremeloes. David Hamilton was the compere.

August 6
Springfield Ballroom, St Saviour, Jersey.
   The Beatles relaxed by go-karting and swimming. It was while in the Channel Islands that John Lennon met up again with Royston Ellis and Ellis introduced him to a late-night party attended by a strange woman called 'Polythene Pam'.

August 7
Springfield Ballroom, St Saviour, Jersey.

August 8
Auditorium, Candie Gardens, Guernsey.
   The Beatles flew to Guernsey in a 12-seater plane.

August 9
Springfield Ballroom, St Saviour, Jersey.

August 10
Springfield Ballroom, St Saviour, Jersey.

August 11
ABC Theatre, Blackpool.
   Mal Evans met the group in the van when they arrived at Manchester Airport after their week in the Channel Islands. It was his first day as a full-time employee of the group. The pressure of work and the need for personal security had led Brian Epstein to ask Mal to work as a combined roadie/bodyguard for the group.

August 12
Odeon Cinema, Llandudno.
   The first night of a six-night season at the seaside, with two houses each night.

August 13
Odeon Cinema, Llandudno.
   After the second show the group returned to Liverpool for the night.
   EMI confirmed that The Beatles' *Twist And Shout* EP had now qualified for a silver disc, for more than 250,000 sales – the first EP release to achieve this distinction.

August 14
Odeon Cinema, Llandudno.
   In the morning they drove to Granada TV Centre, Manchester, to record two songs;
'Twist And Shout' and 'She Loves You' for *Scene*. The first was transmitted that night.

August 15
Odeon Cinema, Llandudno.

August 16
Odeon Cinema, Llandudno.

August 17
Odeon Cinema, Llandudno.

August 18
Alpha TV Studios, Birmingham, to record an appearance for ABC TV's *Lucky Stars
(Summer Spin)* presented by Pete Murray. They mimed 'She Loves You' and 'I'll Get
You', the A- and B-sides to their next single
   Princess Theatre, Devon.

August 19
Gaumont Cinema, Bournemouth, with Billy J. Kramer & The Dakotas and Tommy
Quickly. Another summer seaside residency.
   The Beatles held a 20th birthday party for Billy J. Kramer in their dressing room
between the two houses.
   Granada transmitted The Beatles singing 'She Loves You' on *Scene*.

August 20
Gaumont Cinema, Bournemouth.

August 21
Gaumont Cinema, Bournemouth.

August 22
While in Bournemouth, The Beatles stayed at the Palace Court Hotel where, probably
on this day, Robert Freeman shot the famous monochrome photograph for the *With The
Beatles* album.

THE *WITH THE BEATLES* COVER
Robert Freeman: "I suggested a black and white photograph . . . The boys liked
the idea and the session was set up for noon the following day in the hotel
dining room. The large windows let in a bright sidelight and the dark maroon
velvet curtains were pulled round as a backdrop . . . We decided to use the
black turtleneck sweaters which they wore at the time, to keep the picture
simple." Ringo was placed in the bottom right corner as he was the last to join
the group and had to kneel on a stool to be comfortable in the right position for
the shot. Freeman received £75 for the cover, rather than the £25 EMI
originally proposed.
   Paul: "He arranged us in a hotel corridor: it was very un-studio-like. The
corridor was rather dark, and there was a window at the end, and by using this
heavy source of natural light coming from the right, he got that very moody
picture which people think he must have worked at forever and ever. But it was
an hour. He sat down, took a couple of rolls, and he had it."

After lunch, The Beatles and Robert Freeman drove to the Southern ITV Centre,
Southampton, where they recorded an appearance for the *Day By Day* programme,
miming 'She Loves You', which was broadcast that evening.
   Gaumont Cinema, Bournemouth.

August 23
Gaumont Cinema, Bournemouth.

The single 'She Loves You'/'I'll Get You' was released in the UK as Parlophone R 5055. Demand for the new single was so great that EMI pressed over a quarter of a million copies in the four weeks before its official release.

SHE LOVES YOU

"People said at the time that this was the worst song we'd ever thought of doing," Paul McCartney mused in 1980, and the reviews of their fourth single were a trifle sniffy, suggesting that the group were struggling for new material. Instead, 'She Loves You' proved to be the anthem of Beatlemania. It's not the strongest song they recorded in 1963, or perhaps the most important (that honour must go to 'I Want To Hold Your Hand', which broke them in America), but more than anything else, it conjures up the exuberance which so entranced the nation in the latter half of 1963.

George Martin regarded the final vocal harmony as a cliché, which it may have been in classical terms, but to the pop audience it was a revelation. What sold the record, and The Beatles, though, was the sheer inane appeal of the chorus. Even now, repeat the phrase 'yeah, yeah, yeah' to almost anyone in the country, and they'll catch the reference to The Beatles.

I'LL GET YOU

Like 'Thank You Girl' this Lennon number came straight off the production line, though this time the melody line wasn't quite catchy enough for a single. Take note of the middle eight, however, where John demonstrated that he was every bit as strong a tunesmith as McCartney.

August 24

Gaumont Cinema, Bournemouth.

The Beatles' July 30 recording for *Saturday Club* with presenter Brian Matthew was transmitted by the BBC Light Programme. The Beatles performing on *Lucky Stars (Summer Spin)* was broadcast by ABC TV.

August 25

ABC Theatre, Blackpool.

August 26

Odeon Cinema, Southport.

Another one-week seaside residency. The Beatles set consisted of 'Roll Over Beethoven', 'Thank You Girl', 'Chains', 'A Taste Of Honey', 'She Loves You', 'Baby It's You', 'From Me To You', 'Boys', 'I Saw Her Standing There' and 'Twist And Shout'.

Paul received his third speeding conviction this year and was fined £31 and disqualified from driving for one year.

August 27

Odeon Cinema, Southport.

The Beatles were filmed playing 'Twist And Shout' and 'She Loves You' on stage, but with no audience, at The Little Theatre in Southport as part of the BBC TV Manchester documentary being made by Don Haworth. After a change of clothes to suggest a different occasion, they played 'Love Me Do'. Audience shots were then dubbed in from the previous night's concert. In the end their commercial recordings of these songs were used in the "documentary", which finished up about as close to reality as their movie *A Hard Day's Night*.

The BBC Light Programme broadcast edition 11 of *Pop Go The Beatles*.

August 28

Odeon Cinema, Southport.

The Beatles were interviewed at the BBC's Manchester studios and also filmed as if backstage making up before a concert, and waiting in the wings with their instruments, all for Haworth's *The Mersey Sound* documentary.

August 29

Odeon Cinema, Southport.

The Beatles acted an airport arrival for the "documentary" and also took a Mersey ferry between the Pier Head and Wallasey, signing autographs and meeting fans.

August 30
Odeon Cinema, Southport.
Ringo was filmed pushing his way through extras outside his childhood home at 10 Admiral Grove in the Dingle for Don Haworth's film.
The BBC Light Programme broadcast the "Pop Chat" interview on *Non Stop Pop*.
Another Brian Epstein signing, The Fourmost, began their professional career with the release of a Lennon/McCartney song, 'Hello Little Girl'.

August 31
Odeon Cinema, Southport.
The final show in Southport.

September 1
ABC TV's Didsbury Studio Centre, Manchester. The group recorded an appearance on the variety show *Big Night Out* presented by comedians Mike and Bernie Winters. They mimed 'From Me To You', 'She Loves You' and 'Twist And Shout' before a studio audience of 600 (broadcast September 7).

September 3
Aeolian Hall, London, to record the last three programmes in the *Pop Go The Beatles* series, presented by Rodney Burke. For the 13th edition The Beatles recorded 'Too Much Monkey Business', 'Love Me Do', 'She Loves You', 'Till There Was You', 'I'll Get You' and 'The Hippy Hippy Shake'. Their guests were Johnny Kidd & The Pirates. For the 14th they played 'Chains', 'You Really Got A Hold On Me', 'Misery', 'A Taste Of Honey' (which was later edited into the preceding programme), 'Lucille' and 'From Me To You'. The Marauders were their guests. For the 15th and final session they played 'She Loves You', 'Ask Me Why', '(There's A) Devil In Her Heart', 'I Saw Her Standing There', 'Sure To Fall (In Love With You)' and 'Twist And Shout'. Their guests were Tony Rivers & The Castaways.
The BBC Light Programme broadcast edition 12 of *Pop Go The Beatles*.

September 4
Gaumont Cinema, Worcester.

September 5
Gaumont Cinema, Taunton.

September 6
Odeon Cinema, Luton.
The EP *The Beatles' Hits* was released in the UK as Parlophone GEP 8880 (mono only). Side A: 'From Me To You', 'Thank You Girl'; Side B: 'Please Please Me', 'Love Me Do'.

September 7
Playhouse Theatre, London, to rehearse and record a session for the BBC Light Programme's fifth birthday edition of *Saturday Club*. The Beatles performed 'I Saw Her Standing There', 'Memphis, Tennessee', 'Happy Birthday Saturday Club', which was written especially for the occasion by John, 'I'll Get You', 'She Loves You' and 'Lucille'.
After the recording, Paul did an interview with Rosemary Hart for the BBC Home Service series *A World Of Sound*.
Fairfield Hall, Croydon.
'She Loves You' reached number one in the charts where it stayed for seven weeks.
The Beatles' appearance on Mike and Bernie Winters' *Big Night Out* was broadcast by ABC TV.

September 8
ABC Theatre, Blackpool.

September 10
John and Paul attended a Variety Club of Great Britain luncheon at the Savoy Hotel where they received the award for 'Top Vocal Group of the Year'.

THE ROLLING STONES

That afternoon, The Rolling Stones' manager, ex-Beatles publicist Andrew Oldham, was walking down Jermyn Street when a taxi pulled up beside him, waiting for traffic lights. The window rolled down and a Liverpudlian voice said, "Get in, Andy". It had been only a few months since he had stopped working as The Beatles' press agent.

In the cab were John and Paul, returning to their hotel after lunch. Knowing that The Beatles liked The Rolling Stones, Andrew told them that he was looking for songs for them to record. John and Paul immediately suggested that he might like to hear one they had just written, called 'I Wanna Be Your Man', which they thought might be suitable.

Andrew was on his way to meet the Stones at Ken Colyer's Studio 51 in Great Newport Street, Soho, and John and Paul said they would join him. At the club they borrowed a couple of guitars from Brian and Keith and launched into the number. There was only one problem: the song didn't have a middle eight.

After a quick conference John and Paul told them that if they really liked the song, they would finish it off for them. They disappeared into a side room and reappeared a few minutes later. "Forget something?" asked Bill Wyman.

"No," said Paul. "We've just finished the middle eight. How does this sound?"

It became the Rolling Stones' first Top 20 hit.

September 10
The BBC Light Programme broadcast edition 13 of *Pop Go The Beatles*.

September 11
Abbey Road, to continue work on the *With The Beatles* album. They worked on 'I Wanna Be Your Man' (Paul has no memory of it being intended as anything other than a vehicle for Ringo), 'Little Child', 'All I've Got To Do' and 'Not A Second Time'. Finally, they made a number of takes of George's 'Don't Bother Me'.

September 12
Abbey Road. In preparation for their Australian tour they recorded three message clips for Bob Rogers, an important DJ on Sydney station 2SM, and an open message to be used by any radio station. After this they continued work on 'Hold Me Tight', 'Don't Bother Me', 'Little Child' and 'I Wanna Be Your Man'.

September 13
Public Hall, Preston.
  Imperial Ballroom, Nelson, Lancashire. After the Preston show Paul drove to Nelson to take his place on the panel of judges at the "Miss Imperial 1963" contest, part of an annual "Young Ones Ball" promotion by local newspaper *The Nelson Leader*.

September 14
Press interviews at NEMS Liverpool offices.
  The Victory Memorial Hall, Northwich.

September 15
Royal Albert Hall, London.
  This was the annual "Great Pop Prom" promoted by *Valentine, Marilyn* and *Roxy* magazines in aid of the Printers' Pension Corporation. The Beatles appeared with 11 other acts. The compere was Alan Freeman.
  The Beatles did a photo session with The Rolling Stones, who were also on the bill, on the steps to the rear of the hall. Paul: "Standing up on those steps behind the Albert Hall in our new gear, the smart trousers, the rolled collar. Up there with The Rolling Stones we were thinking, "This is it – London! The Albert Hall! We *felt* like Gods!"
  The single 'She Loves You'/'I'll Get You' was released in the US as Swan 4152.

September 16

John and Cynthia flew to Paris on holiday, where they were joined later by Brian Epstein. George and his brother Peter visited their sister Louise in Benton, Illinois, USA – George thereby becoming the first of the Beatles to travel to America.

Paul, Jane, Ringo and Maureen went to Greece: Paul: "We used to go to Greece because in Greece they never recognised us. Everywhere else, in Germany, in Italy, in the south of France, it was 'There's The Beatles!' and we had to run for our bloody lives. So we'd go to Greece, and then one year everyone recognised us in Greece too. So we figured, 'Whoa, this is the point of no return'. But then you learn either to get out now or realise that this is fame, this is what happens with fame. This is celebrity. We thought, 'Well, we'd better get on with it, come to terms with it'."

Ringo: "I did a lot of swimming during the day while Paul had a bash at the water skiing. During the evenings we used to join in with the local Greek group called The Trio Athenia. 'Cause they didn't play pop stuff – not until we turned up at any rate. Now they'll have a go at half our Top Ten."

September 17

The BBC Light Programme broadcast the 14th edition of *Pop Go The Beatles*.

September 24

The BBC Light Programme broadcast the final edition of *Pop Go The Beatles*.

October 2

Paul and Ringo arrived back in England via Zürich and Frankfurt. John, Cynthia and Brian flew direct from Paris.

October 3

Abbey Road. Ringo overdubbed his vocal on 'I Wanna Be Your Man' and John and Paul put theirs on 'Little Child'.

George flew in from the USA in time to join the others in an interview with Michael Colley for the BBC Light Programme's *The Public Ear*.

Ringo drove to Southend, Essex, to see The Everly Brothers, Bo Diddley and The Rolling Stones play the Odeon Cinema.

October 4

Associated-Rediffusion's studios at Television House, London, to record their first appearance on *Ready, Steady, Go!* They mimed 'Twist And Shout', 'I'll Get You' and 'She Loves You' live and were interviewed by Keith Fordyce and Dusty Springfield.

October 5

Carnegie Hall, Glasgow.

The first of three Scottish gigs.

The special fifth birthday edition of *Saturday Club* was broadcast by the BBC Light Programme.

October 6

Carlton Theatre, Kirkaldy.

A total of 3,000 fans crowded into the two performances.

October 7

Caird Hall, Dundee.

October 9

BBC Paris Studio, London, to record 'She Loves You' for the BBC Light Programme comedy show, *The Ken Dodd Show*.

Don Haworth's BBC television "documentary", *The Mersey Sound*, was broadcast to great acclaim.

October 11

Ballroom, Trentham.

October 12

The Beatles rehearsed for their appearance the following night on *Sunday Night At The London Palladium*.

October 13

London Palladium.

The Beatles topped the bill at ATV's *Val Parnell's Sunday Night At The London Palladium*, transmitted live from the theatre to an audience of 15 million viewers. They played 'From Me To You', 'I'll Get You', 'She Loves You' and 'Twist And Shout', and joined the other acts, which included Brook Benton and Des O'Connor, as well as compere Bruce Forsyth, to wave goodbye to the audience and viewers from the revolving stage which traditionally ended the show.

THE ORIGINS OF BEATLEMANIA

Outside the Palladium, fans blocked Argyll Street and spilled over into Great Marlborough Street, stopping traffic. Fans in the audience screamed so much that John yelled for them to "Shut up!" It was this manifestation of Beatles fans' adulation that led the following day's newspapers to coin the term "Beatlemania". The event was covered by the late news on ITV.

October 14

The British press discovered Beatlemania with headline coverage of The Beatles' appearance on *Sunday Night At The London Palladium* and the mass hysteria that the group caused in its fans. The *Daily Herald*, for example, reported: "Screaming girls launched themselves against the police – sending helmets flying and constables reeling."

Unaware that similar scenes had been surrounding the group's performances for many months, the press dated this event as the birth of Beatlemania, and later came to believe that they had invented the phenomenon themselves.

October 15

Floral Hall, Southport.

It was announced that The Beatles had been invited to appear on the Royal Variety Show, prompting the London press to follow the group to Southport in anticipation of another 'riot'.

October 16

Playhouse Theatre, London, to record their final session for BBC Light Programme's *Easy Beat*. They played 'I Saw Her Standing There', 'Love Me Do', 'Please Please Me', 'From Me To You' and 'She Loves You'.

The Beatles were interviewed about the Royal Variety Show announcement by Peter Woods for BBC Light Programme's *Radio Newsreel*.

October 17

Abbey Road. The Beatles recorded both sides of their next single – 'I Wanna Hold Your Hand' and 'This Boy' – using EMI's new four-track machine for the first time. (EMI was very backward technologically and it is entirely typical that they were only just installing four-track equipment when American studios, such as Atlantic Records in New York, had been using eight-track equipment since the Fifties.)

The Beatles also worked on 'You Really Got A Hold On Me', and made 'The Beatles' Christmas Record' for their fan club members.

Fans blocked Bond Street when Paul arrived to take a girl out to lunch who had won a "Why I Like The Beatles" magazine competition.

October 18

Granada Television Centre, Manchester, to mime 'She Loves You' for that evening's edition of *Scene at 6.30*.

October 19

Pavilion Gardens Ballroom, Buxton. The performance was preceded by another frenetic struggle between fans and police.

October 20
Alpha TV Studios, Birmingham, to record a headline appearance for ABC TV's *Thank Your Lucky Stars*. They mimed 'All My Loving', 'Money (That's What I Want)' and 'She Loves You' while 3,000 fans blocked the streets and attempted to storm the studios.

The BBC Light Programme broadcast the final appearance by The Beatles on *Easy Beat*.

October 23
Abbey Road. The Beatles completed work on 'I Wanna Be Your Man', Ringo's track for the new album.

That afternoon The Beatles flew BEA to Stockholm International Airport, Arlanda, arriving to a scene of screaming fans and uncharacteristic Swedish chaos. Bouquets of flowers were thrust at them from all directions as they posed for pictures in their overcoats on the tarmac. Hundreds of girls had taken the day off school to be there to welcome them, and the press later described the scene as "The Battle of Stockholm Airport". On the state radio station, Sveriges Radio, a DJ called Klas Burling (the Swedish Brian Matthew) played nothing but Beatles records.

The police managed to escort the group to the Hotel Continental where the girls took up their position outside. Many of them managed to get inside The Beatles' suite as well, and everyone partied late into the night.

October 24
The Beatles held a chaotic press conference. Surrounded by heavy security because of the crowds of fans, they attempted to do a little sightseeing, and were taken, rather unnecessarily, to an English-style pub.

Karlaplansstudion, Stockholm, to record (without rehearsal) an interview and a live set for Klas Burling's Sveriges Radio show, *Pop '63*, which for this edition was renamed *The Beatles popgrupp från Liverpool på besök i Stockholm* (The Beatles pop group from Liverpool visiting Stockholm). The group played a lively seven numbers: 'I Saw Her Standing There', 'From Me To You', 'Money (That's What I Want)', 'Roll Over Beethoven', 'You Really Got A Hold On Me', 'She Loves You' and 'Twist And Shout'. The local group Hasse Rosen & The Norsemen also appeared on the show.

That night they visited the Nalen, the main teenage dance hall. It happened to be celebrating its 75th anniversary, so all the local celebrities were there.

Ringo: "A bit more elegant than the Cavern."

George: "But I sense the atmosphere here too. You know, you can always tell the places where they've got living people."

October 25
Nya Aulan, Karlstad, with local group The Phantoms.

This venue was a secondary school hall and the group played two performances of their standard set for the tour: 'Long Tall Sally', 'Please Please Me', 'I Saw Her Standing There', 'From Me To You', 'A Taste Of Honey', 'Chains', 'Boys', 'She Loves You' and 'Twist And Shout'. As in England, their performance was almost entirely drowned by screams.

October 26
Kungliga Tennishallen, Stockholm, where The Beatles were billed second to Joey Dee & The Starlighters for the two shows. The audience clearly thought otherwise.

ABC TV's *Thank Your Lucky Stars* premiered 'All My Loving' and 'Money (That's What I Want)'.

October 27
Cirkus, Gothenburg.

The Beatles played an afternoon show as well as two houses in the evening.

October 28
Waidele record shop, Borås, where they spent half an hour signing records.

Boråshallen, Borås.

October 29

Sporthallen, Eskilstuna, with Jerry Williams, The Violents, Trio Me' Bumba, The Telstars and Mona Skarström.

In London, Brian Epstein signed an agreement with United Artists for the Beatles to star in a full-length feature film. Hearing the news, John responded: "After this film, they'll find out that we're not actors and that will be that".

October 30

Narren-teatern, Stockholm, to record an appearance on the Sveriges Television show *Drop In* before a live audience in a small theatre in the Grona Lund amusement park. They were persuaded by presenter Klas Burling to extent their set from two to four numbers and performed 'She Loves You', 'Twist And Shout', 'Long Tall Sally' and 'I Saw Her Standing There'. Also on the bill were Gals & Pals and the young singer Lill-Babs who appeared in many photographs with the group.

October 31

The Beatles flew SAS back to London where hundreds of screaming teenage girls had gathered on the roof of the Queen's Building at Heathrow Airport to welcome them back to Britain. The scenes are broadcast on national TV news, heightening the media frenzy about 'Beatlemania'. By coincidence, Ed Sullivan happened to be passing through the airport at that time and witnessed the scene. It impressed him very much and led him to book the group for his show when they were still virtually unknown in the USA.

November 1

Odeon Cinema, Cheltenham.

The first night of The Beatles' Autumn Tour, their first series of concerts as unchallenged headliners, with support from The Rhythm & Blues Quartet, The Vernons Girls, The Brook Brothers, Peter Jay & The Jaywalkers and The Kestrels. The compere was Frank Berry. The Beatles' standard set for the tour was 'I Saw Her Standing There', 'From Me To You', 'All My Loving', 'You Really Got A Hold On Me', 'Roll Over Beethoven', 'Boys', 'Till There Was You', 'She Loves You', 'Money (That's What I Want)' and 'Twist And Shout'.

The EP *The Beatles (No.1)* was released in the UK as Parlophone GEP 8883 (mono only). Side A: 'I Saw Her Standing There', 'Misery'; Side B: 'Anna (Go To Him)', 'Chains'.

The single 'I Wanna Be Your Man' by The Rolling Stones, written by Lennon & McCartney, was released in the UK as Decca F 11764.

November 2

City Hall, Sheffield (Autumn Tour).

The *Daily Telegraph* responds to the recent outbreak of 'Beatlemania', with a leader column decrying the rampant hysteria of their fans, and drawing parallels between Beatles concerts and Hitler's Nuremberg rallies.

November 3

Odeon Cinema, Leeds (Autumn Tour).

The Beatles appeared on *The Ken Dodd Show*, broadcast by The BBC Light Programme.

The Beatles' interview on *The Public Ear* was aired by the BBC Light Programme.

November 4

Prince Of Wales Theatre, London, for the Royal Command Performance, in the presence of Their Majesties the Queen Mother and Princess Margaret, accompanied by Lord Snowdon.

Bernard Delfont risked offending the crustier members of the establishment and press by inviting The Beatles to appear at the Royal Variety Performance along with more traditional acts. The Beatles were seventh to perform but were clearly the headline act. On the bill were Marlene Dietrich, Max Bygraves, Harry Secombe, Buddy Greco, Wilfred Bramble & Harry H. Corbett, Charlie Drake, Michael Flanders & Donald Swann, Joe Loss & His Orchestra, Susan Maughan, Nadia Nerina, Luis Alberto Del Parana & Los Paraguayos, Tommy Steele, Eric Sykes & Hattie Jacques, The Clark

Brothers, Francis Brunn, the Billy Petch Dancers, Pinky & Perky and The Prince of Wales Theatre Orchestra.

"RATTLE YER JEWELLERY"

The Beatles wore fancy new black outfits for the occasion: high V-necks, black ties and blindingly white shirts. The curtains opened and they went straight into 'From Me To You' with not one scream from the audience. This was followed by 'She Loves You', and then Paul announced that they would sing something from *The Music Man*: "This one's been covered by our favourite American group – Sophie Tucker," he cracked and they played 'Till There Was You'. John introduced 'Twist And Shout' with his famous remark: "In the cheaper seats, you clap your hands. The rest of you, just rattle your jewellery," a comment which had worried Brian Epstein a great deal in rehearsal, when John had said, "rattle your fucking jewellery". No encores were allowed but the applause went on so long it delayed Dickie Henderson's announcement of the next act.

Afterwards they met the Queen Mother, who asked them where they would be playing next. When told their next concert was in Slough, she remarked, "Oh, that's near us" (meaning Windsor Castle, just two miles from Slough). Later the Queen Mother announced that she found them "most intriguing".

November 5

An Associated-Rediffusion television crew filmed The Beatles in the back of a car driving around London for a documentary called 'The Beatles and Beatlemania', to be included in their current affairs programme *This Week*.

Adelphi Cinema, Slough (Autumn Tour). Watched by 30 policemen waiting to cope with the expected crowds, Ringo led an on-stage jam session with George and several Jaywalkers before the concert.

EMI claimed that 500,000 advance orders had been received for The Beatles' forthcoming single, 'I Want To Hold Your Hand', in a single day.

November 6

ABC Cinema, Northampton (Autumn Tour).

November 7

The Beatles flew to Dublin, for their only appearance in Ireland. They were interviewed at the airport by Frank Hall for Radio Telefis Eireann's television programme *In Town*, shown that evening. They were accompanied by playwright Alun Owen, who remained with them for three days, making notes for their projected first film. At that time, it still had not been decided whether the film should be fact or fiction, nor did it have a name. The resulting film was fiction but based so completely on their lives that it had a strong documentary feel. Alun Owen: "It's most important to get to know The Beatles, to find out exactly what makes them tick. And also to ascertain which things cause those fantastic crowd receptions."

Adelphi Cinema, Dublin (Autumn Tour). Peter Jay wrote in *Record Mirror:* "Dublin was fantastic. The fans there really do go mad. Girls who fainted in the crowds outside the theatre were carried into their seats by attendants. Outside there was the biggest riot yet. It's a fact that cars were overturned and the police had to make several arrests. Inside it was incredible for noise and appreciation."

November 8

The Beatles filmed an interview with Jimmy Robinson of Ulster TV near the Irish border which was included in that evening's edition of *Ulster News*.

Broadcasting House, Belfast to record an interview with Sally Ogle for that evening's *Six Ten* programme.

November 9

Granada Cinema, East Ham, London (Autumn Tour).

The crowds outside the venue were so great that when The Beatles sent out for food, it had to be given a police escort to reach them. They watched through the windows as it was marched across the road through the crowd.

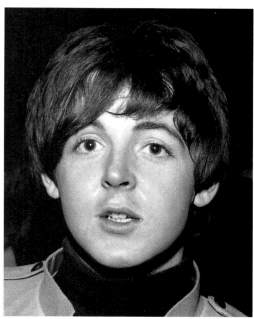

The Fab Four.
(Clockwise, from top left: *Rex, Hulton-Getty, LFI & Hulton-Getty*)

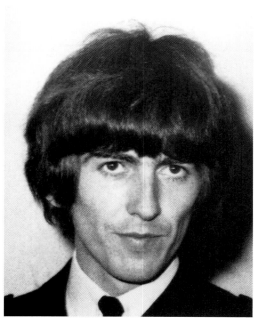

Clockwise, from top left: schoolboy John outside his Aunt Mimi's house in Liverpool (*Camera Press*); Paul, aged 6, with his brother Michael (*Hulton-Getty*); George with his first guitar (*Hulton-Getty*): and Ringo, aged 13, in fancy dress for the 1953 Coronation (*Hulton-Getty*).

John on stage with The Quarrymen, July 6, 1957, at St Peter's Church Garden Fete. It was the day he met Paul for the first time. Left to right: Eric Griffiths, Colin Hanton, Rod Davies, John, Pete Shotton, Len Garry. (*Hulton-Getty*)

The Beatles on stage at the Star Club, Hamburg, in 1960. Left to right: Paul, Pete Best, Stuart Sutcliffe, George and John. (*Redferns/Astrid Kirchherr*)

The Beatles at the Cavern, 1963. (*Rex*)

The Beatles rehearsing on the set *Ready Steady Go!*, October 1963.
On the show they performed 'She Loves You' and 'I'll Get You'. (*Redferns*)

The Beatles during their first American trip, February 1964. (*Rex*)

The Beates return to Heathrow Airport from their first US visit, February 22, 1964, with Brian Epstein and Epstein's lawyer David Jacobs. (*LFI*)

John with Cynthia, holidaying in St Moritz in January 1965. (*Hulton-Getty*)

George with his future wife Patti Boyd during the filming of *A Hard Day's Night* in March 1964. (*Redferns/Kirchherr*)

Paul with Jane Asher in 1967. (*Bettmann-Corbis*)

Ringo and Maureen at the Plaza Theatre, London, for the premiere of the movie *Alfie*, on March 25, 1966. (*Hulton-Getty*)

George and John at London Airport, returning from America, September 1965. (*Hulton-Getty*)

The Beatles on stage the Circus Krone, Munich, Germany, June 124, 1966. (*Rex*)

The Beatles on stage for the second of their momentous Shea Stadium concerts, August 23, 1966. (*Bettman-Corbis*)

November 10
Hippodrome Theatre, Birmingham (Autumn Tour). So thick was the crowd of fans outside the Hippodrome that The Beatles had to don police uniforms to make their way into the theatre.

The Royal Variety Show was transmitted by ATV and on the radio by the BBC Light Programme.

November 11
The Beatles pupgrupp från Liverpool på besök i Stockholm was broadcast on Sveriges Radio.

During a meeting in New York, Brian Epstein persuaded American TV mogul Ed Sullivan to book The Beatles for two performances on his national variety show in February, despite the fact that they have yet to score a hit record in the US.

November 12
Paul had gastric flu, which caused their Portsmouth Guildhall concert to be postponed until December 3.

They were interviewed at the Guildhall by Jeremy James for Southern TV's *Day By Day* programme that evening.

BBC TV's *South Today* programme broadcast an interview with the band by John Johnston recorded at their hotel, The Royal Beach in Southsea.

November 13
Westward TV Studios, Plymouth. The Beatles were interviewed by Stuart Hutchison for *Move Over, Dad* (a local teenagers' programme). So many fans blocked the streets outside that an ingenious route, using interconnecting tunnels, had to be devised to get them to the studio.

ABC Cinema, Plymouth (Autumn Tour).

November 14
ABC Cinema, Exeter (Autumn Tour).

November 15
Colston Hall, Bristol (Autumn Tour).

The Fourmost followed up their début hit with 'Hello Little Girl' by releasing another new Lennon/McCartney song, 'I'm In Love'.

November 16
Winter Gardens, Bournemouth (Autumn Tour).

The three rival American television networks – NBC, CBS and ABC – were permitted to film the hysterical audience and part of the show. Paul and John were interviewed by John Darsa for the CBS coverage. *Life* magazine photographer Terence Spencer with his assistant also arrived at their hotel, the Branksome Towers, outside Bournemouth and was quickly accepted into the inner circle. Brian Epstein was particularly keen on the publicity that a large spread in *Life* would produce. However, The Beatles did not turn up for the shoot that would have given them the January 31, 1964 cover, which went to Geraldine Chaplin instead. Terence Spencer: "The Beatles must be the only people in showbiz ever to have turned down a *Life* cover."

The Beatles interview on *Move Over, Dad* was transmitted by Southern TV.

November 17
Coventry Theatre, Coventry (Autumn Tour).

November 18
EMI House, London, to receive silver discs for *Please Please Me* and the not yet released *With The Beatles* from EMI Chairman Sir Joseph Lockwood. They also received silver EPs for *Twist And Shout* from George Martin and a silver EP and single for *Twist And Shout* and 'She Loves You' from Gerald Marks, the editor of *Disc*. After the presentation there was a cocktail party followed by a formal lunch in the boardroom with company executives and their guests.

That afternoon, Brian Epstein agreed to meet a South African promoter, who was keen to book a Beatles tour in his country, but Epstein rejected the offer when he discovered that the group would be expected to play to racially segregated audiences.

November 19
Gaumont Cinema, Wolverhampton (Autumn Tour).

November 20
ABC Cinema, Manchester (Autumn Tour).
Backstage at the ABC were news crews from Pathé News, Granada TV and BBC Radio. Pathé filmed part of the concert to be screened in British cinemas as *The Beatles Come To Town* during Pathé News. The Granada TV crew filmed the group at the same time and interviewed them about their forthcoming tour of the US.
Michael Barton did a two-minute interview broadcast that same evening on the BBC North Home Service programme *Voice Of The North*. Barton also interviewed George about the Liverpool and Hamburg rock scenes for a North Home Service programme called *Wacker, Mach Schau.*
Another visitor backstage was *Daily Express* reporter Derek Taylor, who had a brief conversation with George.

November 21
ABC Cinema, Carlisle (Autumn Tour).
Paul's interview on *The World of Sound* was broadcast by the BBC Home Service.

November 22
Globe Cinema, Stockton-on-Tees (Autumn Tour).
The album *With The Beatles* was released in the UK as Parlophone PMC 1206 (mono) and PCS 3045 (stereo). Side A: 'It Won't Be Long', 'All I've Got To Do', 'All My Loving', 'Don't Bother Me', 'Little Child', 'Till There Was You', 'Please Mister Postman'; Side B: 'Roll Over Beethoven', 'You Really Got A Hold On Me', 'I Wanna Be Your Man', '(There's A) Devil In Her Heart', 'Not A Second Time', 'Money (That's What I Want)'.

WITH THE BEATLES
By the time their second album was released, The Beatles were the hottest product in British show-business. Second time around, there was no need to sell the album on the reputation of a recent hit single: with Christmas on the horizon, EMI knew the fans would buy anything The Beatles released. What they didn't realise, though, was that *With The Beatles* would prove to be such a giant step beyond their hastily assembled début.
The cover artwork immediately revealed that more thought had gone into this album than its predecessor. Whereas *Please Please Me* used the standard smiling pop pose as its cover design, *With The Beatles* boasted a much artier Robert Freeman photo, with the group's heads arranged in careful line, shot in half-light. It emerged later that this trick was simply borrowed from much earlier pictures of the group, taken by the German photographer Astrid Kirchherr. But as far as the public was concerned, the artwork was startlingly new.
Musically, too, *With The Beatles* announced that the revolution had arrived. The Beatles kept faithfully to the same mix of originals and outside songs that had filled their first long-player, but they were already beginning to play the studio as an instrument. On *Please Please Me*, they'd briefly discovered the potential joys of overdubbing. Now, with more time on their hands, they went to town.
"The first set of tricks was double-tracking on the second album," John Lennon admitted many years later. "We were told we could do it, and that really set the ball rolling. We double-tracked ourselves off the second album." And they did it without sacrificing an ounce of the freshness and exuberance that had become The Beatles' hallmark – audible most clearly on the mono mix of the record, which was again favoured by George Martin for the CD release.

IT WON'T BE LONG
Throughout their career, The Beatles never lost sight of the importance of having hit singles. Certainly in 1963, their continued production of hits was their passport to the future, and

they blatantly concocted potential chartbusters as and when required. Lennon and McCartney competed for the honour of winning an A-side, with only pride and prestige at stake – the songwriting royalties for all their songs were split equally between them, after all.

Like 'She Loves You', the single they recorded a month earlier, Lennon's 'It Won't Be Long' was built around a 'yeah, yeah' chorus. Two singles with the same gimmick would have become a straitjacket, so 'It Won't Be Long' was 'relegated' to the position of lead track on the album, where it was every bit as effective a hook as 'I Saw Her Standing There' had been on 'Please Please Me'.

ALL I'VE GOT TO DO
Compare this song to 'Ask Me Why', written around a year earlier, and the rapid maturity in Lennon's songwriting is immediately apparent. John singled out Arthur Alexander (the man who'd written 'Anna', plus several other Beatles stage favourites) as his prime inspiration for this soulful ballad. He stretched the word 'I' over seven syllables in the opening line, using all the melismatic flair of Sam Cooke or Jackie Wilson, and proved how well he understood the power of melody by shifting into a higher register for the final chorus as a cry of passion. It was a remarkably assured performance, which would have been beyond anyone else in the group at this early stage of their career.

ALL MY LOVING
While Lennon was converting emotion into music, McCartney was writing unforgettable melodies. Classical students claim there's a tune of Tchaikovsky's buried in 'All My Loving', but it's an irrelevant point, as the finished song is pure Beatles – the most commercial song they recorded in 1963 that wasn't issued as a single. Often maligned as musicians, The Beatles prove their worth on this song: Harrison's lead break is beautifully tidy and restrained, while Lennon's lightning rhythm guitar playing is the powerhouse of the arrangement.

DON'T BOTHER ME
"That was the first song that I wrote, as an exercise to see if I could write a song," George Harrison confessed in his autobiography, I Me Mine. "I don't think it's particularly good." Faced by two prolific bandmates, Harrison was envious of their ability and their royalty cheques. Liverpool friend Bill Harry nagged George on the subject while he was ill in bed during a Beatles tour, and Harrison responded by turning his reaction into a slightly clumsy but reasonably accomplished song. Interestingly, it didn't sound anything like his own musical heroes, Carl Perkins or Goffin and King, but came out as a facsimile of what Lennon and McCartney were writing – just as beat groups across the country were doing in their bedrooms.

LITTLE CHILD
Even The Beatles occasionally sounded like tired hacks, though this early in their career, they could always summon the enthusiasm to hide their lack of inspiration. Five years later, this contrived but chirpy pop tune would have been classed as bubblegum. But on With The Beatles, Lennon and McCartney's dynamic vocals and Lennon's chest-expanding harmonica solo turned a piece of hackwork into 106 seconds of pure energy.

TILL THERE WAS YOU
Standards time again, as Paul filled the 'A Taste Of Honey' slot with the hit song from the Broadway musical, The Music Man. He sang the song as if he meant every word, and George Harrison contributed an accomplished acoustic guitar solo – so accomplished, in fact, that some cynics have questioned whether he actually played it. But the solo on the rendition they recorded onstage in Hamburg was equally dextrous, so unless they'd smuggled a session man into the Star-Club, George was the man.

PLEASE MISTER POSTMAN
During 1963, the American stable of Motown labels, owned by Berry Gordy, began to enjoy regular distribution for their youthful soul records in Britain. The Beatles were instant fans, to the extent that three of the tracks on 'With The Beatles' were covers of recent Motown hits.

On their first album, 'Chains' and 'Anna' had been enthusiastic renditions of outside songs, without threatening to become definitive. On 'Twist And Shout', however, and again with The Marvelettes' 'Please Mister Postman', Lennon's performance was so magical that it made the original sound like an imitation. The Beatles tightened up The Marvelettes' vocal arrangement, while Lennon's lead dripped with authority and self-confidence. It was a *thrilling conclusion to the first side of the album, which had already seen the group tackling everything from soul to rock to balladry with ease.*

ROLL OVER BEETHOVEN
Even before there was a Beatles, Lennon, McCartney and Harrison had been performing this Chuck Berry rock'n'roll standard from 1956. During 1961, the song passed from John's hands to George, who also had to double as lead guitarist – fine in the studio, when he could overdub the solo, but prone to being more erratic on stage. Despite their heritage as a rock'n'roll band, The Beatles sounded strangely uncomfortable the first time they cut an authentic American rock song in the studio, hurrying the pace to the point that George had problems fitting all the words into each line.

HOLD ME TIGHT
During the sessions for their first album, The Beatles had taped and then abandoned a version of this self-composed beat number – and the tape was subsequently destroyed. If the take that was considered good enough for release is anything to go by, the original must have been disastrous, as this remake has a McCartney vocal that strays way off key, to the point that neighbouring dogs are likely to howl with distress. Only a handful of Beatles recordings can be said to be below par, but this is one of them.

YOU REALLY GOT A HOLD ON ME
Not so 'You Really Got A Hold On Me', Lennon's second brilliant hijacking of a Motown song. Sublime though The Miracles' original is, it's easily outclassed by The Beatles' effortless interpretation. John's vocal could be used as a dictionary definition of reluctant infatuation, while the decision to dramatise the phrase 'tied up' with a repeated break in the rhythm was a stroke of genius. The response vocals challenged George's limited range to the hilt, but sheer enthusiasm won the day, as The Beatles stole another American song for their own.

I WANNA BE YOUR MAN
By the time The Beatles finished work on this song, they knew that The Rolling Stones were issuing it as their second single. The Stones played the song as an R&B tune; The Beatles gave it to Ringo, whereupon it became his usual concert showcase for the next three years. Amusingly, on the road Ringo usually managed to forget that the song had all of two verses, and ended up repeating the first one over and over again.

DEVIL IN HER HEART
Aficionados of the American girl-group sound, The Beatles borrowed this tune from The Donays – probably the most obscure song they ever covered in the studio. It was George Harrison's choice, and he responded with an energetic if not always convincing lead vocal, backed by the superb chorus harmonies of Lennon and McCartney.

NOT A SECOND TIME
'Not A Second Time' reinforced John Lennon's status as the most adventurous of The Beatles when it came to composing. The rhythm of this piano-based song seemed to be on the verge of imminent collapse, but whereas this was a flaw on 'Ask Me Why', it suited the emotional disruption of the lyric this time around. Usually, John sounded completely in control of every romantic situation, even when the lyrics asserted otherwise, but everything about 'Not A Second Time' announced that Lennon was simply a pawn in her game – predating the more blatant emotional masochism of 'Norwegian Wood' by two years.

MONEY (THAT'S WHAT I WANT)
The third and last of the Motown classics moulded into pure John Lennon songs, Barrett Strong's hit 'Money' took on a new life in this interpretation. The tentative delivery of the original was knocked off the pavement by Lennon's steamroller vocal, every bit as tonsil-shredding as 'Twist And Shout' had been. As on 'I Wanna Be Your Man', George Martin came into his own on keyboards: on the earlier track, he'd played Hammond organ, while this time he supplied the piano which was the root of the song.

But the piano wasn't the only difference between this performance, and the far less convincing version of the same tune at The Beatles' January 1962 audition. At Decca, Lennon had simply been singing Barrett Strong's song. At EMI nearly two years later, he was living it, howling the lyrics as a piece of psychotherapy. And as many critics have noticed, he widened the context of the song by adding a single, throwaway phrase to the final choruses: "I wanna be free", he cried, a prisoner to the passion that the rest of the song denied.

Trivial note: mono and stereo mixes of this song once again have slightly different Lennon vocals. And once again, the definitive version is included on the mono-only CD.

November 23
City Hall, Newcastle upon Tyne (Autumn Tour).

November 24
ABC Cinema, Hull (Autumn Tour).

November 25
Granada TV Centre, Manchester. The Beatles mimed 'I Want To Hold Your Hand' and 'This Boy' and were later interviewed with Ken Dodd by Gay Byrne for Granada's *Scene* and *Late Scene Extra* programmes.

November 26
Regal Cinema, Cambridge (Autumn Tour).

Jean Goodman interviewed The Beatles in their dressing room for the local BBC TV show *East At Six Ten*. "How long do you think The Beatles will last?", Lennon was asked. "About five years", he replied. "Will the group stay together?" "Don't know."

Between their two performances, producer Peter Yolland recorded the group delivering the dialogue intended to be broadcast over the PA during The Beatles' Christmas Show, rather than forcing the group to shout their lines over the screams of their fans every night.

The group spent the night at the University Arms Hotel, three miles outside Cambridge, where they were interviewed by US journalist Michael Braun, who was researching a book on their rise to fame.

November 27
Rialto Theatre, York (Autumn Tour).

All the lights in the theatre fused and the curtains would not work and had to be parted manually. Before the first show, The Beatles were interviewed by two female fans.

The BBC North Home Service programme *Wacker, Mach Schau* was broadcast.

Granada's *Late Scene Extra* with The Beatles miming to 'I Want To Hold Your Hand' was broadcast.

November 28
ABC Cinema, Lincoln (Autumn Tour).

Ringo had earache and had to cut short rehearsals to go to hospital and have his ear syringed but was back in time for the show.

After the show, the group were driven to a hotel near Doncaster. Their chauffeur's driving proved to be so erratic that The Beatles rang Brian Epstein when they arrived at the hotel, insisting that he was replaced.

November 29
ABC Cinema, Huddersfield (Autumn Tour).

Between sets The Beatles gave individual interviews to Gorden Kaye for *Music Box*, a record request show for local hospitals.

The single 'I Want To Hold Your Hand'/'This Boy' was released in the UK as Parlophone R 5084. Advance sales passed the million mark before it was released, the first time this had ever happened in Britain.

I WANT TO HOLD YOUR HAND
"We wrote that together," John admitted after The Beatles split up, in a rare nod of the head to his ex-partner. "It's a beautiful melody – the kind of song I like to sing." And it broke The Beatles as a worldwide phenomenon, becoming their first No. 1 in America, and indeed topping the charts in almost every part of the globe. Cunningly structured, with a drop in tension in the middle section leading to the climactic "I can't hide" (memorably misheard by

Bob Dylan as "I get high"), the song was the culmination of a solid year of experimentation and learning by The Beatles' creative axis.

THIS BOY

The first great three-part harmony vehicle in The Beatles catalogue was written by John Lennon around the standard doo-wop chord changes that had fuelled hundreds of hit records in the Fifties. What made the song was not just the tightness of the harmonies, but the sheer liberation of the middle section – Lennon stretching out the final syllable over several bars. The Beatles accentuated the drama of the moment less on record than they did subsequently on stage, where it rivalled the two-heads-shaking-at-one-microphone routine for audience response. 'This Boy' made an ideal underbelly for the 'I Want To Hold Your Hand' single.

November 30

Empire Theatre, Sunderland (Autumn Tour).

The Beatles made their escape from the theatre by running from the stage into the fire station next door, and then down the firemen's poles into a waiting fire engine. At their hotel, they carried out a telephone interview with a disc jockey in Melbourne, Australia.

December 1

De Montfort Hall, Leicester (Autumn Tour).

The supporting cast on the tour acted as decoys after the show, as fans chased their coach away from the theatre, leaving The Beatles free to return to their hotel by police car.

December 2

Elstree Studio Centre, Borehamwood, to record an appearance on Associated-Rediffusion's *Morecambe And Wise Show*. The group sang 'This Boy', 'All My Loving' and 'I Want To Hold Your Hand' live before a small studio audience and did comedy sketches with Eric and Ernie. The Beatles, Eric and Ernie, all dressed in striped blazers, closed the show with 'Moonlight Bay'. "The show won't be aired for a couple of months," the TV producer was heard to mutter to a colleague. "Let's hope they're still popular then."

The Ballroom, Grosvenor House Hotel, Park Lane, in aid of a charity for the handicapped. The group was part of a cabaret-style floor show and the audience wore evening dress – which didn't prevent them rushing the stage as The Beatles' performance ended.

December 3

Guildhall, Portsmouth (Autumn Tour).

The concert that had been postponed in November because of Paul's gastric 'flu.

December 7

Empire Theatre, Liverpool. George and Ringo travelled to Liverpool by train, while John and Paul flew from Heathrow Airport.

The Beatles comprised the entire panel for a special edition of BBC TV's *Juke Box Jury* before an audience of 2,500 members of The Beatles' Northern Area Fan Club. As usual, the compere was David Jacobs:

The Chants: 'I Could Write A Book' [Liverpool group]
John: "It's gear. Fabulous. Fab. It's it."
Paul: "I talked to The Chants recently about the disc. They said it's powerful. It is."
Ringo: "I'll buy it."
George: "It's great. Enough plugs and they've got a hit."
David Jacobs: "Are they being too generous?"
Unanimous hit.
Elvis Presley: 'Kiss Me Quick'
Paul: "What I don't like about Elvis are his songs. I like his voice. This song reminds me of Blackpool on a sunny day."
Ringo: "Last two years Elvis has been going down the nick."
George: "If he's going back to old tracks, why not release 'My Baby Left Me'? It'd be a number one. Elvis is great, his songs are rubbish."

John: "It'll be a hit. I like those hats with 'Kiss Me Quick' on."
Unanimous hit.
Swinging Blue Jeans: 'Hippy Hippy Shake'
Ringo: "Good, but not as good as the original by Chan Romero."
George: "It's a popular song around Liverpool. We used to do it. Could be a hit."
John: "The boys nearly made it before. I like Bill Harry's version as well!"
Paul: "Doesn't matter about Chan Romero's disc. Nobody remembers. It's as good as a new song."
Unanimous hit.
Paul Anka: 'Did You Have A Happy Birthday?'
George: "Yes I did, thank you."
Paul: "I don't like people with a crack in their voice."
John: "It's in his head."
Unanimous miss.
Shirley Ellis: 'The Nitty Gritty Song'
John: "I like it."
Paul: "I like this kind of record, but it doesn't say anything."
Ringo: "We all like this sort of thing but it won't be a hit."
George: "Won't be a hit in England. We haven't got around to that sort of thing yet."
David Jacobs: "You mean British teenagers are behind the Americans?"
George: "We've liked this type of thing for years but it hasn't really caught on."
Unanimous miss.
Steve and Eydie: 'I Can't Stop Talking About You'
Paul: "People will whistle this one."
Ringo: "SHE carries him, actually!"
George: "It could easily make the twenty. So relaxed."
John: "They're relaxed because they're getting on a bit. I don't like it."
Three to one hit.
Billy Fury: 'Do You Really Love Me?'
Ringo: "Not for me. I've never bought one of his records."
George: "Okay. But I wouldn't buy it. Guitar phrasing is like that on Cliff's latest."
John: "Tune's not bad, but I don't like gallop tunes."
Paul: "I quite liked it."
Unanimous miss.
Bobby Vinton: 'There, I've Said It Again'
George: "Quite nice, but I don't think the public will buy it."
John: "Get an old song and everybody does it again at the same time."
Paul: "Secretly, teenagers don't want old songs brought back."
Ringo: "Nice and smooth, 'specially if you're sitting in one night – and not alone."
Unanimous miss.
The Orchids: 'Love Hit Me'
John: "Just a big con – a pinch from The Crystals and Ronettes."
Paul: "It's good for a British record."
Ringo: "It'll sell a few, but not many."
George: "I'd rather have British groups pinch from The Crystals than the other stuff."
A three to one miss. Then it was revealed that The Orchids were there in the audience.
John: "A lousy trick."
The Merseybeats: 'I Think Of You'
[No time for discussion, only a vote. Unanimous hit.]

Next, the Fan Club audience saw a special concert, shown later the same day as *It's The Beatles!* For this they played 'From Me To You', 'I Saw Her Standing There', 'All My Loving', 'Roll Over Beethoven', 'Boys', 'Till There Was You', 'She Loves You', 'This Boy', 'I Want To Hold Your Hand', 'Money (That's What I Want)', 'Twist And Shout' and 'From Me To You'.
The BBC Light Programme then recorded a two-minute interview to use on their Christmas Day special *Top Pops of 1963*.
Finally, protected by a police cordon, they made a dash to the nearby Odeon Cinema.
Odeon Cinema, Liverpool (Autumn Tour).

December 8
Odeon Cinema, Lewisham, London (Autumn Tour).

December 9
Odeon Cinema, Southend-on-Sea (Autumn Tour).
 A BBC TV news crew interviewed the group in their dressing room.

December 10
Gaumont Cinema, Doncaster (Autumn Tour).
 Backstage, The Beatles gave an interview to the Australian radio journalist Dibbs Mather for the BBC Transcription Service, during which John recited his poem, 'Neville Club', and announced his intention to publish a collection of his humorous writing.

December 11
Futurist Theatre, Scarborough (Autumn Tour).

December 12
Odeon Cinema, Nottingham (Autumn Tour).

December 13
Gaumont Cinema, Southampton, the last concert on the Autumn Tour.

December 14
Wimbledon Palais.
 The Beatles' Southern Area Fan Club concert. An afternoon performance, after which The Beatles sat behind the Palais bar and shook hands with all 3,000 of their SFC members. Most of them stood in an orderly line to shake hands with the group but a few girls fainted. They very soon had to stop giving autographs as the line grew too long. Some girls managed to tousle their hair or kiss their hands.
 Their live performance was completely drowned out by screams. Worried that the fans might cause damage to their stage, the Palais management enclosed it in a steel cage, prompting John to quip, "If they press any harder they'll come through as chips."

December 15
Alpha TV Studios, Birmingham, to record ABC TV's *Thank Your Lucky Stars*. The group arrived at the studios during a snowstorm, but several hundred fans still gathered to greet them. An all Merseyside show. The Beatles mimed 'I Want To Hold Your Hand', 'All My Loving', 'Twist And Shout' and 'She Loves You' and were presented with two gold discs.
 The Beatles' Christmas flexi-disc was sent out to the 28,000 members of their fan club.

December 17
Playhouse Theatre, London, to record a Christmas edition of *Saturday Club* for the BBC Light Programme. They played 'All My Loving', 'This Boy', 'I Want To Hold Your Hand', 'Till There Was You', 'Roll Over Beethoven' and 'She Loves You'. Then they parodied Dora Bryan's recent hit 'All I Want For Christmas Is A Beatle' with 'All I Want For Christmas Is A Bottle'. This was followed by a half-minute medley entitled 'The Chrimble Mudley' which combined 'Love Me Do', 'Please Please Me', 'From Me To You', 'I Want To Hold Your Hand' and 'Rudolph The Red-Nosed Reindeer'.

December 18
BBC Paris Studio, London, to record *From Us To You*, a two-hour Beatles Boxing Day bank holiday special for the Light Programme. 'From Me To You' was recorded as 'From Us To You' as the signature tune to begin and end the programme, and the show was hosted by Rolf Harris. Guests were Susan Maughan, Jeanie Lambe, Kenny Lynch, Joe Brown & The Bruvvers, The Kenny Salmon Seven and Alan Elsdon's Jazzband with Mick Emery. The Beatles and Rolf Harris joined together for a version of 'Tie Me Kangaroo Down, Sport' and the group performed 'She Loves You', 'All My Loving', 'Roll Over Beethoven', 'Till There Was You', 'Boys', 'Money (That's What I Want)', 'I Saw Her Standing There' and 'I Want To Hold Your Hand'.
 Proof of The Beatles' increasing cultural acceptance into the mainstream came when

Mods And Rockers, a ballet based around their music, opened at the Prince Charles Theatre in London's West End.

December 21

Gaumont Cinema, Bradford.

The first of two special previews of *The Beatles' Christmas Show*, performed as a concert without costume or comedy sketches.

Chris Charlesworth, who in 1970 would become a music writer on *Melody Maker*, attended this show with his father: "There were very few boys in the audience. It was almost all girls and they just screamed like crazy. Rolf Harris was the compere and he had to come on for ten minutes just before The Beatles closed the show because, unlike the other acts, they used their own equipment and it had to be set up behind the curtains. Harris was completely drowned out by the screams but he asked for it by drawing sketches of the four Beatles on his easel pad. The Beatles were only on for about 25 minutes and they were also drowned out. I couldn't hear a note they sang or played, even though I was quite near the front, on Paul's side, but it was the most exciting thing I'd ever seen in my life – an unbelievable experience. The next day all I could think about was getting a guitar."

The Christmas Special edition of *Saturday Club* was broadcast by the BBC Light Programme.

December 22

Empire Theatre, Liverpool.

Second of *The Beatles' Christmas Show* previews.

December 23

It's The Beatles, a 15-part weekly series of 15-minute spots presented by Peter Carver, began transmission on Radio Luxembourg.

December 24

Astoria Cinema, Finsbury Park, London, with The Barron Knights & Duke D'Mond, Tommy Quickly, The Fourmost, Billy J. Kramer & The Dakotas, Cilla Black and Rolf Harris.

The show ran for 16 nights, with two houses per night, finishing on January 11, 1964, and was seen by almost 100,000 people.

THE BEATLES' CHRISTMAS SHOW

Peter Yolland designed the show for children. It opened with a speeded up film made from stock clips while the soundtrack announced: "By land, by sea, by air, come the stars of The Beatles Christmas Show . . ." The curtains parted to reveal a large cardboard helicopter landing on the stage. Compere Rolf Harris played the role of airline ticket collector and introduced each member of the cast individually as they stepped off. Naturally, the final passengers to leap out were The Beatles, carrying BEA tote bags and wearing glasses.

In one sketch, a follow spot picked up four men in white coats on a blacked out stage. Three of them hurried away as the commentator, imitating a current toothpaste advertisement, said, "Three out of four doctors . . ." The remaining "doctor" was John Lennon who completed the phrase, ". . . leaves one doctor!" This was the level of scriptwriting and The Beatles were very disappointed with it.

Tommy Quickly threw cotton wool stage snowballs at the audience and The Fourmost played a version of 'White Christmas', at one point doing a Beatles imitation by switching one of their guitars to the left hand.

One awful sketch was called 'What A Night', written by Peter and Ireland Cutter who wrote most of Laurel and Hardy's material. John played Sir John Jasper, a moustache twirling, top hatted, whip carrying villain who threw Ermyntrude, the pathetic heroine, played by George in drag, into the path of an express train, named the "Beeching Express" after the current transport minister, infamous for cutting most of the branch line services in Britain. Ringo danced across the stage and sprinkled everyone with paper snow before George was saved by the timely arrival of Fearless Paul the Signalman.

Fortunately, the producer had allowed room after this pantomime parade of sketches for a full concert performance by the group. The Beatles were finally announced by a roll of drums from Ringo. They played 'Roll Over Beethoven', 'All My Loving', 'This Boy', 'I Wanna Be Your Man', 'She Loves You', 'Till There Was You', 'I Want To Hold Your Hand', 'Money (That's What I Want)' and ended, as usual, with 'Twist And Shout' sung by John. This show was repeated 30 times.

December 25
The Beatles flew home to Liverpool for Christmas.

December 26
The Beatles flew from Liverpool to London.
Astoria Cinema, Finsbury Park, London. *The Beatles Christmas Show.*
From Us To You, a two hour Beatles Boxing Day bank holiday special was broadcast by the BBC Light Programme.
The single 'I Want To Hold Your Hand'/'I Saw Her Standing There' was released in the US as Capitol 5112.

December 27
Astoria Cinema, Finsbury Park, London. *The Beatles' Christmas Show.*
In his review of the year's musical highlights, the classical music correspondent of *The Times* saluted John and Paul as "the outstanding English composers of 1963".

December 28
Astoria Cinema, Finsbury Park, London. *The Beatles' Christmas Show.*

December 29
In an excess of post-Christmas hyperbole, the classical reviewer of *The Sunday Times* outdid his daily rival by pronouncing the Beatles as "the greatest composers since Beethoven".

December 30
Astoria Cinema, Finsbury Park, London. *The Beatles' Christmas Show.*

December 31
Astoria Cinema, Finsbury Park, London. *The Beatles' Christmas Show.* (One house only, to allow time for New Year celebrations.)

January 1
The Beatles continued their residency at the Astoria Cinema, Finsbury Park, London, with *The Beatles' Christmas Show.*

A BBC clip of The Beatles singing 'She Loves You' was shown on American TV's *The Jack Paar Show*, the first film of The Beatles shown to US audiences. Brian Epstein was angry with the BBC for selling the clip because it interfered with his own careful marketing strategy.

January 2
Astoria Cinema, Finsbury Park, London. *The Beatles' Christmas Show.*

January 3
Astoria Cinema, Finsbury Park, London. *The Beatles' Christmas Show.*

In Hamburg, Tony Sheridan overdubbed a new vocal on to the recording of 'Sweet Georgia Brown' which he had taped with The Beatles in May 1962. The new vocal track featured lyrics which commented on the length of The Beatles' hair, and their fan following.

January 4
Astoria Cinema, Finsbury Park, London. *The Beatles' Christmas Show.*

The group recorded an 'open-ended' (answers only) interview at the small recording studio in EMI Records' Manchester Square headquarters. The interview was intended to be sent on record to US disc jockeys, to give the impression that the DJs were actually talking to The Beatles themselves. A photographer from *Life* magazine shot several rolls of film while they were at EMI, still aiming for a proposed cover story on the group to coincide with their arrival in America.

January 4
George and Ringo recorded an interview for the BBC Light Programme magazine *The Public Ear* at their Green Street flat.

Astoria Cinema, Finsbury Park, London. *The Beatles' Christmas Show.*

January 6
Astoria Cinema, Finsbury Park, London. *The Beatles' Christmas Show.*

Afterwards The Beatles went to the Talk Of The Town, on Charing Cross Road, to see Alma Cogan, but arrived too late and missed her performance.

Before the evening performance, The Beatles visited the London offices of *Paris Match* magazine, to be interviewed for an article which would appear as they arrived in France.

January 7
The Beatles recorded an appearance for *Saturday Club* at the Playhouse Theatre, London. They performed 'All My Loving', 'Money (That's What I Want)', 'The Hippy Hippy Shake', 'I Want To Hold Your Hand', 'Roll Over Beethoven', 'Johnny B. Goode' and 'I Wanna Be Your Man'. The show was pre-recorded to be aired during their forthcoming tour of the US.

Astoria Cinema, Finsbury Park, London. *The Beatles' Christmas Show.*

January 8
Astoria Cinema, Finsbury Park, London. *The Beatles' Christmas Show.*

January 9
Astoria Cinema, Finsbury Park, London. *The Beatles' Christmas Show.*

January 10
Astoria Cinema, Finsbury Park, London. *The Beatles' Christmas Show.*

January 11
Astoria Cinema, Finsbury Park, London. The final night of *The Beatles' Christmas Show.*

'I Want To Hold Your Hand' entered the American *Cashbox* charts at number 80.

January 12

London Palladium.

The Beatles appeared on the ATV television variety show *Val Parnell's Sunday Night At The London Palladium* with Alma Cogan, Dave Allen and compere Bruce Forsyth. The Beatles played 'I Want To Hold Your Hand', 'This Boy', 'All My Loving', 'Money (That's What I Want)' and 'Twist And Shout'. As before, they appeared on the carousel at the end of the show where, by tradition, all the featured artists stood and waved goodbye as it slowly revolved.

This was their first meeting with Alma Cogan, who invited them back to her flat at 44 Stafford Court in Kensington High Street which she shared with her mother and younger sister. They arrived at her flat long before she did as they made a quick getaway in their Austin Princess, leaving Alma to change in her dressing room, but her sister Sandra was there to greet them. Paul recalled later that Mrs Cogan had encouraged Sandra to pay him as much attention as possible, in the hope that a suitable match might ensue.

George and Ringo's interview on *The Public Ear* was broadcast by the BBC Light Programme.

January 13

The single 'I Want To Hold Your Hand'/'I Saw Her Standing There' was released in the US as Capitol 5112. It went straight into the charts.

January 14

At 5.15pm The Beatles' Comet 4B left for Le Bourget airport, then the main Paris airport, to begin a three-week residency at the Paris Olympia. With them were Brian Epstein, Mal Evans and press representatives but not Ringo who was unable to meet the others in London that day because Liverpool airport was fogbound. London was also blanketed, but by late afternoon it had lifted enough for the rest of the group to get to France. Their departure was watched by several thousand fans.

The Beatles' Austin Princess was at the airport to meet them, as were 60 fans and the press. More fans were waiting at the George V Hotel, filling the lobby. That evening, Bruno Coquatrix, the director of the Olympia, called in to see them, as did a representative from their French record label, Odeon.

John and Paul shared a suite because they were committed to writing six new songs for their forthcoming film, a song for Billy J. Kramer and one for Tommy Quickly. They had a piano brought in and got to work while George had a night out on the town at the Club Eve. He was accompanied by *Daily Express* reporter Derek Taylor, who had been charged with ghosting a regular column for George about the Paris trip.

January 15

John and Paul got up around noon as usual and ate a regular English breakfast of orange juice, cornflakes, scrambled eggs and a pot of tea. A stroll down the Champs Elysées accompanied by select members of the British press brought a crowd of photographers and sightseers but they were driven back to the hotel before it got out of hand. (Already determined to debunk the Beatlemania hype, a cynical *Daily Mail* reporter noted: "Exactly three girls asked them for autographs. One was English.")

Ringo arrived on the five o'clock flight. At London Airport, he was persuaded by British European Airlines staff to pose for a photograph as he boarded his plane – holding a 'TLES' sign alongside the plane's 'BEA' logo.

That night they did a try-out concert at the Cyrano Theatre in Versailles with all the other artists who would be appearing on the Olympia bill: Trini Lopez, Sylvie Vartan and a full music hall variety act including a juggler. Lopez closed the first half. Sylvie Vartan preceded The Beatles, an unenviable position. The show began at nine and lasted until after midnight with French fans dancing in the aisles and chanting for "Les Beat-les!" In France they drew a male crowd rather than female, and because there was much less screaming they could actually hear the music. Next day the press reported their every move.

In New York, DJ Scott Muni reported that he had received more than 12,000 applications for a Beatles fan club.

January 17

Olympia Theatre, Paris.

The afternoon matinée was sold out to fans whereas the evening audience was made up of more expensively dressed, older Parisians who wanted to see what all the fuss was about. The ancient music hall was not equipped for modern amplification and the fuses blew three times as the theatre could not supply enough power for their amps. Mal rushed on stage to make emergency repairs. There were no screams or shrieks, but the audience clapped in time and appreciated the music. George: "We miss the screams, but the audiences are great. Now roll on America."

The audience was well behaved, but backstage a riot was going on. Cameramen were everywhere and an argument erupted when a French photographer was not allowed in to take exclusive pictures. A fight broke out which spilled onto the stage. George had to move quickly to prevent his guitar from being damaged by the brawling mob and Paul stopped singing to call for order. Gendarmes arrived and added to the chaos. No one was allowed backstage for the remaining dates.

The Olympia was in many ways a dry run for Carnegie Hall, Epstein's policy being to book his group into the most prestigious venues possible. The Olympia was the best music hall in France, where the first night guaranteed an audience in full evening dress, minks and diamonds. It was a beautiful, classic theatre with sumptuous furnishings. However, the dressing room was tiny and the Olympia was unused to Beatlemania: people with tickets had been prohibited from entering the theatre, whereas others found someone already in their seats. It was chaos. The theatre was ringed with armed police and beyond them a cordon of fans chanting "Beat-les, Beat-les, Beat-les!" As the group left the stage a few more punches were exchanged. Predictably, French chauvinism showed in the press reports the next day, though *France Soir* suggested that French pop idols must be jealous because never before had the French clapped along so loudly with the beat.

NUMBER ONE IN AMERICA

That evening a telephone call brought the news that 'I Want To Hold Your Hand' had reached number one in America. It had taken only three weeks to reach the top position. Road manager Mal Evans reported that the group went mad: "They always act this way when anything big happens – just a bunch of kids, jumping up and down with sheer delight. Paul climbed on my back demanding a piggyback. They felt that this was the biggest thing that could have happened. And who could blame them? Gradually they quietened down, ordered some more drinks and sat down to appreciate fully what had happened. It was a wonderful, marvellous night for all of them. I was knocked out . . ." Almost immediately, Brian Epstein fielded a phone call from a promoter in Detroit, offering The Beatles $10,000 for a single concert appearance. The Beatles celebrated until 5am.

Up until now, only a handful of British acts had ever made the charts in the US; the UK was a wasteland for popular music as far as American record buyers were concerned. The Beatles changed all that and opened the door for a tidal wave of British acts which transformed the face of American popular music for ever, destroying the old Brill-Building Tin-Pan-Alley tradition and heralding the idea that popular music could be something other than mere "entertainment".

Beatlemania was hotting up in the US in the classic showbusiness manner: a flurry of lawsuits. *Billboard* reported, "The Beatles, the nation's hottest recording property today, are becoming the object of the nation's hottest lawsuits. The rock'n'rolling English group has a series of singles and LPs out on three labels – Capitol, Vee Jay and Swan. And each is becoming involved in a series of suits and countersuits between the various companies." Dealers across the country were receiving telegrams from one or more of the companies threatening that legal action would be taken if they persisted in selling the other's product.

Meanwhile, WABC's Beatles fan club was receiving between 2,000 and 3,000 letters a day and *Cashbox* was predicting, "Won't be long before every group with long hair will be sought by American companies."

January 18
Olympia Theatre, Paris.

January 19
Olympia Theatre, Paris.
Three sets. The matinée was broadcast live on the Paris station Europe-1's *Musicorama* show. The songs performed were 'From Me To You', 'This Boy', 'I Want To Hold Your Hand', 'She Loves You' and 'Twist And Shout'.

January 20
Olympia Theatre, Paris.
Europe-1 broadcast an interview with The Beatles.
The album *Meet The Beatles* was released in the US as Capitol ST 2047, the first of 33 Beatles records issued in America during 1964.
Side A: 'I Want To Hold Your Hand', 'I Saw Her Standing There', 'This Boy', 'It Won't Be Long', 'All I've Got To Do', 'All My Loving'; Side B: 'Don't Bother Me', 'Little Child', 'Till There Was You', 'Hold Me Tight', 'I Wanna Be Your Man', 'Not A Second Time'.

January 22
Olympia Theatre, Paris.

January 23
Olympia Theatre, Paris.
Brian Epstein denies that Paul is about to marry teenage actress Jane Asher: "Paul is definitely not engaged or married, and does not intend to become engaged or married."
In the bathroom of their hotel suite, John and Paul taped a rudimentary demo recording of an equally rudimentary song, 'One And One Is Two', which was intended for their NEMS stablemate, Billy J. Kramer. "Billy J. is finished when he gets this song", Lennon quipped after the taping was completed.

January 24
Olympia Theatre, Paris.
The Beatles recorded an interview for American Forces Network (AFN) in their Paris studio.

January 25
Olympia Theatre, Paris.
AFN broadcast their interview with The Beatles in the show *Weekend World*. *Cashbox* magazine finally hit the stands showing 'I Want To Hold Your Hand' at number one, up from number 43. It was number three in *Billboard*, up from 45.

January 26
Olympia Theatre, Paris.

January 27
The single 'My Bonnie'/'The Saints' by Tony Sheridan & The Beatles was re-released in the US as MGM K 13213.
The album *Introducing The Beatles* was re-released in the US as Vee Jay VJLP 1062, with two tracks substituted in the original track listing of the LP. Side A: 'I Saw Her Standing There', 'Misery', 'Anna (Go To Him)', 'Chains', 'Boys', 'Ask Me Why'; Side B: 'Please Please Me', 'Baby It's You', 'Do You Want To Know A Secret', 'A Taste Of Honey', 'There's A Place', 'Twist And Shout'.

THE GERMAN SINGLES
German EMI, Electrola Gesellschaft, insisted that The Beatles would not get large sales in that country unless the lyrics were sung in German. The Beatles thought this was nonsense, and so did George Martin, but he did not want to give them an excuse for not doing their best to sell Beatles records. He managed to persuade John and Paul to re-record 'She Loves You' and 'I Want To Hold Your Hand' in German. Someone from Electrola Gesellschaft translated the lyrics and was on hand at the recording to make sure the accents

didn't sound like a comedy record. George Martin turned up at the studio but The Beatles did not. After an hour's wait – a not unusual delay for The Beatles – Martin called the Georges Cinq Hotel, but none of them would come to the telephone. They told Neil Aspinall to inform George Martin that they would not be coming. A furious George Martin told Neil, "You just tell them I'm coming right over to let them know exactly what I think of them." Not long afterwards he burst into the drawing room of The Beatles' suite where, as he described it, the scene was one straight out of Lewis Carroll:

"Around a long table sat John, Paul, George, Ringo, Neil Aspinall and Mal Evans, his assistant. In the centre, pouring tea, was Jane Asher, a beautiful Alice with long golden hair. At my appearance, the whole tableau exploded. Beatles ran in all directions, hiding behind sofas, cushions, the piano . . . 'You bastards,' I yelled. 'I don't care if you record or not, but I do care about your rudeness!' "

The Beatles slowly reappeared and muttered sheepish apologies. Two days later they cut the German language version of the songs.

January 28
John and George flew back to London on their second day off from the Olympia. George had dinner with Phil Spector and The Ronettes.

January 29
Olympia Theatre, Paris.

John and George flew to Paris on the early morning flight.

At the Pathé Marconi Studio in Paris, The Beatles recorded 'Can't Buy Me Love' and German language versions of 'I Want To Hold Your Hand' and 'She Loves You'. Despite regular attempts in later years to persuade EMI to let them record in the US, this proved to be The Beatles' only studio session outside the UK.

The single 'Do You Want To Know A Secret'/'Bad To Me' by Billy J. Kramer & The Dakotas, written by Lennon & McCartney, was released in the US as Liberty 55667.

January 30
Olympia Theatre, Paris.

The single 'Please Please Me'/'From Me To You' was released in the US as Vee Jay VJ 581.

January 31
Olympia Theatre, Paris.

The single 'Sweet Georgia Brown' by Tony Sheridan & The Beatles was released in the UK as Polydor NH 52–906. The track was recorded in May 1962 in Hamburg but Sheridan added a new vocal track earlier this month for this release, complete with timely references to the length of The Beatles' hair.

Soon after this date, several of The Beatles' Hamburg recordings were overdubbed by American session drummer Bernard 'Pretty' Purdie, to make them sound punchier for US release. In several interviews since, Purdie has claimed that he was replacing Ringo's drum tracks because they weren't good enough; in fact, the drumming he was overdubbing had been performed by Pete Best.

February 1
Olympia Theatre, Paris.

February 2
Olympia Theatre, Paris.

February 3
The Beatles visited the American Embassy in Paris to obtain visas and work permits for their forthcoming tour.

Olympia Theatre, Paris.

February 4
Olympia Theatre, Paris.

February 5

The Beatles returned to London from Paris and held the usual press conference at the airport.

February 7

The EP *All My Loving* was released in the UK as Parlophone GEP 8891. Side A: 'All My Loving', 'Ask Me Why'; Side B: 'Money (That's What I Want)', 'P.S. I Love You'.

The Beatles flew to New York City on Pan Am flight 101, where 3,000 fans were waiting at JFK airport. Their party consisted of Paul, Ringo, George, John and Cynthia plus Neil Aspinall, Mal Evans, publicist Brian Sommerville, Brian Epstein and record producer Phil Spector. The group was unusually subdued. Ringo told *Liverpool Post* reporter George Harrison (no relation): "They've got everything over there, will they want us too?"

Paul said: "What have we got to give a country like America? Yes, I know that we've got a record at the top of the charts, but that doesn't mean that they'll go for us personally, does it?" They needn't have worried. Ed Sullivan had already received 50,000 applications for tickets to his show which only seated 728, and fans had been gathering at JFK since the previous afternoon.

The Beatles' Boeing 707 touched down at 1.20pm to scenes never before witnessed at Kennedy. It was a cold clear day. Five thousand fans, mostly young girls taking a day off school, were crowded four deep on the upper arcade of the arrivals building, waving "We Love You Beatles" placards and home-made banners welcoming The Beatles to America. An airport official said, "We've never seen anything like this before, ever. Never. Not even for kings and queens." In addition to the screaming teenagers, they were met by over 200 reporters and photographers from radio, television, magazines and newspapers.

The Beatles themselves thought at first that the President's plane was about to land, then it dawned on them: the reception was for them.

For days the radio stations had been whipping the fans into a frenzy, and it was Murray the K at 1010 WINS who first announced the supposedly secret details of their airline, time of arrival and flight number. The information was quickly repeated on WINS rival stations: WABC and WMCA.

Over 100 yelling journalists were waiting for the group as they emerged from immigration, and at first they couldn't see for the flash bulbs. "So this is America," said Ringo. "They all seem to be out of their minds." One of their first interviews on US soil was with Fred Robbins of Radio Luxembourg, who secured twenty priceless minutes of The Beatles' time.

THE ROAD TO NEW YORK

Tom Wolfe, writing in the *New York Herald Tribune* reported on The Beatles' arrival in his customary style, noticing the small details which characterised the event: [Though in fact Paul, George and Ringo took one limo, John another and Brian was left to hail a cab to get to town.]

"The Beatles left the airport in four Cadillac limousines, one Beatle to a limousine, heading for the Plaza Hotel in Manhattan. The first sortie came almost immediately. Five kids in a powder blue Ford overtook the caravan on the expressway, and as they passed each Beatle, one guy hung out the back window and waved a red blanket.

"A white convertible came up second, with the word BEETLES scratched on both sides in the dust. A police car was close behind that one with the siren going and the alarm light rolling, but the kids, a girl at the wheel and two guys in the back seat, waved at each Beatle before pulling over to exit with the cops gesturing at them.

"In the second limousine, Brian Sommerville, The Beatles' press agent, said to one of The Beatles, George Harrison: 'Did you see that, George?' Harrison looked at the convertible with its emblem in the dust and said, 'They misspelled Beatles.'

"But the third sortie succeeded all the way. A good-looking brunette, who said her name was Caroline Reynolds of New Canaan, Conn., and Wellesley College, had paid a cab driver $10 to follow the caravan all the way into town.

She cruised by each Beatle, smiling vainly, and finally caught up with George Harrison's limousine at a light at Third Avenue and 63rd Street.

"'How does one go about meeting a Beatle?' she said out the window.

"'One says hello,' Harrison said out the window.

"'Hellow!' she said. 'Eight more will be down from Wellesley.' Then the light changed and the caravan was off again."

The scene at the Plaza, New York's grandest hotel, was chaotic with hundreds of fans being held at bay by police barricades and 20 mounted police. They kept up a constant mantra-like chant: "We love you Beat-les, oh yes we dooo! We love you Beat-les and we'll be true!" interspersed with shouts of "We want The Beatles!"

That evening a stream of guests visited the ten-room Presidential suite, including The Ronettes, DJ Murray the K and George's sister, Louise, who lived in Illinois but had flown in to see him.

The Beatles recorded an interview with Brian Matthew on the telephone from the BBC in London to be broadcast the next morning on *Saturday Club*. Then they looked at some of their fan mail: 100,000 letters were waiting for them when they arrived in New York.

February 8

Another press conference was held in the Plaza's Baroque Room. Afterwards John, Paul and Ringo went for a photo-opportunity walkabout in Central Park followed by about 400 girls. George had strep throat and stayed inside, tended by his sister Louise Caldwell.

At 1.30pm The Beatles travelled by limousines to CBS studios at 53rd Street for a soundcheck. On the way, fans charged at the cars en masse and it was up to mounted police to get them through. The studios themselves were guarded by 52 police officers and ten mounted police. At the studios The Beatles had to join AFRA (the US equivalent of the Musicians' Union) and sign forms. Neil Aspinall stood in for George at the camera position run-through for the next day's live show. The studio staff were surprised when The Beatles asked to hear a playback of their rehearsal; no other musical act had ever bothered. The Beatles were interviewed by The Ronettes.

That evening John, Paul and Ringo went to the 21 restaurant for dinner with Capitol Records executives. George Martin joined them. The Beatles ate chops whereas executives ate pheasant. Paul ate crepe suzettes. Back at the hotel they listened to the radio till late at night.

That morning The Beatles' recorded telephone interview with Brian Matthew was broadcast on BBC Light Programme's *Saturday Club*.

THE BEATLES PRESS CONFERENCES

By the time The Beatles reached New York, the press conference had become a regular occurrence. Most press conferences with top recording artists were staid affairs but The Beatles changed all this, displaying an irreverent and sometimes cheeky sense of humour which journalists lapped up and often reported verbatim. For this reason The Beatles were often likened to the Marx Brothers, their apparently off-the-cuff wit charming otherwise sceptical cynics. "How did you find America?" John was asked. "Turn left at Greenland," he replied. "What do you do in your hotel rooms all day?" George was asked. "Ice skate," he replied, deadpan. And when Paul was informed that there was a campaign in Detroit to stamp out The Beatles, he replied: "We have a plan to stamp out Detroit."

February 9

Studio 50, West 53rd Street. Rehearsals for *The Ed Sullivan Show* took up the morning. Once again, Neil Aspinall stood in for the ailing George, but The Beatles' guitarist was sufficiently improved to appear for the actual taping of their performances.

In the afternoon The Beatles recorded numbers for another *Ed Sullivan Show* to be broadcast after they had left the country. This would be their third show – their first was to be done live that evening and the second was to be a live show from Florida on February 16. For the "third" show, they recorded 'Twist And Shout', 'Please Please Me' and 'I Want To Hold Your Hand'. There was a different audience for the third show recording than that which attended the live transmission that evening. Other guests included Gordon and Sheila MacRae and The Cab Calloway Orchestra.

That evening, for the 8pm live show, The Beatles performed 'All My Loving', 'Till There Was You' and 'She Loves You' followed by an Anadin advert. Then came Ed's other guests – Georgia Brown & Oliver Kidds, Frank Gorshin, Tessie O'Shea – and the show closed after a Kent cigarette advert with 'I Saw Her Standing There' and 'I Want To Hold Your Hand'. Thirteen-and-a-half minutes of television had changed the face of American popular music. The Nielsen ratings showed that 73,700,000 people had watched The Beatles on Ed Sullivan, not just the largest audience that Sullivan had ever had, but the largest audience in the history of television.

Half an hour before they appeared on stage, Brian Sommerville handed them a telegram: "Congratulations on your appearance on *The Ed Sullivan Show* and your visit to America. We hope your engagement will be a successful one and your visit pleasant. Give our best to Mr. Sullivan. Sincerely, Elvis & The Colonel." George read the telegram and asked, deadpan, "Elvis who?"

After the show Murray the K took The Beatles, minus George who still had a sore throat, to the Playboy Club. Paul: "The bunnies are even more adorable than we are." Protected by a police escort, they risked walking the few blocks to 59th Street where they were quickly ushered up to the Penthouse lounge for dinner. Afterwards they went on to the Peppermint Lounge, home of the Twist, where Ringo excelled at twisting to Beatles tunes with a young dancer called Geri Miller. They left at 4am.

February 10

The day was taken up with press interviews and presentations. At one ceremony, Capitol Records president Alan Livingstone presented The Beatles with golden discs to mark the sale of a million copies of 'I Want To Hold Your Hand' and a million dollars worth of sales of the album *Meet The Beatles*. The evening was spent at clubs. Once again, they returned to the Plaza at 4am.

February 11

A snowstorm blanketed the East Coast and all flights were cancelled so a special carriage was attached to the Pennsylvania Railroad express, the Congressman, to take them to Washington, DC. The carriage, an old Richmond, Fredericksburg and Potomac Railroad sleeper car called The King George, was already filled with press when they arrived, and at each stop, more cameramen poked their lenses through the windows. Two thousand fans braved eight inches of snow to welcome them at Washington's Union Station. There was a press conference, then they visited WWDC, the first American radio station to play a Beatles record, where they were interviewed by DJ Carroll James. He asked about their influences:

John: "Small Blind Johnny."
Carroll James: "Small Blind Johnny?"
John: "Oh yes, he played with Big Deaf Arthur."
Carroll James: "John, they call you the chief Beatle . . ."
John: "Carroll. I don't call *you* names!"
Carroll James: "Excluding America and England, what are your favourite countries you've visited?"
John: "Excluding America and England, what's left?"

The party checked into The Shoreham Hotel, taking the whole of the seventh floor which was sealed off from the fans. One family refused the leave their rooms on the seventh floor so the hotel cut off the central heating, hot water and electricity, telling them that there had been a power failure. The disgruntled family moved.

A total of 8,092 fans, mostly girls, saw the show at the Washington Coliseum, protected by 362 police officers, one of whom found the volume so loud he stuck a bullet in each ear as ear plugs. The Beatles' set consisted of: 'Roll Over Beethoven', 'From Me To You', 'I Saw Her Standing There', 'This Boy', 'All My Loving', 'I Wanna Be Your Man', 'Please Please Me', 'Till There Was You', 'She Loves You', 'I Want To Hold Your Hand', 'Twist And Shout' and 'Long Tall Sally'. Also on the bill were The Chiffons and Tommy Roe.

Paul: "Most exciting yet."

THE EMBASSY INCIDENT

After the show there was a reception at the British Embassy, given by Lady Ormsby-Gore. There had been a formal dance to benefit The National Association for the Prevention of Cruelty to Children, and The Beatles were required to hand out the raffle prizes at the end of the affair. The British community, arrogant debutantes and aristocrats, disgraced themselves, and one woman even snipped off a lock of Ringo's hair just behind his left ear. John pushed all the autograph seekers away saying, "These people have no bloody manners," and grabbing Ringo, said, "I'm getting out of here." Ringo calmed him down, they did their stuff and left. Brian was told firmly never to expose them to that kind of gathering again.

February 12

The Beatles took the two-hour train ride back to New York but their limousine could not get through the waiting crowds of fans. It was Lincoln's birthday, a public holiday, so school was out and 10,000 fans were waiting at Penn Station. They had to be spirited back to the hotel by normal New York City yellow cabs. After a quick shave, shower and change of clothes, they were smuggled out of the Plaza down the back elevator and out through the kitchens in order to get to nearby Carnegie Hall for a double header at the most prestigious venue in the country. The audience was warmed up by a folk'n'roll group called The Briarwoods. Backstage they received a gold disc from Swan Records for selling a million copies of 'She Loves You'. Shirley Bassey, who was herself about to appear at Carnegie Hall later in the week, was among their visitors.

George Martin had requested permission from EMI to record the Carnegie Hall concerts, but hurried negotiations with the American Federation of Musicians failed to produce the required US agreement, so the shows went untaped.

Promoter Sid Bernstein took Brian Epstein outside into the snow-laden air after the show and offered him $25,000 plus a $5,000 donation to the British Cancer Fund for a Madison Square Garden concert in a few days time. Tickets could be printed and would sell out at once, he assured Brian. "Let's leave this for next time," said Brian.

That night, their last in New York City, they left the Plaza at 1.30am to visit the Headliner Club and then the Improvisation coffee house in Greenwich Village. They returned at dawn and a reporter who was still waiting outside asked if it had been a quiet night. Paul: "No. We met Stella Stevens, Tuesday Weld and Jill Haworth – and they're not exactly quiet girls."

Granada Television screened *Yeah, Yeah, Yeah! – The Beatles In New York*, an instant documentary by the Maysles Brothers.

February 13

National Airlines Flight 11 left New York at 1.30pm, and arrived at Miami at 4pm. At Miami there were 7,000 fans waiting, whipped into a frenzy by rival radio stations WFUN and WQAM who announced their arrival time, but The Beatles leapt straight from the plane into a waiting limousine and were off to the Deauville Hotel in Miami Beach. Their convoy of three black limousines had motorcycle outriders front and back and made the eight miles of expressway into the city in record time, going through red lights, driving on the wrong side of the road, as fans lining the streets cheered and waved.

Murray the K accompanied them, and even shared a room with George in their three-bedroom suite, guarded by Pinkerton detectives. (Disgruntled George never figured out how the pushy New York DJ had pulled that one off.) That evening they visited the Mau Mau Lounge where they saw The Coasters and danced the "Mashed Potato". Murray the K took them to see Hank Ballard & The Midnighters at the Miami Peppermint Lounge. There they were besieged by autograph hunters so they didn't stay long.

After being inundated with requests, Granada Television repeated *Yeah, Yeah, Yeah! – The Beatles In New York* by the Maysles Brothers.

February 14

A short rehearsal for *The Ed Sullivan Show*. A photo session for *Life* magazine in the swimming pool at the home of a Capitol Records executive, followed by a tour round Miami Harbour in a luxury houseboat provided by a Bernard Castro. Two reporters were found to have stowed away and the boat returned to shore to put them off. Their private bodyguard, Sgt Buddy Bresner, took them home to meet his wife and kids – Dottie, Barry, Andy and Jeri – and fed them a typical American meal: roast beef, green beans, baked potatoes, peas, salad and a huge strawberry ice cake. That evening they stayed in the hotel, taking in the floor shows in the hotel's nightclubs: first comedian Don Rickells, then Myron Cohen and singer Carol Lawrence. They had no dinner because Bresner's massive lunch had filled them up.

February 15

The group, wearing swimming trunks, rehearsed in the hotel's Napoleon Room. At 2pm The Beatles did a dress rehearsal for *The Ed Sullivan Show* before an audience of 2,500, many of whom had queued outside since early morning. The rest of the day was spent fishing.

ABC TV's *Dick Clark's American Bandstand* broadcast a telephone interview with the group.

February 16

The Ed Sullivan Show was done in the Deauville Hotel itself. CBS gave out 3,500 tickets when the hall only held 2,600. The police had to deal with riots when fans holding perfectly valid tickets were turned away. The group played, 'She Loves You', 'This Boy', 'All My Loving', 'I Saw Her Standing There', 'From Me To You' and 'I Want To Hold Your Hand'. Boxers Joe Louis and Sonny Liston were both in the audience. Mitzi Gaynor topped the bill but the 70,000,000 viewers were mostly tuned in to watch The Beatles.

The owner of the hotel, Maurice Lansberg, gave a small party for the performers and technicians on the show. Self-service: lobster, beef, chicken, and fish.

February 17

The Beatles tried their hand at water-skiing.

The single 'I Wanna Be Your Man' by The Rolling Stones, written by Lennon & McCartney, was released in the US as London 9641.

February 18

On their day off, The Beatles, probably at Paul's instigation, requested a visit to Cassius Clay's training camp where he was preparing for his rematch with the champion, Sonny Liston. The photographers went crazy as ex-heavyweight champ Clay picked up Ringo as if he weighed only a few ounces.

They had a barbecue in the grounds of a millionaire's home, eating the biggest steaks they had ever seen, and tried their hand with speedboats. That evening they went to a drive-in movie, where they saw Elvis Presley's *Fun In Acapulco*.

February 21

The Beatles returned to London from Miami, via New York.

February 22

The Beatles arrived back in London at 8.10am to a tumultuous welcome. They gave a press conference in the Kingsford-Smith suite at the airport which was shown by BBC TV later as part of the sports programme *Grandstand*. News of their return was also featured on radio news and other programmes.

Paul spent the evening in Canterbury, seeing Jane Asher act in *The Jew Of Malta*.

February 23

ABC TV's Teddington Studio Centre. Without even a day off to get over jet-lag, The Beatles taped an appearance for Mike & Bernie Winters' variety show *Big Night Out* before a live audience. They appeared in various skits, including a river cruise which was also filmed by ITN and used in its news bulletin that evening. They mimed to 'All My Loving', 'I Wanna Be Your Man', 'Till There Was You', 'Please Mister Postman', 'Money (That's What I Want)' and 'I Want To Hold Your Hand'.

Afterwards they went to an all-night party at Alma Cogan's apartment in Kensington.

The Beatles' third appearance on *The Ed Sullivan Show* was screened.

February 24

Ringo went to Liverpool to see his family.

February 25
Ringo took the first flight from Liverpool to London to attend a recording session.
Abbey Road. They finished 'Can't Buy Me Love', recorded 'You Can't Do That' (featuring John on lead guitar for the first time on record) and began work on Paul's 'And I Love Her' and John's 'I Should Have Known Better'.
George's 21st birthday. He received 52 mail-sacks holding about 30,000 cards. Two fans sent him a door so that he could use one of the thousands of 21st keys he was sent. At a party after the Abbey Road session, George was given a gold cigarette lighter by Brian Epstein. The Beatles and the other guests dined on turtle soup, smoked salmon and Chateaubriand steak.

February 26
Abbey Road. Further work on 'And I Love Her' and 'I Should Have Known Better'.
The album *Jolly What! The Beatles And Frank Ifield On Stage* was released in the US as Vee Jay VJLP 1085. Despite its title, it featured regular studio recordings by both artists, allowing Vee Jay to extract yet more mileage from the dozen Beatles tracks which they had under licence. This LP featured eight Ifield songs, plus 'Please Please Me', 'From Me To You', 'Ask Me Why' and 'Thank You Girl'.

February 27
Abbey Road. 'And I Love Her' was finished, plus complete recordings made of John's 'Tell Me Why' and 'If I Fell'.
Two of John Lennon's nonsense poems, 'The Tales Of Hermit Fred' and 'The Land Of Lunapots', were published for the first time in *Mersey Beat*.

February 28
BBC Studios at 201 Piccadilly. The Beatles recorded a second *From Us To You* Easter bank holiday special for the Light Programme. The group was interviewed by Alan ("Fluff") Freeman and taped 'You Can't Do That', 'Roll Over Beethoven', 'Till There Was You', 'I Wanna Be Your Man', 'Please Mister Postman', 'All My Loving', 'This Boy' and 'Can't Buy Me Love'. As before they taped their own version of the show's theme tune *From Us To You* to open and close the programme.
The single 'A World Without Love' by Peter & Gordon was released in the UK as Columbia DB 7225. It had been written by John and Paul and given to Jane Asher's brother who had just received a record contract from EMI. Jane Asher: "The song came up one night when Paul and John were round at our home. They hadn't really finished it, but Peter and Gordon were mad keen about it right away. So the boys worked on it."
The single 'Why'/'Cry For A Shadow' by Tony Sheridan & The Beatles (A-side) and The Beatles (B-side) was released in the UK as Polydor NH 52–275.

February 29
ABC TV's Mike and Bernie Winters' *Big Night Out* featuring the jet-lagged Beatles was broadcast.

March 1
Abbey Road. 'I'm Happy Just To Dance With You' was recorded, specially written for George who was not yet writing songs regularly. This was followed by 'Long Tall Sally' with Paul in fine Little Richard form, and 'I Call Your Name'.

March 2
The Beatles began filming *A Hard Day's Night*, directed by Richard Lester, with a screenplay written by Alun Owen. Filming began at 8.30am on Paddington Station, with The Beatles hurriedly joining Equity minutes before boarding the train.
The first week was spent filming on a specially hired train going from Paddington to Minehead and back, covering 2,500 miles in six days. After the crowds on the first day, they boarded the train at Acton station to avoid Paddington. There was a special dining car laid on for The Beatles and crew but when there was a 40-minute break they used the time set aside for eating to sit still instead of rolling from side to side.
Filming started at 8.30, very early for them, and each day they were given a shooting schedule. Since they all had equal parts, there was never a great deal of dialogue to be

learned. On the train, the dialogue was recorded using microphones inside their shirts, but even then there were many retakes because the levels were not high enough. One of the actresses on the train the first day was Patti Boyd, with whom George struck up an immediate friendship.

The single 'Twist And Shout'/'There's A Place' was released in the US as Tollie 9001.

PATTI BOYD
Patti Boyd was a model and actress who had already made a name for herself by the time she met George. By far the most glamorous of The Beatles' girlfriends, George became smitten with her almost immediately and they were soon living together. George and Patti married in 1966. After her and George separated in the early Seventies, Patti became Eric Clapton's girlfriend and, later, wife.

March 3
Filming on location, between London and Minehead.

March 4
Filming on location, between London and Minehead.

March 5
Filming on location, between London and Minehead.
    The group had drinks with Jeffrey Archer at Vincent's, the Oxford Sportsmen's club, before attending a dinner at Brasenose College, Oxford, that Archer had organised to celebrate their fundraising work for Oxfam.
    The single 'Komm, Gib Mir Deine Hand'/'Sie Liebt Dich' was released in Germany as Odeon 22671.

March 6
Filming on location, between London and Minehead.

March 9
Filming on location, between London and Newton Abbott, Devon. This was the last day of railway location filming.

NEMS ENTERPRISES
NEMS Enterprises Limited moved from Liverpool to new headquarters on the fifth floor of Sutherland House, 5 & 6 Argyll Street, London. The press office, previously at 13 Monmouth Street, London, was also moved to the new office suite. A press release, dated March 2, listed the management staff as: J. Alistair Taylor, General Manager; J.B. Montgomery, Accounts; Tony Barrow, NEMS Press Officer; Brian Sommerville, Beatles' Personal Press Representative; Wendy Hanson, Personal Assistant to Brian Epstein.
    NEMS then managed The Beatles, Gerry & The Pacemakers, Billy J. Kramer, The Dakotas, Cilla Black, The Fourmost, Tommy Quickly, Sounds Incorporated and The Remo Four. In Brian's accompanying letter to his staff he said: "First of all as our organisation is very much in the public eye, it is most important that we present the best possible 'front'. By this I mean that all visitors must be treated with utmost courtesy. That work must be carried out smoothly and efficiently without fuss. And most important, that the offices themselves must be kept tidy and clean at all times."

March 10
Filming at The Turk's Head, Twickenham.
    That evening they visited Tony Sheridan at Brian Epstein's apartment.

March 11
Filming at Twickenham Film Studios, miming to 'I Should Have Known Better' in a mock-up of the train's guard's van. Studio technicians rocked the set during filming. At one point Richard Lester stopped the shoot because the technicians were rocking the set in time with The Beatles' music.

March 12
Filming at Twickenham: hotel room sequences.

March 13
The movie's closing sequence was filmed with a helicopter at Gatwick Airport.

March 16
Ringo filmed his canteen sequence at Twickenham Studios.
Ringo was made Vice-President of Leeds University Law Society.
George and Brian Epstein attended a Cilla Black recording session for BBC's *Saturday Club*.
The single 'Can't Buy Me Love'/'You Can't Do That' was released in the US as Capitol 5150.

March 17
Filming at Les Ambassadeurs Club.
John recorded an interview with Jack de Manio for the BBC Home Service programme *Today* to promote his forthcoming book *In His Own Write*.

March 18
Filming at Twickenham.
While on the set they recorded an interview for the BBC Light Programme show *The Public Ear* in which they interviewed each other.
John's interview was broadcast on the *Today* programme.

March 19
The Variety Club of Great Britain 12th Annual Show Business Awards were presented at a luncheon at the Dorchester Hotel. Harold Wilson, Leader of the Opposition, presented The Beatles with the award for "Show Business Personalities of 1963" and, somewhat shrewdly, had his picture taken with them. John referred to his award, a heart shaped shield, as his "purple heart".
The Beatles were filming that morning at Twickenham and returned to the set directly after the luncheon. Later that evening they recorded their first *Top Of The Pops* programme for the BBC. They mimed to 'Can't Buy Me Love' and 'You Can't Do That'.
There had been a lot of discussion about a name for the film. *Beatlemania* was rejected, as was *Moving On*, *Travelling On*, *Let's Go* and Paul's suggestion, *Who Was That Little Old Man?* It was Ringo who came up with *A Hard Day's Night*. After a particularly heavy day he remarked, "Boy, this has been a hard day's night!" Everyone jumped on the idea immediately.

March 20
Filming at Twickenham.
Ringo was interviewed on the set by Peter Nobel for the BBC radio programme *Movie-Go-Round*.
In the late afternoon they drove to the London headquarters of Associated Rediffusion and appeared live on *Ready, Steady, Go!* miming to 'It Won't Be Long', 'You Can't Do That' and 'Can't Buy Me Love'. They were interviewed by Cathy McGowan and took part in sketches.
George took Hayley Mills to the midnight charity showing of *Charade* at the Regal Cinema in Henley-on-Thames.
The single 'Can't Buy Me Love'/'You Can't Do That' was released in the UK as Parlophone R 5114.

CAN'T BUY ME LOVE
The Beatles' first single of 1964 was taped almost as an afterthought, at the end of the group's one and only EMI studio session outside Britain. Their visit to Pathé Marconi Studios in Paris had been arranged so they could reluctantly concoct German-language versions of two of their biggest hits. With less than an hour remaining, the group cut this Paul McCartney song in just four takes – completely reworking the arrangement between their first, R&B-styled attempt and the more polished final version.
'Can't Buy Me Love' came closer than any of The Beatles' singles thus far, to matching

the rock'n'roll music that they'd been playing since the mid-Fifties. Its lyrics neatly reversed the theme of 'Money' from their previous album, and the track gave George Harrison a splendid opportunity to show off his guitar skills. He added his solo as an overdub, having already proved on that tentative first take that unrehearsed improvisation wasn't exactly his forte.

YOU CAN'T DO THAT

Of all the songs on The Beatles' forthcoming A Hard Day's Night album, John Lennon was proudest of this. Not at all coincidentally, it was the roughest, least polished number he'd recorded up to that date. It was blatantly inspired by the R&B songs coming out of Memphis, and (as rock critic Lester Bangs wrote years later), "built on one of the bitterest and most iron-indestructible riffs ever conceived". Lennon handled the lead guitar himself, hammering out a wiry solo which grew into a furious flurry of chords, totally unlike anything that George Harrison performed on the rest of the album.

March 21

In New York, the prestigious *Saturday Evening Post* published a selection of John's whimsical prose and poetry, billing his work as "Beatalic Graphospasms".

March 22

A sequence of The Beatles interviewing themselves was broadcast on *The Public Ear* by the BBC Light Programme.

March 23

Filming at the Scala Theatre, Charlotte Street, London, where they were to remain all week.

IN HIS OWN WRITE

In His Own Write by John Lennon was published by Jonathan Cape on March 23. John: "Some journalist who was hanging round The Beatles came to me and I ended up showing him the stuff. They said, 'Write a book' and that's how the first one came about, and the second was your follow-up. Then I forgot about it." The journalist was Derek Taylor, who introduced John to representatives from Jonathan Cape.

To promote the book, John appeared live on the BBC television *Tonight* programme broadcast from Lime Grove. He was interviewed by Kenneth Allsop and read selections from the book, many of which first saw print in John's 'Beatcomber' column in *Mersey Beat*.

The Duke of Edinburgh presented The Beatles with the Carl-Alan Award for Musical Achievement in 1963 at a ceremony at the Empire Ballroom in Leicester Square as part of the annual Carl-Alan Ballroom Dancing Awards. The presentation was broadcast live by BBC television.

The single 'Do You Want To Know A Secret'/'Thank You Girl' was released in the US as Vee Jay VJ 587.

The EP *The Beatles* was released in the US as Vee Jay VJEP 1–903. Side A: 'Misery', 'A Taste Of Honey'; Side B: 'Ask Me Why', 'Anna (Go To Him)'. The EP format was unusual in the US, but Vee Jay only had a few tracks to play with and so they released them in every possible format.

March 24

Filming at the Scala Theatre, Charlotte Street, London.

Wax effigies of all four Beatles went on display at Madame Tussaud's museum in central London. The original dummies were later included in the montage of faces on the cover of the *Sgt. Pepper* album. The group's shifting visual image during the 60s forced Madame Tussaud's to rework their original designs on several occasions.

John did an interview to promote his new book for *Dateline London*, a BBC Overseas Service magazine programme.

March 25

Filming at the Scala Theatre, Charlotte Street, London.

The Beatles' appearance on *Top Of The Pops* was transmitted.

March 26
Filming at the Scala Theatre, Charlotte Street, London.

March 27
John and Cynthia, and George and Patti left to spend the Easter weekend in Dromolan Castle, County Clare, Ireland. The press reported that the decently married Lennons had accompanied George and his new girlfriend to act as 'chaperons'. Ringo went to spend the weekend at Woburn Abbey as the guest of Lord Rudolph Russell, son of the Duke of Bedford. Paul remained in London.

The press reported that The Beatles now held the first six positions in the Australian singles charts.

March 30
The single 'Bad To Me' by Billy J. Kramer & The Dakotas, written by Lennon & McCartney, was released in the US as Imperial 66027.

The BBC Light Programme broadcast their specially recorded Beatles bank holiday special, *From Us To You*.

March 31
The group filmed a live concert at the Scala Theatre, Charlotte Street, London, for *A Hard Day's Night*. They mimed to 'Tell Me Why', 'And I Love Her', 'I Should Have Known Better' and 'She Loves You'. Thirteen-year old Phil Collins was in the audience as one of the 350 paid child extras.

That evening, The Beatles recorded a session for BBC Light Programme's *Saturday Club*. They did 'Everybody's Trying To Be My Baby', 'I Call Your Name', 'I Got A Woman', 'You Can't Do That', 'Can't Buy Me Love', 'Sure To Fall (In Love With You)' and 'Long Tall Sally'.

John was interviewed about his book by Brian Matthew for the BBC Home Service programme *A Slice of Life*.

April 1
Filming at the Scala Theatre, Charlotte Street, London.

A meeting was arranged at the London offices of NEMS between John and his father, Freddie. It lasted 20 minutes and George and Ringo were also present. Father and son had not seen each other for 17 years.

Paul visited a sick relative at Walton Hospital in Liverpool.

April 2
Filming at the Scala Theatre, Charlotte Street, London.

April 3
Filming at Twickenham Film Studios.

The Beatles filmed answers to viewers' questions for the Tyne Tees Television programme *Star Parade*.

April 4
In the *Billboard* "Hot 100" chart for the week of April 4, The Beatles occupied no fewer than 12 places, including the top five, an unprecedented achievement that is unlikely ever to be equalled. 'Can't Buy Me Love' was at number 1, followed by 'Twist And Shout' (2), 'She Loves You' (3), 'I Want To Hold Your Hand' (4), 'Please Please Me' (5), 'I Saw Her Standing There' (31), 'From Me To You' (41), 'Do You Want To Know A Secret' (46), 'All My Loving' (58), 'You Can't Do That' (65), 'Roll Over Beethoven' (68) and 'Thank You Girl' (79). A week later two more singles entered the chart – 'There's A Place' (74) and 'Love Me Do' (81).

The Beatles' most recent *Saturday Club* session was broadcast on the BBC Light Programme.

Derek Taylor signed a contract with Brian Epstein to ghostwrite The Beatles' manager's autobiography.

April 5
Filming the chase sequence at Marylebone Railway Station.

April 6
Filming at Twickenham.

April 7
Filming at Twickenham.

April 9
Ringo filmed his solo spot for the film on the towpath of the Thames at Kew.
 The Beatles' Q & A session was broadcast on Tyne Tees Television.

April 10
Filming at Twickenham.
 The album *The Beatles' Second Album* was released in the US as Capitol ST 2080. Side A: 'Roll Over Beethoven', 'Thank You Girl', 'You Really Got A Hold On Me', 'Devil In Her Heart', 'Money (That's What I Want)', 'You Can't Do That'; Side B: 'Long Tall Sally', 'I Call Your Name', 'Please Mister Postman', 'I'll Get You', 'She Loves You'. Despite its title, the LP was actually the group's third album release in the US, though only their second on Capitol.

April 12
Filming at Marylebone Station which was closed on Sundays.

April 13
Filming at Twickenham.
 With *A Hard Day's Night* confirmed as the title of their film, John announced his intention to write a title tune to order – which he did that evening.

April 14
Filming at Twickenham.
 John arrived for the day's filming with his song 'A Hard Day's Night', quickly taught it to Paul, who tidied up the middle section, and the pair then played it to film producer Walter Shenson for the first time.

April 15
Filming outside shots at the Scala Theatre, Charlotte Street, London.
 Paul was interviewed by David Frost for a BBC1 television show, *A Degree Of Frost*.

April 16
Filming chase scenes in Notting Hill Gate.
 Abbey Road. Recording 'A Hard Day's Night'.
 Paul: "When George Martin was scoring *A Hard Day's Night* [for the orchestral film soundtrack], he said, 'What is that note, John? It's been a hard day's night and I've been work-? Is it the seventh? Work-*innnngggg*?'
 "John said, 'Oh no, it's not that.'
 " 'Well is it work-*innnggg*?' He sings the sixth.
 "John said, 'No.'
 "George said, 'Well, it must be somewhere in between then!'
 "John said, 'Yeah, man, write *that* down.' And that's what I love! That's what I find interesting about music!"

April 17
Filming at Les Ambassadeurs.
 The group were interviewed by Ed Sullivan in the club's walled garden during a break in filming.
 The title *A Hard Day's Night* was announced as the name of The Beatles' first film.

April 18
The morning was spent at Twickenham Film Studios.

The afternoon was spent in rehearsal at The Hall Of Remembrance, Flood Street, Chelsea, for a TV Special for Rediffusion called *Around The Beatles*.

The Beatles appeared on ATV's *The Morecambe and Wise Show* (recorded December 2, 1963).

April 19

IBC Studios, Portland Place, to record their contribution to *Around The Beatles*. They played 'Twist And Shout', 'Roll Over Beethoven', 'I Wanna Be Your Man', 'Long Tall Sally', 'Boys' (omitted from the final broadcast), 'Can't Buy Me Love' and a greatest hits medley: 'Love Me Do'/'Please Please Me'/'From Me To You'/'She Loves You'/'I Want To Hold Your Hand' and 'Shout!' They would mime to this tape on the actual show.

Burglars broke into George and Ringo's flat in Green Street, Knightsbridge.

Derek Taylor joined Brian Epstein's staff as his personal assistant.

DEREK TAYLOR

Derek was a reporter who worked on the *Daily Express* and was originally sent to do a 'hatchet' job on The Beatles, but he decided he loved the group and instead found himself ghosting a George Harrison column in the *Express*. This led to a lasting friendship with George and a commission to ghost-write Brian Epstein's autobiography, *A Cellarful Of Noise*. He became their press officer and, after a period living in Los Angeles, rejoined The Beatles, again as press officer, during the Apple era. Erudite, eminently literate and with a quirky sense of humour, Taylor was a much loved and respected member of their entourage, a born diplomat who remained unruffled even in the most trying of circumstances.

April 20

Paul was filmed at the Jack Billings TV School of Dance, Notting Hill, in a solo spot that was ultimately cut from the final film.

April 21

Paul's second day of filming at the Jack Billings TV School of Dance.

April 22

Outdoor locations shots were filmed at the Hammersmith Odeon and in Notting Hill and Shepherd's Bush.

The Beatles attended a press reception, hosted by the Rt. Hon. Sir Eric Harrison, Australian High Commissioner, at Australia House. Fans milled around outside in the pouring rain and the 700 guests all scrambled to get autographs. Paul: "Will it be like this in Australia then? Blimey!" The group was finally pushed into a private office containing a huge map of Australia made entirely of apples. Ringo grabbed one and ate it, telling the Ambassador, "It's bonza, mate!" Each member of the group was presented with a hamper of two magnums of Australian champagne, and tins of fruit. John asked, "Where's the Aussie beer we've heard so much about then?" Sir Eric grew more and more irritated at the proceedings and told reporters, "There has never been a reception quite like this in Australia House and I hope there will never be another one. I guess I am what you would call a square but those photographers were just too much. They climbed all over the chairs and then when we went inside a closed office they were thrusting their cameras through the windows and rapping on the glass . . ."

April 23

Filming at Thornbury Playing Fields, Isleworth, Middlesex.

John cut short his day's filming in order to attend a Foyle's Literary Luncheon, given in his honour, at the Dorchester Hotel. The chairman was Osbert Lancaster and other guests included Arthur Askey, Harry Secombe, Millicent Martin, Joan Littlewood, Helen Shapiro, Marty Wilde, Yehudi Menuhin, Victor Silvester, Mary Quant and cartoonist Giles. Brian Epstein was in attendance but, strangely, no other Beatles. Christina Foyle was put out when the severely hungover John restricted his speech to the words, "Thank you very much and God bless you."

April 24
Ringo's Sir Walter Raleigh puddle sequence was filmed in West Ealing. As it was the final day of shooting, The Beatles, the entire crew, and Murray the K, who was visiting, trooped across the road from the studios to the Turk's Head pub nearby where food and drinks had been laid on in a private room in the back.

April 25
Rehearsals for *Around The Beatles* were held at The Hall of Remembrance, Flood Street, Chelsea.

April 26
The Beatles topped the bill at the *New Musical Express* 1963–4 Annual Poll Winners' All-Star Concert held at Empire Pool, Wembley, in the afternoon. Ten thousand fans saw them receive their awards from Roger Moore and perform 'She Loves You', 'You Can't Do That', 'Twist And Shout', 'Long Tall Sally' and 'Can't Buy Me Love'. Their section of the show was introduced in typically exaggerated manner by the self-styled 'Fifth Beatle', Murray the K, who used his introduction to promote the name and call-sign of his New York radio station.

April 27
The Beatles attended a full dress rehearsal before a live audience for the *Around The Beatles* TV Special held at Rediffusion's studios in Wembley.
    The single 'Love Me Do'/'P.S. I Love You' was released in the US as Tollie 9008.
    The single 'A World Without Love' by Peter & Gordon, written by Lennon & McCartney, was released in the US as Capitol 5175.
    The single 'Why'/'Cry For A Shadow' by Tony Sheridan & The Beatles (A- side) and The Beatles (B-side) was released in the US as MGM K 13227.
    John's *In His Own Write* was published in the US by Simon & Schuster.
    NEMS Enterprises increased its share capital to 10,000 £1 shares. Brian gave The Beatles 250 shares each.

April 28
The *Around The Beatles* TV Special was taped at Rediffusion's Wembley Studio. As well as the numbers they had already recorded, The Beatles played Act V Scene 1 of Shakespeare's *A Midsummer Night's Dream* with John taking the female role of Thisbe, Paul as Pyramus, George as Moonshine and Ringo as Lion – their faintly hysterical performances being accompanied by mock-heckling from the gallery. Paul later named his cat Thisbe. The finished show also featured performances from Cilla Black, P.J. Proby and Long John Baldry.

April 29
ABC Cinema, Edinburgh. Stayed overnight at the Roman Camp Hotel, Callander, Perthshire.
    An interview with BBC Radio Scotland was broadcast on *Scottish News*.

April 30
The group was interviewed in the afternoon by BBC Scotland for the news programme *Six Ten*, then they recorded an interview at the Theatre Royal, Glasgow for STV's *Roundabout* programme.
    That evening they played two sets at the Odeon Cinema, Glasgow.

May 1
The Beatles were driven to the BBC's Paris Studio in the West End of London to record their third *From Us To You* bank holiday special for the BBC Light Programme, introduced by Alan Freeman. They played: 'I Saw Her Standing There', 'Kansas City'/'Hey, Hey, Hey, Hey', 'I Forgot To Remember To Forget', 'You Can't Do That', 'Sure To Fall (In Love With You)', 'Can't Buy Me Love', 'Matchbox' and 'Honey Don't'.

May 2

John and Cynthia, George and Patti flew to Honolulu on holiday but despite the fact that they had booked their flights and hotel reservations under pseudonyms, the pressure from the press was relentless and they were forced to leave. They flew on to Papeeti, in Tahiti. A reporter asked John, "Why are you leaving Hawaii so soon?" John snapped back at him, "Why didn't you leave us alone? How would you like a microphone always stuck in your face when you are on holiday?" George was asked, "How long will you stay in Tahiti?" to which he replied, "An hour."

Paul and Jane, Ringo and Maureen, took a holiday in St Thomas, Virgin Islands. They also travelled under aliases: Paul was Mr Manning, Jane was Miss Ashcroft, Ringo was Mr Stone and Maureen Miss Cockroft. They left from Luton Airport and flew to Paris. From there they flew to Lisbon, where they spent the night at the Ritz Hotel.

An exhibition of Stuart Sutcliffe's paintings opened at the Walker Art Gallery in Liverpool.

May 3

From Lisbon, Paul and Jane, Ringo and Maureen, flew to Puerto Rico and from there to the Virgin Islands – a convoluted route designed to avoid the press. In St Thomas, they hired a yacht, complete with crew: Captain Bolyard and his wife Peggy.

Paul: "Fantastic scenery in those islands – we really felt we were in another world. I remember taking the dinghy out to do some spear fishing. I had this clumsy old spear with me – honestly, it was big enough to catch whales. So I dove – or is it dived? – off the boat and started hunting around for fish. There were lots of little fish kicking around down below, but suddenly I saw some barracudas. Miniature sharks. Nasty fellows those! You can annoy other fish but barracudas are NOT for stirring. They're for avoiding. I tried to get them to go away but it didn't work. So I ran for my life – well, swam for it, anyway! You couldn't see me for bubbles. Of course I didn't catch anything that trip."

Paul walked barefoot on the beach and got spines in his feet. He was over-confident out in the sun and got burned. They swam and collected conch shells (with the conch still inside). They went ashore at Little Dix Bay in Virgin Gorda, in the British Virgin Islands and spent the evening listening to a calypso band and having a dance. At the hotel they saw James Garner in *Boy's Night Out*.

Paul: "There was something about the atmosphere there that made me get quite keen on writing new songs in the evenings. I did a couple while I was there which we recorded when we got back, 'The Things We Said Today' and 'Always And Only' ('It's For You') . . . When you went out at night, the moon lit up everything. You could look into the water and actually see the bottom of the bay. Everything clear and cool and clean. Fab! I found myself just wanting to get some ideas down on paper for songs. All that palm beach stuff!

"After a while I decided to buy myself a cheap guitar, just to keep in practice. But I didn't take it away with me – I gave it to Peggy as a little keepsake. It would have been a bit much to take it all the way back to good ol' England."

May 5

STV broadcast the interview they made with The Beatles during their visit to Glasgow.

May 6

Rediffusion's TV Special *Around The Beatles* was screened.

May 8

The single 'One And One Is Two' by The Strangers With Mike Shannon, written by Lennon & McCartney, was released in the UK as Phillips BF 1335. The song had been rejected by Billy J. Kramer, for whom it was originally intended, as being too banal – a verdict justified when Shannon's single failed to chart.

The album *Let's Do The Twist, Hully Gully, Slop, Surf, Locomotion, Monkey* was released in the US: despite being credited to The Beatles, it only featured four songs on which they performed, three of them as support group for Tony Sheridan.

May 10
The Beatles' appearance at the *NME* Poll Winners' concert at Empire Pool, Wembley, was screened by ABC Television as the climax of a special called *Big Beat '64*.

May 11
The EP *Four By The Beatles* was released in the US as Capitol EAP 2121.
Side A: 'Roll Over Beethoven', 'All My Loving'; Side B: 'This Boy', 'Please Mister Postman'.

May 18
Paul's appearance on *A Degree Of Frost* was broadcast by BBC1.
The *From Us To You* Beatles bank holiday special was broadcast by the BBC Light Programme.

May 21
The German-language single 'Sie Liebt Dich'/'Komm, Gib Mir Deine Hand' was released in the US as Swan 4182.

May 24
The Beatles' interview with Ed Sullivan was screened along with a clip filmed for *A Hard Day's Night*, but not used in the film, of them miming to 'You Can't Do That'.

May 26
John and George returned to London from their holiday.

May 27
John and George attended Cilla Black's 21st birthday party, given by Brian Epstein at his London flat. Afterwards they went to the London Palladium to see Cilla's show.
Paul and Jane, Ringo and Maureen returned from their holiday in St Thomas, Virgin Islands.

May 29
Paul attended a Billy J. Kramer recording session to see him work on 'From A Window'.
The single 'Ain't She Sweet'/'If You Love Me Baby', the A-side by The Beatles and B-side by Tony Sheridan & The Beatles, was released in the UK as Polydor NH 52-317.
The single 'Nobody I Know' by Peter & Gordon, written by Paul McCartney, was released in the UK as Columbia DB 7292.

May 30
The Beatles gave a press conference to discuss their world tour at NEMS' London offices presided over by Derek Taylor, their new press representative.

May 31
Prince of Wales Theatre, London, with Kenny Lynch, Cliff Bennett & The Rebel Rousers, The Vernons Girls, The Lorne Gibson Trio, The Chants and The Harlems. Brian Epstein's "Pop's Alive" show. They did two sets, playing 'Can't Buy Me Love', 'All My Loving', 'This Boy', 'Roll Over Beethoven', 'Till There Was You', 'Twist And Shout' and 'Long Tall Sally'.
Before the show Ringo took delivery of a £350 Ludwig drum kit, supplied by Drum City.

June
Paul bought a steel blue Aston Martin DB5 just before leaving for their world tour.

June 1
Abbey Road. The Beatles worked on songs intended to be used on the *A Hard Day's Night* album: 'Matchbox', 'I'll Cry Instead' and 'Slow Down'. Carl Perkins, the composer of 'Matchbox', was in the studio to watch them. George had been so influenced early on by Perkins that on the Johnny Gentle tour he had called himself Carl Harrison.
The single 'Sweet Georgia Brown'/'Take Out Some Insurance On Me Baby' by Tony Sheridan & The Beatles was released in the US as Atco 6302.

June 2
Abbey Road. John's 'Any Time At All' and 'When I Get Home', and Paul's 'Things We Said Today' were recorded.

At the studio The Beatles recorded an interview with Bob Rogers for Australian television ATN 7.

Paul and Jane saw Cilla Black play the London Palladium.

June 3
Ringo collapsed during a morning photo session for *Saturday Evening Post* in Barnes and was taken to University College Hospital suffering from acute tonsillitis and pharyngitis, requiring complete rest and quiet.

JIMMY NICOL
With The Beatles due to leave on a world tour the next morning, a substitute drummer was urgently required. George Martin suggested Jimmy Nicol, who suddenly found himself a temporary member of the most famous group on Earth. The Beatles cancelled a recording session and spent the time at Abbey Road rehearsing with Jimmy Nicol instead.

Jimmy: "I was having a bit of a lie down after lunch when the phone rang. It was EMI asking if I could come down to the studio to rehearse with The Beatles. Two hours after I got there I was told to pack my bags for Denmark."

That evening, with Ringo not there, the remaining Beatles recorded demo versions of their own composition: George did 'You'll Know What To Do' (unreleased until *Beatles Anthology 1*), Paul did a demo of 'It's For You' to give to Cilla Black and John recorded 'No Reply' which he gave to Tommy Quickly for a single before The Beatles used it.

June 4
The Beatles' Austin Princess, driven by their chauffeur "Big" Bill Corbett, took John, Paul, George and Jimmy Nicol to Heathrow Airport for their flight to Denmark. They were swiftly taken aboard their plane ahead of the other passengers, and signed autographs for the captain and crew. Over 6,000 fans were waiting in Copenhagen airport, with most of the yelling coming from boys rather than girls. Fans attempted to storm the doors of the Royal Hotel, opposite the Tivoli Gardens, when they checked in and the crowd of 10,000 fans brought the centre of Copenhagen to a standstill. The crowds were controlled by Danish police assisted by visiting members of the British Royal Fusiliers.

They had to rehearse their repertoire for Jimmy Nicol, Ringo's stand-in, and Mal Evans introduced a new way of getting them to remember the playlist – he taped it onto their guitars.

Before the first of their two shows at the KB Hallen, they were visited by the British Ambassador. They played two packed-out houses, with 4,400 fans in each. The first set consisted of: 'I Want To Hold Your Hand', 'I Saw Her Standing There', 'You Can't Do That', 'All My Loving', 'She Loves You', 'Till There Was You', 'Roll Over Beethoven', 'Can't Buy Me Love', 'This Boy' and 'Long Tall Sally'. For the second set, and the rest of the tour, the order of the first two numbers was switched round. Ringo's 'I Wanna Be Your Man' was left out of the set. There were riotous scenes at the end of the second performance when the MC announced that The Beatles would not be coming back on stage and a potted delphinium was thrown at him.

Back at the Royal The Beatles ate smorrebrodsseddel, a sort of jam sandwich, and Paul sent Ringo a get-well cable: "Didn't think we could miss you so much. Get well soon."

June 5
They arrived at Amsterdam's Schiphol Airport at 1pm and were presented with bunches of flowers and traditional Dutch hats. After the usual press conference they went straight to Hillegom, 26 miles outside Amsterdam, to rehearse and record a television show for VARA TV at the Treslong café-restaurant. They mimed to 'Twist And Shout', 'All My Loving', 'Roll Over Beethoven', 'Long Tall Sally', 'She Loves You' and 'Can't Buy Me Love', but before they could complete the last number, they were engulfed by fans, mostly boys. Mal Evans, Derek Taylor and Neil Aspinall did their best to clear the stage

but eventually Neil signalled the group to leave. John, Paul and George ran for cover, leaving Jimmy Nicol playing along to the music.

After the concert that evening they toured Amsterdam's red-light district, the Walletjes. John: "When we hit town, we hit it, we were not pissing about. You know, there's photographs of me grovelling about, crawling about in Amsterdam on my knees, coming out of whore houses and things like that, and people saying, 'Good morning, John . . .' The police escorted me to the places because they never wanted a big scandal."

The single 'Like Dreamers Do' by The Applejacks, written by Lennon & McCartney, was released in the UK as Decca F 11916.

June 6

The Beatles made a highly publicised tour of the Amsterdam canals in one of the glass-topped tourist boats. Some fans dived into the canal and the police used very rough tactics in getting them out. All police leave was cancelled and 15,000 police were on duty for The Beatles' canal trip, watched by 50,000 fans.

The concerts were held at the Exhibition Hall in Blokker, about 36 miles from Amsterdam. They travelled there in two white Cadillacs with motorcycle outriders which, curiously, had sidecars. In between sets they managed to get a bit of rest in their dressing room but inadvertently insulted the good people of Blokker. They were expected at a civic reception at a local restaurant and a visit to a traditional Dutch village had also been laid on. No one told them and they slept peacefully while everyone waited for them to appear.

The fans were particularly boisterous, since many were boys. Paul: "Sometimes we thought they were going to get out of hand but nobody ever started any real trouble."

June 7

The 10.15am BEA flight to Hong Kong from London, Heathrow, was held up for an hour to enable The Beatles to make the connection from their flight from Amsterdam, which caused some grumbles in the British press later. The plane stopped to refuel at Zürich, Beirut, Karachi, Calcutta and Bangkok. In Beirut, police turned fire fighting foam on the hundreds of fans who invaded the runway. In Karachi Paul attempted to buy a few souvenirs at the airport but even at 2am shrieking fans appeared from nowhere and he was forced back on to the plane. They managed a 6am cup of tea in the terminal building at Calcutta with no trouble but at Bangkok about 1,000 fans, mostly in school uniforms, rampaged through the airport chanting, "Beatles come out!" They did go down the ramp to sign autographs and be kissed. John and Paul had a pillow fight on board, filmed by Australian TV cameraman Mayo Hunter and transmitted on The Seven Network shortly after the plane landed in Australia.

June 8

The Beatles arrived at Kai Tak Airport in Hong Kong and were quickly transferred to the 15th floor of the President Hotel in Kowloon, by-passing customs and immigration formalities. Paul and Neil ordered a couple of the famous 24-hour suits. That evening, tired and jet-lagged, The Beatles were expected to attend the Miss Hong Kong Pageant, held in the hotel. When they refused there were so many tears that John went down to the Convention Hall to make an appearance. He shook the contestants' hands and made a few choice remarks about the beauty of oriental girls.

George: "The best flight I remember was the one to Hong Kong. It took several hours and I remember them saying, 'Return to your seats because we're approaching Hong Kong' and I thought, 'We can't be there already.' We'd been sitting on the floor drinking and taking Preludins for about 30 hours and so it seemed like a ten-minute flight.

"On all those flights we were still on uppers and that's what helped us get through, because we'd drink a whisky and coke with anyone, even if he was the Devil, and charm the pants off him."

June 9

Princess Theatre, Kowloon, Hong Kong with The Maori Hi-Five. The Beatles played two shows, but since the Chinese promoter had charged outrageous ticket prices, not all the seats were full, and many of the thousands of fans who greeted them at the airport could not afford to see the shows. A ticket cost the equivalent of one week's pay. They did no sightseeing, thinking it might be too dangerous.

An interview record, *The Beatles' American Tour With Ed Rudy*, was released in the US.

June 11
Ringo was discharged from University College Hospital, London.

THE BEATLES' ARRIVAL IN SYDNEY
The Beatles flew to Sydney, stopping for fuel in Darwin where, at 2.35 in the morning, 400 fans stood waiting at the airport for a glimpse of the group. The Beatles went through customs and immigration and met the press. John: "You men must be from the nose-papers. Well don't blow the story up too big!" It was raining heavily and very cold when they arrived at Sydney's Mascot International Airport, despite which 2,000 fans managed to give them a damp welcome. The Beatles were paraded around the airport in an open-topped milk truck so by the time they reached the Sheridan Hotel they were soaked to the skin. A woman, soaking wet, threw her six-year-old mentally handicapped child up into the back of the truck yelling, "Catch him Paul!" Paul, drenched and unsteady as the truck bumped around the airport, managed to catch the terrified child. "May God bless you!" the woman shouted.

"He's lovely! Great!" shouted Paul. "You take him now." The woman ran after the truck until the driver saw her and slowed. She took her child and kissed it. "He's better! Oh, he's better!" she wept.

They checked into their hotel in Potts Point, Sydney. Their luggage had not yet arrived from the airport but Paul and John had enough dry clothes with them to change. George went out on the balcony to wave to fans dressed only in a bath towel wrapped around his waist.

Once they had dried off and warmed up, they launched straight into a round of interviews, press conferences, photo sessions and meetings with promoters and civic dignitaries.

Adelaide Television screened an interview with The Beatles by Ernie Sigley done in Sydney.

June 12
Ringo, accompanied by Brian Epstein, flew to Australia via San Francisco, Honolulu and Fiji. He forgot his passport and the plane was delayed. Eventually he left without it. He climbed the steps alongside actress Vivien Leigh. Brian introduced her but Ringo didn't know who she was. His passport finally arrived at the airport and was put on another plane to be given to him during his stopover in San Francisco.

THE ADELAIDE RECEPTION
The Beatles flew from Sydney to Adelaide in a chartered Ansett ANA jet, arriving at 11.57am. Police estimated that 200,000 people lined the ten miles route of their motorcade from the airport to the city centre. At least 30,000 blocked the area around the City Hall where they met Mayor Irwin, the City Council and their families who presented them with toy koala bears. John told them, "Wherever we go, anywhere in the world, this reception which Adelaide has given us will stick in our memories." Everywhere they went, they were interviewed by Adelaide DJ Bob Francis from 5DN, even on the balcony of the Town Hall. He had booked the suite next to them in the Southern Australia Hotel and had a landline installed to give his listeners hourly reports.

Centennial Hall, Adelaide, two sets with Sounds Incorporated, Johnny Devlin, Johnny Chester and The Phantoms. The compere was Alan Field. More than 50,000 applications had been made for the four concerts at this 3,000 seater hall. Their set was the same as in Denmark and Holland: 'I Saw Her Standing There', 'I Want To Hold Your Hand', 'You Can't Do That', 'All My Loving', 'She Loves You', 'Till There Was You', 'Roll Over Beethoven', 'Can't Buy Me Love', 'This Boy' and 'Long Tall Sally'.

That night, The Beatles had a private party in their hotel suite, ignoring a society extravaganza held in their honour in the Adelaide Hills.

June 13

In the afternoon Ringo arrived in San Francisco and gave a press conference at the airport while changing planes. The conference turned into chaos as reporters scrambled to get autographs, and Ringo was hurried away to board the Qantas flight to Sydney.

Four thousand fans were still camped outside the South Australia Hotel, Adelaide, when The Beatles woke up just after noon. The group held a small reception for their Fan Club organisers before the show.

Centennial Hall, Adelaide. Two sets.

The Beatles held a private party in their suite.

June 14

Ringo arrived in Sydney to the usual shrieking fans and clamouring pressmen. At the inevitable press conference, Ringo told reporters about his rings, his taste in alcohol ("I've switched from Scotch to Bourbon") and said, "I've heard you've got a bridge or something here. No one ever tells me anything, they just knock on my door and drag me out of bed to look at rivers and things. At the moment I love it all. I mean, wouldn't you, if you got off a plane to all this?" He was asked if he ever had his hair cut, to which he replied curtly: "Of course, it'd be down by my ankles if I didn't."

After 90 minutes in Sydney, Ringo and Brian Epstein flew on to Melbourne where the crowd at the airport was already large, waiting to greet the other members of the group due to arrive five hours later. When Brian and Ringo arrived at the Southern Cross Hotel, a crowd of 3,000 fans were already gathered outside. Police Inspector Mike Patterson decided to make a run for it and hoisted Ringo onto his immense shoulders and charged into the crowd. Unfortunately, he tripped over The Beatles' own PR woman and pitched Ringo into the waiting arms of the crowd. Patterson quickly pulled him free and got him into the hotel but he was as white as a sheet. His first words were: "Give us a drink. That was the roughest ride I've ever had." He went straight to his room to lie down.

The other Beatles left their hotel at 12.15pm and flew from Adelaide to Melbourne in their chartered Ansett ANA Fokker Friendship. They arrived at Essendon Airport to a frenzied welcome from a crowd of 5,000. The crowd outside the hotel was so large that army and navy units had been called in as reinforcements when steel barriers were knocked down and the casualties began to mount up. Their route into the city was lined by 20,000 fans, most of whom moved on to the hotel which was under a state of siege. Protected by 12 motorcycle outriders, the group neared their hotel at 4pm and were driven into a garage entrance while a dummy police car with siren blaring pulled up at the hotel's front door as a diversion. In front of the hotel, 300 police and 100 military battled with the crowd, cars were crushed, people broke bones, fell from trees and more than 150 girls fainted. Fifty people, many of them adults, were taken to hospital with injuries sustained in the crush. Scores of girls had their sweaters torn off and many lost their shoes.

To relieve the crush, The Beatles were asked to show themselves, and all five appeared on the first floor balcony. The roar of the crowd was like that at a Nuremburg rally, prompting John to give them a Nazi salute and shout 'Sieg Heil', holding his finger to his upper lip as a moustache.

Once The Beatles had been properly reunited there was a press conference with all five of them, after which Jimmy Nicol's services were no longer needed. Jimmy: "The boys were very kind but I felt like an intruder. They accepted me, but you can't just get into a group like that – they have their own atmosphere, their own sense of humour. It's a little clique and outsiders just can't break in." The Beatles celebrated their reunion with a party with local girls until 4am. Jimmy Nicol was not present.

June 15

Jimmy Nicol slipped out of The Beatles' Melbourne hotel on Bourke Street at 8am in the morning accompanied by Brian Epstein to drive to the airport, "after 12 fabulous days with the world at my feet". Jimmy didn't say goodbye to The Beatles, who were sleeping off their all-night party. Jimmy: "I don't think I should disturb them." At the airport Brian paid him his agreed fee of £500 and gave him a gold watch, engraved, "To Jimmy, with appreciation and gratitude – Brian Epstein and The Beatles."

EMI held a reception for the group at the Epsilon Room of the hotel, where the wrath of a furious John Lennon was directed on EMI executives when John saw that EMI had designed a different sleeve for *With The Beatles* for Australia. (Australian union rules meant that all album sleeve artwork had to be re-photographed and made up. The *With The Beatles* sleeve would have lost too much detail if subjected to this absurd treatment so they made a different one. John was not in the mood to listen to the convoluted explanation.)

Festival Hall, Melbourne, two sets, after which they attended a private party given by Melbourne socialites in the rich suburb of Toorak.

The single 'Nobody I Know' by Peter & Gordon, written by Paul McCartney, was released in the US as Capitol 5211.

A recording of one of their shows on the 12th was broadcast by 5DN as *Beatles Show*.

June 16
The Beatles attended a civic reception at Melbourne Town Hall. Police closed several streets as 15,000 fans took the day off school to catch a glimpse of the group on the Town Hall balcony. They arrived half an hour late because the ticker tape reception slowed their car down. Mayor Leo Curtis had foolishly given tickets for the reception to any fan who wrote in and the reception, planned for 150 people, had swelled to 350. Ringo was asked to speak and gave them a classic Ringo line: "I wish you'd had this reception a little earlier instead of dragging me out of bed at this early hour." (It was 1.15pm.) The Mayor then asked for autographs, prompting a melée as fans and dignitaries scrambled to touch the group. Ringo demanded that they leave immediately and the Mayor took them to his wife's chambers on the second floor.

Away from the crowds, The Beatles relaxed and sat around listening to a university student play the didgeridoo and joining the Curtis family in a sing-song around the piano which Paul played. They stayed half an hour longer than planned and the event was described by Brian Epstein afterwards as "the most happy, informal moment since the tour began." The press, however, thought The Beatles had stormed out of the reception and ran headlines like: "Beatles Walk Out! Anger At Rude Guests."

Festival Hall, Melbourne, two sets.

June 17
George managed to get out for an afternoon's motoring in an MG in the Dandenong Mountains with tour organiser Lloyd Ravenscroft. Meanwhile, John, Paul and Ringo had a hairdresser come in to cut their hair.

Festival Hall, Melbourne, two sets. Channel Nine filmed the final concert for a TV show: *The Beatles Sing For Shell* (the oil company).

June 18
The Beatles flew into Sydney at 11.40am, where a relatively small crowd of 1,200 fans were waiting for them, guarded by 300 police. They were rapidly transferred to their old suite in the Chevron Hotel before the usual press conference where Ringo got in a few good lines.

Reporter: "I'm from Perth, Western Australia."

Ringo: "Are you bragging or complaining?"

Same Reporter: "I have flown 2,000 miles to record this interview."

Ringo: "Gee, your arms must be tired."

Sydney Stadium, Sydney, NSW. The jelly baby throwing habit, the result of an ill-considered publicity statement, really got out of hand in Australia. George: "Wherever we've been since then – America, Europe and now Australia, that stupid story has gone ahead with the result that we get jelly babies chucked at us till we're really fed up."

Paul stopped the show twice to ask the audience, "Please don't throw those sweets at us. They get in our eyes." Each time his request was met by screams and another hail of jelly babies. Paul shrugged his shoulders, "Well, I asked you, anyway." Afterwards they spoke about it to the press. Paul: "I keep asking them not to chuck those damned things, but they don't seem to have the sense to realise we hate being the target for sweets coming like bullets from all directions. How can we concentrate on our jobs on the stage when we are having all the time to keep ducking to avoid sweets, streamers and the other stuff they keep throwing at us?"

John: "It's ridiculous. They even throw miniature koala bears and gift-wrapped packages while we are going round on the revolving stage. We haven't a chance to get out of the way."

Ringo: "It's all right for you lot. You can jump aside and dodge them, but I'm stuck at the drums and can't move, so they all seem to hit me."

Despite that, The Beatles liked the audience. George: "We can't hear ourselves singing, so how can they hear us? There's never a pause in their screaming. They're great!"

It was Paul's 22nd birthday and his principal guests were 17 beautiful girls, winners of the *Daily Mirror* "Why I Would Like to be a Guest at a Beatle's Birthday Party" competition. At 3am Ringo passed out drunk, but the party was carefully monitored and nothing untoward occurred.

John: "You know, The Beatles' tours were like Fellini's *Satyricon*. I mean, we had that image, but man, our tours were like something else. If you could get on our tours, you were in . . . Australia, what, just everywhere. Just think of *Satyricon* with four musicians going through it. Wherever we went there was always a whole scene going on. We had our four bedrooms separate from . . . tried to keep them out of our room. And Derek's and Neil's rooms were always full of fuck knows what, and policemen and everything . . . they didn't call them groupies then, they called it something else. If we couldn't get groupies, we would have whores and everything, whatever was going."

June 19
Sydney Stadium, Sydney, NSW.

John Lennon's nonsense poetry received an airing in an unlikely location, as Conservative MP Charles Curran read extracts from his work during a debate on education standards in the House Of Commons. Assuming that Lennon's wordplay was evidence of a poor education, Curran noted: "He has a feeling for words and story telling, and yet he is in a state of pathetic near literacy." Another Conservative MP, Norman Miscampbell, jumped to Lennon's defence, perhaps mindful of the possible electoral damage of a public assault on Britain's most popular entertainers.

The EP *Long Tall Sally* was released in the UK as Parlophone GEP 8913. Side A: 'Long Tall Sally', 'I Call Your Name'; Side B: 'Slow Down', 'Matchbox'.

LONG TALL SALLY
In just one magnificent take, with no overdubs, The Beatles recorded the finest rock'n'roll performance of their career – seizing Little Richard's 1956 classic and remaking it as their own. George Harrison's solo was spot-on first time, and George Martin duplicated Richard's piano-thumping. What clinched the track, though, was Paul McCartney's throat-searing lead vocal, his finest uptempo performance ever in a recording studio. The song became the title track of (appropriately enough) the group's best-ever EP.

I CALL YOUR NAME
Already recorded by fellow Brian Epstein protégé Billy J. Kramer the previous year, this Lennon song was forcibly reclaimed by its composer on the Long Tall Sally *EP. John's dogmatic vocals suggested he didn't care whether the girl in question answered his call or not, in stark contrast to Kramer's more submissive delivery. As Lennon remarked in 1980, the group approached the guitar solo as a ska band, loping slightly uncomfortably through the Jamaican rhythm before returning to more solid ground for the next verse.*

SLOW DOWN
Though it didn't quite match the sheer excitement of 'Long Tall Sally', Lennon's ultra-confident handling of the Larry Williams rocker (the first of three the band recorded) ran it close. Aided by George Martin's piano, The Beatles cruised through this 12-bar, though it was the rasp in Lennon's voice that pushed it beyond the reach of their British beat group rivals.

MATCHBOX
The Carl Perkins songbook was raided for the first time on the final Long Tall Sally *EP number. Ringo Starr was showcased on this rockabilly tune, based on lyrical ideas that had been circulating the blues world for decades. The song's composer was on hand to witness the recording, which (alongside the two Perkins covers on 'Beatles For Sale') kept him in royalties for decades to come.*

June 20

Sydney Stadium, Sydney, NSW.

Someone in the audience threw an egg, hitting John on the foot. He looked in the direction it came from and yelled, "What d'you think I am, a salad?" No more eggs were thrown.

The Beatles did a telephone interview with Colin Hamilton for the BBC Light Programme show *Roundabout*.

June 21

As they were packing to leave, a tapping on the windows of suite 801 revealed 20-year-old Peter Roberts, an "exile" from Netherton, Liverpool, who had scaled the drainpipes of the hotel in total darkness to say hello. John: "I knew before he opened his mouth where he was from because I knew nobody else would be climbing up eight floors . . . I gave him a drink because he deserved one and then I took him around to see the others."

Ten thousand fans saw them off at the airport, the biggest turn-out yet. They flew the 1,500 miles to Auckland, New Zealand, where 7,000 screaming fans were waiting at the airport and they received a "traditional" welcome of nose-rubbing kisses from laughing Maori women in native costume. John: "My wife'll kill me when she hears about this!" Three thousand more fans watched them drive to the Hotel St George where they were smuggled in through a bottle shop because of the crush of fans.

June 22

Town Hall, Wellington, North Island, NZ. The sound system was so primitive that as they came off stage, John screamed, "What the fucking hell is going on here?" It turned out that the PA operator had never turned his speakers up before and was scared to do so. The second house was considerably louder but the sound quality was still bad. Paul: "We have sung through worse mics, but not very often; usually during the early days; we expected better here."

Ringo was now recovered sufficiently for his vocal spot, 'Boys', to be put back on the set list.

After the concert, Mal Evans had to get out of the car and use his muscle to clear a way through to the hotel because the local police thought that two men would be enough to control a crowd of 5,000 fans. Auckland Chief Constable, Superintendent Quinn, refused a police escort for The Beatles between their hotel and the Town Hall because: "We provide such escorts only for royalty and other important visitors". This smug attitude by the authorities caused problems throughout New Zealand.

A female fan broke into The Beatles' Wellington hotel, but slashed her wrists in Mal Evans' room when she was unable to talk her way into the group's suites. Police had to break down the locked door to take her to a local hospital.

June 23

Town Hall, Wellington, North Island, NZ.

June 24

Town Hall, Auckland, North Island, NZ.

The Beatles' tour encountered more hostility from the smug local establishment in Auckland. The Inspector of Police, ignoring the wishes of the public he was paid to serve, greeted the tour management with, "We didn't want 'em here and I don't know why you brought 'em." Because so few police were on duty, The Beatles' Cadillac was stuck 30 feet from the Royal Continental Hotel where they were staying. Mal, Neil and Lloyd Ravenscroft had to lock The Beatles in the car and push it to the garage door, fighting off fans all the way. It took 20 minutes and about 200 fans managed to get into the garage with them. They then had to throw the fans out one by one before The Beatles could go to their rooms.

John later told an American interviewer: "It was a bit rough. I thought definitely a big clump of my hair had gone. I don't mean just a bit. They'd put about three policemen on for three or four thousand kids and they refused to put more on. 'We've had all sorts over 'ere, we've seen them all,' they said, and they had seen them all as we went crashing to the ground." After this incident John lost his temper and refused to play any more unless more police were provided.

June 25
Town Hall, Auckland, North Island, NZ.

Mayor Robinson hosted a civic welcome for the group, against vocal opposition from other members of the council. A crowd of 7,000 fans gathered outside the Town Hall to see The Beatles rub noses with three Maori girls in native costumes and pretend to attack Mayor Robinson with Maori pois.

June 26
Town Hall, Dunedin, South Island, NZ.

The local authorities ignored the advice from the tour managers and only allocated three policemen to control the thousands of fans who gathered outside the New City Hotel. When they arrived the police had only left a three-foot hole in their barrier outside the hotel through which The Beatles literally had to fight their way as fans easily overwhelmed the three Dunedin constables. Paul's face was scratched and John lost some of his hair as Mal and Neil fought back the crowd to get the group through. John Lennon's expressed opinion of the Dunedin local authorities was rich and colourful.

That night John, Ringo and DJ Bob Rogers played a joke on Paul involving a nude girl which Paul did not find at all amusing.

The album *A Hard Day's Night (Original Soundtrack Album)* was released in the US as United Artists UAS 6366. Side A: 'A Hard Day's Night', 'Tell Me Why', 'I'll Cry Instead', 'I Should Have Known Better' (by George Martin & Orchestra), 'I'm Happy Just To Dance With You', 'And I Love Her' (by George Martin & Orchestra); Side B: 'I Should Have Known Better', 'If I Fell', 'And I Love Her', 'Ringo's Theme (This Boy)' (by George Martin & Orchestra), 'Can't Buy Me Love', 'A Hard Day's Night' (by George Martin & Orchestra).

June 27
Majestic Theatre, Christchurch, South Island, NZ.

A crowd of 5,000 fans turned out to watch the group land and drive to the Clarendon Hotel in the city centre. En route a 13-year-old girl threw herself at their limousine, bouncing off the bonnet onto the road. She got what she wanted because the group took her into the hotel and gave her a cup of coffee.

The BBC Light Programme show *Roundabout* broadcast the telephone interview done with The Beatles in Sydney.

June 28
The group flew to Brisbane, via Auckland and Sydney. They arrived in Sydney on a TEAL flight at 9.35pm. A crowd of 4,000 fans watched them walk a short distance to their chartered Ansett ANA Fokker Friendship aircraft and half an hour later they were gone.

June 29
The Beatles arrived in Brisbane just after midnight where 8,000 fans were waiting. The group were driven past the crowd in an open-topped truck but hiding in the crowd was a vocal core of Beatles haters who pelted the group with eggs, tomatoes and bits of wood. The group were taken quickly to Lennon's Hotel where they declared, "No more unscheduled appearances. For as long as we're in Brisbane, it's the hotel and hall for us."

Festival Hall, Brisbane. The two houses of 5,500 were sold out but once again a gang of egg throwers had managed to get in and marred the concert for others. The Beatles made a few well-known gestures to the crowd but played on. That night The Beatles and 20 Brisbane girls partied till the early hours, dancing to Motown records.

June 30
Festival Hall, Brisbane.

The Beatles secretly left the hotel in two hire cars and spent the day on the Gold Coast, mostly on the huge sweep of white sand between Broadbeach and Surfers' Paradise. As he had been for several days, John was accompanied by a young Japanese fan, with whom he had struck up an intense rapport.

July
Paul bought his father a five-bedroom house called "Rembrandt" on the Wirral, 15 miles from Liverpool. Paul's brother Michael moved in with his father.

July 1
Early in the morning a Rolls Royce delivered the group to Brisbane airport to catch a plane for Sydney. Then began the long Qantas-V flight home, refuelling in Singapore – where Paul and Ringo disembarked to wave to the 600 waiting fans – and Frankfurt.
Australian Channel Nine broadcast *The Beatles Sing For Shell*.

July 2
The Beatles arrived at Heathrow Airport, London, at 11.10am.
Paul played piano and John watched when Cilla Black recorded 'It's For You' at Abbey Road. Cilla: "Paul was at the recording session when I made 'Anyone Who Had A Heart'. He said that he liked the composition and he and John would try to produce something similar. Well they came up with this new number, but for my money it's nothing like the 'Anyone' composition. That was some session we had when I made the new recording. John and Paul joined me, and George Martin. We made one track and then everyone had a go at suggesting how they thought it should be recorded. And everyone had different ideas. George said it should be one way, Paul and John another and I just added my suggestions while they were thinking of what else they could do with the composition."

July 3
Former Beatles drummer Pete Best released his single, 'I'm Gonna Knock On Your Door'.

July 6
The premiere of *A Hard Day's Night*. Piccadilly Circus was closed for traffic as Princess Margaret, Lord Snowdon, The Beatles, their wives and girlfriends attended the world premiere of the film at the London Pavilion. The premiere was a charity event, in support of the Docklands Settlements and the Variety Club Heart Fund, with top seats costing fifteen guineas (£15.75). 12,000 fans filled Piccadilly Circus, which had been closed to traffic for the occasion, for a glimpse of The Beatles.
Afterwards, The Beatles and their guests, including the royal party and members of The Rolling Stones, adjourned to the Dorchester Hotel for a champagne supper party. The group ended the night at the Ad Lib Club, staying there long enough to read the reviews of *A Hard Day's Night* in the first editions of the morning papers.
John: "*A Hard Day's Night* was sort of interesting, since it was the first time. We loathed the script because it was somebody trying to write like we were in real life. In retrospect Alun Owen didn't do a bad job, but at the time we were self-conscious about the dialogue. It felt unreal."
The single 'Like Dreamers Do' by The Applejacks, written by Lennon & McCartney, was released in the US as London 9681.
The single 'Ain't She Sweet'/'Nobody's Child' by The Beatles on the A-side and Tony Sheridan & The Beatles on the B-side was released in the US as Atco 6308.

July 7
Lime Grove Studios, London. The Beatles mimed 'A Hard Day's Night', 'Things We Said Today' and 'Long Tall Sally' for BBC TV's *Top Of The Pops*.
After this, they went to Rediffusion's studios at Television House to record an interview about the film, which was broadcast that evening on Granada Television's *Scene At 6.30*.
John was interviewed by journalist Chris Hutchins about *A Hard Day's Night* for the BBC Light Programme's *The Teen Scene*.
Brian Epstein bought Ringo a pair of diamond cufflinks for his birthday. Ringo spent the evening celebrating with his parents.
Paul presented his father with a £1,200 racehorse, Drake's Drum, for Jim's 62nd birthday. His father unwrapped a parcel containing a picture of the horse, and said, "That's very nice, son, but what do I need a picture of a horse for?" "That's not the

present! I bought you the bloody horse!" It placed second in its first race. Paul remarked, "There you are, I told you my dad was the best jockey in the business."

July 8

BBC TV's *Top Of The Pops* aired The Beatles' performances of the A- and B-sides of their new single taped the previous day.

July 10

3,000 screaming fans were waiting in the bright sunshine at Speke Airport when The Beatles landed to attend the Northern premiere of *A Hard Day's Night* and appear as guests of honour at a civic reception. After struggling through the crowd of photographers, The Beatles held a brief press conference. They were then driven to the Town Hall in a police cavalcade led by motorcycle police, while an estimated 200,000 people (a quarter of the entire population of Liverpool) lined the route, restrained by hundreds of police officers. On a dozen occasions the screaming girls managed to break through the police cordons and bring their motorcade to a screeching halt.

They arrived at the Town Hall at 6.55pm, 25 minutes behind schedule, where an estimated 20,000 fans had gathered to see them. They were welcomed by Elizabeth "Bessie" Braddock, MP for Liverpool's Exchange Division, wearing her Cavern Club membership badge. They all hugged her and she said, "It's great to see you love." After a meal they made an appearance on the balcony overlooking Castle Street to be greeted by screaming crowds and the Liverpool City Police Band playing 'Can't Buy Me Love'. John enlivened proceedings by making a series of Hitler salutes to the crowd.

The Lord Mayor, Alderman Louis Caplan, addressed the 714 guests from the Minstrel Gallery of the Town Hall's large ballroom with The Beatles and a large group of their relatives at his side: 14 members of the Lennon family and 16 from Ringo's. He said how proud Liverpool was of the group and what great ambassadors they were for the city. Each Beatle then said, "Hello" from the gallery, as they were presented with the keys to the city.

They had not expected such a warm reception. John was quoted in the *Liverpool Echo* as saying, "It beats our reception at Adelaide – our previous best – by miles. The boys are flabbergasted. This is the proudest moment of our lives. We never expected so many people would turn out. We thought there would only be a few people standing on the odd street corner.

"What really delighted us more than anything is that everybody here, from the top nobs down to the humblest Scouser, has been so nice and sung praise after praise, which I'm sure we really don't deserve."

Everyone was there, from Lord and Lady Derby and the Bishop of Liverpool to members of the local rock bands and friends from the Cavern days. Everyone needed a pass as the Liverpool police put on the biggest security operation in their history.

Shortly before 9pm they left in an Austin Princess limousine for the Odeon Cinema for the charity premiere of *A Hard Day's Night*. The *Echo* reported a battle by police to clear the milling crowds sufficiently for them to get away and, "even when they did get through, thousands flocked behind them like the tail of a comet".

At the Odeon the Liverpool City Police Band struck up the 'Z-Cars Theme', a popular television police show set in Liverpool, following it with a rather more restrained medley of Beatles hits. Compere David Jacobs introduced The Beatles and everyone went wild. The *Echo* said, "The Odeon Cinema last night had more of the atmosphere of a big family show than a glittering premiere. It was an occasion when the distinguished relatives in the dress circle joined their younger brethren in the stalls for a night out with the city's favourite sons."

After the premiere, the group returned by limousine to Speke Airport, for another round of civic ceremonies, and finally the return flight to London.

BBC1's *Look North* news programme broadcast part of their press conference and an interview with the group conducted by Gerald Harrison.

Granada Television's *Scene At 6.30* broadcast their own interview, done at the airport, as well as film of the balcony ceremony.

John: "We're satisfied with the film, but we're not self-satisfied. There's a lot which is embarrassing for us. The first bit is a drag as far as we're concerned, because that was the first sort of acting we had done, and it looks like it.

"But we enjoyed writing the music for the film, though we've always been the kind of people who didn't like musicals because they were embarrassing when all of a sudden a song started. We all tried to get away from that in our film, but we could only do it to an extent. That's probably why George doesn't want any numbers in the next film. But there will be numbers in the next film, because that's what we sell."

AN UNPLEASANT INCIDENT

The only sour note to the day came from the uncle of Anita Cochrane, who plastered Liverpool with 30,000 leaflets recounting his niece's affair with Paul and its outcome. Anita, an 18-year-old Beatles fan, discovered that she was pregnant after partying with Paul at Stuart Sutcliffe's flat in Gambier Terrace. Unable to contact him by registered letters and telegrams, she eventually retained a lawyer who threatened legal action. Allegedly, it was only then that NEMS responded, offering her £5 a week maintenance. Brian Epstein is said to have intervened personally and offered £5,000 in exchange for renouncing all claims on Paul (published figures vary depending on source). The agreement said that Anita must never bring Paul to court or say or imply that he was the father of her child, Philip Paul Cochrane, nor must she ever reveal the terms of the agreement. All seemed to be well until today's civic reception for The Beatles when her outraged uncle intervened.

The single 'A Hard Day's Night'/'Things We Said Today' was released in the UK as Parlophone R 5160.
   The album *A Hard Day's Night* was released in the UK as Parlophone PCS 3058. Side A: 'A Hard Day's Night', 'I Should Have Known Better', 'If I Fell', 'I'm Happy Just To Dance With You', 'And I Love Her', 'Tell Me Why', 'Can't Buy Me Love'; Side B: Anytime At All', 'I'll Cry Instead', 'Things We Said Today', 'When I Get Home', 'You Can't Do That', 'I'll Be Back'.
   The single 'I'll Keep You Satisfied' by Billy J. Kramer & The Dakotas, written by Lennon & McCartney, was released in the US as Imperial 66048.
   The Beatles' first appearance on *The Ed Sullivan Show* was repeated by CBS-TV.

A HARD DAY'S NIGHT

The transition from pop stars to film actors was already a well-trodden route by 1964. The pop business hadn't yet cottoned on to the potential riches of international merchandising, but a hasty and cheap black-and-white movie was the next best thing. It also enabled The Beatles to be seen in towns and countries that they had no intention of visiting in person. It's probably not a coincidence that The Beatles staged only one further lengthy UK tour after the *A Hard Day's Night* film was released.
   Although the film grossed millions of dollars in America, it was originally conceived as an entirely British phenomenon. The Beatles had been approached in the autumn of 1963, at which stage their fame had scarcely spread beyond their native land. Hence the low budget and black-and-white film: if United Artists had realised the movie would ever be shown in America, they would almost certainly have ensured it was made in colour.
   "We were a bit infuriated by the glibness of it and the shittiness of the dialogue," John Lennon complained in 1970. But Alun Owen's script was a work of remarkable realism by the previous standards of British pop films. The Beatles played caricatures of themselves, in caricatures of their everyday situations – on the road, in concert, and rehearsing for a TV show. Several scenes in the movie featured the group's earlier hits, but the contract called for the band to supply director Dick Lester with seven new songs; and EMI soon made the decision to release a soundtrack album, which would feature the film songs alongside another batch of new recordings.
   Returning from their first visit to the States, The Beatles were faced with a ridiculously tight schedule. They had less than two weeks to write and record the songs for the film; then, during the subsequent shooting, they had to knock off the remaining numbers for the album. If ever there was an excuse for recording cover versions, this was it: instead, for the first and only time in The Beatles' career, John Lennon and Paul McCartney wrote the entire album between them. "Between them" was hardly correct, in fact, as Lennon

contributed no fewer than ten of the thirteen tracks, dominating the LP more than any one Beatle was ever allowed to do thereafter.

Once again, The Beatles okayed the mono mix of the album, and then left George Martin to prepare a hasty stereo version; and once again, Martin utilised the mono tracks on EMI's CD release.

A HARD DAY'S NIGHT

Ringo Starr, recalling some wordplay of John Lennon's, inadvertently christened The Beatles' first film, saving it from the fate of going into history as Beatlemania. Once the title was fixed, The Beatles had to provide a song to match, and quickly: within a week, Lennon (with help from McCartney on the middle section) had prepared this sturdy piece of songwriting-to-order.

The unforgettable opening – George Harrison striking a G suspended 4th chord on his 12-string Rickenbacker – took a few takes to get right, but eventually made this record one of the few that can be recognised by its opening two seconds alone.

For the first time, Lennon and McCartney settled into the pattern they would follow for the rest of the group's lifetime, each man singing the section of the song he'd written. Fans had an early chance to distinguish between McCartney's in-born lyrical optimism, and Lennon's grudging cynicism. And there was another revolution in the air, as The Beatles discovered the joys of fading their singles out, rather than ending in a single climactic chord. After double-tracking and overdubbing, fade-outs became the next favourite toy in The Beatles' studio cupboard.

I SHOULD HAVE KNOWN BETTER

Even when he was functioning as an admitted hack writer, composing Beatles songs to a tight deadline, the John Lennon of 1964 succeeded effortlessly in concocting memorable melody lines. 'I Should Have Known Better' was built around the simplest of two-chord rhythms, with puffing harmonica to match, but it had an effervescence that touched everything The Beatles recorded in the heady spring of 1964.

IF I FELL

In 1964, no one had yet noticed any split in songwriting styles between Lennon and McCartney, so this delicate and melodic ballad was greeted as just another Beatles song. Only in retrospect was it seen as early proof that there was more to John Lennon's armoury than rock'n'roll, acid imagery and cynical wit. In structural terms, this was by far the most complex song John had written to date, and its terrifyingly high harmony line briefly floored McCartney, whose voice cracked under the strain on the mix released on the stereo album. On the CD and the mono LP, however, Paul walked the tightrope without missing a note.

I'M HAPPY JUST TO DANCE WITH YOU

John Lennon wrote this song, but thought so little of it that he passed it over for George Harrison to sing – The Beatles' lead guitarist having failed to meet with group approval for any of his latest efforts at songwriting. Lennon would no doubt have regarded the song's theme as too tame for his more rugged image – though he had just reached the top of the American charts by saying he wanted to hold his girl's hand – but Harrison's charmingly naïve vocal delivery caught the mood of the song perfectly. As usual, The Beatles patched up the thinnest of material with a superlatively commercial arrangement.

AND I LOVE HER

Even under pressure, The Beatles refused to settle for anything but the best when recording this McCartney love song for his girlfriend of the time, actress Jane Asher. For three days running, they attempted different arrangements, eventually nailing it in the same three-hour session in which they cut 'Tell Me Why'. Simple, evocative and gentler than any Lennon/McCartney song they'd recorded up to that point, 'And I Love Her' was treated to a predominantly acoustic arrangement.

Trivia note: several different edits of this song were released in different parts of the world, the variations coming in the number of times the closing guitar riff was repeated.

TELL ME WHY

Another delicious piece of hackwork, 'Tell Me Why' was almost Beatles by numbers – a beefy chorus, a wonderfully cool Lennon vocal, even a self-mocking falsetto section towards the end, and all wrapped up in a fraction over two minutes.

CAN'T BUY ME LOVE
See March 20.

ANY TIME AT ALL
Tight for time, as they were at every session in 1964, The Beatles began recording this song before John Lennon had finished writing it. Thankfully, they eventually realised the fact, though not before they'd attempted seven takes. Lennon added a gentle middle section to this otherwise tough rocker during their afternoon tea-break, and the song was in the can well before bedtime.

I'LL CRY INSTEAD
Though The Beatles' sound is commonly regarded as a mix of American rock'n'roll, pop and R&B, country music became a vital part of the equation from 1964. Under a constant barrage of encouragement from Ringo Starr, the rest of the group started listening to records by Buck Owens, George Jones and other Nashville stars, and the influence began to filter through to the songwriting – particularly Lennon's.

For such a simple song, 'I'll Cry Instead' proved tough to record. Eventually The Beatles gave up trying to perform it live, and divided it into two sections, which George Martin edited together as the final record. Its divided nature explains why it was so easy for the song to be artificially extended for the US album release.

'I'll Cry Instead' inadvertently spawned a genre of Beatles and solo songs: lyrics which had Lennon, usually the masterful romantic hero, sitting head in hands, indulging himself in an ocean of self-pity. For much of the last decade of his life, this pose of guilt and sorrow became something of a straitjacket around his songwriting.

THINGS WE SAID TODAY
McCartney's contributions to A Hard Day's Night *may have been few in number, but they were impressively strong. Like John, Paul was experimenting with writing around minor chords, and quickly realised that they lent themselves to lyrics that were reflective rather than celebratory. John took the formula a stage further by writing almost all his songs for this album in the key of G.*

WHEN I GET HOME
Like much of Lennon's work on this album, 'When I Get Home' doesn't bear too much critical examination – except that from a hastily assembled song, The Beatles were able to make a state-of-the-art pop record by 1964 standards. The track began as if in mid-performance, with a catchy vocal hook, and then romped along merrily enough for another two minutes, without ever suggesting that Lennon meant a word he was singing.

YOU CAN'T DO THAT
See March 20.

I'LL BE BACK
At the end of a record that was a brilliant collection of sometimes less than brilliant songs, John Lennon's 'I'll Be Back' harked back to the strange construction of some of his earlier efforts. Like 'Ask Me Why' and 'All I've Got To Do', it was pure Lennon, owing nothing to what was happening in the pop world around him. For the moment, he hadn't hit on the knack of combining these unsettling melodies with words that carried any emotional weight, so 'I'll Be Back' ended up another superb song about a fictional romance. But the moment of liberation wasn't far away.

July 11
The Beatles flew from Liverpool to London in the early hours of the morning to appear live on ABC TV's *Lucky Stars (Summer Spin)*. They mimed to 'A Hard Day's Night', 'Long Tall Sally', 'Things We Said Today' and 'You Can't Do That'. The appearance took place at ABC's Teddington Film Studios, and was documented by a photographer from *The Beatles Book*.

July 12
Hippodrome Theatre, Brighton, with The Shubdubs, featuring Jimmy Nicol.

On his way there, George's new E-Type Jaguar was involved in a minor road accident in the New Kings Road, Fulham. Pedestrians collected bits of the broken glass as souvenirs.

July 13
The single 'A Hard Day's Night'/'I Should Have Known Better' was released in the US as Capitol 5222.

July 14
Broadcasting House, Portland Place, London, to appear on the first edition of *Top Gear*, the BBC's new rock programme. They played 'Long Tall Sally', 'Things We Said Today', 'A Hard Day's Night', 'And I Love Her', 'I Should Have Known Better', 'If I Fell' and 'You Can't Do That'. The presenter was Brian Matthew.

Paul was interviewed by Michael Smee for the BBC Overseas Service programme *Highlight*.

July 15
John and Cynthia bought "Kenwood" in Saint George's Hill, Surrey. The mock-Tudor mansion in a private estate next to the golf course cost him £20,000, and allowed the couple to escape from their virtual imprisonment at their Kensington flat, which had been under constant siege from fans and the media.

ATV in Britain screened the documentary, *The Road To Beatlemania*.

July 16
The first edition of *Top Gear* was broadcast by the BBC Light Programme.

July 17
The Beatles recorded their fourth bank holiday special *From Us To You* for the BBC Light Programme. They played 'Long Tall Sally', 'If I Fell', 'I'm Happy Just To Dance With You', 'Things We Said Today', 'I Should Have Known Better', 'Boys', 'Kansas City'/'Hey, Hey, Hey, Hey'. John read the closing credits.

The single 'From A Window' by Billy J. Kramer & The Dakotas, written by Lennon & McCartney, was released in the UK as Parlophone R 5156.

July 18
The Beatles flew to Blackpool to spend the day rehearsing for the next day's live broadcast of Mike and Bernie Winters' *Big Night Out* from the ABC Theatre, Blackpool.

July 19
ABC Theatre, Blackpool.

The Beatles appeared in a live transmission of Mike and Bernie Winters' *Big Night Out*. They played 'A Hard Day's Night', 'And I Love Her', 'If I Fell', 'Things We Said Today' and 'Long Tall Sally' as well as participating in various sketches with Mike and Bernie.

July 20
The single 'I'll Cry Instead'/'I'm Happy Just To Dance With You' was released in the US as Capitol 5234.

The single 'And I Love Her'/'If I Fell' was released in the US as Capitol 5235.

The album *Something New* was released in the US as Capitol ST 2108. Side A: 'I'll Cry Instead', 'Things We Said Today', 'Anytime At All', 'When I Get Home', 'Slow Down', 'Matchbox'; Side B: 'Tell Me Why', 'And I Love Her', 'I'm Happy Just To Dance With You', 'If I Fell', 'Komm, Gib Mir Deine Hand'.

July 23
The Night Of A Hundred Stars, London Palladium, with Judy Garland, Sir Laurence Olivier, et al. The Beatles took part in a sketch and played a brief set for this benefit concert in aid of the Combined Theatrical Charities Appeals Council.

July 25
BBC Television Centre, Shepherd's Bush. George and Ringo each made appearances as members of the *Juke Box Jury* panel. George's edition was transmitted live that evening, while Ringo's was taped and screened the following week.

July 26
Opera House, Blackpool.

July 27
To coincide with The Beatles' brief visit to Sweden, *A Hard Day's Night* was premiered in Stockholm, complete with Swedish subtitles. The theme song from the film had also been issued as a single in Sweden, two weeks before it appeared in Britain or America.

July 28
The Beatles flew to Stockholm, Sweden, on the 11.10am flight from Heathrow Airport, London. Despite the fact that the airport was situated more than 25 miles from the centre of Stockholm, more than 3,000 fans assembled to welcome the group to Sweden.

Johanneshovs Isstadion, Stockholm, with The Kays, The Moonlighters, The Streaplers, Jimmy Justice, The Mascots and The Shanes. The group did two houses each night in the ice hockey stadium.

During one of their performances on this night, John received a minor electric shock from a stage microphone. Ringo dislodged his vocal microphone during his vocal cameo on 'I Wanna Be Your Man', forcing him to mime manfully through most of the song.

July 29
Johanneshovs Isstadion, Stockholm.

The Beatles also made a fleeting appearance on Swedish TV, discussing their future plans. John used the occasion to recite his poem 'Good Dog Nigel', to the undoubted bafflement of his Swedish audience.

July 30
The Beatles flew from Stockholm to London, arriving mid-afternoon.

July 31
The single 'It's For You' by Cilla Black, written by Lennon & McCartney, was released in the UK as Parlophone R 5162.

August 1
Ringo's appearance on *Juke Box Jury* was broadcast by BBC TV.

August 2
Gaumont Cinema, Bournemouth, with The Kinks, Mike Berry and Adrienne Poster (later known as Posta).

August 3
The BBC Light Programme broadcast The Beatles' fourth bank holiday special *From Us To You.*

A documentary, *Follow The Beatles,* filmed while they were making *A Hard Day's Night,* was screened by BBC1.

Beatles producer George Martin released a US album of instrumental interpretations of The Beatles' music, *Off The Beatle Track.*

August 7
Plans for Brian Epstein protégé Tommy Quickly to release a new Lennon/McCartney song, 'No Reply', were cancelled when The Beatles decided that they wanted to keep the tune for their own next album.

August 9
Futurist Theatre, Scarborough.

August 10
The single 'Do You Want To Know A Secret'/'Thank You Girl' was released in the US as Oldies 45 OL 149.

The single 'Please Please Me'/'From Me To You' was released in the US as Oldies 45 OL 150.

The single 'Love Me Do'/'P.S. I Love You' was released in the US as Oldies 45 OL 151.

The single 'Twist And Shout'/'There's A Place' was released in the US as Oldies 45 OL 152.

August 11
Abbey Road. The Beatles began work on what was to be the *Beatles For Sale* album. They recorded John's 'Baby's In Black'.

August 12
The film *A Hard Day's Night* opened simultaneously in 500 American cinemas.

The *New York Times*: "This is going to surprise you – it may knock you right out of your chair – but the film with those incredible chaps, The Beatles, is a whale of a comedy."

The *New York World-Telegram & Sun*: "*A Hard Day's Night* turns out to be funnier than you would expect and every bit as loud as the wildest Beatle optimist could hope."

The *New York Herald Tribune*: "It is really an egghead picture, lightly scrambled, a triumph of The Beatles and the bald."

The *New York Daily News*: "The picture adds up to a lot of fun, not only for the teenagers but for grownups as well. It's clean, wholesome entertainment."

The *New York Journal-American*: "The picture turned out to be a completely wacky, off-beat entertainment that's frequently remindful of the Marx Brothers' comedies of the '30's."

The *New York Post*: "*A Hard Day's Night* suggests a Beatle career in the movies as big as they've already been in stage and dancehall. They have the songs, the patter, and the histrionic flair. No more is needed."

The *Washington Post*: "The main thing about it is that you can't hear it because the audience sort of over-participates."

The *Washington Evening Star*: "The film appears to be a genuinely funny British comedy; though nobody may ever really know. Its stars seem agreeable personalities with a zest for spoofing themselves and their idolaters and it looks as if it might be fun if you could hear it as well as see it."

The single 'From A Window'/'I'll Be On My Way' by Billy J. Kramer & The Dakotas, written by Lennon & McCartney, was released in the US as Imperial 66051.

Ringo was interviewed by Chris Hutchins for the BBC Light Programme's *The Teen Scene*, during one of Brian Epstein's "At Home" parties at his flat in Whaddon House, William Mews. All four Beatles attended the party, alongside Judy Garland, members of The Rolling Stones, Cilla Black and Lionel Bart.

August 14
Abbey Road. The Beatles worked on 'I'm A Loser', 'Mr Moonlight' and 'Leave My Kitten Alone', which was not released until the 1995 *Anthology 1* CD.

August 16
Opera House, Blackpool.

Among the support acts were The Who, then known as The High Numbers, and The Kinks.

August 17
John invited interior designer Ken Partridge to transform the Lennons' Weybridge mansion – to the horror of Cynthia, who realised that John's elaborate plans would ensure that the couple would be living in chaos for many months to come.

August 18
The Beatles set off on their 25-date American Tour. Their Clipper took them first to Winnipeg, Canada, where 500 fans stood screaming on the airport roof as the group did a couple of *Hello America* radio interviews from the plane. The plane stopped again in Los Angeles, where there were 2,000 fans and even more interviews. Finally, at 6.24pm The Beatles touched down at San Francisco International Airport to mass hysteria from 9,000 screaming West Coast fans. The plan was for them to make a brief appearance at "Beatlesville" before being taken by limousine to the Hilton Hotel. Beatlesville was a small platform, about a mile northwest of the main airport buildings, surrounded by a cyclone fence and guarded by 180 San Mateo County Sheriffs. However, the chaos and

screaming was so intense when they arrived that The Beatles remained in their limousine and held a quick strategy conference.

Eventually they decided it was worth the risk and, after a considerable delay, they entered the compound to wave to the crowd. Ringo was the first in but his presence caused mass hysteria: thousands of girls pushed forward, some trying to scale the fence as other fans charged a barrier of parked cars but were driven back by counter-attacking deputies. No sooner had Paul, George and John mounted the stage than the deputies herded them all back to their limousine and rushed them away from the hysterical scene. The link fences were being pushed over by the sheer weight of fans, those in front crushed against the links, with only the burly police straining with all their weight to keep the fences upright.

That night, John, Ringo, Derek Taylor, Billy Preston (Little Richard's organist, whom they had met during the rock'n'roller's 1962 UK tour, and later an Apple artist) and Diana Vero, Brian Epstein's secretary, spent a few hours in a small club in Chinatown called The Rickshaw, where they met Dale Robertson, the cowboy actor.

August 19

Cow Palace, San Francisco, California, with The Bill Black Combo, The Exciters, The Righteous Brothers and Jackie DeShannon.

The group's standard set for the tour was 'Twist And Shout', 'You Can't Do That', 'All My Loving', 'She Loves You', 'Things We Said Today', 'Roll Over Beethoven', 'Can't Buy Me Love', 'If I Fell', 'I Want To Hold Your Hand', 'Boys', 'A Hard Day's Night' and 'Long Tall Sally'. Sometimes they would open with 'I Saw Her Standing There' and close with 'Twist And Shout'.

The Beatles played a total of 29 minutes. The gross was $91,670, the net take $49,800. They left behind an astonished populace, 17,130 delirious fans, 19 schoolgirls so overcome with emotion that first aid was necessary and one boy with a dislocated shoulder. The *San Francisco Examiner* reported "Although it was publicised as music, all that was heard and seen of the Mersey Sound was something like a jet engine shrieking through a summer lightning storm because of the yelling fans. It had no mercy, and afterwards everyone still capable of speech took note of a ringing in the ears which lasted for as long as The Beatles had played.

"The eerie scene of four young men with shaggy hairdos wiggling on the stage and moving their lips inaudibly was exaggerated by the flashes from a hundred cameras like sheet lightning in the Midwest."

Thousands of cameras would have been a more accurate assessment. "You can figure it this way," shouted a deputy sheriff. "That's 16,000 kids who aren't out stealing hubcaps."

The Cow Palace was nearly filled by 7pm, an hour before showtime. When The Beatles appeared the girls screamed for a solid four minutes forty-five seconds. The *San Francisco Examiner* reported: "As soon as they left, the screaming stopped abruptly." Fifty fans were hurt and two arrested, fifty more were forcibly prevented from climbing on stage. At the end of the set, The Beatles dropped their instruments on stage, ran for the waiting car and were gone before the audience knew they had finished playing. Even so, some fans managed to crowd round their car as it left the Cow Palace complex, and almost succeeded in crushing the group under the sagging car roof.

On the 15th floor of the hotel, 35 girls were rounded up all together trying to sneak past the guards. Some of the girls were dressed as maids. The Beatles did not stay to party, but flew straight to their next venue instead.

August 20

Convention Center, Las Vegas, Nevada.

At 1am The Beatles' chartered plane touched down at Old McCarran Field in Las Vegas, and they were promptly driven to the Sahara Hotel where, despite a curfew, 2,000 fans were waiting to scream a welcome. The fans were dispersed by police using dogs. They spent the morning in their penthouse suite on the 18th floor of the hotel while fans attempted to scale the walls, climb the garbage shoot and use the freight elevator. The group left for the 8,000-seater Convention Center at 2.30 for a sound check. The afternoon show opened at 4pm but it was not until 5.30 that The Beatles took the stage to the usual screams, shrieks and showers of jelly babies – plus, as Brian Epstein remembered, constant chants of "Ringo For President!"

Between the afternoon and evening concerts, local police received a telephoned bomb warning aimed at The Beatles. Their initial response was that the evening show should be cancelled, but they soon realised that the potential violence that could be inflicted by 8,000 disappointed fans outweighed the danger of a bomb explosion, and the performance went ahead as planned.

After the concert the police used brutal tactics to force the fans away from backstage when The Beatles made their exit. One reporter had her foot run over by a police motorcycle, another girl was bruised in the ribs by a cop's night-stick. The Beatles made $30,000 for their trouble. The police were concerned that underage fans would enter gambling casinos if The Beatles visited them so they were requested to stay away. The Beatles had two slot machines in their rooms, but otherwise did no gambling.

August 21
Seattle Center Coliseum, Seattle, Washington.

The group stayed at the Edgewater Inn, later to become legendary as a rock star/groupie hangout, immortalised by Frank Zappa. All four of them dropped fishing lines out of their windows but no one caught anything. At the press conference before their show, Paul criticised some of the American magazines, "that have printed some pretty terrible stories about us".

The *Seattle Post-Intelligencer* reported on the concert: "The original plan was for 16 Seattle police officers to escort the British quartet down a corridor, across 18 feet of open space and onto the stage. As The Beatles and their cortege whipped from the corridor, a phalanx of youngsters swept down a ramp from the balcony. The officers nearest the ramp pivoted like grid-iron tackles. Youngsters bounced off blue clad soldiers. Ringo, John, Paul and George were gone like gazelles, down a short tunnel toward the stage. Out of the chute like Brahma bulls, they bounced to their places as the Coliseum rose in one vast adolescent moan. Then the screams split the vaulted ceiling."

The band hit the stage at 9.25 and all 14,720 girls in the audience seemed to have brought their cameras. The auditorium was illuminated with sheet lightning from the flash bulbs. While the band was onstage, the police recruited Navy volunteers from the audience and formed them in a double chain from the stage exit to the dressing room corridor. During the performance, one female fan who had climbed high over the stage fell from her perch, landing a few feet in front of Ringo's drumkit. The Beatles played their final note, dropped their instruments, leaped to the back of the stage and out through the door. Hundreds of teenagers swept down the ramps straight into the cordon of United States Navy officers, standing with locked arms. The Beatles put their heads down and ducked their way through the narrow passage between the straining bodies and made it to the corridor mouth which the police promptly plugged after them.

The car that was to have taken The Beatles back to the hotel was so badly damaged by fans that it had to be abandoned and it was another hour before the crowds had thinned enough for the group to be spirited out of the building in an ambulance. The next day, a hotel maid discovered two 16-year-old girls hiding under the bed in a fourth floor room and another in the closet.

August 22
Empire Stadium, Vancouver, British Columbia, Canada.

The show began at 8.14 and The Beatles came on at 9.23. Despite the long show, many reporters still thought that The Beatles' 29-minute set was too short. William Littler, in a grumpy piece in the *Vancouver Sun*, said, "Seldom in Vancouver's entertainment history have so many (20,261) paid so much ($5.25 top price) for so little (27 minutes) as did the audience which screamed at The Beatles in Empire Stadium Saturday night."

Three attempts were made to smash the ten-foot high stadium gates, and it finally buckled under the strain seconds after The Beatles began their performance, but only a dozen or so fans managed to get in before police and ushers got it closed again and held it shut with their bodies. Their exit was timed to perfection. They completed 'Long Tall Sally', bowed low while unstrapping their guitars, bolted from the stage into waiting limousines and with motorcycle outriders, they were out of the stadium fewer than 30 seconds from their last note. The Beatles drove straight to the airport where they caught a plane to Los Angeles.

Thousands of teenagers left their seats and rushed the stage, crushing hundreds of young girls against the restraining fence. Dozens of girls suffered broken ribs and hundreds were treated for hysteria and shock.

August 23

The Hollywood Bowl, Hollywood, California.

18,700 people filled the Bowl, sold out four months earlier, for their concert, which was recorded for posterity by a team of engineers representing Capitol Records. Outside 600 teenagers who were unable to get tickets shrieked, shouted and pushed to get in. Police made several arrests for disturbing the peace, trespassing and destroying property. A compact car was parked alongside the stage in which the group made their getaway as the concert ended at 10pm. About 60 teenagers ran to the closest gate to see them drive off and used a photographer's car as a vantage point; the roof and bonnet of which were caved in. There was a huge traffic jam in the neighbourhood afterwards as thousands of parents converged on the Bowl to take their children home after the show. Police and firemen had set up roadblocks and closed off the whole Bowl area; local residents were given passes in order to get to their homes.

After the concert there was a private party for the movie colony in the Bel Air home of Mr & Mrs Alan Livingstone, president of Capitol Records. More than 500 attended the $25 a ticket affair which raised about $10,000 for the Haemophilia Foundation of Southern California. In the *San Fernando Valley Citizen-News*, Paul was photographed holding Rebel Lee Robinson, granddaughter of Edward G. Robinson.

Before the show, there was a press conference in which the group received five gold records and the key to California. When asked what they thought of Goldwater they gave a thumbs down sign. Dozens of teenage girls had managed to sneak into the conference and one of them asked Paul if he would like to learn to fly. It turned out her father had his own plane and she would be happy to teach him.

The Beatles stayed in a rented house at 356 St. Pierre Road, in Brown Canyon, Bel Air. That night, West Los Angeles police took more than 50 adolescents into technical custody for violating a 10pm curfew as over 400 fans milled around at the junction of Sunset Boulevard and Bel Air Road hoping to see The Beatles. St. Pierre Road itself was blocked by police. Over $5,000 worth of damage was done to shrubs and flowers by the fans and many residents turned on their sprinkler systems to try to ward off the teenagers, but to no avail.

August 24

John managed to sneak out with Derek Taylor and Neil Aspinall for a few hours' shopping, but the outing was cut short when he was recognised.

The single 'Slow Down'/ 'Matchbox' was released in the US as Capitol 5255.

August 25

Paul and George visited Burt Lancaster's house to watch a private screening of Peter Sellers' *A Shot In The Dark*. Ringo was watching a Jack Good TV show when Jayne Mansfield turned up at the doorstep. (Paul had said he would like to meet her.) John greeted her and she tugged at his hair and asked, "Is this real?"

That evening John and Jayne went to the Whiskey A-Go-Go where they were joined by George. George asked photographers to leave them alone and when one of them refused, George threw water at him. George: "I finally decided to baptise him by chucking the ice-water at the bottom of my glass over him." When no one could see, Jayne put her hand on John's thigh and scared him.

August 26

Red Rocks Amphitheater, Denver, Colorado.

Though 2,000 seats remained empty, the 7,000 fans who bought tickets created a box-office record for this open-air stadium.

August 27

Cincinnati Gardens, Cincinnati, Ohio.

The press conference before the show was more animated than usual. The *Cincinnati Enquirer* reported: "A newspaperman from Dayton, who said the four ought to be able to handle a crowd of 30,000 without police protection, was told by Lennon, 'Well, maybe you could. You're fatter than we are.' . . . Teenagers stand up and scream piercingly –

and painfully – when The Beatles appear. Why? They were asked. McCartney said none of them knew, but he had heard teenagers pay to go to their shows just to scream. 'A lot of them don't even want to listen,' he said, 'because they have got the records.'

"A reporter asked what they thought of the psychiatrist who drew an analogy between the hysteria generated by their beat and the speeches of the Nazi dictator Adolf Hitler. Lennon said abruptly, 'Tell him to shut up. He's off his head.'

"A questioner asked McCartney what he thought of columnist Walter Winchell. McCartney answered bluntly, 'He said I'm married and I'm not.' 'Maybe he wants to marry you,' Harrison suggested.

"The four answered a question admitting that the show that comes after the show is sometimes the one to see. They said they whooped it up until 4 or 5 in the morning, depending on how much sleep they need."

There were 17,000 in the audience, girls fainted and one went into convulsions. As usual, the show itself was drowned out by screaming. The *Cincinnati Enquirer* ran a headline: "Teenagers Revel In Madness: Young Fans Drop Veneer Of Civilisation For Beatles." The newspaper reported: "The estimated 115 degree temperature melted bouffant hairdos as well as inhibitions. Well groomed girls who had hoped, without really hoping, that they would attract the eye of a Beatle, began to look like Brillo pads. A priest turned around in the crowd, looked at a reporter with tears in his eyes and said, 'I don't believe it. Just look at them. Look at their faces!' A technician from a television station was trying to measure the sound with an instrument. He gave up when the instrument recorded its maximum reading and broke."

The Beatles ran from the stage, straight to their Cadillac limousines and headed to Lunken Airport where their chartered plane was waiting to take them to New York. They took off shortly after midnight.

August 28
Forest Hills Tennis Stadium, Forest Hills, New York.

When The Beatles' plane touched down at 3.02am at Kennedy Airport, 3,000 fans were waiting for them, and another few hundred were stationed outside the Delmonico Hotel, at Park Avenue and 59th Street, where they were staying, even though their hotel was supposed to be a secret. By the next morning there were thousands of fans there. The girls overturned a concrete plant tub outside the hotel and tried all manner of ingenious ways to get in: pretending they lived there and delivering fake packages. Two girls arrived dressed as nurses to tend The Beatles. Deputy Police Inspector Thomas Renaghan, chief of Manhattan North detectives said the damage wasn't too bad. "We slipped them in pretty easily. They're just four little bits of fellas. If they hadn't been dressed so crazily, we would never have known them."

As The Beatles pushed through the police barricades to reach the hotel, one fan managed to snatch Ringo's St Christopher medal from his neck. Fans stayed outside until 4am, screaming every time anyone came near any of the windows in the hotel. Many of them carried portable radios tuned in to the various Beatles stations. Police used bullhorns to ask hotel guests to stay away from the windows. The girls were restrained by police barricades erected on the other side of Park Avenue, but anyone appearing at a window caused screams and chaos as the girls spilled out into the street, disrupting the traffic. They were encouraged by radio reporters who thrust microphones in front of their faces and yelled, "Okay, let's hear it for The Beatles!"

At the press conference, heavily infiltrated with fans, a reporter said, "Some Long Island fans in the crowd outside say they are switching to The Rolling Stones because you didn't wave to them from the hotel windows." Someone in The Beatles' party mumbled, "If they want to go away for that reason, let them," but Paul responded, "The police said no. They told us to stay away from the windows, boys. After all, we can't get into trouble with the police chief."

The Beatles were asked what they thought of the "oversized roughnecks" who appeared at the airport scene the previous night. "That was us," replied Paul.

John said at the press conference: "I don't mind not being as popular as Ringo, or George or Paul because if the group is popular that's what matters." The girl who stole Ringo's medal, Angie McGowan, returned it and posed for photographs while first Ringo, then Paul, kissed her on the cheek.

The stadium's 15,983 seats were sold out and extra field seats were added at $6.50 each, a steep price in those days. The fans were kept from The Beatles by an eight-foot-high fence topped with barbed wire. The group flew to the stadium by helicopter from the Wall Street heliport.

Heavily critical of the crowd mayhem witnessed at the Forest Hills show, a reporter for the *New York Times* noted: "The Beatles have created a monster in their audience. If they have concern for anything but the money they are earning, they had better concern themselves with controlling their audiences, before this contrived hysteria reaches uncontrollable proportions."

Bob Dylan, accompanied by his road manager and journalist Al Aronowitz, came to visit the group at their hotel after the show, and turned The Beatles and Brian Epstein on to marijuana for the first time.

THE BEATLES SMOKE DOPE

By all accounts, Bob Dylan was more than a little surprised to discover that The Beatles were not already familiar with the effects of marijuana. He'd been under the impression that the bridge of 'I Wanna Hold Your Hand' closed with the line "I get high" when in reality The Beatles sang "I can't hide". When the misunderstanding was cleared up The Beatles and Brian proved keen converts. Damp towels were placed at the bottom of the doors to their suite so that the smell of burning grass didn't permeate the outer rooms. John suggested Ringo be the first to try a joint, Ringo having been elected fall guy, and Ringo went ahead. But Ringo was unfamiliar with the dope smoking etiquette of taking a few puffs from a joint and passing it on, and he smoked almost the whole of the first joint himself. More were hastily rolled and everyone enjoyed the experience. Paul was affected most profoundly and became convinced that such was the genius of his insight that his every thought and word should be written down for posterity. Mal Evans dutifully followed him around with a notebook and pen.

John: "I've never been so excited about meeting any other musician before. I suppose I'd have felt the same if it had been Elvis, but nobody else. Once we met Dylan, we fell into conversation so easily it surprised us all. Beatlemania is something Dylan can understand and relate to. His experiences have been the same, but very different. He tried to explain what his fans were like, how they acted. Then we talked about music, especially about writing lyrics, how he got started with a new song, how the ideas came. That man's a true poet. He gets inspired. It shows in the stuff he writes. You couldn't perform Dylan songs as he does on his records unless you believed in every word."

August 30

Convention Hall, Atlantic City, New Jersey.

The Beatles stayed at the Lafayette Motel in Atlantic City. At 2.15pm, in order to get through the crowds of fans, the group had to sneak out of the motel in the back of a fish truck. Six miles west of Atlantic City they transferred to the tour bus which took them straight to the Philadelphia Convention Hall.

There were 19,000 fans in the audience. Five ambulances were on hand to treat casualties among the 500 teenagers outside the auditorium, and a police sergeant collapsed from exhaustion.

Brian Epstein lowered his guard with an American reporter for the first time, naming John as "the most brilliant" of The Beatles, and adding: "Paul McCartney also qualifies as brilliant; he is extremely intelligent. Ringo Starr has blossomed tremendously. I think he will prove to have great acting ability, perhaps the greatest of the four. George Harrison is actually the most practically musical of the group."

August 31

The group spent their rest days holed up at the Lafayette Motel. Paul used the time to get through to Elvis on the phone.

Ringo: "Paul had a nice talk with him . . . Though we haven't met him, we consider ourselves good friends and appreciate what each of us is doing. El and his manager were very generous to us, showering us with presents and keepsakes. These include some very expensive silver guns and holsters which the four of us and our manager Brian received."

September
Brian Epstein bought the Liverpool pop paper, *Mersey Beat*, from its original proprietor, Bill Harry.

September 2
Convention Hall, Philadelphia, Pennsylvania, before an audience of 13,000 fans.

Before the show there was the usual press conference where 50 police, 25 VIPs and 25 reporters crowded into a meeting room near the hall.

September 3
State Fair Coliseum, Indianapolis, Indiana.

At the obligatory press conference, this one held at the State Fair Radio Building, a reporter asked The Beatles if teenagers screamed at them because they were revolting against their parents. Paul: "They've been revolting for years." John: "I've never noticed them revolting." Paul was asked if he was anti-religious. "I'm not religious, but I'm not anti-religious. I'm not an atheist; I'm agnostic. I just don't know." They were asked if they would like to be able to walk down the street without being recognised. John: "We used to do this with no money in our pockets. There's no point in it."

The Beatles spent two nights in Indianapolis in all, staying at the Speedway Motel on West 16th Street. Before the first concert, Ringo was discovered to be "missing" from The Beatles' hotel, in a strange parallel to the plot of *A Hard Day's Night*. He returned only minutes before the show was due to begin, explaining that he'd lost track of the time while driving a police car round and round a nearby race track.

The group all agreed that the shows at the Coliseum were "quite quiet" compared to other venues. They set foot on the Coliseum stage at 6.21 before an audience of 12,413 screaming fans, mostly girls. After the press conference they did an evening show, this time to 16,924 fans. Thirty girls were treated for hysteria, one fan cut his arm when he was shoved against a glass door and a girl cut her hand while climbing a fence. When The Beatles boarded their chartered plane at Weir Cook Municipal Airport, they were $85,231.93 the richer. ($1,719.02 had already been deducted for state gross income tax. There was some debate in the press as to whether The Beatles [NEMS Ltd] counted as a foreign corporation – if not, then they owed the federal government a further $42,000.)

Mrs Jeane Dixon, the psychic who forecast the assassination of President Kennedy, predicted that The Beatles' plane would crash on take-off from Indiana en route to Denver, Colorado, and that three Beatles would die and the fourth be seriously maimed. She was wrong.

September 4
Milwaukee Auditorium, Milwaukee, Wisconsin.

Both Rolf Harris and The New World Singers issued singles entitled 'Ringo For President'.

September 5
International Amphitheater, Chicago, Illinois.

There had been plans for a civic welcome and 100,000 people were expected but Special Events Director Colonel Jack Reilly cancelled the arrangements saying he did not have sufficient police to spare "for a bunch of singers". Paul commented on TV and radio, "So we shall have to go in by the back door again and the fans won't get a chance to see us or we to see them. It's a great big drag."

Nonetheless Chicago was ready for The Beatles. The Andy Frain Organisation sent ten of its ushers to The Beatles' concert the previous night in Milwaukee to scout the tactics of The Beatles' fans, and the 170 ushers and 35 usherettes were specially selected as being non-Beatles fans so that they would not succumb to the hysteria. Stationed around the auditorium were 320 Chicago cops. One of them, patrolman Anthony Dizonne, remembered the Frank Sinatra days. "This is kind of like Sinatra multiplied by 50 or 100," he observed. "These Beatles make about fifty million bucks a year and they don't even have to buy a haircut in this country."

The Beatles' plane flew into the rarely used Midway Airport an hour late. They were due at 3.40pm but by the time they arrived over 5,000 fans were waiting for them. The girls were kept behind a chain-link fence as the group were bundled into a long black limousine and roared off to the Stock Yard Inn attached to the amphitheater at 42nd Street and Halsted. The crowds outside were so thick that the group had to enter through the kitchens. The *Chicago Sun-Times* reported only one casualty at the airport, a 14-year-old girl who was treated for a cut finger.

At the concert, fans were frisked and all large signs confiscated because they would block the view for others. Jelly beans, candy kisses and anything else that the fans were likely to throw at the group were also confiscated. Despite this, Paul was hit in the face by a spent flashbulb.

After the show half a dozen fans were taken to Evangelical Hospital in various states of emotional and physical exhaustion. One girl was poked in the eye but left the ambulance to rejoin the audience.

After the show, they hurried into waiting cars and drove straight back to the airport where they flew on to Detroit. A police guard was mounted on their hotel room to prevent fans from tearing it apart for souvenirs.

September 6
Olympic Stadium, Detroit, Michigan.

Two shows in the home of Tamla Motown. The sheets used by The Beatles at the Whittier Hotel in Detroit were bought by a radio station, cut into thousands of small squares, and then sold to avid fans.

September 7
Maple Leaf Gardens, Toronto, Canada.

The Beatles flew into town in their charter Electra and parked at the old airport terminal. The first people on board were two immigration nurses who were only interested in getting the group's autographs. They were followed by an immigration officer who had the same thought in mind. George told a reporter from the *Toronto Daily Star*, "We don't like being asked for autographs by the officials. Everywhere we go it's always the police guarding us, or the journalists or the relatives of the promoters who ask us to sign."

They barely made it into the King Edward Hotel. Paul's shirt was ripped and torn: "I thought I was for it, but an immense copper lifted me up and shoved me into the elevator."

Ringo: "We got separated from John and George coming in but the police were very good."

John: "The best view of the country is over the blue shoulder of a policeman."

In order to get them from the hotel to the gig, the police used a paddy wagon and fooled the fans by leaving from the back of the hotel. Paul told the *Daily Star* reporter that they had amused themselves by making sign language at a group of office girls in the National Trust building across from their hotel. "Normally we don't look out the windows because fans go a little potty but we were amazed at seeing the girls there on Labor Day and gave them a cheery wave or two."

The paper ran another news item headed "Beatles' Blonde Snubs Mayor": "Mayor Philip Givens couldn't get to see The Beatles. The mayor and his wife called at the singers' hotel suite at 1.30pm today to pay their respects. According to the Mayor, they got 'a very rude reception'. When they knocked, the mayor said, a blonde answered and took his card. 'Then she said, "Two of them are asleep and two of them are with relatives. Nobody gets in," and slammed the door in my face'."

There were 35,522 paying customers at the two shows, which resulted in a cheque for $93,000 for the group. Some 4,000 men and women police and Mounties were on duty at the Maple Leaf Gardens and a five block area around the Gardens was roped off and patrolled for 12 hours before the group was due to arrive.

Showtime for the first set was 4pm but The Beatles did not appear before 5.30, introduced by Jungle Jay Nelson of station CHUM. A thoughtful review in the *Toronto Telegram* said, "They don't rely on obvious sexuality, either in movement or song, but obviously there is a large element of sexuality in their appeal. Any sexuality is once removed: it occurs in the eye of the beholder rather than from any overt action by The Beatles."

Between sets there was the usual press conference. First The Beatles posed with local disc jockeys, fan club presidents and Miss Canada, then the questions began:

"What time do you get up in the morning?"

John: "Two o'clock in the afternoon."
They were asked if they thought they were setting a good example by smoking.
George: "We don't set examples."
Paul: "Why should we?"
Ringo: "We even drink."
It has been said that you appeal to the maternal instinct in these girls . . .
John: "That's a dirty lie."
They were asked why they didn't record all the songs that they write.
Paul: "It's just not good policy to flood the market with records like they did in America. Naughty them."
How long do you think you'll last?
John: "Longer than you."

September 8

The Forum, Montreal, Quebec, Canada. The two houses were seen by 21,000 fans.
On the plane from Montreal to Jacksonville, Florida, after the concert, Ringo, who was normally ill-at-ease on planes, relaxed and threw a cushion at someone. Immediately a pillow fight ensued with all the first-class pillows winging through the air. Suddenly a voice came over the intercom, "You're behaving like a bunch of children. This plane is in danger of crashing unless you sit quietly. It is vital that you fasten your seat belts . . ." Everyone froze, then returned to their seats and quietly fastened themselves in. Then Paul appeared, returning to his seat, a huge grin on his face at pulling one over on his mates.

September 9

The Beatles' plane was re-routed by Hurricane Dora, and landed instead at Key West at 3.30am. Even in the middle of the night hundreds of teenagers were waiting to scream a welcome.

September 10

During their rest day, The Beatles played a jam session at their hotel with New Orleans R&B star Clarence 'Frogman' Henry, and members of The Bill Black Combo and The Exciters.

September 11

Gator Bowl, Jacksonville, Florida.
After a rest day in Key West, mostly spent drinking, The Beatles finally got to Jacksonville. Once there, they had a hard time reaching the Gator Bowl. After a press conference at their hotel, The George Washington, two dozen police battled about 500 Beatles fans for 15 minutes in the hotel's parking garage at the intersection of Julia and Monroe Streets trying to get The Beatles out of the elevator and into their limousine. It took the group 15 minutes to move 25 feet. Eventually the police drove a flying wedge through the crowd with motorcycle outriders and managed to transfer the group to their trailer at the Gator Bowl by 7.15.
Despite the screaming girls, The Beatles had to refuse to go on until newsreel and television cameramen had left the arena. Newsreel footage, and particularly footage of the group playing, was a valuable commodity and the cameramen refused to leave. Eventually Derek Taylor stepped up to the microphone, shirt-sleeved, and issued an ultimatum. "The Beatles are 100 feet away," he said. "They came thousands of miles to be here. The only thing preventing their appearance is cine cameramen." He said that the film made as newsreels was ultimately sold and shown in cinemas with no royalties paid to The Beatles.
After the announcement Captain C. L. Raines and Captain I. L. Griffin gave the order to end the movie-making. Police officers physically restrained eight cameramen, covered their camera lenses with their hands and led them by the arm from the performance area.

HURRICANE DORA
The concert ran smoothly, though a strong wind, the aftermath of Hurricane Dora, whipped their hair and threatened their instruments as they played. Fans charged the stage after the last number but were restrained by a police

blockade and a six-foot fence. Although 30,000 tickets had been sold, only 23,000 showed up. Around 7,000 out-of-town fans who bought tickets were unable to see the concerts because Hurricane Dora had destroyed roads and bridges. President Johnson was in Jacksonville inspecting the damage as The Beatles played. That evening, a few minutes after midnight, their aircraft took off for Boston from Imeson Airport. No fans had discovered their travel plans, so for once there was no hysteria at the airport.

Derek Taylor spoke to a *Florida Times-Union* reporter on the plane who reported, "Taylor was somewhat apologetic for the showdown he had brought about over the cameramen, but he said a great deal of money was involved. He said this was the first time in the tour history he'd had to make such a speech."

In Detroit, earlier, The Beatles had announced that they would refuse to appear on stage in Jacksonville if the audience was segregated. They had heard that blacks in Florida were only allowed to sit in the balconies at concerts. Their statement read, "We will not appear unless negroes are allowed to sit anywhere." It turned out that there never were plans for the concert to be segregated.

The single 'I Don't Want To See You Again' by Peter & Gordon, written by Paul McCartney, was released in the UK as Columbia DB 7356.

September 12
Boston Garden, Boston, Massachusetts.

September 13
Civic Center, Baltimore, Maryland.

The Beatles stayed at the Holiday Inn, where mounted police were required to restrain the fans. At the Civic Arena, two girls had themselves delivered in a large cardboard box labelled "Beatles Fan Mail" but were discovered by a guard checking all deliveries.

September 14
Civic Arena, Pittsburgh, Pennsylvania.

The Beatles' Lockheed Electra arrived at Greater Pittsburgh Airport half an hour late at 4.36pm to the screams of 4,000 fans, mostly girls, some of whom had been waiting since 9.00am. The plane parked at Gate 16 and the girls began to scream. The organisers were taking no chances and private detectives boarded the plane, then followed the group out and into the waiting limousine which sped quickly away, surrounded by motorcycle police. There were 120 police at the airport including 15 on horseback, a security force even more elaborate than that used by presidents. Teenagers lined Parkway West to see The Beatles' motorcade drive into town. Five thousand fans surrounded the Civic Arena where The Beatles gave a press conference, then ate a catered meal before showtime.

The paid attendance was 12,603, the City Amusement tax was $6,251 and the Federal Levy $5,001.

The promotional album *Hear The Beatles Tell All*, consisting of recently recorded interviews with the group, was distributed to 7,000 radio stations across America by Vee Jay Records. Another new promotional release, this time prepared by Capitol Records, was *The Beatles Introduce New Songs*, featuring John and Paul announcing forthcoming singles by Peter & Gordon, and Cilla Black.

September 15
Public Hall, Cleveland, Ohio. In Cleveland The Beatles stayed at the Sheraton-Cleveland which, as usual, was inundated with fans: a girl of 11 showed up with a stolen key to a $35-a-night room, a boy hid in a packing case being trucked in, an underage fan tried to get into the Kon Tiki Bar, saying he had reservations for cocktails and one girl fainted on the sidewalk outside but recovered enough to say that she thought the nearest first aid station was in the hotel.

The police requested that they stay on the floor on which the press conference was to be held, rather than the presidential suite because too many fans knew they were registered to stay in those rooms. On Public Square outside the only time the police cordons broke was when The Beatles appeared at a window and waved. Traffic was restricted to one mile an hour in case fans surged forward, but the rush hour proceeded smoothly without too much delay.

Shortly after The Beatles took the stage a great wave of teenagers began pushing to the front, slowly taking the police line with them. More than 100 police leaned into the crowd but they were steadily forced back towards the stage, threatening the safety of the group. Inspector Michael Blackwell and Deputy Inspector Carl C. Bare panicked and decided to stop the show.

Bare charged out of the wings onto the stage, shouldered The Beatles aside, grabbed a microphone and bellowed, "Sit down! The show is over!" The Beatles, however, were in the middle of 'All My Loving' and carried on playing. Bare turned and walked towards John, who instead of stopping, did a little dance and made a face at him. Then Inspector Blackwell came storming out, gesturing to the group to get off the stage. He grabbed George by the elbow and steered him to the wings. George turned on him, "What the hell do you think you are doing? Get your hands off me!" The crowd shouted in protest but the music stopped and The Beatles slowly left the stage. The steel safety curtain came down and Blackwell and Bare stared down the booing fans.

In their dressing room The Beatles complained to the news director of local radio station KYW, Art Schreiber. "This has never happened to us before," said John. "We have never had a show stopped. These policemen are a bunch of amateurs." In the wings Brian diplomatically sided with the police. "The police were absolutely right. This has never happened before, but it was clear to me from the start that there was something very wrong. The enthusiasm of the crowd was building much too early."

After lecturing the audience, Blackwell allowed the show to continue after a ten-minute delay, but only on condition that the audience remained in their seats and that the house lights stayed up. Derek Taylor asked them to remain in their seats and the fans began to chant, "DON'T STAND UP, DON'T STAND UP, DON'T STAND UP". The curtain rose again and the group picked up where they left off and the rest of the show went well.

Later, Blackwell said, "I don't blame the children. They're young and they can't be expected to behave like adults. And I don't blame The Beatles – there is nothing wrong with their act. But if we hadn't stopped it there would have been serious injury. One little girl was knocked down in the charge and there were 300 other youngsters about to trample her." One girl was trampled but not seriously hurt. Another fainted.

Afterwards 500 fans attacked the stage door, but to no avail. The Beatles were already speeding away, using back roads, to their waiting aircraft at Cleveland Hopkins Airport. The police had cleverly run a riot bus, a converted paddy wagon, at high speed out of the hall while The Beatles escaped through the back door. The riot bus had been on duty all through the day, running between the Sheraton-Cleveland Hotel and Public Hall. At first the fans were fooled into thinking The Beatles were in it, but soon realised it was a decoy. In the end they ignored it. Just before showtime it made the trip again, this time with The Beatles as passengers, and the fans dismissed it.

The Sheraton-Cleveland Hotel refused to sell the bed linen that The Beatles had used, "because the idea seems to be against good taste," said the manager.

September 16

City Park Stadium, New Orleans, Louisiana.

The Beatles were scheduled to arrive at New Orleans Lakefront Airport where they were to be flown by helicopter to the Congress Inn. However, that was not what happened. First of all the helicopter blew a tyre, so limousines were ordered instead, but they went to Moisant Field, New Orleans International Airport by mistake. It turned out that this was to the good because that was where The Beatles' charter plane landed. They piled into the limousines and were off, complete with flashing blue lights and screaming sirens, at 3am. Unfortunately The Beatles' car got separated from the rest of the motorcade and followed a different route. There were a few hundred fans near the hotel, standing along the road designated their official route, and when they saw The Beatles in an unguarded car they quickly surrounded it, screaming hysterically.

Police soon arrived and forced the fans aside, but as The Beatles' car was backing up, it hit a Kenner police patrol car, causing slight damage. Finally The Beatles made it to the motel, ran through the lobby, the laundry room then outside and to their motel rooms: a three room suite – Room 100. By 4am most of the crowd had faded away. Two of The Beatles were sleeping, the other two were preparing to eat.

At the concert some 700 teenagers broke away from the stand and attempted to crash through the barriers keeping them from the stage. It took 225 New Orleans police more than 20 minutes to restore order. Mounted police patrolled the area around the stage while the fans who broke through onto the football field were roped off to one side. More than 200 fans collapsed and had to be revived with smelling salts and one girl had her arm broken but refused to go to hospital until after the show.

September 17
Municipal Stadium, Kansas City, Missouri.

THE KANSAS CONCERT

This was originally supposed to be a rest day but after seeing the amazing reception the group received elsewhere in the country, a wealthy promoter, Charles O. Finley, approached Brian Epstein with an offer of $100,000 to add Kansas City to their tour. Brian asked The Beatles if they would mind and without even looking up they said, "Whatever you think, Brian." Brian turned the offer down, despite the fact it was an enormous figure for the time. But Finley saw it as a matter of civic pride and was determined that Kansas City should see The Beatles. He offered $150,000, a higher figure than an American artist had ever received and almost guaranteed to show a loss. The 41,000 seater stadium was half full, with 20,280 paying spectators. Finley, the owner of Kansas City Athletics, lost between $50,000 and $100,000 for sponsoring the show. Despite this he donated a further $25,000 to Mercy Hospital. He said, "I don't consider it any loss at all. The Beatles were brought here for the enjoyment of the children in this area and watching them last night they had complete enjoyment. I'm happy about that. Mercy Hospital benefited by $25,000. The hospital gained, and I had a great gain by seeing the children and the hospital gain." An Athletics official said that ticket sales of 28,000 were needed to break even.

The Beatles flew in at 2am in pouring rain. About 100 fans waited, staring at them from behind a wall of wet policemen. George slipped on the wet runway apron on his way to the limousine which transferred them to the Muehlebach Towers where they had the $100-a-day, 18th-floor terrace penthouse. It took seven bellmen to carry in the 200 items of luggage The Beatles party had with them. A Kansas City actress had sent up a Missouri country ham, apple cider, a mincemeat pie and a watermelon.

To commemorate this extraordinary concert, The Beatles added 'Kansas City'/'Hey, Hey, Hey, Hey' to their repertoire, which the local fans loved. Excitement ran so high that the concert had to be stopped, with a threat of cancellation, if the audience did not calm down. They did and The Beatles played on.

The Muehlebach Towers sold the group's bed linen–16 sheets and eight pillow cases – to a Chicago man for $750. As in Detroit a few days earlier, these were later chopped into small pieces and turned into instant souvenirs.

September 18
Memorial Coliseum, Dallas, Texas.

In Dallas the stage was three times higher than was normally used, which put Ringo some 15 feet above the ground. Before the show there was a press conference, as usual, mostly attended by 13-year-old girls from radio stations no one had ever heard of before. Ringo was asked about the girls who had fallen to their knees and eaten the grass The Beatles walked upon. Ringo: "I hope they don't get indigestion."

Someone arranged for Paul to telephone Methodist Hospital to encourage Cheryl Howard, the 10-year-old victim of a hit-and-run driver who was fighting for her life. "A pity you can't be with us tonight at the programme," he told her.

There were the usual scenes outside their hotel, the Cabana, where fans jumped into the fountain after finding all doors to the hotel blocked. When the group returned to the hotel they jumped from their car but were cut off from the back entrance by several hundred fans. George was knocked to his knees and Ringo almost went under but they made it through. During the struggle a girl was pushed through a glass door and was severely cut about the face. Several others were injured. After the show they drove straight to Dallas Love Field where their plane took off at 11.08, taking The Beatles to a ranch in Missouri for a rest. During the flight, Paul led the entire Beatles entourage in a chorus of "Happy Birthday" for their manager, Brian Epstein. The Beatles then presented him with several gifts, including a vintage telephone and a rather impractical set of glassware.

September 19
The Beatles transferred planes on a small Missouri airstrip, and were transported to a ranch home in the Ozark Mountains on a seven-seater plane. During their 36 hours at this residence, the group swam, went riding, and indulged in some shooting and fishing.

Oxfam printed half a million Christmas cards featuring a design specially drawn by John Lennon.

September 20
Paramount Theater, Broadway, New York City, "An Evening With The Beatles" with Steve Lawrence and Eydie Gorme.

One of the few charity concerts The Beatles gave, this on behalf of the United Cerebral Palsy Fund of New York, this performance was attended by 3,682 members of society, who paid up to $100 a ticket. Ed Sullivan visited the dressing room, Gloria Steinem was there, valiantly trying to obtain a story for *Cosmopolitan* (her finished article captured much of the media madness surrounding the group, to which The Beatles replied with polite non-cooperation). Bob Dylan and his manager Albert Grossman went back to their motel with the band after the show. They stayed at the Riviera Motel, near Kennedy Airport, ready for the next morning's departure. That evening Brian Epstein accused press officer Derek Taylor of taking his limousine from outside the Paramount and called him a swine. Derek replied in kind and resigned, both as The Beatles' press officer and as Brian's personal assistant. He worked for a further three months showing his successor the ropes and was later to return to run the Apple press office.

Derek Taylor: "(Brian) handed me a note, which said that he might have been hasty and maybe I had too and if it could be forgiven and forgotten he would be happy if I would take back my resignation. Then he started to cry . . . But I needed to get away from all the hysteria and become normal again and stop having rows and leaving the family for months at a time. I had to stick to my decision."

September 21
The Beatles' Flight BA 510 landed at Heathrow Airport, London, at 9.30pm by which time thousands of fans had gathered on the roof of the Queen's Building to greet them. Continuous Beatles music had been playing throughout the building and regular flight reports were announced, as their Boeing 707 crossed the Atlantic.

The single 'I Don't Want To See You Again' by Peter & Gordon, written by Paul McCartney, was released in the US as Capitol 5272.

September 24
Brickey Building Company Limited was formed by Ringo, to give himself and his fellow Beatles a reliable building and decorating service.

September 27
Prince Of Wales Theatre, London. Ringo acted as one of a panel of celebrity judges in the final of The National Beat Group Competition, a charity event in aid of Oxfam. The second half of the show was broadcast live by BBC2 as *It's Beat Time*.

Paul and Jane attended a party given to celebrate the first anniversary of The Pretty Things.

September 29
Abbey Road. The Beatles worked on 'Every Little Thing', 'I Don't Want To Spoil The Party' and 'What You're Doing'.

September 30
Abbey Road. The Beatles finished 'Every Little Thing' and worked on 'What You're Doing' and 'No Reply'.

October

A Hard Day's Night was shown in Prague as part of a cultural exchange week between Britain and Czechoslovakia – the first time a Western pop film had been screened behind the Iron Curtain. The film was also released in Portugal, although only after several scenes had been censored, to avoid inflaming the passions of local teenagers.

Brian Epstein recorded spoken-word extracts from his autobiography, *A Cellarful Of Noise*, under the supervision of George Martin at Abbey Road studios.

October 1

Paul went to see *Goldfinger*, the new James Bond movie.

Alf Bicknell, The Beatles' new chauffeur, started work. He was to be their driver until August 1966 when they stopped touring.

With their licence to The Beatles' early recordings due to expire early in New Year, the US label Vee Jay Records were frantically trying to exploit this material as exhaustively as possible. They re-released the *Introducing The Beatles* LP alongside a collection of hits by The Four Seasons, as part of a two-record package, imaginatively titled *The Beatles Vs. The Four Seasons* (VJDX 30).

October 2

Rehearsals at the Granville Theatre, Fulham, for Jack Good's American TV show *Shindig*.

That evening Paul attended an Alma Cogan recording session and played tambourine on the track 'I Knew Right Away' (the B-side of her single 'It's You').

October 3

Shindig recorded live before a lively audience of Beatles Fan Club members at the Granville Theatre, Fulham. The Beatles performed 'Kansas City'/'Hey-Hey-Hey-Hey', 'I'm A Loser' and 'Boys'. They also took part in the finale with the Karl Denver Trio.

October 5

The *Ain't She Sweet* album is released in the US as Atco SD 33-169. Despite being credited to The Beatles, it actually contains eight songs by The Swallows, and only four of The Beatles' Hamburg recordings, 'Ain't She Sweet', 'Sweet Georgia Brown', 'Take Out Some Insurance On Me Baby' and 'Nobody's Child'.

October 6

Abbey Road. The Beatles arrived just after 2.30pm. The entire session was spent recording 'Eight Days A Week' until 7.00pm. Between takes, John toyed with the guitar riff which would soon power a new song, 'I Feel Fine'.

After the session John, Paul and Ringo went to the Ad-Lib where they spent the evening with Cilla Black, Mick Jagger and The Ronettes.

October 7

Shindig shown by ABC-TV in the USA.

October 8

That morning Ringo took his driving test in Enfield in order to avoid unwanted publicity. He passed first time. (He had previously been driving a Ford Zephyr around Liverpool, presumably without a licence.)

Abbey Road. The Beatles were in studio two recording Paul's 'She's A Woman', which he had begun to write that morning while walking around St. John's Wood, and then finished at home before leaving for the studio.

October 9

Gaumont Cinema, Bradford.

Opening of The Beatles' four-week tour of Britain. They were delayed by heavy traffic and by police on the A1 who flagged them down in order to get autographs, and arrived in Bradford two hours late. Also on the bill were The Rustiks, Sounds Incorporated, Michael Haslam, The Remo Four, Tommy Quickly and Mary Wells. The MC was Bob Bain.

The Beatles' set for this tour consisted of 'Twist And Shout', 'Money (That's What I Want)', 'Can't Buy Me Love', 'Things We Said Today', 'I'm Happy Just To Dance With You', 'I Should Have Known Better', 'If I Fell', 'I Wanna Be Your Man', 'A Hard Day's Night' and 'Long Tall Sally'. Sixty police guarded the stage area, there were 40 firemen and 60 St John Ambulance men and nurses on hand to deal with fainting fans. Outside, the crowds were controlled by mounted police brought in from Wakefield. There were a few arrests and a firework was thrown.

During a brief soundcheck before the first performance, The Beatles ran through John's new song, 'I Feel Fine', for the first time.

The group spent the night at the Raggles Inn in Queensbury, celebrating John's 24th birthday, before leaving for Leicester the following morning.

October 10
De Montfort Hall, Leicester (British Tour).

Ringo spent most of the day looking for cars. He eventually bought a Facel-Vega, which he tried out by driving at 140 mph up the M1.

The music press reported that the next Beatles album was to have a gatefold cover with a picture of The Beatles standing beneath the Arc de Triomphe at night with lighted matches held under their chins. It didn't happen.

October 11
The Odeon Cinema, Birmingham (British Tour).

October 12
The album *Songs, Pictures And Stories Of The Fabulous Beatles* was released in the US as Vee Jay VJLP 1092. Side A: 'I Saw Her Standing There', 'Misery', 'Anna (Go To Him)', 'Chains', 'Boys', 'Ask Me Why'; Side B: 'Please Please Me', 'Baby, It's You', 'Do You Want To Know A Secret', 'A Taste Of Honey', 'There's A Place', 'Twist And Shout'.

This album, effectively a reissue of *Introducing The Beatles*, brought to an end Vee Jay's merciless recycling of The Beatles' early 1963 recordings, which they had now released on five separate LPs.

Wendy Hanson joined The Beatles' backroom team as Brian Epstein's personal assistant.

October 13
The ABC Cinema, Wigan (British Tour).

October 14
The group spent the day at Granada Television studios in Manchester miming 'I Should Have Known Better' and conducting an interview for the show *Scene At 6.30*.

The ABC Cinema, Ardwick, Manchester (British Tour). Backstage The Beatles were interviewed by David Tindall for BBC1 news magazine *Look North*.

October 15
The Globe Theatre, Stockton-on-Tees (British Tour).

The group were interviewed by Tyne Tees Television for *North-East Newsview*.

October 16
The ABC Cinema, Hull (British Tour).

The single 'If I Fell'/'Tell Me Why' was released in Europe as Parlophone DP 562 (a few hundred copies were accidentally released in the UK on January 29, 1965).

The Beatles on *Scene At 6.30* was broadcast by Granada Television.

Tyne Tees Television broadcast their interview with The Beatles on *North-East Newsview*.

October 17
The group drove back to London from Hull.

October 18
Abbey Road. The Beatles finished 'Eight Days A Week'. They then worked on 'Kansas City'/'Hey-Hey-Hey-Hey', followed by 'Mr Moonlight', 'I Feel Fine' and Paul's 'I'll Follow

The Sun'. George sang Carl Perkins' 'Everybody's Trying To Be My Baby' which they followed with 'Rock And Roll Music' and 'Words Of Love'.

The recording of 'I Feel Fine' marked the first occasion on which guitar feedback had been deliberately incorporated into a pop song. EMI's press department claimed at the time that the novel sound effect had simply been an accident, but the session tapes prove that John devoted much effort to perfecting the sonic whine which introduced the record.

October 19
The group drove from London to Edinburgh to play the ABC Cinema (British Tour).

October 20
Caird Hall, Dundee (British Tour).

June Shields from Grampian Television interviewed The Beatles in their dressing room for the programme *Grampian Week*.

October 21
Odeon Cinema, Glasgow (British Tour).

October 22
Odeon Cinema, Leeds (British Tour).

October 23
The group drove back to London, then played the Gaumont State Cinema, Kilburn (British Tour).

Grampian Television broadcast the Caird Hall interview on *Grampian Week*.

October 24
Granada Cinema, Walthamstow, London (British Tour).

Press conference to announce that The Beatles' new single was to be 'I Feel Fine'/'She's A Woman'.

October 25
Hippodrome Theatre, Brighton (British Tour).

Before the show, The Beatles were interviewed by a *Melody Maker* reporter about their taste in musical instruments, and also took part in a photographic session for *The Beatles Book*. George also had his fortune told and his palms read by a local psychic. After the performance, the group were visited in their dressing room by actor Richard Harris and his wife.

The annual Ivor Novello Awards for contributions to the British Music Industry are announced, and The Beatles win in five separate categories – including a special award for 'Most Outstanding Contribution To Music In 1963'.

October 26
Abbey Road. The morning was spent listening to previous recordings. In the afternoon Ringo recorded his vocal for 'Honey Don't'. During the evening session the group recorded some material for a Christmas flexi-disc.

Afterwards Paul and Ringo, accompanied by Jane and Maureen, went to the Ad-Lib Club.

The latest issue of the monthly magazine *Rave* was published, featuring the first appearance in print of photographs taken by Ringo Starr.

October 28
ABC Cinema, Exeter (British Tour).

Afterwards the group took their chauffeur, Alf Bicknell, for a night out on the town to celebrate his 36th birthday.

October 29
ABC Theatre, Plymouth (British Tour).

October 30
Gaumont Cinema, Bournemouth (British Tour).
The single 'It's You'/'I Knew Right Away' by Alma Cogan, with Paul on tambourine on the B-side, was released in the UK as Columbia DB 7390.

October 31
Gaumont Theatre, Ipswich (British Tour).

November 1
Astoria Theatre, Finsbury Park, London (British Tour).

November 2
An extra date was added to the British Tour and The Beatles flew to Aldergrove Airport in Northern Ireland to play the King's Hall, Belfast.
George Martin released his second US album of instrumental covers of Beatles songs, *A Hard Day's Night*.

November 3
The Beatles flew back to London from Belfast.

November 4
Ritz Cinema, Luton (British Tour).
BBC producer Joe McGrath visited John backstage to invite him to contribute to a new Dudley Moore television show, then unnamed, but eventually called *Not Only . . . But Also*. John had previously run into Dudley Moore in a studio and told him, "I like what you're doing and I'd like to be in on it."
The EP *Extracts From The Film A Hard Day's Night* was released in the UK as Parlophone GEP 8920. Side A: 'I Should Have Known Better', 'If I Fell'; Side B: 'Tell Me Why', 'And I Love Her'.

November 5
Odeon Cinema, Nottingham (British Tour).

November 6
Gaumont Cinema, Southampton (British Tour).
They were interviewed in their dressing room by Tony Bilbow for the Southern Television programme *Day By Day*, broadcast that evening.
The EP *Extracts From The Film A Hard Day's Night (Volume Two)* was released in the UK as Parlophone GEP 8924. Side A: 'Anytime At All', 'I'll Cry Instead'; Side B: 'Things We Said Today', 'When I Get Home'.

November 7
The Capitol Cinema, Cardiff (British Tour).

November 8
Empire Theatre, Liverpool (British Tour).
After the concerts, which are attended by a stellar line-up of local luminaries and entertainers, John Lennon accompanied *Mersey Beat* editor Bill Harry on a visit to Stuart Sutcliffe's parents, taking away a blue abstract painting as a memento of his late friend.

November 9
City Hall, Sheffield (British Tour).

November 10
Colston Hall, Bristol.
The last date of the British Tour was enlivened by a student prank. As The Beatles finished singing 'If I Fell', and bowed to take the applause of the crowd, four students perched in the lighting gantries over their head emptied bags of flour over their heads. After shaking the powder out of their instruments, the visibly amused group completed their performance.

November 13
CBS-TV broadcast *The Beatles In America* – a full-length version of the Maysles Brothers documentary *Yeah, Yeah, Yeah! The Beatles On Tour* which covered their whole tour.

Parlophone released 'America', a single by Liverpool singer Rory Storm, which was produced by Brian Epstein and featured Ringo on backing vocals.

November 14
Television studios, Teddington, where they recorded a *Thank Your Lucky Stars* show, renamed *Lucky Stars Special* in their honour. They mimed to 'I Feel Fine', 'She's A Woman', 'I'm A Loser' and 'Rock And Roll Music'.

Afterwards George and Paul went home while John and Ringo went with friends to the Flamingo Club in Soho to see Georgie Fame and The Blue Flames.

November 15
The *Around The Beatles* TV special was screened in the US for the first time.

November 16
The Beatles recorded 'I Feel Fine' and 'I'm A Loser' at Riverside Studios, London, for an edition of BBC TV's *Top Of The Pops* presented by Brian Matthew. They mimed to both sides of their new single: 'I Feel Fine' and 'She's A Woman'.

November 17
The Beatles recorded a *Top Gear* show for the BBC Light Programme at the Playhouse Theatre, London. Brian Matthew interviewed them and they recorded 'I'm A Loser', 'Honey Don't', 'She's A Woman', 'Everybody's Trying To Be My Baby', 'I'll Follow The Sun' and 'I Feel Fine'.

November 20
John filmed a surreal film sequence with Dudley Moore and Norman Rossington on Wimbledon Common, to accompany his reading from *In His Own Write* on Moore's new BBC2 programme *Not Only . . . But Also*.

November 21
ABC Television broadcast *Lucky Stars Special*.

November 23
Wembley studios. An appearance on *Ready Steady Go!* to promote their new record. They mimed to 'I Feel Fine', 'She's A Woman', 'Baby's In Black' and 'Kansas City'/'Hey, Hey, Hey, Hey'. They also chatted on camera with presenter Keith Fordyce.

The single 'I Feel Fine'/'She's A Woman' was released in the US as Capitol 5327.

The album *The Beatles' Story* was released in the US as Capitol STBO 2222 (a 48-minute documentary double album containing one live cut from The Beatles, recorded August 23, 1964, at the Hollywood Bowl). Side A: 'On Stage With The Beatles', 'How Beatlemania Began', 'Beatlemania In Action', 'The Man Behind The Beatles – Brian Epstein', 'John Lennon', 'Who's A Millionaire?'; Side B: 'Beatles Will Be Beatles', 'Man Behind The Music – George Martin', 'George Harrison'; Side C: 'A Hard Day's Night – Their First Movie', 'Paul McCartney', 'Sneaky Haircuts And More About Paul'; Side D: 'Twist And Shout' (live), 'The Beatles Look At Life', 'Victims of Beatlemania', 'Beatle Medley', 'Ringo Starr', 'Liverpool And All The World!'.

Despite the blatantly exploitative nature of this 'official' release, *The Beatles' Story* still sold well enough to reach the US Top Ten.

November 24
Paul attended the marriage of his father, James, aged 62, to Angela Williams, aged 35.

November 25
The Beatles recorded a Boxing Day special edition of BBC Light Programme's *Saturday Club* show. The broadcast consisted of six songs: 'Rock And Roll Music', 'I'm A Loser', 'Everybody's Trying To Be My Baby', 'I Feel Fine', 'Kansas City'/'Hey, Hey, Hey, Hey' and 'She's A Woman', but four of these, all except the first and 'Kansas City' were

previously recorded versions. It is possible that only two songs were taped this day, or that the new versions were not up to scratch. The programme also included banter with presenter Brian Matthew.

November 27
The single 'I Feel Fine'/'She's A Woman' was released in the UK as Parlophone R 5200.
   The Beatles' final appearance on *Ready Steady Go!* was shown by Rediffusion.

I FEEL FINE
From the opening buzz of feedback (not a studio accident, as claimed at the time, but a conscious decision to use this electronic howl) to the cool passion of John Lennon's vocal, the group's final single of 1964 oozed quality and control. Lennon based the finger-twisting guitar riff on Bobby Parker's R&B record, 'Watch Your Step', which had been covered by The John Barry Seven as early as 1961, and was well known among British blues fans. But the smooth power of the song was Lennon's own, and hinted at The Beatles' development of the original beat-group sound which would follow in 1965.

SHE'S A WOMAN
For once on a Beatles record, Lennon sounded more sophisticated than McCartney when 'I Feel Fine' was supported by the raucous 'She's A Woman'. Little more than an R&B jam with words, the track was hastily and erratically recorded – the stabbing rhythm guitar drops out a couple of times midway through – but it triumphed on sheer willpower.

November 28
Chris Hutchins visited John at Kenwood and interviewed him for the BBC Light Programme's *Teen Scene*, to help promote the *Beatles For Sale* album.
   Afterwards John and Cynthia went Christmas shopping in London.

November 29
John read from his book, *In His Own Write* on Dudley Moore's BBC2 programme *Not Only . . . But Also*. He was apparently shy and self-conscious about reading aloud, but this was quickly dispelled by the antics of Moore and *A Hard Day's Night* star Norman Rossington.
   John and George had a few drinks afterwards, then went to the Crazy Elephant where they spent the evening with two members of The Miracles.
   Chris Hutchins' interview with John was broadcast by the BBC Light Programme's *Teen Scene*.

November 30
Ringo gave an interview to *Melody Maker* about his forthcoming operation to have his tonsils removed. While in their office, he saw the weekly charts compiled and 'I Feel Fine' enter at number one.
   Comedian Jack Dorsey released a novelty single about The Beatles' drummer, 'Ringo's Dog'.

December 1
Ringo booked into University College Hospital to have his tonsils removed. He gave a brief press conference at the hospital before going to the ward.

December 2
Ringo's tonsils were removed. A record player and records were delivered to his bedside.

December 3
Ringo was still in hospital, but doing well and making a fast recovery.
   BBC's *Top Of The Pops* broadcast The Beatles miming both sides of their new single.

December 4
The album *Beatles For Sale* was released in the UK as Parlophone PCS 3062. Side A: 'No Reply', 'I'm A Loser', 'Baby's In Black', 'Rock And Roll Music', 'I'll Follow The Sun', 'Mr

Moonlight', 'Kansas City'/'Hey, Hey, Hey, Hey'; Side B: 'Eight Days A Week', 'Words Of Love', 'Honey Don't', 'Every Little Thing', 'I Don't Want To Spoil The Party', 'What You're Doing', 'Everybody's Trying To Be My Baby'.

Many of the tracks were oldies, played by The Beatles at the Cavern and in Hamburg. John: "The numbers on this LP are different from anything we've done before and you could call our new one a 'Beatles Country and Western LP'."

BEATLES FOR SALE

It's been noted before that the tired, glazed expressions of the four Beatles on the cover of their fourth album was a simple response to circumstances. Unlike the pampered stars of the Nineties, they had no chance between 1963 and 1965 to bask in their wealth and fame. Into that schedule had to be squeezed the recording of the aptly titled *Beatles For Sale*. It was thrown together on off-days between concerts over a period of almost three months, so it wasn't altogether surprising when the record seemed to take a step back from the stylistic unity of their earlier LPs. The return to a blend of original material and covers hinted at the strain the group were under; the generally perfunctory nature of their covers rammed the message home. But the eight Lennon/McCartney songs on the album displayed a growing maturity, and betrayed a new set of influences which would very soon whisk The Beatles beyond the reach of their beat group contemporaries.

One of the prime inspirations for the *Beatles For Sale* songs was country music – first noted on 'I'll Cry Instead' on the third album, and a constant point of reference through their work in 1965. The group had grown up on rockabilly, itself deeply rooted in country, but it took Ringo's continual championing of Nashville's contemporary stars to inspire songs like 'I Don't Want To Spoil The Party' and 'Baby's In Black'.

More lasting was the creative impact of Bob Dylan, to whom The Beatles had been listening since the end of 1963. At first, Lennon, McCartney and Harrison picked up on the style and sound of Dylan's records. Once the American singer had introduced them to the pleasures of dope, however, they began to respond to the artistic freedom that his songwriting made possible. Without Dylan, or drugs, the path from *Beatles For Sale* to *Revolver* might have been too tangled for The Beatles to follow.

NO REPLY

"I remember Dick James coming to me after we did this one," John Lennon recalled shortly before his death, "and saying, 'You're getting much better now – this is a complete story'. Apparently, before that he thought my songs tended to sort of wander off." Music publisher Dick James soon found his own tastes outstripped by the adventurous spirit of The Beatles; by 1966, no one was looking to their songs for "a complete story". But James was right on one score: even though the song was plainly a piece of romantic fiction, it had a watertight structure and a powerful melody, and The Beatles' skills as vocal arrangers were on open display. On tracks like this, Beatles For Sale *sounds like the pinnacle of British beat music, polished to an icy sheen in preparation for being shattered by The Beatles and the Stones, among others, over the next 12 months.*

'No Reply' would go on to become the favoured track for owners of answerphones to record on their machines 20 years later.

I'M A LOSER

Looking back at this song, Lennon recognised it as a milestone. "Instead of projecting myself into a situation," he explained, "I would try to express what I felt about myself. I think it was Dylan who helped me realise that." And the Dylan influence was obvious in other ways, too, from the acoustic guitars powering the song to the use of the harmonica as a statement of passion.

Like 'I'll Cry Instead', 'I'm A Loser' soon drifted into naked self-pity – and anyway, the raw emotions of the song were dressed up in a strong pop format. But for a while, at least, Lennon was delighted at his discovery that he could channel his innermost thoughts into music, as well as the free-form linguistic pleasures of his books. As for the song's message, Lennon summed up his ambivalence perfectly in 1970: "Part of me thinks I'm a loser and part of me thinks I'm God Almighty".

BABY'S IN BLACK

A heavy waltz with a vague country influence, 'Baby's In Black' was one of the last genuine Lennon/McCartney collaborations – composed during a head-to-head session over acoustic guitars, the way they'd been doing since the late 50s. Its rather maudlin lyric suggests that it might originally have been a Lennon idea, but the performance is pure Beatles – and pure 1964. Numbers like this, which invested a little romantic difficulty with the importance of a world crisis, gradually faded from The Beatles' repertoire over the next twelve months.

ROCK AND ROLL MUSIC

Not for the first time, The Beatles took a classic American record and cut it to shreds. Chuck Berry's original Chess recording – which set up rock'n'roll as an antidote to boredom with every other musical style – only hinted at the raw power of the genre. With Lennon, McCartney and producer George Martin trebling up the keyboard part, The Beatles made every hint of that promise into reality. Berry wrote and performed brilliant rock songs, but it took Lennon to sing this one the way it was meant to be heard.

I'LL FOLLOW THE SUN

As early as 1960, the pre-Beatles Liverpool band, The Quarry Men, were experimenting with a tentative arrangement of this McCartney song, making it just about the earliest Lennon/McCartney composition which they ever recorded. Simple but effortlessly melodic, it proves that Paul was born with the gift of writing memorable tunes, while John Lennon's ability as a tunesmith evolved only with practice.

MR. MOONLIGHT

On Friday August 14, 1964, The Beatles recorded one of the strongest rock'n'roll performances of their career. Sadly, this wasn't it. But it could have been: the group eventually decided to jettison their electrifying interpretation of Little Willie John's R&B standard, 'Leave My Kitten Alone' (which remained officially unreleased until 1995) in favour of this bizarre, mediocre version of another song from black America, Dr. Feelgood & The Interns' 'Mr. Moonlight'.

John Lennon had taken to the song immediately he heard it, and it was swiftly incorporated into their Cavern repertoire. But the recorded version, which required two separate sessions to 'perfect', had none of the spontaneity or humour of their live performances. It shambled along rather apologetically, and the half-hearted vocal support from McCartney and Harrison left Lennon's impassioned lead sounding faintly ridiculous. Asked to pick the weakest track The Beatles ever recorded, a fair percentage of fans would opt for 'Mr. Moonlight'.

KANSAS CITY/HEY, HEY, HEY, HEY

Like Little Richard before them, The Beatles covered Leiber & Stoller's early Fifties R&B song and added a frenetic call-and-response routine to the end. Richard had already reworked the original arrangement to his own specifications, and Paul McCartney followed that revamp to the letter. For this recording, The Beatles simply blasted the song the way they did on stage. This late 1964 rendition may be tighter than the performance from December 1962 captured on the 1962 Live Recordings CD, but the approach is almost identical.

EIGHT DAYS A WEEK

A few months earlier, The Beatles had been delighted by the discovery that they could fade their recordings out. Now they went a stage further, and made pop history by fading this song in. Ironically, the track had a conventional ending – though that was edited onto the tape after the basic recording was finished.

Like 'Baby's In Black', 'Eight Days A Week' was a Lennon/McCartney collaboration, though again with Lennon's influence to the fore. It would have made a perfect hit single, and may even have been written with that idea in mind, as its title obviously has some link with the working name of their second movie, scripts for which had already been submitted by October 1964: Eight Arms To Hold You.

WORDS OF LOVE

Two standards from The Beatles' pre-fame live repertoire went through a change of ownership during these sessions. Back at the Cavern in 1961 and 1962, it had been Lennon and Harrison who shared the close harmony vocals on this Buddy Holly song – the only number by one of their favourite writers that they ever recorded. On the record, though, which kept strictly to Holly's arrangement, McCartney elbowed Harrison out of the limelight. Nevertheless, George's contribution – the lovely chiming guitar licks throughout – is pretty impressive.

HONEY DON'T
The second change came with this Carl Perkins rockabilly favourite – traditionally sung by John Lennon on stage, but passed over amiably to Ringo Starr as his token vocal cameo on the album. The switch gave Ringo the chance to utter one of his trademark invitations to George as Harrison launched into the guitar solo.

EVERY LITTLE THING
Though it's one of the least well-known songs they ever recorded, John Lennon's 'Every Little Thing' was as impressive as anything on Beatles For Sale, *with all the trademarks of their 1964 work – a laconic, yet affectionate Lennon vocal, some Harrison guitar that looked forward to the as-yet-unrecorded sound of The Byrds, and a stunningly melodic chorus that stuck instantly in the brain. Ripe for rediscovery by someone like Tom Petty (and covered in 1969 by Yes, of all people), it justifies the claim that almost every Lennon/McCartney song on The Beatles' early albums would have made a convincing hit single.*

I DON'T WANT TO SPOIL THE PARTY
Influenced partly by rockabilly, partly by mainstream country, and partly by the general air of melancholy that seeped into several of his songs in 1964, John Lennon wrote this vaguely self-pitying account of romantic disappointment. Proof of The Beatles' increasing sophistication as arrangers came with the middle eight, on which Paul's harmony moved subtly away from the simple line he might have sung a year earlier.

WHAT YOU'RE DOING
With 'I'll Follow The Sun' having been written in the late Fifties, 'What You're Doing' proved to be Paul McCartney's only new solo contribution to the Beatles For Sale *album. After out-stripping Lennon as a songwriter in the group's early years, Paul was now going through a fallow period, just when John was at his most prolific. A couple of years later, the situation would be dramatically reversed.*

The song itself was built around a simple guitar riff, but as often proves to be the case, simplicity proved difficult to perfect. The Beatles devoted two sessions to taping the song before junking the results and then re-cutting it on the last possible day of recording.

EVERYBODY'S TRYING TO BE MY BABY
Cut in a single, echo-swamped take, this second Carl Perkins cover allowed George Harrison the chance to pay his respects to one of his all-time musical heroes. The combination of the disorientating echo and Harrison's scouse drawl made Perkins' overtly Tennessean lyrics almost impossible to decipher: without access to a lyric sheet, in fact, Harrison may simply have been reproducing the sound of what the American rocker was singing, rather than exactly the same words. Either way, it made for a strange ending to a disjointed album.

December 8
George visited Ringo in hospital, adding to the security problem caused by fans trying to sneak in.

The *Daily Express* reported that Paul had told them he would marry Jane Asher.

December 9
George and Patti flew to the Bahamas for a break before *The Beatles' Christmas Show*.

Paul visited Ringo in hospital, attracting even more press and fans.

December 10
Ringo was finally released from University College Hospital.

December 11
The results of the annual *New Musical Express* readers' poll were published. The Beatles topped both the "World Vocal Group" and "British Vocal Group" categories.

December 15
The album *Beatles '65* was released in the US as Capitol ST 2228. Side A: 'No Reply', 'I'm A Loser', 'Baby's In Black', 'Rock And Roll Music', 'I'll Follow The Sun', 'Mr. Moonlight'; Side B: 'Honey Don't', 'I'll Be Back', 'She's A Woman', 'I Feel Fine', 'Everybody's Trying To Be My Baby'.

December 18
The flexi-disc, *Another Beatles' Christmas Record*, was sent out free to members of The Beatles Fan Club.

December 19
George and Patti flew back to London from Nassau.

December 20
Brian Epstein bought number 24 Chapel Street, Belgravia, London.
   Paul and Jane visited Liverpool singer Rory Storm.

December 21
The first day of rehearsals for *Another Beatles' Christmas Show* at the Hammersmith Odeon.

December 22
The complete cast of *Another Beatles' Christmas Show* assembled on stage at the Hammersmith Odeon for a rehearsal.
   During a break in rehearsals, Jimmy Savile (who was appearing in the show) recorded a brief interview with the group for BBC's *Top Of The Pops '64* Christmas show.

December 23
Rehearsals for the *Christmas Show*.

December 24
The Beatles opened their twice-nightly *Another Beatles' Christmas Show* at the Hammersmith Odeon, London.

ANOTHER BEATLES' CHRISTMAS SHOW
The show was compered by Jimmy Savile, who brought fans to The Beatles' dressing room before the shows. The Mike Cotton Sound playing Georgie Fame's 'Yeh, Yeh!' opened. They were joined by Michael Haslem, a Brian Epstein protégé – one of those who didn't make it – who came on stage to sing 'Scarlet Ribbons'. The Yardbirds were on next followed by a pantomime sketch involving The Beatles dressed as Antarctic explorers looking for the Abominable Snowman, compered by Liverpudlian Ray Fell. So excruciating was this section of the show, both for the group and their fans, that The Beatles resolved never to take part in a similar enterprise again. The first half ended with Freddie and The Dreamers, beginning with 'Rip It Up', 'Bachelor Boy' and including 'Cut Across Shorty'.
   The second half opened with Elkie Brooks followed by Sounds Incorporated, then finally Jimmy Savile introduced The Beatles dressed in blue Mohair suits and singing 'She's A Woman' with Paul taking vocals. John sang 'I'm A Loser', George did 'Everybody's Trying To Be My Baby' then John and Paul duetted on 'Baby's In Black'. Ringo sang 'Honey Don't' followed by John on 'A Hard Day's Night' and their current hit, 'I Feel Fine'. 'Long Tall Sally' was the finale. The drawings on the front and back covers of the programme were by John.

The Beatles performing 'A Hard Day's Night', recorded in July, was broadcast on BBC TV's *Top Of The Pops '64*.

December 25
John and Cynthia spent Christmas Day at home with their son Julian; Paul was with his girlfriend Jane Asher at her family home; and Ringo joined George for Christmas lunch at the latter's home.

December 26
Hammersmith Odeon, London: *Another Beatles' Christmas Show.*

December 28
Hammersmith Odeon, London: *Another Beatles' Christmas Show.*

December 29
Hammersmith Odeon, London: *Another Beatles' Christmas Show.*
(One performance instead of the usual two.)

December 30
Hammersmith Odeon, London: *Another Beatles' Christmas Show.*

December 31
Hammersmith Odeon, London: *Another Beatles' Christmas Show.*
Afterwards Paul, Jane, George and Patti attended EMI producer Norman Newell's New Year's Eve party at his London flat. They also made a fleeting visit to another party, held by EMI boss Sir Joseph Lockwood.

January 1
Hammersmith Odeon, London: *Another Beatles' Christmas Show*.
   Radio Luxembourg began a regular weekly show entirely devoted to The Beatles' music, introduced by Chris Denning.

January 2
Hammersmith Odeon, London: *Another Beatles' Christmas Show*.

January 4
Hammersmith Odeon, London: *Another Beatles' Christmas Show*.
   Paul attended a special luncheon at the Café Royal in London's Regent Street, in honour of music publisher Dick James. At the event, James revealed that John and Paul had earned more than £1 million as songwriters alone during 1964.

January 5
Hammersmith Odeon, London: *Another Beatles' Christmas Show*.

January 6
Hammersmith Odeon, London: *Another Beatles' Christmas Show*.

January 7
Hammersmith Odeon, London: *Another Beatles' Christmas Show*.

January 8
Hammersmith Odeon, London: *Another Beatles' Christmas Show*.
   After this evening's performance, The Beatles were given a private view of the Boat Show at the nearby Earl's Court Exhibition Hall. By midnight they were paddling around an artificial lake in a rubber dinghy and trying out the radio-controlled mini-powerboats.

January 9
Hammersmith Odeon, London: *Another Beatles' Christmas Show*.
   The album *Beatles '65* reached number one in the US charts.
   John read from *In His Own Write* on Dudley Moore's BBC2 programme *Not Only . . . But Also*.

January 11
Hammersmith Odeon, London: *Another Beatles' Christmas Show*.

January 12
Hammersmith Odeon, London: *Another Beatles' Christmas Show*.

January 13
Hammersmith Odeon, London: *Another Beatles' Christmas Show*.

January 14
Hammersmith Odeon, London: *Another Beatles' Christmas Show*.

January 15
Hammersmith Odeon, London: *Another Beatles' Christmas Show*.
   After that evening's performance, Ringo and George spent the evening at a party given by *Melody Maker* journalist Bob Dawbarn.

January 16
Hammersmith Odeon, London: *Another Beatles' Christmas Show*. Final performance.

January 20
Ringo Starr proposed to Maureen Cox at the Ad-Lib Club in London. Maureen accepted.

January 21
The US Music Publishers Association names John and Paul "Top Songwriters Of 1964".

January 25
John and Cynthia flew to the Alps to join George Martin and his future wife Judy Lockhart-Smith on a skiing holiday.

January 26
George Martin was injured during his skiing holiday with the Lennons. To ease his recuperation, John played him the bare bones of a new song he was writing during the holiday, provisionally entitled 'This Bird Has Flown'.

January 27
The music publishing company Maclen Limited was formed with John, Paul and Brian Epstein as directors.

Brian Epstein held a press conference in London to announce The Beatles' plans for 1965. These included a European tour in July, at the centre of which would be a live TV broadcast from Paris, seen all over Europe (although not in Britain). Also on the agenda was an American tour in August, which was set to include at least one concert in Mexico.

Epstein also confirmed that The Beatles hoped to begin work on a third feature film project before the end of 1965.

January 28
George and Patti flew to Europe on holiday.

January 29
The European-only pressing of the single 'If I Fell'/'Tell Me Why' was released in the UK as Parlophone DP 562 to a few record stores by accident. The single was pressed by EMI for foreign export only but these copies were sold by sales reps in error.

February 1
The EP *4 By The Beatles* was released in the US as Capitol R 5365. Side A: 'Honey Don't', 'I'm A Loser'; Side B: 'Mr. Moonlight', 'Everybody's Trying To Be My Baby'.

February 3
Ringo and Maureen attended a special lunch function for the millionaire, Paul Getty Jr.

February 4
Paul and Jane flew to Hammamet, Tunisia, for a holiday, staying at a free villa provided by the British Embassy.

February 7
John and Cynthia, George Martin and Judy returned to England from their holiday. George Martin was hobbling because he had broken a toe on the ski slopes on his first day.

February 8
Music publisher Dick James was reported to have taken out £500,000 worth of life insurance on his two most lucrative clients, John and Paul.

The Beatles' accountant Walter Hofer, informed the press that both the UK and US tax authorities were seeking payment from the group. "We are not at all resisting the tax," Hofer explained, "but we don't want to have to pay it twice."

February 10
Brian Epstein named the third Beatles' feature film project as *A Talent For Loving*, based on a novel by Richard Condon. He announced that the movie would be financed by his own newly formed company, Pickfair Films.

February 11
Ringo married Maureen Cox at Caxton Hall Register Office, London; registrar Mr D.A. Boreham. John, George and Brian Epstein attended but Paul was still in North Africa.

MAUREEN

Ringo had known Maureen, a hairdresser, since the Cavern days and they had been going out together virtually ever since. "This means two married and two unmarried Beatles – two down and two to go," commented George. They drove to Hove, Sussex, for a brief honeymoon at the home of their solicitor David Jacobs on Princes Crescent. Maureen would have three children by Ringo, Zak, Jason and Lee.

February 12
Ringo and Maureen gave a press conference in David Jacobs' back garden.

February 14
Ringo and Maureen returned to London from their honeymoon.
    Paul and Jane returned to London from Tunisia.

February 15
That morning John passed his driving test in Weybridge.
    Abbey Road. The group arrived at 2.30 and spent the afternoon recording John's 'Ticket To Ride'. The evening session from 7 until 10.30 was spent recording Paul's 'Another Girl' and George's 'I Need You'.
    The single 'Eight Days A Week'/'I Don't Want To Spoil The Party' was released in the US as Capitol 5371.

February 16
Abbey Road. An afternoon session completing 'I Need You' and 'Another Girl'. From 5 until 10pm they recorded John's 'Yes It Is' but the session did not go well. John was unhappy with the results and swore a lot.
    During a break in recording, The Beatles collected various awards from EMI, presented by Sir Joseph Lockwood. Among them was the Carl Alan Award, given to the "Best Group Of 1964". The group were also given a set of traditional Japanese dolls, gifts from the Japanese arm of the EMI empire.

February 17
Abbey Road. An afternoon session from 2 until 7 was spent recording Paul's 'The Night Before', after which they worked until 11pm on George's 'You Like Me Too Much'.

February 18
Abbey Road. The Beatles arrived at 10am and spent the morning mixing. John's 'You've Got To Hide Your Love Away' was recorded during the afternoon session. John: "This was written in my Dylan days for the film *Help!* When I was a teenager I used to write poetry, but was always trying to hide my real feelings." Ringo recorded 'If You've Got Trouble' during the evening session but John and Paul, who wrote the song specifically for Ringo, were not happy with the results and the track was not used. The remainder of the evening session was spent recording Paul's 'Tell Me What You See'.
    The rest of the evening was spent in the clubs.
    Northern Songs was launched on the stock exchange. Two million of the company's five million shares were made available to the public, at seven shillings and ninepence apiece (39p). The share price immediately dropped to below six shillings (30p), but soon recovered to fourteen shillings (70p).

February 19
Abbey Road. The group made a late start. John's 'You're Going To Lose That Girl' was recorded in a three-hour afternoon session beginning at 3.30.
    That evening The Beatles attended a private party given in their honour at The Connaught Hotel, Carlos Place, by the chairman of EMI, Sir Joseph Lockwood.

February 20
Abbey Road. The group arrived around midday and recorded the unreleased 'That Means A Lot'. Work finished at 6pm to allow them to pack for the flight to the Bahamas.

February 21
The Beatles' baggage was collected, ready for the flight.

February 22
The Beatles flew to the Bahamas from Heathrow in a chartered Boeing 707 to begin filming *Help!*; 1,400 fans waved goodbye. Actress Eleanor Bron, the female lead in their movie, travelled with the group. There was a refuelling stopover in New York en route but The Beatles did not leave the aircraft, despite US Customs and Immigration insisting that they should pass through US Customs. They lit up immediately after take-off and didn't stop giggling until the plane landed. In the Bahamas they stayed in a house in the grounds of the Balmoral Club near Cable Beach. The hotel consisted of several large houses set in luxurious gardens, complete with an Olympic-sized swimming pool.

The Beatles' arrival in Nassau was watched by thousands of local fans, while media interest meant that a press conference had to be hastily arranged at the airport. Having checked in to their suites at the Balmoral Club, the group went for a midnight swim in the ocean.

February 23
Filming on New Providence Island, Bahamas.

February 24
Filming on New Providence Island, Bahamas. The Beatles usually began work at 8.30 to get in a full day's shooting.

February 25
Filming on New Providence Island, Bahamas.

February 26
Filming on New Providence Island, Bahamas.

February 27
Filming on New Providence Island, Bahamas.

February 28
Filming on New Providence Island, Bahamas.

March 1–9
Filming on New Providence Island, Bahamas. The Beatles worked solidly during their stay in the Bahamas with no days off.

John: "The most humiliating experiences were like sitting with the Mayor of the Bahamas, when we were making *Help!* and being insulted by these fuckin' junked up middle-class bitches and bastards who would be commenting on our work and commenting on our manners. I was always drunk, insulting them. I couldn't take it. It would hurt me. I would go insane, swearing at them."

Among their visitors in the Bahamas was their former press officer Derek Taylor, who had been given the unenviable task of exploiting his friendship with The Beatles to obtain exclusive interviews for Los Angeles radio station KRLA.

March 3
George Martin's contribution to The Beatles' remarkable success was finally acknowledged by his EMI superiors; he received a promotion, and a small pay increase.

March 6
Brian Epstein announced that plans for The Beatles' July concert in Paris to be televised across Europe had been cancelled. Instead, a camera team would be filming their performance at Shea Stadium in New York during August.

Epstein also confirmed that the plan for John to release a spoken-word album of extracts from *In His Own Write* had now been abandoned.

March 10
The Beatles began the journey back to London.

March 11
The Beatles arrived at Heathrow Airport at 7.05am from the Bahamas.

March 13
The Beatles took the 11am flight to Salzburg, Austria to continue filming *Help!*. At Salzburg Airport, 4,000 fans were waiting to greet them, as well as the press. They gave a press conference in a nearby hotel before checking into the Hotel Edelweiss in Obertauern where all the filming took place.

Paul turned out to be very good on skis and was said by their instructor to have the makings of a professional. John had spent a couple of weeks trying to learn before they went to Austria but never really got the hang of it. Many of the people on the set had legs in plaster which The Beatles naturally had to sign.

'Eight Days A Week' reached number one in the US charts.

March 14–17
Filming at Obertauern.

Eight Arms To Hold You was announced as the working title for The Beatles' new film.

The Grammy Awards committee in New York nominated The Beatles for six awards: "Record Of The Year" (for 'I Want To Hold Your Hand'); "Best Rock'N'Roll Recording Of The Year" (also 'I Want To Hold Your Hand'); "Best New Artist Of 1964"; "Song Of The Year" (for 'A Hard Day's Night'); "Best Original Score Written For A Motion Picture Or TV Show" (for *A Hard Day's Night*); and "Best Performance By A Vocal Group" ('A Hard Day's Night' once again).

In addition, three other acts – The Chipmunks, The Boston Pops Orchestra and The Hollyridge Strings – were nominated for their albums of Beatles compositions.

March 18
Filming at Obertauern.

Hayling Supermarkets Limited was incorporated to control a supermarket on Hayling Island, Hampshire, run by John's old school friend Pete Shotton. The directors were Shotton, John and George Harrison.

Drummer Jimmy Nicol made a vain attempt to cash in on his brief membership of The Beatles the previous summer, by issuing a single, 'Clementine'.

March 19
Filming at Obertauern.

The Beatles gave a party for the cast after the day's filming.

Brian Matthew interviewed the group for the BBC Light Programme's *Saturday Club* by telephone from their hotel at 8pm.

March 20
Final day's shooting at Obertauern.

BBC Light Programme's *Saturday Club* broadcast Brian Matthew's interview recorded the previous evening.

John and Ringo were interviewed on the telephone by Chris Denning for his weekly Radio Luxembourg show, *The Beatles*.

March 22
The Beatles flew back to London from Austria.

The album *The Early Beatles* was released in the US as Capitol T-2309 (mono) and ST–2309 (stereo). Side A: 'Love Me Do', 'Twist And Shout', 'Anna (Go To Him)', 'Chains', 'Boys', 'Ask Me Why'; Side B: 'Please Please Me', 'P.S. I Love You', 'Baby, It's You', 'A Taste Of Honey', 'Do You Want To Know A Secret'.

March 24
With the location shooting completed, The Beatles continued to film *Help!* at Twickenham film studios.

March 25
Filming at Twickenham.

March 26
Filming at Twickenham.
    Brian Epstein's office revealed that the proposed soundtrack album from the *Eight Arms To Hold You* movie would follow the style of the US edition of the *A Hard Day's Night* soundtrack, by mixing Beatles recordings with specially recorded orchestral material.

March 27
Around this date, John and Cynthia were introduced to the chemical stimulus of LSD by their dentist, who spiked their late-night cups of coffee with impregnated sugar cubes. The now hallucinating party made their way from the dentist's home to The Pickwick Club in central London, where John interpreted a red light bulb as being the site of a raging inferno of fire, and then on to George's house. There John drew his first psychedelic cartoons, portraying The Beatles as a hydra-like creature, with each head pronouncing: "We all agree with you". Thereafter Lennon became a keen ambassador for the mind-expanding virtues of the drug, while his wife vowed never to experiment with the chemical again.

March 28
The Beatles were driven to the Alpha Studios at Aston in Birmingham, where they recorded their final ever appearance on the ABC TV show *Thank Your Lucky Stars*. They were interviewed by Brian Matthew and mimed to 'Eight Days A Week', 'Yes It Is' and 'Ticket To Ride'.

March 29
Filming at Twickenham.

March 30
Filming at Twickenham during the day.
    Abbey Road in the evening where they did five more takes of Paul's 'That Means A Lot' but Paul was not happy with the results and at 10pm they called it a day.

March 31
Filming at Twickenham.

April
Ringo bought a newly built bungalow in Liverpool, fully fitted and furnished, for his parents.
    An offer from American playwright Wolf Mankowitz for John and Paul to collaborate with him on a project was politely refused.

April 1
Brian Epstein took a lease on the Saville Theatre on Shaftesbury Avenue to use as a showcase for his many showbusiness interests, even opening it as a rock venue on Sunday evenings when the theatre was normally dark.
    The Beatles filmed at Twickenham.
    Before John left for the film studio, he received an unexpected visit from his long estranged father, Freddie Lennon. Rather than displaying the delight for which his father had been hoping, John exhibited immediate hostility, asking: "Where have you been for the last twenty years?" Freddie was allowed to stay in the Lennon household for three days, until John and Cynthia became convinced that he had contacted his son for financial, rather than sentimental, reasons.

April 2
Filming at Twickenham.

April 3
ABC TV transmitted the edition of *Thank Your Lucky Stars* recorded on March 28.

April 5
The Beatles filmed the "Rajahama" Indian restaurant sequence at Twickenham.

George: "We were waiting to shoot the scene in the restaurant when the guy gets thrown in the soup and there were a few Indian musicians playing in the background. I remember picking up the sitar and trying to hold it and thinking, 'This is a funny sound.' It was an incidental thing, but somewhere down the line I began to hear Ravi Shankar's name. The third time I heard it, I thought, 'This is an odd coincidence.' And then I talked with David Crosby of The Byrds and *he* mentioned the name. I went and bought a Ravi record; I put it on and it hit a certain spot in me that I can't explain, but it seemed very familiar to me. The only way I could describe it was: my intellect didn't know what was going on and yet this other part of me identified with it. It just called on me . . . a few months elapsed and then I met this guy from the Asian Music Circle organisation who said, 'Oh, Ravi Shankar's gonna come to my house for dinner. Do you want to come too?'"

April 6
At a break in filming at the Twickenham studios, TV talk show host Simon Dee presented the group with the Radio Caroline Bell Award for "Most Consistent and Best Recording Artistes of the Past Year". The Beatles managed to disrupt the inevitable speeches by ringing the bell at appropriate moments throughout the proceedings.

The EP *Beatles For Sale* was released in the UK as Parlophone GEP 8931 (mono only): Side A: 'No Reply', 'I'm A Loser'; Side B: 'Rock And Roll Music', 'Eight Days A Week'.

April 7
Filming at Twickenham.

The Beatles' office announced that Maureen Starkey was already expecting the couple's first child.

April 8
Filming at Twickenham.

The Beatles all attended the opening night of Downstairs At The Pickwick, a new London nightclub. Michael Crawford was among the other guests.

April 9
The single 'Ticket To Ride'/'Yes It Is' was released in the UK as Parlophone R 5265.
Filming at Twickenham.

TICKET TO RIDE
John Lennon once described this song, The Beatles' first single of 1965, as the precursor to heavy metal. "It was pretty fucking heavy for then," he boasted, "if you go and look at what other people were making. It doesn't sound too bad." Indeed not: from Lennon's brilliantly deadpan vocal to Ringo's cross-beat drumming and McCartney's lead guitar flourishes, 'Ticket To Ride' was musically the strongest record The Beatles had made up to that point.

YES IT IS
George Harrison made the most of his first tone-pedal (alias 'wah-wah') in February 1965, using it on every possible song he could. It was one of several striking factors to this 1965 B-side, a successor to 'This Boy' as a vehicle for three-part harmony. In retrospect, it might have been better if they'd junked this initial attempt at the song and spent the time on rehearsals instead, as the beauty of the melody is rather undercut by the flat vocals on several lines.

April 10
A promotional film of the group performing 'Ticket To Ride' and 'Yes It Is' was filmed at Riverside Studios for use on *Top Of The Pops*.

April 11
The Beatles topped the bill at the Empire Pool, Wembley, at the *New Musical Express* Poll Winners Show. They played 'I Feel Fine', 'She's A Woman', 'Baby's In Black', 'Ticket To Ride' and 'Long Tall Sally' to an audience of 10,000 people, and received their award from Tony Bennett.

Afterwards they drove to the ABC Television studios at Teddington where they appeared on *The Eamonn Andrews Show* to promote their new single.

April 12
Filming at Twickenham.

April 13
At Twickenham where they were filming The Beatles did a live interview for BBC Light Programme's *Pop Inn* to promote 'Ticket To Ride'. This was followed by a late-night session at Abbey Road to record the title song to *Help!* John's original acoustic version was slow, but George Martin thought the fans would prefer a faster number. John went along with the idea but later said, "I don't like the recording that much; we did it too fast trying to be commercial."

Paul bought a three-storey Regency house at 7 Cavendish Avenue in St Johns Wood, London, for £40,000.

April 14
Location filming for *Help!* in Ailsa Avenue, not far from the Old Deer Park in Twickenham.

Help! was announced as the title of the new film, replacing *Eight Arms To Hold You*. Among the rejected suggestions for the title were *Who's Been Sleeping In My Porridge* (by George), and *The Day The Clowns Collapsed* (the film's producer, Walter Shenson).

April 15
The *Top Of The Pops* session recorded on the 10th was broadcast by BBC TV.

April 16
George and John were interviewed live by Cathy McGowan on *Ready, Steady, Go!* at the Rediffusion Television Studios in Wembley.

April 17
Paul spent the day in disguise – cloth peaked cap, glasses, moustache and a big overcoat – in order to go furniture shopping in the Harrow Road and Portobello Road for his new house. A bartender in Ladbroke Grove was not fooled and recognised Paul when he asked for "A drop o' the hard stuff", in an Irish accent.

April 18
A part of their recorded appearance at the *New Musical Express* Poll Winners Show was broadcast on the *Big Beat '65* television special.

The movie *Pop Gear* went on limited release in the UK, featuring clips of The Beatles performing 'Twist And Shout' and 'She Loves You', shot in late 1963.

April 19
The single 'Ticket to Ride'/'Yes It Is' was released in the US as Capitol 5407.

April 20
Filming at Twickenham.

April 21
Brian Epstein sent a telegram to Elvis Presley in The Beatles' names to congratulate him on his first decade in the music business.

Filming at Twickenham.

April 22
Filming at Twickenham.

April 23
Filming at Twickenham.

April 24
Filming in Chiswick.

April 27
Filming at Twickenham.

April 28

Filming at Twickenham.

Peter Sellers arrived on set to present the group with a Grammy Award, issued by the US National Academy of Recording Arts and Sciences. *A Hard Day's Night* had won the award in the "Best Vocal Performance by a Group" category. The Beatles were pipped to the award for "Best Rock'N'Roll Recording" by Petula Clark's 'Downtown'.

April 29

Filming at Twickenham.

Chris Denning interviewed all four Beatles for his weekly Radio Luxembourg show, *The Beatles*.

Jimmy Nicol, the drummer who stood in briefly for Ringo during the Australian tour of 1964, appeared in the London Bankruptcy Court with debts of £4,066 and assets of a nominal £50.

April 30

Filming at Twickenham.

May 2

Plans were announced for The Beatles' 1965 Christmas Show to be broadcast to cinemas across Britain by closed-circuit TV.

Brian Epstein's office also confirmed that the premiere of the group's new movie would be held at the London Pavilion cinema on July 29.

Paul denied US press reports that he had been dating a former Miss Ireland, Marlene McKeown, for several months. "Rubbish!", he told a journalist. "I don't even know her."

May 3

The Beatles spent the day filming on Salisbury Plain with the assistance of the British Army's Third Tank Division. The Beatles, Eleanor Bron (with whom John had already struck up a strong rapport), Victor Spinetti, Roy Kinnear, Leo McKern and the other actors and film crew all stayed at the Antrobus Arms in Amesbury.

May 4

Filming on Salisbury Plain. They spent the night at the Antrobus Arms.

May 5

Filming on Salisbury Plain. Another night at the Antrobus Arms.

May 6

Filming at Twickenham.

May 7

Filming at Twickenham.

John gave instructions for a television set to be fitted in the back of his Rolls Royce car.

May 9

Filming in New Bond Street. John and Ringo filming at Twickenham.

Quizzed about their plans for the 1965 Christmas Show, John, George and Paul angrily denied that they would be taking part in any such event. "That just leaves Ringo," John added sarcastically. "Perhaps he and Brian Epstein could do a Christmas show together."

BOB DYLAN

That evening The Beatles went to see Bob Dylan play the Royal Festival Hall. Afterwards they visited Dylan in his suite at the Savoy Hotel. The four Beatles filed into his reception room, accompanied by keen Dylan fan Alma Cogan, but the atmosphere remained tense until Allen Ginsberg broke the ice by falling off the arm of a settee into John Lennon's lap and asking him if he knew William Blake. "Never heard of him," snapped John but Cynthia spoke up, "Oh John,

you liar, of course you have!" and everyone laughed. The rest of the evening was spent nightclubbing.

May 10
Filming at Cliveden House, near Maidenhead in Berkshire.

Abbey Road. The Beatles recorded two old rock'n'roll numbers, 'Dizzy Miss Lizzy' and 'Bad Boy', aimed at the American market.

May 11
Filming at Cliveden House, for the 'Buckingham Palace' scenes in the movie.

May 16
John attended a party given for Johnny Mathis by Norman Newell.

May 18
Twickenham for post-synchronisation work on the soundtrack to *Help!*

NBC-TV in the USA showed a pre-recorded interview with The Beatles by Peter Sellers in their Grammy Awards show *The Best On Record*. The programme also showed a clip of The Beatles playing 'I'm Happy Just To Dance With You' from *A Hard Day's Night*.

Paul and Jane saw Gene Barry play the Talk Of The Town and visited him after the show. Afterwards they went on to Downstairs at the Pickwick Club.

May 21
George and Patti spent the day shopping.

May 22
'Ticket To Ride' reached number one in the US charts.

A brief clip of The Beatles singing 'Ticket To Ride' appeared in an episode of *Doctor Who* on BBC TV.

May 25
John and Cynthia returned to London from Cannes, where they had attended the Film Festival. That afternoon, before leaving, John recorded an interview with Martin Ogronsky for the CBS-TV *Merv Griffin Show*.

The publishers of the US edition of the reference book *Who's Who* revealed that The Beatles would be included in the next printing of the book, for the first time.

May 26
The Beatles drove to the BBC's Piccadilly Studios where they recorded their last radio show for the BBC, a bank holiday special. They insisted that the name be changed from the usual *From Us To You*, to *The Beatles (Invite You To Take A Ticket To Ride)* which they thought was more suitable for their maturing image. They recorded live versions of 'Ticket To Ride', 'Everybody's Trying To Be My Baby', 'I'm A Loser', 'The Night Before', 'Honey Don't', 'Dizzy Miss Lizzy' and 'She's A Woman'.

May 27
All The Beatles flew off on their holidays. Paul and Jane went to Portugal where they stayed in Bruce Welch's villa in Albufera. Paul wrote the lyrics to 'Yesterday' in the car on the way from the airport and completed them over the next two weeks. Paul: "I fell out of bed. I had a piano by my bedside and I must have dreamed it because I tumbled out of bed and put my hands on the piano keys and I had a tune in my head. It was just all there, a complete thing. I couldn't believe it, it came too easy. In fact I didn't believe I'd written it. I thought maybe I'd heard it before, it was some other tune, and I went round for weeks playing the chords of the song for people, asking them, 'Is this like something? I think I've written it.' And people would say, 'No, it's not like anything else. But it's good . . .'"

John: "That was a good 'un."

June 1

The interview with John recorded at the Cannes Film Festival was shown on the CBS-TV *Merv Griffin Show*.

June 2

John, George and Ringo were among the celebrities who attended the premiere of Dick Lester's new film, *The Knack (And How To Get It)*, at the London Pavilion cinema.

June 3

John and George, accompanied by Cynthia and Patti, attended Allen Ginsberg's 39th birthday party held in a basement flat in Chester Square, London. When they arrived, Ginsberg was wearing nothing but his birthday suit. The two Beatles looked around anxiously in case any photographers were present then quickly departed. "You don't do that in front of the birds!" hissed John to one of the organisers. Ginsberg and John later became quite good friends and John himself was to appear naked on his *Two Virgins* album sleeve.

June 4

The EP *Beatles For Sale 2* was released in the UK as Parlophone GEP 8938 (mono only). Side A: 'I'll Follow The Sun', 'Baby's In Black'; Side B: 'Words Of Love', 'I Don't Want To Spoil The Party'.

June 7

The Beatles (Invite You To Take A Ticket To Ride) was broadcast by the BBC Light Programme as a Whit Monday special.

June 11

Paul and Jane flew back from their holiday a day early at Brian Epstein's request in order to be in Britain when it was announced that The Beatles had been awarded the Member of the Order of the British Empire (MBE).

The embargo on the news was lifted that evening and Paul was interviewed by telephone by Ronald Burns for the BBC Radio *Late Night News Extra* which also included an interview with Brian Epstein.

Ringo: "There's a proper medal as well as the letters, isn't there? I will keep it to wear when I'm old. It's the sort of thing you want to keep."

John: "I thought you had to drive tanks and win wars to win the MBE."

George: "I didn't think you got this sort of thing for playing rock'n'roll."

Paul: "I think it's marvellous. What does this make my dad?"

June 12

THE MBE FURORE

Prime Minister Harold Wilson's decision to include The Beatles on his list of MBEs for the Queen to approve caused many outraged previous recipients to return their medals in protest. One of them was Hector Dupuis, a member of the Canadian House of Commons who claimed that he had been placed on "the same level as vulgar nincompoops". Dupuis received his medal for running the Canadian Selective Service, calling up young men for the armed services.

George: "If Dupuis doesn't want the medal, he had better give it to us. Then we can give it to our manager, Brian Epstein. MBE really stands for 'Mister Brian Epstein'."

The Beatles gave a press conference at Twickenham Film Studios, which was used in news bulletins around the world. John was 70 minutes late, to the annoyance of Brian Epstein, who had to fetch him personally by car to make him attend. John: "I set the alarm for eight o'clock and then just lay there. I thought, well, if anyone wants me they'll phone me. The phone went lots of times, but that's the one I never answer. My own phone didn't go at all. So I just lay there."

John was always uneasy about accepting the award. John: "We had to do a lot of selling out then. Taking the MBE was a sellout for me. You know, before you get an MBE the Palace writes to you to ask if you're going to accept it,

because you're not supposed to reject it publicly and they sound you out first. I chucked the letter in with all the fan-mail, until Brian asked me if I had it. He and a few other people persuaded me that it was in our interests to take it, and it was hypocritical of me to accept it. But I'm glad, really, that I did accept it – because it meant that four years later I could use it to make a gesture. When my envelope arrived marked OHMS I thought I was being called up . . . I shall stick it on the wall or make it into a bell." In fact, he gave it to his Aunt Mimi who kept it on top of her television until he asked for it back in order to return it as a protest against Britain's involvement in the Biafra War.

June 13
Holders of MBE medals began to return their awards in protest at the honour being given to The Beatles.

June 14
Abbey Road. Paul recorded 'Yesterday' entirely solo on his acoustic guitar, followed the gentle ballad with the up-tempo rocker, 'I'm Down' and finished the session with 'I've Just Seen A Face'.

Afterwards Paul and Jane went to the Cromwellian Club.

The album *Beatles VI* was released in the US as Capitol T–2358 (mono) and ST–2358 (stereo). Side A: 'Kansas City'/'Hey, Hey, Hey, Hey', 'Eight Days A Week', 'You Like Me Too Much', 'Bad Boy', 'I Don't Want To Spoil The Party', 'Words Of Love'; Side B: 'What You're Doing', 'Yes It Is', 'Dizzy Miss Lizzy', 'Tell Me What You See', 'Every Little Thing'.

June 15
Abbey Road. John's 'It's Only Love' was recorded during an afternoon session. Afterwards they spent a night in the clubs.

June 16
John and Ringo spent the day at John's house, sorting out songs for Ringo to sing. They were unhappy with the way that 'Troubles' had turned out and were thinking of changing it. They decided that Ringo should record 'Act Naturally'.

The band did more post-synchronisation work at Twickenham for the film and later, at the Argyll Street office of NEMS, John did an interview and read "The Fat Budgie" section from *A Spaniard In The Works* to promote his new book on the BBC Radio show *The World Of Books*. He was also interviewed by Tim Matthews for the BBC Home Service news magazine *Today*, during which he also read the section of the book called "The National Health Cow".

Brian Epstein shelved plans for The Beatles to begin filming their third movie, *A Talent For Loving*, in October, after learning that the climate in Spain at that time of the year might jeopardise the location work.

June 17
Abbey Road. Ringo recorded 'Act Naturally'. This was followed by the group recording 'Wait'. That night they were driven round the nightclubs.

During this session, George Martin also recorded a string quartet playing the accompaniment to Paul's bare version of 'Yesterday'. Paul later revealed that he had also made a tentative approach to The BBC Radiophonic Workshop, with the suggestion that they might be able to produce an electronic backing for the song, but that he never followed the idea through.

George's sister, Louise Harrison, who lived in the US and had only had occasional contact with him in recent years, released a bizarre spoken-word album about her brother's success, *All About The Beatles* (Recar 2012).

June 18
The Beatles were interviewed at the NEMS offices by the Italian-language section of the BBC World Service to coincide with their upcoming Italian dates.

Later, at the BBC's Lime Grove Studios, John appeared on BBC1's *Tonight* programme where he was interviewed by Kenneth Allsop and read two extracts from his book, 'The Wumberlog' and 'We Must Not Forget The General Erection'.

June 20

The Beatles' European Tour opened in Paris. The venture began controversially, when the authorities at London Airport turned away Beatles fans who were arriving to wave the group goodbye, claiming that The Beatles themselves had asked them not to attend. This was angrily denied by both the group and manager Brian Epstein.

The Beatles arrived at Paris-Orly at 10am and checked in to the George Cinq. Their reception was quiet by Beatles standards with only about 50 fans waiting outside their hotel. This pattern was repeated throughout the tour, as the group regularly played to less than capacity audiences.

In Paris, they played two concerts to 6,000 people each at the Palais des Sports, topping a bill which also featured The Yardbirds. The second show was broadcast on both French radio and television.

Afterwards Françoise Hardy visited them at the George Cinq.

The night was spent at Castell's nightclub, where they stayed until dawn.

The Beatles' set during the European tour consisted of: 'Twist And Shout', 'She's A Woman', 'I'm A Loser', 'Can't Buy Me Love', 'Baby's In Black', 'I Wanna Be Your Man', 'A Hard Day's Night', 'Everybody's Trying To Be My Baby', 'Rock And Roll Music', 'I Feel Fine', 'Ticket To Ride' and 'Long Tall Sally'.

June 21

Another night spent in Castell's.

John's interview and reading from "The National Health Cow" was broadcast on the BBC Home Service *Today* programme.

June 22

The Beatles and their entourage flew to Lyons in the afternoon and played two shows at the Palais d'Hiver.

June 23

The Beatles took the train to Milan.

June 24

The Beatles played their first Italian show in Milan at the Velodromo Vigorelli, a 22,000-seater open-air arena. Brian Epstein was not pleased at all the empty seats, particularly during the afternoon show when many of the fans were at school or work and only 7,000 people attended. The press suggested that a combination of high prices and a heat wave had kept the fans away.

John's book *A Spaniard In The Works* was published in the UK by Jonathan Cape at 10s 6d.

June 25

The Alfa Romeo Racing Team drove the group to Genoa in four cars. There they played the Palazzo dello Sport, a 25,000 seater arena where, once again, there were many empty seats. The afternoon show attracted only 5,000 fans.

June 26

The group travelled to Rome by special train from Genoa.

June 27

Two shows in Rome at the Teatro Adriano. While The Beatles were playing 'I Wanna Be Your Man,' which Ringo always sang, Paul for some reason or other was laughing so hard he had to leave the stage. George was not amused and his displeasure was obvious. When Paul returned to the stage the microphone fell over and he continued laughing. This made John start laughing as well but George remained irritated by it all. At the end of the shows, Paul thanked the audience in Italian.

After the evening show, Paul met playwright Noel Coward, who had attended the concert, at their hotel.

Noel Coward: "The noise was deafening throughout and I couldn't hear a word they sang or a note they played. I went backstage and was met by Brian Epstein, who told me they had gone back to the hotel and would I go there. I was told The Beatles refused to see me. I thought this graceless in the extreme, but decided to play it with firmness and dignity. I told Wendy [Hanson, Epstein's personal assistant] to go and fetch one of them, and she finally reappeared with Paul McCartney. The poor boy was quite amiable and I sent messages of congratulation to his colleagues, although the message I would have liked to have sent them was that they were bad-mannered little shits."

June 28
Beatles producer George Martin began work on an album of comic interpretations of their songs by actor Peter Sellers.

June 29
Two more shows at the Teatro Adriano, Rome, though none of the shows there was more than half full.

June 30
The group arrived in Nice where they stayed at the Gresta Hotel and played at the Palais des Expositions.
    After the show they spent the evening at La Fiesta nightclub. At 2am The Beatles were still racing each other and members of their crew on the club's own go-kart track.

July 1
The Beatles flew to Madrid where they visited the Jerez de la Frontera vineyard, while Brian Epstein saw a bullfight in the same arena in Madrid that the group were to play the next night.
    John's *A Spaniard In The Works* was published in the USA.

July 2
Plaza de Toros de Las Ventas, Madrid. The Beatles were growing increasingly worried by the level of violence shown to the fans by the police and security in Italy and particularly in Spain.

July 3
The group flew to Barcelona in the afternoon to play the Plaza de Toros Monumental at 10.30 that evening. This was followed by nightclubbing.
    John's interview for *The World of Books* was transmitted on the BBC Home Service.

July 4
When the group arrived home at London Heathrow at midday, 1,000 fans were waiting to greet them.

July 5
A pre-recorded interview with John was broadcast on the BBC Light Programme's *Teen Scene*.
    The single 'That Means A Lot' by P.J. Proby, written by Lennon & McCartney, was released in the US as Liberty 55806.

July 7
Paul and Jane, George and Patti went to a party given by The Moody Blues in Roehampton.

July 9
Klaus Voormann, a close friend of The Beatles while they were in Hamburg, released his first UK single as a member of the beat group Paddy, Klaus & Gibson, 'I Wanna Know'. The group were managed by Brian Epstein, who was encouraged to sign them by John and Paul.

July 11
The album *Beatles VI* reached number one in the US album charts.

July 13
Paul accepted five Ivor Novello Awards, presented by David Frost, on behalf of John and himself at a luncheon at the Savoy. John refused to attend. He had been upset by the press comments about their receiving the MBE and did not want to put himself on show again. Paul was 40 minutes late because he had forgotten about the engagement. On receiving the award he quipped, "Thanks. I hope nobody sends theirs back now."

July 14
John, Cynthia, George, Patti, Ringo and Maureen spent the evening at the Bastille Night party at the Scotch St James's.
   Paul watched Jane in a repertory performance at the Palace Theatre, Watford.

July 15
A film of Paul receiving the Ivor Novello Awards on the 13th was shown on Rediffusion Television's *Pick Of The Songs,* illustrated by clips of the various winners playing *Ready Steady Go!*

July 17
ABC TV's *Lucky Stars Anniversary Show* showed a film clip of The Beatles playing 'Help!'

July 19
Ringo and Maureen bought "Sunny Heights" in Weybridge for £37,000. They moved in just before Christmas.
   The single 'Help!'/'I'm Down' was released in the US as Capitol 5476.

July 21
500,000 copies of Al Hine's paperback novelisation of *Help!* were distributed to American bookstores. The book featured several scenes which were cut from the final edit of the film.

July 23
The single 'Help!'/'I'm Down' was released in the UK as Parlophone R 5305.
   John: "When 'Help!' came out in '65, I was actually crying out for help. Most people think it's just a fast rock'n'roll song. I didn't realise it at the time; I just wrote the song because I was commissioned to write it for the movie. But later, I knew I really was crying out for help. It was my fat Elvis period. You see the movie: he – I – is very fat, very insecure, and he's completely lost himself. And I am singing about when I was so much younger and all the rest, looking back at how easy it was. Now I may be very positive – yes, yes – but I also go through deep depressions where I would like to jump out the window . . . Anyway I was fat and depressed and I was crying out for help."

HELP!
"The only true songs I ever wrote were 'Help!' and 'Strawberry Fields'," John Lennon claimed in December 1970. *"They were the ones I really wrote from experience and not projecting myself into a situation and writing a nice story about it, which I always found phoney. The lyric is as good now as it was then. It makes me feel secure to know that I was that sensible, aware of myself back then. But I don't like the recording that much, we did it too fast, to try to be commercial." In the same week he gave that interview, Lennon actually attempted to re-record the song, slowing it to funereal pace as a piano ballad. His efforts merely exposed what a smooth and powerful piece of work The Beatles' rendition was – to the point that the surface sheen and production expertise successfully disguised any hint of authentic anguish in Lennon's vocal. The record turned out nothing more or less than a perfect Beatles single, and an ideal theme tune for their movie.*
   Trivia note: the single and LP versions of this song feature slightly different Lennon vocals.

I'M DOWN
On the same day that McCartney recorded the folk-rocker 'I've Just Seen A Face' and the gentle ballad 'Yesterday', he also cut this raucous rock'n'roll song – the flipside of 'Help!' and a blatant attempt to write his own 'Long Tall Sally'. Indeed, 'I'm Down' replaced 'Long Tall Sally' as The Beatles' final song at almost every show they played in their last year as a live

band. Despite having all the required ingredients, from Paul's raw vocal to George's stinging guitar solo, it never quite gelled as well as the Little Richard blueprint, and the lyrics seem rather misogynistic from the standpoint of the Nineties. But it's a powerful piece of work nonetheless.

July 25
The Beatles staged a day of rehearsals in London for their forthcoming US tour.

July 26
Television Wales and West screened a clip from the film *Help!* on *Discs A Gogo*.

July 29
Ten thousand fans gathered in Piccadilly Circus outside the London Pavilion on a humid summer evening for the royal premiere of *Help!* The Beatles arrived in a black Rolls Royce and were presented to Princess Margaret and Lord Snowdon (who had delayed their summer holiday so they could attend the premiere). Jane Asher wore a pure white Edwardian-style evening dress. There was a party afterwards at the Orchid Room of the Dorchester Hotel.

John: "The best stuff is on the cutting room floor, with us breaking up and falling about all over the place."

Paul: "Filming *Help!* stretched us a bit, giving us more than one line at a time to say."

John: "*Help!* was too Disneyland. Later there was a rash of films similar to *Help!* and I could see what Richard Lester, the director, was doing. But he didn't really utilise us in that film. He forgot about who and what we were, and that's why the film didn't work. It was like having clowns in a movie about frogs."

Simultaneous with the premiere in London, *Help!* also went on general release in a selection of English seaside towns, including Barnstaple, Brighton, Canterbury, Clacton, Lowestoft, Plymouth, Ramsgate, Weymouth and Worthing.

United Artists revealed that they had manufactured more prints of *Help!* than of any previous colour film, anticipating unprecedented demand from countries all over the world.

BBC's *Top Of The Pops* showed a film clip from *Help!*

July 30
The Beatles spent the day rehearsing on stage at Brian Epstein's Saville Theatre. They did two BBC interviews: one with Dibbs Mather for the British Information Service and the other with Lance Percival for his *Lance A Gogo* show on the BBC Light Programme.

Later John, Paul and George drove to Blackpool in John's black-glass Rolls Royce. Ringo and Brian Epstein took the plane. The car was parked in the police station car park to keep it safe from fans but in the morning the windows were all cracked. John was angry, but it turned out that the windows had been fitted too tightly and had cracked with the movement of the car, not because they had been tampered with.

July 31
Rehearsals for ABC TV's *Blackpool Night Out* and the upcoming American tour were held in Blackpool.

Singer Suzy Cope issued her début single, 'You Can't Say I Never Told You'. By mistake, the music sheet for the song, released to the trade on the same day, credited John and Paul as its composers, although they had no connection with the song, the record or Cope.

August 1
The Beatles appeared on ABC TV's *Blackpool Night Out* along with Pearl Carr and Teddy Johnson, Mike and Bernie Winters, and Lionel Blair and his dancers. They performed 'I Feel Fine', 'I'm Down', 'Act Naturally', 'Ticket To Ride'. Paul sang 'Yesterday' and they closed with 'Help!'

That evening Ringo and Brian flew back to London while the others followed in the Rolls Royce.

Much press criticism ensued from Brian Epstein's decision that The Beatles should make only this one TV appearance to promote their new single.

August 2

Brian Epstein announced that The Beatles would not be doing a British tour this year. (They did play a nine-date tour in November/December.)

Paul and Jane, Marianne Faithfull and several other friends spent an evening on the town in London using The Beatles' Austin Princess to get around. They first met up with The Byrds at their hotel then continued to the Scotch St James's club in Mason's Yard.

The BBC2 TV show *Music International* broadcast a pre-recorded interview with John.

August 3

John took his Aunt Mimi down to Poole, in Dorset, to choose a bungalow overlooking Poole Harbour.

August 5

United Artists announced that takings at UK cinemas screening *Help!* during its first week of release were 37% higher than those for *A Hard Day's Night* the previous year.

August 6

The album *Help!* was released in the UK as Parlophone PMC 1255 (mono) and PCS 3071 (stereo). Side A: 'Help!', 'The Night Before', 'You've Got To Hide Your Love Away', 'I Need You', 'Another Girl', 'You're Going To Lose That Girl', 'Ticket To Ride'; Side B: 'Act Naturally', 'It's Only Love', 'You Like Me Too Much', 'Tell Me What You See', 'I've Just Seen A Face', 'Yesterday', 'Dizzy Miss Lizzy'.

HELP!

A vastly increased budget, colour stock, exotic overseas locations, and a lavish publicity campaign – The Beatles' second feature film had everything except the one quality which had made its predecessor so successful, realism. John Lennon later dismissed *Help!* as "bullshit", which was unjustly harsh. But though its script crackled with jokes and The Beatles wisecracked their way through the full 100 minutes, complete with striking musical interludes, *Help!* didn't have the magic of *A Hard Day's Night*.

That's not to say it wasn't a successful movie by its own lights. It grossed an impressive figure, in Britain and around the world, and it stands up today as a glossy, semi-satirical period piece, perfectly in keeping with the wacky Beatles image that the world initially mistook for the real thing. By 1965, though, The Beatles were losing interest in refuelling their image. Through the use of soft drugs, they were beginning to glimpse an artistic purpose beyond Beatlemania and the production line of hit records. John Lennon, in particular, managed in 1965 to find his own lyrical voice, and started to use The Beatles as a vehicle to express his increasingly confused feelings about his role in the group, and his personal relationships.

In one important respect, the preparations for *Help!* were identical to those for the previous year's movie. The decision was made in advance to divide the 'soundtrack' album between one side of songs that would appear in the film, and another of non-movie tunes. And as before, the film songs had to be completed before the shooting began. The Beatles' flight for the Bahamas left on February 22: just seven days earlier, the group arrived for their first movie session at Abbey Road. By the time their plane set off for their film location, they had recorded no fewer than 11 songs — although two of these, 'If You've Got Trouble' and 'That Means A Lot', were destined to remain unreleased until the Nineties.

At that stage, the film was still untitled, and it wasn't until The Beatles had returned to Britain at the end of March that they were informed that it would be called *Help!* A title song was commissioned and delivered almost overnight, while the soundtrack album was eventually completed during breaks in the filming, just six weeks before its release date. Tracks unreleased on singles are as follows:

THE NIGHT BEFORE

Studio finesse was second nature to The Beatles by February 1965 – and so too was commercial songwriting. John Lennon's first flirtation with electric piano (which was a constant feature on this album) was the only novel moment on this fluent and ultra-appealing McCartney pop song.

YOU'VE GOT TO HIDE YOUR LOVE AWAY

After the tentative Dylan-isms of 'I'm A Loser', John Lennon made his debt to the American singer-songwriter entirely clear on this song. Too self-pitying for Dylan himself, it was nonetheless a piece of personal expression for its composer, who still automatically equated writing from the heart with songs about romantic disappointment.

For two musical reasons, this track stood out from earlier Beatles recordings. First of all, it was an entirely acoustic performance from an electric rock'n'roll band. Secondly, it featured a guest musician from outside The Beatles' circle. George Martin had been adding keyboards to the group's records from the start, but this song featured a flute solo by arranger John Scott, though his contribution wasn't noted on the sleeve.

I NEED YOU

For only the second time, The Beatles recorded a George Harrison composition – earlier efforts like 'You'll Know What To Do' having been rejected by Lennon/McCartney. An otherwise unexceptional song was punctuated by brief, slightly hesitant bursts of guitar noise, controlled by a foot pedal soon to become famous as the wah-wah.

ANOTHER GIRL

Though the songs themselves broke few boundaries, the recording sessions for the Help! album found The Beatles gradually exploring new techniques and instrumental combinations. On his own 'Another Girl', for instance, Paul played the twisting lead guitar line – as he did on 'Ticket To Ride', recorded at the same session. George Harrison's misgivings about his diminished role on these tracks were presumably dampened by the fact that the third song taped that day was one of his own.

YOU'RE GONNA LOSE THAT GIRL

A beautifully compact piece of songwriting, 'You're Gonna Lose That Girl' illustrated that Lennon was every bit McCartney's match when it came to producing quality pop tunes to order. Tempted though he must have been, Paul let George play lead guitar this time around, contenting himself with adding piano to the basic track.

ACT NATURALLY

Ringo's usual vocal appearance on this album was originally supposed to be 'If You've Got Trouble', a dire Lennon/McCartney composition which The Beatles attempted twice before recognising its canine qualities. By way of compensation for being saddled with such a loser, Ringo was allowed to record an American country hit, co-written by comedian Johnny Russell, and recently debuted by one of the giants of the Bakersfield sound, Buck Owens. With its "they're gonna put me in the movies" lyric, the song fitted the bill perfectly. More than two decades later, Ringo and Buck combined forces to re-record the number.

IT'S ONLY LOVE

Asked to select his least favourite Beatles songs, John Lennon went unerringly for 'Run For Your Life' and this mawkish number – which was still considered strong enough to qualify for heartfelt cover versions by vocalists as diverse as Bryan Ferry and Gary 'US' Bonds. Listen out again for George Harrison on wah-wah guitar, this song being one of the least likely candidates for such an effect in the entire Beatles catalogue.

YOU LIKE ME TOO MUCH

American rock critic Lester Bangs noted that this George Harrison composition was "probably the first song in rock history whose lyrics admitted that neither party loved the other but neither had the guts to call it quits". Harrison's unsentimental attitude to love resurfaced on the next album with 'If I Needed Someone'. At the time, though, more attention was paid to George's increasing confidence as a vocalist, and to the two-men-at-one-piano trick of Paul and George Martin.

TELL ME WHAT YOU SEE

More electric piano, and another McCartney pop tune, slightly more laboured than its contemporaries on this record. The Help! album was the last occasion on which The Beatles felt able to indulge themselves in a set of entirely fictional teen-romance songwriting. By the time they reconvened for the Rubber Soul sessions at the end of 1965, the concept of lyric-writing as a form of intimate confession had taken hold.

I'VE JUST SEEN A FACE

A folk song taken at bluegrass tempo, 'I've Just Seen A Face' was a McCartney gem, given an entirely satisfactory acoustic arrangement. The fact that it was taped during the same three-hour session as Paul's screaming rocker, 'I'm Down', makes its discreet assurance even more remarkable.

Paul resurrected this song during the Wings' tours of the mid-Seventies.

YESTERDAY

"I really reckon 'Yesterday' is probably my best song," said Paul McCartney in 1980. "I like it not only because it was a big success, but because it was one of the most instinctive songs I've ever written. I was so proud of it. I felt it was an original tune – the most complete thing I've ever written. It's very catchy without being sickly."

Despite his initial misgivings about the song's sentimentality, John Lennon eventually agreed, picking 'Yesterday' as one of Paul's strongest compositions. Its origins have passed into the realms of legend: McCartney awoke one morning with the melody in his head, set some nonsense words to the tune to make sure he remembered it (working title: 'Scrambled Egg') and then played it to all and sundry, convinced that a song which had come so easily must have been stolen from something else. No one could identify the source, and Paul was eventually convinced that 'Yesterday' had sprung fully formed from his own imagination.

In 1965, the song evoked some controversy, when it was revealed to the press that Paul had recorded it without any help from the rest of the group, the only instrumental support coming from his own acoustic guitar and a string quartet arranged by George Martin. American magazines listed the song as a McCartney solo release, and when it topped the US singles charts there was speculation that Paul would soon opt for a career outside the group. So he did, but not for another five years.

DIZZY MISS LIZZY

Larry Williams emerged from the same Specialty Records stable as Little Richard, and his best records shared Richard's frenetic marriage of rock'n'roll and R&B. McCartney handled the Little Richard covers in The Beatles, while the Larry Williams songs became Lennon's responsibility. The group had been performing 'Dizzy Miss Lizzy' on stage since their first trip to Hamburg in 1960, though Harrison's slightly erratic guitar fills showed that they hadn't played it for a while before this session. But Lennon cruised through the vocal like the natural rock'n'roller he was.

He illustrated his love for the song by reviving it at his first major post-Beatles concert appearance in Toronto four years later. Meanwhile, 'Dizzy Miss Lizzy' became the last cover version that The Beatles ever released.

John and George attended The Byrds' late night show at Blaises' nightclub in London, and then spent several hours after the gig with the group.

August 8

John, Cynthia, George and Patti made a secretive trip to the Richmond Jazz Festival to see Eric Burdon and The Animals. They were unable to stay for long because they were recognised by fans and almost mobbed.

The album *Help!* reached number one in the UK charts.

August 9

Brian Epstein's new signing, The Silkie, recorded John's 'You've Got To Hide Your Love Away' under John's supervision. Paul played guitar and George the tambourine during the six-hour session.

August 11

The film *Help!* was premiered in New York, without any of The Beatles being present.

August 13

The Beatles arrived at JFK Airport to begin their third US tour. Their TWA flight touched down at 2.30pm and was met by a huge battery of press, radio and TV reporters, but the police had the plane parked two miles from the main terminal so the thousands of waiting fans were unable to see them. They went straight to the Warwick Hotel at 6th Ave and 54th Street where they gave the obligatory press conference to about 250 reporters, fielded by their press officer Tony Barrow. The Beatles had the whole 33rd floor to themselves, with guards at all entrances to keep out unwanted visitors.

The album *Help!* was released in the US as Capitol MAS–2386 (mono) and SMAS–2386 (stereo). It contained fewer songs and included music from Ken Thorne's film score. Side A: 'The James Bond Theme' (The George Martin Orchestra), 'Help!', 'The Night Before', 'From Me To You Fantasy' (The George Martin Orchestra), 'You've Got To Hide Your Love Away', 'I Need You', 'In The Tyrol' (The George Martin Orchestra); Side B: 'Another Girl', 'Another Hard Day's Night' (The George Martin Orchestra), 'Ticket To Ride', 'The Bitter End'/'You Can't Do That' (The George Martin Orchestra), 'You're Going To Lose That Girl', 'The Chase' (The George Martin Orchestra).

August 14
The police cleared the streets for a convoy of limousines to take The Beatles to rehearsals for *The Ed Sullivan Show* at CBS Studio 50 where they began work at 11am. The group did not like the sound balance and continued rehearsals through the afternoon, watching playbacks until they were satisfied it was right. The final tape was made at 8.30 that evening. They performed 'I Feel Fine', Paul did 'I'm Down', then Ringo introduced himself and sang 'Act Naturally'. 'Ticket To Ride' was followed by Paul singing 'Yesterday' to a string quartet from the Ed Sullivan orchestra, and they ended with 'Help!', during which John forgot some of the words. Paul: "I had to sing 'Yesterday' live in front of all those people. It was pretty nerve-wracking but it was very exciting. I know I was nervous. We'd recorded 'Yesterday' but I'd never really had to perform it anywhere."

August 15
The Beatles played Shea Stadium.

SHEA STADIUM
The police feared that fans would jam the tunnels in and out of Manhattan so the group was first escorted by limousine to the Manhattan East River Heliport and from there they flew to the World Fair site in Queens – taking in a sightseeing tour of Manhattan's skyscrapers, to provide some spectacular introductory footage for the film crew. There they transferred from the helicopter to a Wells Fargo armoured van where they were each given a Wells Fargo agent badge. As usual for those days, there was a full bill, and 55,600 fans sat through the King Curtis Band, Cannibal and The Headhunters, Brenda Holloway, The Young Rascals and Sounds Incorporated before Ed Sullivan finally walked on stage to announce The Beatles: "Now, ladies and gentlemen, honoured by their country, decorated by their Queen, loved here in America, here are The Beatles!" They did their standard 30-minute set of a dozen numbers then jumped straight back into the Wells Fargo van, $160,000 richer – amounting to $100 per second of their performance.

The usual set for this tour was: 'Twist And Shout', 'She's A Woman', 'I Feel Fine', 'Dizzy Miss Lizzy', 'Ticket To Ride', 'Everybody's Trying To Be My Baby', 'Can't Buy Me Love', 'Baby's In Black', 'I Wanna Be Your Man', 'A Hard Day's Night', 'Help!' and 'I'm Down'. Mick Jagger, Keith Richards and Andrew Loog Oldham were in the audience.

The concert was filmed by Brian Epstein's Subafilms organisation, and released as a documentary film called *The Beatles At Shea Stadium*.

That evening Bob Dylan visited their hotel.

August 16
This day had been left open as a rain check for Shea Stadium. They stayed in their hotel where visitors included The Supremes, The Exciters, The Ronettes, Del Shannon and Bob Dylan. They also taped a few interviews with DJs.

August 17
The Beatles flew to Toronto, Canada, in the Lockheed Electra hired by Brian Epstein from American Flyers for the tour. Years later, George was on a flight from New York to

Los Angeles and met the pilot. He said, "George, you don't remember me, I'm the pilot from the American Flyers Electra plane that you did the tours on. You'd never believe that plane! It was just full of bullet holes, the tail, the wings, everything – just full of bullet holes. Jealous fellows who would be waiting around, knowing that The Beatles were arriving at such-and-such a time. They'd all be there trying to shoot the plane!"

Maple Leaf Gardens, two shows to an audience of 35,000 fans each. News had leaked that the group were staying at the King Edward Sheraton and dozens of fans had booked themselves in, causing a difficult security problem.

August 18

The Beatles flew in to Atlanta that morning and did just one concert, to 35,000 people at the Atlanta Stadium. The new baseball stadium had a very fine sound system which the group talked about for days after, since at most venues they could rarely hear themselves play. Their plane arrived at Houston airport at 2am, having left Atlanta immediately after the gig. Local police had made no arrangements and fans swarmed out onto the runway as the plane taxied in to the terminal. Fans began climbing over the plane before it had even stopped moving, some of them smoking cigarettes next to the plane's fuel tanks. The group and Brian Epstein were unable to leave the plane until a forklift truck arrived for them.

August 19

The Beatles played two sets to a total of 25,000 fans at the Sam Houston Coliseum. They were restrained performances in very hot weather with complete chaos backstage and no dressing room facilities. The group travelled to and from the show by armoured van.

BBC's *Top Of The Pops* showed a film clip from *Help!*

August 20

The Beatles and entourage flew through the night from Texas, arriving in Chicago at three in the morning at Midway Airport. The police had heard of the trouble in Houston and had forbidden them to land at O'Hare because of the disruption it would cause. They put up at the O'Hare Sahara which had foolishly announced that The Beatles were to stay there, so the place was swarming with fans who made so much noise that no one was able to get any sleep that night. Nonetheless their two sets at the huge White Sox Park Stadium before a total of 50,000 fans went very well.

August 21

In the afternoon The Beatles flew from Chicago to Minneapolis, Minnesota, for one show before 22,000 people at the Twin Cities Metropolitan Stadium. Parts of the show were almost drowned out by a press helicopter circling above the crowd which particularly annoyed John. They stayed at the Leamington Motor Inn, which, like the hotel in Chicago, had announced that The Beatles were staying there. George had the best time in Minneapolis because someone gave him a new guitar. Brian Matthew arrived at the BBC straight from the airport to give the *Saturday Club* radio audience a first-hand report on the opening dates of The Beatles' American tour.

John revealed that he had been approached to write a film script around the contents of his two books, *In His Own Write* and *A Spaniard In The Works*, and that he would be starting work on the project after the US tour.

August 22

The Beatles held a press conference at Minneapolis airport, before leaving for the next stop of their tour. The usual round of media questions was interrupted by a teenage fan, who had managed to gatecrash the event. He asked Ringo for advice on how to play the drums. "You'll never get anywhere listening to me," Ringo replied. "And he's been playing drums for thirty years," John added.

Flying to Portland from Minneapolis, the group's Lockheed Electra flew through a deep gorge and, shortly before landing, one of the plane's four engines caught fire and they arrived belching black smoke and flames. The incident was serious enough for John to scrawl a quick self-obituary on a piece of paper, which he then folded inside a small film canister to ensure that it would survive any crash. The local press had a field day with this story, blowing it up out of all proportion, though it could undoubtedly have proved dangerous had it occurred earlier.

NME reporter Chris Hutchins, who travelled with The Beatles, reported that during the crisis, George quipped: "Now perhaps people will stop joking about how long we're going to last." When the plane landed, John shouted: "Beatles, women and children first!"

The Beatles played two shows at the Portland Memorial Coliseum. Carl Wilson and Mike Love of The Beach Boys visited them backstage. Allen Ginsberg was in the audience and was greeted by John Lennon from the stage. He wrote a poem about the concert called "Portland Coliseum": "A single whistling sound / of ten thousand children's / larynxes a singing / pierce the ears . . .".

August 23
The Beatles left Portland after their concert. With the Electra out of commission, they flew in a Constellation which lengthened the flight so they did not arrive in Los Angeles until a few hours before dawn. They rented a house at 2850 Benedict Canyon, Beverly Hills, but in fewer than ten hours the press and radio stations were giving out the supposedly secret address over the air. While The Beatles relaxed by the pool, the Beverly Hills police force had their work cut out keeping fans from invading their privacy. A dozen police were on duty plus a group of Burns Agency security men.

August 24
Eleanor Bron, who had starred with the group in *Help!*, and The Byrds both visited The Beatles. Peter Fonda also came by when John was on an acid trip.

John: " 'She Said She Said' was written after an acid trip in LA during a break in The Beatles' tour, where we were having fun with The Byrds and lots of girls . . . Peter Fonda came in when we were on acid and he kept coming up to me and sitting next to me and whispering, 'I know what it's like to be dead.' He was describing an acid trip he'd been on."

That evening, the head of Capitol Records, Alan Livingstone, threw a party for the group during which they were presented with various awards. The guests included Edward G. Robinson, Jack Benny, Vince Edwards, Gene Barry, Richard Chamberlain, Jane Fonda, Rock Hudson, Groucho Marx, Dean Martin, Hayley and Juliet Mills and James Stewart. The party ended with a screening of *What's New Pussycat* but Paul and George left before the end to attend a Byrds recording session in the early hours. The Byrds were recording 'The Times They Are A Changin''.

The routine at Benedict Canyon consisted of breakfast at around 2pm, sunbathing and swimming during the afternoon, then dinner followed by a private screening of the latest films. The house had a magnificent view across the canyon and was the perfect place for them to unwind.

Perhaps emotionally weakened by his regular consumption of drugs during this period, John wrote an anguished letter home to his wife, expressing his disillusionment with his life.

John: "I spend hours in dressing rooms and things, thinking about the times I've wasted not being with Julian – and playing with him – you know I keep thinking of those stupid bastard times when I keep reading bloody newspapers and other shit whilst he's in the room with us and I've decided it's ALL WRONG! . . . I'll go now because I'm bringing myself down thinking what a thoughtless bastard I seem to be – I really feel like crying – it's so stupid – and I'm choking up now as I'm writing – I don't know what's the matter with me. I'm having lots of laughs, but in between the laughs there is such a drop."

August 25
Two girl fans hired a helicopter to fly over the Benedict Canyon mansion and jumped from it into the swimming pool. Brian complained to the police and no further helicopters came to bother them.

August 27
The group remained trapped in their house but Paul put on his disguise and accompanied by Alf Bicknell, managed to do a bit of sightseeing.

MEETING ELVIS

That evening they met Elvis Presley at his home on Perugia Way in Bel Air next to the Country Club. They arrived at 11pm to find Elvis waiting on the doorstep. He took them through a huge circular lobby lit with his favourite red and blue lights into an enormous living room dominated by a giant colour television set with the sound turned off. Brian Epstein and Colonel Tom Parker stood together at the side and watched the meeting.

The atmosphere was stilted at first, with no one saying anything until Elvis blurted out, "If you damn guys are gonna sit here and stare at me all night I'm gonna go to bed."

This broke the ice. Elvis produced guitars and he and The Beatles played along to rock records from Elvis' collection. Paul played piano and guitar while Elvis played bass. They found they had things in common, discussing incidents with fans and problems of being on the road. George told Elvis how their plane caught fire while landing in Portland and Elvis remembered a similar episode when his aircraft engine failed in Atlanta.

He said that it normally took him about 28 days to shoot one of his films which amazed The Beatles who thought their six-week shooting schedule had been rushed. John made a terrible gaffe by asking Elvis, "Why don't you go back to making rock'n'roll records?" To Elvis this implied that his career had been all downhill but rather than argue the case, he blamed his film career:

"It's my movie schedule. It's so tight! I might just do one soon, though."

"Then we'll buy that!" John told him. It seemed to The Beatles later that Elvis had been stoned on something throughout the meeting. The visit lasted three hours and they left shortly after two in the morning. As Elvis waved them goodbye he called out, "Don't forget to come and see us again in Memphis if you're ever in Tennessee." As The Beatles' limo pulled away, John turned to the others and asked, "Where's Elvis?" He later said: "It was like meeting Engelbert Humperdinck."

Mal, Neil and Alf, their road managers, were also present during the visit and were amazed to find that Elvis had ten road managers, complete with their wives, living with him in the house, whereas The Beatles made do with three roadies for the four of them.

The Beatles were each given a complete set of Elvis albums, gun holsters with gold leather belts and a table lamp shaped like a wagon.

August 28

The Beatles travelled from Beverly Hills to San Diego in a luxury touring coach with ten seats, a fridge, bathroom, shower and plenty of food and drink. They took the coast highway for the two-hour journey. The Balboa Stadium was filled with 20,000 fans. The bus broke down on the way back to LA and they had to stop at a mortuary to transfer to limousines for the remainder of the journey. Fans caught up with them and jumped all over the cars, ruining them.

American folk singer Joan Baez, a former girlfriend of Bob Dylan's, had now joined The Beatles' entourage, and was apparently enjoying a close friendship with John.

August 29

In the afternoon there was a large press conference at the Capitol Tower at Hollywood and Vine, during which Alan Livingstone presented The Beatles with gold discs for *Help!*

An armoured truck took them from there to the Hollywood Bowl for the first of their concerts. The show was watched by 18,000 fans and one of them gave birth to a boy in the car park outside.

August 30

The last night of their nine days in Beverly Hills. Their second concert at the Bowl was a success and was (like its predecessor) taped by Capitol Records for a possible future live record. The group gave a pool-side party for the dozen or so press men and women who had accompanied them on the tour.

BBC Radio broadcast *The Beatles Abroad*, a 45-minute programme of interviews recorded by Brian Matthew during the early days of the US tour.

August 31

A total of 30,000 people saw the two shows at the San Francisco Cow Palace. The Beatles did their standard 12-number set and the show made news around the world because scores of fans fainted when loose seating allowed fans to push forward and rush the stage. The crowd got so out of hand at one point that the group had to leave the stage and wait in their backstage caravan until the situation had calmed down before returning to play. Johnny Cash and Joan Baez visited backstage. George played 'Greensleeves' and they both joined in the vocals.

September 1

The Beatles flew back to London from the US.

September 2

The Beatles arrived at London Airport.

September 4

The single 'Help!' reached number one in the US charts.

September 6

Paul and Jane went to see the play *The Killing Of Sister George* starring Beryl Reid at the Duke of York's Theatre. They were driven by Alf Bicknell whom they invited in to watch with them. Paul enjoyed it, Jane was critical. Afterwards they cruised a few nightclubs.

September 10

The single 'You've Got To Hide Your Love Away' by The Silkie, written by Lennon & McCartney, was released in the UK as Fontana TF 603.

September 11

John, Paul and George returned to Liverpool to visit relatives for a few days.

September 12

The album *Help!* reached number one in the US charts.

The Beatles' August 14 recording for *The Ed Sullivan Show* was transmitted.

September 13

Maureen gave birth to Zak Starkey at Queen Charlotte's Hospital, Hammersmith, London.

John, Paul and George returned from Liverpool.

The single 'Yesterday'/'Act Naturally' was released in the US as Capitol 5498. 'Yesterday' was not released as a single in the UK until long after The Beatles split up.

September 17

The single 'That Means A Lot' by P.J. Proby, written by Lennon & McCartney, was released in the UK as Liberty 10215.

September 20

The single 'You've Got To Hide Your Love Away' by The Silkie, produced and written by Lennon & McCartney, was released in the US as Fontana 1525.

September 23

The charity Oxfam announced that, for the second year running, they would be printing a special Christmas card featuring a John Lennon cartoon – this time the drawing which accompanied 'The Fat Budgie' in his book, *A Spaniard In The Works*.

September 25

The Beatles cartoon series, *The Beatles,* made by King Features began broadcasting in the US. The series featured genuine Beatles songs and cartoon characters with voices by Paul Frees (John and George) and Lance Percival (Paul and Ringo). The series was produced by Al Brodax who later produced the cartoon film *Yellow Submarine.* The series was not screened at the time in the UK.

September 27

John jolted the promotional campaign for the *Help!* movie by revealing to a journalist that the film had been "a mistake".

EMI revealed that recording sessions for The Beatles' next album, due for release before Christmas, would begin in late October.

October 1

The single 'Yesterday' reached number one in the US. It remained unreleased in the UK because the group did not want their image as a rock'n'roll band damaged by the release of a solo ballad.

A 'YESTERDAY' TALE

In Eric Burdon's autobiography, he says that Paul originally offered Chris Farlowe the song:

"One day he phoned me at my Duke Street pad. 'Hey Eric, how ya doin', it's Chris Farlowe here,' he said in his hoarse voice. I asked how he was getting on. 'Oh, I'm OK. 'Ere listen, you'll never guess what happened. Paul McCartney – you know Paul out of The Beatles?' Yes, I had heard of him. 'Well he came round to our house in the middle of the night. I was out doing a show, but me mum was in and he left her a demo disc for me to listen to.' This was wonderful news. When was Chris going into the studio to cut this gift from the gods? 'Ah,' he growled. 'I don't like it. It's not for me. It's too soft. I need a good rocker, you know, a shuffle or something.' 'Yeah, but Chris,' I said. 'Anything to give you a start, man, I mean even if it's a ballad, you should go ahead and record it.'

" 'No, I don't like it,' he insisted. 'Too soft.'

" 'So what are you gonna do with the song?'

" 'Well, I sent it back, didn't I?'

" 'What was the title of the song?'

" ' "Yesterday",' he retorted."

October 3

Paul and Jane Asher attended a London cabaret performance by Frances Faye at The Talk Of The Town.

October 4

Paul and John visited the recording studio to watch Alma Cogan record 'Eight Days A Week'.

October 7

Former Beatles drummer Pete Best was reported to have taken a legal action for libel against his successor, Ringo Starr, over comments attributed to Ringo in a recent *Playboy* magazine interview with The Beatles.

October 9

All four Beatles attended a party given to celebrate the London opening of Lionel Bart's new musical *Twang*.

Afterwards they celebrated John's birthday.

October 11

Paul visited Decca Records Studios to watch Marianne Faithfull record 'Yesterday'. Marianne's version charted in the UK but came second to that by Matt Monro.

The single 'Twist And Shout'/'There's A Place' was released in the US as Capitol Starline 6061.

The single 'Love Me Do'/'P.S. I Love You' was released in the US as Capitol Starline 6062.

The single 'Please Please Me'/'From Me To You' was released in the US as Capitol Starline 6063.

The single 'Do You Want To Know A Secret?'/'Thank You Girl' was released in the US as Capitol Starline 6064.

The single 'Roll Over Beethoven'/'Misery' was released in the US as Capitol Starline 6065.

The single 'Boys'/'Kansas City'/'Hey, Hey, Hey, Hey' was released in the US as Capitol Starline 6066. This was the only one of these six 'reissue' singles to reach the US chart, albeit no higher than No. 102.

October 12

Abbey Road. John's 'Run For Your Life' was recorded in an afternoon session, leading straight into 'Norwegian Wood', then still known as 'This Bird Has Flown'. George played sitar for the first time on a Beatles' recording; a cheap model bought at Indiacraft. John: "I was trying to write about an affair without letting my wife know I was writing about an affair."

October 13

Abbey Road. The recording of 'Drive My Car' was the first time that The Beatles had recorded past midnight – something which would soon become the norm.

October 14

John and Paul had a songwriting session at Kenwood.

Paul: "We've written some funny songs – songs with jokes in. We think that comedy numbers are the next thing after protest songs. We don't like protest songs, because we're not the preaching sort, and we leave it to others to deliver messages of that kind."

October 15

Paul and Jane saw Ben E. King play at the Scotch St James's. George, Patti, John and Cynthia arrived at the Scotch too late and missed the show.

October 16

Abbey Road. 'Day Tripper' was recorded during an afternoon and evening session, followed by work on George's 'If I Needed Someone'.

October 18

Abbey Road for the afternoon only, during which they completed 'If I Needed Someone' and worked on John's 'In My Life'.

October 20

Abbey Road. Two extended sessions produced 'We Can Work It Out'.

October 21

Abbey Road. The Beatles were in the studio from 2.30 until after midnight working on 'Norwegian Wood' and 'Nowhere Man'.

October 22

Abbey Road. The Beatles were driven to Abbey Road at 10am where they stayed until midnight working on 'Nowhere Man'.

The Beatles refused the invitation to repeat their 1963 performance at the Royal Variety Show next month, despite being promised that they would headline the event. Brian Epstein denied that this was a snub to the Royal Family, insisting that the group's tight recording schedule made it impossible for them to attend.

Paul: "We're not trying to dodge doing something for charity – we're making a contribution with a show of our own soon. But it's just not our audience. If we went on and people didn't like us, everyone would say, 'Ha, ha, The Beatles failed, they're on the slide.' As it is, they'll fill the theatre without any help from us, and at the same time we shan't suffer."

October 24

Abbey Road. The Beatles began work at 2.30pm, working on Paul's 'I'm Looking Through You' and stayed until midnight. Afterwards all of them except John continued to the Scotch St James's where Brian was holding a party.

October 26
The Beatles were invested with their MBEs.

The Beatles arrived at Buckingham Palace in John's black glass Rolls Royce in time for the 11am honours ceremony in the Great Throne Room. Wearing dark suits and ties, they stood in a row while the Queen pinned the medals to the narrow lapels of their jackets. "How long have you been together now?" she asked.

"Oh, for many years," said Paul.

"Forty years," said Ringo, and everyone laughed.

"Are you the one that started it all?" the Queen asked Ringo.

He told her that the others started it. "I'm the little one," he said.

The Queen wore a pale gold gown. The room in Buckingham Palace was decorated in cream and gold, with six chandeliers overhead and an organ at one end. The band of the Coldstream Guards quietly played tunes from 'Humoresque' and 'Bitter Sweet'. Paul later described it as "a keen pad".

The Lord Chamberlain, Lord Cobbold, read out The Beatles' names. They stepped forward and bowed. The Queen shook hands, spoke to each, and pinned on the medals. They then stepped back into place and bowed again.

Paul described the Queen as, "Lovely. Great! She was very friendly. She was just like a mum to us."

At the investiture 189 people received awards, including six who were knighted. The Beatles were awarded the MBE, the lowest of the five divisions of the order, for service to their country. It ranks 120th of the 126 titles of precedence and is the most widely given honour.

Outside, 4,000 Beatles fans chanted "Yeah, yeah, yeah" and jostled with police who managed to hold them back, but could not prevent them climbing the gates and lamp-posts outside the palace.

Immediately afterwards there was a press conference arranged in the downstairs bar of the Saville Theatre for The Beatles to discuss their MBEs and give their reaction to the protests.

October 27
A recording session booked for this date was cancelled because John and Paul had not yet written sufficient new material.

George Martin: "We hope to resume next week. We are not waxing songs by other composers. We want this to be an all Lennon/McCartney album."

October 28
Abbey Road. Mixing session for 'We Can Work It Out'.

John Lennon arrived at the Ad-Lib with a crowd of friends, driven in his Rolls Royce by The Beatles' chauffeur Alf Bicknell. When he learned that it was Alf's birthday he insisted on giving him a night out on the town. One of the entourage, John's friend Terry Doran, took charge of the car and after the Ad-Lib, John took the whole party to dinner at the Savoy where Françoise Hardy was in cabaret.

October 29
Abbey Road. A new vocal track was added to 'We Can Work It Out'.

October 31
Box offices at cinemas and theatres across Britain opened, selling tickets for The Beatles' December tour.

November 1
The Beatles drove to Manchester to record *The Music Of Lennon And McCartney,* a special for Granada Television. Paul began 'Yesterday' and after 22 seconds the cameras cut away to a pregnant Marianne Faithfull performing her version. The group mimed to 'We Can Work It Out' and 'Day Tripper'. Other artists performed their own versions of Beatles songs.

John became a director of Drutsown Limited, a company set up to control his literary income.

November 2
The Beatles finished recording at Granada and returned to London.

November 3
Abbey Road. An afternoon and an evening session ending at midnight recording Paul's 'Michelle'.

November 4
Abbey Road. A 7pm until 3am session recording Ringo's 'What Goes On'.

November 6
Abbey Road. A 7pm until 3am session working on Paul's 'I'm Looking Through You', but no one was satisfied with the results.

November 7
Capitol Records withdrew promotional support for their US Beatles single, 'Boys', after being advised by the group that they no longer thought it was representative of their sound.

November 8
Abbey Road. The group rehearsed George's 'Think For Yourself' and at about 3am recorded *The Beatles Third Christmas Record*, a flexi-disc issued free to fan club members only.

November 10
Abbey Road. A 9pm to 3am session for John's 'The Word' and more work on 'I'm Looking Through You'.

November 11
Abbey Road. A late-night session beginning at 6pm and ending at 7am working on 'Wait', recording Paul's 'You Won't See Me' and John's 'Girl'. They put the finishing touches to 'I'm Looking Through You' and their new album, *Rubber Soul* was finished.

November 12
Parlophone's Italian office released an album entitled *The Beatles In Italy* – not, as its title suggested, a live recording from their recent European tour, but a collection of previously released studio tracks.

November 15
The afternoon was spent sequencing songs for the new album with George Martin.
   EMI announced that 'We Can Work It Out' would be the A-side of The Beatles' next single.

November 16
Paul saw Gene Pitney play in Slough and acted as MC, making the announcements from behind the stage curtains so that no one in the audience knew it was him: "And to start the show in swinging style: The Mike Cotton Sound!" He was there because Peter Asher's group, Peter & Gordon, were on the bill. Between houses, when the curtain was down, Paul played drums on stage.

November 17
George and Patti spent the day shopping.
   John contradicted EMI's announcement two days earlier by insisting that, as far as he was concerned, 'Day Tripper' was the A-side of the next single. He also revealed that he had been approached by film director Tony Richardson to write the script for a proposed movie adaptation of the book, *In The Words Of The Hornet*.

November 18
John and Cynthia spent the day shopping.

November 23
The Beatles filmed their own promotional film clips to promote the new album. This way they would be able to appear on television in the US, Japan and the rest of the world instead of being restricted to just a few British TV shows. They filmed all day at Twickenham Film Studios. Film versions were made of 'We Can Work It Out', 'Day Tripper', 'Help!', 'Ticket To Ride' and 'I Feel Fine' which were shown all over the world during the Christmas period.

Press agent Tony Barrow: "The boys would normally have appeared on television themselves to plug their new single, but they have been busy preparing an entirely new stage act, featuring all new numbers from their forthcoming album, for the tour which begins in Glasgow."

November 25
Harrods opened for three hours in the evening to enable The Beatles to do late-night Christmas shopping in private. Both Ringo and George purchased items of furniture, while John bought a giant slide for his son Julian to use in the garden.

November 27
Paul saw his brother Michael in his group The Scaffold perform at the Granada, East Ham where they were on the bill of a Manfred Mann/Yardbirds concert, and attended the party after the show.

November 29
The Beatles taped an interview with Brian Matthew at the BBC Aeolian Hall for use on the Christmas Day edition of the BBC Light Programme's *Saturday Club*.

November 30
Brian Matthew interviewed George and John separately at NEMS Argyll Street office for the BBC Overseas Service.

December 1
The Beatles spent the day practising at Mal and Neil's apartment in order to be on form for their upcoming British tour.

An art exhibition at the Nell Gwynne Club, London included some of John's drawings.

The December issue of the US magazine *McCall's* included a short story by John called 'The Toy Boy'. The piece had been written for the proposed follow-up to *In His Own Write* and *A Spaniard In The Works*. John had already signed a contract with Jonathan Cape for a third book, but abandoned the idea in 1966, feeling that this form of expression was no longer necessary now that The Beatles had expanded the range of their lyric writing.

December 2
The Beatles drove to Berwick-on-Tweed. One of George's guitars fell off the back of the car en route and was smashed to pieces by following traffic.

BBC TV's *Top Of The Pops* premiered the new promo films for 'Day Tripper' and 'We Can Work It Out'.

John's company, Drutsown Limited, changed its name to Lennon Books Limited.

December 3
The single 'Day Tripper'/'We Can Work It Out' was released in the UK as Parlophone R 5389. 'We Can Work It Out' was originally intended as the A-side of the single, but at John's insistence, both sides were given equal prominence in the press and on the radio.

The album *Rubber Soul* was released in the UK as Parlophone PMC 1267 (mono) and PCS 3075 (stereo). Side A: 'Drive My Car', 'Norwegian Wood (This Bird Has Flown)', 'You Won't See Me', 'Nowhere Man', 'Think For Yourself', 'The Word', 'Michelle'; Side B: 'What Goes On', 'Girl', 'I'm Looking Through You', 'In My Life', 'Wait', 'If I Needed Someone', 'Run For Your Life'.

EMI made an initial pressing of 750,000 copies to cope with the expected demand.

The Beatles began their last UK tour in Glasgow, playing two sets at the Odeon Cinema. Also on the bill were their friends The Moody Blues. The Beatles' set consisted of: 'Dizzy Miss Lizzy', 'I Feel Fine', 'She's A Woman', 'If I Needed Someone', 'Ticket To Ride', 'Act Naturally', 'Nowhere Man', 'Baby's In Black', 'Help!', 'We Can Work It Out', 'Day Tripper' and 'I'm Down'.

Bad weather made Brian Epstein change their hotel from a small one just out of town to a grand hotel in the centre of Glasgow which posed a security problem.

DAY TRIPPER

For once, the guiding rule that you can tell which Beatle wrote a song by the identity of the lead vocalist breaks down with this song, originally issued as a double A-sided single in December 1965. 'Day Tripper' was a Lennon composition – the title apparently meant "a weekend hippie" – but it was McCartney who sang the verses, while Lennon handled the chorus. Like 'I Feel Fine' and 'Ticket To Ride', the song was built around a rock-solid guitar riff, which suggested that Lennon was responding to the inspiration of The Rolling Stones, who'd strung a series of singles around similar instrumental hook-lines since the middle of 1964.

WE CAN WORK IT OUT

Supporting 'Day Tripper' was this collaboration of two unfinished songs, taken by The Beatles themselves as revealing the diverse approaches of Lennon and McCartney to music and to life. EMI immediately tried to push this as the A-side of the single, only for John Lennon to intervene and insist that the rockier 'Day Tripper' be given equal, if not superior, status. Not that Lennon wanted to denigrate 'We Can Work It Out', to which he made a vital instrumental contribution on harmonium; he simply didn't wish to see the softer side of the group's music exposed at the expense of their rock'n'roll roots.

RUBBER SOUL

"I think *Rubber Soul* was the first of The Beatles' albums which presented a new Beatles to the world," reckons George Martin, who was close enough to the proceedings to know. "Up till then, we had been making albums rather like a collection of singles. Now we were really beginning to think about albums as a bit of art on their own. And *Rubber Soul* was the first to emerge that way."

John Lennon concurred: "We were just getting better, technically and musically, that's all. We finally took over the studio. On *Rubber Soul*, we were sort of more precise about making the album, and we took over the cover and everything. It was Paul's album title, just a pun. There is no great mysterious meaning behind all this, it was just four boys, working out what to call a new album."

There's no real disagreement, among fans, musicians and critics alike. *Sgt. Pepper* may have been The Beatles' production extravaganza, and *Revolver* their first post-acid celebration, but *Rubber Soul* was the record on which they revealed clear signs of fresh thinking – not just in musical or lyrical terms, but also philosophically. If *Beatles For Sale* marked the pinnacle of British beat, and *Help!* a consolidation of the past, *Rubber Soul* was a step into the future.

It's important to remember that The Beatles weren't pioneers in their quest for new artistic experiences. Bob Dylan had already recorded and released *Bringing It All Back Home* and *Highway 61 Revisited* by the time the group began work on *Rubber Soul*. But The Beatles were the first to introduce Dylan's free-form wordplay into the tight constraints of the three-minute pop song. Weeks before The Byrds discovered the joys of being 'Eight Miles High', the Liverpudlians announced that "the word is love".

Equally important to remember is that, unlike *Pepper* or *The White Album*, *Rubber Soul* wasn't a carefully considered studio creation. As they had been the previous autumn, The Beatles were trapped on a deadline-powered treadmill. When they arrived at Abbey Road studios on October 12, they knew that their next single, and album, had to be ready for release at the start of December. In the event, they cut it right to the bone: the final songs weren't written or recorded until mid-November. Just 18 days after the album was mixed, copies were on sale in the shops.

Despite the determinedly trend-setting approach of the album, one thing hadn't changed: The Beatles still intended *Rubber Soul* to be heard in mono, rather than stereo. In order to make both this record and *Help!* acceptable for modern digital audiences, George Martin remixed them both into 'proper' stereo for the CD releases.

DRIVE MY CAR

For all John Lennon's reputation as a rock'n'roller, it was Paul McCartney who wrote The Beatles' most raucous songs of 1965 – 'I'm Down' (the flipside of the 'Help!' single) and then this sly piece of sexual innuendo. What's most noticeable about the song at this distance, though, is the sparseness of the production. At a time when their nearest rivals, The Rolling Stones, were experimenting with dense, murky soundscapes, The Beatles cut this album with the maximum of separation between individual instruments, creating a feeling of space rather than tension.

NORWEGIAN WOOD (THIS BIRD HAS FLOWN)

At the time it was released, Paul McCartney described this Lennon composition as "a comedy song". In the same debunking spirit, George Harrison admitted that the arrangement was "an accident as far as the sitar part was concerned". And not until 1970 did John Lennon explain: "I was trying to write about an affair without letting my wife know I was writing about an affair."

The sitar wasn't an accident, as George had played the instrument on the first still-unreleased version of the song on October 12. And the lyrics certainly weren't comedy, though they had their moments of humour. In oblique, memorable imagery, Lennon conjured up a romantic encounter that rapidly moved beyond his control – a theme that would soon become an obsession in his work.

YOU WON'T SEE ME

From reality to fantasy, in one fell swoop: no one would claim McCartney's 'You Won't See Me' as a piece of self-revelation. But it was a supreme piece of commercial songwriting, recorded during the last, frantic day of sessions to complete the album. Note the superb falsetto harmonies, and McCartney's confident piano playing.

NOWHERE MAN

Sitting bored in his Surrey home suffering writer's block, John Lennon suddenly envisaged himself as the "nowhere man, thinking all his nowhere plans for nobody". As the composer, Lennon wrote himself a message of hope: "nowhere man, the world is at your command". The Beatles translated the song into gorgeous Byrdsian 1965 pop, showing off another set of delicious vocal harmonies.

THINK FOR YOURSELF

George Harrison's spiritual investigations would soon initiate an entire genre of songwriting. 'Think For Yourself' was the first sign that he had a voice of his own, every bit as cynical as Lennon's about the trappings of everyday life, but holding out the study of the mind and the universe as a panacea. "Try thinking more, if just for your own sake," he sang, in a line which summed up his philosophy for the next few years.

THE WORD

Meanwhile, John and Paul considered that "the word is love" – their first tentative step into the shimmering waters of drug-enhanced freedom and meditation. At the time, McCartney was more impressed by the song's simple musical form: "To write a good song with just one note in it – like 'Long Tall Sally' – is really very hard. It's the kind of thing we've wanted to do for some time. We get near it in 'The Word'."

MICHELLE

Songs become standards when they sound as if they've been around forever the first time you hear them. 1965 saw Paul McCartney unveiling the two songs that have been more covered than anything else he has ever written – first 'Yesterday' and then this romantic Gallic ballad, complete with in-built French translation. Every bit as much a hook as the chorus was the descending bass-line, as Paul explained to Mark Lewisohn: "I'll never forget putting the bass line in because it was a kind of Bizet thing. It really turned the song around."

WHAT GOES ON?
"That was a very early song of mine," John Lennon explained, "but Ringo and Paul wrote a new middle eight together when we recorded it." That gave Ringo his first ever composing credit, the group having turned down his solitary composition up to that point, 'Don't Pass Me By'. On Rubber Soul, *'What Goes On' performed exactly the same function as 'Act Naturally' had on* Help! *– opening the second side of the LP with a lightweight, country song in preparation for the meatier fare to follow.*

GIRL
Written overnight for the last session of the album, 'Girl' was the song that illustrated just how far John Lennon had travelled since 'I Feel Fine' a year earlier. "'Girl' is real," he explained in 1970." It was about that girl, who happened to be Yoko in the end, the one that a lot of us were looking for. And I was trying to say something about Christianity, which I was opposed to at the time." With its biting attack on Catholic values, and its thinly veiled mixture of lust and disgust, 'Girl' was Lennon's most personal statement of disillusionment to date.

I'M LOOKING THROUGH YOU
For almost the first time, Paul McCartney used this song as a vehicle for a personal message, rather than an attempt to write a hit single. He'd fallen out with his girlfriend of the time, Jane Asher, and 'I'm Looking Through You' was his response – half apology, half accusation. The Beatles first recorded the song without its melodic middle section, substituting a harsh guitar solo. Ever the tunesmith, Paul had written the missing lines by the time they finally recorded the released version.

IN MY LIFE
"In the early days, George Martin would translate for us," Lennon remembered in 1970. "In 'In My Life', there's an Elizabethan piano solo. He would do things like that." In musical terms, that was the most striking thing about 'In My Life'. But it acquired a new resonance in the wake of Lennon's death in 1980, when it took on the role of a personal epitaph, a warm-hearted salutation to friends and lovers down the years. That's the way it was intended in 1965, as well, with John feeling sufficiently removed from his upbringing to be able to feel nostalgic about the world he'd left behind.

WAIT
Desperate needs require desperate remedies, and for the second time ('Hold Me Tight' being the first) The Beatles plugged a gap on a new album by returning to a reject from a previous session. At least 'Hold Me Tight' had been re-recorded, though: for 'Wait', the group called up the tape of a song which they'd attempted during the sessions for 'Help!', and decided wasn't up to scratch. With more vocal harmonies, percussion and vocals, they salvaged it, though the song's naïve enthusiasm still sounds out-of-place amid the more worldly lyrics of other Rubber Soul *songs.*

IF I NEEDED SOMEONE
By far the best song George Harrison had written up to that point, 'If I Needed Someone' left its mark for several reasons. It boasted stunning three-part harmonies, the tightest they'd yet achieved on record; it had a jingle-jangle guitar sound obviously borrowed from The Byrds, in exactly the same way as The Byrds had developed their sound from listening to The Beatles; and it featured lyrics that were not so much anti-romantic as totally realistic. 'If I Needed Someone' may be the first pop song written from the jaded, though not quite exhausted, viewpoint of a man who had women lined up outside his hotel door in every city of the world.

RUN FOR YOUR LIFE
The first song to be recorded for Rubber Soul *appeared last on the album – and on its composer's list of preferences. "I always hated that one," John Lennon admitted in later years. "It was one I knocked off just to write a song, and it was phoney." It was also a mildly nasty rocker with a central threat stolen from an Elvis Presley classic. The line, "I'd rather see you dead little girl than to be with another man", first surfaced on Elvis' revolutionary revamp of the blues standard 'Baby, Let's Play House' back in 1955. Lennon never sought to disguise the theft; but in 1965, most reviewers and fans hadn't been schooled in Elvis' Sun sessions, which were then available only scattered across long-deleted albums, and the lyrical debt went unnoticed.*

December 4
The group had a bad journey through snow to Newcastle for a concert at the City Hall (British Tour).

December 5
Liverpool Empire (British Tour).

All their friends and relatives attended the concert which turned out to be the last time The Beatles played their home town. During the second show, Paul joined support act The Koobas on stage to play drums on 'Dizzy Miss Lizzy'.

The double A-side single, 'We Can Work It Out'/'Day Tripper', reached No. 1 in the UK charts.

The album *Rubber Soul* reached number one in the UK album charts.

George savagely criticised The Hollies' rendition of his song, 'If I Needed Someone', which was released today, describing it as "rubbish" and complaining: "They've spoilt it. The Hollies are alright musically, but the way they do their records, they sound like session men who've just got together in a studio without ever seeing each other before."

Hollies leader Graham Nash responded: "Not only do these comments disappoint and hurt us, but we are sick of everything The Beatles say or do being taken as law. The thing that hurts us most is George Harrison's knock at us as musicians. And I would like to ask this. If we have made such a disgusting mess of his brainchild song, will he give all the royalties from our record to charity?"

December 6
The Beatles spent the day with friends and family in Liverpool.

The album *Rubber Soul* was released in the US as Capitol T–2442 (mono) and ST–2442 (stereo). As usual it contained fewer tracks than the UK original: Side A: 'I've Just Seen A Face', 'Norwegian Wood (This Bird Has Flown)', 'You Won't See Me', 'Think For Yourself', 'The Word', 'Michelle'; Side B: 'It's Only Love', 'Girl', 'I'm Looking Through You', 'In My Life', 'Wait', 'Run For Your Life'.

The single 'Day Tripper'/'We Can Work It Out' was released in the US as Capitol 5555.

The EP *The Beatles Million Sellers* was released in the UK as Parlophone GEP 8946. (mono only). Side A: 'She Loves You', 'I Want To Hold Your Hand'; Side B: 'Can't Buy Me Love', 'I Feel Fine'.

December 7
The group drove to Manchester with no trouble but the city was covered in thick fog and it took them four hours to find the venue, arriving at the ABC Cinema, Ardwick, after they should have been on stage. Walter Shenson visited them backstage to discuss their third film.

Paul: "We've had a few ideas for writing our own film scripts, like the one about Jesus Christ coming back to earth as an ordinary person. But I think we're now resigned to the fact that we will just not have the time to work on a full-scale musical until The Beatles as a group are finished.

"We have always wanted to write a number about the places in Liverpool where we were born. Places like Penny Lane and The Docker's Umbrella have a nice musical sound, but when we strung them all together in a composition, they sounded so contrived, we gave up."

December 8
Gaumont Cinema, Sheffield (British Tour).

After the show, The Moody Blues joined them for dinner at their hotel.

December 9
The band drove to Birmingham through torrential rain and played the Odeon Cinema (British Tour).

December 10
The Beatles returned to London and played the Hammersmith Odeon (British Tour).

Britain's best-selling music paper, the *New Musical Express*, printed the results of its annual Readers Poll. The Beatles won the "Best British Group" and "Best World Group" categories, while John deposed Cliff Richard as "British Vocal Personality".

December 11
The band played the Finsbury Park Astoria (British Tour) to a tremendous London audience.

George: "This is one of the most incredible shows we've done. Not just because of the audience, but because they're Londoners. This is the funny thing. It's always been the other way round – fantastic in the North but just that little bit cool in London. It's incredible. It seems like the Beatlemania thing is happening all over again."

December 12
The UK tour ended with a concert at the Cardiff Capitol Cinema. Ringo drove back to London after the show in order to go to the Scotch St James's Christmas party.

December 13
John, Paul and George returned to London. They met with Brian to discuss their projected third film. The meeting ended in disagreement with the group turning down the script for Richard Condon's *A Talent For Loving* for which Brian had already bought the rights.

December 14
John and Cynthia did Christmas shopping.

December 16
Granada Television screened the *Songs Of Lennon And McCartney* special in London; viewers across the rest of Britain saw the show the following day.

John: "There are only about 100 people in the world who really understand what our music is all about. Ringo, George, and a few others scattered around the globe. That's all. The reason so many people use our numbers and add nothing at all to them is that they do not understand the music. Consequently they make a mess of it.

"We try and find a truth for ourselves, a real feeling. You can never communicate your complete emotion to other people, but if we can convey just a little of what we feel, then we've achieved something."

December 17
The Beatles Third Christmas Record flexi-disc was sent to 65,000 members of The Beatles fan club.

December 18
John spent the night in the clubs.

December 19
Paul and Jane saw a performance of Lionel Bart's musical *Twang* at the Shaftesbury Theatre.

December 23
Paul did last-minute Christmas shopping. Among his Christmas gifts to the other Beatles were acetates of a special record called *Paul's Christmas Album* made in an edition of four copies only. On it Paul acted as a DJ playing his favourite tracks.

December 25
BBC Light Programme's *Saturday Club* broadcast clips from a specially recorded interview.

The pirate ship Radio Caroline broadcast a specially recorded Christmas message by the group who had always given their support to pirate stations.

BBC TV's *Top Of The Pops* showed film clips of the group performing 'I Feel Fine', 'Help!', 'Ticket to Ride' and 'Day Tripper'.

December 26

George was driven to Liverpool to pay a surprise visit to his mother and family in their new bungalow on Boxing Day. George and chauffeur Alf Bicknell had to sleep on camp beds in the attic.

Radio Caroline broadcast a pre-recorded interview with Paul on its *Pop's Happening* programme.

Paul was also in Liverpool to see his family, bringing his friend, Guinness heir, Tara Browne, with him. While they were out for a ride in country lanes in the Wirral, Paul fell off his moped and cut his lip badly enough to require several stitches.

December 31

Paul, Jane, George and Patti attended a big New Year's party with EMI executives. John and Cynthia spent the evening at a party given by Norman Newell.

John's father, Freddie Lennon, released a single, 'That's My Life (My Love And My Home)' on Pye Records. This desperate piece of self-promotion did little to reconcile Freddie with his estranged son.

FREDDIE LENNON

John: "I never saw him until I made a lot of money and he came back. I opened the *Daily Express* and there he was, washing dishes in a small hotel or something very near where I was living in the stockbroker belt outside London. He had been writing to me to try and get into contact. I didn't want to see him. I was too upset about what he'd done to me and to my mother and that he would turn up when I was rich and famous and not bother turning up before. So I wasn't going to see him at all, but he sort of blackmailed me in the press by saying all this about being a poor man washing dishes while I was living in luxury. I fell for it and saw him and we had some kind of relationship. He died a few years later of cancer. But at 65 he married a secretary who had been working for The Beatles, age 22, and they had a child, which I thought was hopeful for a man who had lived his life as a drunk and almost a Bowery bum."

January
John installed a home studio at Kenwood, and over the next months he experimented with creating many avant-garde sounds, plus one-man demos of his new compositions.

January 1
The album *Rubber Soul* entered the *Billboard* Hot 100 charts.

January 2
Motown Records in Detroit claimed that their top writing and production team, Holland, Dozier & Holland, had been asked by The Beatles to compose several songs for their next album.

January 4
Brian Epstein travelled to New York to sign contracts for the next Beatles US tour, scheduled to take place in the summer.

January 5
CTS Studios: The Beatles re-recorded and overdubbed sections of *The Beatles At Shea Stadium* soundtrack because the audience screaming and technical problems meant that the live sound was not up to exhibition standard. 'I Feel Fine' and 'Help!' were re-recorded from scratch.

John and Cynthia entertained P.J. Proby at their home then drove back to London in John's black Rolls Royce to Proby's house off the King's Road, Chelsea, where he was giving a party. John returned home at dawn.

January 7
John and Ringo met at John's to discuss The Beatles' next film.

January 8
Paul went to Liverpool to visit his family.

John, George and Ringo went to a party given by Mick Jagger at his home.

The album *Rubber Soul* reached number one on the *Billboard* Hot 100 charts.

The single 'We Can Work It Out' reached number one in the *Billboard* singles charts.

January 9
Brian Epstein flew from New York to the Bahamas, to discuss the handling of The Beatles' offshore bank accounts, officially based in that country.

January 12
John, Cynthia, Ringo and Maureen flew to Port of Spain, Trinidad, for a winter holiday.

January 13
George and Patti met up with Mick Jagger and Chrissie Shrimpton for a night of dancing at Dolly's nightclub on Jermyn Street, in the West End.

January 20
Folk singer Donovan revealed that his next single would be a tribute to The Beatles, entitled 'For John And Paul'.

January 21
George married Patricia Anne Boyd at the Leatherhead and Esher Register Office, Surrey. Paul and Brian Epstein were the Best Men; John and Ringo were still away on holiday, and unable to attend.

That evening, the couple celebrated with a party at "Kinfauns", George's American-style villa in Esher.

January 22
George and Patti gave a press conference before being driven to Heathrow to fly to Barbados for their honeymoon. "How did you manage to keep it a secret?", a reporter asked George. "Simple," he replied. "We didn't tell anyone."

January 23
John and Cynthia, Ringo and Maureen returned from Trinidad.

January 27
Tickets went on sale for the *New Musical Express* Pollwinners Concert on May 1, at which it had already been confirmed that The Beatles would headline. All the seats were sold within three days.

January 31
Peter Sellers' send-up of 'A Hard Day's Night'/'Help!' was released in the US.

February
John returns the advance he's been given by Jonathan Cape for his third book, effectively cancelling the project.
    John: "I should have finished a new book. It's supposed to be out this month. But I've only done one page. I thought, why should I break my back getting books out like records?"
    Actor David McCallum announced his plan to record an album of John's poetry.
    Barry Miles and John Dunbar opened the Indica Bookshop in London's Covent Garden; Paul designed the promotional flyers for the shop, and also the wrapping paper.
    Paul and art dealer Robert Fraser flew to Paris for a few days, so that Paul could meet artists and purchase work to hang in his new St. John's Wood home.

February 3
Paul saw Stevie Wonder perform at the Scotch St James's and visited with him backstage afterwards. Paul was very pleased to see him because he had always been one of his favourite Motown acts.

February 10
'Woman' by Peter & Gordon, written by Paul as Bernard Webb, entered the *Billboard* charts at number 83.

February 12
John and Ringo spent a night at the Scotch St James's.

February 13
The Grammy Awards Committee in New York nominated The Beatles for ten awards – divided between six nominations for 'Yesterday', and a further four for 'Help!'

February 21
The single 'Nowhere Man'/'What Goes On' was released in the US as Capitol 5587.

February 24
Paul attended a lecture and taped performance by Luciano Berio at the Italian Institute. He and Berio spoke afterwards but there were too many press and Italian embassy people present for them to relax.

February 26
The single 'Woman' by Peter & Gordon, written by Paul as Bernard Webb, entered the UK charts at number 47.

February 28
The Cavern was closed by the Official Receiver with debts of £10,000. The Police had to break down barricades to evict fans who had holed up inside to resist the closure.

March
Paul placed an advertisement in the underground magazine *Global Moon Edition Of The Long Hair Times* under the pseudonym 'Ian Iachimoe', requesting script ideas for an experimental film.

March 1
The Beatles At Shea Stadium was given its world premiere on BBC1 in black and white. It was originally filmed in colour, designed for the American market where it was shown in cinemas. Press advertisements for the show were designed by The Beatles' old friend from Hamburg, artist and musician Klaus Voormann.

March 3
Brian Epstein announced The Beatles' plans to tour Britain, Japan, the US and Germany during 1966.

March 4
The London *Evening Standard* published an interview with John Lennon by his friend Maureen Cleave. John: "Christianity will go. It will vanish and shrink. I needn't argue about that. I'm right and I will be proved right. We're more popular than Jesus now. I don't know which will go first – rock'n'roll or Christianity. Jesus was alright but his disciples were thick and ordinary. It's them twisting it that ruins it for me." His words upset no one in Great Britain but when they were reprinted in the US, Christian fundamentalists reacted with hate and outrage.

The EP *Yesterday* was released in the UK as Parlophone GEP 8952 (mono). Side A: 'Yesterday', 'Act Naturally'; Side B: 'You Like Me Too Much', 'It's Only Love'.

March 6
Paul and Jane went skiing in Klosters, Switzerland.

March 16
The Beatles failed to win any of the ten Grammy awards for which they had been nominated. Capitol Records boss Allan Livingstone launched an official protest about the fact that 'Yesterday' had not been selected as "Song Of The Year". "It makes a mockery of the whole event," he complained.

March 18
NEMS had to confirm that Peter & Gordon's hit song, 'Woman' was written by Paul McCartney, though it was credited to Bernard Webb. Paul said he put a false name on it to see if it would still make the charts.

March 20
Paul and Jane returned from their holiday in Klosters.

Almost a year after he had purchased the house, his home in Cavendish Avenue, St. John's Wood was now finally ready for him and Jane to move in.

March 23
Photo session to provide new pictures of the group to publicise their next American album.

March 24
All of The Beatles and their wives and girlfriends attended the premiere of Lewis Gilbert's film *Alfie*, starring Jane Asher.

March 25
The Beatles did a photo session for Bob Whitaker at his studio at 1 The Vale, off the Kings Road, Chelsea.

THE 'BUTCHER' SLEEVE
The Beatles posed in white coats, using sides of meat and broken dolls as props.

John: "Bob was into Dali and making surreal pictures . . . it was inspired by our boredom and resentment at having to do another photo session and another Beatles thing. We were sick to death of it . . . That combination produced that cover."

**The image was used as the sleeve for their next American album,
Yesterday . . . and Today but provoked a very negative reaction and was
withdrawn. It was used in the UK in ads for the single 'Paperback Writer'.**

While at Whitaker's studio, The Beatles posed for a second, more conventional photo
session for Nigel Dickson, working for *The Beatles Book* fan magazine. They also
recorded an interview with Radio Caroline DJ Tom Lodge which was released as a
flexi-disc called *Sound Of The Stars* given away free in a promotion by *Disc And Music
Echo*, part-owned by Brian Epstein.

March 26
Drake's Drum, the racehorse that Paul bought for his father, won the Hylton Plate at the
Aintree Racecourse in Liverpool, coming in at 20–1. Paul, his father and his brother
Michael watched the race.

March 27
The *Sunday Express* newspaper announced that The Beatles had now sold the equivalent
of 159 million singles all over the world.

March 28
Ringo and George met Roy Orbison backstage before his performance at the Granada
Cinema, Walthamstow.

March 30
Despite heavy press speculation beforehand, which bolstered the attendance for the
event, The Beatles did not make an unannounced appearance at the 1966 Top Pop
Festival held in Lincoln.

April 1
Paul and John visited Indica Books and Gallery in Mason's Yard. John bought a copy of
Timothy Leary's *The Psychedelic Experience* and a reworking of the *Tibetan Book Of The
Dead,* in the introduction of which he found the first line of 'Tomorrow Never Knows'.

April 6
Abbey Road. An 8pm until 1.15am session recording the backing tracks for John's
'Tomorrow Never Knows'.

John: "That's me in my *Tibetan Book of the Dead* period. I took one of Ringo's
malapropisms as the title, to sort of take the edge off the heavy philosophical lyrics.

"Often the backing I think of early on never comes off. With 'Tomorrow Never Knows'
I'd imagined in my head that in the background you would hear thousands of monks
chanting. That was impractical, of course, and we did something different. It was a bit of
a drag, and I didn't really like it. I should have tried to get near my original idea, the
monks singing; I realise now that was what it wanted."

Paul: "That was an LSD song. Probably the only one."

John: "The new album could include literally anything – electronic music, jokes. One
thing's for sure, it will be very different. We wanted to have the last record so that there
was no space between the tracks – just continuous music throughout the whole LP. But
EMI wouldn't wear it.

"Paul and I are very keen on this electronic music. You make it clinking a couple of
glasses together, or with bleeps from the radio, then you loop the tape so that it repeats
the same noises at intervals. Some people build up whole symphonies from it. It would
have been better than the background music we had for the last film."

April 7
Abbey Road. Paul's looped tapes were added to provide the unique solo on 'Tomorrow
Never Knows'. They began work on Paul's 'Got To Get You Into My Life'.

John: "I think that was one of his best songs, too, because the lyrics are good and I
didn't write them."

April 8

Abbey Road. An afternoon and evening session resulted in the completion of a backing track for 'Got To Get You Into My Life.'

Afterwards they spent an evening in the clubs to unwind.

April 11

Abbey Road. First they did more work on 'Got To Get You Into My Life' and then spent most of the afternoon and evening sessions on George's 'Love You To'.

George: "'Love You To' was one of the first tunes I wrote for sitar . . . this was the first song where I consciously tried to use sitar and tabla on the basic track. I overdubbed the guitars and vocal later."

April 13

Abbey Road. During the first session of the day they completed 'Love You To', then after a break for dinner, they recorded the backing tracks for 'Paperback Writer', finishing up at 2.30am. A photographer from the group's official fan magazine, *The Beatles Book*, was on hand to document the session.

April 14

Abbey Road. The afternoon was spent completing 'Paperback Writer' and the evening, until 1.30am, working on the future B-side 'Rain'.

April 16

Abbey Road. An afternoon and evening session during which they completed 'Rain'.

John: "I got home from the studio and I was stoned out of my mind on marijuana and, as I usually do, I listened to what I'd recorded that day. Somehow I got it on backwards and I sat there transfixed with the ear-phones on, with a big hash joint. I ran in the next day and said, 'I know what to do with it. I know . . . Listen to this!' So I made them all play it backwards. The fade is me actually singing backwards – 'Sharethsmnowthsmeaness'."

Ringo: "My favourite piece of me is what I did on 'Rain'. I think I just played amazing. I was into the snare and hi-hat. I think it was the first time I used this trick of starting a break by hitting the hi-hat first instead of going directly to a drum off the hi-hat . . . I think it's the best out of all the records I've ever made. 'Rain' blows me away. It's out of left field. I know me and I know my playing, and then there's 'Rain'."

April 17

Abbey Road. The Beatles laid down the backing tracks for John's 'Doctor Robert'.

April 18

John and George saw The Lovin' Spoonful play The Marquee, and then attended a London nightclub with Spencer Davis, Stevie Winwood, Tom McGuinness and Brian Jones.

The Cavern Club was sold by a court receiver after going bankrupt.

April 19

Abbey Road. 'Doctor Robert' was completed.

April 20

Abbey Road. A 12-hour session from 2.30pm until 2.30am working on John's 'And Your Bird Can Sing', and rehearsals for George's 'Taxman'.

April 21

Abbey Road. 'Taxman' was finished, with Paul adding his distinctive guitar solo. George: "I was pleased to have him play that bit on 'Taxman'. If you notice, he did like a little Indian bit on it for me."

April 22

Abbey Road. The Beatles worked on 'Taxman' and 'Tomorrow Never Knows'.

April 23
Paul spent the day at John's, songwriting and discussing the album.

April 26
Abbey Road. The Beatles spent a 12-hour session, ending at 2.24am, working on 'And Your Bird Can Sing'.

April 27
Abbey Road. John's 'I'm Only Sleeping' was virtually finished when they called it a day at 3am.

April 28
Abbey Road. The session was spent recording the eight-piece string section for Paul's 'Eleanor Rigby'.

Paul: "That started off with sitting down at the piano and getting the first line of the melody, and playing around with words. I think it was 'Miss Daisy Hawkins' originally, then it was her picking up the rice in a church after a wedding. That's how nearly all our songs start, with the first line just suggesting itself from books or newspapers.

"At first I thought it was a young Miss Daisy Hawkins, a bit like 'Annabel Lee', but not so sexy, but then I saw I'd said she was picking up the rice in church, so she had to be a cleaner; she had missed the wedding, and she was suddenly lonely. In fact she had missed it all – she was the spinster type.

"Jane Asher was in a play in Bristol then, and I was walking round the streets waiting for her to finish. I didn't really like 'Daisy Hawkins' – I wanted a name that was more real, and I got the name from a shop called 'Rigby'."

April 29
Abbey Road. The day was spent adding vocals to 'Eleanor Rigby' and to 'I'm Only Sleeping'.

May
Larry Taylor, manager of American crooner Tony Bennett, requested that John and Paul would write some new material for his client.

May 1
NME Poll Winners concert at Empire Pool, Wembley, with The Spencer Davis Group, Dave, Dee, Dozy, Beaky, Mick & Titch, The Fortunes, Herman's Hermits, Roy Orbison, The Overlanders, The Alan Price Set, Cliff Richard, The Rolling Stones, The Seekers, The Shadows, The Small Faces, Sounds Incorporated, Dusty Springfield, Crispian St Peters, The Walker Brothers, The Who and The Yardbirds. The Beatles played a 15-minute set, for which they had staged a brief rehearsal the previous day, but Brian Epstein would not allow ABC TV to film it because they had not reached an agreement over the terms. They were permitted to film them receiving their Poll Winners Awards. This was The Beatles' last live appearance in the UK.

May 2
BBC Playhouse Theatre, London. The Beatles were interviewed by Brian Matthew for the 400th edition of *Saturday Club*.

Afterwards Paul and Ringo were interviewed separately for the BBC Overseas Service programme *Pop Profile*.

May 5
Abbey Road. George spent from 9.30pm until 3am recording the backwards guitar solo on 'I'm Only Sleeping'.

May 6
Abbey Road. The session was spent adding vocals to 'I'm Only Sleeping'.

The Liverpool poetry and music group, Scaffold, which included Paul's brother Mike, released their first single, '2 Days Monday'. Mike McCartney adopted the pseudonym 'Mike McGear' for his work with Scaffold, to avoid accusations that he was cashing in on his brother's success.

May 9
Abbey Road. Paul and Ringo worked on Paul's 'For No One'.

May 13
The Beatles had a night out at the Scotch St James's.

May 14
Melody Maker reported that The Beatles had sold over 1,000,000 records in Denmark.

May 15
ABC TV showed their film of The Beatles receiving their *NME* Poll Winners Awards.

May 16
Abbey Road. Paul added his vocal to 'For No One'.

May 18
Abbey Road. 'Got To Get You Into My Life' was recorded, using Eddie Thornton, Ian Hamer and Les Condon on trumpets and Peter Coe and Alan Branscombe on tenor saxes.

May 19
Abbey Road. Beginning at 10am The Beatles taped promotional clips of 'Paperback Writer' and 'Rain' in both colour and black and white for television stations around the world. Director Michael Lindsay-Hogg had worked with them before at *Ready Steady Go!* and they were to use him again in the future.
     They had lunch at the Genevieve restaurant on Thayer Street, near EMI, and taped more film in the afternoon. That evening Alan Civil recorded his celebrated French horn solo on 'For No One'.

May 20
The day was also spent shooting promotional films for 'Paperback Writer' and 'Rain', this time on location at Chiswick House, London.
     That evening John and Cynthia went to an all-night party with Mick Jagger and Chrissie Shrimpton.

May 21
Early the next morning John, Cynthia, Mick and Chrissie went to Portobello Road market, getting there before the tourists.

May 26
Abbey Road. The backing track for 'Yellow Submarine' was recorded.
     Paul: "I wrote that in bed one night. As a kids' story. And then we thought it would be good for Ringo to do."

May 27
Accompanied by Keith Richards and Brian Jones, Paul and Neil Aspinall went to Dolly's Club on Jermyn Street to meet Bob Dylan the day his European tour reached London. Afterwards they all went back to Dylan's room at the Mayfair Hotel to listen to a set of test pressings he had with him from his most recent sessions.
     Later that evening John and George attended Dylan's concert at the Albert Hall and watched as a faction of the audience jeered and booed when Dylan switched to electric instruments for the second half and, backed by The Band, gave them some rock'n'roll.
     John made a guest appearance in D.A. Pennebaker's film documentary of Bob Dylan's UK tour *Eat The Document*. John and Dylan were filmed talking in the back of a limousine, which had picked John up in Weybridge. Out-take footage revealed that both singers, Bob especially, were suffering from the adverse effects of recent drug-taking.

May 28
The Beatles spent the day in Bob Dylan's hotel room, watching D.A. Pennebaker's film *Don't Look Back*.

May 29
The Beatles spent another day with Bob Dylan at the Mayfair.

May 30
The single 'Paperback Writer'/'Rain' was released in the US as Capitol 5651.

May 31
Ringo allowed photographer Leslie Bryce to shoot an "At Home" session at his house in Weybridge for *Beatles Monthly*.

June
Allen Klein, the US businessman who had recently been appointed as the manager of The Rolling Stones, boasted that by the end of 1966 he would also be handling The Beatles' business affairs.

June 1
Abbey Road. The sound effects were added to 'Yellow Submarine', assisted by Brian Jones, Marainne Faithfull, Beatles roadies Mal and Neil and various other friends.
　　That evening George saw Ravi Shankar play a recital at the Albert Hall.
　　In the US, an album of material by The Pete Best Group was released by Savage Records, under the cunning title, *Best Of The Beatles*.

June 2
Abbey Road. Most of the session was spent recording George's as-yet-untitled 'I Want To Tell You'.
　　BBC television's *Top Of The Pops* premiered The Beatles' promotional films of 'Paperback Writer' and 'Rain'.

June 3
Abbey Road. 'I Want To Tell You' was finished and 'Yellow Submarine' mixed in a session ending at 2.30am.
　　The British popular press reacted with suitable outrage at the photographs of The Beatles covered with meat and dolls, which were used in the advertisements in the pop papers for the new single.

June 4
The Beatles pre-recorded interview for the 400th edition of the BBC Light Programme's *Saturday Club* was broadcast.

June 5
The promotional films for 'Paperback Writer' and 'Rain' were aired on NBC TV's *Ed Sullivan Show*.

June 6
Abbey Road. Most of the session was spent mixing. Paul added a vocal overdub to 'Eleanor Rigby'.

June 7
A day spent at George's house rehearsing.

June 8
Abbey Road. Paul's 'Good Day Sunshine' recorded.

June 9
Abbey Road. 'Good Day Sunshine' completed.
　　The 'Paperback Writer' promo film was screened on BBC TV's *Top Of The Pops*.

June 10
'Paperback Writer'/'Rain' was released in the UK as Parlophone R 5452.

PAPERBACK WRITER

Widely greeted as a disappointment – a brash, insubstantial throwaway – at the time it was released, the first Beatles single of 1966 remains one of the jewels of The Beatles' crown, especially when coupled with its flipside, 'Rain'. It's true that Paul McCartney was writing a snapshot of fictional life rather than a confessional masterpiece or a straightforward teen romance, but the instrumental and vocal complexity of the song – plus its dazzling conceptual ambition – forced the ever-competitive Beach Boys to respond with the even more complex 'Good Vibrations'. The limits of EMI's studio technology were stretched to produce the richest, toughest sound of any Beatles record to date. Listen out for Lennon and Harrison's 'Frère Jacques' vocal refrain during the final verse, incidentally.

RAIN

Experimentation with drugs exploded John Lennon's creative potential. In place of the semi-fictional love songs that had been The Beatles' stock-in-trade, 1966 saw him introducing a series of numbers that explored the workings of the mind, and captured the hazy insight of the psychedelic experience.

'Rain' was one of the first, and perhaps the best, of his acid songs. Half dream, half nightmare in the wings, it combined the earthy, rich rock sound of its companion-piece, 'Paperback Writer', with an other-worldly lyric. The Beatles knew almost by instinct how to achieve that atmosphere in sound: they taped the backing track, complete with what Ringo regards as his best-ever drumming on record, at breakneck speed, then slowed the tape. Lennon's vocal went through the opposite process: it was recorded on a machine running slowly, and then speeded up for the final track. The juxtaposition of speed and laziness – plus the final burst of backwards vocals, an idea claimed by both Lennon and George Martin – heightened the unearthly tension of this brilliant record.

June 11

The British pop magazine *Disc* appeared with a full-colour, front cover photograph taken from the so-called 'butcher' session.

June 12

Media disquiet begins to spread in the US over The Beatles' plans to use one of the 'butcher' photographs as the cover of their next album.

June 14

Abbey Road. The Beatles began work on Paul's 'Here, There And Everywhere'.
John: "This was a great one of his."

June 15

The day was spent rehearsing for their appearance on *Top Of The Pops* to promote 'Paperback Writer'.

The album *Yesterday . . . and Today* was released in the US as Capitol T–2553 (mono) and ST–2553 (stereo). Side A: 'Drive My Car', 'I'm Only Sleeping', 'Nowhere Man', 'Doctor Robert', 'Yesterday', 'Act Naturally'. Side B: 'And Your Bird Can Sing', 'If I Needed Someone', 'We Can Work It Out', 'What Goes On', 'Day Tripper'.

June 16

The Beatles went to the BOAC Air Terminal in Victoria to receive vaccinations against cholera in preparation for their forthcoming Far Eastern tour.

After this they travelled in John's black Rolls Royce to BBC Television Centre where they recorded their first live appearance on *Top Of The Pops*, which was also their last live television appearance playing music.

Abbey Road. The band worked until 3am on 'Here, There And Everywhere'.

The 'Butcher' sleeve on the *Yesterday . . . and Today* album was withdrawn in the US. A new bland sleeve was pasted on top of the withdrawn copies and all new pressings just had the new sleeve. Collectors carefully peeled the replacement sleeves off and mint copies of the 'Butcher' sleeve are now sold at rare record auctions for huge sums of money.

The Beatles appeared live on *Top Of The Pops* performing both sides of their new single.

June 17
Abbey Road. 'Here, There And Everywhere' was completed and more work was done on 'Got To Get You Into My Life'.
Paul bought a 183-acre dairy farm in Machrihanish, Kintyre, Scotland.
Paul: "It's 200 acres and a farmhouse as well. It was well worth the money as far as I'm concerned. But don't think I'm a big property tycoon. I only buy places I like."

June 20
Abbey Road. A short visit to the studio after tea for the mixing of 'Got To Get You Into My Life'.
The album *Yesterday . . . and Today* was re-released in the US with a new innocuous sleeve.

June 21
Abbey Road. John's 'She Said She Said' was recorded between 7pm and 3.45am.

June 22
The Beatles attended a pre-opening party at Sibylla's nightclub on Swallow Street in which George had a financial stake.

June 23
The Beatles took the 11am flight to Munich where they were met by the press and a small number of fans, before a fleet of white Mercedes whisked them off to the Bayerischer Hof Hotel. They arrived late for a press conference at the hotel because they were trapped in the lift for ten minutes on the way down from their floor. Later, when no one was about, they took a late-night dip in the pool.

June 24
Circus-Krone-Bau, with Cliff Bennett & The Rebel Rousers, The Rattles and Peter & Gordon. Two sets, at 5.15 and 9.00pm, the second of which was filmed by ZDF, German television. Unusually, The Beatles staged an afternoon rehearsal to prepare for the TV performance.
Their set for the tour consisted of: 'Rock'n'Roll Music', 'She's A Woman', 'If I Needed Someone', 'Day Tripper', 'Baby's In Black', 'I Feel Fine', 'Yesterday', 'I Wanna Be Your Man', 'Nowhere Man', 'Paperback Writer' and 'I'm Down'. Among their guests at the hotel was Bettina Derlien, the barmaid from the Star-Club.

June 25
Early in the morning, The Beatles arrived at Munich railway station in a fleet of Mercedes with motorcycle police guarding them. They boarded the Royal train, previously used by the Queen of England, to take them to Essen. They each had their own suite of rooms, and were on board in time for breakfast.
Grugahalle, Essen. They gave a press conference between their two shows and had a meal in their dressing room. They got back to their train, which travelled through the night to Hamburg, arriving at about 2am.
The promotional film for 'Paperback Writer' was shown in the UK on the final edition of ABC TV's *Thank Your Lucky Stars*.

June 26
Their train arrived in Hamburg at 6am and they moved into the Schloss Hotel in Tremsbüttel, 30 miles away from Hamburg and the fans. They slept until 1.30pm then made a balcony appearance for the several hundred fans gathered outside. John visited Astrid Kirchherr, who gave him several letters written by Stuart Sutcliffe. Dr Bernstein, their Reeperbahn days doctor, and their Hamburg record producer Bert Kaempfert were among their many visitors. The Beatles played two sets at Ernst Merck Halle with the usual press conference in between. During one of the shows, John remarked to the crowd: "Don't listen to our music. We're terrible these days." Afterwards John and Paul went for a walk around the Reeperbahn after midnight, revisiting their old haunts.

June 27

The Beatles returned to Heathrow airport, then left for Tokyo on the inaugural flight by Japanese Airlines over the North Pole. Unfortunately, a typhoon warning caused the plane to be grounded at Anchorage, Alaska, where they spent the night at the Westwood Hotel. That evening The Beatles visited the hotel's club, 'The Top Of The World' on the top floor, and a local DJ gave them a quick tour of Anchorage.

June 28

The Beatles continued their flight to Tokyo. Ringo had recently bought himself one of the first portable cassette recorders, and took great delight in taping the conversations going on around him on the plane.

June 30

The Beatles arrived at Haneda airport, Tokyo at 3.40am (having lost a day by crossing the date line). They stayed at the Tokyo Hilton where they had their own floor, occupying the Presidential Suite. Hotel security was the tightest that The Beatles had yet endured, preventing them from making unplanned sightseeing trips around the Tokyo streets.

Nippon Budokan Hall, Tokyo, with Yuya Uchida and Isao Bitoh.

The Beatles played one concert to 10,000 fans. There was considerable right-wing opposition – including death threats – to The Beatles playing at Nippon Budokan Hall (Martial Arts Hall), because the building was regarded as a national shrine to Japan's war dead, and it was therefore seen as sacrilegious for a rock'n'roll group to play there. Because of these threats, the Japanese lined the route from the airport and the perimeter of the hotel with 30,000 uniformed men. It went on to become one of the main rock venues in Tokyo.

July 1

Nippon Budokan Hall.

Japanese television filmed the first of today's two concerts.

July 2

Nippon Budokan Hall.

The final day of concerts. Fan hysteria was so great and the army security so tight that The Beatles were unable to leave their hotel. In order to buy some souvenirs, local tradesmen were brought to their suite and The Beatles bought a variety of kimonos, bowls and other goods at suitably inflated prices. They also purchased a brush painting set, which they used to collaborate on an elaborate abstract design, later presented to the president of the local branch of The Beatles Fan Club.

July 3

The Beatles flew to Hong Kong, where they rested in the VIP lounge while their plane refuelled, before continuing to Manila in the Philippines (then under the dictatorship of Ferdinand Marcos) where a crowd of 50,000 fans was waiting to greet them. The Filipinos, having noted the behaviour of the Japanese authorities, were not to be outdone. With typical heavy-handedness, military police burst into the plane and seized The Beatles, dragging them down the stairs and into protective custody.

George wrote: "These gorillas, huge guys, no shirts, short sleeves, took us right off the plane. They confiscated our 'diplomatic bags'. They took all four of us, John, Paul, Ringo and me, without Brian or Neil or Mal. Then they removed us in a boat to Manila Bay surrounded by a ring of cops, guns everywhere . . . straight away we thought we were all busted because we thought they would find all the dope in our bags."

Two army battalions in full combat gear met The Beatles and took them to navy headquarters before transferring them to a private yacht where a wealthy Filipino, Don Manolo Elizalde, showed them off to a party of rich friends. It was not until 4am that Brian Epstein was able to regain control of the situation and The Beatles finally reached their suite at the Hotel Manila.

THE MANILA INCIDENT

On July 4 The Beatles were exhausted and slept late. Unfortunately, Imelda Marcos had organised a lunch party for 300 sons and daughters of top army

officers and businessmen at the Malacanang Palace to introduce them to The Beatles. The group were still asleep after the previous night's debacle when officials came looking for them. Brian Epstein claimed to know nothing of the invitation and refused to allow any further indignities to be perpetrated upon them. Naturally this was taken as a grave insult, with potentially dangerous repercussions.

That afternoon they played the Rizal Memorial Football Stadium, before 30,000 fans, and again in the evening to 50,000 fans.

The next day the hotel provided no room service. They found that their front man, Vic Lewis, had been questioned by high ranking military officials until dawn, and all military security had been withdrawn. The Beatles and their entourage had to run the gauntlet to get to their plane. They were spat at, insulted and jostled. At the airport Alf Bicknell was thrown to the floor and kicked by military security men and the escalator was turned off so that they had to struggle up with all their equipment. Mal Evans and Brian Epstein had to get off the plane again to sort out a passport and tax problem which officials suddenly invented before KLM flight 862 was finally allowed to leave Manila at 4.45pm.

George summed up The Beatles' feelings succinctly: "The only way I'd ever return to the Philippines would be to drop an atom bomb on it."

July 6

Returning home, there was a refuelling stop in Bangkok after which The Beatles arrived in New Delhi, India, where they hoped to take a peaceful three day break. Unfortunately, 600 fans were already waiting at the airport when they landed and the Oberoi Hotel was soon under siege. They managed to sneak out the back way and do some shopping and sightseeing. They all bought Indian instruments from Rikhi Ram & Sons, on Connaught Circle.

George: "It turned out to be a good trip, except that when we went out of town, in old Fifties Cadillacs, and walked around the villages, I realised that the Nikon cameras given to us in Tokyo were more than an Indian villager could earn in a lifetime."

July 8

The Beatles arrived back in London at 6am. There was a short press conference when they landed and George and Ringo appeared on the morning edition of the BBC Home Service's radio show *Today*.

George: "We're going to have a couple of weeks to recuperate before we go and get beaten up by the Americans."

The EP *Nowhere Man* was released in the UK as Parlophone GEP 8952 (mono). Side A: 'Nowhere Man', 'Drive My Car'; Side B: 'Michelle', 'You Won't See Me'.

July 10

British pop group Freddie & The Dreamers cancelled their proposed concerts in the Philippines in protest at the treatment The Beatles received in that country.

July 12

The Beatles were awarded Ivor Novello Awards for 'We Can Work It Out' (top selling single of 1965), 'Yesterday' (most outstanding song of the year) and 'Help!' (second best selling single of 1965).

Mid-July

John purchased an expensive suite of film editing equipment, which allowed him to make abstract movies as an accompaniment to his experiments in *musique concrete*.

July 23

The Cavern Club reopened in Liverpool under new ownership. The Beatles sent a telegram and the opening ceremony was attended by Prime Minister Harold Wilson, whose constituency was in Liverpool.

July 24
Ill health forced Brian Epstein to cancel a trip to America, to make final arrangements for The Beatles' US tour.

July 29
The American magazine *Datebook* published Maureen Cleave's interview with John in which he said, "We're bigger than Jesus now." American Christian fundamentalists reacted with outrage. A DJ in Birmingham, Alabama, organised an immediate boycott of The Beatles' music, and broadcast his intention to conduct a 'Beatle-burning' bonfire of the group's records.

July 30
The album *Yesterday . . . and Today* reached number one on the *Billboard* Hot 100 charts where it stayed for five weeks.

July 31
Zealots in Birmingham, Alabama, were shown on BBC television news burning Beatles records just as the Nazis had burned books.

August 1
Paul recorded an interview for the BBC Light Programme's *David Frost At The Phonograph*.

August 2
George and Patti drove to Stoodleigh in Devon for a few days' holiday with Patti's mother, Diana Jones, in her 18th century farmhouse.

August 5
'Yellow Submarine'/'Eleanor Rigby' was released in the UK as Parlophone R 5493.

The album *Revolver* was released in the UK as Parlophone PMC 7009 (mono) and PCS 7009 (stereo). Side A: 'Taxman', 'Eleanor Rigby', 'I'm Only Sleeping', 'Love You To', 'Here There And Everywhere', 'Yellow Submarine', 'She Said She Said'; Side B: 'Good Day Sunshine', 'And Your Bird Can Sing', 'For No One', 'Doctor Robert', 'I Want To Tell You', 'Got To Get You Into My Life', 'Tomorrow Never Knows'.

REVOLVER
The Beatles were supposed to begin 1966 by making their third feature film in as many years. But no one could agree on a script, or even a theme, and instead The Beatles enjoyed an unprecedented three-month break at the start of the year.

They were already convinced that their enervating routine of tour-film-record-tour had to be broken, and had completed their British tour at the end of 1965, assuming it would be their last. They were already contracted to undertake one final jaunt around the world in June, but mentally they were beginning to metamorphose into post-touring states of mind.

With the exception of their last British concert at the *NME* Pollwinners' Show on May 1, The Beatles had more than two months on their schedule to record their next LP. They began on April 6th with the most revolutionary track on the album, Lennon's 'Tomorrow Never Knows', and ended just over eight weeks later with one of the two most brilliant pop albums ever recorded up to that point. Its rival was The Beach Boys' *Pet Sounds*, a masterpiece of melody, harmony and orchestral arrangement that undoubtedly affected the final sound of The Beatles' LP.

What time and mental space in the studio gave The Beatles was the chance to experiment (although most of the *Revolver* songs went through remarkably little change of approach once the sessions began), and the freedom to choose exactly the right sound for each track. *Revolver* was where The Beatles became a consummate studio band – ironically enough, in the same year that they proved completely unable (or maybe unwilling is closer to the point) to perform their more complex material on stage. Listen to *Revolver*, and then to the

tuneless performances they gave on tour a few weeks later, and it's hard to imagine that they are the same band.

The Beatles' state of mind during that final tour is aptly summed up by this quote from Paul McCartney: "I was in Germany on tour just before *Revolver* came out. I started listening to the album and I got really down because I thought the whole thing was out of tune. Everyone had to reassure me that it was OK." And so it was.

TAXMAN

"'Taxman' was when I first realised that even though we had started earning money, we were actually giving most of it away in taxes." So said George Harrison, cementing forever the public perception of him as the Beatle most obsessed with money (an interesting sideline to his other clichéd role as the mystic Beatle). Groomed for years by manager Brian Epstein to stay out of political controversy, The Beatles began in 1966 to comment on issues like the war in Vietnam. 'Taxman' was a more universal protest – George fingered both the Conservative and Labour leaders in his lyrics – but the song had a political message, nonetheless. It also had a remarkably powerful lead guitar riff, played (ironically enough) not by George but by Paul.

ELEANOR RIGBY

"I wrote a good half of the lyrics or more," claimed John Lennon in later years of this archetypal Paul McCartney song. True or not, it was a sign that Lennon realised the strength of what Paul had written. It was a short story with a moral, all packaged within little more than two minutes. Aside from the backing vocals, McCartney was the only Beatle featured on the track, accompanied by a string section scored by George Martin – one of his most obvious and effective contributions to a Beatles record. The song later inspired the most memorable segment of the Yellow Submarine *movie, as the craft drifts above the lonely, dingy streets of Liverpool.*

I'M ONLY SLEEPING

Half acid dream, half latent Lennon laziness personified, 'I'm Only Sleeping' was a joyous celebration of life without pressure. It also conformed to one of the key instructions of the acid trippers, that explorers of the mind should relax and let thoughts come to them, rather than forcing them to appear.

The other-worldly feel of the song was created by artificial means – first speeding up Lennon's vocal to make it sound as if he was singing from beyond the physical plane, and then playing the tape of Harrison's guitar interjections backwards. During the editing process, a fistful of different mixes were prepared, and variations on the basic stereo CD version can be found on vinyl releases scattered around the globe.

LOVE YOU TO

Lester Bangs called it "the first injection of ersatz Eastern wisdom into rock", but George Harrison's translation of the Buddhist spiritual texts he'd been reading in recent months simply reinforced the message of 'Think For Yourself' on the previous album. As far as the public were concerned, though, Harrison had "gone Indian" overnight, an impression reinforced as he took sitar lessons from Ravi Shankar, encouraged the rest of the group to study under the Maharishi Mahesh Yogi, and offered Eastern-sounding songs to the group for the next 18 months.

'Love You To' sounded astonishing alongside the electrifying pop of the Revolver *album, where it proved that The Beatles could tackle any genre they wanted. It also inaugurated a less happy tradition, of John Lennon not contributing to the recording of Harrison's songs. One man who did appear, however, was Indian tabla player Anil Bhagwat.*

HERE, THERE AND EVERYWHERE

For the third album running, Paul McCartney turned up with a song that became an instant standard. He credited its original inspiration to multiple hearings of The Beach Boys' Pet Sounds *LP, though there's little melodic similarity between them. But the romantic simplicity of the song shone like a beacon through the cynicism and uncertainty that fuelled most of the album.*

YELLOW SUBMARINE

A simple children's song intended for the equally simple public persona of Ringo Starr, 'Yellow Submarine' still received the full-scale studio treatment. Mark Lewisohn's definitive account of *The Beatles'* sessions documents the various effects and gimmicks that were recorded for the song, and then rejected. 'Yellow Submarine' was, in business terms, the most important song on the Revolver *LP*, as it inspired the cartoon movie which solved the enduring problem of the third film that The Beatles had owed United Artists since the summer of 1965.

SHE SAID SHE SAID
Another major Lennon song on an album dominated by his paranoid acid visions, 'She Said She Said' was inspired by the doom-laden, LSD-driven remark by actor Peter Fonda, who buttonholed Lennon in The Beatles' LA hideaway with the words, "I know what it's like to be dead". 'Tomorrow Never Knows' captured the horror of that statement; 'She Said She Said' turned it into an early piece of Lennon autobiography, the first step on the journey to his Plastic Ono Band *album. And all this turmoil and angst was contained within a brilliant three-minute pop song.*

GOOD DAY SUNSHINE
Perfect summer pop for the era, McCartney's 'Good Day Sunshine' had enough melodic twists and turns (note the harmonic shifts in the final chorus) to put it beyond the reach of most would-be cover artists. Simple, effective and stunning, it was the ideal complement to the darker Revolver *songs.*

AND YOUR BIRD CAN SING
John Lennon described this song as "another horror", and he wrote it, so he should know. It's full of the fake wisdom of those philosophically lightweight days when it seemed as if the world could be turned on its axis by a tab of acid and a few seconds' thought. Musically, though, it's one of the highlights of the album, powered by a twisting, insidious guitar riff and featuring one of Lennon's most deadpan, off-hand vocals. Rich and mysterious, the track may have been fancy paper round an empty box, but the package sounded so good that no one cared.

FOR NO ONE
Just two Beatles appeared on McCartney's 'For No One', Ringo playing percussion, and Paul singing and playing keyboards and the lovely descending bass line. The French horn, allowed a lengthy solo in George Martin's score, was performed by Alan Civil from the London Philharmonia. The song itself was another remarkable McCartney ballad, melodically sophisticated and lyrically mature.

DOCTOR ROBERT
Named without any hint of disguise after a London 'doctor' who could be guaranteed to supply rock stars with exotic drugs on demand, John Lennon's 'Doctor Robert' was hinged around the same rough-edged guitar as 'And Your Bird Can Sing'. And once again, his lead vocal oozed cynicism and emotional distance, like the world-weary survivor of three years' hard Beatlemania that he was.

I WANT TO TELL YOU
Allowed three songs on any Beatles album for the first time (and also the last, with the exception of the double White Album*), George Harrison had the chance to expose several different facets of his songwriting talent. Like 'If I Needed Someone', 'I Want To Tell You' was hinged around The Beatles' superb harmonies (Lennon and McCartney seemed to relish the role of backing singers, relieved of the pressure to carry the song). Once again, Harrison unwrapped an awkward, determinedly realistic view of relationships, in which failed communication was the order of the day. Throughout The Beatles' career, George never wrote a straightforward love song: all his portrayals of romance were surrounded in misunderstanding and the dreadful prospect of boredom, and this was no exception.*

GOT TO GET YOU INTO MY LIFE
Revolver revealed The Beatles as master of any musical genre they cared to touch. Having satirised white musicians' desire to play black musical styles in the title of Rubber Soul, *Paul McCartney turned his hand to the 1966 soul boom with ease, concocting this fabulous piece of mock-Stax, with five brassmen providing the final Memphis-style touches. The hand of control was evident throughout, with the brass sound deliberately 'limited' to create a faintly unreal sound.*

Trivia note: compare the fade-outs of the mono and stereo versions of this song, and you'll find entirely different McCartney ad-libs.

TOMORROW NEVER KNOWS

Almost five months after The Beatles added their final vocals to the charming 'I'm Looking Through You', they were back in the studio – to create three minutes of turmoil that envisaged the death of the conscious mind and the triumph beyond death of the universal spirit. What had happened between November 1965 and April 1966? John Lennon had been on a dual voyage of discovery – experimenting with the hallucinogenic powers of LSD, and finding that it was possible to match the chaotic visions he saw on his chemically fuelled trips with collages of sound.

Both Lennon and McCartney began creating mind movies at their home studios, extended webs of noise that were based around tape loops and 'found sounds'. McCartney was the pioneer in this regard, and it was he who supervised the addition of the almost supernatural squawks and howls that punctuated the song. But the concept was Lennon's, taken from his reading of The Tibetan Book Of The Dead. *Like Harrison, Lennon noted the similarity between the imagery of Eastern spirituality, and the beyond consciousness experiences of the acid trip. 'Tomorrow Never Knows', with its eerie 'treated' vocal, droning drums and terrifying soundscape, was the ultimate expression of his discovery – and of the enormous change in The Beatles since they'd finished* Rubber Soul.

August 6

Despite the fact he was still suffering from severe exhaustion after a recent bout of glandular fever, Brian Epstein flew to the US to try to sort out the problems caused by John's remarks about Jesus. There were fears that the entire American tour might have to be cancelled. By August 6 a total of 30 American radio stations had banned Beatles records.

Paul and John recorded an hour-long interview about songwriting for the BBC Light Programme at Paul's new house in Cavendish Avenue. It was broadcast as *The Lennon And McCartney Songbook*.

Paul's interview with David Frost was broadcast on the BBC Light Programme's *David Frost At The Phonograph*.

August 8

Beatles records were banned by the South African Broadcasting Corporation after John's supposedly irreligious remarks offended the apartheid regime. The ban lasted five years, until after The Beatles broke up. After that Paul, George and Ringo's solo albums were allowed, but not John's, a ban which survived until well after his death.

The single 'Eleanor Rigby'/'Yellow Submarine' was released in the US as Capitol 5715.

The album *Revolver* was released in the US as Capitol T–2576 (mono) and ST–2576 (stereo). As usual it had fewer tracks than the UK release. Side A: 'Taxman', 'Eleanor Rigby', 'Love You To', 'Here, There And Everywhere', 'Yellow Submarine', 'She Said She Said'; Side B: 'Good Day Sunshine', 'For No One', 'Doctor Robert', 'I Want To Tell You', 'Got To Get You Into My Life', 'Tomorrow Never Knows'.

August 11

The Beatles flew to the US, landing first at Boston, then at Chicago, where they arrived at 4.18pm.

JOHN AND JESUS

The press and all three television networks were waiting in Chicago and talked of nothing but John's remarks about Jesus. The Beatles had to do a live press conference from the 27th floor of the Astor Towers Hotel where they were staying. John was obviously very uncomfortable, being forced to apologise for something which the Americans had taken out of context.

John: "Look, I wasn't saying The Beatles are better than God or Jesus. I said 'Beatles' because it's easy for me to talk about Beatles. I could have said 'TV' or 'the cinema', 'motorcars' or anything popular and I would have got away with it . . .

"I'm not anti-God, anti-Christ or anti-religion. I was not saying we are greater or better. I believe in God, but not as one thing, not as an old man in the sky. I believe that what people call God is something in all of us. I believe that what Jesus, Mohammed, Buddha and all the rest said was right. It's just the translations have gone wrong.

"I wasn't saying whatever they're saying I was saying. I'm sorry I said it, really. I never meant it to be a lousy anti-religious thing. From what I've read, or observed, Christianity just seems to me to be shrinking, to be losing contact."

Reporter: "A disc jockey in Birmingham, Alabama, who actually started most of the repercussions, has demanded an apology from you."

John: "He can have it, I apologise to him."

August 12

International Amphitheater, Chicago, with The Remains, Bobby Hebb, The Cyrkle and The Ronettes.

They played two sets, each to 13,000 people. They played the same set on this US tour as on their European and Japanese tour: 'Rock'n'Roll Music', 'She's A Woman', 'If I Needed Someone', 'Day Tripper', 'Baby's In Black', 'I Feel Fine', 'Yesterday', 'I Wanna Be Your Man', 'Nowhere Man', 'Paperback Writer' and 'I'm Down', sometimes adding 'Long Tall Sally'.

August 13

Olympic Stadium, Detroit. Two sets.

Station KLUE in Longview, Texas, getting on the bandwagon a bit late, organised a public burning of Beatles' records. The station manager said, "We are inviting local teenagers to bring in their records and other symbols of the group's popularity to be burned at a public bonfire on Friday night, August 13."

The Grand Dragon of the South Carolina Ku Klux Klan attached a Beatles record to the large wooden cross which he then set on fire as part of their ritual.

Spanish Radio was reported to have banned the airplay of Beatles records "for ever" because of John's 'blasphemous remark' and in Holland there were moves to ban The Beatles from playing in the country and to have their records banned from the airwaves.

John: "When they started burning our records . . . that was a real shock, the physical burning. I couldn't go away knowing I'd created another little piece of hate in the world . . . so I apologised."

George: "They've got to buy them before they can burn them."

Ringo was asked why neither 'Eleanor Rigby' nor 'Yellow Submarine' featured in the group's live repertoire. " 'Eleanor Rigby' is not suitable for the stage," he replied, "and would need to be re-arranged. I don't know how Paul would make up for the loss of the strings. 'Submarine' sounds like a good singalong thing, so I'd like us to do it on stage sometime, perhaps in the autumn. But to be honest, we've kept the same list of titles we used last month in Germany and the Far East. We haven't had the chance to rehearse any new numbers since then."

The album *Revolver* entered the UK charts at number one, and remained there for nine weeks.

After the second set in Detroit they left by bus for Cleveland, Ohio, arriving at 2am.

August 14

Municipal Stadium, Cleveland, Ohio.

Two sets to 20,000 fans. When 2,500 fans got into the arena area, the show was stopped midway through a performance of 'Day Tripper', and The Beatles retired backstage for about 20 minutes until order was restored.

Radio station KLUE in Longview, Texas, was taken off the air the day after their Beatles records bonfire when a lightning bolt struck their transmission tower, destroying electronic equipment and knocking their news director unconscious.

August 15

DC Stadium, Washington, DC to 32,000 fans – and a handful of members of the Ku Klux Klan, who picketed the concert.

The Beatles flew into the capital that afternoon and travelled to Philadelphia by coach as soon as their one show was over.

The album *This Is Where It Started* by Tony Sheridan and The Beatles was released in the US.

August 16
Philadelphia Stadium, Philadelphia.

One evening show held before a crowd which filled little more than a third of the 60,000 seater stadium. The performance was staged amid the beginnings of an electric storm with almost continuous lightning. The rain did not start until just after their set had finished. They flew straight to Canada after the show.

George: "Our performances over the last two years have deteriorated to such an extent that our 1966 stage shows are terrible compared to, say, the Cavern days or Hamburg. The audience can't hear it and we can't, which is why it's terrible. We used to play best in the old days when a larger proportion of our fans were boys. The more fame we got, the more girls came to see us, everybody making a noise so that nobody could hear us."

August 17
Maple Leaf Gardens, Toronto, Canada.

At a press conference before the show, John aroused another controversy by expressing his support for American draft-dodgers who had fled over the border into Canada to escape being sent to Vietnam.

The Beatles did two shows and stayed overnight before flying to Boston.

August 18
Suffolk Downs Racetrack, Boston.

The bleachers were filled by 25,000 fans, while the stage was specially constructed in the middle of the racetrack.

August 19
Mid South Coliseum, Memphis.

An already tense atmosphere in the Deep South was heightened when a spokesman for the Memphis city authorities announced that "The Beatles are not welcome in Memphis". A local preacher, the Reverend Jimmy Stroad, organised a mass rally outside the stadium, to protest against the presence of the "blasphemous" John Lennon within a municipal arena. Six Ku Klux Klansmen also picketed the stadium in their costumes. A small number of fanatics threw rubbish on stage and exploded a firecracker. Outside, decoy cars were used to fool protestors, but The Beatles' coach was still surrounded by hordes of Christian demonstrators screaming abuse. Paul: "They were zealots. It was horrible to see the hatred on their faces."

August 20
Crosley Field, Cincinnati.

This show was postponed because of heavy rain and re-scheduled for the next day. The local promoter originally insisted that the show should go ahead, despite the danger of electrocution, but The Beatles refused to perform unless he could guarantee their safety.

August 21
Crosley Field, Cincinnati.

A midday concert, after which they flew 350 miles to St. Louis.

Busch Stadium, St. Louis, Missouri.

The Beatles played at 8.30pm during a heavy rain-storm to a very wet audience of 23,000 fans. The group were protected by a flimsy tarpaulin which dripped water on the amps. It was this gig which finally convinced Paul McCartney that The Beatles should stop live performances. The other Beatles had decided this long before.

August 22
The Beatles flew to New York, where John Lennon sparked further controversy at their airport press conference by speaking out against US participation in the Vietnam War.

August 23
Shea Stadium, New York.

There were 44,000 fans at the show (compared with 55,000 the previous year), which earned the group $200,000. Once again, 'Day Tripper' prompted several thousand fans to try to invade the stage, although they were beaten back by security guards before they reached The Beatles. The group flew straight to Los Angeles after they left the stage.

Before the show, The Beatles took part in two press conferences. The first was organised by the Official Fan Club, and featured an invited audience of 160 fans – who were later congratulated by the group on the intelligence of their questioning. A professional press conference immediately afterwards was less successful, having to be cut short when arguments arose between journalists over The Beatles' opposition to the Vietnam War.

August 24
The Beatles arrived in Los Angeles in the early hours of the morning and rested up at 7655 Carson Road, the private house in Beverly Hills that Brian Epstein had rented for them. Among their visitors were their former press agent, Derek Taylor, plus members of The Byrds and The Mamas and The Papas.

August 25
Seattle Coliseum, Seattle.

The Beatles flew in that morning and stayed at the Edgewater Inn, where the expected press conference was held. Paul was repeatedly quizzed about a rumour that he was about to marry Jane Asher the next day.

Their flight back to Los Angeles from Seattle was delayed for five hours because one of the plane's wheels was discovered to be worn right down to the canvas and had to be replaced.

August 27
The Beatles were visited at their Beverly Hills vacation home by Beach Boys members Brian Wilson and Carl Wilson.

The BBC screened the TV film of the 1965 Shea Stadium performance for the second time.

August 28
Dodger Stadium, Los Angeles.

There were 45,000 fans for this show and only 102 security men. Dozens of fans were injured and 25 people detained during clashes between police and fans. The Beatles' limousine was besieged by fans and had to turn back. They eventually made their escape in an armoured van.

Faced by continued press criticism of poor attendances at The Beatles' shows, Brian Epstein issued a special statement: "This tour compares phenomenally well with last year's. It's much better all round this year, from the point of view of increased interest and we are actually playing to bigger audiences. Here in Los Angeles, for example, 36,000 people saw The Beatles at the Hollywood Bowl. Today's concert at Dodger Stadium is attracting 10,000 more. People have been saying things about diminishing popularity, but all one can go by is attendances, which are absolutely huge. By the time we leave, 400,000 thousand people will have seen this series of shows, and Sid Bernstein has already delivered his formal invitation to The Beatles to return to Shea Stadium for him in the summer of 1967."

Before the show, John enlivened the customary press conference by repeating the "blasphemous" remarks he had made about Jesus several months earlier – this time without apology.

August 29
Candlestick Park, San Francisco.

THE LAST EVER BEATLES CONCERT
This was the last time The Beatles performed before a paying audience. It was seen by 25,000 fans. Their last number on stage was 'Long Tall Sally', one of their Hamburg show-stoppers.

By this time the whole group, even Paul who had held out the longest for a continuation of touring, knew that the concerts had to stop. With posterity in

mind, he asked the Beatles press officer to tape the performance on his hand-held cassette recorder. George expressed his relief on the plane home: "That's it. I'm no longer a Beatle," he announced.

John: "On our last tour people kept bringing blind, crippled and deformed children into our dressing room and this boy's mother would say, 'Go on, kiss him, maybe you'll bring back his sight.' We're not cruel. We've seen enough tragedy in Merseyside, but when a mother shrieks, 'Just touch him and maybe he'll walk again,' we want to run, cry, empty our pockets. We're going to remain normal if it kills us."

The radio show *The Lennon and McCartney Songbook* was transmitted by the BBC Light Programme.

August 30
The Beatles left Los Angeles for London.

August 31
The Beatles arrived back in London from Los Angeles, to be greeted by several thousand screaming fans.

September 5
John flew to Hanover, Germany, to begin filming his part in *How I Won The War* with director Richard Lester on a NATO tank range in Celle, outside Hanover. John: "There were many reasons for doing it: a) it was Dick Lester and he asked me; b) it was anti-war; and c) I didn't know what to do because The Beatles had stopped touring and I thought if I stopped and thought about it I was going to have a big bum trip for nine months so I tried to avoid the depression of the change of life by leaping into the movie. The thing I remember is that Dick Lester had more fun than I did."

September 6
John had his hair cut short for his role as Private Gripweed. The momentous event occurred in the breakfast room of the bar The Inn On The Heath in Celle. In addition to an army haircut, he wore small round "granny" glasses, which his use made fashionable.

September 8
For the fourth year running, The Beatles were offered the chance to appear at the Royal Variety Show; for the third year running, Brian Epstein declined on their behalf.

September 10
The album *Revolver* reached No. 1 on the *Billboard* Hot 100 charts, where it remained for six weeks.

September 14
George and Patti flew to Bombay, India, for George to take sitar lessons with Ravi Shankar and study yoga. They checked into the Taj Mahal, Bombay, under the names Mr and Mrs Sam Wells.

September 15
Paul attended a performance of free-form music given by AMM with Cornelius Cardew at the Royal College of Art. The audience of a dozen or so people was invited to join in and Paul made occasional sounds on the radiator and a beer mug. Paul: "You don't have to like something to be influenced by it."

John and Neil Aspinall took the train to Paris.

September 16
Paul and Brian Epstein joined John and Neil Aspinall for a weekend break in Paris.

September 18
John and Neil Aspinall went to Spain where the filming for *How I Won The War* was due to continue the next day in Carboneras, Spain. John and Cynthia shared a villa in Almeria – owned by Sam Spiegal – with the actor Michael Crawford and his family.

September 19
Location filming began again. John had to get up at 6 each morning for his driver to take him to the film set in his black Rolls.

The press discovered that George and Patti were staying in India and George had to give a press conference at the Taj Mahal in which he explained he had come to India to study and get some peace and quiet.

September 26
Brian Epstein was hospitalised in a London clinic, officially for "a check-up", although he was apparently suffering from an overdose of prescribed drugs. The drama forced him to cancel another proposed visit to see John in Spain.

September 28
Japanese artist Yoko Ono made her first public appearance in Britain, during a symposium on 'Destruction In Art'. She staged two 'concerts' at the Africa Centre in Covent Garden, London.

October
Paul's friend, art dealer Robert Fraser, staged an exhibition by painter Richard Hamilton at his London gallery. Paul helped to hang some of the work, bought a piece at the opening, and also encouraged John to see the exhibition when he returned from Spain.

October 3
Brian Epstein was compelled to emerge from his recuperation clinic, to deny persistent press reports that Paul was about to announce he was leaving The Beatles. Instead, he was able to reveal that while John was filming in Spain, Paul was composing the soundtrack to a movie entitled *Wedlocked, Or All In Good Time.*

October 4
Ringo and Maureen flew to Almeria to spend a few days visiting John on the film set of *How I Won The War.*

October 17
The US record label Clarion became the latest company to recycle some of The Beatles' 1961 Hamburg recordings, on an album entitled *The Amazing Beatles And Other Great English Group Sounds.*

October 21
George did an interview with the BBC correspondent in Bombay, Donald Milner, about his reasons for spending five weeks in India.

A charity Christmas card designed by John went on sale in the UK, with proceeds going to the Polio Research Fund.

October 22
George and Patti returned to London from Bombay.

October 26
When Ravi Shankar arrived at London Airport from India, George was there to meet him, dressed in Indian clothes. Ravi Shankar, European educated, was wearing a Western suit.

October 27
Penguin Books published *The Penguin John Lennon,* a double volume of John's two books.

October 31
Donovan arrived to spend a week at George's house in Esher.

November
Ringo Starr was reportedly offered a small role in the next James Bond film, *You Only Live Twice*.

November 4
NEMS finally vacated 13 Monmouth Street, Brian Epstein's first London office. Most of the operation had been in Argyll Street since 1964.

November 6
The Beatles turned down a request to appear on a TV special in aid of victims of the disaster in Aberfan, where dozens of school children had been killed or injured when a wave of mud and coal slurry had demolished their school.

Paul put his Aston Martin DB5 on the plane-ferry at Lydd, Kent, and flew to France. Wearing a disguise (though his car was hardly inconspicuous), he spent a week driving slowly through the chateaux of the Loire, before he met up with Beatles roadie Mal Evans under the grand clock in Bordeaux. He kept a journal during his trip, and also shot a quantity of film.

November 7
John celebrated his return from his film duties in Spain by indulging in a three-day orgy of LSD, during which he made several avant-garde recordings with the Mellotron that had recently been installed in his home studio at Kenwood.

November 9
John met Yoko Ono at the Indica Gallery, Mason's Yard, London.

YOKO
The day before the opening of her show, *Unfinished Paintings And Objects*, Yoko was introduced to John by the co-owner of the gallery, John Dunbar. John: "I got the word that this amazing woman was putting on a show next week and there was going to be something about people in bags, black bags, and it was going to be a bit of a happening and all that. So I went down to a preview of the show, I got there the night before it opened. I went in – she didn't know who I was or anything – I was wandering around, there was a couple of artsy type students that had been helping lying around there in the gallery, and I was looking at it and I was astounded. There was an apple on sale there for 200 quid, I thought it was fantastic – I got the humour in her work immediately. I didn't have to have much knowledge about avant-garde or underground art, but the humour got me straight away. There was a fresh apple on a stand, this was before Apple – and it was 200 quid to watch the apple decompose.

"But there was another piece which really decided me for-or-against the artist, a ladder which led to a painting which was hung on the ceiling. It looked like a blank canvas with a chain with a spyglass hanging on the end of it. This was near the door where you went in. I climbed the ladder, you look through the spyglass and in tiny little letters it says 'yes'.

"So it was positive. I felt relieved. It's a great relief when you get up the ladder and you look through the spyglass and it doesn't say 'no' or 'fuck you' or something. It said 'yes'.

"I was very impressed and John Dunbar sort of introduced us – neither of us knew who the hell we were, she didn't know who I was, she'd only heard of Ringo I think, it means apple in Japanese. And she came up and handed me a card which said 'Breathe' on it, one of her instructions, so I just went (pant). That was our meeting."

In fact Yoko knew very well who The Beatles were. She had approached Paul several weeks before, hoping to solicit some original Lennon and McCartney manuscripts to give to John Cage for his 50th birthday celebrations as Cage collected original scores of modern music. Paul said no but told her that John might let her have one.

November 11
John and Cynthia saw Ben E. King play the Scotch St James's.

November 12
Paul and Mal drove from Bordeaux to Spain, making home movies en route. Paul originally intended to meet John in Almeria but John finished shooting his part early and was already home. Paul decided on a safari instead and arranged to meet Jane in Africa. Paul and Mal drove to Seville and organised someone to drive the Aston back to London. They flew to Madrid and from there to Nairobi. They had a ten-hour stopover in Rome which they spent sightseeing at St Peter's and the usual sights.

Over the next week, they toured Ambosali Park, which is overlooked by Mount Kilimanjaro, and stayed at the royal family's customary Kenyan lodgings, at the Treetop Hotel.

November 13
The Four Tops played the Saville Theatre with a backdrop supposedly designed by Paul.

November 18
The single 'From Head To Toe'/'Night Time' by The Escorts, produced by Paul McCartney, was released in the UK as Columbia DB 8061.

November 19
Paul, Jane and Mal flew back to London from Kenya.

During this plane trip, Paul first came up with the concept for the *Sgt. Pepper's Lonely Hearts Club Band* album.

Paul: "I thought, let's not be ourselves. Let's develop alter egos, so we're not having to project an image which we know. It would be much more free. What would really be interesting would be to actually take on the personas of this different band . . . So I had this idea of giving The Beatles alter egos simply to get a different approach. Then when John came up to the microphone or I did, it wouldn't be John or Paul singing, it would be the members of this band . . . so we'll be able to lose our identities."

November 20
Brian Epstein gave a party for The Four Tops in his home in Chapel Street. John and George attended.

November 24
Abbey Road. The Beatles reconvened to start work on a new album, beginning with John's 'Strawberry Fields Forever'.

John: "The awareness apparently trying to be expressed is – let's say in one way I was always hip. I was hip in kindergarten. I was different from the others. I was different all my life. The second verse goes, 'No one I think is in my tree.' Well I was too shy and self-doubting. Nobody seems to be as hip as me is what I was saying. Therefore, I must be crazy or a genius – 'I mean it must be high or low,' the next line. There was something wrong with me, I thought, because I seemed to see things other people didn't see.
I thought I was crazy or an egomaniac for claiming to see things other people didn't see."

The Beatles attended the opening of an exhibition at the Indica Gallery by the Greek sculptor Takis Vasilakis.

November 25
The Beatles' fourth Christmas record *Pantomime: Everywhere It's Christmas* was recorded in the demo studio in the basement of the New Oxford Street offices of Dick James, their music publisher.

November 27
John made a filmed appearance in Peter Cook and Dudley Moore's BBC Television show *Not Only . . . But Also* in which he played a uniformed nightclub doorman. The filmed location for the club was the underground gentlemen's lavatory on Broadwick Street, near Berwick Street market, Soho. John was shown wearing his new "granny" glasses.

November 28
Abbey Road. The group recorded three more takes of 'Strawberry Fields Forever'.

November 29
Abbey Road. More work on 'Strawberry Fields Forever'.

December
John and Yoko met for the second time, at the opening of a Claes Oldenburg exhibition. Encouraged by his apparent interest in her work, Yoko mailed him a copy of her book of conceptual art 'instructions', *Grapefruit*.

December 1
Paul saw The Young Rascals make their UK début at the Scotch St James's.

December 2
Paul was so impressed by The Young Rascals that he saw them a second time, this time at Blaises.

December 6
Abbey Road. Work began on 'When I'm Sixty Four'. The Beatles also taped Christmas greetings for the pirate stations Radio London and Radio Caroline.

December 8
Abbey Road. Paul added his vocal to 'When I'm Sixty Four' in the afternoon and all four Beatles arrived for an evening session working on 'Strawberry Fields Forever' again.

December 9
Abbey Road. The Beatles continued to work on 'Strawberry Fields Forever'.

December 10
The album *A Collection of Beatles Oldies* was released in the UK as Parlophone PMC 7016 (mono) and PCS 7016 (stereo). Side A: 'She Loves You', 'From Me To You', 'We Can Work It Out', 'Help!', 'Michelle', 'Yesterday', 'I Feel Fine', 'Yellow Submarine'; Side B: 'Can't Buy Me Love', 'Bad Boy', 'Day Tripper', 'A Hard Day's Night', 'Ticket To Ride', 'Paperback Writer', 'Eleanor Rigby', 'I Want To Hold Your Hand'. The album marked the first UK release of the group's version of the Larry Williams rocker, 'Bad Boy'.

BAD BOY
On the same day in 1964 that The Beatles recorded 'Dizzy Miss Lizzy', they also cut a more obscure Larry Williams rocker, 'Bad Boy'. Once again, John Lennon was to the fore, whooping his way through the tale of a pre-juvenile delinquent (told in true American slang). The group's instrumental support wasn't quite in the same league, which is probably why this track was reserved initially for an American LP, Beatles VI, and only appeared in Britain on this compilation.

December 11
The BBC Home Service programme *The Lively Arts* broadcast an interview done with George in India in which he discussed philosophy and Indian music.
George: "Too many people have the wrong idea about India. Everyone immediately associates India with poverty, suffering and starvation, but there's much more than that. There's the spirit of the people, the beauty and the goodness. The people there have a tremendous spiritual strength which I don't think is found elsewhere. That's what I've been trying to learn about."

December 15
Abbey Road. The Beatles continued work on 'Strawberry Fields Forever'.

December 16
Members of The Beatles fan club were sent copies of The Beatles' fourth Christmas flexi-disc called *Pantomime: Everywhere It's Christmas*. Side One: 'Song; Everywhere It's

Christmas', 'Orowanyna', 'Corsican Choir And Small Choir', 'A Rare Cheese', 'Two Elderly Scotsmen', 'The Feast', 'The Loyal Toast'; Side Two: 'Podgy The Bear And Jasper', 'Count Balder And Butler', 'Felpin Mansions (Part Two)', 'The Count And The Pianist', 'Song; Please Don't Bring Your Banjo Back', 'Everywhere It's Christmas', 'Mal Evans', 'Reprise: Everywhere It's Christmas'.

Ringo: "We worked it out between us. Paul did most of the work on it. He thought up the 'Pantomime' title and the two song things."

Paul: "I drew the cover myself. There's a sort of funny pantomime horse in the design if you look closely. Well I can see one there if you can't."

December 18

Paul and Jane attended the premiere of the film *The Family Way* at the Warner Theatre which had an incidental soundtrack written by Paul and arranged by George Martin.

John: "I copped money for *The Family Way*, the film music that Paul wrote when I was out of the country filming *How I Won The War*. I said, 'You'd better keep that.' He said, 'Don't be soft.' It's the concept. We inspired each other so much in the early days. We write how we write now because of each other."

John and Paul's friend Tara Browne was killed in a car crash, on his way to visit another friend of Paul's, David Vaughan. John later said that the tragedy inspired them to write the line "He blew his mind out in a car" in 'A Day In The Life', although Paul has since challenged that idea.

December 19

The design team Binder, Edwards and Vaughan announced that Paul had agreed to make an experimental electronic tape to be played at the *Carnival of Light* to be held at the Roundhouse, Chalk Farm, in January.

December 20

Abbey Road. More vocals were added to 'When I'm Sixty Four.'

The Beatles recorded interviews with John Edwards for the ITN (Independent Television News) programme *Reporting '66* and were filmed arriving at Abbey Road and working on a song together.

December 21

Abbey Road. Woodwind was added to 'When I'm Sixty Four' and John added more vocals to 'Strawberry Fields Forever'.

The single 'Love In The Open Air'/'Theme From *The Family Way*' by The George Martin Orchestra and written by Paul McCartney was released in the UK as United Artists UP 1165.

December 25

All four Beatles remained in London and the Home Counties for Christmas.

December 26

John's appearance on Peter Cook and Dudley Moore's BBC Television show, *Not Only . . . But Also,* was screened.

December 29

Abbey Road. Paul working alone in the studio recorded the backing track to his 'Penny Lane', finishing up at 2.15am.

Paul: "'Penny Lane' is a bus roundabout in Liverpool and there is a barber's shop . . . There's a bank on the corner so we made up the bit about the banker in his motor car. It's part fact, part nostalgia for a place which is a great place – blue suburban skies as we remember it, and it's still there."

December 30

Abbey Road. Further work done on 'When I'm Sixty Four' and 'Penny Lane'.

December 31

George and Patti, Brian Epstein, Eric Clapton and others were refused admittance to Annabel's Night Club because George was not wearing a tie. He refused the one offered to him by the doorman. They saw in the New Year at the Lyon's Corner House Restaurant on Coventry Street.

January

Paul asked his housekeepers, the Kellys, to leave after he found that they had written an article about his home life for an Australian magazine.

Paul: "Mr and Mrs Kelly are looking for another place and I'm getting another couple to replace them. There have been disagreements over the running of the household. I haven't asked them to leave instantly because that would be unreasonable."

They were replaced by Mr and Mrs Mills. ("She still hasn't given me a tune yet," quipped Paul, referring to popular pianist Mrs Mills.)

January 4

Abbey Road. *Sgt. Pepper* sessions. Continued work on 'Penny Lane'.

January 5

Abbey Road. *Sgt. Pepper* sessions. Paul's vocal track on 'Penny Lane' was followed by a free-form, "Freak Out", The Beatles' only combined effort at producing "a bit of random". David Vaughan, of the design team Binder, Edwards and Vaughan, had asked Paul for some music for a sound and light rave to be held at the Roundhouse, Chalk Farm. Paul obliged, and at 13 minutes, 14 seconds, produced the longest Beatles track ever completed. There was no rhythm track, just heavily echoed bursts of percussion, shouts and random bits of piano and guitar. George refused to allow it onto the *Anthology* series of CDs in 1996.

January 6

Abbey Road. *Sgt. Pepper* sessions. More work on 'Penny Lane'.

The album *The Family Way (Original Soundtrack Album)* by The George Martin Orchestra and written by Paul McCartney was released in the UK as Decca SKL 4847. Side One: 'Love In The Open Air' (cuts one to six); Side Two: 'Love In The Open Air' (cuts one to seven).

The Beatles' German friend, Hans-Walther Braun, appeared on the German TV programme *Damals In Hamburg*, and played an extract from a 1960 recording by the group which they had given him that year, featuring the earliest known rendition of Paul's song, 'I'll Follow The Sun'. Remarkably, this event passed unnoticed by Beatles fans outside Germany, and nothing more was heard of Braun's tape until similar material surfaced on bootleg albums in the early 1980s.

January 7

The *Daily Mail* newspaper published adjacent stories about the inquest into the death of John and Paul's friend, Tara Browne, and a report on the poor state of the roads in Blackburn, Lancashire, where 4,000 holes needed to be filled. Both themes found their way into the lyrics of 'A Day In The Life'.

January 8

Paul and John attended a fancy-dress party thrown by Georgie Fame at the Cromwellian Club.

January 9

Abbey Road. *Sgt. Pepper* sessions. Wind instruments added to 'Penny Lane.'

January 10

Abbey Road. *Sgt. Pepper* sessions. More work on 'Penny Lane'.

American ABC TV broadcast the 1965 recording of *The Beatles At Shea Stadium*.

January 11

Paul saw the BBC2 programme *Masterworks*, on which David Mason played piccolo trumpet on Bach's *Brandenburg Concerto No 2 in F Major* with the English Chamber Orchestra from Guildford Cathedral. Paul realised that this was the sound he wanted on 'Penny Lane'.

Later that evening Paul and Ringo saw Jimi Hendrix perform for the first time, at one of his regular London club gigs at the Bag O'Nails.

January 12
George Martin telephoned David Mason and booked him for a session on the 17th to play piccolo trumpet on 'Penny Lane'.

Abbey Road. *Sgt. Pepper* sessions. More work on 'Penny Lane'.

Afterwards Paul and Jane had a "candlelit dinner" at Paul's house in Cavendish Avenue before Jane left to tour the US with the Bristol Old Vic Repertory Company.

January 14
It was reported in the London press that Paul had turned down an offer from the National Theatre to write music for the songs in Kenneth Tynan's production of Shakespeare's *As You Like It* which would have been staged at the Old Vic and starred Sir Laurence Olivier. Paul told them that he could not write contemporary music to go with Elizabethan words, but he would write 'The Larry O Stomp' if they wanted.

January 15
John had a minor car accident but was not hurt.

Paul and George saw Donovan at the Royal Albert Hall.

January 17
Abbey Road. *Sgt. Pepper* sessions. David Mason added his famous piccolo trumpet solo to 'Penny Lane'. Paul improvised the part by singing it to George Martin, who then wrote it out on score paper for Mason to play.

Paul: "I got the idea of using trumpets in that pizzicato way on 'Penny Lane' from seeing a programme on television. I didn't know whether it would work, so I got the arranger for the session into the studio, played the tune on the piano and sang how I wanted the brass to sound. That's the way I always work with arrangers." The song was now complete.

January 18
Paul was interviewed in London by Jo Durden-Smith for a Granada Television documentary on the London underground scene, of which Paul was part. The film, for the *Scene Special* programme, was subtitled *It's So Far Out, It's Straight Down* (whatever that meant).

January 19
Abbey Road. *Sgt. Pepper* sessions. The basic track for 'A Day In The Life' was recorded with Mal Evans counting off the 24 empty bars in the middle and marking the end with an alarm clock.

January 20
Abbey Road. *Sgt. Pepper* sessions. Vocal tracks added to 'A Day In The Life'.

John: "Well, it was a peak. Paul and I were definitely working together, especially on 'A Day In The Life' that was real . . . The way we wrote a lot of the time: you'd write the good bit, the part that was easy, like 'I read the news today', or whatever it was, then when you got stuck or whenever it got hard, instead of carrying on, you just drop it; then we would meet each other, and I would sing half, and he would be inspired to write the next bit and vice versa. He was a bit shy about it because I think he thought it's already a good song. Sometimes we wouldn't let each other interfere with a song either, because you tend to be a bit lax with someone else's stuff, you experiment a bit. So we were doing it in his room with the piano. He said, 'Should we do this?' Yeah, let's do that. But *Pepper* was a peak all right."

January 21
Paul attended a party given by Julie Felix at her flat in Old Church Street, Chelsea.

George gave Donovan his first lesson on the sitar.

January 25
Abbey Road. *Sgt. Pepper* sessions. Paul supervised a new mix of 'Penny Lane' because he was not satisfied with the old one.

Brian Epstein signed a deal allowing *Sunday Times* newspaper journalist Hunter Davies to write an authorised biography of The Beatles, granting their co-operation in exchange for a percentage of the royalties.

January 27

The Beatles and Brian Epstein signed a new nine-year worldwide recording contract with EMI Records, updating their previous deal, which had expired the previous day.

January 28

Paul and George went to see The Four Tops, presented by Brian Epstein, at the Royal Albert Hall.

January 29

John and Paul saw The Jimi Hendrix Experience and The Who at Brian Epstein's Saville Theatre.

January 30

EMI were desperate to release a new Beatles single, so Brian Epstein asked George Martin for two tracks from the *Sgt. Pepper* sessions. George reluctantly gave him 'Penny Lane' and 'Strawberry Fields'.

The Beatles began filming the promotional films for 'Strawberry Fields Forever' and 'Penny Lane' at Knole Park, Sevenoaks in Kent where director Peter Goldmann filmed them next to a dead oak tree in the park.

January 31

Pirate station Radio London became the first station to play 'Penny Lane' on the air.

John bought an 1843 circus poster in an antique shop in Sevenoaks, near where they were filming. The poster provided him and Paul with almost the complete lyrics for 'Being For The Benefit Of Mr. Kite', which they wrote together at Kenwood, where John had hung the poster on the wall of his den.

Filming was completed for the 'Strawberry Fields' promo at Knole Park.

February 1

Abbey Road. *Sgt. Pepper* sessions. The 'Sgt. Pepper's Lonely Hearts Club' theme was recorded.

Paul: "I had come to the conclusion that The Beatles were getting a little bit safe, and we were a little intimidated by the idea of making 'the new Beatles album'. It was quite a big thing: 'Wow, follow that!' So to relieve the pressure I got the idea, maybe from some friends or something I'd read, that we shouldn't record it as The Beatles. Mentally we should approach it as another group of people and totally give ourselves alter egos. So I came up with the idea of Sgt. Pepper's Lonely Hearts Club Band and the song 'It Was Twenty Years Ago Today'."

February 2

Abbey Road. *Sgt. Pepper* sessions. Further work on 'Sgt. Pepper's Lonely Hearts Club Band'.

February 3

Abbey Road. *Sgt. Pepper* sessions. Work on 'A Day In The Life'. Ringo added his wonderful drum track, replacing the previous one.

February 5

Part of the horse-riding scene for the 'Penny Lane' promotional film was made at Angel Lane in Stratford, East London.

February 7

The Beatles returned to Knole Park, Sevenoaks, Kent, to shoot more horse-riding and the candelabra scenes for their 'Penny Lane' promotional film.

Monkee Micky Dolenz and his road manager, Ric Klein, spent an evening at Paul's house in Cavendish Avenue.

February 8
Abbey Road. *Sgt. Pepper* sessions. Work began on John's 'Good Morning, Good Morning', which he had written the previous week (inspired by a TV commercial for breakfast cereal) and demoed in his home studio.

February 9
The Beatles recorded three takes of 'Fixing A Hole' at Regent Sound Studios, Tottenham Court Road, instead of at Abbey Road. It was their first time away from EMI's own studio facility. Paul brought a visitor to the session, who had turned up unannounced at his home just as he was about to leave for the studio, and declared that he was Jesus Christ.

February 10
Abbey Road. *Sgt. Pepper* sessions. The famous orchestral chord on 'A Day In The Life' was recorded. To encourage the classical musicians to let down their hair, Paul ensured that they were kitted out in full evening dress, masks and false noses.

Guests at the session included Mick Jagger and Marianne Faithfull, Keith Richards, Donovan, Micky Dolenz, Patti Harrison, clothes designers Simon Postuma and Marijke Koger of The Fool, and various friends.

Paul: "Once we'd written the main bit of the music, we thought, now look, there's a little gap there and we said oh, how about an orchestra? Yes, that'll be nice. And if we do have an orchestra, are we going to write them a pseudo-classical thing, which has been done better by people who know how to make it sound like that – or are we going to do it like we write songs? Take a guess and use instinct. So we said, right, what we'll do to save all the arranging, we'll take the whole orchestra as one instrument. And we just wrote it down like a cooking recipe: 24 bars; on the ninth bar, the orchestra will take off, and it will go from its lowest note to its highest note."

February 11
BBC's *Juke Box Jury* showed part of the 'Penny Lane' promotional film.

February 12
Sussex police raided the home of Keith Richard of The Rolling Stones, having been tipped off that illegal drugs were being consumed on the premises. Richard, bandmate Mick Jagger and art connoisseur Robert Fraser were arrested. Subsequently, rumours spread that George and Patti Harrison had also attended the party, and that the police had waited for them to depart before making their arrests.

February 13
Abbey Road. *Sgt. Pepper* sessions. George's 'Only A Northern Song' was begun. (Not used on *Sgt. Pepper*, but finally released on the *Yellow Submarine* soundtrack album.)

The single 'Penny Lane'/'Strawberry Fields Forever' was released in the USA as Capitol 5810.

PENNY LANE
" 'Penny Lane'/'Strawberry Fields Forever' was the best record we ever made," reckoned Beatles producer George Martin. McCartney's nostalgic 'Penny Lane' didn't have the psychic tension of Lennon's 'Strawberry Fields', but it was every bit as imaginative and lyrical. No other single displays the complementary talents of the Lennon/McCartney pairing so well.

While John's song was locked in the mind, Paul's roamed the streets of Liverpool with a smile on its face. The music matched that sense of freedom, with the crowning touch supplied by David Mason's piccolo trumpet solo. A closing Mason flourish was removed from the song in the final mix, though only after an early mix had been sent to the States, for use on promo copies of the single.

STRAWBERRY FIELDS FOREVER
The greatest pop record ever made? Almost certainly it is, though it shares with its partner, 'Penny Lane', the less glorious fate of having broken a run of Beatles No. 1 hits that went all the way back to 'Please Please Me' four years earlier. In what is arguably the most disgraceful statistic in chart history and to the eternal shame of the British record buying

public, Engelbert Humperdinck's vacuous ballad 'Release Me' prevented The Beatles' double sided slab of genius from reaching the top.

Ostensibly inspired by a Liverpool children's home familiar from his boyhood, 'Strawberry Fields Forever' was actually an attempt by John Lennon to chart the process of consciousness and understanding, through fragmented lyrical images. The story behind the finished record is familiar: two different renditions of the song, in entirely different moods and keys, were cleverly edited together by George Martin via the use of variable tape-speed. If ever a song deserved such serendipity, it was this one – a record that never dates, because it lives outside time.

February 14
Abbey Road. *Sgt. Pepper* sessions. More work on 'Only A Northern Song'.

February 16
Abbey Road. *Sgt. Pepper* sessions. Work on 'Good Morning, Good Morning'.

BBC Television's *Top Of The Pops* showed the 'Penny Lane' and 'Strawberry Fields Forever' promotional clips.

February 17
Abbey Road. *Sgt. Pepper* sessions. Work on 'Being For The Benefit Of Mr. Kite'.

The single 'Penny Lane'/'Strawberry Fields Forever' was released in the UK as Parlophone R 5570.

John: "We don't often write entirely on our own – I mean, I did bits of 'Penny Lane' and Paul wrote some of 'Strawberry Fields'."

Paul played Mellotron on the opening of 'Strawberry Fields' using the flute setting and getting it in one take. George and Paul played timpani and bongo drums while Ringo played electronic drums.

February 19
Another Brian Epstein presentation at the Saville Theatre: John and Ringo saw Chuck Berry and Del Shannon perform.

February 20
Abbey Road. *Sgt. Pepper* sessions. Fairground sounds were added to 'Being For The Benefit Of Mr. Kite'.

George Martin: " 'For The Benefit Of Mr. Kite' was an attempt to create atmosphere. John wanted a circus fairground atmosphere and said he wanted to hear sawdust on the floor, so we had to try and provide that! I wanted a backwash, a general melange of sound, the kind you would hear at a fairground if you closed your eyes. To achieve this we found a load of old steam organ tapes which played things like 'Stars And Stripes Forever'. I chopped them up into foot-long sections and joined them together, sometimes back to front. The whole thing was to create a sound that was unmistakably a steam organ, but which had no particular tune at all."

February 21
Abbey Road. *Sgt. Pepper* sessions. 'Fixing A Hole' was completed.

February 22
Abbey Road. *Sgt. Pepper* sessions. The giant piano chord was added to 'A Day In The Life'. Paul, John, Ringo and Mal Evans, seated at three pianos, all played E major. After overdubbing the chord lasted for 53 seconds. The recording levels were turned up so high in the mix that the sound of Abbey Road's air conditioning system could be heard.

February 23
Abbey Road. *Sgt. Pepper* sessions. Work began on Paul's 'Lovely Rita'.

February 24
Abbey Road. *Sgt. Pepper* sessions. More work on 'Lovely Rita'.

February 26
Brian Epstein bought Rushlake Green Mansion in Sussex. It was always a great joke with Brian that in order to get to his country house he had to drive through the village of Black Boys.

February 27
A story in the *Daily Mail* newspaper about a missing teenager, headlined "A-Level Girl Dumps Car And Vanishes", inspired Paul to begin writing 'She's Leaving Home'.

Paul: "That was enough to give us a storyline. I started to get the lyrics: she slips out and leaves a note and then the parents wake up . . . It was rather poignant. When I showed it to John, he added the Greek chorus, long sustained notes. (The lines) 'We gave her most of our lives, we gave her everything money could buy' may have been in the runaway story, it might have been a quote from the parents."

February 28
Abbey Road. *Sgt. Pepper* sessions. The day was spent in studio two rehearsing 'Lucy In The Sky With Diamonds'. Three-year-old Julian had brought home a drawing from school showing a schoolmate and some diamond shaped stars in the sky. Julian's teacher had asked him what it was, and was told "Lucy In The Sky With Diamonds". The teacher then carefully wrote the title across the top of the drawing, which is where John found the title for his song.

Paul: "So we had a nice title. We did the whole thing like an *Alice in Wonderland* idea, being in a boat on the river, slowly drifting downstream and those great Cellophane flowers towering over your head. Every so often it broke off and you saw Lucy in the Sky, with Diamonds all over the sky. This Lucy was God, the big figure, the white rabbit. You can just write a song with imagination on *words* and that's what we did.

"It's like modern poetry, but neither John nor I have read much. The last time I approached it I was thinking 'This is strange and far out', and I did not dig it all that much, except Dylan Thomas who I suddenly started getting, and I was quite pleased with myself because I got it, but I hadn't realised he was going to be saying exactly the same things.

"It's just that we've at last stopped trying to be clever, and we just write what we like to write. If it comes out clever, OK. 'Love Me Do' was our greatest philosophical song. For it to be simple and true means that it's incredibly simple."

March 1
Abbey Road. *Sgt. Pepper* sessions. Work on 'Lucy In The Sky With Diamonds'.

March 2
Abbey Road. *Sgt. Pepper* sessions. Work on 'Lucy In The Sky With Diamonds'.

March 3
Abbey Road. *Sgt. Pepper* sessions. Four French horns were added to the 'Sgt. Pepper's Lonely Hearts Club Band' track. As usual, Paul hummed the melody, George Martin transcribed it and the session musicians played it. Afterwards they mixed 'Lucy In The Sky With Diamonds'.

March 6
Abbey Road. *Sgt. Pepper* sessions. Sound effects of audience laughter and applause were added to the title track.

March 7
Abbey Road. *Sgt. Pepper* sessions. More work on 'Lovely Rita'.

Peter Blake and Jann Howarth had supper with Paul and Jane at Cavendish Avenue and Paul played them an acetate of 'Lovely Rita'.

Granada Television transmitted *It's So Far Out, It's Straight Down* in their *Scene Special* programme.

March 9

Abbey Road. *Sgt. Pepper* sessions. Work began on Paul's 'Getting Better', which had been inspired when he remembered how stand-in Beatles drummer Jimmy Nicol always used the expression "It's getting better" whenever he was asked how things were going during his brief time on tour with The Beatles in 1964.

March 10

Abbey Road. *Sgt. Pepper* sessions. More work on 'Getting Better.'

March 11

The Beatles won three Grammy Awards for their releases in 1966: "Best Vocal Performance" for 'Eleanor Rigby'; "Best Song" for 'Michelle'; and "Best Cover Artwork" for Klaus Voormann's *Revolver* design.

March 13

Abbey Road. *Sgt. Pepper* sessions. The brass section was added to 'Good Morning, Good Morning'.

March 15

Abbey Road. *Sgt. Pepper* sessions. Work began on George's 'Within You Without You' using four Indian musicians on tabla, dilruba, swordmandel and tamboura. The other Beatles did not play on this track but were there.

Afterwards Peter Blake and Jann Howarth had dinner with John and Paul.

March 17

Abbey Road. *Sgt. Pepper* sessions. The orchestral track for Paul's 'She's Leaving Home' was recorded. George Martin had been unavailable to orchestrate it (he was producing a Cilla Black record), so Paul used Mike Leander as an arranger instead, which upset George Martin considerably. The Beatles themselves did not actually play on the finished track.

March 20

Abbey Road. *Sgt. Pepper* sessions. John and Paul recorded the vocal track for 'She's Leaving Home'.

While at the studio, Brian Matthew interviewed the group for the BBC Transcription Service programme *Top Of The Pops* (no relation), and recorded acceptance speeches for three 1966 Ivor Novello Awards to be edited into the BBC Light Programme's *The Ivor Novello Awards For 1966* programme which John and Paul did not want to attend in person. During these interviews, the two Beatles hinted strongly that they would not be touring in the future.

March 21

Abbey Road. *Sgt. Pepper* sessions. The piano solo was added to 'Lovely Rita' but vocals on 'Getting Better' were interrupted when John found himself on an accidental acid trip. John: "I never took it in the studio. Once I did, actually. I thought I was taking some uppers, and I was not in the state of handling it . . . I suddenly got so scared on the mike. I said, 'What is it? I feel ill.' "

Because so many fans were gathered outside the studios, George Martin took John up onto the flat roof to get some air. When Paul and George realised what was happening they ran up the stairs after them. They knew that the studio roof had just a low parapet and were worried that John might try to fly. Paul and Mal Evans took John back to nearby Cavendish Avenue and Paul decided to keep him company on the trip – Paul's second.

Paul: "Me and John, we'd known each other for a long time. And we looked into each other's eyes, which is fairly mind-boggling. You dissolve into each other. And it was amazing. You would want to look away, but you wouldn't, and you could see yourself in the other person. It was a very freaky experience, and I was totally blown away."

March 22

Abbey Road. *Sgt. Pepper* sessions. George continued work on 'Within You Without You' while the others listened to playbacks.

March 23

Abbey Road. *Sgt. Pepper* sessions. Further work on 'Getting Better'.

March 25

It was announced that The Beatles had won two Ivor Novello Awards for 1966.

March 28

Abbey Road. *Sgt. Pepper* sessions. John added the lead vocal to 'Good Morning, Good Morning'. The animal noises were added to it, and further work was done on 'Being For The Benefit Of Mr. Kite'.

March 29

Abbey Road. *Sgt. Pepper* sessions. Work began on 'With A Little Help From My Friends'.

The title of The Beatles' next album was announced as *Sgt. Pepper's Lonely Hearts Club Band,* a name which Paul and Mal Evans came up with on a plane flight, when Mal asked Paul what the "P" on the paper packet with the in-flight meal meant.

Paul: "I was just thinking nice words like Sergeant Pepper and Lonely Hearts Club, and they came together for no reason. But after you have written that down you start to think, 'There's this Sergeant Pepper who has taught a band to play, and got them going so that at least they found one number. They're a bit of a brass band in a way, but also a rock band because they've got the San Francisco thing.' We went into it just like that; just us doing a good show."

March 30

Abbey Road. *Sgt. Pepper* sessions. Further work was done on 'With A Little Help From My Friends'.

THE *PEPPER* SLEEVE

During the afternoon, the sleeve for *Sgt. Pepper* was shot at Michael Cooper's photographic studio at 4 Chelsea Manor Studios, Flood Street, off the King's Road, with a number of friends present.

Paul: "I came up with the title and went to Robert with some drawings for the idea of the cover."

Robert Fraser: "The whole concept of the cover was Paul McCartney's. He asked me if I knew anybody who could execute this idea. It was my suggestion to put it through Peter Blake and his wife and Michael Cooper, as I knew they were the only people who would understand. It was built in Michael's studio in Flood Street and everybody came up with ideas – all The Beatles, all of us – it became a collaboration."

Peter Blake: "We had an original meeting with all four Beatles, Robert Fraser and Brian Epstein; most of the subsequent talking was done with Paul at his house and with John there sometimes."

Paul: "The original idea was to be a presentation from the mayor and corporation, like a Northern thing. There'd be a floral clock and there'd be us, and then on a wall or something, we'd have photos of all the band's heroes – they were going to be on a photo. So I said to everyone, 'Who are your favourites? Make a list.' Marlon Brando was one of the first choices, Brigitte Bardot, Monroe, James Dean – all obvious ones. Then George came up with a list of gurus, and all sorts of other things came in."

The original list of "Heroes" made by The Beatles before the *Sgt. Pepper* sleeve was given to Robert Fraser and Peter Blake was as follows (sic throughout): "Yoga's; Marquis de Sade; Hitler; Neitch; Lenny Bruce; Lord Buckley; Alistair Crowley; Dylan Thomas; James Joyce; Oscar Wilde; William Burroughs; Robert Peel; Stockhausen; Auldus Huxley; H.G.Wells; Izis Bon; Einstein; Carl Jung; Beardsley; Alfred Jarry; Tom Mix; Johnny Weissmuller; Magritte; Tyrone Power; Carl Marx; Richard Crompton; Tommy Hanley; Albert

Stubbins; Fred Astaire". In addition, Paul's original sketch for the sleeve featured Brigitte Bardot six times larger than anyone else.

Paul "I took the idea of the floral clock, and the heroes and the presentation by a mayor to Robert and he and I went to Peter Blake and Peter developed it all from there. The lists were his idea, and all the cut-outs instead of using real people, and the floral clock got changed around; but basically it was the original theme."

The list grew enormously, with Robert adding in his favourite LA painters, and Peter and Jann adding their favourites. The final line-up on the sleeve was: Stuart Sutcliffe; Aubrey Beardsley; five gurus; two anonymous women; drawings of three girls; Sonny Liston; George (in wax); John (in wax); Ringo (in wax); Paul (in wax); "Cheeky" Max Miller; Sir Robert Peel; Aleister Crowley; Mae West; Lenny Bruce; Aldous Huxley; Dylan Thomas; Marlon Brando; Tom Mix; Terry Southern; Karlheinze Stockhausen; W.C. Fields; Dion; Tony Curtis; Oscar Wilde; Wallace Berman; C.G. Jung; Tyrone Power; Edgar Allan Poe; Tommy Handley; Marilyn Monroe; Dr Livingstone (in wax); Larry Bell; Johnny Weismuller; Fred Astaire; William Burroughs; Stephen Crane; Issy Bonn; Merkin; Stan Laurel; George Bernard Shaw (in wax); Richard Lindner; Oliver Hardy; Albert Stubbins (footballer); Karl Marx; Huntz Hall (of The Bowery Boys); H.G. Wells; Einstein; Bobby Breen (singing prodigy); Marlene Deitrich; Simon Rodia (creator of Watts-Towers); Robert Allen Zimmerman (Bob Dylan); Lawrence of Arabia; Lewis Carroll; an American legionnaire; Diana Dors; and Shirley Temple.

Paul: "Jesus and Hitler were on John's favourites list but they had to be taken off. John was that kind of guy but you couldn't very well have Hitler and so he had to go. Gandhi also had to go because the head of EMI, Sir Joe Lockwood, said that in India they wouldn't allow the record to be printed. There were a few people who just went by the wayside."

April 1
Abbey Road. *Sgt. Pepper* sessions. The 'Sgt. Pepper's Lonely Hearts Club Band (Reprise)' was recorded and mixed all in one session.

April 3
Paul flew to Los Angeles with Mal Evans. Shortly after midnight, Mal Evans took his bags around to Paul's house in Cavendish Avenue. Paul went to bed at 3.30am but was up early because decorators arrived to begin working on the house. Two Air France officials arrived to collect Paul and Mal and not long afterwards they flew into Paris-Orly Airport. From there they took a flight to Los Angeles. Paul had intended to bring a copy of the photograph for the front of *Sgt. Pepper* to show Jane when he met up with her in Denver but he forgot. Paul's American visa turned out to have expired but American customs and immigration at Los Angeles sorted it out in 30 minutes. Then a private Lear jet, hired from Frank Sinatra, took them to San Francisco.

Abbey Road. *Sgt. Pepper* sessions. George added his lead vocal to 'Within You Without You'.

April 4
Paul and Mal Evans flew in to San Francisco which had had its first snow in 42 years and was much colder than they had been expecting. They did the sights, photographed the Golden Gate Bridge and bought records. They stopped by the Fillmore Auditorium and found Jefferson Airplane rehearsing there. They returned to their house, where Paul jammed with them, and played them the acetate of *Sgt. Pepper* which he'd brought over from England. Paul smoked pot with them but declined the DMT he was offered, despite the stories to the contrary still circulating in San Francisco.

April 5
Paul flew into Denver, Colorado, where Jane Asher was playing Shakespeare with the Bristol Old Vic company, to pay a surprise visit on her 21st birthday.

Paul's Lear jet covered the journey from San Francisco to Denver quickly: 650 mph at 41,000 feet. At Denver Airport Paul was met by Bert Rosenthal who had lent Paul his house. Mal booked into the Driftwood Motel. Later in the day, Paul and Jane were collected by Rosenthal and taken to the hotel where Jane's 21st was to be held. The Bristol Old Vic people laid on a wonderful party.

April 6
Mal hired a Hertz rental car and drove Paul and Jane up into the Rockies. They parked off the road among the trees and walked down a rocky gorge to the river where they ended up paddling in the cold water. They walked barefoot in the drifts of snow in the crisp air. That evening they demolished a huge meal and fell asleep in front of Rosenthal's colour television.

April 7
Mal took Paul's camera to be fixed, then went to the park to see the Greek Theatre. Paul filmed Jane walking among the trees and it was then that Paul thought of the *Magical Mystery Tour* as an idea for a TV special.

April 8
Jane had a matinée performance, so Paul and Mal drove into the mountains, past Central City to the old Boodle Mine, complete with its own graveyard. Both Paul and Mal got stuck in snow and mud and finished up looking pretty scruffy. Back in Central City they found "Paul's Café" and went in to refresh themselves and eat. Across the street, in the Gilded Garter bar, they had a few drinks and listened to a local country singer. The singer approached them and asked if they were folk singers because he was sure he knew their faces. They returned to Denver in time to see Jane in *Romeo and Juliet*.

In Chertsey, Surrey, John visited the workshops of coach builders J.P. Fallon Limited to discuss the possibility of having his Rolls Royce repainted in a psychedelic pattern. They were happy to oblige and the car was driven to the workshop a few days later.

April 9
The Old Vic company flew out of Denver to continue their tour of America. In the afternoon, Paul and Mal went to see the Red Rocks Stadium, scene of a memorable Beatles concert three years before. Paul signed a lot of autographs and really enjoyed himself. Then Bert Rosenthal drove them to the airport. The Lear Jet was late in arriving but they were soon in Los Angeles and ensconced in the home of Mr and Mrs Derek Taylor.

April 10
Paul and Mal spent the day shopping at Century Plaza, surprising the locals. Mal bought a talking pillow. Afterwards they visited John and Michelle Phillips of The Mamas and The Papas and sat around watching the rain. It was a very friendly visit but Paul also wanted to visit The Beach Boys, and drove off leaving Mal beside the Phillips' log fire.

Brian Wilson was producing the track 'Vegetables' released on The Beach Boys' *Smiley Smile* album. Paul is said to have had a hand in its production.

April 11
After playing guitar on 'On Top Of Old Smokey' at The Beach Boys session, Paul arrived back at John and Michelle Phillips' house at midnight, bringing Brian Wilson and his wife with him. John and Michelle got out their collection of instruments. At Paul's request, John brought out a tray of glasses, filled with different amounts of water, which he demonstrated how to play. Paul played cello and even flugelhorn. The jam session lasted most of the night. They arrived at Derek Taylor's house in time for breakfast and to pack. Paul spent the flight back to London working on new songs and on the idea of a *Magical Mystery Tour* film.

April 12
Paul and Mal arrived at Heathrow airport.

Paul: "The Beatles are definitely not splitting up. We have never even thought of splitting up. We want to go on recording together. The Beatles live!"

April 19
The Beatles' tax lawyers had suggested that they form an umbrella company controlling all their subsidiary interests. This company, later known as Apple, would have them

under an exclusive contract. The Beatles themselves would become a legal partnership, sharing all their income, whether from group, live or solo work (except songwriting) and The Beatles & Co. was created to bind them together legally for ten years on a goodwill share issue of £1 million.

April 20

Abbey Road. *Sgt. Pepper* sessions. Standing around a single microphone, The Beatles recorded several minutes of gibberish which was then overdubbed, reversed and edited to make the final run-out groove on the album. While recording this, Ringo felt faint. "I think I'm going to fall over," he said and toppled backwards, to be caught by the ever resourceful Mal Evans.

John also suggested that a high-pitched note, beyond the range of the human ear, be added especially for dogs and considerable time was spent with all The Beatles, several friends, and George Martin, seeing how high they could hear. All of them still had good hearing, due in part to the fact that stage foldback had not yet been introduced, so the volume at their concerts was low by modern standards. Also, mixing and playback was then conducted at relatively low levels compared to the practice in the Seventies and Eighties.

April 24

The single 'Love In The Open Air' by George Martin & His Orchestra, written by Paul McCartney, was released in the US as United Artists UA 50148.

All four Beatles attended the first night of Donovan's week-long engagement at the Saville Theatre.

April 25

Abbey Road. Work began on the 'Magical Mystery Tour' theme song. Despite the fact that *Sgt. Pepper* was not yet released, The Beatles moved straight on to another project: Paul's idea for *Magical Mystery Tour* which Brian Epstein thought was a fine vehicle for all four Beatles.

John: "*Magical Mystery Tour* was something Paul had worked out with Mal and he showed me what his idea was and this is how it went, it went round like this, the story and how he had it all . . . the production and everything. Paul had a tendency to come along and say well he's written these ten songs, let's record now. And I'd say, 'well, give us a few days and I'll knock a few off', or something like that."

April 26

Abbey Road. Further work on 'Magical Mystery Tour'.

April 27

Abbey Road. Vocals were added to 'Magical Mystery Tour'.

April 29

The 14 Hour Technicolour Dream benefit party for the underground newspaper *International Times* was held at Alexandra Palace – The Ally Pally. John Lennon and John Dunbar saw a news clip about it on the television at John's house in Weybridge while they were on an acid trip, and John immediately called his driver and had them driven there. John was filmed at the event. Coincidentally, Yoko Ono was one of the 41 performers.

May 1

The single 'I Don't Want To See You Again' (Lennon & McCartney)/'Woman' (Paul McCartney) by Peter & Gordon was released in the US as Capitol Starline 6155.

May 3

Abbey Road. The trumpets were added to 'Magical Mystery Tour'.

May 4

Abbey Road. A mixing session for 'Magical Mystery Tour' which Paul and possibly other Beatles attended.

May 7
Ringo saw The Jimi Hendrix Experience at the Saville Theatre.

May 9
Abbey Road. The Beatles recorded an instrumental jam which was probably intended for the film of 'Magical Mystery Tour', but was never completed or used.

May 11
'Baby You're A Rich Man' session held at Olympic Sound Studios in Barnes, intended for the cartoon film *Yellow Submarine* but in fact used on their next single. Mick Jagger was among their guests at the session.

May 12
Pirate station Radio London became the first station to play *Sgt. Pepper* in its entirety – before copies had even been pressed.
  Abbey Road. 'All Together Now', for the *Yellow Submarine* film, was recorded and mixed all in one session. The Beatles were committed to providing three exclusive new songs for the film.

May 15
Brian Epstein held a dinner party for The Beatles to mark the imminent release of *Sgt. Pepper's Lonely Hearts Club Band*. Afterwards, Paul went to see Georgie Fame at the Bag O'Nails nightclub on Kingly Street, Soho. There he met Linda Eastman, who was there with Chas Chandler and The Animals. Afterwards they went on to The Speakeasy Club, on Margaret Street, where Procol Harum's 'A Whiter Shade Of Pale' was being played for the first time.

LINDA EASTMAN
Linda Eastman was an accomplished photographer when she met Paul. Raised in a wealthy household in Scarsdale, New York, her father Lee Eastman was a successful entertainment business attorney who also represented various painters, including the noted abstract artist Willem de Kooning, and she majored in art history at the University of Arizona. Contrary to popular belief she was not related to the Eastman family of Eastman-Kodak fame. Initially a receptionist at *Town And Country* magazine, Linda was assigned to photograph a number of musical acts beginning with The Dave Clark Five. Married first to geophysicist John Melvyn See, she had one daughter, Heather, by him before marrying Paul, the last Beatle bachelor, in 1969. She produced three further children, Mary, Heather and James, by McCartney.
  Paul: "She passed our table. I was near the edge and stood up just as she was passing, blocking her exit. And so I said, 'Oh, sorry. Hi. How are you? How're you doing?' I introduced myself, and said, 'We're going on to another club after this, would you like to join us?'
  "That was my big pulling line! I'd never used it before, but it worked this time!"

May 17
Abbey Road. Work began on 'You Know My Name, Look Up The Number', the lyrics to which John had found written on the front of the London Telephone Directory while visiting Paul at Cavendish Avenue. ("You know their name, look up the number.")
  John Lennon and John Dunbar made a brief appearance on BBC2's *Man Alive,* a television documentary about the 14 Hour Technicolour Dream.

May 18
Photo session in Hyde Park with Marvin Lichtner from *Time* magazine.
  Paul and John sang backing vocals on The Rolling Stones' single 'We Love You' at Decca Studios. Allen Ginsberg attended the recording session and described them as "two young princes in their finery".

May 19

Sgt. Pepper's Lonely Hearts Club Band was launched with a small press party held at Brian Epstein's house at 24 Chapel Street. Brian had only recently emerged from several weeks of seclusion at a private clinic called the Priory in Surrey, where he had been treated for his drug problems.

Linda Eastman was invited to the party as a press photographer and met Paul again. Around a dozen reporters attended the event, at which they were served champagne, poached salmon and caviar.

George Martin: "Obviously Paul and John were the prime movers of *Sgt. Pepper*, Paul probably more than John. But their inspiration, their creation of original ideas was absolutely paramount, it was fundamental to the whole thing. I was merely serving them in helping them to get those ideas down, so my role had become that of interpreter. In John's case, his ideas weren't all that concise so I had to try to realise what he wanted and how to effect it, and I would do this either by means of an orchestra or sound effects or a combination of both. This role was an interesting one because it presented many challenges for me. I would come up to new problems every day because the songs themselves presented those problems. The songs in the early days were straightforward and you couldn't play around with them too much. Here we were building sound pictures."

Paul: "Whereas we'd just been The Beatles and songwriters, I now started to sort of nudge with the avant-garde and said, 'Hell, we could do this'. The whole idea of taking on a new identity came out of all this. The idea that we didn't have to be The Beatles any more. We could be The Enlightened Beatles or we could be somebody altogether different – Sgt. Pepper's Band.

"It seemed obvious to us that peace, love and justice ought to happen. We were opening ourselves to millions of people's influences, things that arrived in the form of, say, 'A Day In The Life'."

May 20

Ringo invited John, Cynthia, George, Patti and Brian Epstein to take afternoon tea with Maureen, Zak and himself at "Sunny Heights".

DJ Kenny Everett officially previewed *Sgt. Pepper* on his BBC Light Programme show *Where It's At*. He was unable to play the final track, however, because BBC censors had banned 'A Day In The Life' on the grounds that it advocated the use of drugs. The show also featured pre-recorded interviews with John, Paul and Ringo about the album.

May 24

All four Beatles went to the Speakeasy to see Procol Harum.

May 25

The Beatles recorded 'It's All Too Much' at the De Lane Lea recording studio on Kingsway.

John took delivery of his Rolls Royce, now painted with psychedelic fairground patterns like a gypsy caravan. Rolls Royce launched a formal objection.

May 28

All four Beatles attended a party at Brian Epstein's new country house near Heathfield in Surrey. John took the opportunity to convert former Beatles press officer Derek Taylor to the delights of LSD.

May 31

Further work was done on 'It's All Too Much' at the De Lane Lea recording studios.

June

The Beatles' office announced that the group were planning to begin work on their long-delayed third feature film this autumn, probably a vehicle called *Shades Of A Personality* in which the four Beatles would display four different sides to the same man's character. The film was set to be made in Spain.

June 1

An unstructured instrumental jam was recorded at De Lane Lea studios in Kingsway.

The album *Sgt. Pepper's Lonely Hearts Club Band* was released in the UK as Parlophone PMC 7027 (mono) and PCS 7027 (stereo). Side A: 'Sgt. Pepper's Lonely Hearts Club Band', 'With A Little Help From My Friends', 'Lucy In The Sky With Diamonds', 'Getting Better', 'Fixing A Hole', 'She's Leaving Home', 'Being For The Benefit Of Mr. Kite'; Side B: 'Within You Without You', 'When I'm Sixty Four', 'Lovely Rita', 'Good Morning Good Morning', 'Sgt. Pepper's Lonely Hearts Club Band (reprise)', 'A Day In The Life'.

Paul: "We recorded *Sgt. Pepper* to alter our egos, free ourselves and have a lot of fun."

John: "The people who have bought our records in the past must realise that we couldn't go on making the same type forever. We must change,"

The amazing thing was that *Sgt. Pepper* was recorded on an antique Studer J37 4-track. In 1981 it was auctioned by Jackson Music Ltd. for £500.

SGT. PEPPER'S LONELY HEARTS CLUB BAND

"The biggest influence on *Sgt. Pepper* was *Pet Sounds* by The Beach Boys," said Paul McCartney in 1980. "That album just flipped me. When I heard it, I thought, 'Oh dear, this is the album of all time. What the hell are we going to do?' My ideas took off from that standard. I had this idea that it was going to be an album of another band that wasn't us – we'd just imagine all the time that it wasn't us playing. It was just a nice little device to give us some distance on the album. The cover was going to be us dressed as this other band in crazy gear; but it was all stuff that we'd always wanted to wear. And we were going to have photos on the wall of all our heroes."

That's the standard view of *Sgt. Pepper*, from the man who almost single-handedly created the album, and its legend. In this reading, *Pepper* is the best pop record of all time – the album that customarily wins critics' polls, the masterpiece that first persuaded 'serious' musical critics pop was worth their consideration.

There's a rival view of the whole affair, however, and it was put forward most cogently by McCartney's supposed partner, John Lennon. "*Paul* said 'come and see the show' on that album," he moaned a few years after its release. "I didn't. I had to knock off a few songs so I knocked off 'A Day In The Life', or my section of it, and 'Mr. Kite'. I was very paranoid in those days. I could hardly move."

More than any other Beatles album bar *Abbey Road*, *Sgt. Pepper* was a Paul McCartney creation. He it was who dreamed up the concept, the title, the idea behind Peter Blake's remarkable cover, the orchestrations, and the device of pretending that the entire LP was the work of another band entirely – which in turn became one of the major themes of the *Yellow Submarine* movie, then in its pre-production stages.

Meanwhile, John Lennon was deep in a creative trough. For the first time, Lennon and McCartney appeared – to Lennon, at least – to be in competition rather than on the same side. Since The Beatles had played their final live shows in August, McCartney had been composing – first the musical themes for the film *The Family Way*, then the songs that would appear on the next Beatles album. Lennon had also been involved in film work, but as an actor, in Dick Lester's *How I Won The War*. Required for the part to shed his Beatle locks, he adopted the granny specs that soon became his trademark, stared into the mirror, and wondered what the future might bring for an unemployed Beatle. Back in England at the end of the filming, Lennon regarded McCartney's enthusiasm to get into the studio as a threat. Aware that he was likely to be outnumbered in the songwriting stakes, he raised the emotional barriers and took against the *Pepper* album from the start.

In the end, Lennon came up with the requisite number of songs for the album, but he never warmed to the concept. On *Revolver*, and again on the majestic 'Strawberry Fields Forever', cut early in the sessions, he'd experienced the relief and satisfaction of writing from the heart. For *Pepper*, he was back where he'd been in 1964, writing songs to order. Hence the sarcastic, dismissive comments he reserved for this album throughout the rest of his life.

Whatever else *Sgt. Pepper* may or may not have been, it was certainly an event. It unified British pop culture in a way no other occasion could match. Maybe in hindsight it wasn't The Beatles' strongest album, but it had an impact unlike any record before or since. It literally revolutionised the direction of pop, helping to divide it between those who were prepared to follow the group along the path of experimentation (thus creating 'rock') and those who mourned the loss of the less significant Beatles of yore (the champions of 'pop'). After *Pepper*, nothing was ever the same again – within or without The Beatles.

SGT. PEPPER'S LONELY HEARTS CLUB BAND
Complete with the appropriate sound effects, the album's up-tempo title track introduced the record, the concept and the Club Band. It performed the function of an overture in an opera, preparing the audience for what was to follow, and introducing the themes that supposedly unified the piece.

WITH A LITTLE HELP FROM MY FRIENDS
Beatles official biographer Hunter Davies watched Lennon, McCartney and their associates completing work on Paul McCartney's original idea, aware from the start that this would be a vehicle for Ringo Starr – or 'Billy Shears', as he was billed in the opening seconds of the song. Though the song's theme was tailored towards Ringo's warm public image (right down to the line "what would you say if I sang out of tune", a real possibility), at least one observer saw a hidden meaning. Speaking in 1970, US Vice-President Spiro Agnew told an audience that he had recently been informed that the song was a tribute to the power of illegal drugs – news to its composers, perhaps.

Not often did other performers outclass The Beatles with cover versions of their songs, but Joe Cocker's gut-wrenching version of 'Friends' in 1968 left Ringo floundering.

LUCY IN THE SKY WITH DIAMONDS
The minor furore over the meaning of 'Friends' had nothing on the frenzied response to this piece of whimsy from the pen of John Lennon. "I was consciously writing poetry," he admitted, shifting blame for the line about "newspaper taxis" to his nominal co-writer. But the Alice In Wonderland style imagery, supposedly inspired by a drawing John's son Julian had brought home from nursery school, was widely believed to be a description of an acid trip. As soon as someone noticed the initials of the song's title (LSD), that seemed to clinch the story – except that Lennon continued to deny it until his dying day. Having owned up to so much else down the years, there was no reason for him to lie – especially over a song which he always felt was "so badly recorded".

GETTING BETTER
Based on a favourite saying of Beatles stand-in drummer Jimmy Nicol, 'Getting Better' was a McCartney song augmented by Lennon, who contributed the self-accusing verse that began "I used to be cruel to my woman". Ever since Lennon's death, McCartney has bemoaned his inability to find a co-writer who, like John, would answer a line like "it's getting better all the time" with "can't get much worse". Even in the midst of what was intended to be a concept album, McCartney could turn out a song that was clever, melodic, memorable and universal in its application.

FIXING A HOLE
For the first time in England, The Beatles left Abbey Road studios for the session that provided the basic track for this fine McCartney song, often overlooked by critics and fans alike. EMI's studio was fully booked for the night, so the group moved to Regent Sound in the West End, where The Rolling Stones' early hits had been taped.

While John Lennon's writing veered between fantasy and obvious self-revelation, McCartney's skirted from the romantic to the delightfully oblique. This song definitely fell into the latter category, with lyrics that unveiled as many mysteries as they solved. Instrumentally, too, 'Fixing A Hole' was a minor classic, from McCartney's opening trills on the harpsichord to Harrison's lyrical guitar solo.

SHE'S LEAVING HOME
"Paul had the basic theme for this song," said John Lennon, "but all those lines like 'We sacrificed most of our life . . . We gave her everything that money could buy', those were the

things Mimi used to say to me. It was easy to write." Paul's rather precious piece of fictional writing wasn't helped by Mike Leander's ornate score for the song, one of the few occasions when The Beatles were left sounding pretentious. It took the realism of Lennon's answer-lines to cut through the sweetness of the piece.

BEING FOR THE BENEFIT OF MR. KITE
A masterpiece of ingenuity rather than inspiration, 'Mr. Kite' was written when John transcribed the wording from a vintage circus poster into verse form, and recorded with the help of scores of small segments of fairground organ tape, tossed into the air and then stuck back together to produce the eerie noise that dominates the instrumental sections. Lennon dismissed it as a throwaway – which, when you remember how it was made, is pretty apt.

WITHIN YOU WITHOUT YOU
Though it was John Lennon who resented Paul McCartney's domination of the Pepper *sessions, George Harrison probably had more cause to be aggrieved. He was restricted to just one number on the LP, his other contribution ('Only A Northern Song') being rejected.*
Like 'Love You To', 'Within You Without You' blatantly displayed George's infatuation with Indian culture. Recorded with the assistance of several Indian musicians, plus Beatles aide Neil Aspinall on tamboura, the song required no help from any other member of the group. "It was written at Klaus Voorman's house in Hampstead, one night after dinner," George explained a decade later. "I was playing a pedal harmonium when it came, the tune first, then the first sentence." Some thought it a masterpiece, some a prime example of mock-philosophical babble. Either way, it was pure Harrison.

WHEN I'M SIXTY-FOUR
Paul began writing this song when he was a teenager, needing only to add the middle sections for this revival of a ten-year-old melody. Within the concept of the album, it fitted the image of the Edwardian Pepper band, whereas it would have seemed mawkish on any of the group's earlier LPs. The addition of clarinets to the mix heightened the pre-First World War feel.

LOVELY RITA
The anthem for traffic wardens ("meter maids") everywhere, 'Lovely Rita' was a glorious throwaway, full of musical jokes and brimming with self-confidence. Nothing on the record expressed that as fully as the piano solo, ironically played by keyboard maestro George Martin.

GOOD MORNING, GOOD MORNING
Using a TV commercial for Kellogg's cereal as his starting point, John Lennon concocted a wonderfully dry satire on contemporary urban life. Several points to watch out for here: the reference to the popular BBC TV sitcom, Meet The Wife; *the ultra-compressed brass sound provided by members of Sounds Incorporated; a stinging Harrison guitar solo; and the cavalcade of animals, in ascending order of ferocity, which segues into the next track.*

SGT. PEPPER'S LONELY HEARTS CLUB BAND (REPRISE)
For the first but definitely not the last time, Paul McCartney topped and tailed a set of songs by reprising the opening melody, in true Hollywood musical fashion.

A DAY IN THE LIFE
Delete 'A Day In The Life' from Sgt. Pepper *and you'd have an elegant, playful album of pop songs. With it, the LP assumes some kind of greatness. Some might vote for 'Hey Jude' or 'Strawberry Fields Forever' as the finest ever Beatles recording, but 'A Day In The Life' would run anything close – and it's certainly the best ever collaborative effort between Lennon and McCartney.*
Lennon wrote the basic song, its verses a snapshot from his own life and the world around him – the death of a friend in a car crash, a newspaper cutting about the state of the roads in Blackburn, Lancashire. The tag line "I'd love to turn you on" brought a broadcasting ban in Britain: more importantly, it led twice into an overwhelming orchestral assault, with 40 musicians headed helter-skelter up the scales towards a crescendo of silence. First time around, the barrage leads into McCartney's stoned middle-eight, another day in another life; second time, there's a pause, and then a piano chord that resounds for almost a minute. Then bathos: a whistle only dogs could hear, followed by the locked-groove gibberish that brought the side to a close, and is sampled briefly at the end of the CD. Stunning, magnificent, awesome: there's nothing in rock to match it.

June 2

Work on 'It's All Too Much' at De Lane Lea.

Yellow Submarine film producer Al Brodax: "The numbers they have been recording this month for the movie are brilliant – incredible! They are using sounds I have never heard, nor could ever have imagined before."

The album *Sgt. Pepper's Lonely Hearts Club Band* was released in the US as Capitol MAS 2653 (mono) and SMAS 2653 (stereo) with the same track list as the UK release.

After the jailing the previous day of *International Times* founder John 'Hoppy' Hopkins on a charge of possessing cannabis, luminaries from the British underground met to discuss registering a protest. Barry Miles rang Paul to solicit his support, and Paul promised that the Beatles would finance an advertisement in *The Times* deploring the laws on 'soft' drugs.

June 3

Barry Miles and drug researcher Steve Abrams visited Paul in St. John's Wood to discuss the campaign against the drug laws.

June 4

Paul and Jane, George and Patti were in the audience at Brian Epstein's Saville Theatre to see The Jimi Hendrix Experience headline a bill which included Denny Laine & His Electric String Band, The Chiffons and Procol Harum. Jimi Hendrix opened his set with the title track from *Sgt. Pepper*. Paul described it as among the greatest honours he ever had bestowed upon him, particularly as Jimi had only three days to rehearse the piece.

June 7

Abbey Road. Another take of 'You Know My Name, Look Up The Number' was made.

The animated *Yellow Submarine* film was announced.

June 8

Abbey Road. Paul invited Brian Jones from The Rolling Stones to attend the recording session, thinking he might bring along a guitar and play some rhythm. Brian arrived with an alto saxophone, which used to be his instrument in the pre-Rolling Stones Ramrods. He played a sax solo for them on 'You Know My Name, Look Up The Number' which remains one of Paul McCartney's favourite Beatles' numbers.

June 9

Abbey Road. 'You Know My Name, Look Up The Number' was mixed.

June 12

The album *The Family Way (Original Soundtrack Album)* by The George Martin Orchestra and written by Paul McCartney was released in the USA as London MS 82007 with the same tracks as the UK release.

June 14

The backing track for 'All You Need Is Love' was recorded at Olympic Studios, Barnes, for use on the first live worldwide satellite link-up which was expected to be seen by 200 million people. George Martin pleaded with them, "You can't just go off the cuff. We've got to prepare something." John came back with 'All You Need Is Love' and Martin orchestrated it. George Martin: "When it came to the end of their fade-away as the song closed, I asked them: 'How do you want to get out of it?' 'Write absolutely anything you like, George,' they said. 'Put together any tunes you fancy, and just play it out like that.'" Martin came up with the 'Marseillaise', a Bach two-part invention, 'Greensleeves' and a short quote from 'In The Mood' (which EMI ultimately had to pay copyright on).

June 16

The Monterey International Pop Festival began at the Monterey County Fairgrounds in California. Despite constant speculation throughout the weekend, none of The Beatles was in attendance. But the group did provide festival co-ordinator Derek Taylor with an original piece of artwork, which was printed in the festival programme.

June 17
Life magazine ran an interview with Paul McCartney in which he revealed that he had taken acid.

June 19
Abbey Road. Further work done on 'All You Need Is Love'.

PAUL AND LSD
After Paul's admission in *Life* Magazine, the British press besieged him to make a statement. Paul gave an interview to Independent Television News for broadcast on the 9pm news that evening.
Reporter: "How often have you taken LSD?"
Paul: "Um, four times."
Reporter: "And where did you get it from?"
Paul: "Well, you know, I mean, if I was to say where I got it from, you know, it's illegal and everything, it's silly to say that so I'd rather not say it."
Reporter: "Don't you believe that this was a matter which you should have kept private?"
Paul: "Well the thing is, you know, that I was asked a question by a newspaper and the decision was whether to tell a lie or to tell the truth, you know. I decided to tell him the truth but I really didn't want to say anything because if I'd had my way I wouldn't have told anyone because I'm not trying to spread the word about this but the man from the newspaper is the man from the mass medium. I'll keep it a personal thing if he does too, you know, if he keeps it quiet. But he wanted to spread it so it's his responsibility for spreading it. Not mine."
Reporter: "But you're a public figure and you said it in the first place. You must have known that it would make the newspapers."
Paul: "Yes, but to say it, you know, is only to tell the truth. I'm telling the truth. I don't know what everyone is so angry about."
Reporter: "Well, do you think you have encouraged your fans to take drugs?"
Paul: "I don't think it will make any difference. You know, I don't think my fans are going to take drugs just because I did. But the thing is, that's not the point anyway. I was asked whether I had or not and from then on the whole bit about how far its going to go and how many people it's going to encourage is up to the newspapers and up to you, you know, on television. I mean, you're spreading this now, at this moment. This is going into all the homes in Britain and I'd rather it didn't, you know. But you're asking me the question and if you want me to be honest I'll be honest."
Reporter: "But as a public figure, surely you've got a responsibility to not say any . . ."
Paul: "No, it's you who've got the responsibility. You've got the responsibility not to spread this now. You know, I'm quite prepared to keep it as a very personal thing if you will too. If you'll shut up about it, I will!"

June 21
Abbey Road. 'All You Need Is Love' was mixed.

June 23
Abbey Road. The orchestral track was added to 'All You Need Is Love'.

June 24
Abbey Road, preparing for the satellite link-up. The Beatles, the 13-man orchestra and their conductor did a full run-through for the BBC cameramen. More than 100 journalists and photographers were allowed into the studio for a late-morning photocall.

June 25
The Beatles performed 'All You Need Is Love' on the BBC *Our World* live worldwide TV link-up live from EMI's massive studio one.
The studio was filled with potted flowers and The Beatles wore uniforms of green, pink and orange, similar to the *Sgt. Pepper* cover. Waist long flowing scarves wafted from

their necks but the medieval look was marred slightly by the headphones they all wore, as well as the usual studio clutter of microphones, headphone leads, instruments and music stands. Among the guests were Keith Richards, Eric Clapton, Graham Nash and Gary Leeds. Keith Moon fooled around on the drums with Ringo during the long wait before transmission. Simon, Marijka and Joshi, from The Fool, wore the flowing patchwork patterns and headscarves they would shortly market through the Apple boutique. The Small Faces sat close to each other in new Granny Takes A Trip clothes. Mick Jagger sat on the floor with Marianne Faithfull, close by Paul's high stool, wearing a silk jacket with a pair of psychedelic eyes painted on it, smoking a very fat joint in front of the 200 million viewers, the day before he was to be busted for drugs. "All You Need Is Love!" streamers and balloons floated down from the ceiling and the audience all sang along. Placards with the message ALL YOU NEED IS LOVE written large in many languages were paraded before the cameras. The vocals, Paul's bass, Ringo's drums, George's solo and the orchestra were all mixed live on the air. In the control room afterwards George Martin played back the tape. "Another big hit!" said Paul.

Paul: "We had one message for the whole world – love. We need more love in the world. It's a period in history that needs love."

June 26
Abbey Road. Ringo added the opening drum roll to 'All You Need Is Love' and the record was mixed, ready for instant release.

June 28
George was fined £6 at South Western Court, London, for speeding in Roehampton Lane, Putney in his black Mini Cooper.

The Family Way, the film for which Paul had composed the soundtrack, was premiered in New York.

June 29
The Beatles' Book Monthly photographer, Leslie Bryce, photographed John at Kenwood, his mock-Tudor mansion in Weybridge, for an "at home" session.

July 1
The BBC Light Programme show, *Where It's At* broadcast a pre-recorded interview with Paul talking about 'All You Need Is Love'.

July 3
Vic Lewis gave a private party for The Monkees at the Speakeasy. The guests included John and Cynthia, George and Patti, Paul and Jane, The Who, Eric Clapton, the Manfred Mann group, Lulu, Procol Harum, The Fool, Micky Most, Vicki Wickham, Dusty Springfield, and Monkees Peter Tork, Mike Nesmith and Micky Dolenz (Davy Jones and Ringo were both away).

The Fool were commissioned by Brian Epstein to redesign the interior of his Saville Theatre, in a similar style to their recent psychedelic transformation of John's Rolls Royce.

July 4
George and Patti travelled to Liverpool to spend several days with his family.

July 5
John and Cynthia saw Marmalade at the Speakeasy.

July 7
The single 'All You Need Is Love'/'Baby You're A Rich Man' was released in the UK as Parlophone R 5620. It was only decided 24 hours before the TV show that 'All You Need Is Love' should be their next single, based on the demand that the worldwide viewing would cause.

Paul: "It does sound like we used to sound. But it's really next time round on the spiral. I'd sum it up as taking a look back with a new feeling."

'Baby You're A Rich Man' was originally intended for the soundtrack of the full-length Beatles cartoon, *Yellow Submarine*. It was originally called *One Of The Beautiful People*.

ALL YOU NEED IS LOVE

With both the Our World *programme on June 25 and universal appeal in mind, John Lennon wrote 'All You Need Is Love', one of the anthems of the Sixties. The decision was made to broadcast the actual recording of the song live – or so the public were informed, though Lennon and the other Beatles sang and played along to a pre-recorded backing track, and John actually re-cut his lead vocal a few hours later. The broadcast passed without incident, and remains one of the strongest visual impressions of the summer of love, as a mini-orchestra and many of the group's friends from the pop aristocracy congregated in the cavernous Studio One at Abbey Road.*

BABY YOU'RE A RICH MAN

"We just stuck two songs together for this one," admitted John Lennon, "the same as 'A Day In The Life'." The final effect wasn't quite as grandiose, but 'Baby You're A Rich Man' certainly took less time to record – being started and finished in a single six-hour session. Rumours that the song's final choruses contain a hidden 'tribute' to Brian Epstein – "baby you're a rich fag Jew" – appear to be groundless. But it is true that the number was originally intended for the Yellow Submarine *soundtrack, though it ended up being released a year before the film on the flipside of 'All You Need Is Love'. The instrument punctuating the song that sounds like a manic trumpet is a primitive synthesiser called a Clavioline, incidentally.*

July 9

London painter John McDonnell exhibited 'The Musicians', a reworking of a work by Caravaggio, with the faces of The Beatles replacing the original subjects of the painting. The work was later sold to an American tourist for 100 guineas (£105).

July 12

George and Patti returned to London from Liverpool.

July 17

The single 'All You Need Is Love'/'Baby You're A Rich Man' was released in the USA as Capitol 5964.

July 19

The four Beatles met in London to discuss their next film project, and also their plans to purchase an island hideaway in Greece.

July 20

Paul and Jane attended a Chris Barber recording session at the Chappell Recording Studios to see him record Paul's instrumental 'Catcall'. Paul played piano, along with Brian Auger, and can be heard yelling in the chorus at the end.

John had long had the idea that The Beatles should all live together on an island with a recording studio/entertainment complex in the middle, surrounded by four separate villas. Beyond that would be housing for their friends and the staff. Alex Mardas, a TV repairman whom John had dubbed "Magic Alex", had friends in the Greek Military Junta, and arranged for The Beatles to island-seek there. Though the authorities had already banned both long hair and rock'n'roll, they felt that The Beatles visiting Greece might help prop up their tourist industry and undermine some of the bad press they had been getting for torturing dissidents. Alex flew to Greece and came up with the island of John's dreams: the island of Leslo, about 80 acres surrounded by four habitable islands, one for each Beatle. The island was for sale for £90,000, including a small fishing village, four ideal beaches and 16 acres of olive groves.

George and Patti, Ringo and Neil Aspinall flew to Athens where they were met by Alex and his father, who was in the military police. They stayed at the Mardas house in suburban Athens until the remaining members of the party arrived.

July 22

John and Cynthia with Julian, Paul and Jane, Patti's 16-year-old sister Paula, Mal Evans and Alistair Taylor from the NEMS office, who was in charge of buying the island, set off for Greece. Their hired yacht, the MV *Arvi*, was stuck near Crete in high winds and did not get to Athens until the 25th, so they all stayed in Athens.

The Fab Four, circa 1967.
(Clockwise, left to right: *Bettmann-Corbis, MSI, Hulton-Getty, Hulton-Getty*)

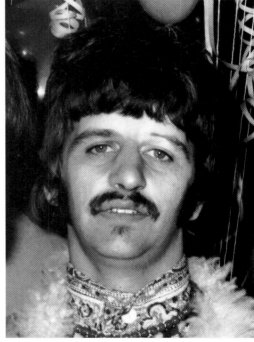

The Beatles at their *Sgt Pepper* launch party, at Brian's Epstein's Belgravia home, May 19, 1967.
(*Bettmann-Corbis*)

The four Beatles in the back yard of Abbey Road Studios, holding 'All You Need Is Love' posters, June 24, 1967.
(*Jane Bown/Camera Press*)

George with Ravi Shankar in Los Angeles, August 3, 1967. (*Popperfoto*)

August 26, 1967: Listening to the Maharishi's words of wisdom in Bangor, left to right: Mike McGear, Ringo, Maureen, John and, in the foreground, Paul and Jane Asher. (*Hulton-Getty*)

The Beatles at the Royal Hotel, Torquay, during the filming of *Magical Mystery Tour*, September 12, 1967. (*Hulton-Getty*)

July 8, 1968, three Beatles and a virtual John the opening of the *Yellow Submarine* movie. (*LFI*)

John and Yoko in June, 1968. (*Jane Bown/Camera Press*)

George in Golden Gate Park, San Francisco, August 9, 1968. (*Bettmann-Corbis*)

Paul and John on their way to New York to launch Apple, May 1968. (*LFI*)

On the day of their marriage, March 12, 1969, Paul and Linda pose for photographers outside his home in Cavendish Avenue, St John's Wood. Also in the frame are Mal Evans (left), Peter Brown (right) and Heather, Linda's daughter from her previous marriage, in the foreground. (*Camera Press*)

Ringo and Maureen in 1969. (*LFI*)

December 11, 1968: John at The Rolling Stones' *Rock And Roll Circus* TV show, where he performed in a band with Keith Richards, Eric Clapton and Mitch Mitchell. (*Andrew Maclear/Redferns*)

George on stage with Delaney & Bonnie at John and Yoko's 'War Is Over' concert, December 12, 1969. (*LFI*)

From Moptops to Men of the World: The Beatles in 1963, with George Martin, and in front of John's Rolls-Royce in 1969. (*News International & LFI*)

July 23

In a convoy of a Mercedes and two huge American taxis, the party went out into the country. Paul, Jane and Neil's taxi caught fire in the extreme heat and when the others turned back to look for them they were found walking along the road, back towards the village where the party had eaten lunch.

Alex arranged a few sightseeing trips to prevent them from getting bored, but he also kept the Greek tourist authorities informed of their timetable so wherever they went there were crowds of people following. Alistair Taylor wrote, "Once on a trip to a hill village, we came round a corner of the peaceful road only to find hundreds of photographers clicking away at us."

July 24

The Oxford University drama company invited The Beatles to attend a performance of *Agamemnon* by Aeschylus, at the theatre at Delphi, but Alex had informed the tourist authorities who broadcast the fact they would be there on Athens Radio. They arrived in Delphi to an enormous crowd of fans and pushy journalists. They climbed back into their Mercedes and headed straight back to Athens.

THE 'POT' AD

The Times ran a full-page advertisement on July 24 headed, "The law against marijuana is immoral in principle and unworkable in practice" which was signed by, among others, all four Beatles and Brian Epstein. The petition's arguments included the following: that the smoking of cannabis on private premises should no longer constitute an offence; cannabis should be taken off the dangerous drugs list and controlled, rather than prohibited; possession of cannabis should either be legally permitted or at most be considered a misdemeanour and that all persons now imprisoned for possession of cannabis or for allowing cannabis to be smoked on private premises should have their sentences commuted.

It was signed by 65 eminent names including Francis Crick, the co-discoverer of the DNA molecule and a Nobel laureate, novelist Graham Greene, and MPs Brian Walden and Tom Driberg, as well as future MP Jonathan Aitken, but the four MBEs caused the most press concern. Questions were asked in the House, and a chain of events set off, which did actually result in the liberalisation of the laws against pot in Britain. The £1,800 advertisement was paid for by The Beatles at Paul McCartney's instigation.

July 25

George and Paul stayed in, playing guitars and relaxing while John, Ringo and the others went shopping for instruments, attracting a large crowd of sightseers and fans.

The yacht finally arrived. It had 24 berths and a crew of eight including the captain, a chef and two stewards.

July 26

Ringo and Neil Aspinall flew back to London from Athens. Maureen was pregnant and with the baby nearly due Ringo did not want to be away too long.

The others boarded the yacht. The first few days were spent swimming, sunbathing, and taking LSD. Then they set off to inspect Leslo, where they were to build their commune. After a full day of exploring the island, planning where the recording studio would be located and who would live on which island, Alistair Taylor was instructed to fly straight back to London and make the arrangements to buy it.

Export controls meant that The Beatles had to buy special export dollars and then apply to the government for permission to spend them. Taylor eventually got the clearance but by then no one was interested in the idea any more and he was told to sell the property dollars back to the government. In the meantime, their value had increased so The Beatles made £11,400 profit on the deal.

July 27

Music publishers KPM Music approached Northern Songs, claiming that copyright in the tune 'In The Mood' had been infringed by the incorporation of a few bars from the song in the fade-out of The Beatles' 'All You Need Is Love'.

July 29
George, Patti and Mal Evans returned from Greece to prepare for a trip to Los Angeles.

July 31
Paul, Jane, John, Cynthia, Julian, Paula and Alex flew back to London from Athens.
Ringo recorded a farewell message at pirate station Radio London, broadcast on their last day on the air before the government stamped them out and replaced them with their own anodyne version of pop radio.

August 1
George, Patti, "Magic" Alex Mardas and Neil Aspinall flew from London to Los Angeles where they had rented a house on Blue Jay Way. George and Patti flew as Mr and Mrs Weiss, taken from Nat Weiss, the director of Nemperer Artists in New York, who was to meet them at the airport and look after them.
That evening George called Derek Taylor and gave him directions to get there but Derek got lost in the LA fog trying to find their house. While he was waiting, George wrote a song with the street name as the title.

August 2
George, Patti, Neil and Alex visited Ravi Shankar's Music School and watched him teach. Afterwards they had a meal with Shankar on Sunset Strip.

August 3
George, Alex and Neil went to Ravi Shankar's Music School where George and Ravi Shankar held a press conference to promote Shankar's Hollywood Bowl concert set for the following day. Patti and her sister Jenny, who flew down from San Francisco to join them, went sightseeing.
That evening they attended a Mamas And Papas recording session with Derek Taylor.

August 4
George and his party attended Ravi Shankar's concert at the Hollywood Bowl.
Polydor reissued their album of 1961 Hamburg recordings, *The Beatles' First*.

August 5
George and company attended a recording session by Alla Rahka, after which they went for a meal in Alvira Street with Derek Taylor and his entire family.

August 6
George visited Ashish, Ali Akbar Khan's son, the sarod player, while the others visited Disneyland. That evening they dined at Ravi Shankar's house.

August 7
After flying along the coast from Los Angeles, George, Patti, Jenny, Derek Taylor and Neil Aspinall walked around the Haight-Ashbury district of San Francisco, attracting a huge crowd of hippies and beggars.

August 9
Neil, Alex, George and Patti flew back to London, via New York.

August 11
The Beatles were photographed by Richard Avedon at the penthouse photographic studio in Thompson House. Avedon used the images for a series of four psychedelic posters which appeared first in *Look* magazine before being published separately and adorning thousands of student bedrooms around the world.

August 13
EMI announced that the *Sgt. Pepper* album had now sold more than 500,000 copies in the UK alone.

August 16
The first press screening of *How I Won The W*ar, the film starring John, was held in London.

August 18
The single 'We Love You' by The Rolling Stones, with backing vocals by John Lennon and Paul McCartney, was released in the UK as Decca F 12654.

August 19
Maureen Starkey gave birth to a second son, Jason, at Queen Charlotte's Hospital, London.

August 20
John and Paul visited Maureen Starkey in hospital. Later they returned to Paul's home in St. John's Wood to discuss The Beatles' future plans.

August 22
The Beatles began work on 'Your Mother Should Know' at Chappell Recording Studios, London.

August 23
The Beatles finished work on 'Your Mother Should Know' at Chappell. Brian Epstein was on hand to watch part of the session, the last time he visited the group in the recording studio.

August 24
John and Cynthia, Paul and Jane, George and Patti attended a lecture by the Maharishi Mahesh Yogi at the London Hilton on Park Lane. After the lecture they had a private audience with the Maharishi and arranged to attend his seminar which was to be held in Bangor that weekend.

August 25

THE MAHARISHI
The Beatles, their wives and girlfriends, Mick Jagger and Marianne Faithfull took the train from Euston Station to Bangor to attend the Maharishi's teaching seminar. Cynthia Lennon got caught in the crush and a policeman refused to let her through the barrier onto the platform until it was too late and the train pulled away without her. Neil Aspinall drove her there.

For the four Beatles, it was the first time in five years that they had ever travelled anywhere without the protective cordon supplied by Brian, Neil or Mal.

John: "Bangor was incredible, you know. Maharishi reckons the message will get through if we can put it across. What he says about life and the universe is the same message that Jesus, Buddha and Krishna and all the big boys were putting over. Mick came up there and he got a sniff and he was on the phone saying: 'Keith, send Brian, send them all down.' You just get a sniff and you're hooked.

"There's none of this sitting in the lotus position or standing on your head. You just do it as long as you like. (In a heavy accent) Twenty minutes a day is prescribed for ze workers. Twenty minutes a morning and twenty minutes after verk. Makes you happy, intelligent and more energy. I mean look how it all started. I believe he just landed in Hawaii in his nightshirt, all on his own, nobody with him, in 1958.

"The main thing is not to think about the future or the past, the main thing is to just get on with *now*. We want to help people to do that with these academies. We'll make a donation and we'll ask for money from anyone we know with money, anyone that's interested, anyone in the so-called establishment who's worried about kids going wild and drugs and all that. Another groovy thing: everybody gives one week's wages when they join. I think it's the fairest thing I've heard of. And that's all you ever pay, just the once.

"Even if you go into the meditation bit just curious or cynical, once you go into it, you see. We weren't so much sceptical because we'd been through that phase in the middle of all the Beatlemania like, so we came out of being sceptics a bit. But you've still got to have a questioning attitude to all that goes on. The only thing you can do is judge on your own experience and that's what this is about."

August 26

The Beatles informed the national press, who were besieging the Maharishi's meditation centre in Bangor, that they had renounced the use of hallucinogenic drugs.

2,000 fans gathered at Shea Stadium in New York, to protest that The Beatles had not played any concerts in the US during the summer of 1967.

August 27

Brian Epstein was found dead in his London house.

Jane Asher received the telephone call which brought The Beatles the news in Wales, and gave the receiver to Paul. Saddened, worried and confused, the group gave a brief press conference then departed for London.

John: "I can't find words to pay tribute to him. It is just that he was lovable, and it is those lovable things we think about now."

Paul: "This is a great shock. I am deeply upset."

George: "He dedicated so much of his life to The Beatles. We liked and loved him. He was one of us."

Ringo: "We loved Brian. He was a generous man. We owe so much to him. We have come a long way with Brian along the same road."

Jimi Hendrix cancelled his evening show at Brian's Saville Theatre in honour of his memory.

BRIAN'S DEATH

In the afternoon of August 25 Brian had driven down to his Sussex country home, dined with two companions then driven back to London late, evidently disappointed that expected houseguests had failed to arrive. He remained in his room throughout the following day and, on the Sunday morning, his housekeepers became concerned at his non-appearance. Eventually the door to Brian's bedroom was forced open by a doctor and Brian's assistant. His lifeless body was on the bed. At an inquest the cause of death was found to be accidental, resulting from 'incautious self-overdoses', with the drug Carbitol, taken to assist sleep, mentioned specifically.

John: "We were in Wales with the Maharishi. We had just gone down after seeing his lecture first night. We heard it then. I was stunned, we all were, I suppose, and the Maharishi, we went in to him. 'What, he's dead' and all that, and he was sort of saying oh, forget it, be happy, like an idiot, like parents, smile, that's what the Maharishi said. And we did.

"I had that feeling that anybody has when somebody close to them dies: there is a sort of little hysterical, sort of hee, hee, I'm glad it's not me or something in it, the funny feeling when somebody close to you dies. I don't know whether you've had it, but I've had a lot of people die around me and the other feeling is, 'What the fuck? What can I do?'

"I knew we were in trouble then. I didn't really have any misconceptions about our ability to do anything other than play music and I was scared. I thought, 'We've fuckin' had it.'

"I liked Brian and I had a very close relationship with him for years, because I'm not gonna have some stranger runnin' things, that's all. I like to work with friends. I was the closest with Brian, as close as you can get to somebody who lives a sort of 'fag' life, and you don't really know what they're doin' on the side. But in the group I was closest to him and I did like him.

"We had complete faith in him when he was runnin' us. To us, he was the expert. I mean originally he had a shop. Anybody who's got a shop must be all right. He went round smarmin' and charmin' everybody. He had hellish tempers and fits and lock-outs and y'know he'd vanish for days. He'd come to a crisis every now and then and the whole business would fuckin' stop cause he'd go on sleepin' pills for days on end and wouldn't wake up. Or he'd be missin', y'know, beaten up by some old docker down the Old Kent Road. But we weren't too aware of it. It was later on we started findin' out about those things.

"We'd never have made it without him and vice versa. Brian contributed as much as us in the early days, although we were the talent and he was the hustler. He wasn't strong enough to overbear us. Brian could never make us do what we didn't really want to do."

Derek Taylor: "It was like two movies: The Beatles in full colour, meditating in Bangor with The Rolling Stones; Brian in stark black and white, sprawled dead on his bed. Then the two films merged, but I still couldn't pick up the plot. The news was too much, the first crack in the marble of our wonderful temple of the mind wherein we would all dwell in perfect harmony."

August 28
Brian's sudden death dominates the newspaper headlines in the UK and US. The Beatles confirmed that they intended to continue their study of meditation with the Maharishi.

The single 'We Love You' by The Rolling Stones (John Lennon and Paul McCartney on backing vocals) was released in the US as London 905.

August 29
The inquest into Brian Epstein's death was adjourned, although the coroner gave permission for the burial to go ahead at a Jewish cemetery in Liverpool.

Brian Epstein's funeral was a strictly family affair with none of his groups, not even The Beatles, in attendance.

August 30
Brian Epstein's brother Clive was elected as the new chairman of the family company, NEMS Enterprises, with Robert Stigwood as managing director.

August 31
The Beatles announced that they would continue to be managed by NEMS Enterprises until further notice, but that Clive Epstein would not be taking over his brother's role as their personal manager. "No one could possibly replace Brian," Paul commented. An official statement issued to the press added: "The Beatles would be willing to put money into NEMS if there was any question of a takeover from an outsider. The Beatles will not withdraw their shares from NEMS. Things will go on as before."

EMI announced that worldwide sales of 'All You Need Is Love' had now topped three million.

September 1
The Beatles met at Paul's house on Cavendish Avenue to discuss their future. They decided to continue with the *Magical Mystery Tour* project and put everything else on hold.

Before the other Beatles arrived, Paul held a separate meeting with publicist Tony Barrow, to discuss the special storybook which he wanted to accompany the *Magical Mystery Tour* album.

Tony Barrow: "Paul wanted me to surround the making of *Magical Mystery Tour* with a massive new publicity campaign, designed to keep The Beatles in the newspapers at home and abroad all through September. Without that, he thought, Epstein's death would look like the end of an era. In Paul's eyes, *Magical Mystery Tour* could be sold to the world as the beginning of a bright new era in The Beatles' history."

September 2
The Beatles dispatched their aide Alistair Taylor to the seaside, to check, before they began work in earnest on the *Magical Mystery Tour* project, that coach companies still operated mystery tours. They did.

September 4
NEMS announced that The Beatles would be travelling to the Maharishi Mahesh Yogi's camp in Rishikesh, India, in early October to study transcendental meditation.

September 5
Abbey Road. *Magical Mystery Tour* sessions. Work began on John's 'I Am The Walrus'.

September 6
Abbey Road. *Magical Mystery Tour* sessions. Further work done on 'I Am The Walrus', including John's vocal. Paul recorded a demo version of 'The Fool On The Hill' and the basic tracks were recorded for George's 'Blue Jay Way'.

September 7
Abbey Road. *Magical Mystery Tour* sessions. Work on 'Blue Jay Way'.

September 8
Abbey Road. *Magical Mystery Tour* sessions. The instrumental 'Flying' was recorded. At this time the track was called 'Aerial Tour Instrumental' and was meant for a flying sequence in which The Beatles intended to have the coach actually fly, using special effects.

Westminster coroner Gavin Thurston recorded a verdict of "accidental death" on Brian Epstein, ruling that The Beatles' manager had become confused about the quantity of sleeping tablets that he had taken in his final hours.

September 11
The coach for the *Magical Mystery Tour* was still being painted with its psychedelic livery and was delayed for two hours in leaving Allsop Place, where rock'n'roll package tours always started. Paul went in search of a cup of tea in the nearby London Transport canteen above Baker Street station. There he signed a few autographs and chatted until the bus arrived. Discovering that there were no uniforms for the bus driver and courier to wear, Paul walked down to Soho with Mal Evans to buy some appropriate clothing.

The other three Beatles were picked up in Virginia Water, Surrey, near their homes. All 43 seats in the coach were filled with technicians, Beatles, Mal, Neil and even a few fan club secretaries. They drove to Teignmouth, Devon, stopping for lunch at the Pied Piper restaurant in Winchester en route. In Teignmouth the entire party stayed at The Royal Hotel where 400 local fans were waiting for them in the pouring rain. Paul gave a short press conference about the film.

John: "Paul made an attempt to carry on as if Brian hadn't died by saying, 'Now, now, boys, we're going to make a record.' Being the kind of person I am, I thought well, we're going to make a record all right, so I'll go along, so we went and made a record. And that's when we made *Magical Mystery Tour*.

"Paul said, 'Well, here's the segment, you write a little piece for that,' and I thought, 'Bloody hell,' so I ran off and I wrote the dream sequence for the fat woman and all the things with the spaghetti. Then George and I were sort of grumbling about the fuckin' movie and we thought we'd better do it and we had the feeling that we owed it to the public to do these things."

September 12
The coach got stuck on a bridge on its way to Widecombe Fair, blocking the road, and had to back half a mile up the road to turn around. The AA redirected traffic. John was filmed losing his temper but the footage was not used. They abandoned plans to visit the fair and stopped at the Grand Hotel in Plymouth for lunch.

John and Paul gave an interview to Hugh Scully for the local BBC1 news magazine programme *Spotlight South West* and posed for a photo call.

The coach continued to Newquay, Cornwall, with several stops to film en route. In Newquay they stayed at the Atlantic Hotel, where they held a meeting with the film crew to discuss how they could bring the shooting back on schedule.

September 13
John directed a film sequence in which Scottish "funny walks" specialist Nat Jackley chased bikini-clad girls around the Atlantic Hotel swimming pool. Simultaneously, Paul and Ringo directed a scene filmed on the beach at Newquay.

Spencer Davis was staying in Cornwall and saw a news item showing the AA and local police trying to push The Beatles' bus round the narrow bend and off the bridge. He phoned the Atlantic Hotel and spoke with Mal Evans who invited him over.

George was interviewed by Miranda Ward for the BBC's new Radio One programme *Scene and Heard*.

BBC TV's *Spotlight South West* aired their interview with John and Paul.

Paul: "We're not going to turn out records or films just for the sake of it. We don't want to have to talk unless we have something to say. We enjoy recording, but we want to go even further. I would like to come up with a completely new form of music, invent new sounds. But at the moment I'm thinking things out. There seems to be a pause in my life right now – a time for re-assessment."

September 14
Filming in various locations.

Miranda Ward joined The Beatles' party and interviewed Ringo for *Scene And Heard*.

Spencer Davis returned The Beatles' hospitality of the previous evening and invited them over to Perranporth where he and his family were on holiday. Ringo, Paul, Neil and Miranda Ward went with several other coach passengers. Spencer Davis: "I invited some of them back to the pub in the evening and Ringo and Paul came, but George and John were doing something else. There was a piano in the corner and Paul stuck a pint of beer on the top and started playing and people hadn't even noticed that he was in there. There was one girl who looked and said, 'The piano player, look who it is!' It was so funny to see the reaction on their faces." Paul led the sing-song around the pub piano until 2am but refused to play the pub standard, 'Yellow Submarine'.

September 15
Filming in front of the hotel and various locations en route to London. They stopped for lunch at a small fish and chip shop in Taunton (in Somerset) and filmed there.

September 16
Abbey Road. *Magical Mystery Tour* sessions. More work done on 'Your Mother Should Know'.

The Beatles decided to postpone their upcoming visit to India until all work on *Magical Mystery Tour* was completed.

September 18
The Beatles filmed at the Raymond Revue Bar in Soho with the Bonzo Dog Doo-Dah Band and stripper Jan Carson whose bare breasts were covered in the film with a superimposed CENSORED sign.

September 19
The Beatles filmed at West Malling Air Station, Maidstone, Kent, when they found that you needed to book film studios ahead of time.

Steve Winwood's group Traffic were approached by Paul to film a special clip of them performing 'Here We Go Round The Mulberry Bush' for inclusion in *Magical Mystery Tour*.

September 20
Filming at West Malling Air Station, Maidstone, Kent.

September 21
Filming at West Malling Air Station, Maidstone, Kent.

September 22
Filming at West Malling Air Station, Maidstone, Kent.

The Beatles were granted the honour of a cover story in the American news magazine, *Time*.

September 23
Filming at West Malling Air Station, Maidstone, Kent.

September 24
Filming at West Malling Air Station, Maidstone, Kent. The grand finale, with The Beatles trooping down the staircase singing 'Your Mother Should Know', was filmed with the aid of the 160 members of The Peggy Spencer Formation Dancing Team and two dozen Women's Royal Air Force cadets. Paul: "That was the shot that used most of the budget."

September 25
The Beatles had allowed two weeks for editing, but in the end it took 11. Editing began immediately and was done by Roy Benson in a rented Soho editing suite: Norman's Film Productions at the corner of Old Compton Street and Wardour Street. Paul was present throughout all 11 weeks, unless he was recording, and the others appeared to a lesser degree.
Abbey Road. *Magical Mystery Tour* sessions. Work began on Paul's 'The Fool On The Hill'.

September 26
Abbey Road. *Magical Mystery Tour* sessions. More work on 'The Fool On The Hill'.

September 27
Abbey Road. *Magical Mystery Tour* sessions. The orchestra and the Mike Sammes Singers' parts were added to 'I Am The Walrus'. Paul added a new vocal to 'The Fool On The Hill'.
John was one of the subscribers to a postal art event staged by Yoko Ono. The "13 Days Do It Yourself Dance Festival" cost £1 to join, in return for which subscribers received an instructional postcard from Yoko every morning. Her first missive tells her followers to "Breathe at midnight".

September 28
Abbey Road. *Magical Mystery Tour* sessions. Work done on 'I Am The Walrus' and 'Flying'. Yoko Ono has already told John and his fellow subscribers to "Breathe at dawn".

September 29
John and George appeared on Rediffusion Television's *The Frost Programme*, discussing transcendental meditation with David Frost.
John: "Buddha was a groove, Jesus was all right."
George: "I believe in reincarnation. Life and death are still only relative to thought. I believe in rebirth. You keep coming back until you have got it straight. The ultimate thing is to manifest divinity, and become one with The Creator."
Abbey Road. *Magical Mystery Tour* sessions. The sound effects were added to 'I Am The Walrus' including the fragment of Shakespeare's *King Lear*. Paul's 'Your Mother Should Know' was also finished.

September 30
The first edition of BBC Radio1's *Scene And Heard* broadcast its interview with George.

October 1
A further one-day shoot at West Malling.

October 2
Abbey Road. Work began on The Beatles' next single, Paul's 'Hello Goodbye'.

October 4
John and George made a follow-up appearance on *The Frost Programme* continuing their discussion of transcendental meditation.

October 6
Abbey Road. *Magical Mystery Tour* sessions. 'Blue Jay Way' completed.

October 7
The Beatles turned down New York promoter Sid Bernstein's offer of $1 million for two concerts in the US.

October 9
Yoko Ono's "13 Days Do It Yourself Dance Festival" ended on John's 27th birthday, when he was instructed to: "Colour yourself. Wait for the spring to come. Let us know when it comes."

October 11
Yoko's one-woman show, *Yoko Plus Me*, opened at the Lisson Gallery in London. *Me* was the anonymous John Lennon, who also underwrote the cost of the exhibition, which was subtitled "Half A Wind" and featured objects which had been painted white and then chopped in half.

John: "She gave me her *Grapefruit* book and I used to read it and sometimes I'd get very annoyed by it; it would say things like 'Paint until you drop' or 'bleed' and then sometimes I'd be very enlightened by it and I went through all the changes that people go through with her work – sometimes I'd have it by the bed and I'd open it and it would say something nice and it would be alright and then it would say something heavy and I wouldn't like it.

"There was all that and then she came to me to get some backing for a show and it was half a wind show. I gave her the money to back it and the show was, this was a place called Lisson Gallery, another one of those underground places. For this whole show everything was in half; there was half a bed, half a room, half of everything, all beautifully cut in half and painted white. And I said to her, 'Why don't you sell the other half in bottles?' having caught on by then what the game was and she did that – this was still before we had the nuptials – and we still have the bottles from the show, it's my first. It was presented as *Yoko Plus Me* – that was our first public appearance. I didn't even go to see the show, I was too uptight."

October 12
George's 'It's All Too Much' was mixed at De Lane Lea Studios, where it was recorded.

Abbey Road. *Magical Mystery Tour* sessions. Mixing 'Blue Jay Way' followed by John producing a recording of 'Shirley's Wild Accordion', a Lennon and McCartney composition played by Shirley Evans (accordion) and Reg Wale (percussion), for use in the film. (Not in fact used.)

October 13
The single 'How I Won The War', by Musketeer Gripweed (John Lennon) and The Third Troop (Ken Thorne) was released in the UK as United Artists UP 1196. John's only contribution to the single was a few words of dialogue from the soundtrack of *How I Won The War*.

October 14
Miranda Ward's interview with Ringo was broadcast on Radio1's *Scene And Heard*.

October 17
The Beatles, plus other NEMS artists like Cilla Black, Gerry Marsden, The Fourmost and Billy J. Kramer, attended a memorial service for Brian Epstein held at 6pm at the New London Synagogue, 33 Abbey Road, London.

Mick Jagger revealed that he and Paul had had talks about The Rolling Stones and The Beatles setting up a jointly owned recording studio. But he dismissed any idea of a permanent business collaboration with The Beatles as "premature".

October 18
John and Cynthia attended the Motor Show, held at the Earl's Court Exhibition Hall.

That evening all four Beatles, their wives and girlfriends attended the premiere of Richard Lester's film *How I Won The War,* starring John Lennon, held at the London Pavilion. John and George both sported psychedelic jackets, while Paul and Ringo opted for normal evening suits. Also in attendance were celebrities like Jimi Hendrix, David Hemmings and his actress wife Gayle Hunnicut, and singers Anita Harris, Cilla Black and Cass Elliot.

Afterwards they went to Cilla Black's flat at 9b Portland Place for a celebration party.

October 19
George and Ringo flew to Sweden, via Copenhagen, to visit the Maharishi Mahesh Yogi at his Transcendental Meditation Academy in the coastal resort of Falsterbohus. They flew back to London the same day.

Abbey Road. *Magical Mystery Tour* sessions. Further work on 'Hello Goodbye'.

October 20
Abbey Road. *Magical Mystery Tour* sessions. The flute passage was added to 'The Fool On The Hill' and the viola to 'Hello, Goodbye'.

The single 'Catcall' by The Chris Barber Band, written by Paul McCartney, was released in the UK as Marmalade 598005.

October 21
Ravi Shankar told reporters at a US press conference that George was making encouraging progress with his sitar playing.

Ravi Shankar: "George is still just a beginner, but he is an enthusiastic and ambitious student, because he realises that the sitar itself is an evolution from Indian culture. It might take a lifetime of learning before he is a great master of the instrument. But if he progresses in the same way that he has been doing, his understanding will lead him to a medium of greatness on the sitar. But it takes a lifetime to learn. I have been studying since I was a very little boy in India, and I am still learning."

October 24
A Hard Day's Night received its world television premiere, broadcast across the US by NBC-TV.

October 29
Paul and Mal Evans flew to Nice with cameraman Aubrey Dewar and engaged a taxi driver to wake them and take them to the mountains overlooking Nice before the break of dawn. Paul left home without his passport, but persuaded immigration authorities that as they knew who he was, he could travel without it.

Ringo filmed the getting-on-the-bus sequence for *Magical Mystery Tour* in Lavender Hill, London.

October 30
Paul and Aubrey Dewar filmed the sunrise in the mountains behind Nice, and Paul mimed 'Fool On The Hill' for the *Magical Mystery Tour* film. They stayed on the mountain for most of the day, though only the dawn footage was eventually used.

Music publisher Dick James announced that Northern Songs had made £842,000 profit in the previous year.

November 1
Paul flew back to London from Nice.

George and John attended a reception for the group Family at Sybilla's.

November 2
Abbey Road. Paul added an extra bass line to 'Hello Goodbye'.

November 3
George's 'Blue Jay Way' sequence was filmed at Ringo's house, "Sunny Heights", in Weybridge, Surrey.

November 6
Abbey Road. Mixing session which The Beatles probably attended.

The group held a photo session in London, posing with a cut-out submarine as advance publicity for the *Yellow Submarine* film.

November 7
Abbey Road. Paul added a new vocal to 'Magical Mystery Tour'.

November 8
How I Won The War received its US premiere in New York.

November 10
Paul directed three separate versions of the promotional film for 'Hello Goodbye' on stage at the Saville Theatre, Shaftesbury Avenue, one of them complete with dancing girls in grass skirts, another featuring The Beatles wearing their 1963 collarless suits.

November 12
The 'Hello Goodbye' promotional films were edited, with Paul supervising operations.

November 17
The Beatles Limited changed its name to Apple Music Limited, and Apple Music Limited became The Beatles Limited.

Neil Aspinall flew to New York to personally deliver copies of the 'Hello Goodbye' promotional film to the producers of such television programmes as *The Ed Sullivan Show* and *Hollywood Palace*.

November 19
Paul and Jane went to see The Bee Gees, The Bonzo Dog Doo-Dah Band, The Flowerpot Men and Tony Rivers & The Castaways at the Saville Theatre.

November 20
'I Am The Walrus' was banned by both BBC Television and BBC Radio, although no announcement was made. The BBC clearly felt that there must be a drug reference there somewhere, and anyway the reference to knickers was obscene.

November 21
The Musicians' Union closed shop prohibited miming, so The Beatles' promotional films for 'Hello Goodbye' were not shown in Britain. An attempt was made to include the promo clip as a piece of footage being edited by The Beatles in the Soho cutting room, but it didn't work and was scrapped.

November 22
George worked on his solo *Wonderwall* film project at Abbey Road, with two flautists and a tabla player.

The film company Peacock Productions applied to the High Court for an injunction to prevent release of the *Yellow Submarine* movie, alleging that they had not been paid for their work on the project. The injunction was somewhat premature, as the film was still some months from completion.

November 23
George continued work on the *Wonderwall* soundtrack at Abbey Road.

ITV also banned The Beatles' film and a plan to screen one of the three films in colour on BBC2's *Late Night Line Up*, was also abandoned. Instead, *Top Of The Pops* played 'Hello Goodbye' over a clip from *A Hard Day's Night,* much to The Beatles' annoyance.

November 24
The single 'Hello Goodbye'/'I Am The Walrus' was released in the UK as Parlophone R 5655.

John and Paul attended the first recording session by Apple's new signing, Grapefruit, held at the IBC Recording Studio on Portland Place.

John worked on a compilation of his home tapes at Abbey Road.

HELLO GOODBYE

To John Lennon's disgust, his epic 'I Am The Walrus' was issued on the flipside of this commercial but rather inconsequential McCartney composition – three minutes of contradictions and meaningless juxtapositions, with a tune that was impossible to forget. More interesting than the song were The Beatles' four promotional films, shot at London's Saville Theatre, none of which was able to be shown on British TV at the time because of union rules about miming.

I AM THE WALRUS

"I was the Walrus, whatever that means. The Walrus was a big capitalist that are all the fucking oysters, if you must know. I always had this image of the Walrus in the garden and I loved it, so I didn't ever check out what the Walrus was. But he's a fucking bastard, that's what he turns out to be. Everybody presumes that means something, that just because I said I am the Walrus, it must mean I am God or something, but it's just poetry."

That's John Lennon in 1970, attempting to debunk all the theories that had been inspired by the oblique lyrical stance of his sole contribution to the Magical Mystery Tour *soundtrack. He revealed many years later that 'Walrus' had been a deliberate effort to mystify his critics and followers alike, by stringing together violently dissimilar images without a shred of continuity. Lennon enjoyed watching the outside world interpreting his nonsense verse, and relished the recording of the song, which – like 'Blue Jay Way' – became the vehicle for another bout of studio experimentation. (As was often the case with The Beatles' most unusual recordings, several slightly different mixes of 'Walrus' were issued aound the world.)*

Among the delights on offer were a mellotron, heavily used by Lennon at home and in the studio in 1967; a 12-piece string section; 16 members of the Mike Sammes Singers, chanting "Oompah, oompah, stick it up your number"; and several lines of Shakespeare's King Lear, *lifted from a BBC radio drama production being broadcast during the mixing session.*

November 25

Radio 1's *Where It's At* programme transmitted an interview done with John Lennon by Kenny Everett and Chris Denning. The whole of the *Magical Mystery Tour* double EP was played, the only time 'I Am The Walrus' was broadcast by the BBC, which had unofficially banned it because the lyrics included the word "knickers". The song was also banned from the airwaves in the US.

John: "It always seems to happen now that people misinterpret what we write or say. We're happy with the words and I don't see how they can offend anyone. Do you think they're obscene?"

November 26

The 'Hello Goodbye' promotional film was screened on *The Ed Sullivan Show* in the US, where there were no Musicians' Union restrictions on mimed performances.

November 27

The single 'Hello Goodbye'/'I Am The Walrus' was released in the USA as Capitol 2056.

The album *Magical Mystery Tour* was released in the US as Capitol MAL 2835 (mono) and SMAL 2835 (stereo). Side A: 'Magical Mystery Tour', 'The Fool On The Hill', 'Flying', 'Blue Jay Way', 'Your Mother Should Know', 'I Am The Walrus'; Side B: 'Hello Goodbye', 'Strawberry Fields Forever', 'Penny Lane', 'Baby You're A Rich Man', 'All You Need Is Love'.

November 28

Abbey Road. The Beatles recorded *Christmas Time (Is Here Again)*, their fifth Christmas record to be sent out to members of their fan club.

Afterwards John worked on sound effects tapes for his upcoming stage version of *The Lennon Play: In His Own Write.*

December 3

Ringo flew to Rome to begin work on his cameo role in the movie, *Candy,* directed by Christian Marquand and based on the Olympia Press novel by Terry Southern and Mason Hoffenberg. Ringo played the Mexican gardener.

Paul and Jane drove to Paul's farm in Campbeltown, Scotland, for a break.

December 5
John and George represented The Beatles at a party to celebrate the impending opening of the Apple Boutique at 94 Baker Street, London.

THE APPLE BOUTIQUE
John: "Clive Epstein or some other such business freak came up to us and said you've got to spend so much money, or the tax will take you. We were thinking of opening a chain of retail clothes shops or some barmy thing like that . . . and we were all thinking that if we are going to open a shop let's open something we're interested in, and we went through all these different ideas about this, that and the other. Paul had a nice idea about opening up white houses, where we would sell white china and things like that, everything white, because you can never get anything white, you know, which was pretty groovy, and it didn't end up with that, it ended up with Apple and all this junk and The Fool and all those stupid clothes and all that."

December 7
Ringo's first day before the cameras in Rome filming *Candy*.
　The Apple Boutique opened its doors to the public.

December 8
The EP *Magical Mystery Tour* was released in the UK as Parlophone MMT I (mono) and SMMT1 (stereo). Side A: 'Magical Mystery Tour', 'Your Mother Should Know'; Side B: 'I Am The Walrus'; Side C: 'The Fool On The Hill', 'Flying'; Side D: 'Blue Jay Way'.

MAGICAL MYSTERY TOUR
Early in April 1967, with *Sgt. Pepper* not yet complete, Paul McCartney flew to America for a week's holiday. On his return flight, he drafted out his idea for a TV special which would involve a mystery tour on a coach – not the usual British seaside trip to a less than exotic location twenty miles down the coast, but a voyage into the imagination.

By mid-April, McCartney had written the title tune for the project, and the four Beatles had agreed a tentative format for the programme. What with the intervention of the Maharishi Mahesh Yogi, and the unexpected death of Brian Epstein, the project wasn't completed until almost the end of the year. When it was ready for public screening, it was scheduled for prime-time viewing on BBC TV, as part of the programming for Boxing Day 1967. Used to a stodgy diet of sitcoms and variety shows, the great British public responded to the frequently bizarre and often amateurish *Magical Mystery Tour* with bewilderment bordering on anger. The professional reviewers were equally damning, and the film passed into history as The Beatles' first major flirtation with public disapproval.

The reasons for the failure were varied. The film was originally shown in black-and-white, thereby losing the visual impact of many of the sequences. The public hadn't known what to expect, and many viewers were assuming that the show would be the kind of song-and-dance spectacular that the closing 'Your Mother Should Know' sequence satirised. Mostly, though, the criticisms were justified. For all its brilliant set pieces, *Magical Mystery Tour* desperately required professional editing and direction. Self-indulgent and unrestrained, it showed The Beatles that they didn't have an automatic lock on the public's taste.

As usual with a McCartney idea post–1966, John Lennon felt resentful about the entire project. "Paul had a tendency to come along and say, well, he's written his ten songs, let's record now," he moaned in 1970. "And I said, well, give us a few days and I'll knock a few off. He set *Magical Mystery Tour* up and had worked it out with (Beatles roadie) Mal Evans, and then he came and showed me what his idea was, the story and how he had it all, the production and everything. George and I were sort of grumbling, you know, 'Fuckin' movie, oh well, we better do it'."

Six new songs were written and recorded for the film. The Beatles finally elected to release them as a double-EP package, at twice the normal single price, complete with a cartoon book vaguely telling the story of the film. The American market wasn't geared up for EPs, however, so Capitol turned the two EPs into an LP, adding in the earlier Beatles singles from 1967. In that format, the album was heavily imported into Britain, and eventually won a full release here in the late Seventies. When EMI prepared The Beatles' albums for CD, *Magical Mystery Tour* automatically took its place in the line-up, between *Pepper* and *The White Album*.

MAGICAL MYSTERY TOUR

Aside from some vocal additions in November, the title track from the Magical Mystery Tour *film was completed before* Sgt. Pepper *was released. It was a McCartney effort from start to finish, embellished by the use of session brass players, and with Paul himself acting as a carnival barker at the start to drag the punters in.*

No fewer than three different versions of the track were made available to the public at the end of 1967. The film mix remains unavailable on record, but both the mono and stereo versions were included when EMI issued a boxed set of The Beatles' EPs on compact disc. The CD album, meanwhile, has the stereo version.

YOUR MOTHER SHOULD KNOW

Simple and nostalgic alongside the calculated experimentation of the other film soundtrack songs, 'Your Mother Should Know' inspired one of the great Magical Mystery Tour *set pieces, as The Beatles waltzed down a huge staircase in white suits, like refugees from a Thirties Hollywood musical.*

I AM THE WALRUS

See November 24.

THE FOOL ON THE HILL

Maintaining his record of writing an instant standard on every mid-Sixties Beatles album, Paul McCartney composed this touching, beautiful ballad late in the proceedings, cutting a solo demo at the piano, and then concocting a deliciously light and airy arrangement for the final version. Three flute players added to the atmosphere (once again the mono and stereo mixes differ, most notably in their placement of the flute interjections).

FLYING

No other Beatles recording underwent such drastic editing as this instrumental with vocal backing. Intended to support a psychedelic section of the film, rich in shifts of colour and texture, it was suitably eerie – and bizarre, apparently ending with a jazz section borrowed from elsewhere in The Beatles' collective record library. All that was removed as the track was sliced from ten minutes to little more than two, leaving 'Flying' as an off-the-wall EP-filler – the only instrumental The Beatles issued on EMI, and also their first four-man composition.

BLUE JAY WAY

George Harrison was at his rented home on Blue Jay Way in Los Angeles, waiting for former Beatle aide Derek Taylor to arrive for dinner. Taylor, fortuitously, was late, and Harrison turned his mild concern and irritation into this song. What could have been a simple, maudlin ditty was transformed by The Beatles' studio prowess into an exotic, almost mystical journey. Harrison's vocal was treated until it sounded as if it was coming from beyond the grave, though with none of the ghostly threat of Lennon's similarly altered voice on 'Tomorrow Never Knows'. Backwards tapes, droning organs, and a cello combined to heighten the Eastern atmosphere – without a single Indian instrument being employed.

December 9

Ringo filmed with Ewa Aulin, the former Miss Teen Sweden, who was playing Candy.

As usual, The Beatles were voted "Top World Group" and "Top British Vocal Group" in the readers' poll held by the New Musical Express.

December 11

Ringo filmed with Ewa Aulin.

Paul and Jane Asher travelled to Paul's farm in Scotland for a brief holiday.

Apple Music signed its first group. John named them Grapefruit, coincidentally the name of Yoko's book. Most of the group were former members of Tony Rivers & The Castaways, one of Brian Epstein's groups.

December 12
Ringo filmed with Ewa Aulin.

December 13
Ringo filmed his sex scene with Ewa.
Speaking on behalf of The Beatles, a NEMS Enterprises spokesman dismissed as "guesswork" the idea that The Beatles would form their own record label in 1968 under the aegis of their new Apple organisation.

December 14
Ringo filmed more of his sex scene with Ewa.

December 15
The Beatles' fan club flexi-disc *Christmas Time (Is Here Again)* was released.
Ringo filmed at a "love-in".

December 16
John and George flew to Paris to attend a UNICEF gala at the Palais de Chailloy with Maharishi Mahesh Yogi.
Ringo's last day of filming.

December 17
Ringo flew back to London from Rome, his role in the film *Candy* completed.
John and George flew back to London where they acted as hosts at the *Magical Mystery Tour* party for the area secretaries of the Official Beatles Fan Club, at the Hanover Grand Film and Art Theatre, London. An advance copy of *Magical Mystery Tour* was shown as well as *The Beatles At Shea Stadium*.
Paul: "Film-making isn't as difficult as many people imagine. It's a matter of common sense more than anything. We'd never directed anything before and we didn't know about editing, but we're learning. *Magical Mystery Tour* was an experiment, and so far it's been successful."

December 19
Seven investment companies were registered and formed in London on behalf of The Beatles: Apricot Investments Ltd., Blackberry Investments Ltd., Cornflower Investments Ltd., Daffodil Investments Ltd., Edelweiss Investments Ltd., Foxglove Investments Ltd. and Greengage Investments Ltd.

December 20
Paul and Jane returned to London from Campbeltown.

December 21
A fancy dress party was held for the complete crew of *Magical Mystery Tour* including all the technical staff, plus relatives and a few friends. Robert Morley was Father Christmas. The Bonzo Dog Doo Dah Band played. Paul and Jane arrived as a cockney pearly king and queen, Ringo as a Regency dandy, George as a cavalier and John dressed as a teddy boy. John paid close personal attention to Patti during the party, until being reminded by fellow guest Lulu that he was supposed to be escorting his own wife for the evening.

December 25
Paul and Jane announced that they were engaged to be married.

December 26
Magical Mystery Tour was given its world premiere in monochrome on BBC Television at 8.35pm.

December 27
In order to answer and counter the adverse press criticism of *Magical Mystery Tour* Paul appeared live on Rediffusion's *The Frost Programme* where he discussed the film and wider issues with David Frost.

December 29
John and his friend, the actor Victor Spinetti, were talking about Morocco. John suggested that they go there immediately and they collected their passports and took the next flight from London Airport that day.

December 31
The Beatles (except for John, who was still in Morocco) saw in the New Year at Cilla Black's flat on Portland Place.

January 1
Paul and Jane Asher visited the McCartney family in Liverpool.

January 5
John got together with his father Freddie once more, this time at Kenwood, John's House in Weybridge. Freddie had been washing dishes in a nearby hotel. John told the *Daily Mirror* that he had ended his feud with his father: "From now on I hope we'll be in close contact all the time."
George worked on the soundtrack to the film *Wonderwall* at Abbey Road.
Magical Mystery Tour was repeated on BBC2, this time as it was originally intended to be seen, in colour.

January 6
The *Daily Telegraph* reported that Brian Epstein had left £486,032 (£266,032 net) and that his mother was to control the estate.

January 7
George flew from London to Bombay, with stopovers in Paris, Frankfurt and Teheran, to record the *Wonderwall* film soundtrack using local Indian musicians.

January 9
George began work at EMI's Bombay recording studios.

January 11
George recorded the backing track for 'The Inner Light'.

January 12
The Beatles Film Productions Limited changed its name to Apple Film Limited and Apple Music Limited changed its name to Apple Corps Limited.
George completed the recordings needed for *Wonderwall* and began recording ragas and other traditional pieces of music for possible use on Beatles records, one of which was the basic track for 'The Inner Light'.

January 17
John, Ringo and Paul attended a press reception organised by RCA Records to celebrate the release of 'Dear Delilah', the first single by the Apple-managed group Grapefruit.

January 18
George flew back to London from Bombay with the *Wonderwall* tapes.

January 19
The single 'Dear Delilah' by Grapefruit was released in the UK. The press were informed that John and Paul helped produce the session.

January 22
Apple Corps opened offices at 95 Wigmore St, London.
Paul attended Diana Ross & The Supremes' opening night of their season at the Talk Of The Town club in London.

January 25
Twickenham Film Studio. The Beatles filmed their cameo appearance that was featured at the end of the animated cartoon *Yellow Submarine*. Afterwards John and George attended Ossie Clark's fashion show in London.

January 26
Paul joined his brother Mike McGear and poet Roger McGough for a recording session at Abbey Road.

January 27
John was interviewed by Kenny Everett at Kenwood, Weybridge, for BBC Radio 1's *The Kenny Everett Show*.

January 28
Paul taught Cilla Black 'Step Inside Love', the hastily composed song he'd written for her forthcoming TV series. At this point, the song only consisted of one verse and a chorus.

January 30
Cilla Black's television series *Cilla* went on the air using Paul's 'Step Inside Love', sung by Cilla, as its signature tune.
　　George completed work on the soundtrack for the film *Wonderwall* at Abbey Road.

February 1
Ringo attended rehearsals at the BBC Rehearsal Rooms in North Acton, London, for his live appearance on Cilla Black's new television show, *Cilla*.

February 2
Ringo attended a second day of rehearsals for *Cilla*. Meanwhile, Paul completed his song 'Step Inside Love', ready for Cilla to record a full-length rendition as her next single.

February 3
Abbey Road. Work began on Paul's 'Lady Madonna'.

February 4
Abbey Road. Work began on John's 'Across The Universe'. Two fans, waiting outside, were brought into the studio to provide the high falsetto harmonies needed.
　　John's interview on BBC Radio 1's *The Kenny Everett Show* was broadcast.

February 5
Ringo attended camera position rehearsals for his appearance on *Cilla* at the BBC Television Theatre, Shepherd's Bush, London.
　　Paul appeared at a press conference held at the Royal Garden Hotel, London to publicise the Leicester Arts Community Festival. He was persuaded to do it by a student who managed to talk his way into Paul's Cavendish Avenue house.

February 6
Ringo appeared live on BBC Television's *Cilla*, taking part in sketches, singing and even tap dancing.
　　Abbey Road. The other three Beatles worked on 'The Inner Light' and completed 'Lady Madonna' (taking a break to watch Ringo's appearance on *Cilla*). 'Lady Madonna' featured the saxophone talents of Ronnie Scott, Harry Klein, Bill Povey and Bill Jackman. Paul played all the piano, and the comb and paper routine was actually just him singing through cupped hands.

February 8
Abbey Road. 'The Inner Light' was completed and most of the session was spent working on 'Across The Universe'. John remained unsatisfied with the results. Spike Milligan, who watched the session as George Martin's guest, asked if he could use 'Across The Universe' on a wildlife charity record he was organising and The Beatles agreed.

February 9
The *New Musical Express* carried the first of a series of ads, carrying the one-word message "Apple", and intended to raise public awareness of The Beatles' latest business venture.

February 10
Paul and Jane saw Paul's brother Michael in a Scaffold concert at Queen Elizabeth Hall, London.

February 11

Abbey Road. The Beatles intended to shoot footage of the recording of 'Lady Madonna', their next single, as a promotional film, but chose instead to record a new song, 'Hey Bulldog'. The filming was directed by Tony Bramwell, head of Apple Films.

Yoko Ono attended a Beatles session for the first time as John's guest, and embarrassed her host by demanding to know why all The Beatles' songs used exactly the same rhythm, and why they didn't attempt something more adventurous.

February 14

Mal Evans collected luggage belonging to George and Patti, her sister Jenny, John and Cynthia, and took Qantas flight 754 to Delhi. The excess baggage charge was £195.19.6d. He went a day early in order to organise transport for John and George when they arrived on the 16th to begin their much delayed study of transcendental meditation with Maharishi Mahesh Yogi.

February 15

George, Patti, John and Cynthia flew from London Airport to India.

February 16

George, Patti, John and Cynthia arrived in Delhi at 8.15am, on the overnight flight. Mal met them at the airport with Mia Farrow, who had already decided that she was part of The Beatles' entourage. Mal had organised three cars for the 150-mile drive from Delhi to Rishikesh.

February 18

On the eve of his departure for India, Paul was interviewed by the London *Evening Standard* newspaper.

February 19

Paul, Jane, Ringo and Maureen flew from London Airport to India.

February 20

INDIA

Paul, Jane, Ringo and Maureen arrived in Delhi, attracting much more press attention as the media were now alerted to what was going on. A film crew was on hand as they stepped from the plane after the exhausting 20-hour flight, jet-lagged from the five time zones. Mal Evans and Raghvendra, from the ashram, placed garlands of red and yellow flowers around their necks as a traditional token of greeting. Ringo's arm was giving him pain from the required injections so they set off to find a hospital. Their driver lost his way and finished up in a dead end, followed by a whole convoy of press cars, one of which came to the rescue and led them to the hospital.

The Academy of Transcendental Meditation was built 150 feet above the Ganges surrounded on three sides by jungle-covered mountains. The students lived in six stone cottages. Each room had twin beds and modern bathroom facilities though the water supply sometimes broke down.

Breakfast from 7 until 11am consisted of porridge, puffed wheat or cornflakes; fruit juice, tea or coffee, toast, marmalade or jam. Breakfast was followed by meditation practice, with no rules or timetable. Lunch and dinner both consisted of soup followed by a vegetarian main dish, tomato and lettuce salads, turnips, carrots with rice and potatoes on the side. John and George were already vegetarians so the diet was nothing strange, but Ringo found the spices too hot for his taste. Mal assembled a stock of eggs so that he could cook Ringo fried, boiled, poached or scrambled eggs.

The Beatles were three weeks behind the other students so the Maharishi gave them extra tuition and lectures in the afternoons. These took place in the open air, sometimes on his flat sun roof. If it was a cool day, they would go to his bungalow and sit on cushions. Mal had his own chair because he was unable to cross his legs comfortably.

The Beatles were on a TM teachers' course: there were 90-minute lectures at

3.30 and 8.30pm with questions and answers, and progressively longer meditation sessions. Other students included Paul Horn, Mike Love and Donovan.

February 23
The *Daily Express* newspaper in London published colour photographs of each of The Beatles, taken by Richard Avedon, and offered readers the chance to buy enlargements of the set, plus a special Beatles poster.

February 24
The London *Evening Standard* ran an interview with Paul in which he said, "Instead of trying to amass money for the sake of it, we're setting up a business concern at Apple – rather like a Western Communism . . . we've got all the money we need. I've got the house and the cars and all the things that money can buy."

February 29
Yoko Ono appeared at the Royal Albert Hall with avant-garde jazz trumpet player Ornette Coleman. Both the performance and the afternoon rehearsal were recorded.
　　Within a few days, Yoko had separated from her husband, fellow performance artist Tony Cox. Having been given an address for John in India, she began to write regularly to him. Slowly the tone of her correspondence turned from artistically intriguing to flirtatious. Among the 'instructional' pieces she sent him was one enticingly titled "John Lennon As A Young Cloud".

March 1
Ringo and Maureen left Rishikesh much earlier than anticipated. They were unhappy away from their children and did not like the food. Ringo told the press it was like a Butlin's holiday camp.

March 3
Ringo and Maureen arrived back in London, and immediately parcelled up several rolls of 16mm cine film to be sent out to the other Beatles.

March 8
The single 'Step Inside Love' by Cilla Black, written for her by Paul McCartney, was released in the UK as Parlophone R 5674.
　　The single 'And The Sun Will Shine' by Paul Jones, featuring Paul on drums, was released in the UK as Columbia DB 8379.

March 9
Sgt. Pepper's Lonely Hearts Club Band won four Grammy awards at the annual ceremony in Los Angeles: Best Album of the Year, Best Contemporary Album, Best Engineered Record and Best Album Cover.

March 13
Ringo gave an interview to the *New Musical Express*, to explain why he had returned from India before the rest of The Beatles, and to talk about their long-delayed third feature film.
　　Ringo: "We plan to start in June. Scripts are being considered right now. I don't know which one we'll choose, but I'd like it if we all played more than one role. The ideas we considered for a film western, and for us to play the split personality of one person, were fine in theory. But they just didn't work out as a 90-minute script.
　　"So far, no one seems to have thought very much about using us more as individuals than as a group. For instance, if we could all take several roles, one minute I could pop up as a chauffeur and the next as King Kong. I hope people wouldn't recognise me."

March 14
Tony Bramwell's promotional film for 'Lady Madonna' (which actually showed them recording 'Hey Bulldog') was shown on BBC TV's *Top Of The Pops*.

March 15

The single 'Lady Madonna'/'Inner Light' was released in the UK as Parlophone R 5675.

The promotional film for 'Lady Madonna' was shown on BBC Television's *All Systems Freeman* presented by Alan Freeman.

LADY MADONNA

From its piano intro (lifted almost directly from Humphrey Lyttleton's mid-Fifties British jazz classic, 'Bad Penny Blues') to its rock'n'roll horn section, 'Lady Madonna' was the first Beatles single of 1968. It made a perfect introduction to a year when Fifties rock'n'roll made a reappearance in the charts and the concert halls. The song itself was a more oblique piece of social comment than 'She's Leaving Home' the previous year, but its vague air of concern for a single mother fitted in with the contemporary trend for kitchen-sink drama in the theatre and on TV.

A bunch of Britain's top jazzmen were dragooned at short notice to play on the track, while Lennon, McCartney and Harrison faked one brass solo by blowing air through their cupped hands like children.

THE INNER LIGHT

After several commentators had accused George Harrison of 'stealing' the lyrics to this, his final Indian-flavoured Beatles song, from the teachings of the Tao Te Ching, George put the matter straight in his autobiography. In that book, he printed a letter from Juan Mascaró, who translated the Tao, and actually sent George a copy of his translation of section XLVII, inviting him to set it to music.

Harrison duly did just that, composing perhaps the most beautiful melody of any of his Sixties songs – which deserved a better fate than to languish on the flip of 'Lady Madonna'. The basic track for 'The Inner Light' was recorded at the same sessions as George's soundtrack music for the film Wonderwall, *many thousands of miles away from Abbey Road – at EMI's studio in Bombay, India, to be exact. Various Indian musicians provided the instrumental backing. Several other raga-styled pieces were taped at the same session, but they remain unreleased.*

March 18

The single 'Lady Madonna'/'The Inner Light' was released in the USA as Capitol 2138.

March 26

Paul, Jane and Neil Aspinall flew back to England from Rishikesh, leaving George and Patti, John and Cynthia and "Magic" Alex who had come out to join them.

March 27

Paul, Jane and Neil Aspinall touched down at London Airport.

March 31

The Beach Boys announced that they would soon be staging a joint concert tour with the Maharishi, under the banner 'World Peace 1', and hinted that one or more of The Beatles would also be taking part.

April

Paul spent much time at his farm in Scotland.

April 2

A new Beatles music publishing company, Python Music Limited, was formed.

April 8

Paul directed a promotional film for 'Elevator', the next single by Grapefruit, the group contracted to Apple Music. The filming took place at and around the Albert Memorial in London's Kensington Gardens.

Derek Taylor began work as Apple and Beatles press officer, having been persuaded by The Beatles to return to Britain from Los Angeles.

April 12

John and Cynthia, George and Patti and "Magic" Alex left in a hurry from Rishikesh,

India, after "Magic" Alex convinced John and George that the Maharishi was using his position to gain sexual favours from at least one of the female meditators. The Maharishi had never claimed to be celibate, and since he was not given a chance to explain or deny the charge, the reasons for their departure remain unclear. Alex Mardas certainly did not want to relinquish his claim to be John's "guru" and it would appear that he engineered the whole thing. At Delhi Airport, John wrote 'Sexy Sadie', at that time called 'Maharishi'.

John: "There was this big hullaballoo about him trying to rape Mia Farrow or somebody and trying to get off with a few other women and things like that. We went to see him after we stayed up all night discussing was it true or not true. When George started thinking it might be true, I thought well, it must be true; because if George started thinking it might be true there must be something in it.

"So we went to see Maharishi, the whole gang of us, the next day, charged down to his hut, his bungalow, and as usual, when the dirty work came, I was the spokesman – whenever the dirty work came, I actually had to be leader – and I said, 'We're leaving.'

"'Why?' he asked, and all that shit and I said, 'Well, if you're so cosmic, you'll know why.' He was always intimating, and there were all these right-hand men always intimating, that he did miracles. And I said, 'You know why,' and he said, 'I don't know why, you must tell me,' and I just kept saying, 'You ought to know' and he gave me a look like, 'I'll kill you, you bastard,' and he gave me such a look. I knew then. I had called his bluff and I was a bit rough to him."

While John and Cynthia returned to London, George and Patti flew to Madras to visit Ravi Shankar.

During the flight back to London, John informed his wife of the extent of his unfaithfulness during the Beatlemania years.

April 16
Apple Publicity Limited was formed.

Apple 17
George and Ravi Shankar were filmed playing sitars, in a clip intended for the documentary movie *Raga*.

April 18
John and Ringo went to the launch party of Bell Records at the Revolution Club, London.

April 19
Apple Music published an advertisement in the *New Musical Express* soliciting tapes from unknown artists. Apple was promptly inundated and only a tiny percentage of them were actually played.

Apple's advert: "This man has talent. One day he sang his songs to a tape recorder (borrowed from the man next door). In his neatest handwriting he wrote an explanatory note (giving his name and address) and, remembering to enclose a picture of himself, sent the tape, letter and photograph to Apple Music, 94 Baker Street, London W1. If you were thinking of doing the same thing yourself – do it now! This man now owns a Bentley!"

April 21
George and Patti returned to London from India.

April 25
George spoke to newspaper reporters in London about his experiences in India.

April 28
John and Ringo attended a performance of the musical *Charlie Girl* in London, starring their NEMS stablemate Gerry Marsden.

May 5
Twiggy saw Mary Hopkin on the television talent show *Opportunity Knocks* and telephoned Paul to suggest she would be a good person for Apple to sign.

May 6

The single 'Step Inside Love' by Cilla Black and written by Lennon and McCartney was released in the US as Bell 726.

May 9

John and Ringo held a meeting at Apple with Derek Taylor and Alex Mardas, plus John's former schoolfriend Ivan "Ivy" Vaughan, to discuss the possibility of an Apple children's school, which would be run by Vaughan, now a qualified teacher. Vaughan was hired at £50 a week ("the average wage for a Headmaster", according to the minutes of the meeting) to investigate accommodation, staffing, and the cost of books and equipment.

During the meeting, John insisted that "there should be no discrimination regarding background", and that "all the arts including music, dancing, theatre, films etc. should be in the school timetable. The art of propaganda in the advertising field must also be taught."

May 11

John and Paul, accompanied by "Magic" Alex, Neil Aspinall, Mal Evans, Ron Kass and Derek Taylor, flew to New York to launch Apple in the US. They stayed with their lawyer, Nat Weiss, at his apartment at 181 East 73rd Street but conducted most of their interviews from hotels.

May 12

John and Paul had an Apple "business meeting" with the newly appointed US head of the company, record executive Ron Kass, while cruising round the Statue of Liberty in a Chinese junk.

May 13

John and Paul conducted interviews with The *New York Times* and other newspapers all day from a suite at the St. Regis Hotel.

May 14

John and Paul gave a press conference at the Americana Hotel on Central Park West.

John: "The aim of the company isn't a stack of gold teeth in the bank. We've done that bit. It's more of a trick to see if we can't get artistic freedom within a business structure; to see if we can create things and sell them without charging three times our cost. "

At the Americana press conference Paul met up once again with Linda Eastman, who wrote her telephone number on an unused cheque and gave it to him.

The Beatles taped an interview with Mitchell Krause for WNDT, the non-commercial Channel 13's programme *Newsfront*.

That evening they appeared on NBC's *The Tonight Show* where they were interviewed by Joe Garagiola as Johnny Carson was away. As well as discussing their plans for Apple, John used the opportunity to denounce the Maharishi.

John: "We made a mistake. He's human like the rest of us."

May 15

Accompanied by Linda, Nat Weiss drove John, Paul and "Magic" Alex to the airport for their flight back to London.

George, Patti, Ringo and Maureen flew to Cannes, in the south of France to attend the premiere of *Wonderwall* at the Cannes Film Festival.

Channel 13 in New York screened their interview with John and Paul.

May 16

John, Paul and "Magic" Alex arrived in London on TWA's early flight.

Apple Management Limited was incorporated.

May 17

The album *McGough & McGear* by Roger McGough and Mike McGear, produced by Paul McCartney, was released in the UK as Parlophone PCS 7047. The album was launched with a small lunch party, and the copies given to those attending had a typed (multiple carbons) press release enclosed written by Derek Taylor in very stoned mode, which has become very collectable. It read:

HELLOW.

Thank you for coming to lunch.

It is very nice of you and we are your friends.

Now then, what do you want to know about it all?

"Oh well of course" you may say "How do we know what we want to know; surely you would be the best judge of that. After all is said and done, what is there to know?"

It is so much a case of guessing, for there's no knowing what anyone would want to know.

No.

Let us guess.

Eyes down.

"Our father, all the eights, 88 . . . . . ."

We are already confusing the issue.

This approach is what the psychiatrists call "maze making" or "problem posing" or "crisis creating" brought about in order to find a solution, or an exit line.

Now . . . . some names . . . .

Jane and Mrs. Asher . . . William I Bennet (WIB) . . . Spencer Davies (is) . . . Barry Fantoni . . . Mike Hart . . . Jimi Hendrix . . . Vera Kantrovitch . . . Gary Leeds . . . Dave Mason and Carol . . . MIKE McGEAR . . . ROGER McGOUGH . . . John Mayall . . . Paul McCartney . . . John Mitchell . . . Zoot . . . Graham Nash . . . Viv Prince (yes) . . . Andy Roberts . . . Prince "Stash" de Rola . . . Paul Samwell-Smith . . . Martin Wilkinson . . .

What have they in common? What have they not? They are all beautiful. The two in capital letters are here today. They made the album. You have in your hand or adjacent. They are in the Scaffold. (The capital letters were mine not theirs. McGear and McGough have no egos.)

The other people are friends. Friends. Friends who all contributed to the album in one way or many or all or a little.

At any rate they all went into the recording session and sang or played or beat some tangible thing or simply waved their arms to create in the air some benign (we mean, of course, benign) turbulence

McGear and McGough are from Liverpool poetic and funny, concerned and open . . ..

Well listen, we are all here together now aren't we? In circumstances such as these, who needs a press release?

Have we not tongues to speak.

You are kind.

Thank you.

Derek.

The world premiere of *Wonderwall* was given at the Cannes Film Festival, France with George, Patti, Ringo and Maureen in attendance.

May 19

With Cynthia taking a short holiday, John called Yoko Ono and invited her out to Kenwood. They made a random sound tape, which was later issued as *Two Virgins* with the notorious sleeve showing them both naked. When Cynthia returned, she found Yoko ensconced in the bedroom, wearing Cynthia's dressing gown.

JOHN & YOKO

John: "I'd never known love like this before, and it hit me so hard that I had to halt my marriage to Cyn. And don't think that was a reckless decision, because I felt very deeply about it and all the implications that would be involved. When we are free – and we hope that will be within a year – we shall marry. There is no need to marry – as Mick and Marianne say – but there's nothing lost in marrying either.

"Some say my decision was selfish. Well, I don't think it is. Are your children going to thank you when they're 18? There is something else to consider, too – isn't it better to avoid rearing children in a strained relationship?

"My marriage to Cyn was not unhappy. But it was just a normal marital state where nothing happened and which we continued to sustain. You sustain it until you meet somebody who suddenly sets you alight.

"With Yoko I really knew love for the first time. Our attraction was a mental one, but it happened physically too. Both are essential in the union – but I never thought I would marry again. *Now the thought of it seems so easy.*

"When we got back from India we were talking to each other on the phone. I called her over, it was the middle of the night and Cyn was away, and I thought well now's the time if I'm gonna get to know her anymore. She came to the house and I didn't know what to do; so we went upstairs to my studio and I played her all the tapes that I'd made, all this far out stuff, some comedy stuff, and some electronic music, She was suitably impressed and then she said well let's make one ourselves so we made 'Two Virgins'. It was midnight when we started 'Two Virgins', and it was dawn when we finished, and then we made love at dawn. It was very beautiful."

George, Patti, Ringo and Maureen returned to London from Cannes. George and Patti drove immediately to Warrington, to attend the christening of George's nephew Ian.

May 21
Paul and Jane had lunch with Andy Williams and his French wife Claudine Longet. That evening they attended his final Royal Albert Hall show and the end of the show party afterwards.

May 22
George and John, accompanied by Yoko, attended the press launch and press conference for Apple's second boutique, Apple Tailoring (Civil and Theatrical) housed at 161 New King's Road, London and run by designer John Crittle.

George: "We bought a few things from him, and the next thing I knew, we owned the place!"

May 23
Apple Tailoring opened its doors to the public.

Paul and Ringo were interviewed at Abbey Road for Tony Palmer's BBC Television *Omnibus* documentary on pop music called *All My Loving*.

May 26
Paul directed a promotional film for Grapefruit's new single, 'Elevator', at the Albert Memorial in Hyde Park, London.

Cynthia returned home from a brief holiday in Greece, to discover Yoko Ono in residence with John.

Cynthia: "Facing me was John sitting relaxed in his dressing gown. With her back to me, and equally as relaxed and at home, was Yoko. The only response I received was "Oh, hi", from both parties. They looked so right together, so naturally self-composed under the unusual circumstances. I felt totally superfluous. I was a stranger in my own home. All I could think of saying was, 'We were all thinking of going out to dinner tonight. We had lunch in Rome and we thought it would be lovely to have dinner in London. Are you coming?' It sounded so stupid in the light of the changed circumstances. The only reply I received was "No thanks". And that was it. I wanted to disappear, and that is just what I did."

Towards the end of May, The Beatles gathered at George's American-style bungalow "Kinfauns" in Esher, to record a demo tape of songs from which they would choose what to put on their next album. Most of the songs had been written during their visit to India. They first recorded John's songs: 'Cry Baby Cry', 'Child Of Nature', 'The Continuing Story of Bungalow Bill', 'I'm So Tired', 'Yer Blues', 'Everybody's Got Something To Hide Except Me And My Monkey', 'What's The New Mary Jane' and 'Revolution'. Then came George's new compositions: 'While My Guitar Gently Weeps', 'Circles', 'Sour Milk Sea', 'Not Guilty' and 'Piggies'. They returned to John's notebook for 'Julia', then came Paul's songs: 'Blackbird', 'Rocky Racoon', 'Back In The USSR', 'Honey Pie', 'Mother Nature's Son', 'Ob-La-Di, Ob-La-Da' and 'Junk'. They finished with two more of John's: 'Dear Prudence' and 'Sexy Sadie'.

George: "There's about 35 songs we've got already, and a few of them are mine. God knows which one will be the next single. I suppose we've got a vague overall conception of the kind of album we want to do, but it takes time to work out. We could do a double album, I suppose – or maybe a triple album. There's enough stuff there."

May 30
Abbey Road. Work began on what was to become the double album *The Beatles*, usually known as *The White Album*. The first song worked on was John's 'Revolution 1'.

May 31
Abbey Road. *The White Album* sessions. Work continued on 'Revolution 1' and the last six minutes was removed to form the basis of the chaotic 'Revolution 9'. Yoko screamed on the track, her first appearance on a Beatles recording.

Paul and Jane were in the audience as Scaffold recorded a live LP at their concert at the Lewisham Odeon in South London. Also on the bill were The Hollies and Paul Jones.

June 4
Abbey Road. *The White Album* sessions. Further work on 'Revolution 1'.

Paul began seeing Francie Schwartz.

June 5
Abbey Road. *The White Album* sessions. Recording began on Ringo's 'Don't Pass Me By', his first composition used on a Beatles record.

June 6
Abbey Road. *The White Album* sessions. Further work on 'Don't Pass Me By'.

Kenny Everett visited the studio to record an interview for his BBC Radio 1 programme *The Kenny Everett Show*.

John and Victor Spinetti were filmed for the BBC2 arts programme *Release* discussing *The John Lennon Play: In His Own Write,* directed by Victor Spinetti, which was due to open in London on the 18th.

Around this time, Cynthia returned from a brief holiday abroad, to be informed by Magic Alex that John intended to divorce her, and that he wanted her and their son Julian to move out of Kenwood.

June 7
George, Patti, Ringo, Maureen and Mal Evans flew to California to enable George to film a guest appearance in Ravi Shankar's film *Raga*.

June 8
Paul was the best man at his brother Michael's wedding to hair stylist Angela Fishwick, held at St. Bridget's Parish Church in Carrog, Merioneth, North Wales – the same church where Paul and Mike's father Jim married his second wife in 1966. The other Beatles sent congratulatory telegrams. The reception was held at Jim McCartney's home in Gayton, Cheshire, and featured a family sing-song, led by Paul at the piano.

George and Ringo visited folksinger Joan Baez at her home in Carmel, California.

June 9
BBC Radio One broadcast The Beatles' interview on *The Kenny Everett Show*.

George and Ringo played golf in Monterey.

June 10
Abbey Road. *The White Album* sessions. John worked on 'Revolution 9', adding more sound effects.

June 11
Abbey Road. *The White Album* sessions. John did further work on 'Revolution 9', while Paul, in a separate studio, recorded and mixed 'Blackbird', without the aid of the other Beatles.

Tony Bramwell from Apple Films shot a colour promotional film of Paul with Mary Hopkin, to help in the launch of her record.

In California, George and Ravi Shankar were filmed walking along the coast-cliffs in Big Sur, and taking part in a "teach-in".

June 13
George and Ringo jammed with David Crosby, Peter Tork and Peter Asher at Tork's Los Angeles home.

June 15
John and Yoko held their first public event by planting acorns for peace at Coventry Cathedral. Their intended site had to be altered because Canon Verney refused to allow an unmarried couple to bury anything in consecrated ground. The original acorns were soon stolen by Lennon fans, and the replacements sent by John and Yoko had to be placed under 24-hour guard.

George and Ringo flew from Los Angeles to New York, where Ringo and Maureen met Eric Clapton and Jeff Beck, and attended a Jimi Hendrix show at the Scene on 46th Street.

June 16
Intertel TV Studios, Wembley. David Frost interviewed Paul before a live audience for an all-British Frost programme taped for transmission in America. The programme was called *David Frost Presents . . . Frankie Howerd*, and on it, Howerd interviewed Paul about Apple, then Paul introduced Mary Hopkin and she sang two songs.

June 18
George, Patti, Ringo and Maureen flew back to London from New York. The National Theatre production of *The John Lennon Play: In His Own Write,* directed by Victor Spinetti, opened at the Old Vic Theatre, London. John and Yoko's arrival together at the theatre was seized upon by the press, several of whom called out to John, "Where's your wife, Mr Lennon?"

Paul celebrated his 26th birthday at the Apple offices, inviting several fans inside to join him for lunch. That evening, while the other Beatles were at the Old Vic, Paul attended another theatrical performance, the opening of a new play starring Jane Asher.

June 19
John had lunch with Victor Spinetti and Derek Taylor to reflect on the aftermath of the *In His Own Write* premiere.

June 20
Paul, Tony Bramwell and Ivan Vaughan flew to Los Angeles where Paul was due to address the Capitol Records Sales Conference (Capitol were the American distributors of Apple records). He contacted Linda Eastman who flew out from New York the next day to join him.

Abbey Road. *The White Album* sessions. John and Yoko utilised three studios to continue the assembly of loop tapes for 'Revolution 9'. One was made from a Royal Academy of Music examination tape in which an anonymous man, asking question number nine, had his voice turned into an endless loop which John and Yoko faded in and out at will.

June 21
Abbey Road. *The White Album* sessions. 'Revolution 1' was finished with the addition of the horn section and guitar solo.

In Los Angeles, Paul addressed a Capitol Records Sales Conference and announced that in future all Beatles records would appear on the Apple label, although the group technically was still on EMI/Capitol.

June 22
John and Victor Spinetti appeared on the BBC2 arts programme *Release*, discussing the *In His Own Write* play.

Paul attended a Capitol Records staff barbecue in Los Angeles, and then watched a concert by Albert King at the Whiskey-A-Go-Go in Hollywood.

Apple paid half a million pounds for a new headquarters building at 3 Savile Row, the former home of Nelson's Lady Hamilton.

June 24
Abbey Road. George began work as a producer, recording 'Sour Milk Sea' with new Apple signing, Jackie Lomax, an old friend from Liverpool.
The White Album sessions. John and Yoko worked on the stereo mixes of 'Revolution 9'.
Paul gave impromptu renditions of some of the songs that The Beatles were about to record, for a party of fans gathered outside his Los Angeles hotel. Later, he flew back to London, via New York.

June 25
Abbey Road. George continued work with Jackie Lomax on 'Sour Milk Sea'.
The White Album sessions: John and Yoko cut one minute from 'Revolution 9', though it was to remain the public's least favourite "Beatles" track.
Paul, Tony Bramwell and Ivan Vaughan returned to London from Los Angeles.

June 26
Abbey Road. *The White Album* sessions: work on John's 'Everybody's Got Something To Hide Except Me And My Monkey'.

June 27
Abbey Road. *The White Album* sessions. Further work on John's 'Everybody's Got Something To Hide Except Me And My Monkey'.

June 28
Abbey Road. *The White Album* sessions. Recording began on 'Good Night', John's lullaby for five-year-old Julian. John sang it through in the studio several times so that Ringo would get the phrasing but declined to record it himself, thinking it was too "soft" for his hard image. Unfortunately no recording of John's acoustic version was made.

June 29
NEMS executive Vic Lewis flew to Moscow, to discuss the possibility of The Beatles playing a series of live concerts in the USSR.

June 30
Paul recorded The Black Dyke Mills Band in Saltaire, near Bradford, playing one of his own compositions, 'Thingumybob' (which he wrote as the theme tune for a London Weekend Television comedy series of the same name) and 'Yellow Submarine' as a B-side.
While in Saltaire he was interviewed by Tony Cliff for the local BBC Television programme *Look North*.
On the way home Paul, with Derek Taylor and Peter Asher, stopped in Harrold, a small Bedfordshire village, where Paul entertained the locals at the piano in the village pub – premiering, among other songs, his new composition 'Hey Jude'.

July 1
Abbey Road. *The White Album* sessions. John added the lead vocal to 'Everybody's Got Something To Hide Except Me And My Monkey'.
Before the session, John and Yoko arrived dressed in white at the opening of John's first full art exhibition, *You Are Here*, at the Robert Fraser Gallery, London, which consisted mostly of charity collecting boxes. The exhibition was subtitled: "To Yoko from John Lennon". John marked the opening by releasing 365 helium-filled balloons over London. John: "I declare these balloons high." Each balloon was launched with a postcard attached, and a message asking the finder to return them to Apple. John was discouraged to learn that a high percentage of finders chose to decorate their cards with racist comments about Yoko.
BBC1's Yorkshire local news programme *Look North* broadcast the interview with Paul.

July 2
Abbey Road. *The White Album* sessions. Ringo recorded more vocals for 'Good Night'.

Paul had lunch with Sir Joseph Lockwood, chairman of EMI, and Lord Poole at Lazards, the City merchant bank, to discuss Apple.

July 3

Abbey Road. *The White Album* sessions. Work on Paul's 'Ob-La-Di, Ob-La-Da'.

July 4

Abbey Road. *The White Album* sessions. More work on 'Ob-La-Di, Ob-La-Da'.

July 5

Abbey Road. *The White Album* sessions. Horns added to 'Ob-La-Di, Ob-La-Da'.

July 8

Abbey Road. *The White Album* sessions. Paul did not like the results so far on 'Ob-La-Di, Ob-La-Da' and started afresh – to the disgruntlement of John and George, who had already made their lack of enthusiasm for the song clear.

Rehearsals began for 'Revolution', intended by John as an A-side for the next single (but ultimately used as the B-side).

The actor David Peel approached Paul about Apple paying for a children's beach show at Brighton. David Peel: "He agreed to help straight away, as well as suggesting our title." The Punch and Judy puppet shows were called Apple Peel.

Paul, George and Ringo attended a press screening of *Yellow Submarine* at the Bowater House Cinema in Knightsbridge. This was the first time any of The Beatles had seen the animated movie.

July 10

Abbey Road. *The White Album* sessions. More work on John's 'Revolution'. Both Yoko Ono and Paul's American friend Francie Schwartz attended the session.

July 11

Abbey Road. *The White Album* sessions. Piano and bass added to 'Revolution' and horns added to 'Ob-La-Di, Ob-La-Da'.

John and Yoko attended the London wedding of "Magic" Alex Mardas.

July 12

Abbey Road. *The White Album* sessions: 'Don't Pass Me By' was virtually completed and from midnight on, a new bass and guitar part was added to 'Revolution'.

July 13

During a break in The Beatles' sessions at Abbey Road, John introduced Yoko to his Aunt Mimi at her home in Poole.

July 15

Abbey Road. *The White Album* sessions. Paul added a new vocal to 'Ob-La-Di, Ob-La-Da' and John remixed 'Revolution'. After this they rehearsed 'Cry Baby Cry'.

July 16

Abbey Road. *The White Album* sessions. More work done on 'Cry Baby Cry'.

Balance engineer Geoff Emerick finally quit working with the group. He could no longer tolerate the swearing and ill-mannered attitude shown towards the engineers (particularly from John), and the tense atmosphere in the studio.

July 17

The world premiere of the animated *Yellow Submarine* film was held at the London Pavilion in Piccadilly Circus. Fans as usual brought traffic to a standstill and blocked the streets. Ringo and Maureen, John and Yoko and George and Patti were present but Paul attended alone.

Afterwards they attended the celebration party at the Royal Lancaster Hotel, where the discotheque had been renamed Yellow Submarine for the occasion (and was to remain so for several years after). At the party, Paul spent some time talking to Clem Curtis, lead singer of The Foundations, and promised to write the group a song.

July 18
Abbey Road. *The White Album* sessions. More work on 'Cry Baby Cry' and rehearsals for Paul's 'Helter Skelter', including the taping of a legendary 27-minute rendition of the latter song.

July 19
Abbey Road. *The White Album* sessions. Work began on John's send-up of the Maharishi, 'Sexy Sadie'.

The BBC's TV arts programme *How It Is* focused on John's *In His Own Write* play and the forthcoming *Yellow Submarine* cartoon film, broadcasting extracts from them both.

July 20
Jane Asher, appearing on Simon Dee's BBC Television show *Dee Time*, said that her engagement to Paul was off – but that it was not she that had broken it. She told Dee that they had been engaged for seven months, after knowing each other for five years. (She had arrived back at Cavendish Avenue one day to find Paul in bed with a girl named Francie Schwartz.)

July 22
Abbey Road. *The White Album* sessions. 'Don't Pass Me By' was completed, then a new version of 'Good Night' was recorded with the orchestra and Mike Sammes Singers. Ringo did his vocal track just after midnight.

July 23
Abbey Road. *The White Album* sessions. 'Everybody's Got Something To Hide Except Me And My Monkey' was completed.

July 24
Abbey Road. *The White Album* sessions. More work on John's 'Sexy Sadie'.

July 25
Abbey Road. *The White Album* sessions. Work began on George's 'While My Guitar Gently Weeps'.

July 28
The Beatles spent almost the entire day in and around London on various promotional photographic assignments, as part of what came to be known as their 'Mad Day Out'. Photos were taken in Hyde Park, in London's Docklands, and in the garden of Paul's St. John's Wood home.

July 29
Abbey Road. Work began on Paul's 'Hey Jude', destined to become the next single.

July 30
Abbey Road. More work done preparing 'Hey Jude' for final recording which was to take place in an independent studio.

The Beatles were filmed at work by James Archibald for a documentary film intended for cinematic exhibition called *Music*.

The Beatles decided to close down the Apple Boutique from tomorrow, giving away all the stock, having taken their choice of items off the shelves.

Paul: "We decided to close down the shop last Saturday – not because it wasn't making any money, but because we thought the retail business wasn't our particular scene. We want to be free to devote more time to recording and films. So we went along, chose all the stuff we wanted – I got a smashing overcoat – and then told our friends. Now everything that is left is for the public."

July 31
Trident Studios, Soho. The backing track for 'Hey Jude' was laid down.

Queues formed all night around the block for a chance to grab free clothing from the Apple Boutique. The shop was completely stripped, with people taking away shop fittings and even the carpet. Apple gave the other boutique at 161 King's Road to the store manager.

Paul's official press release: "We decided to close down our Baker Street shop yesterday and instead of putting up a sign saying, 'Business will be resumed as soon as possible', and then auction off the goods, we decided to give them away. The shops were doing fine and making a nice profit on turnover. So far, the biggest loss is in giving the things away, but we did that deliberately. We're giving them away – rather than selling them to barrow boys – because we wanted to give rather than sell.

"We came into shops by the tradesman's entrance but we're leaving by the front door. Originally, the shops were intended to be something else, but they just became like all the boutiques in London. They just weren't our thingy. The staff will get three weeks' pay but if they wish they'll be absorbed into the rest of Apple. Everyone will be cared for. The Kings Road shop, which is known as Apple Tailoring, isn't going to be part of Apple anymore but it isn't closing down and we are leaving our investment there because we have a moral and personal obligation to our partner John Crittle, who is now in sole control. All that's happened is that we've closed our shop in which we feel we shouldn't, in the first place, have been involved.

"Our main business is entertainment – communication. Apple is mainly concerned with fun, not with frocks. We want to devote all our energies to records, films and our electronics adventures. We had to re-focus. We had to zoom in on what we really enjoy, and we enjoy being alive, and we enjoy being Beatles."

August
John and Yoko collaborated on their first film projects, *Film No. 5 (Smile)* (a slow-motion record of John doing just that) and *Two Virgins* (in which the couple's faces merged into one).

Yoko: "They were done in a spirit of home movies. In both films, we were mainly concerned about the vibrations the films send out – the kind that was between us. Imagine a painting that smiles just once in a billion years. John's ghostly smile in *Film No. 5* might just communicate in a hundred years' time, or maybe, the way things are rolling, it may communicate much earlier than that. I think all the doors are just ready to open now."

August 1
Trident Studios, Soho. The orchestra, bass and lead vocals were added to 'Hey Jude' using Trident's eight-track facility (EMI still used 4-track). There were fierce arguments between John and Paul about who was to get the A-side of the new single, their first on the Apple label, but Paul eventually won and 'Hey Jude' became the first Apple release (and the biggest selling Beatles single of all time).

August 2
Trident Studios. 'Hey Jude' was completed with overdubs and mixed.

The London Weekend Television series *Thingumybob*, starring Stanley Holloway and with Paul's title tune, began transmission.

August 3
Paul and Francie Schwartz spent an evening at the Revolution Club. She later wrote a kiss-and-tell biography about her brief relationship with him called *Body Count*.

August 4
Yellow Submarine went on general release across the UK.

August 6
Trident Studios. 'Hey Jude' was mixed from stereo to mono.

John, Patti Harrison and fashion editor Suzy Menkes attended a fashion show at Revolution. John was interviewed by Matthew Robinson for that evening's edition of the BBC Radio programme *Late Night Extra*.

August 7
Abbey Road. *The White Album* sessions. Work continued on George's 'Not Guilty'.

The session didn't end until 5.30am, after which Paul went with Francie Schwartz to the now empty Apple Boutique and traced the name of The Beatles' new single on the whitewashed windows: 'Hey Jude' and 'Revolution'. When local Jewish traders misunderstood the title 'Hey Jude' and complained, Paul said he was sorry if he offended them, it was nothing to do with Jews and told the *Evening Standard*: "We thought we'd paint the windows for a gas. What would you do if your shop had just closed?"

August 8
Abbey Road. *The White Album* sessions. George's 'Not Guilty' reached take 101. It was not included on the final album.

August 9
Abbey Road. *The White Album* sessions. More work on 'Not Guilty'.
After the session, Paul alone recorded 'Mother Nature's Son' which the other Beatles did not play on.

August 10
Paul gave a controversial interview to Alan Smith of the *New Musical Express*. He admitted: "The truth about me is that I'm pleasantly insincere."
Paul: "Starvation in India doesn't worry me one bit, not one iota. It doesn't, man. And it doesn't worry you, if you're honest. You just pose. You've only seen the Oxfam ads. You can't pretend to me that an Oxfam ad can reach down into the depths of your soul and actually make you feel for those people – more, for instance, than you feel about getting a new car."

August 11
Apple Records was officially launched with "National Apple Week". The press received a special pack, labelled "Our First Four", containing copies of 'Hey Jude' by The Beatles, 'Sour Milk Sea' by Jackie Lomax, 'Thingumybob' by The Black Dyke Mills Band and Mary Hopkin's 'Those Were The Days'. 'Hey Jude' became the biggest selling Beatles single ever, selling six million copies in four months (ultimately eight million worldwide). In addition, Mary Hopkin's 'Those Were The Days' sold four million copies worldwide in four months, getting Apple Records off to a good start.

August 12
Abbey Road. *The White Album* sessions: George's vocal on 'Not Guilty' was taped in the control booth, with the microphone plugged straight into the board.
John and Yoko attended an Ossie Clark fashion show in Chelsea.

August 13
Abbey Road. *The White Album* sessions. 'Sexy Sadie' was remade and John's 'Yer Blues' begun. The group crowded into a small tape room off the main studio to try and re-create the cramped Cavern feeling for 'Yer Blues' and were very pleased with the acoustics there. Worries about leakage proved unfounded.

August 14
Abbey Road. *The White Album* sessions. 'Yer Blues' was virtually finished, then, after Paul and Ringo left, John and George recorded 'What's The New Mary Jane', one of John's "experimental", Yoko-influenced numbers.
John: "That was me, George and Yoko, out of our heads on the floor at EMI."

August 15
Abbey Road. *The White Album* sessions. Paul's 'Rocky Raccoon' recorded.

August 16
Abbey Road. *The White Album* sessions. New version of George's 'While My Guitar Gently Weeps'.

August 17
George and Patti flew to Greece for a short break with Mal Evans.

August 20

Abbey Road. *The White Album* sessions continued in George's absence. 'Yer Blues' finished off.

Paul added the brass overdubs to 'Mother Nature's Son'. After this he recorded the short 'Wild Honey Pie' and 'Etcetera' (for use as a demo by Marianne Faithfull – she declined to record it). The tension in the studio between the members of the group was reported as being very bad at this point.

August 21

Abbey Road. *The White Album* sessions. John added a new lead vocal to 'Sexy Sadie'.

George and Patti returned to London from Greece.

August 22

Abbey Road. *The White Album* sessions. They recorded 'Back In The USSR' – without Ringo, and with Paul playing drums.

RINGO QUITS

The bad feelings between the group reached crisis point and Ringo announced he was quitting. He left to consider his future. The actual incident that caused him to storm out was a fluffed tom-tom fill. Ringo flew to the Mediterranean to spend a fortnight on Peter Sellers' yacht. It was there, after refusing to eat the squid served to him, that Ringo wrote 'Octopus's Garden'.

Cynthia filed for divorce, citing John's adultery with Yoko as the reason. John did not contest the order.

August 23

Abbey Road. *The White Album* sessions. 'Back In The USSR' was finished.

In what had now become an annual event, New York Beatles fans gathered at Shea Stadium to commemorate the anniversary of the group's last live appearance in the city.

August 24

John and Yoko appeared live, talking about art, happenings and peace, on David Frost's London Weekend Television programme *Frost On Saturday,* broadcast from Wembley.

Ronan O'Rahilly, the former head of Radio Caroline (before the government closed the pirate ships down), joined Apple as a "business adviser". Derek Taylor's press release said, "John admires him very much for what he did with Radio Caroline."

August 26

The single 'Hey Jude'/'Revolution' was released in the US as Apple (Capitol) 2276.

The single 'Thingumybob'/'Yellow Submarine' by John Foster & Sons Ltd., Black Dyke Mills Band, written and produced by Paul McCartney, was released in the US as Apple 1800.

The single 'Those Were The Days'/'Turn! Turn! Turn! (To Everything There Is A Season)' by Mary Hopkin, and produced by Paul McCartney, was released in the US as Apple 1801.

The single 'Sour Milk Sea' by Jackie Lomax and written and produced by George Harrison was released in the US as Apple 1802.

HEY JUDE

A couple of verses, a middle section or two, a fade-out: you can't explain the impact of 'Hey Jude' by analysing the song. McCartney wrote the lyrics as a message of encouragement to young Julian Lennon, while his parents were in the throes of a very public separation. At times, the words veered into meaninglessness – "the movement you need is on your shoulder" indeed – and the tune was nothing complex. Neither was the production, which started simple and built towards an orchestral finale.

So why was 'Hey Jude' so important? Partly because of its length, though it was still shorter than another major 1968 hit, 'MacArthur Park' by Richard Harris. Mostly, though, 'Hey Jude' sounded like a community anthem, from the open-armed welcome of its lyrics to its instant singalong chorus. The fact that it didn't come with a controversial political message made its universal application complete.

At Trident Studios, The Beatles and a 36-piece orchestra recorded this remarkable record in two days – plus two beforehand for rehearsals. George Harrison's idea to answer McCartney's vocal lines with his electric guitar was vetoed, but John Lennon made his own distinctive contribution to the record with a four-letter word, hidden deep in the mix around the three-minute mark.

REVOLUTION

'Revolution 1' (see 'THE BEATLES') was meant to be a single, but wasn't immediate enough. So John Lennon persuaded The Beatles to try again, setting his noncommittal response to the worldwide uprisings of May 1968 to a fierce electric rhythm. With fuzzy, distorted guitars and a screaming vocal, 'Revolution' cut to the bone; it remains by far the toughest rock song The Beatles ever issued on a single. But Lennon's ambitions for the track weren't quite fulfilled, because the emergence of McCartney's 'Hey Jude' a month later made it quite clear what the lead track of The Beatles' first single on the Apple label would be. Still, John did have the compensation of knowing his song was on the flipside of the best-selling Beatles 45 of all time.

August 27
While visiting his family, Paul went to a Liverpool v. Everton football match.

August 28
Trident Studios, Soho. *The White Album* sessions. The Beatles, minus Ringo, began work on John's 'Dear Prudence'.

August 29
Trident Studios, Soho. *The White Album* sessions. Overdubs were added to 'Dear Prudence'.

August 30
Trident Studios, Soho: *The White Album* sessions. The completed 'Dear Prudence' was mixed.

Presentation copies of the 'Our First Four' press pack were delivered to politicians and members of the royal family.

The single 'Hey Jude'/'Revolution' was released in the UK as Apple (Parlophone) R 5722.

The single 'Those Were The Days'/'Turn! Turn! Turn! (To Everything There Is A Season)' by Mary Hopkin and produced by Paul McCartney was released in the UK as Apple 2.

The single 'Sour Milk Sea' by Jackie Lomax and written and produced by George Harrison was released in the UK as Apple 3.

Neil Aspinall married Susan Ornstein at Chelsea Register Office. The Beatles gave them a house as a wedding present, but Paul was the only member of the group to attend the ceremony.

August 31
Private Eye announced that John and Yoko's forthcoming album would have a full-frontal nude cover.

September 3
Abbey Road. *The White Album* sessions.

RINGO RETURNS
Having decided to remain in the group, Ringo returned to the studio to find his drum kit smothered in flowers. In fact he did not record that day; the time was spent "liberating" EMI's new eight-track machine which was still being "evaluated" by EMI technical experts. Ringo: "I felt tired and discouraged . . . took a week's holiday, and when I came back to work everything was all right again." However, he added, "Paul is the greatest bass guitar player in the world. But he is also very determined; he goes on and on to see if he can get his own way. While that may be a virtue, it did mean that musical disagreements inevitably arose from time to time."

September 4
Twickenham Film Studios. Promotional films, directed by Michael Lindsay-Hogg, were made for both 'Hey Jude' and 'Revolution'. While at the film studios, David Frost taped an introduction to the clips to use on his *Frost On Sunday* programme, giving the viewers the illusion that The Beatles were playing live on his show and fooling the Musicians' Union into believing that no miming was involved. On the promotional films, an orchestra was present and The Beatles had their instruments, but it was only the lead vocals that were actually live – and even they were taped on top of the existing vocals on the track, to guard against mistakes.

September 5
Abbey Road. *The White Album* sessions. More work done on George's 'While My Guitar Gently Weeps'. John played the original lead guitar part on this song.

September 6
Thames Television filmed Paul and Mary Hopkin at the Apple Building, 3 Savile Row, for their new children's series, *Magpie*.

Abbey Road. *The White Album* sessions. Eric Clapton added his famous solo to George's 'While My Guitar Gentle Weeps', wiping out John's less proficient effort of the previous day, with Ringo on percussion and Paul playing fuzz bass and doing vocal harmonies as George recorded his lead vocal.

The single 'Thingumybob'/'Yellow Submarine' by John Foster & Sons Ltd., The Black Dyke Mills Band, written by Lennon & McCartney and produced by Paul McCartney was released in the UK as Apple 4.

September 8
The film clip of 'Hey Jude' was given its premiere performance on London Weekend Television's *Frost On Sunday*.

September 9
Abbey Road. *The White Album* sessions. A new version of Paul's 'Helter Skelter' was recorded.

September 10
Abbey Road. *The White Album* sessions. Overdubs added to 'Helter Skelter'.

Thames Television's children's programme *Magpie,* showing Paul and Mary Hopkin with the show's presenter Pete Brady, was broadcast.

September 11
Abbey Road. *The White Album* sessions. Work began on John's 'Glass Onion'.

EMI announced that 'Hey Jude' has already sold more than two million copies around the world.

September 12
Abbey Road. *The White Album* sessions. More work on 'Glass Onion'.

September 13
Abbey Road. *The White Album* sessions. Drums and piano for 'Glass Onion'.

September 15
Around this date, John and Yoko photographed themselves in the nude, from the front and rear, intending to use the shots as cover artwork for their first collaborative album.

September 16
Abbey Road. *The White Album* sessions. Recording began on Paul's 'I Will' and overdubs were added to 'Glass Onion'.

September 17
Abbey Road. *The White Album* sessions. Paul's 'I Will' was completed.

September 18

Abbey Road. *The White Album* sessions. Paul arrived at the session early and had already blocked out 'Birthday' before the others arrived. By mid-evening most of it was finished. All of The Beatles, plus Yoko, Patti Harrison, acting producer Chris Thomas and others, walked round the corner to Paul's house to see *The Girl Can't Help It*, Jayne Mansfield's first film, featuring Little Richard, Fats Domino, The Platters, Gene Vincent and Eddie Cochran which was screened on BBC2 at 9.05pm. Afterwards they returned to the studio and by 5am they had finished and mixed the song.

George was interviewed by Alan Smith for BBC Radio 1's *Scene And Heard*.

John was interviewed by Jonathan Cott for *Rolling Stone* magazine.

September 19

Abbey Road. *The White Album* sessions. George's 'Piggies' was recorded, with producer Chris Thomas on harpsicord.

The promotional film for 'Revolution' is screened for the first time in the UK on BBC TV's *Top Of The Pops*.

September 20

Abbey Road. *The White Album* sessions. 'Piggies' was completed.

September 22

Apple announced that The Beatles' next album would be a 24-song, two-record set.

September 23

Abbey Road. *The White Album* sessions. Work began on John's 'Happiness Is A Warm Gun', which he had written with uncredited assistance from Apple press officer Derek Taylor.

September 24

Abbey Road. *The White Album* sessions. More work was done on the rhythm track for 'Happiness Is A Warm Gun'.

September 25

Abbey Road. *The White Album* sessions. Recording of 'Happiness Is A Warm Gun' was completed.

September 26

Abbey Road. *The White Album* sessions. 'Happiness Is A Warm Gun' was mixed and John spent most of the session making a sound effects tape for 'Glass Onion' which went unused.

Apple booked the Royal Albert Hall for several days in December, in preparation for a possible live performance by The Beatles, alongside other Apple artists like Mary Hopkin and Jackie Lomax.

September 28

George's interview for *Scene And Heard* was broadcast by BBC Radio 1.

George: "It would be great if The Beatles and Elvis Presley could get together for an album."

September 30

Hunter Davies's authorised biography of The Beatles, *The Beatles*, was published in the UK by William Heinemann Limited.

Throughout September Paul's father, James, was ill in hospital. Paul visited Liverpool frequently to see him.

October 1

Trident Studios, Soho. *The White Album* sessions. Paul's 'Honey Pie' was virtually completed.

October 2
Trident Studios, Soho. *The White Album* sessions. Paul added the lead vocal and guitar to 'Honey Pie'.

George joined a Cream recording session to add backing vocals and rhythm guitar to 'Badge', a song he had written with guitarist Eric Clapton.

October 3
Trident Studios, Soho. *The White Album* sessions. George's 'Savoy Truffle' was begun. It was inspired by the contents of a box of Mackintosh's Good News chocolates – Eric Clapton's favourite.

October 4
Trident Studios, Soho. *The White Album* sessions: Paul and a 14-piece orchestra recorded 'Martha My Dear' and added the finishing touches to 'Honey Pie'.

October 5
Trident Studios, Soho. *The White Album* sessions. George added the lead vocal, and Paul the bass and drums to 'Savoy Truffle'.

October 7
Abbey Road. *The White Album* sessions. A long session, from 2.30pm until 7 the next morning, was spent on the rhythm track for George's 'Long Long Long'. John was not there.

October 8
Abbey Road. *The White Album* sessions. Another long session, 4pm until 8am the following morning, during which John's 'I'm So Tired' and 'The Continuing Story Of Bungalow Bill' were both recorded and finished, and more work was done on George's 'Long Long Long'. Yoko Ono made a cameo vocal appearance on 'The Continuing Story Of Bungalow Bill'.

October 9
Abbey Road. *The White Album* sessions. Final work was done on 'The Continuing Story of Bungalow Bill' and 'Long Long Long'. While this was going on, Paul quickly recorded 'Why Don't We Do It In The Road' in the next door studio. Once again, John was absent.

The *David Frost Show* on US TV broadcast a clip of Paul introducing Mary Hopkin to the American audience.

October 10
Abbey Road. *The White Album* sessions. 'Piggies' and 'Glass Onion' were completed, and Paul again slipped away, this time with Ringo, and the two of them completed 'Why Don't We Do It In The Road'.

George Harrison formed a new music publishing company, Singsong Limited.

Paul told reporters that The Beatles were planning to stage a live show in the near future, which would be filmed for subsequent TV transmission.

October 11
Abbey Road. *The White Album* sessions. Six saxophones were added to 'Savoy Truffle'.

The single 'I'm The Urban Spaceman' by The Bonzo Dog Doo Dah Band, produced by Paul McCartney as Apollo C. Vermouth, was released in the UK as Liberty LBF 15144.

October 12
Abbey Road. *The White Album* sessions. The whole evening was spent mixing various tracks.

Jane Asher told the London *Evening Standard:* "I know it sounds corny but we're still very close friends. We really are. We see each other and we love each other, but it hasn't worked out. That's all there is to it. Perhaps we'll be childhood sweethearts and meet and get married when we're about seventy."

October 13
Abbey Road. *The White Album* sessions. John recorded and mixed his ballad, 'Julia', without the aid of the other Beatles.

October 14
Abbey Road. *The White Album* sessions. Overdubs were added to 'Savoy Truffle' and the rest of the session was spent mixing the tracks for the now complete double album.

No longer needed for the final mixing and sequencing of the album, Ringo went for a holiday in Sardinia with Maureen.

October 15
Abbey Road. *The White Album* sessions. Mono and stereo mixing sessions.

October 16
Abbey Road. *The White Album* sessions. Paul, John and George Martin held a 24 hour session, beginning at 5pm and ending at 5pm the following day, choosing the songs and working out the sequencing of the four sides of the double album. They were up against a tight deadline, and every studio and listening room at Abbey Road was used for this marathon task: studios one, two and three as well as listening rooms 41 and 42. In the end 30 songs were presented to the public as *The Beatles* (and, as usual, the two sides of their new single was not included).

George was not involved in the final selection and sequencing because he flew to Los Angeles that day to continue working with Jackie Lomax on his forthcoming Apple album.

October 18

JOHN BUSTED

The Drugs Squad raided John and Yoko who were living at 34 Montagu Square, London, on loan to them from Ringo. John had earlier received a tip-off from a member of the press that the police were planning to raid his home, and had 'springcleaned' the flat to make sure that it was clear of drugs.

They found 219 grains of cannabis resin and took the couple to Paddington Green police station where they also charged them with obstructing the police in the execution of a search warrant.

John: "So all of a sudden like, there was this knock on the door and a woman's voice outside and I look around and there is a policeman standing in the window wanting to be let in. We'd been in bed and our lower regions were uncovered like. Yoko ran into the bathroom to get dressed with her head poking out so they wouldn't think she was hiding anything. And then I said, 'Ring the lawyer, quick', but she went and rang Apple, I'll never know why. So then they got us for obstruction which was ridiculous because we only wanted to get our clothes on."

October 19
John and Yoko appeared at Marylebone Magistrates' Court. They were remanded on bail and their case was adjourned until November 28.

October 20
Paul and Linda travelled to New York for a brief holiday.

George produced a session for Apple artist Jackie Lomax in Los Angeles.

October 24
London advertising agency J. Walter Thompson, who had been invited by Apple to handle the promotion of *The Beatles*, recommended a campaign of TV advertising featuring Paul talking about the record; adverts in all the national newspapers every day during the week leading up to the launch; and hiring London buses which could be painted white and then decorated with portraits of The Beatles. None of these suggestions was accepted.

October 25
The single 'Quelli Erand Giorni'/'Turn! Turn! Turn! (To Everything There Is A Season)' by Mary Hopkin and produced by Paul McCartney was released in Italy as Apple 2.
John and Yoko announced that Yoko was pregnant and they were expecting a baby in February 1969.

October 28
Cynthia Lennon's divorce petition was officially listed.
Ringo and Maureen returned to London from their Sardinian holiday.

October 30
John and Ringo attended Tiny Tim and The Bonzo Dog Band in concert at the Royal Albert Hall in London.
Paul and Linda returned to London from New York, having taken an overnight stop in Jamaica.

October 31
Linda Eastman moved to London to live with Paul, bringing her daughter Heather with her and enrolling her in a local private school.
Tony Palmer's BBC Television documentary on pop music, called *All My Loving*, was screened.

November
George spent nearly seven weeks in Los Angeles recording six more tracks with Jackie Lomax for the album *Is This What You Want?* at Sound Recorders Studio, using the best of the Los Angeles session men including Hal Blaine on drums, Larry Knechtel on keyboards and Joe Osborn on bass.

November 1
The album *Wonderwall Music (Original Soundtrack Album)* by George Harrison & Band/Indian Orchestra, written and produced by George Harrison, was released in the UK by Apple as SAPCOR 1. Side One: 'Microbes', 'Red Lady', 'Medley', 'Tabla and Pakavaj', 'In The Park', 'Medley', 'Greasy Legs', 'Ski-ing and Gat Kirwani', 'Dream Scene'; Side Two: 'Party Seacombe', 'Medley', 'Love Scene', 'Crying', 'Cowboy Museum', 'Fantasy Sequins', 'Glass Box', 'On The Bed', 'Wonderwall To Be Here', 'Singing Ohm'.

November 3
George recorded his synthesiser 'composition', 'No Time Or Space', with the assistance of Moog maestro Bernie Krause in California.

November 4
Yoko Ono was admitted to Queen Charlotte's Hospital in London, after doctors feared that the stress of her recent arrest, and the press backlash which has been affecting the Lennons, might endanger her unborn child. John remained by her bedside, and over the next fortnight the couple made a series of *vérité* recordings in the hospital.

November 5
Paul and Linda drove to Scotland for a long rest on his farm.

November 6
The Apple press office announced that The Beatles had booked the Roundhouse theatre in Chalk Farm, London, from December 14th to 23rd, to play one or more live concerts.

November 7
John penned a cartoon strip entitled 'A Short Essay On Macrobiotics' for the health magazine *Harmony*.

November 8
Cynthia was granted a decree nisi in the London Divorce Court because of John's admitted adultery with Yoko. She retained custody of their son, Julian.

It was reported that George's five-year songwriting contract with Northern Songs Limited had expired in March and not been renewed.

John and Yoko financed newspaper advertisements for the Peace Ship, a radio station run by Ronan O'Rahilly and intended to end the conflict in the Middle East.

November 11

The album *Unfinished Music No.1 – Two Virgins* by John Lennon and Yoko Ono and written and produced by John and Yoko was released in the US as Apple T 5001. Side One: 'Two Virgins No.1', 'Together', 'Two Virgins (numbers 2 to 6)'. Side Two: 'Two Virgins', 'Hushabye Hushabye', 'Two Virgins (numbers 7 to 10)'.

The photograph of the two of them in the nude on the sleeve caused offence in some quarters, and EMI refused to distribute it. Track Records did the job instead. In the US, Capitol also refused to have anything to do with it, for fear that the Bible Belt would react with their customary prurience. A small label called Tetragrammaton, mostly known for spoken word records, took up the challenge but even they felt obliged to put the record into a brown paper sleeve, with a cut-away allowing John and Yoko's faces to peer through.

John: "Originally, I was going to record Yoko, and I thought the best picture of her for an album would be naked. So after that, when we got together, it just seemed natural for us both to be naked. Of course, I've never seen my prick out on an album before."

November 15

While in Los Angeles, George made a short, unannounced appearance on the CBS TV show *The Smothers Brothers' Comedy Hour* before a live audience in Hollywood.

November 13

The *Yellow Submarine* movie was belatedly premiered in the US. Despite staying only a few hundred yards from the Hollywood cinema which hosted the event, George declined to attend. "I've already seen it twice", he explained.

November 17

George's appearance on *The Smothers Brothers' Comedy Hour* was broadcast on the CBS network in the US.

November 19

Ringo, Maureen and their children moved from "Sunny Heights" in Weybridge to a new home, "Brookfields" near Elstead.

November 20

Paul was interviewed at his home in Cavendish Avenue, St John's Wood, by Tony MacArthur for a two-hour Radio Luxembourg special, *The Beatles*.

November 21

Yoko suffered a miscarriage of her baby at Queen Charlotte's Hospital, London, caused almost certainly by the stress of being arrested. John stayed at her side, sleeping overnight in a spare hospital bed. When the bed was needed for a patient, John slept on the floor.

The unborn child was named John Ono Lennon II, and was buried by the couple in a secret location.

November 22

The album *The Beatles* (known as *The White Album*) was released in the UK as Apple (Parlophone) PMC 7067-7068 (mono) and PCS 70677068 (stereo). Side One: 'Back In The USSR', 'Dear Prudence', 'Glass Onion', 'Ob-La-Di, Ob-La-Da', 'Wild Honey Pie', 'The Continuing Story Of Bungalow Bill', 'While My Guitar Gently Weeps', 'Happiness Is A Warm Gun'; Side Two: 'Martha My Dear', 'I'm So Tired', 'Blackbird', 'Piggies', 'Rocky Raccoon', 'Don't Pass Me By', 'Why Don't We Do It In The Road', 'I Will', 'Julia'; Side Three: 'Birthday', 'Yer Blues', 'Mother Nature's Son', 'Everybody's Got Something To Hide Except Me And My Monkey', 'Sexy Sadie', 'Helter Skelter', 'Long Long Long'; Side Four: 'Revolution 1', 'Honey Pie', 'Savoy Truffle', 'Cry Baby Cry', 'Revolution 9', 'Good Night'.

Robert Fraser proposed that, since Peter Blake had art directed *Sgt. Pepper*, Richard Hamilton, another leading figure in British Pop Art, should do the next. He was asked to meet The Beatles at the Apple office in Savile Row, and after being kept waiting for an hour or more he was ushered in. By then Hamilton was having second thoughts about getting involved with the pop music business and asked Paul, "Why don't you do it yourself? You don't need me. I'm the wrong sort of artist for you." He said that as *Sgt. Pepper* was so over the top, he would be inclined to do a very prissy thing, almost like a limited edition, and went on to propose a plain white album. He also suggested that they number each copy, a joke numbered edition of something like five million copies. Paul thought this was an amusing idea and agreed. Richard Hamilton: "Then I began to feel a bit guilty at putting their double album under plain wrappers; I suggested it could be jazzed up with a large edition print, an insert that would be even more glamorous than a normal sleeve.

"That's why the album ended up the way it did. Most people, among them Yoko, think it was Yoko's idea. I've no doubt that she would have been very supportive – from what I knew of her work and Fluxus background, the approach would have been right up her street. It was at the time when Yoko was really moving into the Beatle business and putting her oar in strongly. But my contact with the project was only through Paul – even EMI was held off."

Paul: "Richard and I worked together on the collage for The Beatles' *White Album*. Richard and I sat down all week while he did the collage from childhood photos of us all. The thing that impressed me at the end of the week was that after he'd filled the whole board with pictures and got his composition right, his final move was to take pieces of white paper and place them strategically to give space through the whole thing so that it wasn't just crammed with pictures. It was beautiful and I remember being very impressed with the way he put this negative space on – it was the first time that I'd ever seen that idea."

THE BEATLES (THE WHITE ALBUM)

On one hand, *The Beatles – The White Album*, as all but pedants call it – was the most diverse record that The Beatles, or probably any pop band in history, has ever made. On the other, as Paul McCartney remembered, "That was the tension album. We were all in the midst of that psychedelic thing, or just coming out of it. In any case, it was weird. Never before had we recorded with beds in the studio and people visiting for hours on end: business meetings and all that. There was a lot of friction during that album. We were just about to break up, and that was tense in itself."

Lester Bangs described it perfectly: "The first album by The Beatles or in the history of rock by four solo artists in one band". In doing that, he was simply following John Lennon's lead: "If you took each track, it was just me and a backing group, Paul and a backing group – I enjoyed it, but we broke up then."

Although Ringo quit the group for more than a week, he is unlikely to have been at the centre of the dissension in the ranks: the main arguments were between George and Paul (Harrison reckoning that McCartney was treating him as a junior member of the band) and John and the rest of the band (over, on one side, Lennon's insistence on Yoko Ono joining the group in the studio and, on the other, her treatment at the hands of Paul and George).

There were plenty of other pressures at work. The lack of central management in the group's career since the death of Brian Epstein in August 1967 had presented them with additional financial and business decisions to worry about, ignore and occasionally even make. McCartney's keen interest in maintaining a steady ship rubbed up against Lennon and Harrison's more *laissez-faire* attitude to events.

The creation of Apple, their multi-genre business empire that was intended as a fantasy come true but rapidly disintegrated into chaos, took its toll on the group's unity and enthusiasm. So too did the aftermath of the Maharishi episode, with even the most meditation-friendly of The Beatles suffering extreme disillusionment after their idyll with the Indian guru mutated into farce. Most of all, though, the group were individually and collectively aware that without leadership or a definite direction, they had no unifying purpose. From the start of 1968 onwards, they seemed to work to a 'two steps forward, three steps back, one step into another dimension' policy – with results that were often inspired, and just as often muddle-headed.

It's some kind of proof of their genius, then, that *The White Album* was so brilliant, and so vast. Producer George Martin always wanted the group to throw away the chaff and trim the 30-track, 90-minute epic into a tight 40-minute LP of polished gems. But half the attraction of *The White Album* is its sprawling chaos. Such a giant canvas allowed The Beatles, more often one at a time than not, to show off every aspect of their music. For the first and probably last time in pop history, a group demonstrated on one release that they could handle rock'n'roll, reggae, soul, blues, folk, country, pop and even the avant-garde with consummate ease – and still come out sounding like The Beatles. As a handy history of popular music since 1920, or simply a rich mine of battered gems, *The Beatles* is impossible to beat.

For the last time, both mono and stereo mixes of this double album were prepared, and The Beatles took great delight in making them as different from each other as possible. Almost every song on *The White Album* has variations between the two mixes: in one extreme case, the mono version is 20 seconds shorter than the stereo.

BACK IN THE USSR

For many of the White Album *sessions, The Beatles were able to work on separate, individual projects at the same time, and keep their four-man performances – and the resulting tension they caused – to a minimum. But on August 22, 1968, when all of The Beatles assembled to record Paul McCartney's 'Back In The USSR', tempers frayed, and it was Ringo Starr – pegged by the world as the least opinionated of the group – who walked out, announcing he'd quit the band.*

In his place, McCartney played drums, with a little assistance from Lennon and Harrison; and the entire song was cut without Ringo. The result was a magnificent Beach Boys pastiche, which that group's lead singer, Mike Love, later claimed to have helped write. Hunter Davies's official Beatles biography, published in 1968, offered another story.

DEAR PRUDENCE

Prudence Farrow, sister of the actress Mia, was the subject of this generous, warm-hearted Lennon song. It was inspired by her behaviour at the Maharishi's Indian retreat, when Lennon was deputed to entice her out of her self-enforced hiding in her quarters. Lennon widened the song to take in a pantheistic vision of the world's beauty, one of the few positive statements to emerge from his stay in India. (Another, a song called 'Child Of Nature', wasn't considered for this album; instead, it was rewritten three years later as 'Jealous Guy' for John's Imagine *LP, its original spirit of universal harmony replaced by fear and guilt.)*

This was another of the recordings done during Ringo Starr's departure from the group: strange that The Beatles should open their album with two tracks that were both recorded by a three-man line-up.

GLASS ONION

Like 'I Am The Walrus', 'Glass Onion' was written by John Lennon as a deliberate riposte to critics and fans who thought they were discovering the Holy Grail in some of his more recherché lyrical imagery. "I wrote 'The Walrus was Paul' in that song," John explained many years later. "At that time I was still in my love cloud with Yoko, so I thought I'd just say something nice to Paul – you did a good job over these few years, holding us together. I thought, I've got Yoko, and you can have the credit."

Besides the deliberately obtuse lyrics 'Glass Onion' boasted a searing Lennon vocal, and a mournful string coda that cut against the mood of the song.

OB-LA-DI, OB-LA-DA

Day after day, Paul McCartney dragged The Beatles through take after take, and arrangement after arrangement, of a throwaway, mock-reggae tune about a singer and a man who "has a barrow in the marketplace". Was it worth it? Well, the song has humour on its side, especially with the other Beatles throwing in the off-the-cuff comments that were fast becoming a trademark on their 1968 recordings. And 'Ob-La-Di, Ob-La-Da' did become a No. 1 hit for Marmalade. But rarely in The Beatles' career did they spend so much time on something so ephemeral.

WILD HONEY PIE

During the White Album *sessions, Paul McCartney felt comfortable enough for the first time to capture some of his one-minute moments of madness on tape. He recorded this strange, whimsical ditty as a one-man band, overdubbing several vocal parts and guitars, and emerging with 53 seconds of music that would never have been considered for release on any Beatles album but this one.*

THE CONTINUING STORY OF BUNGALOW BILL

Anything went for this one-day session – a Spanish guitar intro borrowed from a sound effects tape, a vocal cameo from Yoko Ono, harmonies from Ringo's wife, Maureen Starkey, and mellotron from producer Chris Thomas. Lennon's lyrics told the semi-humorous story of a fellow Meditation convert, addicted to big game hunting, and everyone in the vicinity of the studio contributed to the singalong chorus.

WHILE MY GUITAR GENTLY WEEPS

George Harrison won such acclaim for this song that he was tempted to write a much less successful follow-up, 'This Guitar (Can't Keep From Crying)'. Ironically, the most famous guitar solo on any Beatles record was played by an outsider – Cream guitarist Eric Clapton, a close friend of Harrison's, who was invited to the session both for his musical skills and in an attempt to cool the frequently heated passions in the studio.

As it was originally written, and demoed via a solo performance at Abbey Road, Harrison's song had an additional verse, which didn't survive beyond this initial (and quite magical) acoustic performance.

HAPPINESS IS A WARM GUN

The song's original title – 'Happiness Is A Warm Gun In Your Hand' – left its social message perfectly clear. But besides reflecting John Lennon's moral outrage at the American firearms lobby, it also had a second function, as John explained: "It's sort of a history of rock and roll." And a third inspiration for the track was confirmed later, when he revealed that much of the most direct imagery in the song conveyed his sexual passion for Yoko Ono. Beatles and Apple Corps press officer Derek Taylor contributed some of the song's most mysterious lines.

Musically, the track was a tour de force, albeit without the theatrics and orchestrations of the Pepper *album. It moved swiftly from a dream state to an air of menace, then a frenetic middle section, and finally a repeated four-chord chorus which somehow combined erotic fervour with an affectionate pastiche of Fifties rock'n'roll.*

MARTHA MY DEAR

What began as a McCartney solo piece, a deliciously romantic piano piece in his utterly distinctive style, ended up with the accompaniment augmented by a troupe of brass and string musicians. Thankfully, they didn't bury the whimsical charm of the song, whose heroine took her name from McCartney's near-legendary sheepdog.

I'M SO TIRED

Like 'Yer Blues', 'I'm So Tired' wins the Lennon prize for irony, this paean of self-doubt and boredom having been composed in the supposedly spiritual surroundings of the Maharishi Mahesh Yogi's Indian retreat. The ennui and desolation of Lennon's vocal filled in the tiny fragments of obliqueness in one of his most direct songs, and made for an eerie counterpoint to the optimistic, joyous McCartney numbers which surrounded it.

BLACKBIRD

Nature song? Love ballad? Message of support for the black power movement? McCartney's gently beautiful 'Blackbird' supported several interpretations, but required nothing more than appreciation for its flowing melody and its stark visual imagery. The recording was a solo performance, aided only by bird sounds borrowed from the EMI tape library. Paul never wrote a simpler or more effective song.

PIGGIES

With the aid of his mother, who wrote the "damn good whacking" line, George intended 'Piggies' as humorous social satire – though its title soon meant that the counterculture adopted it as an anti-police anthem. Continuing the animal theme of 'Blackbird', pig noises were added to the basic track (Lennon's sole contribution to the song), which was also augmented by a hefty orchestral arrangement, and a harpsichord played by the man who produced several White Album *sessions, Chris Thomas.*

ROCKY RACCOON

Anyone scouring The Beatles' catalogue for early signs of the playfulness in which Paul McCartney indulged – some would say overindulged — during his solo career could find plenty of evidence on the White Album. *With the assistance of George Martin on saloon-bar piano, the group (minus Harrison) completed this attractive but lightweight mock-Western ditty in just one session.*

DON'T PASS ME BY

After five years of trying, Ringo Starr finally got his first solo composition on a Beatles album. It turned out to be a country hoedown with playful lyrics and a generally lugubrious air, with some off-the-cuff fiddle playing by Jack Fallon, who'd met The Beatles six years earlier when he promoted one of their concerts in Stroud.

For some reason – maybe because they felt it was one of the least important songs on the album – Lennon and McCartney chose to experiment with the mixing of this track, emerging with mono and stereo versions that run at recognisably different speeds, and have variations in the instrumental overdubs.

WHY DON'T WE DO IT IN THE ROAD?

John Lennon called this near-solo McCartney performance "one of his best", which was either sarcasm or showed that he always valued his partner's off-the-cuff moments more than his controlled ones. Ringo added his drums to a basic piano, guitar and vocal track that Paul had recorded without the assistance or knowledge of the other group members. Raucous and good-humoured, it was a rare moment of levity from the man increasingly left to direct the group's activities.

The song's (very) slightly risqué lyric, all two lines of it, heightened the vague air of controversy surrounding the album. McCartney was already in trouble with the press for allowing a minuscule nude picture of himself to be included on the set's free poster.

I WILL

It took 67 takes for Lennon, McCartney and Starr to come up with a basic track for this gentle love song which met its composer's expectations. McCartney then added his tuneful vocal, sang his bass part rather than playing it, and still found time during the session to ad-lib a dreamy song called something like 'Can You Take Me Back', which duly found its way onto the finished album as an uncredited snippet between 'Cry Baby Cry' and 'Revolution 9'.

JULIA

It was Donovan who taught John Lennon the finger-picking style that he used on this song, as well as 1969 recordings like 'Sun King' and Yoko Ono's 'Remember Love'. For the first and last time in The Beatles' career, this was an entirely solo performance by John – dedicated both to his late mother (Julia Lennon) and to Yoko. Translated into English, her name apparently means 'ocean child', a phrase which was incorporated into Lennon's lyric.

BIRTHDAY

Either side of repairing to McCartney's house to watch the classic rock'n'roll movie, The Girl Can't Help It, *on TV, The Beatles recorded this riff-based rocker – one of the last genuine Lennon/McCartney collaborations. Two Beatle partners, Patti Harrison and Yoko Ono, sang the answer vocals in the chorus, while the band rocked out as if they hadn't a care in the world. It was a rare show of old-style unity during a difficult few months of recording.*

YER BLUES

Written from the supposed haven of the Maharishi's camp in Rishikesh, 'Yer Blues' was an anguished confession of loneliness and pain, wrapped in a deliberately self-mocking title. "There was a self-consciousness about suddenly singing blues," Lennon explained in 1970. "I was self-conscious about doing it."

With its references to Bob Dylan and rock'n'roll, 'Yer Blues' was obviously intended to be a definitive statement of Lennon's boredom with his role – definitive, that is, until the "I don't believe in Beatles" cry in 'God' on his Plastic Ono Band *album. The song meant enough to him to be reprised both at The Rolling Stones' Rock'N'Roll Circus TV show in December, and at the Toronto festival the following year.*

MOTHER NATURE'S SON

Like 'Blackbird', 'Mother Nature's Son' was a gentle, pastoral acoustic song which captured McCartney's writing at its most inspired. Augmented by a subtle horn arrangement, it epitomised the devastating switch of moods and tempos that made this album – and indeed The Beatles' work in general – so remarkable.

EVERYBODY'S GOT SOMETHING TO HIDE EXCEPT ME AND MY MONKEY

Playing with lyrical opposites, then lapsing into nonsense for the chorus, John Lennon concocted a rock'n'roll song that suggested more than it meant. Such a tongue-in-cheek number deserved an appropriate arrangement, and The Beatles set out to enjoy the process of recording it – speeding up the tape of the backing track to heighten the frantic feel, and then hurling a motley collection of screams, cries and even some singing into the fade-out.

SEXY SADIE

"That was about the Maharishi," explained John in 1970, when quizzed about the identity of the mysterious Ms Sadie. "I copped out and wouldn't write 'Maharishi, what have you done, you made a fool of everyone'."

In the studio, Lennon briefly demonstrated the song's obscene original lyrics, which made no attempt to shield the Maharishi by the use of poetry. On the record, though, the insult was softened by the sheer beauty of the music, which hinged around McCartney's brilliant piano playing, and some acerbic singing from John. Eight bars of instrumental work were removed from the fade-out during the final mix, incidentally.

HELTER SKELTER

"That came about because I read in Melody Maker *that The Who had made some track or other that was the loudest, most raucous rock'n'roll, the dirtiest thing they've ever done," Paul McCartney explained. "I didn't know what track they were talking about but it made me think, 'Right. Got to do it.' And I totally got off on that one little sentence in the paper."*

On July 18, then, The Beatles gathered at Abbey Road to match that description, and emerged with a 27-minute jam around a menacing guitar riff. Unreleased until 1995, and then only as a four and a half minute edit, this live-in-the-studio recording was the heaviest track The Beatles ever made. Played live by all four Beatles, on two guitars, bass and drums, it was a slow, lumbering McCartney song, moody and sombre.

Seven weeks later, they tried again, this time aware that they needed to make their statement in five minutes, not 27. Having cut the basic track, they added a chaotic barrage of horns, distortion and guitar feedback, and then prepared two entirely different mixes of the song – the stereo one running almost a minute longer than the mono, which omitted Ringo's pained shout, "I've got blisters on my fingers."

A year later, Charles Manson's followers wrote the words 'Helter Skelter' in blood as they killed actress Sharon Tate and her friends in her Hollywood home. Bizarrely, John Lennon (rather than McCartney, the song's composer) was called as a witness in the trial, but refused to attend. "What's 'Helter Skelter' got to do with knifing somebody?" he complained. "I've never listened to the words properly, it was just a noise."

LONG LONG LONG

Without John Lennon, who as usual was mysteriously absent when a Harrison song appeared on the agenda, The Beatles managed 67 takes of this delicately lyrical number. Then they capped a low-key, almost inaudible performance with a few moments of chaos – capturing the sound of a wine bottle vibrating on top of a speaker cabinet, and matching it with a flurry of guitars, groans and drums.

REVOLUTION 1

For the first and last time, The Beatles succeeded on May 30, 1968 in recording the basic backing for two different tracks at exactly the same time. How? It was quite simple. At the first session for their new album, they recorded a ten-minute rendition of John's latest song – best interpreted as an overt political statement, backing the stance of the main Communist Parties in the debates over the student riots in Paris, rather than the calls from ultra-left parties for immediate revolution. (Later, Lennon would take entirely the opposite political position.)

The first four minutes became 'Revolution 1', originally planned as a single but eventually deemed too low-key, and subsequently re-recorded in an entirely electric arrangement; the last six minutes, a cacophony of feedback and vocal improvisation, was transported to become the basis of 'Revolution 9'.

HONEY PIE

Not a revival of a flappers' favourite from the Twenties but a McCartney original, 'Honey Pie' must have owed something to the music of his father Jim McCartney's jazz band. Scratches from an old 78rpm record were added to one of the opening lines of the song, to boost its period flavour. George Martin scored the brass and woodwind arrangement, and that arch experimentalist, John Lennon, was quite happy to add electric guitar to a song that was the total opposite of all his contributions to the album.

SAVOY TRUFFLE

George Harrison wrote this playful song, inspired by a close friend: "Eric Clapton had a lot of cavities in his teeth and needed dental work. He ate a lot of chocolates – he couldn't resist them. I got stuck with the two bridges for a while, and Derek Taylor wrote some of the words in the middle." Taylor therefore collected his second anonymous credit on the White Album, *but no royalties. Harrison, meanwhile, borrowed most of the lyrics from the inside of a chocolate box, while John Lennon commented on proceedings by not turning up for any of the sessions where the song was recorded.*

CRY BABY CRY

Consult Hunter Davies's book to find John Lennon's rather apologetic description of how he wrote this song – which in one of his final interviews he denied ever having been involved with, the two days of sessions obviously struck from his mental record.

Using characters that sounded as if they'd been borrowed from a Lewis Carroll story, Lennon spent some time (but not too much) working up a song which he seems to have regarded from the start as a blatant piece of filler.

REVOLUTION 9

On the raucous collage of sounds that was the second half of the original 'Revolution 1' (see above), John Lennon and Yoko Ono built an aural nightmare, intended to capture the atmosphere of a violent revolution in progress. By far the most time-consuming White Album *track to complete, and then the most controversial when the record was released, 'Revolution 9' was John and Yoko's most successful venture into the world of sound-as-art.*

The track began bizarrely enough, with a snippet of an unreleased Paul McCartney song (see 'I Will'), then an EMI test tape repeating the words "Number nine" over and over again. After that, there was chaos – a cavalcade of tape loops, feedback, impromptu screams and carefully rehearsed vocal overdubs, sound effects recordings and the noise of a society disintegrating. Reportedly, Paul McCartney agreed to the inclusion of the track only with severe misgivings, which George Martin expressed more forcibly.

GOOD NIGHT

The composer of this lush and sentimental ballad was not the lush and sentimental Paul McCartney, but the acerbic and cynical John Lennon, whose contributions to The White Album *therefore ranged from the ultra-weird to the ultra-romantic within two consecutive tracks. Fast becoming the children's favourite of The Beatles, Ringo Starr sang this lullaby, to a purely orchestral accompaniment. None of the other three Beatles appears on the track.*

November 23

In the wake of the controversy aroused by John and Yoko's nude album sleeve, the press were quick to seize upon a tiny nude photograph of Paul, which formed part of the collage on the poster accompanying *The Beatles*. Apple press officer Derek Taylor retorted: "All this work, all these tracks, all this talent – and all their dirty little minds focus on is one tiny picture."

November 24

Paul confirmed that Yoko's recent miscarriage might force the postponement of The Beatles' return to live performances.

The group Grapefruit left Apple. Their manager, Terry Doran, told *The People*: "I like The Beatles as friends, but not bosses . . . there's too much driftwood at Apple."

November 25
The album *The Beatles* (*White Album*) was released in the US as Apple (Capitol) SWBO 101 (stereo only) with the same tracks as the UK release.

November 27
Invited to contribute an original piece of writing to *Aspen* magazine, John filled out a nonsensical version of 'My Diary', repeating the same banal information for each day's entry.

November 28
John pleaded guilty to the charge of unauthorised possession of cannabis resin at Marylebone Magistrates' Court. In an effort to gain sympathy for the couple, John's solicitor told the court that after the raid, Yoko had lost her baby and that this had been a terrible blow to them. John was fined £150 and ordered to pay costs of 20 guineas. He and Yoko were found not guilty on the charge of obstructing the police in execution of a search warrant. In court it was reported that while being questioned after the raid, in an effort to protect Yoko, whom he feared might be deported because she was not a British citizen, John asked, "Can I just ask a question? As this stuff is all mine, will it be me only who is involved?" This drug conviction was to haunt John for years and was used by the Nixon administration in repeated attempts to deny him a Green Card for residence in the US.

November 29
The album *Unfinished Music No.1 – Two Virgins* by John Lennon and Yoko Ono and written and produced by John and Yoko was released in the UK as Apple SAPCOR 2 with the same tracks as the US release.

November 30
New Musical Express reported that 'Hey Jude' was approaching sales of six million worldwide.

December
During December and January, John and Yoko made the film *Rape* for Australian television. A camera team hounded a young woman until she was near to tears. John: "We are showing how all of us are exposed and under pressure in our contemporary world . . . what is happening to this girl on the screen is happening in Biafra, Vietnam, everywhere."

December also saw a continued media backlash against John and Yoko, inspired by the controversial *Two Virgins* album sleeve. Most US record stores refused to stock the record, even when its offending artwork was concealed beneath a brown paper bag. In the UK, EMI declined to distribute the LP, which was handled instead by the independent label Track Records.

John's new songs reflected his darkening mood: they included 'A Case Of The Blues', 'Everybody Had A Hard Year', and 'Oh My Love', the initial draft of which was a love song to the child that the couple had lost.

During this period, John and Yoko sank into the morass of heroin addiction, a burden which left its mark on his demeanour and enthusiasm for The Beatles over the next two months.

December 2
The album *Wonderwall Music (Original Soundtrack Album)* by George Harrison & Band/Indian Orchestra, written and produced by George Harrison, was released in the US as Apple ST 3350 with the same tracks as the UK release.

December 4
George circulated a memo to the staff of Apple warning them that he had invited a group of Californian Hell's Angels over to stay at 3 Savile Row:

"Hell's Angels will be in London within the next week, on the way to straighten out Czechoslovakia. There will be 12 in number complete with black leather jackets and motor cycles. They will undoubtedly arrive at Apple and I have heard they may try to make full use of Apple's facilities. They may look as though they are going to do you in but are very straight and do good things, so don't fear them or uptight them. Try to assist them without neglecting your Apple business and without letting them take control of Savile Row."

December 6
The readers of the *New Musical Express* gave The Beatles their customary victories in the "Best British Group" and "Best World Group" categories of the annual poll. 'Hey Jude' was voted "Best Single Of 1968".

The album *James Taylor* by James Taylor and featuring Paul McCartney on bass guitar (first track side two: 'Carolina On My Mind') was released in the UK as Apple SAPCOR 3.

December 7
The American correspondent for *Disc and Music Echo* reported that Paul had been going out with New York photographer Linda Eastman.

December 10
"Kenwood", John and Cynthia's house in the St George's Hill Estate in Weybridge, was put up for sale.

John and Yoko attended rehearsals at Wembley Studios for the next day's filming of The Rolling Stones' extravaganza: *Rock And Roll Circus*. John sang 'Yer Blues', and also took part in a jam session on some 50s rock'n'roll standards with Taj Mahal's guitarist, Jesse Ed Davis.

December 11
On the spur of the moment, Paul and Linda with Linda's daughter, Heather, flew to Praia da Luz in the Algarve, Portugal, to stay with Hunter Davies who had casually sent a postcard inviting them. They decided too late for a commercial flight, so Neil Aspinall hired a private jet. They arrived at Davies's rented villa at night and banged on the door, waking him up. They had no Portuguese currency so Davies had to pay the taxi.

John and Yoko, with John's son, Julian, spent the day and most of the night at Wembley Studios filming the all-star jam session: The Rolling Stones' *Rock And Roll Circus*. John led a band that called themselves The Dirty Macs and included Yoko, Eric Clapton, Keith Richards (on bass) and Mitch Mitchell (drums), performing 'Yer Blues' and a free-form jam that featured Yoko's unusual vocals and guest violinist Ivry Gitlis. In the event, Jagger thought The Stones were outperformed by The Who and the project was shelved until 1997 when it was released on video. Around midnight John and Yoko drove back to central London to appear live on BBC Radio's *Night Ride* where they talked to DJ John Peel about their *Two Virgins* album and played a few minutes of the new *The Beatles* album.

December 12
The arrival of a private jet at tiny, newly opened Faro Airport had attracted press attention and Paul had to conduct a press conference on the beach.

December 17
Candy, with Ringo in a starring role, was premiered in New York.

December 18
The single 'I'm The Urban Spaceman' by The Bonzo Dog Doo Dah Band (Paul as Apollo C. Vermouth) and produced by Paul McCartney was released in the US as Imperial 66345.

John and Yoko appeared on stage in a large white bag as part of a Christmas happening, the Underground Christmas Party, at the Royal Albert Hall. The bag, they explained, was a vehicle to ensure "total communication". During their brief appearance, a protestor ran to the edge of the stage, holding a banner complaining about the British government's involvement in the civil war afflicting Nigeria. "Do you care, John Lennon, do you care?", the demonstrator shouted to the figures in the bag.

Apple confirmed that The Beatles' long-awaited return to the concert stage had now been postponed until January 18.

John: "It's unfortunate that all the publicity came out about doing live shows when it did. We were only thinking about it vaguely, but it kind of got out of hand."

December 20

The fan club flexi-disc, *The Beatles' 1968 Christmas Record*, was released. It included John reciting a satirical poem, 'Jock And Yono', which contained a thinly veiled attack on the other members of The Beatles.

December 23

Apple's first Christmas party was held at 3 Savile Row, complete with what its suppliers assured everyone was the Largest Turkey in the World, Hell's Angels, and members of a visiting Californian hippie commune. John and Yoko, who had hardly been seen at Apple since it opened its new headquarters, dressed up as Father and Mother Christmas and handed out presents to all the children attending.

December 25

All the Beatles spent Christmas with their families in the UK, except George, who stayed with Bob Dylan in Woodstock, USA.

1969

January

The Federal Bureau of Investigation opened a file on John, having been alerted to his "subversive" nature by the furore surrounding the nude sleeve for *Two Virgins*.

During an interview with the magazine *Nova*, Yoko coined the memorable phrase, "Woman is the nigger of the world", subsequently turned into a song by John.

January 1

George returned to London from New York.

January 2

Filming *Get Back* at Twickenham Studios.

Under pressure from Paul to return to live performance, the other Beatles had reluctantly agreed to make an appearance before a live audience, which would be filmed and released as a one-hour television show. However, it proved impossible to agree upon a venue: The Roundhouse in Chalk Farm was booked and cancelled, the idea of a Roman amphitheatre in Tunisia, filmed at dawn, empty of people, and slowly filling up with all races and creeds for the concert, was given serious consideration before Ringo vetoed it on the grounds that he wouldn't like the food.

Since they all agreed on the idea of the television film, Apple Films producer Denis O'Dell proposed that they begin rehearsing and suggested that they film the rehearsals for inclusion in the proposed film. He had Twickenham Film Studios booked from February 3 for use on Ringo's *Magic Christian* film, and he proposed they use the time until then to film on the sound stage in full 16mm. It was a disaster. They were still exhausted from the marathon *The Beatles* sessions. Paul bossed George around; George was moody and resentful. John would not even go to the bathroom without Yoko at his side and for her part Yoko made sure she was in every shot. The tension was palpable, and it was all being caught on film.

The Beatles were scheduled to arrive every morning at 10am, a target they only achieved on the first day of shooting. Thereafter, Paul and Ringo endeavoured to keep to the schedule; John and George simply ignored it, and arrived at Twickenham when they felt like it.

"It's like hard work to do it," George complained during an early Twickenham session. "I don't want to work, really. It's a drag to get your guitar at eight in the morning, when you're not ready for it."

On the first day of the filming, the group swapped fragments of their new songs. John unveiled 'Don't Let Me Down' and 'Dig A Pony'; George introduced 'All Things Must Pass' and 'Let It Down'. Eventually they worked on two Lennon songs, 'Don't Let Me Down' and 'Everybody Had A Hard Year', which Paul swiftly incorporated into his own song, 'I've Got A Feeling'.

January 3

Filming *Get Back* at Twickenham Studios. After Paul had played them 'Let It Be' for the first time, and Ringo had demonstrated his own songs-in-progress, The Beatles worked on George's 'All Things Must Pass' and their own oldie 'One After 909'. "Are we going to do any oldies on the show?", George asked the others. "It would be nice, and it would get over that initial thing of us hitting them with all new stuff."

Police in New Jersey, US, impounded 30,000 copies of John and Yoko's *Two Virgins* album on the grounds that the cover was pornographic.

John: "We were both a bit embarrassed when we peeled off for the picture – so I took it myself with a delayed action shutter. The picture was to prove that we are not a couple of demented freaks, that we are not deformed in any way and that our minds are healthy. If we can make society accept these kind of things without offence, without sniggering, then we shall be achieving our purpose. There has got to be law and order, but that doesn't mean we should suffer bad, out of date laws. If laws weren't changed they would still be jumping on queers and putting them away. So there is a case for us all to put society right – and that is basically why there is unrest all over the world; because revolution must come."

January 6

Filming *Get Back* at Twickenham Studios. The Beatles arrived late and unenthusiastic, but some work done on 'Don't Let Me Down' and 'Two Of Us'. John, strung out on heroin, was mostly silent and withdrawn, leaving Yoko to do most of the talking. George made his lack of excitement over the entire project plain: "I think we should forget the whole idea of the show." As the discussion about the proposed live concert progressed, Yoko suggested that The Beatles should perform to a conceptual audience in an empty auditorium, while director Michael Lindsay-Hogg waxed lyrical about the idea of a concert in front of thousands of torch-lit Arabs.

As the session declined, Paul and George bickered over minor details in the songs. "I always hear myself trying to annoy you," Paul said apologetically. "You're not annoying me," George replied coldly, "you don't annoy me anymore." The argument slipped into the conflict glimpsed in the final *Let It Be* film, as George snapped: "I'll play what you want me to play. I won't play at all if you don't want me to. Whatever it is that will please you, I'll do it."

The Apple press office announced that George would shortly begin collaborating with Derek Taylor on a musical inspired by daily life inside the Apple building.

Derek Taylor: "George has already written an outline and some of the music. I'm in charge of ideas and lyrics. We started last Wednesday after Mike Connor, who is in charge of Apple offices in Los Angeles, suggested we got together on a musical."

January 7
Filming *Get Back* at Twickenham Studios. Poor rehearsals of 'Maxwell's Silver Hammer' and John's 'Across The Universe', during which John forgot his own words. In an argument between George and Paul, George suggested that The Beatles should break up. "I don't want to do any of my songs on the show," he admitted, "because they'll turn out shitty, they'll come out like a compromise." Finally, Paul lost his cool: "I don't see why any of you, if you're not interested, get yourselves into this. Why are you here?" George closed the argument with a threat of a separation: "Maybe we should get a divorce".

That evening, George wrote 'I Me Mine', inspired by the pettiness and selfishness that he felt were afflicting The Beatles.

January 8
Filming *Get Back* at Twickenham Studios. The main feature of this day was an argument between John and George, with John putting down George's songwriting. "I don't care if you don't want it on your show," George snarled after he'd played them 'I Me Mine' for the first time.

January 9
Filming *Get Back* at Twickenham Studios. Jam session on 'Suzy's Parlour', after Paul had introduced 'Her Majesty' and 'Another Day' to the sessions. George also arrived with a new song, 'For You Blue'.

January 10
Filming *Get Back* at Twickenham Studios.

GEORGE QUITS
George's feeling that Paul was treating him as an inferior, combined with the tension he felt at always having Yoko present, reached breaking point. After a fierce argument with John, criticising him for contributing nothing to the sessions and showing no interest in the project, George walked off the set from the studio canteen telling the others he'd "see them round the clubs", and drove to Liverpool to see his parents. George thus became the second Beatle to leave the group.

The Beatles finished their lunch. On return to the studio, Yoko took up position on George's blue cushion and finally got the remaining Beatles to back her on an extended "wailing" session. "If George doesn't come back by Monday or Tuesday," John noted at one point, "we'll have to get Eric Clapton to play with us. If George leaves, do we want to carry on The Beatles? I do. We should just get other members and carry on."

Ringo: "George had to leave because he thought Paul was dominating him. Well, he was."

George: "I didn't care if it was The Beatles. I was getting out."

January 12

The *Wonderwall* film opened at the Cinecenta cinema. George was the only Beatle in attendance.

The Beatles met at Ringo's house to try to iron out their difficulties but the feud between John and George remained intractable.

January 13

Filming *Get Back* at Twickenham Studios. Paul and Ringo were the only Beatles to attend and spent the session discussing what to do about John's decision to let Yoko do all his talking for him. John made a brief appearance in the late afternoon, but no work was done.

Paul sent Derek Taylor a curt but graphic postcard to his home, bearing the message: "Up yer". The card was Taylor's reward for attempting to heal the rift within The Beatles.

The album *Yellow Submarine* was released in the US as Apple (Capitol) SW 385 (stereo only). Side A: 'Yellow Submarine', 'Only A Northern Song', 'All Together Now', 'Hey Bulldog', 'It's All Too Much', 'All You Need Is Love'; Side B: Seven soundtrack instrumental cuts by The George Martin Orchestra.

YELLOW SUBMARINE

The decision to base a cartoon film on a fictionalised version of the 1967 Beatles, named after one of their best-loved songs and featuring characters loosely taken from several others, brought to an end a stand-off which had been threatening to become embarrassing. Ever since they'd completed *Help!* in the summer of 1965, The Beatles had owed United Artists another film. Initially, they'd swallowed their lack of enthusiasm for another comic romp, and considered various scripts submitted in late 1965 and early 1966. A year after that, Brian Epstein was still promising the outside world that the movie would shortly begin production – though no final script or concept was ever agreed.

One of Epstein's last important deals before his death was his agreement to assist with the making of *Yellow Submarine*, which would require little or no active involvement from The Beatles, bar the submission of several new songs. The group did not even have to supply the voices for their cartoon selves, actors taking over that role, and creating a minor press 'scandal' in the process. As it turned out, The Beatles were so delighted by the finished cartoon – having expected crassness and been shown something close to art – that they agreed to appear in a final real-life scene, giving their public approval to the movie.

Until then, however, their contribution had been minimal. Until the film company's schedule demanded final delivery of the songs, they'd mentally set aside any rejects from 1967 sessions for the movie. The balance of power in the group dictated that two of the four rejects were George Harrison compositions – one of them the most striking piece of psychedelia The Beatles ever recorded.

These four new songs were originally planned for release as an EP. This was considered unsuitable for the American market, however, and so an album was concocted, combining the new items with two old songs from the soundtrack, plus twenty minutes of George Martin's incidental music. The group presumably decided against an LP made up of all their film songs because it would have repeated too many of the numbers from the *Sgt. Pepper* and *Magical Mystery Tour* albums.

YELLOW SUBMARINE

Unchanged from its appearance on Revolver, *the title song from the* Yellow Submarine *cartoon was one of two songs making its second appearance on a Beatles record.*

ONLY A NORTHERN SONG

"A joke relating to Liverpool, the Holy City in the North of England," is how George Harrison described this song – bizarrely never issued in 'true' stereo. The joke, incidentally, refers to Northern Songs, the company who published compositions by Lennon, McCartney and (in 1967, at least) Harrison. The lyrical non sequiturs and lugubrious musical backing made this one of the more unusual Beatles recordings, even by 1967 standards.

ALL TOGETHER NOW
Written with the film very much in mind, McCartney's singalong ditty became a children's favourite, completed in just over five hours of studio work. It's hard to imagine a song this slight being considered for any of the other Beatles albums.

HEY BULLDOG
"I went to see The Beatles' recording, and I said to John, 'Why do you always use that beat all the time, the same beat, why don't you do something more complex?'" Yoko Ono's question mightn't have been the most tactful way of greeting her first sight of her husband-to-be at work. On this occasion, in fact, simplicity was bliss. Gathered in the studio to shoot a promo film for the 'Lady Madonna' single, The Beatles made use of the opportunity to complete their obligations to the film company. Like 'I Am The Walrus', 'Hey Bulldog' defied detailed lyrical analysis, but its wonderfully chaotic production and raw Lennon vocal made it a minor classic. The Beatles enjoyed it, too, as a listen to the fade-out makes clear.

IT'S ALL TOO MUCH
This song, said composer George Harrison, was "written in a childlike manner from realisations that appeared during and after some LSD experiences and which were later confirmed in meditation." It was also a wonderfully inventive piece of psychedelia, a spirit-of-'67 freak-out that won fresh acclaim from a later wave of acid-rock adventurers in the late Seventies and early Nineties. Discordant, off-beat and effortlessly brilliant, the song was (alongside 'Taxman') Harrison's finest piece of Western rock music to date. Sadly, it was edited before release, losing one verse in its reduction from eight minutes to six.

ALL YOU NEED IS LOVE
The mix of this song included on the Yellow Submarine *album was marginally different from the original hit single.*

The remaining tracks by George Martin were: 'Pepperland', 'Sea Of Time & Sea Of Holes', 'Sea Of Monsters', 'March Of The Meanies' and 'Pepperland Laid Waste', together with 'Yellow Submarine In Pepperland' which was an orchestral revamp of the film's title song. These attractive instrumental numbers had no connection with The Beatles. Their presence on the CD makes *Yellow Submarine* **the least inspiring of The Beatles' albums for all but the determined completist.**

January 14
Filming *Get Back* at Twickenham Studios. John showed up but complained that he had been up all night on drugs and wasn't feeling well. They played 'Madman' and 'Watching Rainbows', watched for part of the session by actor Peter Sellers.

January 15
Filming *Get Back* at Twickenham Studios. George returned from Liverpool, and during a five-hour meeting, made up his difficulties with John. He told the others that he would leave the group unless the idea of a live performance was dropped. He was prepared, however, to be filmed making an album, but for that he suggested they use their own state-of-the-art 72-track recording studio that "Magic" Alex was supposed to be building for them at Savile Row.

January 16
Apple announced that The Beatles' live show at the Roundhouse, scheduled for the 18th, had been postponed. They also confirmed that a Beatles EP would be released shortly, including the 'new' songs from the *Yellow Submarine* album alongside the previously unreleased Lennon song, 'Across The Universe'.

January 17
The album *Yellow Submarine* was released in the UK as Apple (Parlophone) PMC 7070 (mono) and PCS 7070 (stereo) with the same tracks as the US release.

January 18
In an off-the-record remark on the stairs at Apple, John told the editor of *Disc And Music Echo*, Ray Coleman, "Apple is losing money every week . . . if it carries on like this, all of us will be broke in the next six months." Coleman printed the quote, causing consternation among Apple's bankers and The Beatles' tax advisers.

January 20
Part of George's terms for returning to the group was to cancel plans for a live concert, and end the filming at Twickenham. The *Get Back* film project was switched to Apple's new basement recording studios at 3 Savile Row where John's guru, "Magic" Alex, had supposedly built them a 72-track recording facility.

Unfortunately, Alex did not have the slightest idea how a recording studio actually worked and had not even provided a conduit connecting the studio with the control room so microphone leads and instruments could be connected to the desk. Confronted with an unusable studio, The Beatles called on George Martin to rescue them. He borrowed a pair of four-track machines from EMI, the leads were trailed in through the control room door, and two days later The Beatles began work.

George: "Alex's recording studio was the biggest disaster of all time. He was walking around with a white coat on like some sort of chemist, but he didn't have a clue what he was doing. The whole thing was a disaster, and it had to be ripped out."

January 21
Ringo was interviewed by David Wigg for the BBC Radio1 programme *Scene And Heard*. In 1976 Wigg released all of his BBC interviews with The Beatles on a double album, *The Beatles Tapes*. Legal moves by The Beatles failed to prevent its release.

George Martin and Glyn Johns continued to work on turning the Apple recording studio into a workable environment for The Beatles' session the next day.

January 22
Get Back sessions. With cameras and tapes rolling, The Beatles began work on the album and film which would have broken up any normal group. On the first day they ran through 'All I Want Is You' (later called 'Dig A Pony'), 'I've Got A Feeling', 'Don't Let Me Down', 'She Came In Through The Bathroom Window' and a few cover versions including The Drifters' 'Save The Last Dance For Me' and Canned Heat's 'Going Up The Country'. To musical accompaniment, Paul also recited a critical article on The Beatles from the *Daily Sketch* newspaper: "The awful tension of being locked in each other's arms snapped last night at TV rehearsal. Drugs, divorce and a slipping image played desperately on their minds . . . They will probably never be the same again."

Billy Preston, a friend of The Beatles since Hamburg days, was visiting Apple and was recruited by George to play on The Beatles' sessions and in the film in order to help ease the tension between the four of them. By the end of the session, John was asking Preston: "Why don't you be on the album?"

January 23
Get Back sessions. Work on Paul's 'Get Back'.

January 24
Get Back sessions. Work on Paul's 'On Our Way Home' (later called 'Two Of Us'), 'Teddy Boy', 'Maggie May', John's 'Dig It', 'Dig A Pony' and 'I've Got A Feeling'. The session began with a group discussion about how great a role Billy Preston should play in the sessions. John and George pushed for him to be included as a full member of The Beatles; "I'd like a fifth Beatle," John said. "It's bad enough with four!" Paul replied.

After the session was completed and The Beatles had left, Glyn Johns prepared a rough tape of the songs they'd been working on.

January 25
Get Back sessions. Glyn Johns played the group the tape he'd prepared of their work to date, which persuaded all The Beatles that despite the fact they weren't satisfied with anything they'd recorded to date, it was still worth continuing with the sessions. After

jamming on the Everly Brothers' 'Bye Bye Love' they worked on Paul's 'Let It Be' and 'George's Blues' (later retitled 'For You Blue').

David Wigg's interview with Ringo was broadcast by BBC Radio1's *Scene And Heard*.

January 26
Get Back sessions. Work on 'Dig It' was followed by a long rock'n'roll jam to loosen themselves up: 'Shake Rattle And Roll', 'Kansas City', 'Miss Ann', 'Lawdy Miss Clawdy', 'Blue Suede Shoes', 'You Really Got A Hold On Me' and 'Tracks Of My Tears'. Then they were ready to work on Paul's 'Long And Winding Road' and a song of George's which eventually appeared as 'Isn't It A Pity' on his *All Things Must Pass* triple album.

With the filmed live concert cancelled, the director of the film side of the project, Michael Lindsay-Hogg, realised that he might have months of filming ahead of him, judging by how long it took The Beatles to record an album. At a meeting in the board room at Apple, he proposed that they give a live concert, but all they would have to do was walk up one flight of stairs to the roof of their own building. Even this met with resistance, with George reluctant and Ringo determined not to do it. This time John and Paul combined persuaded the others, albeit only minutes before the actual event.

January 27
Get Back sessions. Work on 'Get Back', 'Oh! Darling', 'I've Got A Feeling' and a jammed version of Jimmy McCracklin's 'The Walk'. John's 'Sweet Loretta Fart she thought she was a cleaner . . .' parody of 'Get Back' was also recorded during this session. John received a phone call at the studio, telling him that Yoko's divorce from Tony Cox was about to be finalised.

Lennon Books Limited changed its name to Lennon Productions Limited.

January 28
Get Back sessions. The Beatles recorded both sides of their next single, 'Get Back' and 'Don't Let Me Down', as well as working on a remake of 'Love Me Do', 'The One After 909', 'Dig A Pony', 'I've Got A Feeling' and 'Teddy Boy'.

Derek Taylor gave Allen Klein John's telephone number and John and Yoko met with Klein in the Harlequin suite of the Dorchester Hotel, London. They were very impressed with him, and John decided on the spot to make him his personal adviser. There and then he wrote to Sir Joseph Lockwood, the chairman of EMI: "Dear Sir Joe: From now on Allen Klein handles all my stuff."

ENTER ALLEN KLEIN
Allen Klein had a meeting with all four Beatles. Acting on the advice of John Eastman, Linda's brother, they had been about to buy NEMS for £1m, which EMI was prepared to lend them as an advance against royalties. (NEMS was entitled to take 25% of their record royalties for a further nine years even though Brian Epstein's management contract had expired, something that Epstein slipped into his renewal contract with EMI that The Beatles had not read or noticed.) Klein pointed out that royalties were subject to a high rate of tax, and they would have to earn £2 million to repay the debt. He said that until he had a chance to examine John's financial situation he wouldn't recommend buying NEMS. George and Ringo asked him to examine theirs too. Paul left the meeting.

January 29
Get Back sessions. Work on versions of 'Teddy Boy', 'The One After 909', 'I Want You', Buddy Holly's 'Not Fade Away', 'Mailman, Bring Me No More Blues' as well as the old Hamburg and Cavern days standard, 'Besame Mucho'. Despite Paul's last-minute attempt to persuade the other Beatles to agree to a live show in front of an audience at the Saville Theatre, the foursome settled on the Apple rooftop the following morning. "I think it would be daft not to play tomorrow," John finally asserted, "even if it is a grand dress rehearsal." Even George was persuaded: "Let's get it done."

January 30

THE ROOFTOP CONCERT

Mal and Neil set up the instruments, as of old, and The Beatles, with Billy Preston, took up position on the flat roof of their Savile Row headquarters. Traffic was brought to a halt as the lunchtime crowds gathered on the pavement below and all the windows and roofs nearby quickly filled with West End office workers, getting a privileged view of the last ever Beatles live concert. The police tried to put a stop to it, but the combined Apple door security, and reluctance on the part of the police to actually pull the plug on such an extraordinary scene, meant that they played for 42 minutes.

They began with a rehearsal of 'Get Back', 'Don't Let Me Down', 'I've Got A Feeling', 'The One After 909', 'Dig A Pony' (for this, an assistant had to kneel in front of John holding the words on a clipboard), 'God Save The Queen', 'I've Got A Feeling' (again), 'Don't Let Me Down' (again) and 'Get Back' (again). This final version of 'Get Back' was interrupted by the police and Paul ad-libbed, "You've been playing on the roofs again and you know your momma doesn't like it, she's gonna have you arrested!" At the end of the song, Maureen Starkey burst into loud applause and cheers, causing Paul to return to the microphone and acknowledge her, "Thanks, Mo!"

John ended the set, and The Beatles' live career, with the words "I'd like to say thank you on behalf of the group and ourselves and I hope we passed the audition."

January 31

The last day of filming the *Get Back* sessions. Several of Paul's songs ('The Long And Winding Road', 'Let It Be' and 'Two Of Us') were unsuitable for the rooftop concert because they featured a piano or acoustic guitar. These were filmed at this session. A version of 'Lady Madonna' was also recorded. With the project in the can, The Beatles now put it on the shelf, where it would stay for more than a year.

EMI got their tape recorders back and workmen moved in to tear out "Magic" Alex's non-functioning studio.

February 2

The divorce of Yoko and her husband Anthony Cox in the Virgin Islands was ratified and Yoko was granted custody of their child Kyoko, even though Cox had essentially been the one who brought her up. Cox objected to the settlement terms which were obtained by the powerful lawyers that John's money provided, and continued to look after Kyoko. John and Yoko were both now free to remarry.

February 3

Ringo began an intense filming schedule at Twickenham Film Studios, playing support to Peter Sellers in Joe McGrath's *The Magic Christian,* based on the book by Terry Southern (as *Candy* also was). Filming went on from Monday to Friday for 13 weeks and Ringo was at the studio most days.

The Beatles, Allen Klein and John Eastman held a meeting. Allen Klein was appointed as The Beatles' business manager, charged with examining their finances and finding a way to stop NEMS from bleeding them of a quarter of their income.

February 4

As a compromise to Paul, Eastman and Eastman, Linda's father and brother, were appointed as Apple's General Council, to keep an eye on Allen Klein's activities.

February 5

The album *Goodbye* by Cream (featuring George Harrison on 'Badge') was released in the US as Atco SD 7001.

February 7

George entered University College Hospital, London, for treatment of a throat condition.

February 8
In a press report of the news that Klein had joined Apple as a financial adviser, John was quoted as saying: "We know him through Mick Jagger and we trust him – as much as we trust any businessman." In fact Jagger had been lukewarm about the idea, having had very bad experiences with Klein himself. He sent Paul a personal note warning him against using Klein, but when summoned to the board room of Apple, and faced by all four Beatles, he caved in to Lennon's obvious enthusiasm for Klein and simply said, "He's all right, if you like that kind of thing." Klein was to get control of the copyrights of all of Mick Jagger and Keith Richards' early songs.

George's tonsils were removed at University College Hospital.

February 10
George wrote to Derek Taylor from his hospital bed: "You have to be 'IN' to know how good it is 'OUT'. It is O.K. even in here today, so it must be absolutely beautiful at Apple or in the street. I smoked 2 cigs yesterday (naughty) – but could easily manage a joint sometime. (Not hash or tobacco – must be the grass, man.) I believe Krishna took a lot of the load off me, because it was only the day of the operation that I felt like cutting out. Yesterday was too much: Saturday was DEATH."

February 11
Abbey Road. John and Yoko did a mixing session of some of their experimental tapes.

February 12
Paul was made sole director of a new off-the-shelf company, Adagrose Limited, which was later renamed McCartney Productions Limited.

February 13
Mary Hopkin's first album, *Postcard*, produced by Paul, with a sleeve designed by Paul and photographed by Linda, was launched by Apple at a party held in the restaurant on the top of the Post Office Tower in Bloomsbury. Jimi Hendrix and Donovan were among the guests, and Paul and Linda stayed until the end to show support for their new act.

February 14
John Eastman wrote to Clive Epstein, who was now running NEMS after his brother's death: "As you know, Mr Allen Klein is doing an audit of The Beatles affairs vis-à-vis NEMS and Nemperor Holdings Ltd. When this has been completed I suggest we meet to discuss the results of Mr Klein's audit as well as the propriety of the negotiations surrounding the nine-year agreement between EMI, The Beatles and NEMS."

February 15
Clive Epstein replied to John Eastman: "Before any meeting takes place, please be good enough to let me know precisely what you mean by the phrase 'the propriety of the negotiations surrounding the nine-year agreement between EMI, The Beatles and NEMS'."

George, his tonsils successfully removed, left University College Hospital.

February 17
Leonard Richenberg of Triumph Investment Trust, a city merchant bank, acquired a 70 per cent stake in NEMS and Nemperor Holdings. The Beatles were horrified at the idea of merchant bankers collecting their income for them and wrote a letter to EMI, signed by all four Beatles, saying: "We hereby irrevocably instruct you to pay Henry Ansbacher & Co. all royalties payable by you directly or indirectly to Beatles and Co. or Apple Corps." (Henry Ansbacher & Co was their merchant banker and considered OK.) EMI didn't know what to do so they froze the money – £1.3m in royalties – and put it into the nearest branch of Lloyds Bank.

The album *James Taylor* by James Taylor (produced by Peter Asher and featuring Paul McCartney's bass playing on 'Carolina In My Mind') was released in the US as Apple SKAO 3352.

February 19
Ringo was served a writ to quit the premises by Bryman Estates, landlords of 34 Montagu Square, for breaking the terms of his lease by allowing John and Yoko to use drugs there.

February 20
Ringo attended the UK premiere of *Candy* at the Odeon Cinema, Kensington, London.

February 21
The album *Postcard* by Mary Hopkin, produced by Paul McCartney, was released in the UK as Apple SAPCOR 5.
   The single 'Rosetta' by The Fourmost, produced by Paul McCartney, was released as CBS 4041.

February 22
Trident Studios, Soho. Further work done on John's 'I Want You' (with Billy Preston).

February 23
Trident Studios, Soho. John mixed 'I Want You'.
   Soon after this session, John and Paul requested that engineer Glyn Johns, who'd been present throughout the January sessions at Twickenham and Apple, should attempt to compile and sequence a viable album from the unsorted pile of master tapes. Johns subsequently revealed that the task "absolutely petrified" him.

February 24
It was announced that The Triumph Investment group of companies had gained control of NEMS Enterprises.

February 25
Abbey Road. George, working by himself, cut three demo tapes of his latest songs: 'Old Brown Shoe', 'Something' and 'All Things Must Pass'. The recordings were mixed and he was able to take home acetates after a good day's work.

February 26
Allen Klein held a series of business meetings at Apple to determine The Beatles' response to the Triumph Investments takeover of NEMS.

February 28
The album *Goodbye* by Cream (featuring George Harrison on 'Badge') was released in the UK as Polydor 583053.
   The eviction action against Ringo by Bryman Estates was settled out of court, allowing Ringo to sell his leasehold on 34 Montagu Square.

March
The Apple press office announced that The Beatles now owned the film rights to J.R.R. Tolkien's fantasy trilogy, *The Lord Of The Rings*, and that plans were underway for that to become the long-overdue third Beatles movie.
   Dick James and Charles Silver sold their shares in Northern Songs to Lew Grade's ATV, who then announced that they wanted to buy a controlling interest.

March 1
Paul produced both sides of Mary Hopkin's new single, 'Goodbye' and 'Sparrow', at Morgan Studios in Willesden.
   Ringo began work on *The Magic Christian*, at Twickenham Film Studios.

March 2
John and Yoko made an unscheduled appearance, together with John Tchikai and John Stevens, at an evening of avant-garde jazz and experimental music at Lady Mitchell Hall, Cambridge University. They performed a single improvised piece, subsequently titled 'Cambridge 1969'.
   Paul did more work on Mary Hopkin's new single at Morgan Studios.

March 3
The album *Post Card* by Mary Hopkin, produced by Paul McCartney, was released in the US as Apple ST 3351 with the fourth track of side two ('Someone To Watch Over Me' on the UK release) replaced by her number one hit, 'Those Were The Days'.

March 4
Princess Margaret met Ringo when she visited the set of *The Magic Christian* at Twickenham Film Studios to see her friend Peter Sellers. Paul and Linda were also there.

George was interviewed by David Wigg for the BBC Radio 1 programme *Scene And Heard*.

March 8
Part of George's interview with David Wigg was broadcast on BBC Radio 1's *Scene And Heard*.

March 10
Engineer Glyn Johns began a four-day series of mixing sessions, attempting to salvage The Beatles' *Get Back* album.

March 11
Paul produced Jackie Lomax singing 'Thumbin' A Ride', a Lieber and Stoller Coasters B-side that he found in his record collection. Paul played drums, George played guitar and Billy Preston played keyboards.

March 12
Paul and Linda were married at Marylebone Register Office, with his brother Michael and roadie Mal Evans as witnesses. Afterwards they went to St John's Wood Church where their marriage was blessed by the Rev. Noel Perry-Gore. There was a luncheon reception afterwards at the Ritz Hotel given by Rory McKeown. Princess Margaret and Lord Snowdon were there and Patti's sister Paula tried to hand Margaret a joint in full view of everyone.

None of the other Beatles attended the wedding, though George and Patti went to the reception. They arrived very late because the notorious Sergeant Pilcher chose Paul's wedding day to raid George's house for drugs, bringing a large piece of hashish with them (in case they didn't find anything) which they "found" on the floor. George commented, "I'm a tidy person. I keep my socks in the sock drawer and my hash in the hash box. It's not mine." They were taken to Esher Police Station and formally charged with possession of cannabis resin. Pilcher was later found guilty in the police corruption trials of the early Seventies.

After the reception Paul returned to the studio to continue work on 'Thumbin' A Ride'. Abbey Road. John and Yoko recorded 'Peace Song'.

March 13
Ringo shot a grouse-hunting scene on Chobham Common, Surrey, for *The Magic Christian*.

March 14
US promoter Sid Bernstein arrived in London, anxious to persuade The Beatles to perform four shows in the US, at a price of one million dollars per concert. The Beatles gently rejected his offer without agreeing to a meeting.

March 16
Paul and Linda with Heather, Linda's daughter by a previous marriage, flew to New York to spend three weeks with her family.

John and Yoko flew to Paris, intending to get married. They booked into the Plaza Athenée but were unable to get married in France because they had not been in residence long enough.

March 17

The single 'Badge' by Cream, written by George Harrison and Eric Clapton, was released in the US as Atco 6668.

The single 'Carolina In My Mind' by James Taylor, with Paul McCartney on bass, was released in the US as Apple 1805.

March 18

Ringo and Spike Milligan shot the traffic warden scene outside the Star and Garter, in Putney, for *The Magic Christian*.

George and Patti made an initial court appearance on their charges of cannabis possession, and were remanded on bail.

March 20

John and Yoko, still in Paris, had tried to get married on the cross-channel ferry but were refused permission to board *The Dragon* at Southampton because of "inconsistencies in their passports". Peter Brown at Apple found that they *could* get married on the British-governed island of Gibraltar. John, Yoko, Peter Brown and official photographer David Nutter flew to Gibraltar by private jet. They arrived at 8.30am and were at the British Consulate when it opened at 9am. There, registrar Cecil Wheeler married them with Peter Brown and David Nutter as their witnesses. They remained in Gibraltar for just 70 minutes before flying straight back to Paris and their luxury suite.

John: "We chose Gibraltar because it is quiet, British and friendly. We tried everywhere else first. I set out to get married on the car ferry and we would have arrived in France married, but they wouldn't do it. We were no more successful with cruise ships. We tried embassies, but three weeks' residence in Germany or two weeks' in France were required."

March 21

Allen Klein was appointed business manager of Apple. His first task was to sort out the mess caused by Dick James selling his Northern Songs shares without first offering them to The Beatles. Klein told the *Daily Telegraph* that under a three year contract he would receive 20 per cent of all the money collected by Apple but no money from existing recording contracts. He would, however, receive 20 per cent of any increase he negotiated on those contracts. He began firing the staff.

The album *Is This What You Want?* by Jackie Lomax, produced by George Harrison, was released in the UK as Apple SAPCOR 6.

March 23

Ringo flew to New York for a few days' location shooting on *The Magic Christian*.

March 24

John and Yoko had lunch with Salvador Dali in Paris.

Ringo told US reporters that The Beatles would never appear together in public again.

Ringo: "People really have tried to typecast us. They think we are still little moptops, and we are not. I don't want to play in public again. I don't miss being a Beatle anymore. You can't get those days back. It's no good living in the past."

March 25

John and Yoko flew to Amsterdam to begin a seven-day peace bed-in in room 902 of the Hilton Hotel.

JOHN'S BED-IN

John: "We're staying in bed for a week, to register our protest against all the suffering and violence in the world. Can you think of a better way to spend seven days? It's the best idea we've had." They were ridiculed by the world's media but by reporting the event at all, the press was passing on a message about the need for peace, so John and Yoko felt satisfied.

March 28

John was in bed for peace when he read in the newspaper that Dick James, the man they had made into a multi-millionaire, had sold his shares in Northern Songs to ATV without first offering them to The Beatles. John was furious: "I won't sell. They are my shares and my songs and I want to keep a bit of the end product. I don't have to ring Paul. I know damn well he feels the same as I do."

The single 'Goodbye' (Lennon & McCartney)/'Sparrow' by Mary Hopkin, produced by Paul McCartney, was released in the UK as Apple 10.

March 31
The last day of John and Yoko's seven-day bed-in. John and Yoko then flew to Vienna where they held a press conference from inside a white bag at the Hotel Sacher. It received worldwide coverage which a normal press conference would not, despite the fact that no one was sure it really *was* them. They were in Vienna for the world television premiere of *Rape,* which they produced.

George and Patti were found guilty of possession of cannabis at Esher and Walton Magistrates' Court and were fined £250 each with ten guineas' costs each. George: "I hope the police will leave us alone now."

April
John and Yoko sent out "Acorns For Peace": every world leader was sent an acorn and asked to plant it for peace. The idea was John and Yoko's but Apple had to do the work. It took the staff of the press office weeks to find enough acorns, as it was the wrong season, and they finished up digging holes in the London parks trying to find where the squirrels had hidden them. An offer of acorns at £1 each was turned down. Months later some of the boxes had still not been addressed and sent out, as promoting 'Get Back' and Mary Hopkin's new single took precedence.

John: "Yoko and I plan to send one of these envelopes containing two acorns to the head of state of every country in the world. We want them to plant them for peace."

Yoko: "If they want us to, we would go to the countries and plant them ourselves."

John: "Peace can't wait. I think this will be the most positive move for peace yet. It would be much better than all that phoney smiling and shaking hands you see in the papers."

April 1
Ringo and Laurence Harvey filmed a Hamlet striptease scene at the Theatre Royal, in Stratford, East London, for *The Magic Christian*.

John and Yoko returned to London and gave a press conference at Heathrow. Later they appeared live on Thames Television's *Today* programme where they attempted to explain "Bagism" to Eamonn Andrews.

The *Daily Express* reported John as saying: "I am back to work, recording with The Beatles – I need the money . . . I'm scratching the deck, to my way of thinking. Right now, in cash, I have about £50,000."

April 2
John, Yoko and Paul, together with Allen Klein, visited The Beatles' merchant bankers, Henry Ansbacher and Company, to plot a strategy to try and get back Northern Songs for themselves. Their adviser was Mr Bruce Ormrod. It looked an evenly matched fight with ATV and The Beatles controlling about the same number of shares: ATV had acquired 1,604,750 shares from Silver and James, and already held 137,000, giving them nearly 35 per cent of the company. The Beatles between them controlled 29.7 per cent: Paul had the most at 751,000, John had 644,000 and held another 50,000 on trust and Ringo had 40,000. George had sold his but Patti had 1,000. Apple controlled another 30,000 through Subafilms. "Monopoly with real money," John called it. "Businessmen play the game the way we play music, and it's something to see." The Northern Songs saga prompted Paul to write 'You Never Give Me Your Money'.

April 3
John and Yoko appeared on *The Eamonn Andrews Show* live from the Café Royal in Regent Street, where they tried to get Andrews to climb into a white bag with them. Fellow guests Jack Benny and Yehudi Menuhin were not amused.

George was interviewed by Sue McGregor for the lunchtime BBC Radio 1 programme *World At One* in which he discussed Ravi Shankar.

The single 'Badge' by Cream, written by George Harrison and Eric Clapton, was released in the UK as Polydor 2058 285.

April 5
The *Financial Times* reported: "It appears that Dick James, managing director of Northern Songs, has failed to persuade Beatles John Lennon and Paul McCartney to accept the £9 million bid for Northern from ATV."

April 6
The 'Get Back' single is premiered by Radio 1 DJs Alan Freeman and John Peel.

April 7
Disappointed by the way that 'Get Back' sounded on the radio the previous day, Paul oversaw a remix session on the song at Olympic Studios in London.

The single 'Goodbye' (Lennon & McCartney)/'Sparrow' by Mary Hopkin, produced by Paul McCartney, was released in the US as Apple 1806.

April 9
Ringo filmed a boat race scene at Barclays Bank Rowing Club on the Thames Embankment for *The Magic Christian*.

April 10
The Beatles rejected ATV's offer of £9 million for their shares in Northern Songs and announced that they were considering a counter bid (though where they would have obtained the £9.5 million required in real cash is hard to imagine). Lew Grade told the *Daily Telegraph*: "We have 35 per cent of the shares and will not let go of that for anything." The publicity caused market speculators to get in on the act and soon a powerful syndicate of holders of Northern Songs shares was formed known as The Consortium. Between them they had 14 per cent of the shares, enough to swing the outcome, and they met in secret to discuss their strategy.

April 11
The single 'Get Back'/'Don't Let Me Down' by The Beatles, with Billy Preston, was released in the UK as Apple (Parlophone) R 5777.

Paul penned the copy for the press advertisements: " 'Get Back' is The Beatles' new single. It's the first Beatles record which is as live as live can be, in this electronic age. There's no electronic whatchamacallit. 'Get Back' is a pure spring-time rock number. On the other side there's an equally live number called 'Don't Let Me Down'.

"Paul's got this to say about 'Get Back' . . . 'We were sitting in the studio and we made it up out of thin air . . . we started to write words there and then . . . when we finished it, we recorded it at Apple Studios and made it into a song to roller-coast by.'

"P.S. John adds, it's John playing the fab live guitar solo. And now John on 'Don't Let Me Down': John says don't let me down about 'Don't Let Me Down'.

"In 'Get Back' and 'Don't Let Me Down', you'll find The Beatles, as nature intended."

GET BACK
Shortly before his death, John Lennon revealed his long-felt suspicion that this song had been triggered by Paul McCartney's feelings towards Yoko. In fact, as he knew very well, 'Get Back' began life as an ironic comment on British politics. Under its original title of 'No Pakistanis', it satirised the racist views of those who saw Commonwealth immigrants as an invasion force, swamping British culture. Trouble was, the irony was likely to be lost on anyone who wasn't pre-warned, and McCartney regretfully dropped the original lyrics. (His decision was proved right nearly 20 years later when the Sun newspaper got hold of a tape of 'No Pakistanis', and accused The Beatles of racism. Irony is just too complicated for some people.)

In its new form, 'Get Back' was a tight, attractive rocker with lyrics that meant nothing but sounded good – a combination Paul tried to repeat, with rather less success, on Wings' singles like 'Helen Wheels' and 'Junior's Farm'. It featured a rare guitar showcase for John Lennon, who commented wryly: "When Paul was feeling kindly he would give me a solo, and I played the solo on that." Though 'Get Back' was performed on the Apple rooftop on January 30, 1969, the single version was taped in the studio a couple of days earlier, issued as a single in April (after emergency last-minute remixes) and then chopped down for inclusion on the Let It Be *LP* in 1970.

DON'T LET ME DOWN
On the same day as 'Get Back', The Beatles recorded this gloriously spontaneous Lennon love song. For a brief moment, Lennon and McCartney were in perfect synchronisation, both of them keen to escape from the studio trickery and multi-overdubbing of recent Beatles albums. McCartney soon returned to over-production, on Abbey Road, *but Lennon adopted the 'live-in-the-studio' approach as his watchword for the next couple of years.*

April 12
John and Yoko had a meeting at Ansbachers in the City to work out the complicated financing necessary for The Beatles' counter bid for Northern Songs.

The second part of George's interview with David Wigg was broadcast on BBC Radio1's *Scene And Heard.*

April 14
John and Yoko arrived at Paul's house in Cavendish Avenue so that Paul could go over 'The Ballad Of John And Yoko' with John. Despite their business problems, the Lennon and McCartney songwriting partnership was always held in very high regard by both partners, and was a major source of income for both of them. Once the song was complete, they went over to nearby Abbey Road and recorded it, without the aid of the other Beatles (George was abroad and Ringo was filming). Paul played drums, bass, piano and percussion. John did lead vocals and lead guitar.

April 15
More meetings at Ansbachers. At one point Mr Ormrod had persuaded a number of City institutions who owned Northern Songs shares to go in with The Beatles in a deal that would have given The Beatles control but, with the papers all drawn up and waiting for John, Paul, George and Ringo's signature, John announced, "I'm not going to be fucked around by men in suits sitting on their fat arses in the City." The City businessmen decided that they would be better off siding with ATV.

April 16
Abbey Road. The group recorded George's 'Old Brown Shoe' and began work on his 'Something'.

April 17
BBC TV screened a special promo film for 'Get Back' on *Top Of The Pops.*

April 18
Abbey Road. George's 'Old Brown Shoe' completed and further work done on 'I Want You'.

The Beatles, advised by Henry Ansbacher, surprised the City by saying they were bidding for control of Northern Songs only, which caused Northern's share price to drop. Lew Grade announced that he was not considering raising his bid.

April 19
The press found out more details of The Beatles' offer and reported that it was being mounted by three Beatles companies: Apple Corps, Subafilms and John and Paul's Maclen (Music).

April 20
There was a massive row at Ansbacher's because Paul, on Eastman's advice, refused to commit his shares in Northern Songs as part of the collateral required for the loan from Ansbacher's to finance The Beatles' bid. Their offer amounted to £2.1 million of which Ansbacher was lending them about £1.2 million against collateral. John and Paul together could just about manage it, but Paul refused to put up his shares. John's shares in Northern Songs were worth about £1.1 million, Maclen Music was worth just over half a million and Subafilms – which owned rights to *A Hard Day's Night, Help!* and *Yellow Submarine* – was worth about £350,000. Allen Klein had to put in all his shares in MGM:

45,000 shares worth about £650,000. The Beatles were now in a position to finance their bid.

Abbey Road. Work done on 'I Want You' and 'Oh! Darling'.

April 21

John and Yoko formed Bag Productions Limited. The company's affairs were managed by Lennon's assistant, Anthony Fawcett, who later wrote a book about his time with the Lennons.

In the City, the Consortium declared its hand and staged a blocking operation.

April 22

In a short formal ceremony on the roof of the Apple building at 3 Savile Row, John changed his middle name from Winston to Ono by deed poll before Commissioner of Oaths Bueno de Mesquita. John: "Yoko changed her name for me, I've changed mine for her. One for both, both for each other. She has a ring, I have a ring. It gives us nine 'O's between us, which is good luck. Ten would not be good luck." Unfortunately for John, he technically became John Winston Ono Lennon (ten 'O's) as one can never fully revoke a name given at birth.

Abbey Road. John and Yoko taped the heartbeats used on *The Wedding Album*.

April 24

Paul denied a rumour started by an American DJ that he was dead: "I'm as fit as a fiddle," he told *Life* reporters.

In a deal hammered out between Klein and Richenberg, NEMS surrendered its claim to 25 per cent of The Beatles royalties for the next nine years. Instead Triumph received £750,000 cash, 25 per cent of the royalties already frozen by EMI (over £300,000). Triumph received £50,000 for the 23 per cent that NEMS held in The Beatles' film company Subafilms and received 5 per cent of the gross record royalties from 1972 until 1976. This had been a sticking point but in the end Richenberg was satisfied because he knew that Klein would next turn his attention on EMI and obtain a substantial royalty rate increase. The Beatles also received an option on the 4.5 per cent of Northern Songs shares owned by NEMS, useful in the forthcoming battle for Northern Songs, and received 266,000 shares in Triumph in exchange for The Beatles' 10 per cent share in NEMS. Everyone was satisfied with the outcome.

On this same day, The Beatles offered 42s 6d per share for the 20 per cent of Northern Songs shares they needed to gain control. This would have cost them £2,100,000. They also said they would extend their contracts with Northern Songs for a further two years and would add other valuable assets to the company if they gained control. They added that they "would not be happy to continue, let alone renew, their existing contracts with Northern under the aegis of ATV".

BBC1's *Top Of The Pops* showed a clip of The Beatles singing 'Get Back' on the roof of the Apple building.

April 25

John and Yoko attended a showing of their film *Rape* at the Montreux Television Festival in Switzerland.

April 26

Abbey Road. Paul added a lead vocal to 'Oh! Darling' and work began on Ringo's 'Octopus's Garden'.

Dr Richard Asher, Jane Asher's father, was found dead in his Wimpole Street home.

April 27

Abbey Road. John and Yoko made another recording of their heartbeats for use on *The Wedding Album*.

April 29

Abbey Road. Ringo added his lead vocal to 'Octopus's Garden'.

April 30
Abbey Road. New guitar added to 'Let It Be' and the rest of the session spent adding vocals and overdubs to 'You Know My Name (Look Up The Number)'.

The Beatles paid for quarter-page ads in four national newspapers, promising to extend their songwriting services to Northern Songs and saying they would not interfere in its management.

May 1
Abbey Road. A mixing session for 'Oh! Darling' and John and Yoko's heartbeat track 'John And Yoko'.

May 2
Abbey Road. The Beatles worked on George's 'Something'.

John and Yoko were interviewed earlier by Michael Wale at BBC's Lime Grove Studios for the BBC1 television arts programme *How Late It Is*, discussing their film *Rape*. It was broadcast that evening.

ATV claimed that they had support from shareholders holding 45 per cent of the Northern Songs shares and extended their offer until May 15.

May 4
John and Yoko bought a new home, a Georgian mansion in 72 acres of land called "Tittenhurst Park" in Sunninghill in Berkshire, once owned by the tycoon Peter Cadbury. It cost £145,000.

John and Yoko, Paul and Linda, joined Ringo and Maureen at Les Ambassadeurs club in London for a party hosted by Ringo and Peter Sellers to celebrate the completion of the UK filming of *The Magic Christian*. Other guests included Richard Harris, Sean Connery, Stanley Baker, Spike Milligan, George Peppard, Roger Moore and Christopher Lee.

May 5
Olympic Sound Studios, Barnes, London. New bass and guitar added to 'Something'.

The single 'Get Back'/'Don't Let Me Down' by The Beatles with Billy Preston was released in the US as Apple (Capitol) 2490.

John applied for his visitor's visa to the US, withdrawn after his recent drugs conviction, to be reinstated.

May 6
Olympic Sound Studios, Barnes, London. Work began on 'You Never Give Me Your Money', Paul's response to the financial problems at Apple.

May 7
Olympic Studios. The session was spent mixing and listening to playbacks. Earlier, the group met with EMI chief Sir Joseph Lockwood.

John: "A lot of the tracks will be like 'Get Back' and a lot of that we did in one-take kind of things. We've done about 12 tracks, some of them still to be mixed, and Paul and I are working on a kind of montage that we might do as one piece on one side. We've got two weeks to finish the whole thing, so we're really working at it."

May 8
John and Yoko were interviewed by David Wigg for the BBC Radio One programme *Scene and Heard*.

As part of Klein's draconian restructuring of Apple, he sacked Alistair Taylor, the general manager of Apple who had previously been Brian Epstein's personal assistant and who witnessed The Beatles first contract with Epstein. Taylor: "It was a hell of a blow." Paul: "It is not possible to be nice about giving someone the sack."

John, George and Ringo signed a management contract with Allen Klein, in effect making him their manager. Paul held out.

May 9

Olympic Sound Studios, Barnes, London. The Beatles had a very stormy meeting in which Paul continued to hold out against the other three who wanted Allen Klein to manage them for a 20 per cent cut of their earnings. Paul thought 15 per cent would be sufficient ("We're a big act. He'll take 15 per cent"). When Paul refused to sign the relevant documents until he had consulted his lawyer, the others stormed out of the studio, cancelling the planned recording session.

Allen Klein's ABKCO Industries (Allen and Betty Klein Corporation) was duly appointed business manager of The Beatles' companies but Paul all along refused to sign the contract and remained opposed to Klein's involvement in Apple or The Beatles, preferring his own in-laws, The Eastmans. This dispute marked the effective end of The Beatles as a four-man force, despite the fact that they continued to work and record together for a further three months.

Paul stayed behind in the studio and after a long talk with Steve Miller, recorded 'My Dark Hour' with him, on which Paul played drums, bass and did backing vocals. He was credited on the record as "Paul Ramon".

BBC1's *Top Of The Pops* showed a clip of The Beatles singing 'Get Back' on the roof of the Apple building.

May 9

Zapple, Apple Records' new experimental and avant-garde label, was launched with the release of two experimental Beatles solo albums.

The album *Unfinished Music No.2: Life With The Lions* by John Lennon and Yoko Ono, written and produced by John and Yoko, was released in the UK as Zapple 01. Side One: 'Cambridge 1969 ('Song For John', 'Cambridge', 'Lets Go On Flying', 'Snow Is Falling All The Time', 'Mummy's Only Looking For Her Hand In The Snow')'; Side Two: 'No Bed For Beatle John', 'Baby's Heartbeat', 'Two Minutes Silence', 'Radio Play'.

The album *Electronic Sound,* performed and produced by George Harrison was released in the UK as Zapple 02. Side One: 'Under The Mersey Wall'; Side Two: 'No Time Or Space'.

The single 'I Fall Inside Your Eyes' by Jackie Lomax, produced by George Harrison, was released in the UK as Apple 11. (Side A, produced by Jackie Lomax and Mal Evans, featured Ringo on drums.)

May 11

John and Yoko's interview with David Wigg was transmitted by BBC Radio1's *Scene And Heard* programme.

George assisted at the session as former Cream bassist Jack Bruce recorded 'Never Tell Your Mother She's Out Of Tune'.

May 15

Paul was interviewed by Roy Corlett for BBC Radio Merseyside's *Light And Local* programme at his father's house, "Rembrandt", in Heswell, Cheshire.

BBC1's *Top Of The Pops* showed a clip of The Beatles singing 'Get Back' on the roof of the Apple building.

May 16

Ringo and Maureen, Peter Sellers and his wife, director Joe McGrath and producer Denis O'Dell and their wives were given a free trip to New York on the newly launched *Queen Elizabeth II* by Commonwealth United, the backers of *The Magic Christian*, as a reward for bringing in the film on time and under budget.

John and Yoko intended to travel with them but were prevented by the US immigration authorities, who refused to grant John a visitor's visa because of his November 28, 1968 drug conviction.

Paul and Linda flew to Corfu for a holiday, having revealed that Linda was expecting a child later in the year.

BBC Radio Merseyside's *Light And Local* programme transmitted their interview with Paul.

May 18
The second part of John and Yoko's interview with David Wigg was broadcast by BBC Radio 1's *Scene And Heard* programme.

May 19
The album *Is This What You Want?* by Jackie Lomax and produced by George Harrison (except for the third track, 'New Day', with Ringo on drums, which was produced by Jackie Lomax and Mal Evans and replaced the third track, 'How Can You Say Goodbye', on the UK version) was released in the US as Apple ST 3354. All the tracks except the third were the same as the UK release.

LOSING NORTHERN SONGS
Lew Grade's ATV gained control of Northern Songs Limited after a long and bitter battle. John had become disillusioned by the terms of the deal worked out by Ormrod and the Consortium in which the new board would have three representatives from each side with David Platz as the MD. John said he didn't see why The Beatles should bother to take over a company and then be told that they couldn't do what they liked with it. He said that he would rather let Grade have it than be dictated to like this. The company would not have been theirs to play with, of course, since all they were buying was control, and other shareholders were nervous that Klein might finish up running it. The Consortium sided with ATV who got the majority they needed a mere 15 minutes before The Beatles' offer expired. ATV now controlled virtually all of John and Paul's songs, and all future songs until 1973. The Beatles finished up owing Ansbacher's £5,000 for their services.

May 20
John and George had a meeting at Ansbacher's.

May 22
Ringo, Maureen, Peter Sellers and company arrived in New York then flew to the Bahamas for a two-week holiday to celebrate the end of filming.

Hey Jude won the 1968 Ivor Novello Award for top selling British song, while John and Paul also received a special award to mark the popularity of 'Fool On The Hill'.

BBC1's *Top Of The Pops* showed a clip of The Beatles singing 'Get Back' on the roof of the Apple building.

May 23
It was announced that Dick James would continue as MD of Northern Songs and Charles Silver would remain chairman of the board. The Beatles were invited to nominate a board member but declined.

May 24
John and Yoko flew from London to the Bahamas to hold another bed-in for peace at the Sheraton Oceanus Hotel. His choice of the Bahamas was not because Ringo was there, or the pleasant weather, but because it was just off the coast of the US and therefore the American press would be able to cover the event.

May 25
John and Yoko found that the Bahamas were further from the US than they thought, and that 86 degrees Fahrenheit was not the ideal temperature in which to spend a week in bed. They flew instead to Toronto. They were held at the airport for two and a half hours by the immigration authorities but were eventually allowed to enter the country where they spent the night in a Toronto motel.

May 26
The album *Unfinished Music No.2: Life With The Lions* performed, written and produced by John Lennon and Yoko Ono, was released in the US as Zapple ST 3357 with the same tracks as the UK release.

The album *Electronic Sound*, performed and produced by George Harrison was released in the US as Zapple ST 3358 with the same tracks as the UK release.

John and Yoko flew from Toronto to Montreal where they began an eight-day bed-in for peace in room 1742 of the Queen Elizabeth Hotel, handily located for the New York press corps.

May 28

Glyn Johns assembled a working version of the *Get Back* LP for the approval of The Beatles.

John: "We got an acetate each and we called each other and said, 'What do you think? Oh, let it out.' We were going to let it out in really shitty condition. I didn't care. I thought it was good to let it out and show people what had happened to us. 'This is where we're at now, we can't get it together, we don't play together anymore, leave us alone.' But that didn't happen."

May 29

John and Yoko were interviewed by phone over the air by radio station KSAN in San Francisco. They urged peace protestors in the city's People's Park to shun the use of violence.

Among their listeners were members of the psychedelic band Quicksilver Messenger Service, who immediately wrote to the Lennons: "The advice you gave was right on! Violence really does beget violence. It seems as though the issues of the Berkeley Campus over the years have helped make San Francisco the free place it is. But the way the People's Park issue is being handled is not too cool. I know your advice will save a lot of broken bones."

May 30

The single 'The Ballad Of John And Yoko'/'Old Brown Shoe' was released in the UK as Apple (Parlophone) R 5786.

THE BALLAD OF JOHN AND YOKO

"Standing in the dock at Southampton/Trying to get to Holland or France . . ." Songs should be like newspapers, John Lennon said in 1970, and 'The Ballad Of John And Yoko' was just that – a report from the front-line in the battle between, on the one side, the keen-to-be-married Lennons, and on the other, the forces of law and order who didn't want convicted drugs offenders staging bed-ins in their capital cities, thank you very much.

'Instant' was John Lennon's approach to art in 1969 and 1970: his dream was to write a song in the morning, record it that afternoon, mix it at night and have it in the shops by the end of the week. He finally achieved that aim with his own 'Instant Karma!' early in 1970; but 'The Ballad Of John And Yoko' ran it close, being recorded and fully mixed in less than nine hours.

Such was the haste with which the session was arranged that only Paul McCartney was able to meet the call. He played drums to John's acoustic guitar for the basic track, and the two Beatles then overdubbed two lead guitar parts (John), piano (Paul), bass (Paul), percussion (Paul and John) and finally their vocals. The first Beatles song to be mixed solely in stereo – the birth of a new era – also brought another era to an end. Though it was far from the last time Lennon and McCartney worked together in the studio, it was their last major artistic collaboration.

OLD BROWN SHOE

Even when John Lennon was available to play on a Harrison song, an increasingly infrequent event by 1969, his instrumental contribution wasn't used in the final mix – his rhythm guitar losing its place to George's Hammond organ part. Otherwise, George's rocker was a four-man effort, thrown together with seemingly haphazard enthusiasm to create a suitable off-the-cuff flipside for 'The Ballad Of John And Yoko'. Harrison even allowed himself one of his loudest guitar solos on record as a rare moment of self-indulgence.

June

Apple head of A&R, Peter Asher, resigned. He told the press: "When I joined Apple the idea was that it would be different from the other companies in the record business. Its policy was to help people and be generous. It didn't mean actually I had a tremendous amount of freedom; I was always in danger of one Beatle saying : 'Yes, that's a great idea, go ahead,' and then another coming in and saying he didn't know anything about it. But it did mean that it was a nice company to work for. Now that's all changed. There's a new concentrative policy from what I can see and it's lost a great deal of its original feeling."

June 1
John and Yoko's bed-in continued. John, Yoko and a roomful of visitors, including members of the Radha Krishna Temple, Allen Ginsberg, Phil Spector, Abbie Hoffman, rock writer Paul Williams, comedian Tommy Smothers and Timothy Leary, recorded the peace anthem 'Give Peace A Chance'.

George and Patti flew to Sardinia for a holiday.

June 2
The single 'A New Day'/'Thumbin' A Ride' by Jackie Lomax with Ringo on drums on side A, and side B produced by Paul McCartney, was released in the US as Apple 1807.

The last day of John and Yoko's bed-in ended in the afternoon when John and Yoko went to Ottawa for a university conference on peace. In the evening they flew back to London – a journey interrupted in Frankfurt, where the German immigration authorities briefly refused to allow the Lennons to change planes on their soil.

June 4
The single 'The Ballad Of John And Yoko'/'Old Brown Shoe' was released in the US as Apple (Capitol) 2531. Many radio stations refused to air 'The Ballad Of John And Yoko', complaining that its lyrics were "blasphemous".

June 14
John and Yoko pre-recorded an appearance for the US edition of *The David Frost Show* recorded with a studio audience at InterTel Studios, Wembley.

John: "We got a really fantastic movie out of making our next LP. It really is incredible – just the sweat and strain of four guys making an album. It's being pared down to about four hours. It could make a major movie."

Around this time, John announced that Yoko was again pregnant, and that regardless of its sex, the child would be named Amsterdam, in honour of the couple's recent bed-in.

June 16
The single 'My Dark Hour' by The Steve Miller Band with Paul McCartney (as Paul Ramon) on bass guitar, drums and backing vocals, was released in the US as Capitol 2520.

June 17
Paul and Linda returned from their holiday in Corfu.

Kenneth Tynan's musical play *Oh! Calcutta!* opened at the Eden Theater in New York. One of its scenes, a masturbation fantasy entitled 'Four In Hand', was credited in the programme as being based on an idea by John.

June 22
John and Yoko were interviewed about their peace campaign on Radio Luxembourg.

June 23
George and Patti returned from their holiday in Sardinia.

Ringo shot a scene near the National Film Theatre on the South Bank in which paper money was thrown into a huge tank full of slaughterhouse offal and manure.

June 27
Ringo and Maureen flew to the south of France for a holiday.

The single 'That's The Way God Planned It'/'What About You?' by Billy Preston and produced by George Harrison was released in the UK as Apple 12.

June 29
John, Yoko, Kyoko and John's son Julian began a motoring holiday in Scotland.

July 1
Abbey Road. *Abbey Road* sessions. Paul added a new lead vocal to 'You Never Give Me Your Money'.

John and Yoko were involved in a car crash in Golspie, in the north of Scotland, when John let the car go out of control. They were taken to the Lawson Memorial Hospital where John had 17 stitches in a facial wound, Yoko 14 stitches and Kyoko four. John's son Julian was suffering from shock and they were all detained in hospital.

July 2
Abbey Road. *Abbey Road* sessions. Paul recorded the 'Her Majesty' fragment which was to end *Abbey Road*. When George and Ringo arrived they all worked on 'Golden Slumbers'/'Carry That Weight'.

Cynthia Lennon arrived in Scotland to tell John what she thought of him and to take Julian back to London.

July 3
Abbey Road. *Abbey Road* sessions. More work done on 'Golden Slumbers'/'Carry That Weight'.

With John and Yoko still in hospital, Ringo and Maureen substituted for them at the launch party for The Plastic Ono Band's 'Give Peace A Chance' single at the Chelsea Town Hall, London.

July 4
Abbey Road. *Abbey Road* sessions. More work on 'Golden Slumbers'/'Carry That Weight'.

The single 'Give Peace A Chance' (Lennon & McCartney)/'Remember Love' (Yoko Ono) by The Plastic Ono Band and produced by John and Yoko was released in the UK as Apple 13.

John sent Apple's Derek Taylor a mock begging letter from his hospital bed, signed "Jack McCripple (ex-seamen)".

July 5
Paul joined the crowd of more than 250,000 spectators watching The Rolling Stones' free concert in London's Hyde Park. Despite persistent rumours before the event, none of The Beatles joined The Stones on stage.

July 6
John and Yoko chartered a helicopter to transfer them to a private jet for the flight back to London. The helicopter left from the lawn of the Lawson Memorial Hospital with the staff waving goodbye. The smashed car was crushed into a cube and exhibited on the lawn of Tittenhurst Park.

July 7
Abbey Road. *Abbey Road* sessions. The three Beatles, John at home recovering from his car crash, worked on 'Here Comes The Sun'.

The single 'That's The Way God Planned It'/'How About You?' by Billy Preston and produced by George Harrison was released in the US as Apple 1808.

The single 'Give Peace A Chance'(Lennon & McCartney)/'Remember Love' (Ono) was released in the US as Apple 1809.

July 8
Abbey Road. *Abbey Road* sessions. More work on 'Here Comes The Sun'.

July 9
Abbey Road. *Abbey Road* sessions. John arrived back in the studio and worked on Paul's 'Maxwell's Silver Hammer'. Yoko, more seriously injured than John, accompanied him as usual. A double bed was delivered to the studio by Harrods and Yoko lay in it, a microphone suspended above her mouth in case she wanted to add her thoughts.

The first acetate copies of the *Get Back* album were sent out to potential reviewers in the UK.

July 10
Abbey Road. *Abbey Road* sessions. Overdubs added to 'Maxwell's Silver Hammer'.
  John and Yoko's appearance on *The David Frost Show*, recorded on June 14th, was broadcast on US TV.

July 11
Abbey Road. *Abbey Road* sessions. More overdubs added to 'Maxwell's Silver Hammer' (Ringo played anvil), and work done on 'Something' and 'You Never Give Me Your Money'.

July 13
Paul supervised a recording session with Mary Hopkin at Apple Studios. Sessions continued intermittently between Paul's Beatles commitments over the next two weeks.

July 15
Abbey Road. *Abbey Road* sessions. The vocals and chimes were overdubbed and added to 'You Never Give Me Your Money'.

July 16
Abbey Road. *Abbey Road* sessions. More work on 'Here Comes The Sun' and 'Something'.

July 17
Abbey Road. *Abbey Road* sessions. Paul added his lead vocal to 'Oh! Darling' followed by all The Beatles working on Ringo's 'Octopus's Garden'.

July 18
Abbey Road. *Abbey Road* sessions. Paul had another try at the lead vocal to 'Oh! Darling' followed by Ringo's vocal on 'Octopus's Garden.'
  The single 'My Dark Hour' by The Steve Miller Band, with Paul McCartney as Paul Ramon, was released in the UK as Capitol CL 15604.
  The EP *Wall's Ice Cream* with 'Little Yellow Pills' by Jackie Lomax, produced by George Harrison, and 'Happiness Runs (Pebble And The Man)' by Mary Hopkin, produced by Paul McCartney, was released in the UK as Apple CT I, as an Apple special business promotion.
  The single 'Penina' by Carlos Mendes, written by Paul, was released in Portugal as Parlophone QMSP 16459.

July 21
Abbey Road. *Abbey Road* sessions. Work began on John's 'Come Together'.

July 22
Abbey Road. *Abbey Road* sessions. Paul had another try at the vocal on 'Oh! Darling' then the group worked on John's 'Come Together'.

July 23
Abbey Road. *Abbey Road* sessions. Rehearsals and recording of 'The End'.

July 24
Abbey Road. *Abbey Road* sessions. First Paul cut a demo of 'Come And Get It' for Apple band, the Iveys, soon to change their name to Badfinger. Then The Beatles recorded 'Sun King'/'Mean Mister Mustard'.

July 25
Abbey Road. *Abbey Road* sessions. More work on 'Sun King'/'Mean Mr. Mustard' and 'Sun King'. Then they began work on John's 'Polythene Pam' and Paul's 'She Came In Through The Bathroom Window', recording them as one continuous number.

July 26
George gave a short radio interview to promote a forthcoming peace march in Hyde Park.

July 27

To the disappointment of the organisers, George failed to join Patti at the head of the Hyde Park peace march.

July 28

Abbey Road. *Abbey Road* sessions. More work on 'Polythene Pam'/'She Came In Through The Bathroom Window'.

July 29

Abbey Road. *Abbey Road* sessions. Guitar was added to 'Come Together' and work done on 'Sun King'/'Mean Mr. Mustard'.

July 30

Abbey Road. *Abbey Road* sessions. An overdub day working on 'Come Together', 'Polythene Pam'/'She Came In Through The Bathroom Window', 'You Never Give Me Your Money' and 'Golden Slumbers'/'Carry That Weight'. After this they worked on a trial order for the medley, and Paul rejected 'Her Majesty' from the set, asking the tape operator John Kurlander to edit it out and throw it away. EMI threw away nothing so he attached it to the end of the master tape on a long piece of leader tape. When an acetate was cut, the long gap, followed by 'Her Majesty' remained and Paul liked it that way, so it stayed.

July 31

Abbey Road. *Abbey Road* sessions. 'You Never Give Me Your Money' was completed and overdubs added to 'Golden Slumbers'/'Carry That Weight'.

August 1

Abbey Road. *Abbey Road* sessions. Work began on John's ballad 'Because'.

August 3

Ringo and Maureen, accompanied by Mal and Lil Evans, attended a concert at the London Palladium by country singer Hank Snow. After the show, Snow was photographed with Ringo backstage.

August 4

Abbey Road. *Abbey Road* sessions. The three part harmonies on 'Because' were recorded.

August 5

Abbey Road. *Abbey Road* sessions. Paul put the loop tapes for the crossfade from 'You Never Give Me Your Money' to 'Sun King' onto four-track. 'Because' was completed by George playing the Moog synthesiser and vocals were added to 'The End'.

August 6

Abbey Road. *Abbey Road* sessions. George added guitar to 'Here Comes The Sun' and Paul added synthesiser to 'Maxwell's Silver Hammer'.

August 7

Abbey Road. *Abbey Road* sessions. Work on 'The End'. First vocals were added then a guitar track with Paul, George and John trading solos.

August 8

Abbey Road.

THE *ABBEY ROAD* SLEEVE

At 11.35am, with a policeman holding up the traffic, photographer Iain Macmillan climbed up a stepladder in the middle of Abbey Road and shot the now famous photograph of The Beatles walking across the zebra crossing near the recording studio. It was a hot day so Paul was not wearing shoes. The cover had been Paul's idea – he drew a sketch of how he wanted the

photograph to look – and when the transparencies were developed, he was the one who chose which shot to use.

Abbey Road sessions: After lunch, in the studio, new drums and bass were added to 'The End', work was done on 'I Want You' and Paul added lead guitar to 'Oh! Darling'.

August 11
Abbey Road. *Abbey Road* sessions. Further work on 'I Want You', to which 'She's So Heavy' was added. More work was done on 'Oh! Darling' and 'Here Comes The Sun'.
John and Yoko moved into their new mansion at Tittenhurst Park, Ascot.

August 12
Abbey Road. *Abbey Road* sessions. Mixing session.

August 13
Abbey Road. *Abbey Road* sessions. Mixing session.

August 14
Abbey Road. *Abbey Road* sessions. Editing work done on the medley. John was interviewed at the studio by Kenny Everett for his BBC Radio 1 show *Everett Is Here*.

August 15
Abbey Road. *Abbey Road* sessions. Orchestral overdubs were added to 'Golden Slumbers'/'Carry That Weight', 'The End', 'Something' and 'Here Comes The Sun'.

August 17
Paul produced Mary Hopkin's rendition of 'Que Sera Sera' as a possible future single.

August 18
Abbey Road. *Abbey Road* sessions. Paul added piano to 'The End.'

August 19
Abbey Road. *Abbey Road* sessions. 'Here Comes The Sun' and 'Something' were completed.

August 20
Abbey Road. *Abbey Road* sessions. John's 'I Want You (She's So Heavy)' was completed, with its abrupt ending, made by literally cutting the tape. After this The Beatles listened to the tracks in the proposed running order for the album. This was the last time that all four Beatles were together in Abbey Road.

August 21
Abbey Road. *Abbey Road* sessions. A mixing and editing session.
Apple Corps' first annual general meeting was held at 3 Savile Row with all four Beatles in attendance.
Adagrose Ltd. changed its name to McCartney Productions Limited.

August 22
The Beatles posed together for a photo session in the grounds of Tittenhurst Park. It was the last ever Beatles photo shoot, and their last appearance together at any Beatles event.
The single 'Hare Krishna Mantra'/'Prayer To The Spiritual Masters' by Radha Krishna Temple, produced by George Harrison, was released in the US as Apple 1810.
The album *That's The Way God Planned It* by Billy Preston and produced by George Harrison was released in the UK as Apple SAPCOR 9.

August 25
Abbey Road. *Abbey Road* sessions. Final editing on tracks for the medley.

August 26
George and Mal Evans drove to Portsmouth to meet Bob Dylan, who had arrived in the UK for his headlining appearance at the Isle of Wight Festival.

August 27
As part of the deal struck on April 24, The Beatles sold Triumph their shares in NEMS Enterprises Limited.

August 28
Paul and Linda's daughter Mary was born at Avenue Clinic, London.
  George and several bus loads of journalists attended the Apple press launch of the Radha Krishna Temple's first recording 'Hare Krishna Mantra', in the gardens of a large country house in Sydenham, south London. Indian food was served but no alcohol.
  After this event, the Harrisons drove back to Portsmouth, and then caught the ferry to the Isle of Wight, to spend more time with Bob Dylan and his family.

August 29
The single 'Hare Krishna Mantra'/'Prayer To The Spiritual Masters' by Radha Krishna Temple and produced by George Harrison was released in the UK as Apple 15.
  The album *Songs For A Tailor* by Jack Bruce and featuring George Harrison (as L'Angelo Misterioso) on track one, 'Never Tell Your Mother She's Out Of Time', was released in the UK as Polydor 583-058.

August 30
Ringo and Maureen, John and Yoko travelled to the Isle of Wight for the next day's Dylan concert.

August 31
All The Beatles, except Paul, saw Bob Dylan & The Band headline at the Isle of Wight outdoor festival.

September 1
After the Isle of Wight festival, Bob Dylan returned to Tittenhurst Park with John and Yoko but refused to join in a recording session.

September 5
John and George resigned as directors of Hayling Supermarkets Limited.

September 8
Ringo was taken to the Middlesex Hospital, central London, suffering from an intestinal complaint and kept in for observation.

September 10
The album *That's The Way God Planned It* by Billy Preston and produced by George Harrison was released in the US as Apple ST 3359 with the same tracks as the UK release.
  The Institute of Contemporary Arts held an evening of John and Yoko's avant-garde films, including the premiere of *Self Portrait* (an entertaining study of John's penis in the process of becoming erect). Also screened were *Rape, John And Yoko's Honeymoon, Two Virgins, Smile* and *Folding*. John and Yoko sent a couple to sit in a white bag on stage beneath the screen throughout the screening, thought by many people to be the Lennons themselves. The event was billed thus: "John and Yoko's evening of film events will end towards midnight. It will happen once. It will be what they want it to be."
  Around this time, John and Yoko produced another film, *Apotheosis*, capturing the ascent of a helium-filled balloon. A follow-up, logically entitled *Apotheosis 2*, was filmed later in the year.

September 11
John visited Abbey Road to remove the master tape of The Beatles' 'What's The New Mary Jane', with the intention of releasing it as a solo single.

Later that day, during a meeting at Apple, John informed Allen Klein that he was quitting The Beatles.

September 12

Rock promoter John Brower telephoned John and Yoko to invite them to attend the Toronto Rock'n'Roll Revival concert the next day to hear Little Richard, Chuck Berry and Jerry Lee Lewis, offering eight first-class tickets for them and six friends. John immediately agreed provided he and his band could play live. The astonished promoter accepted at once and, since John had no band – The Beatles had not played live in three years – he had to form one quick. He summoned together Eric Clapton, Klaus Voormann and session drummer Alan White. Mal Evans was informed that he was handling the gear. Brower dealt with visas and immigration, still unable to believe that he had attracted a Beatle to his festival.

September 13

PLASTIC ONO BAND LIVE IN TORONTO

John woke up and wanted to back out of the Toronto concert but Clapton said he was keen to play. John just made the plane and during the flight he made a half-hearted attempt to rehearse a few songs with The Plastic Ono Band, as he dubbed them. Meanwhile the Canadian radio stations were going wild and there were several hundred fans waiting at the airport, reminiscent of the old days.

They hastily rehearsed a few songs and before going on stage at the Varsity Stadium of Toronto University, John was so nervous he threw up. The Plastic Ono Band stuck to classics: 'Blue Suede Shoes', 'Money', 'Dizzy Miss Lizzy', 'Yer Blues', 'Cold Turkey' and 'Give Peace A Chance'.

John: "The ridiculous thing was that I didn't know any of the lyrics. When we did 'Money' and 'Dizzy' I just made up the words as I went along. The band was bashing it out like hell behind me. Yoko came up on stage with us, but she wasn't going to do her bit until we'd done our five songs. Then after 'Money' there was a stop, and I turned to Eric and said 'What's next?' He just shrugged, so I screamed 'C'mon!' and started into something else. We did 'Yer Blues' because I've done that with Eric before. It blew our minds. Meanwhile Yoko had whipped offstage to get some lyrics out of her white bag. Then we went into 'Give Peace A Chance' which was just unbelievable. I was making up the words as we went along. I didn't have a clue."

Backstage, John met several of his 1950s rock heroes, including Little Richard, Jerry Lee Lewis and Gene Vincent, who clung drunkenly to his arm, saying: "Remember the old days, John?"

September 16

Maclen (Music) Limited instigated legal proceedings against Northern Songs Limited requesting a re-audit of royalty statements from February 11, 1965 onwards. This was an area that Klein specialised in, and nearly always came up trumps.

September 19

The single 'Que Sera Sera'/'Fields Of St Etienne' by Mary Hopkin and produced by Paul McCartney was released in France as Apple 16.

Paul was interviewed by David Wigg for the BBC Radio1 *Scene And Heard* programme.

BBC2's *Late Night Line-Up* previewed the entire *Abbey Road* album.

Lew Grade's ATV bought sufficient shares in Northern Songs from the Consortium to give it just under 50 per cent. The Beatles had lost control of their publishing but Klein and Grade got on extremely well and got together to work out a new deal to bring The Beatles back into the Northern Songs stable. ATV would buy all their Northern Songs shares in exchange for stock and cash – so they would have stock in ATV, which controlled their songs. They would re-sign as songwriters until 1976. Maclen would be sold back to John and Paul and Apple would get the lucrative sub-publishing rights for the US. It was a very good deal but because The Eastmans would have nothing to do with Klein, it too fell through.

September 20

Allen Klein negotiated a tough new contract for The Beatles with EMI/Capitol giving them an increased royalty rate. Though their contract was not due to expire until 1976, the group had virtually fulfilled the minimum provision of five long-playing records and five singles and so Klein was in a strong bargaining position.

Their previous deal with Capitol was already very good: 17.5 per cent of wholesale in the US, but Klein managed to get them 25 per cent. Paul gave credit where it was due and signed the contract along with Ringo and John. George was in Cheshire visiting his sick mother but he returned a few days later and added his signature.

At the meeting John and Yoko made Klein the business manager of their company, Bag Productions.

JOHN QUITS

John also used the meeting to finally tell the other Beatles that he was leaving the group:

John: "I said to Paul, 'I'm leaving.' I knew on the flight over to Toronto or before we went to Toronto: I told Allen I was leaving, I told Eric Clapton and Klaus that I was leaving then, but that I would probably like to use them as a group. I hadn't decided how to do it – to have a permanent new group or what – then later on, I thought fuck, I'm not going to get stuck with another set of people, whoever they are.

"I announced it to myself and the people around me on the way to Toronto a few days before. And on the plane – Klein came with me – I told Allen, 'It's all over.' When I got back, there were a few meetings, and Allen said well, cool it, cool it, there was a lot to do, business-wise you know, and it would not have been suitable at the time.

"Then we were discussing something in the office with Paul, and Paul said something or other about The Beatles doing something, and I kept saying, 'No, no, no,' to everything he said. So it came to a point where I had to say something, of course, and Paul said, 'What do you mean?'

"I said, 'I mean the group is over, I'm leaving.' Allen was saying don't tell. He didn't want me to tell Paul even. So I said, 'It's out.' I couldn't stop it, it came out. Paul and Allen both said that they were glad that I wasn't going to announce it, that I wasn't going to make an event out of it. I don't know whether Paul said don't tell anybody, but he was darned pleased that I wasn't going to. He said, 'Oh, that means nothing's really happened if you're not going to say anything.'

"So that's what happened. So, like anybody when you say divorce, their face goes all sorts of colours. It's like he knew really that this was the final thing; and six months later he comes out with whatever. I was a fool not to do it, not to do what Paul did, which was use it to sell a record."

Kenny Everett's BBC Radio 1 show *Everett Is Here* broadcast the first part of its interview with John.

September 21

The first part of David Wigg's interview with Paul for the BBC Radio 1 *Scene And Heard* programme was broadcast.

The single 'Badge' by Cream and written by George Harrison and Eric Clapton was reissued in the UK (Polydor 2058–285).

September 25

Abbey Road. John and Yoko supervised stereo mixes of their Toronto concert for release: 'Blue Suede Shoes', 'Money (That's What I Want)', 'Dizzy Miss Lizzy', 'Yer Blues', 'Cold Turkey', 'Give Peace A Chance', 'Don't Worry Kyoko (Mummy's Only Looking For Her Hand In The Snow)' and 'John, John (Let's Hope For Peace)'.

John and Yoko attended a lunch time press reception at Apple Studios for the launch of Trash's new single 'Golden Slumbers', a Lennon & McCartney song taken from *Abbey Road*.

Afterwards John and Yoko, with The Plastic Ono Band (John on guitar and vocals, Yoko on whatever, Eric Clapton on guitar, Klaus Voormann on bass and Ringo on drums) returned to Abbey Road where they recorded 'Cold Turkey'. John had originally offered the song to The Beatles, but Paul had turned it down.

September 26
The album *Abbey Road* was released in the UK as Apple (Parlophone) PCS 7088 (stereo only). Side A: 'Come Together', 'Something', 'Maxwell's Silver Hammer', 'Oh! Darling', 'Octopus's Garden', 'I Want You (She's So Heavy)'; Side B: 'Here Comes The Sun', 'Because', 'You Never Give Me Your Money', 'Sun King'/'Mean Mr. Mustard', 'Polythene Pam'/'She Came In Through The Bathroom Window', 'Golden Slumbers'/'Carry That Weight', 'The End', 'Her Majesty'.

Radio Luxembourg broadcast an interview with Ringo by Kid Jensen, talking about *Abbey Road*.

ABBEY ROAD
The Beatles finished work on *The White Album* in October 1968. It was released in November, followed in January 1969 by the *Yellow Submarine* soundtrack LP. That month, The Beatles also recorded what eventually became the *Let It Be* LP. And three weeks after the end of the basic sessions for that record, the group began work on another new album.

Within the space of a year, then, The Beatles recorded or released around 60 new songs. So you'd expect the last of these albums to suffer in the songwriting stakes. *Abbey Road* may have its throwaways, especially in the lengthy medley on the original second side of the LP, but many fans regard it as the best album The Beatles ever made. It's also their best selling album.

That isn't a view that John Lennon would have backed, though. He regarded the album as contrived, a deliberate repair-job on The Beatles' image after the disastrous *Let It Be* sessions. Producer George Martin had a more balanced view of *Abbey Road*: "That whole album was a compromise. One side was a whole series of titles which John preferred and the other side was a programme Paul and I preferred. I had been trying to get them to think in symphonic terms and think of the entire shape of the album and getting some form to it – symphonic things like bringing songs back in counterpoint to other songs, actually shaped things. And I think if we had gone on making records, that was the way I would have done it. But we were already breaking up. *Abbey Road* was the death knell."

Martin's admission that he sided with Paul's concept for the record rather than John's is a tacit admission that the trio's working relationship had become irretrievably fragile. Lennon's response was virtually to withdraw from the sessions. *Abbey Road* is very much a McCartney album, with strong cameos from George Harrison: Lennon's material either sat uneasily alongside the rest of the songs, or else was little more than hackwork.

And yet: The Beatles never played or sang together more brilliantly than they did on *Abbey Road*. In particular, the much-maligned Side Two medley – assembled from a collection of vignettes – is instrumentally tighter than anything they'd cut since *Revolver*. And never had The Beatles' harmony vocals been more inventive, or stunningly precise, than on this record. Countless times on the album there are moments of pure beauty, proof that art can sometimes force its way to the surface almost against the wishes of its creators.

COME TOGETHER
During the Lennons' Toronto bed-in in May 1969, one visitor to their humble hotel room was Timothy Leary, LSD guru and would-be liberator of the world's collective mind. Leary had decided to run for Congress, or the Senate, or anywhere that would have him, and had decided on a campaign slogan: 'Come together'. Knowing Lennon to have been a keen user of his favourite drug, Leary commissioned John to write a song of that title, which his followers could sing on the campaign trail.

Lennon did as he was asked, and came up with a banal ditty along the lines of "Come together and join the party". Then Leary went to jail. Lennon reckoned his obligations had now expired, and used the "come together" idea for himself. Instead of a political anthem, 'Come Together' became a celebration of marital sex, with verses that free-associated Chuck Berry style. (In fact, Lennon borrowed a little too blatantly from Berry's 'You Can't Catch Me', sparking a legal dispute that was still affecting his career six years later.)

In the studio, Lennon prefaced the song with a whispered refrain of "shoot" – which gained an unwelcome dose of irony 11 years later. The Beatles' version never quite caught fire, however, and Lennon remained fonder of the live remake he taped in 1972 at Madison Square Garden.

SOMETHING

What Frank Sinatra called "the greatest love song ever written", and he'd sung a few in his time, began life in 1968, when George Harrison listened to a track on one of the first batch of Apple Records LPs. The track in question was James Taylor's 'Something In The Way She Moves', and Harrison soon built a song around the phrase – little realising that it would become his best-known and most lucrative composition.

After recording a solo demo of 'Something' in February 1969, Harrison brought it to the Abbey Road sessions in April. An initial attempt to cut the backing track was rejected; so the band, plus Billy Preston, regrouped early in May. At that point, the track lasted nearly eight minutes, ending in a rather low-key instrumental jam which was subsequently edited out of the mix. Sporadically over the next two months, Harrison added to the basic track, the final session featuring overdubs from 21 string players.

As he did later with 'My Sweet Lord' and 'All Things Must Pass', George had already given one of his best songs away to a friend by the time he recorded it himself. The recipient this time was Joe Cocker, though luckily for The Beatles his version appeared only after theirs. The Beatles' rendition, meanwhile, went on to become the first UK single pulled from one of their previously released albums, plus Harrison's first Beatles A-side.

The song reached a wider currency via Sinatra's regular performances. Tailoring the lyric to his own needs, Ol' Blue Eyes rewrote part of the middle section: "You stick around, Jack, she might show". Amused by this bastardisation of his work, George retained Sinatra's phrasing when he performed the song live in the early Nineties.

MAXWELL'S SILVER HAMMER

To judge from the general level of enthusiasm on display when the song is performed in the Let It Be movie, no one had much time for 'Maxwell's Silver Hammer' apart from its composer, Paul McCartney. A novelty song about a serial killer, it was distinguished by its blatant commercial appeal, and for its subtle use of a prototype Moog synthesiser by Paul.

OH! DARLING

To his dying day, John Lennon resented the fact that Paul McCartney didn't ask him to sing the throat-shredding lead vocal on this Fifties-styled rocker. At session after session, in fact, McCartney would arrive early to attempt a take before his voice lost its flexibility. Eventually he nailed it, completing a performance that later inspired a 'tribute' of sorts, in the shape of 10cc's 'Oh Donna'.

OCTOPUS'S GARDEN

As seen in the Let It Be movie, Ringo Starr arrived at the Apple Studios one day with the idea for a song. George Harrison turned it into one, rewriting the chord sequence, and suggesting ways in which the melody could be improved. With no egos at stake when a Ringo song was on the menu, The Beatles lent themselves wholeheartedly to the playful spirit of the song. Ringo revived memories of 'Yellow Submarine' with some suitably aquatic sound effects.

I WANT YOU (SHE'S SO HEAVY)

The first of the Abbey Road songs to be started was one of the last to be finished – and also the only Lennon composition on the album that sounded as if it came from the heart. Deliberately unpoetic, it was a simple cry of love for Yoko Ono, with a bluesy verse (based around the rhythm of the mid-Sixties Mel Torme hit, 'Coming Home Baby') locked to a relentless, multi-overdub guitar riff, concocted by Lennon and Harrison.

Besides the relentless plod of the guitar battalions, the closing minutes of the track resounded to the hiss and moan of the Moog synthesiser, adding an unearthly menace to what began as a simple song of love and lust.

HERE COMES THE SUN

Faced with a day of business meetings at Apple, George Harrison repaired to Eric Clapton's garden, where he wrote this beautiful song around some simple variations on a D-chord. Another instant classic to set alongside 'Something', it revealed Harrison as the dark horse of the group, rapidly rivalling his more prestigious bandmates. Once again, some delicate Moog touches enhanced the final mix.

BECAUSE

Though John Lennon later nailed this track as "a terrible arrangement", most fans regard it as one of the highlights of Abbey Road – both for the beauty of its lyrics (a pantheistic vision that was closer to romantic poetry than acid-inspired fantasy) and for the stunning three-part harmonies of Harrison, Lennon and McCartney. Lennon wrote the song around a piano riff he found when he asked Yoko to play Beethoven's 'Moonlight Sonata' – backwards.

YOU NEVER GIVE ME YOUR MONEY

"Abbey Road was really unfinished songs all stuck together," complained John Lennon in 1980. "Everybody praises the album so much, but none of the songs had anything to do with each other, no thread at all, only the fact that we stuck them together."

That's true, but it ignores the fact that the medley – which began with this song, and climaxed some fifteen minutes later with 'The End' – was great pop music, with a cascade of hooks, mini-choruses and themes interlocking to produce a tapestry of melody and sound.

'You Never Give Me Your Money' is the strongest of the medley songs. It began life as an ironic comment on The Beatles' business disputes, and achieved the same oblique lyrical significance as McCartney's best songs on Pepper. Within four minutes, it moves through five distinct sections without once appearing contrived.

SUN KING

'Sun King' revamped the guitar picking technique Lennon had used on 'Julia' the previous year, matched with the vocal harmonies of 'Because'. The song was a complete throwaway – most of the lyrics were mock-Spanish gobbledegook – but it sounded wonderful.

MEAN MR. MUSTARD

Originally up for consideration for The White Album, 'Mean Mr. Mustard' was a Lennon fantasy which he'd based around a newspaper story about a notorious miser. Though it has an entirely different feel to 'Sun King', the two songs were recorded together as one musical piece, under the working title of 'Here Comes The Sun-King'.

POLYTHENE PAM

Demonstrating that the medley was planned from the start, 'Polythene Pam' and 'She Came In Through The Bathroom Window' were also recorded as one. 'Polythene Pam', showing off John Lennon's best Scouser accent, was based loosely around a character he'd met in a near-orgy the previous year. It led seamlessly into . . .

SHE CAME IN THROUGH THE BATHROOM WINDOW

Like its companion piece, 'She Came In Through The Bathroom Window' was loosely autobiographical – the spur this time being an attempted robbery at Paul McCartney's house, in which a fan had climbed in through aforesaid window in search of first-hand souvenirs. And like 'Something', a cover of this song ended up on Joe Cocker's second album, part of The Beatles' thank-you for Cocker's remarkable interpretation of 'With A Little Help From My Friends'.

GOLDEN SLUMBERS

Thomas Dekker's 17th century lullaby took musical shape in Paul McCartney's hand, with one of those melodies that was entirely original but sounded on first hearing as if you'd known it your entire life. Once again, the song was recorded from the start as part of a medley with . . .

CARRY THAT WEIGHT

Another McCartney composition, this reprised some of the lyrical and musical themes of 'You Never Give Me Your Money', and featured mass vocals from McCartney, Harrison and Starr. Lennon missed the sessions for this song, being otherwise detained in a Scottish hospital after a car crash.

THE END

'Carry That Weight' sounds as if it had been taped at the same time as 'The End', but the latter was actually inserted over the fade-out of 'Carry That Weight' as an entirely separate recording. It features two lines of vocals, the second of which became something of a valediction to The Beatles: "And in the end, the love you make is equal to the love you take".

There was Ringo's one and only drum solo on record, and a lengthy guitar section which featured interplay between Harrison, Lennon and McCartney. An orchestra was added to the final seconds of the song – all part of the extravaganza which provided a fitting finale to The Beatles' longest and most carefully structured suite of songs.

HER MAJESTY

It wasn't quite 'The End', though. At the close of a tape carrying a rough mix of the second side of the album, engineer John Kurlander inserted a brief 20-second ditty which had originally been meant to appear between 'Mean Mr. Mustard' and 'Polythene Pam', until Paul McCartney decided he wanted it removed. When another engineer, Malcolm Davies, cut an acetate of the side, he assumed 'Her Majesty' was meant to be the final track. Paul liked the surprise element of including the song on the album – even though it began with the final chord of 'Mean Mr Mustard', while its own final chord was missing, hidden beneath the opening flurry of 'Polythene Pam'. Just as the chaos of 'You Know My Name (Look Up The Number)' brought The Beatles' singles career to a tongue-in-cheek close, 'Her Majesty' prevented anyone from claiming that the group's lengthy Abbey Road medley was a sign of pomposity.

September 27
Kenny Everett's BBC Radio1 show *Everett Is Here* broadcast the second part of its interview with John.

An interview with John by Kid Jensen was broadcast on Radio Luxembourg.

September 28
Trident Studios, Soho. The Plastic Ono Band, with the same line-up as on September 25, re-cut 'Cold Turkey'.

The second part of David Wigg's interview with Paul for the BBC Radio 1 *Scene And Heard* programme was broadcast.

September 29
Abbey Road. John supervised the mixing of 'Cold Turkey'.

October 1
The album *Abbey Road* was released in the US as Apple (Capitol) SO 383 (stereo only), with the same tracks as the UK release.

The release of the album coincided with a US media frenzy inspired by the rumour that Paul had died in 1966, and had since been replaced by a lookalike imposter, one 'William Campbell'. The more vehemently Apple denied the story, the more it was believed by gullible fans. The net result was to ensure that *Abbey Road* sold more quickly than any album since the height of Beatlemania in 1964.

John watched on TV as demonstrators at the Vietnam Moratorium Day in New York chanted his song 'Give Peace A Chance' – the first time the song had been co-opted as a peace anthem.

October 3
Lansdowne Studios, London. A studio version of Yoko's 'Don't Worry Kyoko (Mummy's Only Looking For Her Hand In The Snow)' was recorded by The Plastic Ono Band as the B-side of 'Cold Turkey'.

October 5
Abbey Road. Overdubs put on The Plastic Ono Band's 'Cold Turkey'.

October 6
The single 'Something'/'Come Together' was released in the US as Apple (Capitol) 2654.

The album *Songs For A Tailor* by Jack Bruce, featuring George Harrison as L'Angelo Misterioso on 'Never Tell Your Mother She's Out Of Time', was released in the US as ATCO SD–306.

October 8
George recorded an interview with David Wigg at Apple for the BBC Radio 1 programme *Scene And Heard*.

October 9
Yoko was taken to King's College Hospital, London, on John's 29th birthday, for emergency blood transfusions when it seemed she might lose another baby. John stayed at her bedside throughout. She and John had not long gone through a cold turkey withdrawal from heroin addiction.

October 12
After four days in hospital, with John still at her side, Yoko miscarried her expected baby.
    The first part of David Wigg's interview with George for the BBC Radio1 programme *Scene And Heard* was broadcast.

October 13
Paul and Linda, Ringo and Maureen attended the opening night of Mary Hopkin's cabaret season at the Savoy Hotel, London.

October 15
Ringo and Maureen flew from London to Los Angeles.
    John and Yoko set out on a brief Mediterranean cruise with "Magic" Alex Mardas, to reinforce their decision to quit heroin, and to allow Yoko to recuperate after her miscarriage.

October 17
The single 'Everything's All Right' by Billy Preston and produced by George Harrison was released in the UK as Apple 19.

October 19
The second part of David Wigg's interview with George for the BBC Radio 1 programme *Scene And Heard* was broadcast.
    John and Yoko returned to London after their cruise.

October 20
Abbey Road. John and Yoko did a new mix of the tapes of the Toronto Plastic Ono Band concert.
    The single 'Cold Turkey' (Lennon)/'Mummy's Only Looking For A Hand In The Snow' (Ono) by The Plastic Ono Band and produced by John and Yoko was released in the US as Apple 1813.
    The album *Wedding Album* by John Ono Lennon and Yoko Ono Lennon, written and produced by John and Yoko, was released in the US as Apple SMAX 3361. Side One: John And Yoko; Side Two: Amsterdam.
    George attended a Ravi Shankar concert at the Royal Albert Hall.

October 21
John was interviewed by David Wigg for the BBC Radio 1 programme *Scene And Heard*.

October 22
Paul and Linda went to Paul's farm in Scotland.
    Ringo and Maureen returned home to London from LA.

October 24
Paul was interviewed on his Scottish farm by BBC journalist Chris Drake who had travelled to Scotland, determined to put an end to the absurd "Paul is dead" rumours coming from the States.
    The single 'Everything's All Right' by Billy Preston and produced by George Harrison was released in the US as Apple 1814.

The single 'Cold Turkey' (Lennon)/'Mummy's Only Looking For A Hand In The Snow' (Ono) by The Plastic Ono Band and produced by John and Yoko was released in the UK as Apple 1001.

October 26
John's interview with David Wigg for the BBC Radio 1 programme *Scene And Heard* was broadcast.

Part of Chris Drake's interview with Paul was broadcast on BBC Radio 4's *The World This Weekend*.

October 27
Abbey Road. Ringo began work on *Sentimental Journey* which, discounting John and Yoko's experimental work, made him the first Beatle to produce a solo album. Ringo and a 17-piece orchestra recorded 'Night And Day'.

Part of Chris Drake's interview with Paul was broadcast on BBC Radio 4's *The World At One*.

Another extract from Chris Drake's interview with Paul was broadcast on BBC Radio 2's *Late Night Extra*.

Contractors began work installing a recording studio at Tittenhurst Park for John and Yoko.

October 31
The single 'Something'/'Come Together' was released in the UK as Apple (Parlophone) R 5814.

George was reported to have recorded with Eric Clapton, Ric Grech and Denny Laine at Olympic Sound Studios, Barnes, London.

November
Journalist and documentary film-maker Tony Palmer was commissioned by John and Yoko to write their authorised biography but given only six days to do it. He knocked out 75,000 words and met the deadline, only to be told that they had changed their mind and no longer wanted the book.

Early in the month, John and Yoko took a Mediterranean cruise with "Magic" Alex, intending to free themselves completely from heroin use – the probable cause of Yoko's miscarriages.

November 3
The ICA screened another evening of John and Yoko's experimental films. The couple did not attend.

November 6
Abbey Road. Ringo's *Sentimental Journey* sessions. Ringo recorded Lena Horne's 'Stormy Weather' with an 18-piece orchestra. It was not included on the final album.

November 7
Abbey Road. Ringo's *Sentimental Journey* sessions. Orchestral tracks were recorded for 'Stardust'. (Paul was credited on the sleeve for the arrangement.)

The album *Wedding Album* by John Ono Lennon and Yoko Ono Lennon, written and produced by John and Yoko, was released in the UK as Apple SAPCOR 11 with the same tracks as the US release.

November 10
A third programme of John and Yoko's short films was presented at the ICA, once again in their absence.

November 13
Back in 1966, John bought Dorinish, an uninhabited island off the coast of county Mayo, Ireland, which he only visited once, on a week-long acid trip. Now he offered free use of it to hippies wishing to establish a commune.

November 14
Abbey Road. Ringo's *Sentimental Journey* sessions. Ringo added his vocal to 'Stardust' and began work on 'Dream'.

November 15
Melody Maker journalist Richard Williams mistakenly reviewed all four sides of the advance pressing he had been sent of John and Yoko's latest experimental offering, *The Wedding Album*. In fact it was a double album and the other two sides consisted of studio EQ test tones. Richard found the infinitesimal variances in pitch of sides two and four interesting.

November 25
John returned his MBE to the Queen. It was delivered by his chauffeur in the morning. He attached the following note:
    "Your Majesty,
    I am returning my MBE as a protest against Britain's involvement in the Nigeria – Biafra thing, against our support of America in Vietnam and against 'Cold Turkey' slipping down the charts.
    With Love,
    John Lennon"
    John was interviewed by David Bellan from BBC Radio 4. As with the original award of The Beatles' MBEs in 1965, his decision to send back his medal evoked a storm of protest from his fellow award-holders.

November 26
Abbey Road. John and Yoko supervised the remix of 'What's The New Mary Jane' and 'You Know My Name (Look Up The Number)' for release as a Plastic Ono Band single because it seemed that The Beatles were not going to release them.
    John's interview with David Bellan was broadcast on BBC Radio 4's *Today* programme.

November 28
Abbey Road. Ringo's *Sentimental Journey* sessions. Ringo recorded 'Blue Turning Grey Over You'.
    Apple announced the December 5 release of 'You Know My Name (Look Up The Number)' by The Plastic Ono Band. It was quickly withdrawn, possibly because it was one of Paul's favourite Beatles tracks and he wanted it out under their name. It finally appeared as the B-side of 'Let It Be' in March 1970.

December 1
Ringo was filmed in various London locations talking with Tony Bilbow for a full-length BBC2 documentary on him for an edition of *Late Night Line-Up* to be broadcast on the day of the world premiere of Ringo's new film, *The Magic Christian*.
    John and Yoko, moved by the persecution of gypsies, offered to buy a 32-foot caravan for use as a school for gypsy children at an unofficial site in Caddington, Bedfordshire.
    The 77th and last issue of *The Beatles Book* monthly magazine was published. Publisher Sean O'Mahony had decided to fold the magazine because it was obvious that there was little likelihood of The Beatles resuming an active musical career. He used the occasion of his final editorial to lambast the group for the way in which they had encouraged drug experimentation among young people. (*The Beatles Book* was revived in May 1976 and passed issue 250 in 1997.)
    George and Patti, Ringo and Maureen went to the first night of the Delaney & Bonnie & Friends tour which opened at the Royal Albert Hall, London. George enjoyed the show so much that he decided to join the tour and played two sets each night with them, standing unobtrusively at the back of the stage.

December 2
John was interviewed by anthropologist Desmond Morris, best known for his BBC Children's Television programme *Zoo Time*, for a programme called *Man Of The Decade*. ATV had asked Alistair Cooke, Mary McCarthy and Morris to choose the Man of the

Decade. Cooke chose JFK, McCarthy chose Ho Chi Minh and Morris went for John. The 20-minute section devoted to John also used archive footage, chosen by John.

The same day, BBC1 began filming John and Yoko – including him being filmed by ATV – for their own *The World of John and Yoko* documentary for the *24 Hours* series, presented by David Dimbleby.

George joined Delaney & Bonnie & Friends on stage at the Colston Hall, Bristol.

December 3

Tim Rice and Andrew Lloyd Webber asked John if he would play the role of Christ in the new musical they had written called *Jesus Christ, Superstar.*

BBC1 filmed John and Yoko for *The World of John and Yoko.*

John was interviewed by American journalist Gloria Emerson. They argued furiously when she questioned his sincerity. BBC Radio 2 broadcast a heavily censored version of the result two weeks later.

George joined Delaney & Bonnie & Friends on stage at the Town Hall, Birmingham.

December 4

Abbey Road. Ringo's *Sentimental Journey* sessions. Ringo and a 17-piece orchestra completed 'Blue Turning Grey Over You'.

Abbey Road. John and Yoko, Mal Evans, Eddie Klein, Anthony Fawcett, Geoff Emerick and many others recorded two experimental tapes. The first was a track on which everyone laughed uproariously and shouted out things which was later given a percussion and chanting backing track. In the second all the participants approached the microphone and whispered a message. John and Yoko announced that this would be the fourth in the series *Two Virgins*, *Life With The Lions* and *The Wedding Album* but it was never released. BBC1 filmed the entire thing for *The World of John and Yoko.*

George joined Delaney & Bonnie & Friends on stage at City Hall, Sheffield.

December 5

BBC1 filmed John and Yoko for *The World of John and Yoko* in the snow-covered Suffolk countryside, where they were filming their second balloon movie, *Apotheosis 2.* John and Yoko, and the BBC *24 Hours* film crew spent the night at The Bull in Long Melford, Suffolk.

George joined Delaney & Bonnie & Friends on the stage at the City Hall, Newcastle Upon Tyne.

The single 'Come And Get It' by Badfinger, written and produced by Paul McCartney, was released in the US as Apple 1815.

December 6

The three stars of *The Magic Christian* – Ringo, Peter Sellers and Spike Milligan – appeared together on *Frost On Saturday* to plug the film. The programme was taped earlier that day at the London Weekend Television studios in Wembley.

The BBC1 crew finished their filming for *The World of John and Yoko* with some footage of John and Yoko in their hotel room at The Bull in Long Melford.

George joined Delaney & Bonnie & Friends on stage at the Empire Theatre, Liverpool.

December 7

John and Yoko appeared on BBC1's religious programme *The Question Why*, in a debate chaired by Malcolm Muggeridge. It was broadcast live from the BBC's Lime Grove Studios.

George joined Delaney & Bonnie & Friends on the stage at the Fairfield Hall, Croydon, for the final night of their tour. Both sets were recorded and released in May 1970 as the live album *Delaney & Bonnie On Tour With Eric Clapton.*

December 8

Abbey Road. A new vocal track for Ringo's 'Octopus's Garden' was recorded so that he could mime it on George Martin's *With A Little Help From My Friends* television show without the Musicians' Union knowing.

December 9

John and Yoko announced through Apple that they intended to make a film about James Hanratty who was hanged for murder. It was described as a gesture of support for Hanratty's parents' campaign to prove their son's innocence. Apple said that the Lennons' film would reveal new evidence to prove his innocence. John: "We spent many hours with the parents. They convinced us that there was a miscarriage of justice without a shadow of a doubt." (The film, called *Hanratty*, financed by John and Yoko, was shown only once, in London.)

December 10

Ringo and Maureen, accompanied by John and Yoko, attended the royal world premiere of *The Magic Christian* at the Odeon Cinema, Kensington, London. John and Yoko startled the queues outside by slowly marching past them carrying a banner proclaiming "Britain Murdered Hanratty".

BBC2's arts programme, *Late Night Line-Up* – this edition just called *Line-Up* – broadcast their full-length documentary on Ringo.

George appeared with Delaney & Bonnie & Friends for all three nights of their residence at the Falkoner Theatre, Copenhagen, Denmark.

December 11

George appeared with Delaney & Bonnie & Friends for their second night at the Falkoner Theatre, Copenhagen, Denmark.

December 12

George appeared with Delaney & Bonnie & Friends for the final night at the Falkoner Theatre, Copenhagen, Denmark.

The album *The Plastic Ono Band – Live Peace In Toronto* by The Plastic Ono Band, produced by John and Yoko, was released in the UK as Apple CORE 2001. Side One: 'Introduction Of The Band', 'Blue Suede Shoes', 'Money (That's What I Want)', 'Dizzy Miss Lizzy', 'Yer Blues', 'Cold Turkey', 'Give Peace A Chance'; Side Two: 'Don't Worry Kyoko (Mummy's Only Looking For Her Hand In The Snow)', 'John, John (Let's Hope For Peace)'.

The album *The Plastic Ono Band – Live Peace In Toronto* by The Plastic Ono Band was released in the US as Apple SW 3362 with the same tracks as the UK release.

The album *No One's Gonna Change Our World* by various artists with the first track 'Across The Universe' by The Beatles was released in the UK as EMI Star Line SRS 5013.

December 14

Ringo taped his contribution to George Martin's *With A Little Help From My Friends* spectacular, alongside The Hollies, Dudley Moore, Lulu, Spike Milligan and the 40-piece George Martin Orchestra at the Talk Of The Town near Leicester Square.

A white bag, labelled "A Silent Protest For James Hanratty" containing two wriggling occupants – possibly John and Yoko but more likely not – was delivered to Speakers' Corner in Hyde Park, London where Hanratty's father called for a public enquiry into his son's murder conviction. Later that day a petition was handed in at 10 Downing Street.

December 15

Ringo taped a two-minute appeal on behalf of the British Wireless for the Blind Fund, to be broadcast by the BBC on Christmas Day.

John and Yoko's Plastic Ono Supergroup played at the *Peace For Christmas* concert at the Lyceum Ballroom, Covent Garden, London, in aid of UNICEF. The musicians only had time for one brief rehearsal, in the afternoon before the show. George Harrison was among the musicians in the hastily assembled group: the first time he and John had appeared together in concert since August 1966. The other members of the line-up were Eric Clapton, Delaney and Bonnie, Alan White, Bobby Keyes, Keith Moon, Klaus Voormann, Jim Gordon and Billy Preston. They performed extended versions of 'Cold Turkey' and 'Don't Worry Kyoko (Mummy's Only Looking For Her Hand In The Snow)'. The entire show was recorded and part of their set was released on John and Yoko's 1972 double album *Sometime in New York City*.

John: "I thought it was fantastic. I was really into it. We play 1984 music. The Plastic Ono Band plays the unexpected – it could be 'Blue Suede Shoes' or it could be Beethoven's Ninth. With Plastic Ono, anything goes."

Alan White: "The crowd must have been absolutely flabbergasted, because there were 15 or 18 people on stage, with two drummers. We just jammed this one riff that developed and developed, and then came to a climax. It was amazing."

Alan Smith (*New Musical Express*): "This same piece of music kept going for a marathon 40 minutes or more, and I'm still not sure why. Without wishing to be offensive, the physical result was that it gave me one of the worst headaches I've suffered."

The BBC *24 Hours* documentary *The World of John and Yoko* was transmitted.

December 16

Huge posters and billboards were erected in 11 cities across the world proclaiming "War Is Over! If You Want It. Happy Christmas from John and Yoko." In some countries the message was translated into the native language.

John and Yoko flew to Toronto, Canada, for their third visit this year. They stayed on Ronnie Hawkins' ranch, where they telephoned radio stations all over the world, giving them a peace message to broadcast. Hawkins got stuck with the phone bill.

December 17

In Toronto, John and Yoko announced plans for a three-day Peace Festival, to be held there from July 3–5 1970. John also began the onerous task of signing all 3,000 copies of *Bag One*, his set of erotic lithographs.

December 19

The fan club album, *The Beatles Seventh Christmas Record,* was released.

December 20

CBS TV (Columbia Broadcasting Corporation) filmed a conversation between John and Marshall McLuhan, author of *The Medium Is The Message*, at his office in the University of Toronto.

John was interviewed live on the CBC (Canadian Broadcasting Corporation) programme *Weekend* by Lloyd Robertson.

December 22

At a press conference at the Château Champlain Hotel in Montreal, John said: "We think this was a positive decade, not a depressing one. This is just the beginning. What we've got to do is keep hope alive, because without it we'll sink."

December 23

John and Yoko had a 51-minute meeting with the Canadian Prime Minister, Pierre Trudeau, in Ottawa. Trudeau had earlier said: "I don't know about acorns, but if he's around, I'd like to meet him. He's a good poet." Afterwards John said: "We spent about 50 minutes together, which was longer than he had spent with any head of state. If all politicians were like Trudeau there would be world peace."

December 24

John and Yoko arrived back in England where they headed for Rochester Cathedral, Kent, to join a sit-in and fast calling for peace and to spotlight world poverty.

December 25

BBC1's *Top Of The Pops '69* showed a clip of The Beatles singing 'Get Back' on the roof of the Apple building, the first time it had been televised in Britain in colour.

Ringo appeared in a BBC Radio 1 charity appeal on behalf of the British Wireless for the Blind Fund.

December 29

John and Yoko flew to the small village of Ålborg in Denmark where they spent the New year with Yoko's previous husband, Anthony Cox, his new wife Melinda, and Kyoko, his daughter by Yoko.

At a press conference they performed a Danish folk song called 'Kristelighed' and pledged to donate all their further record royalties to the peace movement (something which was later discreetly forgotten).

December 30
ATV broadcast *Man of the Decade,* the last 20 minutes of which were devoted to John Lennon, including an interview filmed at Tittenhurst Park.

December 31
George and Patti, Paul and Linda were among the guests at Ringo and Maureen's New Year's party in Highgate, London.

John and Yoko issued a statement, announcing that 1970 was now Year 1 AP (After Peace): "We believe that the last decade was the end of the old machine crumbling to pieces. And we think we can get it together, with your help. We have great hopes for the new year."

January 3
Abbey Road. Paul, George and Ringo worked on overdubs to George's 'I Me Mine' for use on the *Let It Be* soundtrack album (as the *Get Back* film and soundtrack were now called). John was invited to attend the session, but decided instead to remain with Yoko in Denmark.

January 4
Abbey Road. Further overdubs to 'Let It Be'.

January 8
Olympic Sound Studios, Barnes, London. George added a vocal overdub to the Glyn Johns production of 'For You Blue'.

January 12
The single 'Come And Get It' by Badfinger and produced by Paul McCartney was released in the US as Apple 1815.

January 14
Olympic Sound Studios, Barnes, London. Ringo's *Sentimental Journey* sessions. Ringo added his vocals to 'Love Is A Many Splendoured Thing' and 'Sentimental Journey'.

January 15
A two-week exhibition of John Lennon's "Bag One" lithographs opened at the London Arts Gallery in New Bond Street.

January 16
Police detectives raided the London Arts Gallery and confiscated the eight erotic lithographs. The exhibition continued with just six exhibits. On April 27, the gallery got the prints back, having argued in court that Picasso's erotic lithographs had been shown in Britain and not deemed obscene.

January 17
'Come And Get It' by Badfinger entered the *New Musical Express* charts.

January 20
John and Yoko had their hair cropped short in Denmark, described by the *Daily Mirror* as "the most sensational scalpings since the Red Indians went out of business". The couple preserved their shorn locks in a bag for future use.

January 22
John's "Bag One" lithographs were exhibited at the London Gallery in Detroit, Michigan. There were no confiscations.

January 25
John and Yoko flew back to London from Denmark.

January 26
Ringo and Maureen flew to Los Angeles.

January 27
Abbey Road. John and The Plastic Ono Band cut a new single: 'Instant Karma!', which had been written that morning. The song was produced by Phil Spector, working with John for the first time. John took the vocals and played acoustic guitar, with Alan White on drums, Klaus Voormann on bass, Billy Preston on electric piano and George playing lead guitar. By 4am it was finished and mixed.

The session was effectively an audition for Spector, who had requested the opportunity to produce The Beatles from their joint manager, Allen Klein. Delighted with the finished version of 'Instant Karma!', John quickly gave his approval for Spector to be allowed access to the tapes of their January 1969 sessions, in a last effort to complete the *Get Back* project. But Spector had to wait for approval from all four Beatles, which delayed his involvement until late March.

In Los Angeles, Ringo taped an appearance before a live audience for the NBC-TV show, *Rowan and Martin's Laugh In*.

January 28
The London Arts Gallery exhibition of John's "Bag One" lithographs closed.

January 29
Ringo and Maureen attended the American premiere of *The Magic Christian* in Los Angeles.
Allen Klein was convicted of ten tax offences in the New York Federal District Court.

January 30
Ringo and Maureen went to Las Vegas to see Elvis Presley in concert.
The single 'All That I've Got I'm Gonna Give It To You' by Billy Preston, produced by George Harrison, was released in the UK as Apple 21.

January 30
Rolling Stone read between the lines in various John Lennon interviews and published a story under the headline "Beatles Splitting? Maybe, Says John".

January 31
Ringo and Maureen returned to Los Angeles from Las Vegas.

February 1
Ringo and Maureen flew to New York from Los Angeles.

February 2
Ringo and Maureen returned to London from New York.

February 3
Abbey Road. Ringo's *Sentimental Journey* sessions. A 16-piece orchestra recorded the backing track for a remake of 'Love Is A Many Splendoured Thing' and Ringo added his vocal track.

February 4
In another rooftop ceremony, this time with London Black Power leader Michael X (Michael Abdul Malik), John and Yoko swapped their shorn hair – brought back in a bag from Denmark – for a pair of Muhammad Ali's blood stained boxing shorts at the Black House in north London. John and Yoko said they intended to auction the boxing trunks to raise money for peace. The proceeds from their hair were to go to "the Black community". The event was virtually ignored by the UK press.

February 5
Abbey Road. Ringo's *Sentimental Journey* sessions. Ringo recorded a new vocal for 'Love Is A Many Splendoured Thing'.

February 6
John and Yoko were interviewed at Apple by John Bellan for BBC Radio 1's *Scene And Heard*.
The single 'How The Web Was Woven'/'Thumbin' A Ride' by Jackie Lomax produced by George Harrison (A side) and Paul McCartney (B side) was released in the UK as Apple 23.
The single 'Instant Karma! (We All Shine On)' by The Plastic Ono Band/'Who Has Seen The Wind?' by Yoko Ono Lennon (side B produced by John Lennon) was released in the UK as Apple 1003.

February 7
Short-haired John and Yoko were interviewed for London Weekend Television's *The Simon Dee Show*. They brought with them Michael Abdul Malik – Michael X, the Black community leader to whom they had given their hair the previous week.

February 8
The Simon Dee Show transmitted its interview with John, Yoko and Michael X.

February 9
Abbey Road. Ringo's *Sentimental Journey* sessions. Ringo added vocals to 'Have I Told You Lately That I Love You?'

February 11
John and The Plastic Ono Band taped two different live appearances before an audience for BBC1's *Top Of The Pops* to promote 'Instant Karma!'. The line-up consisted of John on vocals and electric piano, Klaus Voormann on bass, Alan White on drums, Mal Evans on tambourine, and Yoko either holding cards or knitting while blindfolded. In fact John's vocal was the only thing performed live, as the entire backing track was the one from the actual single, which had been specially mixed at Abbey Road the day before for the occasion. This was John's second time on *TOTP* – The Beatles had only appeared on the show once, back in June 1966.

John paid outstanding fines amounting to £1,344 imposed on 96 anti-Apartheid protesters demonstrating against a South African rugby team which played a match in Scotland in December 1969.

Abbey Road. Ringo's *Sentimental Journey* sessions. Klaus Voormann conducted a 15-piece orchestra in his own arrangement of 'I'm A Fool To Care', then Ringo added his vocal track.

The album *The Magic Christian (Original Soundtrack Album)* by Ken Thorne & Orchestra (additional tracks by Badfinger) and produced by Paul McCartney, Ringo Starr and Peter Sellers was released in the US as Commonwealth United CU 6004.

February 12
Abbey Road. Ringo's *Sentimental Journey* sessions. A 31-piece orchestra plus nine singers recorded an arrangement of 'Let The Rest Of The World Go By', then Ringo added his vocal track.

Paul had been working on his own solo album since the end of 1969, using a Studer four-track at his home in Cavendish Avenue. He tested the machine by recording 'The Lovely Linda', then recorded 'That Would Be Something', 'Valentine Day', 'Momma Miss America (Rock'n'Roll Springtime)', 'Glasses', 'Oo You', 'Teddy Boy', 'Junk' and an instrumental of the same tune called 'Singalong Junk'. He had to make guesses about the levels because the machine had no properly functioning VU meters so he continued work at Morgan Studios, booking himself in under the name Billy Martin. There he cut 'Hot As Sun' and, on this day, 'Kreen-Akore'. He went on to make eight-track copies of his four-track masters so that he could overdub onto them.

Top Of The Pops screened one of their films of The Plastic Ono Band playing 'Instant Karma!'.

February 13
The single 'Ain't That Cute' (Harrison/Troy), produced by George Harrison/'Vaya Con Dios' (Russell/Starkey/James/Hoff – with George Harrison on guitar) by Doris Troy was released in the UK as Apple 24.

February 15
John and Yoko's interview was broadcast by BBC Radio 1's *Scene And Heard*.

February 16
John and Yoko began editing a film of their Montreal bed-in for peace.

February 18
Abbey Road. Ringo's *Sentimental Journey* sessions. Ringo recorded new vocals for 'Have I Told You Lately That I Love You' and 'Let The Rest Of The World Go By'. This was followed by a midnight recording session for Ringo's composition 'It Don't Come Easy'. George Martin produced the track, George Harrison conducted the musicians: George on acoustic guitar, Klaus Voormann on bass, Ringo on drums and Stephen Stills on piano. Ringo added his vocals to the best take and by 4.40am it was mixed.

February 19
Abbey Road. Ringo recorded another vocal track for 'It Don't Come Easy'.
    BBC TV's *Top Of The Pops* broadcast the second 'Instant Karma!' film.

February 20
The single 'Instant Karma! (We All Shine On)' by The Plastic Ono Band/'Who Has Seen
The Wind?' by Yoko Ono Lennon (side B produced by John) was released in the US as
Apple 1818. The version of 'Instant Karma!' was suitably different to the one on the UK
release, having been subtly remixed by Phil Spector without John's knowledge.

February 21
Abbey Road. Paul's *McCartney* sessions. Once again booked in as Billy Martin, Paul
began mixing his eight-track masters.

February 22
Abbey Road. Paul's *McCartney* sessions. More mixing, then Paul recorded 'Every Night'
and 'Maybe I'm Amazed'.

February 23
NBC broadcast the edition of *Rowan And Martin's Laugh In* in which Ringo appeared.

February 24
Abbey Road. Paul's *McCartney* sessions. Paul had a mixing session in studio two.
    Abbey Road. Ringo's *Sentimental Journey* sessions. In studio one, Ringo added a new
vocal to 'Blue Turning Grey Over You'.

February 25
Abbey Road. Paul's *McCartney* sessions. Paul recorded 'Man We Was Lonely',
completing it and mixing it into stereo. As on all the tracks on the album, Paul played all
the instruments.
    Ringo switched his sessions to De Lane Lee's new studio in Soho, where Johnny
Dankworth conducted a 20-piece orchestra playing 'You Always Hurt The One You Love'
and Ringo added his vocals.
    John and Yoko disassociated themselves from the Toronto Peace Festival, planned
for July 3–5, when they found out that there was to be an admission charge. The festival
didn't happen.

February 26
The album *Hey Jude* was released in the US as Apple (Capitol) SW 385 (stereo only).
Side A: 'Can't Buy Me Love', 'I Should Have Known Better', 'Paperback Writer', 'Rain',
'Lady Madonna', 'Revolution'; Side B: 'Hey Jude', 'Old Brown Shoe', 'Don't Let Me
Down', 'The Ballad Of John And Yoko'. The record was the handiwork of Allen Klein,
who had convinced John, George and Ringo that repackaging The Beatles' back
catalogue in the US would bring them additional income without any effort on their part.

March 5
Yoko once more entered the London Clinic for observation, after discovering that once
again she was pregnant. John stayed at her bedside throughout.
    On Paul's recommendation, Ringo tried out Morgan Sound Studios, where he
completed *Sentimental Journey*. On this day he recorded 'Whispering Grass' and 'Bye
Bye Blackbird' with a 36-piece orchestra.
    BBC1's *Top Of The Pops* showed a January 1969 film of The Beatles recording 'Let It
Be'.

March 6
Ringo completed his *Sentimental Journey* album at Morgan: drums, piano and sax,
played by Johnny Dankworth were added to 'You Always Hurt The One You Love' and
four other tracks were mixed. The album was now ready for release.
    The single 'Let It Be'/'You Know My Name (Look Up The Number)' was released in
the UK as Apple (Parlophone) R 5833.

The single 'Govinda'/'Govinda Jai Jai' by Radha Krishna Temple and produced by George Harrison was released in the UK as Apple 25.

LET IT BE

The Beatles' final single, 'Let It Be' was a rare piece of spiritually inspired writing from Paul McCartney. The 'Mother Mary' in the lyric was universally assumed to be his own mother, the late Mary McCartney, while the conciliatory tone of the song might have been an overt message of peace to the other Beatles.

Originally taped in front of the cameras in January 1969, the song was overdubbed with a lead guitar solo in April; then again with another in January 1970, at the same session in which a George Martin-scored brass section was overdubbed.

The first guitar solo appeared on the single; for the album mix, Phil Spector selected the rawer second effort, and also heightened the sound of Ringo and Paul's percussion, to the point where it threatened to become intrusive.

YOU KNOW MY NAME (LOOK UP THE NUMBER)

The Beatles' career as Britain's greatest singles band ended with this off-the-wall track, issued on the flipside of 'Let It Be'. It began life during the sessions for Magical Mystery Tour, *with Brian Jones of The Rolling Stones playing saxophone, was left to one side for two years, then overdubbed during the recording of* Abbey Road. *Once The Beatles' split was confirmed, towards the end of 1969, Lennon decided to rescue the track, and planned to issue it as a Plastic Ono Band single, alongside another Beatles off-cut, 'What's The News Mary Jane'. That plan was stymied, and so the song ended up as a Beatles recording after all.*

"It's probably my favourite Beatles track," said Paul McCartney, "just because it's so insane. It was just so hilarious to put that record together." And the humour survives, from the deliberately over-the-top repetition of the title, to the Goons-like parade of vocal imitations that Lennon and McCartney unveiled for the last three minutes of the song. More than any other Beatles recording, it captures the sheer pleasure that was their lasting legacy to the world.

John penned an open letter to the readers of *Rolling Stone* magazine about the debacle of the Toronto Peace Festival, printed in the April 16th issue under the title, "Have We All Forgotten What Vibes Are?"

John: "We need help! It is out of our control. All we have is our name. We are sorry for the confusion. It is bigger than both of us. We are doing our best for all our sakes – we still believe. Pray for us."

March 7

An interview with Ringo, done while he was in the States, was screened by American ABC TV's show *Get It Together*.

March 8

Trident Studios, Soho. Ringo did another remake of 'It Don't Come Easy' with George helping in the studio.

March 9

George was interviewed by Johnny Moran for a BBC Radio 1 Easter Monday special called *The Beatles Today*, which they recorded at the BBC's Aeolian Hall in New Bond Street.

That evening, George assisted Ringo in the studio for more work on 'It Don't Come Easy' which for some reason was not released until April 1971.

The single 'How The Web Was Woven'/'I Fall Inside Your Eyes' by Jackie Lomax, produced by George Harrison, was released in the US as Apple 1819.

Yoko, with John, was discharged from the London Clinic.

March 11

The single 'Let It Be'/'You Know My Name (Look Up The Number)' was released in the US as Apple (Capitol) 2764.

March 12
George and Patti moved out of "Kinfauns", their bungalow in Esher, Surrey, and moved to Friar Park, a huge Victorian mansion in Henley-on-Thames, Oxfordshire, which had turrets, an underground boating lake and a scaled down reconstruction of Mont Blanc in its extensive gardens.

March 14
John's "Bag One" lithographs opened at the Denise René Hans Mayer Gallery in Düsseldorf. No pictures were seized. The show also opened without problems at the Lee Nordness Gallery in New York.

March 15
At Talk Of The Town, Ringo shot a promotional film of himself singing the title song from *Sentimental Journey* to promote the album. The shoot was directed by Neil Aspinall before an invited audience and featured the Talk Of The Town Orchestra, conducted by George Martin.
   BBC Radio 1's *Scene And Heard*, broadcast part of Johnny Moran's interview with George.

March 16
Abbey Road. Paul's *McCartney* sessions. Paul attended a playback session of his tapes.
   The single 'Ain't That Cute' (Harrison/Troy), produced by George Harrison with 'Vaya Con Dios' (Russell/Starkey/James/Hoff – with George Harrison on guitar) by Doris Troy was released in the US as Apple 1820.

March 17
Ringo and Maureen attend Patti's birthday party at Friar Park.

March 19
BBC1's *Top Of The Pops* showed a January 1969 film clip of The Beatles recording 'Let It Be'.

March 22
The French magazine *L'Express* carried an interview with John in which he claimed that The Beatles smoked marijuana in the toilets at Buckingham Palace before receiving their MBEs on October 26, 1965. He was exaggerating: what really happened was that they slipped away for a cigarette.

March 23
Abbey Road. Paul's *McCartney* sessions. Paul finished off the master tapes of *McCartney* to his satisfaction and took them away.
   In room four at Abbey Road, at John and Allen Klein's request, Phil Spector was just beginning his remixing of the *Let It Be* tapes. Paul didn't know about this.
   The album *Leon Russell* by Leon Russell with George Harrison on guitar and Ringo Starr on drums was released in the US as Shelter SHE 1001.

March 24
The single 'Govinda'/'Govinda Jai Jai' by Radha Krishna Temple, produced by George Harrison was released in the US as Apple 1821.

March 25
Abbey Road. Phil Spector remixed 'Two Of Us' and Paul's 'Teddy Boy'.
   Ringo was interviewed at Apple by David Wigg for BBC Radio 1's *Scene And Heard*.
   Around this date, psychologist Dr. Arthur Janov, the advocate of Primal Scream Therapy, arrived at Tittenhurst Park at John's invitation to treat the Lennons for their neuroses. Janov had earlier sent John a copy of his book, *The Primal Scream*. The course of treatment, involving isolation from each other and complete freedom from chemical stimulants, soon moved to the Inn On The Park hotel in London, and then in April to Janov's Primal Institute in Los Angeles.

March 26
Abbey Road. Phil Spector continued his remix of *Let It Be*.

March 27
Abbey Road. Phil Spector continued his remix of *Let It Be*.

The album *Sentimental Journey* by Ringo Starr was released in the UK as Apple PCS 7101. Side One: 'Sentimental Journey', 'Night And Day', 'Whispering Grass (Don't Tell The Trees)', 'Bye Bye Blackbird', 'I'm A Fool To Care', 'Star Dust'; Side Two: 'Blue Turning Grey Over You', 'Love Is A Many Splendoured Thing', 'Dream', 'You Always Hurt The One You Love', 'Have I Told You Lately That I Love You', 'Let The Rest Of The World Go By'.

March 28
Five of John's "Bag One" lithographs were confiscated by police from the Merrill Chase Gallery in Oak Brook, near Chicago, Ill.

March 29
Ringo appeared live on David Frost's London Weekend Television show *Frost On Sunday* to promote his new album and show the film clip made at the Talk Of The Town.

John telephoned a message of support to a CND gathering in east London. In it he revealed that Yoko was pregnant again, but in mid-August she miscarried for the third time.

Ringo's interview with David Wigg was broadcast on BBC Radio 1's *Scene And Heard*.

March 30
Abbey Road. Phil Spector continued his remix of *Let It Be*, adding fragments of dialogue from the film footage, none of which made it onto the finished album.

March 31
Ringo appeared live on the BBC Radio Two programme *Open House*, where he was interviewed by Pete Murray.

April 1
Abbey Road. Ringo becomes the last Beatle to play at a Beatles recording session when, working with Phil Spector in studio one, he overdubbed his drum parts on the tracks 'Across The Universe', 'The Long And Winding Road' and 'I Me Mine'.

Spector recorded a 50-piece orchestra and chorus to create a "wall of sound" backing track for 'Across The Universe', 'The Long And Winding Road' and 'I Me Mine'. Spector was his usual temperamental self, and managed to anger and upset everyone involved with the session: the musicians downed instruments – but eventually picked them up again – the conductors and technical staff were all annoyed and Pete Brown, the balance engineer, stormed out of the building and went home. Spector had to call him and apologise before he would return. Ringo – the only Beatle there – had to order Spector to calm down and eventually the session was completed.

John and Yoko issued a hoax press release for April Fool's Day stating they had both entered the London Clinic for a dual sex-change operation.

In the London Arts Gallery prosecution, defence lawyers compared John's lithographs with the later work of Picasso.

April 2
Abbey Road. Spector mixed the three orchestral tracks from the previous day and the *Let It Be* album was finished – at least as far as he was concerned. Acetates were submitted to all four Beatles for their approval. Initially, they all gave the OK for the album to be released.

Ringo: "I spoke to Paul on the phone and said, 'Did you like it?', and he said, 'Yeah, it's OK.' He didn't put it down. And then suddenly he didn't want it to go out. Two weeks after that, he wanted to cancel it."

April 10

Paul had his solo album, *McCartney*, ready for release on April 17, but did not want to do any interviews for it.

PAUL QUITS

Paul asked Peter Brown at Apple to write a questionnaire with the usual sort of things that journalists would want to know and he would answer it. Naturally Peter Brown slipped in the question that journalists had been clamouring to ask for six months: Brown opened up with fairly standard press questions but at question 28 he asked:

Is this album a rest away from Beatles or start of solo career?

Paul: Time will tell. Being a solo album means "the start of a solo career" . . . and not being done with The Beatles means it's a rest. So it's both.

Peter Brown: Have you any plans for live appearances?

Paul: No.

Peter Brown: Is your break with The Beatles temporary or permanent, due to personal differences or musical ones?

Paul: Personal differences, business differences, but most of all because I have a better time with my family. Temporary or permanent? I don't know.

Peter Brown: Do you foresee a time when Lennon-McCartney becomes an active songwriting partnership again?

Paul: No.

The press release was printed and enclosed with advance copies of the album. The media went wild: "The Beatles Break Up!" was headline news around the world.

The final press release for The Beatles, written by Derek Taylor, typed by Mavis Smith, read as folows:

April 10, 1970

Spring is here and Leeds play Chelsea tomorrow and Ringo and John and George and Paul are alive and well and full of hope.

The world is still spinning and so are we and so are you.

When the spinning stops – that'll be the time to worry. Not before.

Until then, The Beatles are alive and well and the Beat goes on, the Beat goes on.

May 8

The album *Let It Be* was released in the U.K. as Apple (Parlophone) PCS 7096 (stereo only). Side A: 'Two Of Us', 'Dig A Pony', 'Across The Universe', 'I Me Mine', 'Dig It', 'Let It Be', 'Maggie May'; Side B: 'I've Got A Feeling', 'The One After 909', 'The Long And Winding Road', 'For You Blue', 'Get Back'.

George Martin: "It was always understood that the album would be like nothing the Beatles had done before. It would be honest, no overdubbing, no editing, truly live . . . almost amateurish. When John brought in Phil Spector he contradicted everything he had said before. When I heard the final sounds I was shaken. They were so uncharacteristic of the clean sounds The Beatles had always used. At the time Spector was John's buddy, mate and pal . . . still is, I don't know. I was astonished because I knew Paul would never have agreed to it. In fact I contacted him and he said nobody was more surprised than he was."

Glyn Johns had edited and mixed a completed album on January 5 but none of The Beatles were entirely happy with it, nor could John understand why Glyn Johns wanted credit as producer, even though he produced most of it.

John: "Phil Spector came in and listened to every take. He changed the takes originally used. He listened to about one thousand million miles of tape, none of which had been marked or catalogued. Which is why The Beatles couldn't face the album, because there was too much shit and nobody was interested enough to pull it together. And Phil pulled it together, remixed it, added a string or two here and there. I couldn't be bothered because it was such a tough one making it. We were really miserable then. Spector has redone the whole thing and it's beautiful."

In an interview published in the London *Evening Standard* on April 21 and 22 Paul said: "The album was finished a year ago, but a few months ago American record producer Phil Spector was called in by John Lennon to tidy up some of the tracks. But a few weeks ago, I was sent a re-mixed version of my song 'The Long And Winding Road', with harps, horns, an orchestra and women's choir added. No one had asked me what I thought. I couldn't believe it. I would never have female voices on a Beatles record. The record came with a note from Allen Klein saying he thought the changes were necessary. I don't blame Phil Spector for doing it but it just goes to show that it's no good me sitting here thinking I'm in control because obviously I'm not. Anyway I've sent Klein a letter asking for some of the things to be altered, but I haven't received an answer yet."

LET IT BE

In November 1968, Paul McCartney finally realised that The Beatles were on the verge of internal collapse. Faced with the alternative of letting the group slip away, or fighting for their future, he made a decisive move. John Lennon and George Harrison had made their opposition to performing live with The Beatles very clear; Ringo Starr, meanwhile, was happy to go with the flow. But for one last time, McCartney persuaded the group to think again – to regain contact with their core audience by performing one, or at most two, live concerts, which would be filmed for a TV special. Maybe there'd be two TV shows in the deal, one covering the rehearsals, the other the concert. And the live performance would in turn become The Beatles' next album – a deliberate opposite to the months-long sessions for *Sgt. Pepper* and *The Beatles*.

Dates were booked at the Albert Hall, then the Roundhouse, for December; but the plans fell through. Harrison's opposition proved to be the crucial factor, but he did agree to film cameras documenting the band at work, with the possibility of a live show if the rehearsals went well enough.

So on January 2, 1969, The Beatles assembled at Twickenham Film Studios for the first of three weeks' of fraught 'private' rehearsals. "It was a dreadful feeling in Twickenham Studio being filmed all the time," said John Lennon after the trauma was over. "I just wanted them to go away. We'd be there at eight in the morning and you couldn't make music at that time. It was in a strange place with people filming and coloured lights."

Towards the end of the month, the venue moved to the group's own, newly opened Apple Studios, where they were joined by Beatle-for-a-fortnight Billy Preston, whose presence helped calm the group's internal friction. There they attempted to record a 'live-in-the-studio' LP, taping hour after hour of ramshackle recordings. On January 30, they played their concert – on the roof of the Apple building, a couple of hundred feet above any possible audience. The next day, they performed several more songs live in front of the cameras, within the safety of the Apple studios. Then they dumped the tapes on engineer Glyn Johns, and told him to go away and come up with an album. Three weeks into February, they had already begun work on *Abbey Road*.

"We didn't want to know," Lennon admitted. "We just left it to Glyn and said, here, do it. It's the first time since the first album that we didn't have anything to do with it. None of us could be bothered going in. We were going to let it out with a really shitty condition, to show people what had happened to us."

Johns completed work on one version of the album, provisionally titled *Get Back*, in May; The Beatles rejected it. *Abbey Road* concentrated their attention for a while; then John Lennon told the others he was quitting the group. In January 1970, the remaining three Beatles taped one more song, and a final batch of overdubs, and Glyn Johns prepared a second *Get Back* LP. It too was turned down by all the group.

Enter legendary American producer Phil Spector, who'd been touting for work with The Beatles. In March 1970, he began an intensive week of remixing and overdubbing. In the first week of May, the LP – retitled *Let It Be*, and packaged with a *Get Back* photo book that had been intended for the original album – was in the shops.

"When Spector came, it was 'go and do your audition'," Lennon explained. "And he worked like a pig on it. He'd always wanted to work with The Beatles and he was given the shittiest load of badly recorded shit with a lousy feeling to it ever, and he made something out of it. He did a great job. When I heard it, I didn't puke."

Paul McCartney did, though, appalled by the orchestral and choral overdubs added to his song, 'The Long And Winding Road'. Critics slated the album, and by the time the documentary film of the original sessions was released, McCartney had announced that he was leaving the group. Lennon's prior decision having been kept out of the media, he was promptly blamed for the break-up. By the end of 1970, Paul was suing the rest of the band in the High Court. As John Lennon put it, the dream was over.

TWO OF US
As the movie demonstrated, 'Two Of Us' began its life as a playful rocker, but quickly mutated into a gentle McCartney acoustic song – its title and duet format a final gesture of affection from Paul to John. The live-in-the-studio recording from January 1969 was brilliantly enhanced by Phil Spector's post-production, which gave the acoustic instruments a richness missing from any previous Beatles recording.

DIG A PONY
Edited down slightly from the rooftop recording, this was a typically obscure Lennon song, full of lines which promised much and never quite delivered. In the early years of the group, he'd concocted fictional love songs at will; in their closing months, he was equally capable of manufacturing lyrics that hinted at a spiritual depth they didn't possess. Understandably, Lennon was sniffy about the song in later years.

ACROSS THE UNIVERSE
John was anything but sniffy about 'Across The Universe', however. "It's one of the best lyrics I've written," he said proudly in 1970, "in fact it could be the best. It's good poetry, or whatever you call it. The ones I like are the ones that stand as words without melody." Composed in a stream-of-consciousness, early-hours lyrical torrent, it belongs in the category of poetry that describes its own creation, standing as a hymn of praise to whatever muse gave it birth. But Lennon never matched that sense of freedom in the recording studio. Originally taped in the same batch of sessions that produced 'Lady Madonna', the song was left to one side while the group decided what to do with it. First it was going to be a single, then a flipside, then an EP cut. It was revived unsuccessfully during the film sessions, but without a hint of inspiration. Finally, it was given away to the World Wildlife Fund for a charity album.

Phil Spector took the original tape, slowed it down a fraction, deleted the overdubbed bird sounds, and added an orchestra and a choir. The result was one of the highlights of The Beatles' career, justification in itself for Spector's involvement in the creative process.

I ME MINE
For the last time, The Beatles gathered together in one place early in January 1970. Only one thing was wrong: The Beatles were now a three-piece, without John Lennon, who was having his hair cut and discovering the secret of how flying saucers worked in Denmark.

Cutting Harrison's tune – half waltz, half rocker – without Lennon wasn't a problem: the three other Beatles had performed it that way in the Let It Be movie, while John and Yoko danced around the studio floor. McCartney, Harrison and Starr ended up with a song barely 90 seconds long: Phil Spector simply copied chunks of the tape and nearly doubled its length.

DIG IT
A brief extract from an improvised three-chord jam session that ran to more than 12 minutes on tape, 'Dig It' was included on the album to boost its vérité credentials. The original Get Back LP would have included a longer chunk of the song, to no one's great benefit. Check the hours of session tapes that have emerged from movie off-cuts, and you'll find that The Beatles were infatuated by the phrase 'dig it' in January 1969. They could have assembled a full album of their jams around the phrase, but thankfully resisted the temptation.

LET IT BE
See March 6.

MAGGIE MAY
Recorded between takes of 'Two Of Us', this was a 30-second, Lennon-led revival of a popular Liverpool folksong – rescued from the session tapes by George Martin and producer/engineer Glyn Johns.

I'VE GOT A FEELING

Mix an unfinished McCartney blues called 'I've Got A Feeling' with an unfinished Lennon acoustic ballad called 'Everybody Had A Hard Year', and you had one of the roughest and most impressive songs on the Let It Be *album – taped during the Apple rooftop concert. This was the last song that Lennon and McCartney actively wrote as a songwriting partnership.*

THE ONE AFTER 909

'The One After 909' joined 'What Goes On', 'When I'm Sixty-Four' and 'I'll Follow The Sun' on the list of pre-1960 Beatles songs released on official albums. Originally composed by John Lennon as an American-style rocker in 1959, the song was revived as a possible single in March 1963, though that version remains unreleased. Six years later, something reminded Lennon of the song, and he re-introduced it to the group's repertoire in time for the Let It Be *film, and the rooftop concert at Apple in particular. Maybe not coincidentally, The Beatles sounded more relaxed playing this oldie in semi-satirical style than anywhere else in the movie.*

THE LONG AND WINDING ROAD

One of the two great McCartney ballads premiered during these ill-fated sessions, 'The Long And Winding Road' began life as a gentle, piano-based performance, with mild accompaniment from the rest of The Beatles. In the hands of producer Phil Spector, however, it became a production extravaganza, with 50 musicians and vocalists overdubbed onto the basic track. McCartney hated the results, complaining that Spector had swamped his work with a Mantovani-style arrangement; Spector's defenders said that Phil had simply responded to the natural romanticism of the song. Paul also moaned about the presence of female vocalists on the track, which was somewhat ironic in view of his subsequent recording career.

FOR YOU BLUE

Harrison's slide-guitar blues – with John 'Elmore' Lennon on slide – was a slight but appealing song that fitted in well with the album's original, live-in-the-studio concept. It was one of the few tracks on the album taken from the early days of recording at Apple, rather than the rooftop concert or the subsequent 'before-the-cameras' session.

GET BACK

'Get Back' ended the Let It Be *film, and the album, in 1970; and the same charming piece of Lennon dialogue ("I hope we passed the audition") followed it on both occasions. But the two versions of 'Get Back' were entirely different, the rooftop performance appearing in the film, while the LP ended with an Apple studios take that was recorded three days earlier. A longer version of the song had already been issued as a single in April 1969.*

May 11

The single 'The Long And Winding Road'/'For You Blue' was released in the USA as Apple (Capitol) 2832.

May 13

The film Let It Be premiered in New York.

May 18

The album *Let It Be* was released in the USA as Apple (Capitol) AR 34001 with the same tracks as the UK release.

May 20

The film *Let It Be* was premiered in Liverpool and London, but none of the Beatles turned up to see it.

THE END OF THE BEATLES

The press release that Paul issued in April attracted headlines around the world. The greatest group in history was no more. Even Derek Taylor's whimsical optimism failed to disguise the awful truth: The Beatles had split into two camps with John, George and Ringo on one side and Paul on the other. The rift was irreversible and The Beatles would not work together again.

Not much was heard from them for the rest of the year. John, Paul and George all worked on solo albums, while Ringo's second solo effort *Beaucoups*

Of Blues, was issued in October. In September George appeared at a press
conference at the Royal Festival Hall, welcoming a group of Indian musicians to
a celebration of Indian art. Like Paul, he'd grown a scruffy beard and like all
his former colleagues he looked desperately tired, as if the trials and
tribulations of the past 12 months had aged them prematurely.

In America a single of 'The Long And Winding Road' (Apple 2832) topped
the charts in June, as did *Let It Be*, the album from which it was taken. Paul
was horrified at the way in which Phil Spector had added lush strings to his
ballad and would cite this interference with his work as a key element in his
forthcoming lawsuit to formally disband the group.

There were, of course, plenty of speculative newspaper stories suggesting
Beatle activity and, it has to be said, these were not discouraged by those who
worked at Apple and whose jobs were on the line in the event of a total
meltdown. One tradition that Apple did maintain was The Beatles' annual
Christmas album, and on December 18 The Beatles' US Fan Club album, *The
Beatles' Christmas Album*, was released in the US as Apple SBC 100
consisting of a compilation of their previous Christmas flexi-discs. Side One:
'The Beatles' Christmas Record' (Dec. 1963), 'Another Beatles' Christmas
Record' (Dec. 1964), 'The Beatles' Third Christmas Record' (Dec, 1965), 'The
Beatles' Fourth Christmas Record' (Dec. 1966); Side Two: 'Christmas Time Is
Here Again!' (Dec. 1967), 'The Beatles' 1968 Christmas Record' (Dec. 1968),
'The Beatles' Seventh Christmas Record' (Dec. 1969). The Beatles' UK Fan
Club album *From Them To Us*, was released in the UK as Apple LYN 2154
featuring the same tracks as the US *The Beatles' Christmas Album*.

On December 31 Paul began proceedings in the High Court of Justice in
London to wind up The Beatles. Paul: "I for one am very proud of the Beatle
thing. It was great and I can go along with all the people you meet on the street
who say you gave so much happiness to many people. I don't think that's corny
. . . I believe that we did bring a real lot of happiness to the times."

Aftermath

And . . . in the end

Regardless of how many rock and pop musicians stand up each year to receive their Grammys, Brits and platinum albums, The Beatles remain the yardstick by which their success is measured. Thanks to the ever increasing size of the global music industry they did so much to establish in the first place, many of the statistical sales records that The Beatles once held have now been eclipsed, but no one has ever really become "bigger than The Beatles" or even the "new Beatles", nor are they ever likely to because becoming "bigger than The Beatles" is simply unattainable. Their achievements will forever remain unique because of the context and the manner in which they were accomplished.

Most of those now compared briefly to The Beatles begin and end their careers as what are today referred to as 'boy bands', but many of these acts don't even play musical instruments, let alone write all their own material. Their stage shows are often limited to displays of athletic formation dancing while they sing or mime along to pre-recorded tapes, and there is a tendency for their back catalogues to stagnate within 12 months of their demise. What price today the back catalogues of The Monkees, The Osmonds, The Bay City Rollers, Duran Duran, Kajagoogoo, Wham!, A-Ha, Bros, New Kids On The Block, Brother Beyond or Take That?

It is equally inconclusive to compare the success of The Beatles with serious stadium filler artists of the calibre of R.E.M., U2 or even Bruce Springsteen, none of whom were actually compared to The Beatles because their careers developed slowly and big success arrived only after several years of hard graft. Although all three have now produced around as many albums as The Beatles and their record sales (and concert ticket sales) certainly measure up, it has taken them at least three times as long to achieve this. Regardless of their integrity in an increasingly profit motivated industry, R.E.M., U2 and Springsteen never really changed anything, or even attract more than a few dozen fans whenever they land at Heathrow Airport.

Any act that becomes very popular very quickly are tagged "the new Beatles", but this overlooks the fact that The Beatles, or at least three of them, played together for almost four years before they saw the inside of a real recording studio. In the meantime, somehow, they scratched a living by performing live. In the modern era it's unlikely that any group, including R.E.M or U2, would stick it out together for four years from formation to recording, though Springsteen certainly paid his dues on the New Jersey shore. Among The Beatles' near contemporaries, only The Who, again just three of them, made a living playing live for four years before recording. But The Who made only four albums in the Sixties, against The Beatles' twelve. By comparison, less than six months elapsed between the formation of The Beatles' biggest rivals, The Rolling Stones, and the recording session that produced their first single.

Of course, the sedulous conditions under which The Beatles produced their work are unlikely ever to be repeated. It seems extraordinary to say it, but for all their modern-day sophistication, today's multi-national record companies are simply not equipped to handle two albums a year from the same artist, nor are they likely to welcome non-album singles which won't act as promotional tools for the triennial album. Perhaps there's a lesson to be learned here: today's Top Five singles often sell less than 100,000; in their heyday The Beatles' singles sold over a million on advance orders alone and that's just in the UK!

No matter how successful other acts may prove to be in the future, it is unlikely that more than 2,000 other artists will record a cover version of any of their songs. Nor do more recent bands have the widespread appeal of The Beatles. Again, looking at the cover versions of their songs, they have been tackled by everyone from Ella Fitzgerald, Sinatra, Ray Charles, Fats Domino and Peggy Lee at one end of the scale, to Laibach's thrash metal version of the entire *Let It Be* album on the other, to say nothing of Cathy Berberian's *Beatles' Arias*, an entire album of Beatles songs given operatic treatment, or the many brass band, string quartet and even steam organ versions of their songs.

The Beatles cast a giant shadow, a shadow so huge that many bands don't even realise they sit within its umbra. At the height of their fame, in the mid-Sixties, they influenced a huge number of their contemporaries: from Brian Jones period Rolling Stones (particularly Jones's use of sitar, and the whole of *Satanic Majesties* which was a *Sgt. Pepper* imitation), through Donovan, The Kinks to all the other pop acts who went on to produce more complex, lasting work, spurred on by the advances and experiments of

The Beatles. Before the end of the Sixties their vocal harmonies were influencing everyone from The Hollies to The Bee Gees and by the end of the decade their impact was spreading out through ELO who took mid-period psychedelic Beatles songs as a blue print for almost everything they did. Another strand of their work, notably the guitar heavy *White Album*, was developed by Led Zeppelin, much more of a Beatles band than most people think; and Syd Barrett took much from The Beatles for the whimsical early Pink Floyd. Their influence was all encompassing. In the USA, one only has to look at the work of The Byrds, The Beach Boys and Buffalo Springfield – to name just those groups whose name also begins with "B" – to see how the Americans coped with the British Invasion.

Interest in their work remains far higher than any of their contemporaries, so much so that their complete repertoire remains in print at full price, and fans still clamour for more. They have become the most collected group of all time and the most bootlegged. In the years since The Beatles disbanded lawyers and managers representing their interests have increased their tight stranglehold on the group's product. Although Paul and John's heir Yoko Ono have lost control of their song publishing, they (and George and Ringo) have effectively turned around the slave and master situation that existed with EMI in the Sixties, i.e. The Beatles are now very much the masters.

All of which probably explains why the three volume *Anthology* series of rarities and outtakes, released in 1996, sold as well as it did and, together with the accompanying eight volume video collection, raised a sum not unadjacent to $400 million for the three surviving Beatles and Yoko. This made them, in 1996, the third highest paid entertainers in the world, after Oprah Winfrey and Steven Spielberg, almost 40 years after John first encountered Paul at the Woolton village fete. Even in 1999, a year when the corporate entity now known as The Beatles released absolutely no CDs, books or other artefacts, only two entertainers in Britain earned more than they did on back catalogue sales alone.

Their musical accomplishments aside, these cold cash statistics alone explain why The Beatles remain the yardstick by which others are and always will be measured.